Tort Law
for Paralegals

Aspen College Series

Tort Law
for Paralegals

Fifth Edition

Neal R. Bevans, J.D.

Western Piedmont Community College

®. Wolters Kluwer

Published by Wolters Kluwer in New York.

Wolters Kluwer serves customers worldwide with CCH, Aspen Publishers,
and Kluwer Law International products. (www.wolterskluwerlb.com)

To contact Customer Service, e-mail customer.service@wolterskluwer.com,
call 1-800-234-1660, fax 1-800-901-9075, or mail correspondence to:

Wolters Kluwer
Attn: Order Department
PO Box 990
Frederick, MD 21705

Printed in the United States of America.

1 2 3 4 5 6 7 8 9 0

ISBN 978-1-4548-5219-3

Library of Congress Cataloging-in-Publication Data

Bevans, Neal R., 1961- author.
  Tort law for paralegals / Neal R. Bevans, J.D., Western Piedmont Community College. — Fifth edition.
    pages cm
  Includes index.
  ISBN 978-1-4548-5219-3
  1. Torts — United States. 2. Legal assistants — United States — Handbooks,
manuals, etc. I. Title.

  KF1250.Z9B48 2015
  346.7303–dc23

                                                                    2015010712

About Wolters Kluwer Law & Business

Wolters Kluwer Law & Business is a leading global provider of intelligent information and digital solutions for legal and business professionals in key specialty areas, and respected educational resources for professors and law students. Wolters Kluwer Law & Business connects legal and business professionals as well as those in the education market with timely, specialized authoritative content and information-enabled solutions to support success through productivity, accuracy and mobility.

Serving customers worldwide, Wolters Kluwer Law & Business products include those under the Aspen Publishers, CCH, Kluwer Law International, Loislaw, ftwilliam.com and MediRegs family of products.

CCH products have been a trusted resource since 1913, and are highly regarded resources for legal, securities, antitrust and trade regulation, government contracting, banking, pension, payroll, employment and labor, and healthcare reimbursement and compliance professionals.

Aspen Publishers products provide essential information to attorneys, business professionals and law students. Written by preeminent authorities, the product line offers analytical and practical information in a range of specialty practice areas from securities law and intellectual property to mergers and acquisitions and pension/benefits. Aspen's trusted legal education resources provide professors and students with high-quality, up-to-date and effective resources for successful instruction and study in all areas of the law.

Kluwer Law International products provide the global business community with reliable international legal information in English. Legal practitioners, corporate counsel and business executives around the world rely on Kluwer Law journals, looseleafs, books, and electronic products for comprehensive information in many areas of international legal practice.

Loislaw is a comprehensive online legal research product providing legal content to law firm practitioners of various specializations. Loislaw provides attorneys with the ability to quickly and efficiently find the necessary legal information they need, when and where they need it, by facilitating access to primary law as well as state-specific law, records, forms and treatises.

ftwilliam.com offers employee benefits professionals the highest quality plan documents (retirement, welfare and non-qualified) and government forms (5500/PBGC, 1099 and IRS) software at highly competitive prices.

MediRegs products provide integrated health care compliance content and software solutions for professionals in healthcare, higher education and life sciences, including professionals in accounting, law and consulting.

Wolters Kluwer Law & Business, a division of Wolters Kluwer, is headquartered in New York. Wolters Kluwer is a market-leading global information services company focused on professionals.

For my sister, Lisa Ford; my niece, Katie Burnett;
and my nephew, Ben Burnett

Summary
of Contents

Contents		*xi*
Preface		*xxxiii*
Chapter 1	An Introduction to Tort Law	1
Chapter 2	Intentional Torts	39
Chapter 3	Defenses to Intentional Torts	73
Chapter 4	Introduction to Negligence	107
Chapter 5	Duty	143
Chapter 6	Breach of Duty Under Negligence Law	181
Chapter 7	Proximate Cause	219
Chapter 8	Damages	267
Chapter 9	Defenses to Negligence	303
Chapter 10	Strict Liability and Products Liability	349
Chapter 11	Defamation	391
Chapter 12	Malpractice	435
Chapter 13	Insurance	477
Chapter 14	Fraud, Misrepresentation, and Business Torts	517
Appendices		*557*
Glossary		*585*
Index		*589*

Contents

PREFACE   xxxiii

CHAPTER 1: AN INTRODUCTION TO TORT LAW   1

I.   INTRODUCTION TO A TORTS CASE   1

A. "Can I Sue?"   2
B. Torts Are Legal Wrongs   3
C. Cause of Action   3
D. The Basis of a Lawsuit Is a Cause of Action   5

II.   TORT LAW COMPARED TO OTHER FORMS OF LAW   5

A. Who Brings the Case?   5
B. The Pleadings   6
C. Civil and Criminal Cases Operate Independently of
    One Another   7
D. Proof in a Civil Case Is Preponderance of Evidence   7
E. Terms Are Different   8

III. TORT LAW COMPARED TO OTHER AREAS OF LAW   8

IV.   A SHORT HISTORY OF TORT LAW   9

A. An Eye for an Eye   9
B. Money for an Eye   9
C. The Development of Tort Law in the United States   10

V.   BRINGING A TORT CASE   10

A. Investigating the Cause of Action: Rule 11   11
B. Litigation Chart   12

C. Sources of Proof   13
D. Filing a Complaint   14

VI.   DISCOVERY IN CIVIL CASES   14

A. Interrogatories   14
B. Depositions   15
C. Request for Production of Documents   15
D. Request to Admit Facts   15
E. Request for Physical and/or Mental Examination of a Party   15

VII. THE TRIAL OF A CIVIL CASE   16

A. Jury Selection   16
B. Opening Statement   17
C. Presentation of the Plaintiff's Case   17
D. Motion for Directed Verdict   18
E. The Defense Case   18
F. Closing Argument   19
G. The Jury Charge   19
H. The Verdict   19

VIII. ALTERNATIVE DISPUTE RESOLUTION   20

A. What Is Alternative Dispute Resolution?   20
B. Arbitration Versus Mediation   20

IX.   APPEALS   21

A. The Importance of Case Law   21
    1. *How Is Case Law Created?*   22
B. Stare Decisis   22
C. An Example of Case Law   24
    Vallejo v. Ebert   24

Chapter Summary   25
Skills You Need in the Real World   26
The Life of a Paralegal   27
Ethical Issues for the Paralegal: An Introduction   27
Relevant Cases   28
Websites   33
Forms and Court Documents   34
Key Terms   36
Review Questions   36
Applying What You Have Learned   36

CHAPTER 2: INTENTIONAL TORTS — 39

I. THE CHUMLEY CASE — 39

II. THE PROBLEM WITH INTENTIONAL TORTS — 40

III. ASSAULT AND BATTERY — 41

A. The Elements of Assault — 41
1. The Defendant's Actions Are Intentional — 42
2. Fear or Apprehension — 42
3. Harmful or Offensive Contact — 43
B. The Elements of Battery — 43
1. Defendant Acted Intentionally — 43
2. What Do We Mean by "Contact"? — 44
   a. Making Contact with Weapons or Other Objects — 44
   b. The Connection Between the Defendant's Actions and Ultimate Harm — 44
3. Harmful or Offensive Contact — 46
4. The Reasonable Person Standard — 46

IV. FALSE IMPRISONMENT — 47

A. The Elements of False Imprisonment — 47
1. Restraint Must Be Intentional — 47
2. Restraint Must Be Unlawful — 48
3. By the Use of Force or Threats — 48
4. Holding Personal Property Hostage — 49
B. Defenses to False Imprisonment — 49
1. Consent — 49
Thompson-El v. Bank of America — 49

V. ALIENATION OF AFFECTIONS — 52

VI. INTENTIONAL INFLICTION OF EMOTIONAL DISTRESS — 52

A. Elements of Infliction of Emotional Distress — 52
1. Intentional or Reckless Conduct — 53
2. Bystander Emotional Distress — 53
3. Causation — 53

B. Emotional Distress: What Is It?   53
1. *The Defendant's Actions Were Outrageous*   54

VII. MALICIOUS PROSECUTION   **55**

A. The Elements of Malicious Prosecution   55
1. *Defendant Brings or Continues a Criminal Charge
   Against the Plaintiff*   55
2. *The Case Terminates in the Plaintiff's Favor*   55
3. *The Defendant Acted with Malice in Bringing the Charge*   56
4. *There Was No Probable Cause for the Charge*   56

VIII. TORT IMMUNITY FOR FAMILIES   **56**

**IX. INTENTIONAL TORTS INVOLVING
PROPERTY: TRESPASS**   **57**

A. Intent   57
1. *Unprivileged*   57
B. Entry onto the Plaintiff's Real Property   58
1. *Proving "Entry"*   58
C. Without Permission   58

X. NUISANCE ACTIONS   **59**

A. Public Nuisance Versus Private Nuisance   59
1. *Private Nuisance*   59
2. *Damages and Injunctions*   60
B. New Lawsuits Under Environmental Theories   60

**XI. TORTS TO PERSONAL PROPERTY:
TRESPASS TO CHATTELS**   **60**

Chapter Summary   61
Skills You Need in the Real World   62
The Life of a Paralegal   64
Ethical Issues for the Paralegal: Statutes of Limitation   64
Relevant Cases   64
Websites   68
Forms and Court Documents   68
Key Terms   70
Review Questions   70
Applying What You Have Learned   70

CHAPTER 3: DEFENSES TO INTENTIONAL TORTS 73

I. WHAT IS A DEFENSE? 73

II. SELF-DEFENSE 74
A. The Response Must Be Equal to the Threat 74
B. Limitations on Self-Defense 75
  1. *No Self-Defense for Aggressors* 75
    a. *Self-Defense Claim if Aggressor Voluntarily Stopped Fighting* 75
  2. *No Self-Defense for Martial Artists* 75
C. Claiming Self-Defense When Defending Others 76
D. Other Limitations on Self-Defense: No Deadly Force to Protect Property 76
E. Mutual Combat 77

III. CONSENT 77

IV. DURESS, NECESSITY, COMPULSION, AND COERCION 78
A. Duress 78
B. Coercion 78
C. Necessity 78
D. Compulsion 79

V. INTOXICATION 79
A. Voluntary Intoxication 79
B. Involuntary Intoxication 80

VI. MISTAKE 80

VII. AGE 80

VIII. INSANITY 81
A. The Insanity Defense 81

IX. IMMUNITY 82

X. PRIVILEGE 83
Carter v. Scott 84

XI.   STATUTES OF LIMITATION   **87**

**XII. DEFENSES AVAILABLE TO
       CODEFENDANTS**   **87**

    A. Joint and Several Liability   88
    B. Vicarious Liability   89
        1. *Employer/Employee Liability* (Respondeat Superior)   90
            a. *Limitations on* Respondeat Superior   90
        2. *Family Purpose Doctrine*   92
        3. *Joint Enterprise*   92

Chapter Summary   93
Skills You Need in the Real World   93
The Life of a Paralegal   94
Ethical Issues for the Paralegal: Avoiding a Claim of
Unauthorized Practice of Law   95
Relevant Cases   95
Websites   102
Forms and Court Documents   102
Key Terms   103
Review Questions   104
Applying What You Have Learned   104

CHAPTER 4: INTRODUCTION TO NEGLIGENCE   **107**

**I.   NEGLIGENCE: WHAT MAKES IT
       DIFFERENT?**   **107**

II.   THE HISTORY OF NEGLIGENCE   **108**

III. THE CHUMLEY CASE   **108**

IV.   THE FOUR ELEMENTS OF NEGLIGENCE   **109**

    A. Duty   109
    B. Breach   111
    C. Causation   112
    D. Damages   112
        TransCare Maryland, Inc. v. Murray   113

**V.   THE LAWYERS WHO REPRESENT
       PLAINTIFFS AND DEFENDANTS**   **117**

    A. Becoming a Lawyer   117
    B. The Economics of Law Firms   117

C. Plaintiffs' Firms 118
D. Defense Firms 119
E. Contracting with a Law Firm 119
F. Contract in the Chumley Case 119

VI. OBTAINING INFORMATION FROM THE CLIENT **123**

A. Authorizations from the Client 123
B. Other Information from the Client: Facts and Photos 123

Chapter Summary 126
Skills You Need in the Real World 128
The Life of a Paralegal 129
Ethical Issues for the Paralegal: Initial Client Meeting ... 130
Relevant Cases 131
Websites 136
Forms and Court Documents 136
Key Terms 139
Review Questions 139
Applying What You Have Learned 139

CHAPTER 5: DUTY **143**

I. THE CHUMLEY CASE: A DANGEROUS INTERSECTION? **143**

II. THE LEGAL DEFINITION OF DUTY **144**

A. When Does a Duty Arise? 145
B. Using Formulas to Determine Duty 145
C. Duty Does Not Depend on Victim's Identity 146
D. Duty as a Legal Obligation 146
E. Duty Does Not Arise from Habit or Custom 147
F. Duty Arising from Professional Status 148
   1. *Different Levels of Duty for Some Professionals* 148
   2. *What Is the Standard of Care for a Professional?* 148
   3. *Specialists* 149
G. Duty Arising Out of Other Factors 149

III. HOW THE COURTS DETERMINE DUTY   **150**

    A.   Relationship Can Determine Duty   151
    B.   Special Relationships   151

IV. DUTY FROM A SOCIAL RELATIONSHIP   **152**

    A.   Are Friends a Special Relationship?   152
    B.   Social Host Liability   153

V. PREMISES LIABILITY   **154**

    A.   Duty Is on Possessor, Not Owner   154
    B.   Classifying Visitors   155
    C.   Classifying Visitors: Trespassers   156
       1.   *Exceptions to the General Rule of No Duty*
          to Trespassers   156
          a. The Attractive Nuisance Doctrine   157
          b. Rescue Doctrine   158
    D.   Classifying Visitors: Licensees   158
    E.   Classifying Visitors: Invitees   158
       1.   *"Economic Benefit" Test*   159
       2.   *Abnormally Dangerous or Ultra-hazardous*
          Conditions   159
    F.   Abolishing the Categories (and Distinctions)
       Between Invitees and Licensees   160
    G.   Guest Statutes   160
       1.   *Automobile Guest Statutes*   160

VI. DUTY TO THIRD PARTIES   **161**

    A.   Foreseeability of Injury to Third Party   163
       Tarasoff v. Regents of University of California   163
    B.   Can a Defendant Waive His Duty?   167

Chapter Summary   167
Skills You Need in the Real World   168
The Life of a Paralegal   169
Ethical Issues for the Paralegal: Keeping Up with
Developments in the Law   169
Relevant Cases   170
Websites   176
Forms and Court Documents   177
Key Terms   178
Review Questions   178
Applying What You Have Learned   178

CHAPTER 6: BREACH OF DUTY UNDER NEGLIGENCE LAW

CHAPTER 6: BREACH OF DUTY UNDER NEGLIGENCE LAW — 181

I.   INTRODUCTION   **181**

II. WHO BREACHED A DUTY IN THE CHUMLEY CASE?   **182**

III. BREACH OF DUTY   **183**

A. The Objective Standard   184
B. The Jury Determines the Standard of Care   186
C. Physical Characteristics   186
D. Emergencies   187
E. Custom or Tradition to Establish Breach of Duty?   187

IV. PROFESSIONALS HAVE A HIGHER STANDARD OF CARE   **188**

V.   COURT DOCTRINES THAT HELP TO DETERMINE BREACH OF DUTY   **188**

A. *Res Ipsa Loquitur*   189
    1. *The Commonsense Element of* Res Ipsa Loquitur   190
    2. *Defenses to a* Res Ipsa *Claim*   190
    3. *Pleading* Res Ipsa Loquitur: *What the Complaint Should Allege*   191
B. Negligence Per Se   191
    1. *What the Complaint Should Say About Negligence Per Se*   193
    Young-Gibson v. Patel   195

VI. EXPERT EVIDENCE AND BREACH OF DUTY   **199**

Chapter Summary   200
Skills You Need in the Real World   200
The Life of a Paralegal   203
Ethical Issues for the Paralegal: Confidentiality   203
Relevant Cases   204
Websites   214
Forms and Court Doctrines   214
Key Terms   215
Review Questions   215
Applying What You Have Learned   216

CHAPTER 7: PROXIMATE CAUSE   219

**I.   PROXIMATE CAUSE IN THE
      CHUMLEY CASE**   219

II. INTRODUCTION   220

   A. Proving Proximate Cause   220
       1. Breach of Duty of Care   220
       2. Breach Was the Cause   220
   B. The Law on Proximate Cause Tends to Be Vague   221

**III. DEVELOPING THE CONCEPT OF
      PROXIMATE CAUSE**   222

   A. Historical Development of Proximate Cause   222
   B. Problems Defining Proximate Cause   223
   C. Working Definition of Proximate Cause   223
       1. Elements of the Working Definition   223
           a. Proof of an Injury Caused by the Defendant   223
           b. In a Natural, Unbroken, and Continuous
               Sequence   224
           c. Uninterrupted by Any Intervening Causes   224
           d. Produced the Plaintiff's Injuries   224
           e. Without Which the Result Would Not Have
               Occurred   224
       2. Restatement's Position on Defining Proximate
           Cause   224
   D. Proximate Cause Requires a Close Connection Between
       the Defendant's Actions and the Plaintiff's Injuries   225
       1. Remote Causes Are Less Likely to Be Considered
           Proximate Cause   226
       2. Remote Causes Are Harder to Prove   226
       3. Proximate Cause Depends on the Facts in the Case   226
       4. Evaluating a Case for Proximate Cause   226
   E. Proximate Cause Must Show That the Defendant Is
       Responsible   227
   F. Foreseeability   228
       1. The Palsgraf Case   229
       Palsgraf v. Long Island R.R. Co.   229
       2. An Analysis of Palsgraf: "Orbit of the Risk"
           Doctrine (Foreseeability)   232
       3. Defining Foreseeability After Palsgraf   233

**IV.   COURT-CREATED TESTS FOR
         PROXIMATE CAUSE**   **233**

A.   "But For" Test   234
B.   "Substantial Factor" Test   234
     Williams v. Rosner   235

V.   PLEADING PROXIMATE CAUSE   **243**

A.   Is Proximate Cause a Defense?   243
B.   In the End, Proximate Cause Is a Jury Question   243
     1. *How Much Evidence Does the Plaintiff Have to
        Produce to Make Proximate Cause a Jury Question?*   244
     2. *On Appeal, Courts Will Leave the Jury's Determination
        Intact, Unless Clearly Wrong*   244

**VI.   MULTIPLE DEFENDANTS AND
         PROXIMATE CAUSE**   **245**

VII.   INTERVENING CAUSES   **247**

A.   Superseding Causes   247
B.   Acts of God or Acts of Nature   248

Chapter Summary   249
Skills You Need in the Real World   249
The Life of a Paralegal   251
Ethical Issues for the Paralegal: Attorney-Client Privilege   251
Relevant Cases   252
Websites   260
Forms and Court Documents   260
Key Terms   262
Review Questions   262
Applying What You Have Learned   263

CHAPTER 8: DAMAGES   **267**

I.   DAMAGES IN THE CHUMLEY CASE   **267**

II.   INTRODUCTION TO DAMAGES   **269**

A.   Compensatory Damages   269
     1. *General Damages*   270
        a. *Pain and Suffering*   271

        b. *Presenting an Argument to the Jury for Pain and*
          Suffering and Other General Damages   271
    2. *Special Damages*   272
       a. *Lost Wages*   272
       b. *Medical Bills*   272
       c. *Future Losses*   273
    3. *Proving Damages*   273
       a. *Why Is the Distinction Between General and Special*
         Damages Important?   274
       b. *Day-in-the-Life Video*   274
       c. *Proving Property Losses*   274
       d. *Collateral Source Rule*   275
       e. *Mitigation of Damages*   276
    4. *Emotional Distress*   276
    5. *Loss of Consortium*   277
    6. *Prior Injuries*   277
    7. *Bad Faith Damages*   278
     Rachal v. Brouillette   278
  B. Punitive Damages   282
    1. *Tort Reform and Punitive Damages*   282
    2. *Tobacco Companies and Punitive Damages*   284
  C. Nominal Damages   284
  D. Equitable Remedies   284

**III. EVALUATING A CASE FOR
POTENTIAL DAMAGES**   **285**

  A. Evaluating a Case   285
  B. Reviewing the Facts of a Case   285
  C. Asset Searches   286
  D. Jury's Function Is Assessing Damages   286
  E. Jury Instructions   287

Chapter Summary   288
Skills You Need in the Real World   288
The Life of a Paralegal   289
Ethical Issues for the Paralegal: National Paralegal
Associations   289
Relevant Cases   290
Websites   297
Forms and Court Documents   298
Key Terms   300
Review Questions   300
Applying What You Have Learned   300

CHAPTER 9: DEFENSES TO NEGLIGENCE 303

I. **THE RAILROAD'S DEFENSE IN THE CHUMLEY CASE** 303

II. **INTRODUCTION TO CONTRIBUTORY NEGLIGENCE** 304

   A. Historical Reasons for the Development of Contributory Negligence 304
   B. Defining Contributory Negligence 307
      1. *Why Study Contributory Negligence?* 308
      2. *Why Does the Doctrine Continue to Exist?* 309
   C. The Doctrine of "Avoidable Consequences" 309
   D. How Much at Fault Must Plaintiff Be? 310
   E. Is There Such a Thing as "Contributory Negligence Per Se"? 310
   F. The "All or Nothing" Element of Contributory Negligence 311
   G. Is Contributory Negligence Doomed? 311
   H. Exceptions to Contributory Negligence 311
      1. *Last Clear Chance* 311
         a. *Proving Last Clear Chance* 312
         b. *Pleading Last Clear Chance* 312
      2. *Sudden Emergency* 312
      3. *Assumption of the Risk* 313
      4. *Other Exceptions to Contributory Negligence* 314
         a. *Plaintiff's Age and Physical Factors* 314
         b. *Mental Incompetence* 314
      5. *The Rescuer Doctrine* 314
   I. Situations in Which Contributory Negligence Does Not Apply 315
   J. Contributory Negligence Is a Jury Question 315

III. **COMPARATIVE NEGLIGENCE** 316

   A. Historical Development of Comparative Negligence 317
   B. The Uniform Comparative Fault Act 317
   C. The Three Models of Comparative Negligence 317
      1. *Pure Comparative Negligence* 318
      2. *Modified Comparative Negligence* 318
      3. *Slight-Gross Comparative Negligence* 318
      4. *Combinations of Approaches* 319
   D. Types of Cases in Which Comparative Negligence Applies 319
   E. Comparative Negligence and Punitive Damages 319

F. How Comparative Negligence Affects Proximate Cause
    Analysis   319
G. Defenses to Comparative Negligence   320
    1. The Rescuer Doctrine   320
    2. Mentally Incompetent Persons   320
H. Pleading Comparative Negligence   321
I. Settlement Issues in Comparative Negligence Cases   321
J. Multiple Defendants and Comparative Negligence   321
K. Motions for Directed Verdict in Comparative
    Negligence Cases   321
L. The Jury's Verdict   322
    Ayala v. Lee   322
    Smith v. Cianelli   327

Chapter Summary   331
Skills You Need in the Real World   332
The Life of a Paralegal   334
Ethical Issues for the Paralegal: Paralegals Who Can
Appear in Court   335
Relevant Cases   335
Websites   343
Forms and Court Documents   343
Key Terms   345
Review Questions   345
Applying What You Have Learned   346

CHAPTER 10: STRICT LIABILITY AND PRODUCTS LIABILITY 349

I.   INTRODUCTION   349

II. A PRODUCTS LIABILITY CASE: TIRE
     BLOWOUT   350

III. STRICT LIABILITY   350

     A. Ultra-hazardous Activity   350
     B. A Short History of Strict Liability   351
         1. Background   351
         2. Developing Strict Liability in the United States   352
     C. Strict Liability for Animal Behavior   353
     D. Strict Liability Has Not Been Adopted in All
         Jurisdictions   353
     E. Statute of Limitations Concerns in Strict Liability
         Lawsuits   353

IV. INTRODUCTION TO PRODUCTS LIABILITY   354

    A. Products Liability in the United States   354
        1. *Privity of Contract Requirement*   354
        2. *The Theory Underlying the Privity Requirement*   355
    B. A New Judicial Approach   355
        1. *The* MacPherson *Case and a Change in Judicial Attitudes*   356
        MacPherson v. Buick Motor Co.   356
        2. *The Significance of the* MacPherson *Case*   358
    C. The Basic Elements of a Products Liability Case   359
    D. Products Liability Cases Do Not Involve Consumer Dissatisfaction   359
    E. Warranties   360
        1. *Warranty of Merchantability*   360
        2. *Warranty of Fitness for Purpose*   360
        3. *Express Warranties*   362
    F. Liability Without Fault Under Products Liability   362
    G. The Standard of Care in Products Liability Cases   363
        1. *Manufacturer's Duty to Test and Inspect Products*   363
          a. *Food*   364
          b. *Compliance with Safety and/or Health Regulations*   364
    H. Products Liability Per Se?   364
    I. Public Policy Arguments for Products Liability Cases   365
    J. Proving a Products Liability Case   365
        1. *Design Defects*   366
        2. *Manufacturing Defects*   366
        3. *Defects in Marketing*   366
        4. *Pleading Products Liability Cases*   366
    K. Model Uniform Products Liability Act   368
    L. Discovery in Products Liability Cases   368
        Ontiveros v. 24 Hour Fitness Corp.   369
    M. Retailers and "Mere Conduits"   374
    N. Inherently Dangerous Objects   375
    O. Defenses to Products Liability Actions   375

V. THE TIRE BLOWOUT HYPOTHETICAL   376

Chapter Summary   376
Skills You Need in the Real World   376
The Life of a Paralegal   377
Ethical Issues for the Paralegal: Frivolous Lawsuits   378
Relevant Cases   378
Websites   386
Forms and Court Documents   386
Key Terms   388

Review Questions   388
Applying What You Have Learned   389

CHAPTER 11: DEFAMATION   391

I.   INTRODUCTION   391

II. DEFAMATION   392

A. What Is Defamation?   392
B. Defamation Comes in Two Forms   393
C. Elements of Defamation   393
   1. *Defamatory Language*   393
     a. Definition   393
     b. Opinions   394
   2. *False Statements*   394
   3. *The Statement Refers to the Plaintiff* 394
     a. Burden of Proof   394
     b. Is It Possible to Defame a Group? 395
   4. *Publication*   395
   5. *Injury to the Plaintiff's Reputation* 396
D. Simple Libel   396
   1. *What Is a Writing?*   398
   2. *Libel Per Quod*   398
   3. *Libel Per Se*   398
E. Slander   399
   1. *Defining Slander*   399
   2. *Slander Per Se*   399
   3. *Special Damages*   400
   4. *Is Libel More Serious than Slander?* 400
F. Defenses to Defamation   401
   1. *The Statement Is Not Defamatory*   401
   2. *The Defamed Person Is Deceased*   401
   3. *Privileges*   401
     a. Absolute Privileges   402
     b. Qualified Privileges   402
   4. *The Statement Is True*   403
   5. *"Good Faith" Statutes*   403
G. Damages in Defamation Cases   404
H. Constitutional Limits on Defamation Actions   404
   1. *Analyzing a Defamation Case for Constitutional Implications* 405
   2. *The* New York Times *Rule*   405
     a. Malice   406
     b. Malice and Negligent Investigation 407

          3. The Shifting Standard Depending on the Plaintiff's
              Notoriety   407
    I.   Defamation in Cyberspace   408
    J.   Invasion of Privacy   408
          1. Intrude on a Person's Privacy   409
          2. Make Public Disclosure of Private Facts   409
          3. Use the Person's Name or Likeness without Permission   409
          Larue v. Brown   409

III.   ANALYZING A CASE OF DEFAMATION   **415**

Chapter Summary   415
Skills You Need in the Real World   416
The Life of a Paralegal   417
Ethical Issues for the Paralegal: Conflicts of Interest   418
Relevant Cases   419
Websites   428
Forms and Court Documents   429
Key Terms   430
Review Questions   430
Applying What You Have Learned   431

CHAPTER 12: MALPRACTICE   **435**

I.   CHUMLEY AND MALPRACTICE   **435**

II.   INTRODUCTION TO PROFESSIONAL
**   MALPRACTICE**   **436**

III.   WHAT IS MEDICAL MALPRACTICE?   **436**

    A. A Brief History of Medical Malpractice   437
    B. Defining Medical Malpractice   438
    C. What Is the Basis for a Medical Malpractice Case?   438
          1. Battery   438
          2. Contract   439
          3. Negligence   439

IV.   THE BASIC ELEMENTS OF A MEDICAL
**   MALPRACTICE CLAIM**   **440**

    A. Duty   440
    B. Breach   440
          1. Defining the Standard of Care   441
          2. Modern Approaches to Standard of Care   441

        a. *Level of Experience*   442
        b. *National Versus Local Standards*   442
        c. *Establishing Standard of Care by Statute*   442
        d. *Elements to Consider in Establishing the Standard
           of Care*   443
      3. *Expert Testimony in Medical Malpractice Cases*   444
      4. *Specialists*   444
   C. Proximate Cause in Medical Malpractice Cases   444
   D. Damages   445
      1. *Specific Types of Injuries*   446
        a. *Wrongful Birth*   446
        b. *Wrongful Adoption*   447
        c. *Wrongful Death*   447
      2. *Punitive Damages*   447
      3. *Punitive Damages and Tort Reform*   447

 V.   INFORMED CONSENT   **449**

   A. Statutory Requirements in Informed Consent   450
   B. Emergencies   451
   C. Scope of Informed Consent   451

 **VI. PLEADINGS IN MEDICAL MALPRACTICE
        CASES**   **452**

 **VII. DISCOVERY ISSUES IN MEDICAL
        MALPRACTICE CASES**   **453**

 **VIII. DEFENSES TO MEDICAL MALPRACTICE
        CLAIMS**   **454**

   A. Statute of Limitations   454
   B. Contributory Negligence of the Patient   454
      Verdon v. Duffy   455

 **IX. THE CHUMLEY CASE: FOLLOW-UP ON
        MEDICAL MALPRACTICE ISSUE**   **457**

 X.   LEGAL MALPRACTICE   **457**

   A. The Attorney's Duty   457
   B. Breach of Duty   458
      1. *Additional Proof of Breach Required*   458
      2. *Expert Testimony*   458
   C. Proving Damages   459
   D. Defenses in Legal Malpractice Cases   459

XI. OTHER TYPES OF PROFESSIONAL MALPRACTICE — 460

Chapter Summary — 460
Skills You Need in the Real World — 461
The Life of a Paralegal — 462
Ethical Issues for the Paralegal: Fee Splitting or Sharing — 463
Relevant Cases — 463
Websites — 470
Forms and Court Documents — 471
Key Terms — 473
Review Questions — 473
Applying What You Have Learned — 474

CHAPTER 13: INSURANCE — 477

I. MR. CHUMLEY AND THE INSURANCE COMPANY — 477

II. INTRODUCTION — 478

III. THE IMPACT OF INSURANCE ON CIVIL SUITS — 478

IV. HISTORY OF INSURANCE — 479

V. WHAT IS INSURANCE? — 480

VI. THE INSURANCE CONTRACT — 480

A. The Insurance Policy — 481
B. State Laws Regarding Insurance Policies — 481

VII. AUTOMOBILE INSURANCE — 483

A. Statutory Minimum Liability Coverage — 483
B. Liability Coverage — 483
C. Bodily Injury — 484
D. Property Damage — 484
E. Medical Payments — 484
F. Uninsured Motorist Coverage — 484
G. Underinsured Motorist Coverage — 485
H. Important Provisions in Typical Automobile Policies — 485
    1. Duty to Defend — 486
    2. Subrogation — 486

      3. *"Stacking" of Policies* 487
         a. *Limit of Liability Provisions and Stacking* 487
   I. *"No-Fault" Insurance* 488
   J. *Exclusions* 489
      1. *Intentional Injuries* 489
      2. *Other Exclusions* 489

VIII. HOW INSURANCE COVERAGE AFFECTS SETTLEMENT **490**

   A. Discovery Issues with Insurance 490
   B. Specialization Among Personal Injury Attorneys 491
      1. *Plaintiffs' Firms* 491
      2. *Insurance Defense Firms* 491
   C. Settlement 492
   D. Releases 493
      State Farm Mut. Auto. Ins. Co. v. Swartz 495
Chapter Summary 498
Skills You Need in the Real World 499
The Life of a Paralegal 500
Ethical Issues for the Paralegal: Insurance Fraud 501
Relevant Cases 502
Websites 510
Forms and Court Documents 511
Key Terms 513
Review Questions 513
Applying What You Have Learned 514

CHAPTER 14: FRAUD, MISREPRESENTATION, AND BUSINESS TORTS 517

I. THE SHAREHOLDER'S SUIT **517**

II. INTRODUCTION **518**

III. FRAUD **518**

   A. Proving Fraud 519
   B. Alleging Fraud in the Complaint 520
   C. Limitations on Fraud Actions 521
   D. Fraud and Criminal Law 521

IV. NEGLIGENT MISREPRESENTATION 523

A. The Restatement Position on Negligent Misrepresentation 523
B. Elements of Negligent Misrepresentation 523
C. Traditional Tort Analysis for Negligent Misrepresentation 524
   1. Duty and Breach of Duty 524
   2. Causation 525
   3. Damages 525
D. Opinions and Negligent Misrepresentation 526
E. Negligent Misrepresentation Versus Mistake 527
F. Pleading Negligent Misrepresentation 527
G. Defenses to Negligent Misrepresentation 528
   1. Truth 528
   2. Opinion 528
   3. Statement That Did Not Concern a Material Fact 528
   4. No Detrimental Reliance on the Statement 528
   5. No Damages 529
   6. Waiver 529
H. Defenses That Are Unavailable in Negligent
   Misrepresentation 529
   1. No Knowledge 530
   2. Lack of Privity 530
   3. Good Faith 530

V. INTERFERENCE WITH CONTRACT 530

A. Elements of Interference with Contract 531

VI. DECEPTIVE TRADE PRACTICES 532

A. Deceptive Trade Practices Act 532
B. Public and Private Enforcement Under DTPA 533

VII. CONSUMER PROTECTION LAWS 533

VIII. SEXUAL HARASSMENT 534

A. Sexual Harassment in the Workplace 534
B. What Is Sexual Harassment? 534
   1. Quid Pro Quo Sexual Harassment 534
   2. Hostile Environment Sexual Harassment 534

IX. DRAM SHOP LIABILITY   **535**

X. WORKERS' COMPENSATION   **535**

    A. The Basic Premise of Workers' Compensation   535
    B. Bringing a Claim Under Workers' Compensation   536
    C. The Issues in Workers' Compensation   536
    D. Assigning Monetary Values to Injuries   537
       Gutierrez v. Devine   537

**XI. FOLLOW-UP ON THE SHAREHOLDER'S
SUIT**   **539**

Chapter Summary   540
Skills You Need in the Real World   541
The Life of a Paralegal   543
Ethical Issues for the Paralegal: Coaching Witnesses   543
Relevant Cases   544
Websites   550
Forms and Court Documents   550
Key Terms   553
Review Questions   553
Applying What You Have Learned   554

APPENDIX A: CLIENT MATERIAL/DOCUMENTS   557
APPENDIX B: CORRESPONDENCE   561
APPENDIX C: PLEADINGS   563
APPENDIX D: DISCOVERY   571
APPENDIX E: MEDICAL   581
GLOSSARY   585
INDEX   589

Preface

INTRODUCTION TO THE FIFTH EDITION

The fifth edition of *Tort Law for Paralegals* has undergone a major rewrite and revision. The author has worked hard to incorporate the most recent changes in tort law and to discuss the growing impact of technology in the day-to-day practice of law, examining the challenges (and benefits) that it provides practitioners. The text begins with a general discussion of civil law and then proceeds through the concepts of intentional torts and defenses, followed by an in-depth examination of negligence law. This examination spans several chapters and includes all elements of a negligence action, as well as defenses to negligence. From there, the author moves on to a discussion of product liability, business torts, and an explanation of the impact of insurance coverage on bringing and defending tort cases.

FEATURES

This fifth edition continues many of the features that have made previous editions so popular. The material attempts to balance theory with practice. It is designed to appeal to various learning styles. Many of the components give the text a solid, visual appeal while also delivering important information about the bases of tort law.

- **Chapter Objectives**
  Each chapter begins with clearly stated learning objectives to guide readers in their studies.

- **Tort Basics at a Glance**
  Scattered throughout each chapter are small synopses of the basics of tort law. Students can see a brief summary of the topic and the critical points to be gleaned from the material.

- **Definitions**
  As each new term is introduced, it is also defined for the student. These contemporaneous definitions help to reinforce the concept under discussion and provide an additional frame of reference for the legal term.

Figures, Tables, and Diagrams

Each chapter has been extensively updated with new figures, tables, and diagrams to assist students in understanding concepts by presenting them in a visual format.

Practical Advice

The text also provides examples and advice about topics as varied as drafting a complaint to billing for time.

Case Excerpts

Almost every chapter in the text has been updated with new cases that reflect the most up-to-date changes in tort law.

Litigation Facts

The text also contains checklists, figures, and tables that allow students to bring the theoretical discussions into a more practical realm by showing how attorneys and paralegals prepare for a wide variety of tort cases.

Skills You Need in the Real World

This feature helps create a balance between theoretical legal discussions and down-to-earth practicality by showing the reader how various activities in the real world are carried out. Whether investigating a claim, billing an account, or preparing legal documents, this section — which comes at the end of each chapter — helps emphasize the day-to-day activities carried out by paralegals who work in tort law.

Life of a Paralegal

Each chapter also contains a profile of a real-life working paralegal. The reader can hear in the paralegal's own words what it is like to work at a private firm or to investigate a claim or to meet with clients, among many other topics discussed by these paralegals. This section also contains practical advice for readers seriously considering a career as a paralegal.

Ethics Issues for the Paralegal

Ethics is a critical concern for attorneys and paralegals, and ethical scenarios and rules are presented throughout the text to help emphasize this point. At the end of each chapter, the author discusses a particular ethical issue in great detail. Examples include how the attorney-client relationship is established to avoid legal malpractice claims.

Tech Topic

The text also contains a new feature: Tech Topic, which updates the discussions to examine technological innovations and how they impact the practice of law.

Chapter Summary

At the conclusion of each chapter, a summary presents a condensed overview of the material covered in the chapter, helping the reader focus on the key points raised.

Websites

The fifth edition of this book has even more broadly expanded its consideration of the Internet and its impact on the day-to-day practice of law. Each chapter contains websites that direct the reader to online resources for more extensive and targeted reading on a particular topic. The chapters have been revised to discuss the impact of the Internet on all areas of tort law.

Forms and Court Documents

Among the many items in the end-of-chapter materials are excerpts from actual court documents. These contain examples of pleadings that range from complaints and answers to interrogatories and motions. This section allows the reader to see how the various legal topics discussed in the chapter are actually put into place by attorneys and paralegals as they pursue (or defend) a civil tort case.

Key Terms

Each of the key terms discussed in the body of the chapter are excerpted and provided to the reader again at the conclusion of the chapter. This allows students to ensure that they have mastered the important concepts discussed throughout the text.

Review Questions

Extensive review questions test the student's understanding of concepts raised in the chapters and also serve as a way to stimulate in class discussion of various tort law concepts.

Applying What You Have Learned

In the author's continuing effort to balance theory and practice, this section allows students to apply the chapter's theoretical concepts to specific, real-world problems and to arrive at solutions for these problems.

Non-Gender-Specific Language

In recognition of the impact of gender-specific language, the author has adopted the following convention in the text: even-numbered chapters use "he" in general discussions and examples, while odd-numbered chapters use "she" for the same purpose.

An Introduction to Tort Law

Chapter Objectives

- Explain the foundations of tort law
- Show the distinction between tort law and other branches of law
- Describe the differences between tort law and criminal law
- Explain the basic steps involved in a civil trial
- Describe the basic court system, including appellate court structure

I   INTRODUCTION TO A TORTS CASE

They had spent the day shopping. Charles Chumley, 60 years old, was driving while Julia, his wife of 35 years, was in the passenger seat beside him. They had visited a larger town about 30 miles away and had spent the day at the mall. Now they were heading home. They had lived in the town of Cling for almost 20 years. Charles had a job nearby as a shift supervisor at a plant that made wooden chairs and tables. Julia had worked at city hall as a secretary until she retired last year. For the past few months, they had enjoyed taking little shopping trips together on the weekends. Charles was looking forward to his retirement. He used to joke to her that they would get a camper and drive all over the country. Julia didn't like driving, especially on long trips, but she would play along with him. Around 4:30 that Saturday afternoon, they reached the outskirts of town and turned down their street. Morgan Street hadn't changed much in 20 years. Just short of their house, a railroad track crossed Morgan Street. There wasn't a stop sign or a mechanical gate, just one "cross-buck" sign that read "Rail Road Crossing." Charles had driven across that track at least twice a day, five days a week for 20 years. The thick evergreen trees that grew near the intersection made it hard for him to see down the track.

What happened next has been pieced together from the facts. There is no dispute that when the Chumley car crossed the tracks, it was struck broadside by a 32-ton train, owned by National Railroad Company. The impact sounded like a small bomb going off, as some neighborhood people said later. The car was impaled on the front of the locomotive engine and pushed about 100 yards down the track, before the car finally rolled off the front of the railroad engine and slid into a ditch. Charles was severely injured, and Julia was killed instantly.

Fortunately for Charles, a fire station was only two blocks away, and it was equipped with an ambulance. Fire and rescue got to the scene in less than three minutes. They cut Charles out of the car, but there wasn't anything they could do for Julia. Charles was airlifted from the scene to a nearby city and spent several months in the hospital there. Although he almost died in intensive care, he managed to pull through. He has no memory of the collision. He walks with a cane now. He has severe, permanent injuries that prevent him from ever returning to work or even driving a car again. His wife is dead. His life has been devastated.

Charles Chumley has just walked into your law office. He wants to sue the railroad.

This is a torts case.

TORT BASICS AT A GLANCE

The term *tort* refers to any case involving a physical, financial, or emotional injury. Many states have gradually phased out this term, replacing it with the more general term *civil injury.*

Throughout this book, we discuss the many fascinating aspects of tort law, but we never stray far from this case. Because no matter how interesting a particular point of law may be, tort law in its final analysis is always about people. People get injured; people bring lawsuits; people win or lose at trial. People, like Charles Chumley, want to know what their legal options are.

A. "CAN I SUE?"

Clients always want an answer to that question. That's what Charles Chumley asks the day he walks into the law office. Mr. Chumley doesn't have any legal training, so he doesn't realize that he is asking the wrong question. The real question is this: Has Mr. Chumley suffered a legal wrong for which he can receive damages? See Figure 1-1 for a list of the various types of civil trials, including tort cases.

B. TORTS ARE LEGAL WRONGS

A tort is a legal wrong or legal injury that entitles the victim to compensation. Later we discuss how a torts case is different from a criminal case and other types of law, but there is one major element to a torts case: If a person has suffered a legally recognized wrong, then he or she may be entitled to compensation from the person who injured him or her. A tort, or a civil injury, gives the injured party a legal right. Having said that, however, not every injury entitles a person to compensation.

C. CAUSE OF ACTION

Before a person can sue, he or she must have a **cause of action.** Simply put, this is an injury that is recognized at law. Say, for instance, that you are going out to your car in the parking lot. It has been a long day, and you're looking forward to getting home and relaxing a bit. However, a strange man is standing close to your car. As you walk up, you begin to feel a little apprehensive. You nod at the man, but he doesn't nod back. Feeling even more apprehensive, you reach for your car keys to unlock your door, and you realize that the man is actually glaring at you. He has a very angry look on his face. You consider asking him a question, but instead you wisely get into your car. The man continues to stare at you as you start your car. You can feel his eyes on you as you back up and leave the area. Throughout this situation, the man has neither said anything nor moved, but you can *feel* his maliciousness. You drive home, and although you never see the man again, you suffer from nightmares that he is coming after you.

Do you have a cause of action? Or, put another way, does the law of your state authorize a lawsuit based on these facts?

The answer, barring any additional facts, is no. Because the man didn't actually do anything and you never saw him again, there is no legally recognized claim you could bring against him. There are some things in life that people simply have to put up with. A glaring stranger is one of them. The law permits people to bring lawsuits against others only when the victim has suffered some legally recognized wrong. The fact that you felt that the man had an evil purpose, or that he gave you a mean look, does not mean that his actions rise to a legally recognized wrong. Without a wrong, or a cause of action, there can be no case. This is as true with evil looks as it is for multi-million-dollar losses. If there is no legal wrong, there is no tort.

Now take the same scenario and change one fact: As you get into your car, the man takes a swing at you and misses, then runs away. Do you have a legally recognized cause of action against him? Yes, absolutely. The man has just

Cause of action
A legal injury on which a lawsuit can be based.

FIGURE 1-1

U.S. District Courts—Civil Cases Commenced, by Nature of Suit and District, During the 12-Month Period Ending March 31, 2014

U.S. Cases

| Circuit and District | Total Civil Cases | Total U.S. Civil Cases | Contract Cases | Real Property | Tort Action | Civil Rights | Prisoner Petitions | | | | | | Habeas Corpus | Forfeitures and Penalties | Labor Suits | Social Security | All Other |
							Motions to Vacate Sentence	Habeas Corpus General	Death Penalty	Prison Civil Rights	Prison Condition	Mandamus and Other	Alien Detainee				
TOTAL	303,820	46,727	2,673	1,057	1,763	1,514	7,549	2,520	3	1,156	390	312	745	2,042	499	19,636	4,868

committed the tort of assault (discussed in Chapter 2). The important point is that the man did something that the law recognizes as a legal wrong. In some cases, as we see in later chapters, when the man fails to act, or fails to act in a reasonable manner, you may also have a cause of action against him for negligence.

D. THE BASIS OF A LAWSUIT IS A CAUSE OF ACTION

Does Charles Chumley have the basis for a lawsuit? On the face of it, the answer would seem to be yes. The state where he was injured, like all states, allows a person injured in a car wreck to sue the person who caused the wreck. The basis of the cause of action is the other person's negligence. In this case, Mr. Chumley claims that a train caused his injuries by acting in a negligent manner. Mr. Chumley is not saying that the railroad engineer deliberately or intentionally set out to hurt him. Instead, Mr. Chumley is saying that he was hurt through the carelessness of the engineer, and through him, the railroad company that he works for. The first answer we can give Mr. Chumley, at this stage, is yes, a lawsuit can be brought on these facts. That doesn't necessarily mean that the lawsuit *should* be brought. That's a different question. First, we must answer this question: How is a torts case different from other kinds of cases? Then we can outline the steps that a torts case follows.

II TORT LAW COMPARED TO OTHER FORMS OF LAW

Tort law is a field of law that is as specialized in its own way as criminal law, tax law, or divorce law. Let's explore the basic differences between a torts case and a criminal case, using the scenario of the glaring stranger that we mentioned earlier.

A. WHO BRINGS THE CASE?

A torts case is brought by the individual who has suffered some legally recognized wrong. If this were a criminal case, for example, a prosecutor would bring the case. Prosecutors are the representatives of the government and seek criminal indictments against people who break the law. The prosecutor does not represent the victims; the prosecutor represents society. Although a prosecutor may work closely with the victims, the victims do not have any authority over the prosecutor. On the other hand, when a victim brings a civil suit, the victim often hires a lawyer to represent his or her interests. This lawyer works directly for the victim and must follow his or her instructions. See

Figures 1-2 and 1-3 for an overview of the differences between torts and criminal cases.

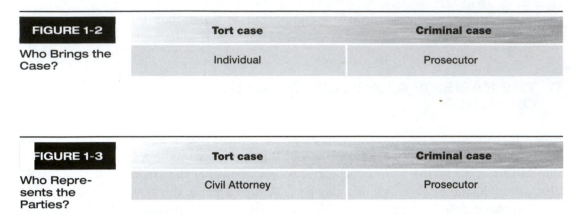

FIGURE 1-2	Tort case	Criminal case
Who Brings the Case?	Individual	Prosecutor

FIGURE 1-3	Tort case	Criminal case
Who Represents the Parties?	Civil Attorney	Prosecutor

In addition to the differences outlined above, the terminology we use to describe these parties is also different. When a person brings a civil suit, he or she is called a *plaintiff*. When the government brings a criminal case, it is usually referred to as the *state,* or the *people*. One thing that often contributes to confusion about these terms is that we use the same term to refer to the other side in civil and criminal cases. That person is called the *defendant*. See Figure 1-4 for the types of claims that are brought.

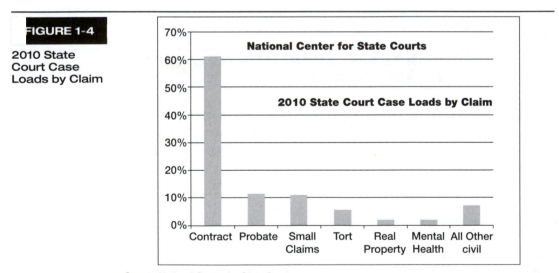

FIGURE 1-4

2010 State Court Case Loads by Claim

Source: National Center for State Courts

Pleadings
Documents that describe the legal injuries and counterclaims raised by the parties in a civil case.

B. THE PLEADINGS

Another important difference between torts cases and criminal cases has to do with the documents that begin the suit, commonly referred to as the **pleadings.**

In a civil case, the plaintiff files a **complaint.** This document sets out the legal wrong that the plaintiff suffered. It also requests that the defendant pay the plaintiff monetary damages.

A criminal case usually begins with a warrant, followed by an **indictment** issued by a grand jury. The indictment details the defendant's actions and how these actions violate the law. The indictment doesn't ask for monetary damages. In fact, if the defendant loses the criminal case, he or she will usually go to prison. See Figure 1-5 for an overview of the differences between torts and criminal pleadings.

Complaint
Document drafted by the plaintiff's attorney and served on the defendant. It details the personal or financial injury suffered by the plaintiff.

Indictment
Official document issued by the grand jury, accusing the defendant of a criminal act.

Torts case	Criminal case
Complaint	Indictment
↓	↓
Details plaintiff's injury	Details defendant's crime

FIGURE 1-5

Bringing the Charges

C. CIVIL AND CRIMINAL CASES OPERATE INDEPENDENTLY OF ONE ANOTHER

When the strange man waiting by the car took a swing at you and missed, he committed the tort of assault. He may also have committed a crime. For example, if you got into your car and called the police, criminal law would be triggered and the man might get arrested. Does this mean that you cannot also sue him? Absolutely not. You can bring your lawsuit whether or not a criminal case has also been brought against the man. Civil cases and criminal cases operate independently of one another. The plaintiff's attorney doesn't work with the prosecutor. The plaintiff's attorney doesn't have to wait until the criminal case is over before bringing a civil suit. A civil suit can be brought before, during, or after a criminal case. One reason why these two cases can proceed independently of one another is that the burden of proof is different in both cases.

When a person chooses to represent himself or herself without an attorney, it is referred to as proceeding pro se *(by oneself). Less than 3 percent of litigants in tort cases represent themselves.[1]*

D. PROOF IN A CIVIL CASE IS PREPONDERANCE OF EVIDENCE

When a plaintiff brings a complaint against a defendant, he or she must prove the case by a preponderance of evidence. This means that the plaintiff has to prove that his or her allegations are "more likely than not" true. Another way of thinking about this standard is to imagine an old-fashioned, two-sided scale. If the plaintiff presents enough evidence to tilt the scales in his or her favor, the plaintiff is entitled to win. However, the proof required in a criminal case is very different.

TORT
BASICS
AT A
GLANCE

The burden of proof in a civil case is preponderance of the evidence, which means that the plaintiff must prove that his or her version of the facts is true "more likely than not."

In a criminal case, the government must prove its case "beyond a reasonable doubt." The problem with this standard is that it is hard to explain. It is certainly higher than the civil requirement of preponderance of evidence, but how much more? Most commentators explain "beyond a reasonable doubt" as the requirement that the government prove its case to the point where the jury would have no commonsense objections to the government's version of what occurred.

Damages
Money that a court orders the losing side in a civil case to pay to the other side.

Liable
A finding that one of the parties in a civil case is obligated to pay damages to the other party.

Guilt
The jury's determination that the defendant in a criminal case is responsible for committing a crime.

E. TERMS ARE DIFFERENT

In addition to a different standard of proof, the terms that we use in a torts case are different from what we use in criminal cases. At the end of a civil case, if the jury decides that the defendant should pay **damages** to the plaintiff, the defendant is held to be **liable.** At the end of a criminal case, if the jury decides that the government has proven its case against the defendant, the defendant is **guilty.** In the case of the man who took a swing at you, he could be prosecuted by the government and sued by you at the same time. Civil torts and criminal cases, although based on the same facts, actually have very little to do with one another.

TORT LAW COMPARED TO OTHER AREAS OF LAW

Obviously, tort law has many differences from (and similarities to) criminal law. How does tort law compare to other forms of civil law—for instance, business law, corporate law, and patent law, to name a few other subspecialties? Tort law is actually quite different from these other areas of law, as well. When parties to a contract sue one another, the cause of action is usually based on some unfulfilled promise contained in the contract. People who are parties to a contract have a relationship with one another, and it is that relationship that gives rise to the suit. In a torts case, on the other hand, there is usually no requirement of relationship. A plaintiff is not even required to know the defendant. The important issue is whether the defendant's actions injured the plaintiff. In corporate law, for example, the focus is on the creation and legal obligations of various forms of businesses, from sole proprietorships to major corporations. In this book we address the topic of business torts, but other than that small overlap, there are few similarities between tort law and corporate law. As you can see, tort law is a distinct subspecialty of law and has its own rules, concepts, and historical roots.

Tort law is often referred to by the more descriptive title of "civil injuries." Actually, that title makes a great deal of sense. Torts involve physical, emotional, or financial injuries. The civil courts provide a framework for victims to attempt to receive compensation for these various injuries. Just as there are various kinds of crimes, there are various kinds of torts. This book focuses on one of the largest areas of tort law: personal injury cases. The reason for this is simple — personal injury cases are common. A paralegal is far more likely to become involved in a car wreck case than a class action product liability case. In fact, many firms limit their entire practice to car wreck cases. There is never a shortage of business.

However, this is not to say that the other kinds of torts are not important. One of the largest jury verdict awards came in a torts case that did not involve a car wreck. That verdict resulted from the foundering of the Exxon *Valdez* off the coast of Alaska. The resulting oil spill ruined miles of beaches and killed untold thousands of fish and animals. The jury that heard the negligence suit awarded punitive damages against Exxon of over $9 billion. To date, that remains the largest jury verdict in history. Whether Exxon will actually have to pay out $9 billion is another matter. At least one appellate court has said that the punitive damage award is too large and should be reduced.

IV. A SHORT HISTORY OF TORT LAW

Although the development of tort law over the past 2,000 years makes an interesting treatise on its own, we dispense with a great deal of it in this book. However, we focus attention on certain historical developments in tort law, if for no other reason than some of these legal concepts are still around today and continue to have an impact on modern lawsuits.

A. AN EYE FOR AN EYE

One of the ancient concepts in tort law had to do with the legal principle of "an eye for an eye." Under this principle, if a person intentionally cut off another person's hand, the injured man would be entitled to require amputation of the offender's hand. The practical difficulties of such a system seem apparent to us and probably became readily apparent to the participants. Such a system does not promote a peaceful society. It also does not encourage people to use the court system to work out their differences.

B. MONEY FOR AN EYE

The concept of "an eye for an eye" quickly changed to a more modern concept of legal payment for injuries. Under this system, the various parts of a person's body were given monetary value, and damage (or loss of use) of any of these parts would require a monetary payment by the offender. Eyes and hands had the greatest value, while toes had the least. Facial scars carried more monetary value than scars on other parts of the body. Although this system seems terribly outdated, it is in fact the system that is in use today in most workers' compensation statutes. Today, when a worker is injured on the job, a dollar amount is set for damage or loss of use of a hand, an arm, or an eye, just as it was done over a thousand years ago.

This system of assigning monetary value to parts of the body also applies to negligence cases. Although there is no printed schedule stating exact amounts for body parts, the idea remains the same. One of the things that the jury will determine during the course of its deliberations is how much value to attach to the plaintiff's injuries caused by the defendant's negligence. This determination is one of the main duties of the jurors when they retire to the jury room to deliberate. First they determine if the plaintiff should win; then they determine how much the plaintiff should receive.

C. THE DEVELOPMENT OF TORT LAW IN THE UNITED STATES

The survivors of the sinking of the RMS Titanic had little success in negligence suits brought against the White Star Line for the disaster that occurred in 1912.

Tort law developed very slowly in the United States. Early legal treatises either neglect it entirely or mention tort law only as a minor consideration. This situation changed dramatically with the coming of the Industrial Revolution to both England and the United States. Suddenly, there were dangerous machines operating everywhere, and they were injuring people. One particular machine, the railroad locomotive, generated more lawsuits than anyone could have imagined. The law of negligence suddenly took center stage, with workers and passengers bringing suits against negligently operated railroad engines. The courts, always slow to recognize massive changes in social institutions, at first sided with the railroad companies. Recoveries were denied in the face of obvious negligence. However, this situation slowly changed over the decades, until the courts developed new theories of negligence to take into account the negligence of a public carrier. In these days of ubiquitous lawsuits brought against airline companies and others for accidents, it is difficult to comprehend that similar railroad disasters of 150 years ago spawned few cases and even fewer recoveries.

BRINGING A TORT CASE

Plaintiff
The legal title of the person who brings a complaint.

Defendant
The legal title of the person who is served with the complaint.

The person or corporation who files a lawsuit is called the **plaintiff.** The person or corporation who is sued is called the **defendant.** Sometimes both parties have claims against one another. How do we determine who is the plaintiff and who is the defendant? The answer is simple: Whoever files a complaint first is the plaintiff. But there is a lot more to a civil case than simply filing a complaint. In our case, before a complaint can be filed, the lawyer representing the plaintiff, Charles Chumley, has to launch an investigation to make sure that the claim Mr. Chumley is raising is valid. See Figure 1-6 for statistics on plaintiffs who win their civil trials.

State	Total Incoming Tort Cases	Percent of Civil Caseload	Tort Cases per 100,000 Population
All Civil Cases Processed in General Tier			
New Jersey	57,653	6.9%	650
Missouri	15,494	5.3%	257
Puerto Rico*	6,105	3.8%	166
Kansas	3,475	2.1%	120
Wisconsin	6,350	2.5%	111
Iowa*	3,106	2.3%	101
Minnesota*	3,946	2.1%	73
Maine*	974	2.4%	73
All Tort Cases Processed in General Tier			
Connecticut	14,336	7.0%	399
Pennsylvania	36,874	7.3%	289
Utah	1,963	1.5%	69
Tort Cases Processed in General and Limited Tiers			
Ohio	25,950	4.0%	225
Texas	53,147	3.4%	204
Washington	11,635	4.0%	169
Kentucky	5,879	2.4%	134
Alaska	937	4.4%	128
Hawai'i	1,422	3.5%	102
North Carolina	8,439	1.1%	87

FIGURE 1-6

Incoming Tort Caseloads and Rates in 18 States, 2012

National Center for State Courts, Data Source: Court Statistics Project, Publication: Examining the Work of State Courts: An Analysis of 2010 State Court Caseloads, 9/24/12, p. 12

A. INVESTIGATING THE CAUSE OF ACTION: RULE 11

Not only is investigating a claim prior to filing a lawsuit a good idea, the rules of civil procedure may require it. For instance, Rule 11 of the Federal Rules of Civil Procedure (a rule that is closely followed in most states) requires that a reasonable inquiry be made into the factual basis of the lawsuit before a complaint is filed. The rule was developed as a way to attempt to reduce the number of frivolous lawsuits. Investigation can take many forms but always focuses on discovering the facts of a claim. See Figure 1-7 for the full text of Rule 11.

FIGURE 1-7
 	
Rule 11, Federal Rules of Civil Procedure
	(a) Signature.
	Every pleading, written motion, and other paper must be signed by at least one attorney of record in the attorney's name — or by a party personally if the party is unrepresented. The paper must state the signer's address, e-mail address, and telephone number. Unless a rule or statute specifically states otherwise, a pleading need not be verified or accompanied by an affidavit. The court must strike an unsigned paper unless the omission is promptly corrected after being called to the attorney's or party's attention.
	
	(b) Representations to the Court.
	By presenting to the court a pleading, written motion, or other paper — whether by signing, filing, submitting, or later advocating it — an attorney or unrepresented party certifies that to the best of the person's knowledge, information, and belief, formed after an inquiry reasonable under the circumstances:
	
	    (1) it is not being presented for any improper purpose, such as to harass, cause unnecessary delay, or needlessly increase the cost of litigation;
	    (2) the claims, defenses, and other legal contentions are warranted by existing law or by a nonfrivolous argument for extending, modifying, or reversing existing law or for establishing new law;
	    (3) the factual contentions have evidentiary support or, if specifically so identified, will likely have evidentiary support after a reasonable opportunity for further investigation or discovery; and
	    (4) the denials of factual contentions are warranted on the evidence or, if specifically so identified, are reasonably based on belief or a lack of information.

B. LITIGATION CHART

One item that helps in investigating a case is a litigation chart. This chart shows all of the essential elements of the lawsuit. Prepared either for the plaintiff or the defense, this chart shows all the elements of the claim, the evidence necessary to support that claim, and the identity of the witness or evidence that will prove the claim.

Obviously the litigation chart will look different depending on which side prepares it. When the plaintiff prepares a litigation chart, the essential elements include all of the basic claims of the complaint. When the defense side prepares a litigation chart, it focuses on disproving the essential elements of the plaintiff's claim and whatever defenses will be raised at trial. See Figure 1-8 for a sample litigation chart.

FIGURE 1-8

Litigation Chart

This is a sample litigation chart from a car wreck case. The allegations come directly from the complaint.

Allegation	Witness	Testimony (summary)	Physical evidence
That, on or about the 19th day of October 2000, at approximately 9:40 A.M., plaintiff was operating a motor vehicle traveling west on Maple Street in Anytown, Mason County, North Carolina	Plaintiff: Jane Smith	That she was driving that day, on that street	None
The defendant driver admitted at the scene that she did not see plaintiff's vehicle before pulling out into the intersection	Officer: John Doe	Taking the statement from defendant after being called to the scene	None
That plaintiff was operating her vehicle below the posted speed limit of 35 mph	Plaintiff: Jane Smith	Ms. Smith's testimony	None
	Accident reconstructionist: Dave Jones	His study of the scene; skid marks, point of impact from glass shards	Photographs, diagrams made by Dr. Jones

C. SOURCES OF PROOF

As the legal team investigates a claim to develop a case for trial, one aspect of the case remains paramount: evidence. Because an attorney cannot testify at trial, the only way to prove or disprove a claim is through testimony or evidence. A witness will testify either through deposition or on the witness stand about the facts of the case. Exhibits will be used to bolster or support this evidence. In other situations, evidence may be presented to disprove a claim. In either event, it is important to know who the witnesses are, what they are going to say, and what type of evidence the attorney intends to introduce at trial. Much of this evidence and witness testimony can be discovered long before a complaint is ever filed. We explore the types of investigations and other trial preparation issues throughout this book.

D. FILING A COMPLAINT

Once the investigation is complete, the next step in a civil suit is drafting the complaint and serving it on the defendant. Keep in mind that not all states use the same terminology. In fact, this is a good place to point out that the law in each state is unique, with its own rules, terminology, and procedures. We address the basic law of torts that can be found in all states, but always remember to check the laws of your state for differences. These differences apply to everything from the names of courts to the titles of documents in a lawsuit. For simplicity's sake, we use the same terminology throughout. We refer to the document that sets out the plaintiff's cause of action — and begins the lawsuit — as the complaint. When the defendant responds to the complaint, he or she files a document that is usually called an **answer.**

Answer
The name of the document that the defendant serves on the plaintiff, outlining his or her defenses and any claims he or she may have against the plaintiff.

VI DISCOVERY IN CIVIL CASES

Once the pleadings have been filed and served on the opposing parties, the case moves into a new phase: discovery. During the discovery phase, both sides are encouraged to learn as much about the claim in the case as possible. Courts have gradually liberalized the rules surrounding civil discovery under the theory that the more that both sides know about the case prior to trial, the more likely they are to settle the case before taking it to a jury. To that end, parties may do any or all of the following:

- Issue interrogatories
- Depose witnesses
- Request the production of documents
- Request that the other side admit to certain facts
- Request a physical and/or mental examination of a party

A. INTERROGATORIES

Interrogatories are written questions posed by one side to the other. These questions can cover a wide range of issues concerning the case and other matters. For instance, a party is permitted to ask the other side for the names, addresses, and telephone numbers of the witnesses the other side plans to call at trial, and about the general nature of the testimony, the existence of written reports about the incident, etcetera. As is true with all discovery requests, courts are very liberal in permitting questions and ordering the other side to provide answers.

B. DEPOSITIONS

Unlike interrogatories, depositions are oral questions of a witness. A deposition occurs weeks or even months prior to trial. At the beginning of the deposition, the witness is sworn and is then asked questions by the attorneys. The entire deposition is conducted before a court reporter, who takes down everything that is said by the witness and the attorneys. Later, the court reporter produces a typed transcript of the questions and answers that the attorneys may review prior to trial.

C. REQUEST FOR PRODUCTION OF DOCUMENTS

Discovery rules also permit both sides to request the other side produce documents. These requests for documents can include reports or almost any other written material relating to the incident that forms the basis of the suit.

D. REQUEST TO ADMIT FACTS

In addition to permitting either side to a suit to ask questions of the opposition, the discovery rules allow one side to request that the other side admit to the truth of certain matters. For instance, the firm representing Mr. Chumley might serve a request to admit on the defendant railroad company requesting that it admit that it is a duly authorized corporation in the state of Placid. When a party admits to certain facts, it means that further proof is no longer required. An admitted fact is taken as true.

E. REQUEST FOR PHYSICAL AND/OR MENTAL EXAMINATION OF A PARTY

When the plaintiff's physical injuries are in dispute in a case, as they usually are in personal injury (tort) cases, the defendant is permitted to request that the plaintiff submit to a physical examination performed by a doctor chosen by the defense. In the case of Mr. Chumley, his extensive injuries are the basis of a substantial monetary claim. In this case, the defendants may very well request a physical examination by their doctor to help them determine Mr. Chumley's health.

Tech Topic
SOCIAL MEDIA AND THEIR EFFECT ON TORTS CASES

Facebook, Twitter, MySpace, YouTube . . . what relevance do social media sites have in today's tort actions? Plenty! While users see social media as a harmless way to share every mundane detail of their lives, attorneys and paralegals see them as gold mines for discovery.

Discovery is the part of the litigation process during which each side can access and review each other's information — including sensitive, private information — as long as it is determined to be relevant to the case. Social media are fast becoming integral parts of the discovery process, particularly in personal injury cases.

A 2007 Pennsylvania case, *McMillen v. Hummingbird Speedway Inc.*, involved a plaintiff who sued to recover damages for substantial injuries he allegedly received when his car was rear-ended by a defendant's

vehicle following a stock car race. During discovery, the defendant found on the public portion of McMillen's Facebook page a description of a recent fishing trip as well as a trip to see the Daytona 500. The defendant then asked McMillen to reveal his username and password so that the entire page could be viewed for evidence that his injuries weren't as serious as he claimed.

Plaintiff McMillen refused on the grounds that the information was confidential. However, the court agreed with the defendant and compelled McMillen not only to reveal his login information but also to refrain from deleting or changing anything on his Facebook account.

The bottom line is that anything posted on social media sites is fair game for discovery in tort actions.

THE TRIAL OF A CIVIL CASE

When it comes to the actual trial of a civil case, there are remarkably few differences between how that type of trial is conducted and the way that any other trial, including a criminal case, is carried out. In fact, if you happened to enter a courtroom on any given day of the week, it might take you several minutes before you could figure out if you were watching a criminal case or a civil case. The reason for this is simple: All jury trials proceed in much the same way. The first phase of a jury trial is the selection of a jury.

A. JURY SELECTION

The parties to a civil case select a jury from a panel of citizens who have been summoned to the court for jury duty. This panel, also called the *venire*, is filled with people who are citizens of the county or state. These people come from all walks of life and all types of backgrounds. The only limitation is that a convicted felon is not allowed to sit on a jury. Short of that, there are very few limitations on who is allowed to sit on a jury.

When jury selection begins, both parties question the panel and use the answers as the basis for removing panel members until 12 jurors remain. This process is called **voir dire** or "striking" the jury, named after the process of striking off a person's name from a list. Each side in a civil case has the right to strike panel members. They usually take turns as each panel member's name is called out, either announcing that they strike or that they accept a panel member. As soon as the requisite number of jurors is selected (in some states, six-person juries can be seated), the rest of the panel is excused. At this point, the people who have been selected to sit on the jury are put into the jury box.

Voir dire
(French) "Look speak"; the process of questioning a juror to discover bias or prejudice, or who would make an acceptable juror to hear a case.

B. OPENING STATEMENT

Once the jurors are seated in the jury box, the next phase in most jury trials is the opening statement. In an opening statement, the attorneys for the plaintiff and the defendant are permitted to address the jury and explain their basic positions in the case. The plaintiff's attorney goes first. He or she often begins by explaining to the jury what the case is about. After that, the attorney explains how the plaintiff was injured by the defendant's actions and how that injury entitles the plaintiff to receive monetary damages from the defendant. Once the plaintiff's attorney has addressed the jury, the defendant's attorney has the right to address the jury. Obviously, the defense opening will be very different from the plaintiff's opening. The defendant's attorney often tells the jury that the plaintiff's case is unjustified and that the plaintiff is not entitled to receive any money from the defendant. The jury has to decide which version of these two diametrically opposed viewpoints is the more reasonable.

C. PRESENTATION OF THE PLAINTIFF'S CASE

Once opening statements are over, the plaintiff presents his or her case. The plaintiff must prove the allegations he or she has raised in the complaint. If the plaintiff has claimed that the defendant was reckless or negligent, the plaintiff has to present evidence to support that claim. Proof comes in the form of witness testimony and physical exhibits. The plaintiff's attorney calls witnesses to the stand and asks them questions under oath. The purpose of this questioning, called direct examination, is to prove the claims in the complaint. The plaintiff's attorney asks the witnesses about what they saw on the day of the accident (if they are eyewitnesses) or about the plaintiff's medical troubles (if they are medical professionals). Whatever claim the plaintiff raises, he or she has to prove it through witnesses and exhibits. These exhibits often consist of items such as photographs, videos, documents, and medical records, among others.

On television, attorneys are often seen screaming and yelling at witnesses, or sometimes at each other. In the real world, this seldom happens. For one thing, most judges would never put up with such behavior. For another, a trial is a very formal affair, conducted by professionals. As a general rule, the attorneys are very courteous to each other and the witnesses.

Once the plaintiff's attorney has finished asking the witness questions, the defendant's attorney has the right to ask questions. This is called cross-examination. The purpose of cross-examination is very different from direct examination. In cross-examination, the defendant's attorney often attempts to show that the witness has a bias for the plaintiff or that the evidence could be interpreted in some other way, etcetera.

The plaintiff's case proceeds from witness to witness, exhibit to exhibit, until the plaintiff has presented all the evidence and the attorney believes that the claim has been proven. At this point, the plaintiff's attorney announces that he or she "rests." This announcement means that the plaintiff's case is over. At this point, the defendant will usually ask for a directed verdict.

D. MOTION FOR DIRECTED VERDICT

Motion for directed verdict
A motion brought by the defense at the end of the plaintiff's case, asking that the case be dismissed because the plaintiff has failed to prove the claims raised in the complaint.

When the plaintiff's case is over and the plaintiff has rested, the defense normally asks the judge for permission to argue a **motion for directed verdict.** At this point the jury is sent out of the courtroom and the defendant's attorney will present an argument to the judge that the plaintiff has failed to prove his or her case. Most defense attorneys make this argument, even if the evidence in the case has been extensive. The defense attorney has nothing to lose by making the request and everything to gain. If the judge agrees with the defense, the case will be dismissed and the defendant will pay no damages. If the judge sides with the plaintiff, the case will proceed and the defendant is in no worse a position than he or she was when the case started.

E. THE DEFENSE CASE

In some cases, the plaintiff may have the opportunity to dispute specific facts raised by the defense during its presentation. This right is called rebuttal.

The case for the defense closely resembles the presentation of the plaintiff's case. The defense is attempting to prove that the plaintiff has no basis for his or her suit, either because the defendant did not do anything wrong, or because the plaintiff was not as injured as claimed, etcetera. The defense calls witnesses to the stand, and these witnesses are questioned in exactly the same way as the plaintiff's witnesses were. The defense may also present exhibits. All of this evidence is designed to disprove the plaintiff's case. The plaintiff's attorney has the same right to cross-examine the defense witnesses as the defense attorney had to cross-examine the plaintiff's witnesses.

When the defendant has presented all his or her testimony and evidence, he or she makes a similar announcement as the plaintiff made when the plaintiff finished his or her case: "Your Honor, the defense rests." At this point, the trial of the case is over. No additional witnesses will testify and no other exhibits will be offered. The case is not over, however. There are still at least two more phases before the trial is complete: the closing argument and jury charge.

F. CLOSING ARGUMENT

When the evidentiary phase of the trial is over, the attorneys have the right to address the jury one more time during closing argument. A closing argument resembles an opening statement, but only superficially. The attorneys speak directly to the jurors, explaining what they believe the evidence in the case proved. Obviously, the plaintiff will argue that the evidence proved his or points. The defense attorney will just as obviously claim that the testimony and exhibits support his or her view of the case. Unlike an opening statement, attorneys are permitted to draw conclusions, appeal to the jurors' emotions, or argue the consequences to the community of a particular verdict.

> **Sidebar**
>
> *Most studies show that jurors make up their minds about a case during the opening statement.*

G. THE JURY CHARGE

Once the closing arguments are complete, the judge addresses the jurors. The judge tells the jurors what they are supposed to do once they retire to the jury room. The judge tells the jurors how they should go about deciding the case. He or she also reads them the crucial legal points that factored in the case. For instance, a judge might instruct the jurors that, "One of your first duties upon retiring to the jury room will be to select one member to act as jury foreperson. This person will conduct the proceedings and alert the court when you have reached a verdict." These instructions are called *jury charges* and provide direction for the jury about what the law on particular points is and what weight they can give to certain types of evidence.

H. THE VERDICT

When the jury charge is complete, the jurors are told to leave the courtroom and sequester themselves in the jury room, where they can talk about the case. The jurors are also told that once they make up their minds, their decision, or **verdict,** should be announced to the court. The jury's verdict in a civil case often boils down to a decision about who should win. If the jury decides that the defendant should win, the verdict will be "We, the jury, find for the defendant." If they decide that the plaintiff should win, the verdict will be "We, the jury, find for the plaintiff." If the jurors find for the plaintiff, they are also instructed to decide how much money the defendant should have to pay to the plaintiff.

> **Verdict**
> The jury's final decision in the case, in which they decide questions of fact raised in the case.

The basic steps in a civil trial are:

Jury selection	Closing arguments
Opening statements	Jury charge
Direct and cross-examination of	Jury deliberation
witnesses	Verdict

TORT
BASICS
AT A
GLANCE

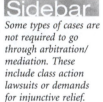

VIII ALTERNATIVE DISPUTE RESOLUTION

So far, our discussion has focused on the stages of a civil trial. This should not create the impression that civil cases are not settled prior to trial. In fact, most civil cases are disposed of prior to trial, either through the efforts of the parties to negotiate some mutually acceptable resolution or through alternative dispute resolution.

A. WHAT IS ALTERNATIVE DISPUTE RESOLUTION?

Over the past two decades, alternative dispute resolution and mediation have become increasingly popular with overwhelmed court systems. The term *alternative dispute resolution,* or ADR, is shorthand for any of a variety of nontrial methods to resolve differences in civil cases. Among these methods are arbitration and mediation.

Arbitration is a process in which two or more parties voluntarily agree to submit their dispute to an impartial third person for resolution. Arbitration can be either binding or nonbinding. When the parties voluntarily submit a case to an arbitrator, there is usually a stipulation in the agreement that the parties agree to be bound by the arbitrator's decisions in the case. Many states also have programs in place that force litigants in most civil cases to go through an arbitration or mediation process. The rules governing arbitration and mediation are set out in the state statutes. In North Carolina, for instance, court-ordered, nonbinding arbitration has been authorized in certain civil cases since 1989.

B. ARBITRATION VERSUS MEDIATION

When parties enter into arbitration, they agree to submit certain disputed issues to a third party. They also agree that they will follow the ruling of the arbitrator, whatever the final decision may be. Mediation, on the other hand, is an informal process designed to assist the parties in resolving their disputes among themselves. Unlike arbitrators, mediators do not make an award or render a judgment on the merits of the action.

TORT BASICS AT A GLANCE

Arbitrators decide contested issues; mediators help the parties resolve their contested issues.

IX APPEALS

When one or more parties to the case are dissatisfied with the jury's verdict, they are permitted to appeal their case. Appellate courts are courts of limited jurisdiction, meaning that they can only address certain issues and make certain, limited rulings. When a party appeals a case, the appeal is not conducted as a new trial. Appellate courts do not hear witness testimony or consider evidence. They review what occurred at the trial and read the briefs submitted by the parties. In almost all cases, an appellate court is limited to three possible decisions on an appeal; the court can **affirm, reverse,** or **remand** a case.

When an appellate court affirms a decision, it agrees with the lower court's decision in the case. If the decision is reversed, it means that the appellate court is changing the decision of the lower court. A reversal at the first appellate court would mean that whoever won the case in the trial court would now be the loser. A remand directs the case back to the trial court for an additional hearing on some issue. Remands are relatively rare, but when they occur, they are usually the result of some new allegation. Because the appellate court has neither the facility nor the legal authority to carry out a hearing, the only option is to send the case to a court that does have such power.

The appellate court's decision means that one party wins and one party loses. In order to justify its decision, and to explain its reasoning, the appellate court publishes its decision in an opinion. The opinion states the important facts, law, and rationale for the court's decision. This published opinion becomes extremely valuable for legal researchers, because it explains the court's view on a particular topic. The body of published decisions is known as case law.

Affirm
The appellate court agrees with the verdict, or some ruling, entered in the trial and votes to keep that decision in place.

Reverse
To reverse a decision is to set it aside; an appellate court disagrees with the verdict, or some ruling, in the trial and overturns that decision.

Remand
The appellate court requires additional information or an evidentiary hearing; it cannot conduct such a hearing itself, so it sends the case back to the trial court for the hearing and then considers the appeal based on that hearing.

A. THE IMPORTANCE OF CASE LAW

When a client asks about the "law" on a particular topic, he or she usually fails to realize that for legal professionals, there are several different kinds of law. For instance, statutes are created by the legislature and signed into existence by the state governor. Administrative rules and regulations are created by governmental agencies and are often considered to be just as binding as a statute. (If you are in doubt about that statement, just consider the rules and regulations of the Internal Revenue Service.) However, most clients are not aware of the fact that prior decided cases are just as binding on the legal system as are statutes.

Case law refers to the body of judicial decisions stretching back for centuries. Appellate courts such as the U.S. Supreme Court have been deciding cases since our legal system was created. This body of legal decisions creates a vast, and sometimes confusing, body of law.

Case law
The body of cases decided by judges who have interpreted statutes and prior cases.

When a case goes up on appeal, the appellate courts are often called upon to interpret statutes. The court's interpretation of a statute is binding on all future litigants. The U.S. Supreme Court makes such rulings many times a year. For instance, when the U.S. Supreme Court rules that a specific type of evidence is admissible (medical narratives, for instance), this ruling is binding on the entire nation. An understanding of judicial interpretations, or case law, is critically important to a legal professional. In an area of law such as tort law, which is rich in case law but has relatively few applicable statutes, case law takes on an even more prominent role.

1. HOW IS CASE LAW CREATED?

To discuss how case law is created, we review the facts of a hypothetical case: John Doe sues Richard Roe over a car wreck. John was sitting in his car at a red light when Richard Roe, who was traveling in the same direction, rear-ended Mr. Doe. This is a pretty straightforward case, but it will help to illustrate how case law is created. At trial, Richard Roe argues a rather novel idea: that John Doe's car, which is an import with a radically different design from any other car in this country, is built so low to the ground that a driver in a more standard car would have trouble seeing it. The judge only allows Richard Roe to offer limited testimony along these lines before cutting him off. Richard Roe is allowed to use this idea as his defense to the jury, but the jury decides against him and finds for the plaintiff, John Doe. Rather than pay the damages assessed by the jury, Richard Roe takes his case up on appeal. In the court of appeals, he argues that the judge unfairly limited his right to produce evidence about the design of John Doe's car. Roe is essentially saying to the court of appeals, "If I had been allowed to present this testimony, I might have won."

B. STARE DECISIS

Stare decisis
The principle that courts will reach results similar to those reached by courts in prior cases involving similar facts and legal issues.

The court of appeals considers this argument. Because all courts are bound by the principle of **stare decisis,** their consideration of this argument takes a standard format. Stare decisis is the Latin term for *stand by decided cases.* It is an old but still very useful concept. When a court states that it will stand by decided cases, it is saying that if there is a prior decision by a court that dealt with this same issue, this court will rule the same way as that prior court, even if this court doesn't like the ruling. Stare decisis is really an issue of continuity. Judges abide by stare decisis to give everyone who appears before them some sense of predictability about what the court will do. If a judge decides that he or she will not follow the decision in the prior case, the judge must show how this case is different from the prior case. With a different case, you can have a different ruling.

Let's get back to the case of *Doe v. Roe.* The court of appeals has been asked to decide if the trial judge unfairly curtailed Roe's ability to present evidence about the design of Doe's car. The first question that the judges in the court of appeals will ask themselves is, "Has this same issue ever come up before?" If it has, the principle of stare decisis dictates that they must rule the same way as that prior case. In researching the law, the judges discover that ten years ago, the state supreme court had a similar case before it in which a party raised a similar claim. In that case, the state supreme court said that there was nothing improper in limiting the presentation of this evidence, so long as the party was allowed to present the defense to the jury.

This case seems similar to the current case on appeal. The judges in the court of appeals decide to affirm.

With an order affirming the trial court's decision, Richard Roe now faces a decision. He can appeal to the state supreme court, but his chances of winning there are much lower. For one thing, most state supreme courts have the requirement of **certiorari,** or cert. Cert refers to that court's power to decide which cases it will hear on appeal. In most states, the court of appeals (or whatever name it is called) lacks the power of cert. However, most state supreme courts, and certainly the U.S. Supreme Court, have the power to decline to hear an appellate case by denying cert. Generally speaking, the state supreme court, like the U.S. Supreme Court, will only decide to hear cases that the court considers to be significant or that will help clear up some cloudy issue of the law.

Richard Roe's attorney files a request for cert with the state supreme court and, as in most cases appealed to that court, cert is denied. At this point, unless Roe thinks that he has a chance with the U.S. Supreme Court, his options are over. See Figure 1-9 for a diagram of the various courts of appeals.

At every stage of this process, Roe's attorney has had his paralegal researching the case law to see if there are any legal issues that she can raise with the court that might be successful. John Doe's legal team has also been busy reviewing the case law, but their focus has been to make sure that the decision stands.

Certiorari (cert)
The power of a court to decide which cases it will hear and which it will not.

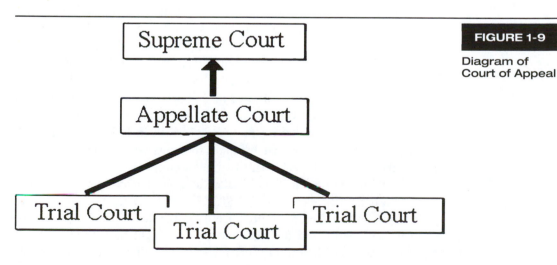

FIGURE 1-9

Diagram of
Court of Appeal

C. AN EXAMPLE OF CASE LAW

In each chapter of this book, you will find at least one case reported. In this first chapter, an appellate case is presented that lays out the basics of what a tort case is and how it proceeds. The first case excerpt to be considered revolves a common occurrence: a dog bite.

VALLEJO V. EBERT
120 A.D.3d 797, 991 N.Y.S.2d 656 (2014)

WILLIAM F. MASTRO, J.P., THOMAS A. DICKERSON, JEFFREY A. COHEN, AND ROBERT J. MILLER, JJ.

In an action to recover damages for personal injuries, the plaintiff appeals (1), as limited by his brief, from so much of an order of the Supreme Court, Kings County (Partnow, J.), dated August 12, 2013, as granted the defendant's cross motion for summary judgment dismissing the complaint and denied those branches of his motion which were to compel the deposition of nonparty witnesses, hold them in contempt for their failure to appear for a deposition, and arrest and detain them until they were deposed, and (2) a judgment of the same court dated September 27, 2013, which, upon the order, is in favor of the defendant and against him dismissing the complaint. The notice of appeal from the order is deemed also to be a notice of appeal from the judgment.

ORDERED that the appeal from the order is dismissed; and it is further,

ORDERED that the judgment is affirmed; and it is further,

ORDERED that one bill of costs is awarded to the defendant.

To recover in strict liability in tort for damages caused by a dog, the plaintiff must establish that the dog had vicious propensities and that the owner knew or should have known of the dog's vicious propensities Evidence tending to demonstrate a dog's vicious propensities includes evidence of a prior attack, the dog's tendency to growl, snap, or bare its teeth, the manner in which the dog was restrained, the fact that the dog was kept as a guard dog, and a proclivity to act in a way that puts others at risk of harm.

Here, the defendant established her prima facie entitlement to judgment as a matter of law. Evidence submitted in support of the motion, including a transcript of the deposition testimony of the defendant, showed that the dog had been living with the defendant's family, which included a small child, without incident, for approximately four or five years before it bit the plaintiff. Prior to the incident, the defendant had not seen the dog exhibit aggressive behavior. In opposition, the plaintiff failed to raise a triable issue of fact as to whether the defendant was aware, or should have been aware, that her dog had vicious propensities. The mere presence of a "Beware of Dog" sign on the defendant's property, and the fact that the dog might have been confined when there was a celebration at the premises, were insufficient to raise a triable issue of fact.

To the extent that the complaint alleged a common-law negligence cause of action, the Supreme Court properly awarded summary judgment to the defendant dismissing the cause of action because "New York does not recognize a common-law negligence cause of action to recover damages for injuries caused by a domestic animal."

Since further discovery would not have affected the outcome of the cross motion for summary judgment, the plaintiff's contentions that the Supreme Court should have granted those branches of his motion which were to compel the deposition of nonparty witnesses, hold them in contempt for their failure to appear for their scheduled depositions, and arrest and detain them until they were deposed have been rendered academic by our determination.

Questions about the case:

1. What is a plaintiff required to show in order to recover under a theory of strict liability in a dog bite case?
2. What kind of evidence would satisfy the requirements for "vicious propensities"?
3. What evidence did the defendant present that showed that the dog had no violent proclivities?
4. Did the defendant's "Beware of Dog" sign show that the defendant was aware of the dog's propensity for violence?

Chapter Summary

A tort is a legal wrong that gives the wronged party the right to seek redress in court. When a person files an action claiming a civil injury, he or she is seeking damages or other compensation for a wrong carried out by another. Tort law is civil in nature and differs from other areas of law, such as criminal law, in several important ways. When a plaintiff initiates a case against a defendant, both the pre-trial procedures and the trial itself follow a predictable pattern, from the filing of the complaint to the jury's verdict. Once the jury has decided the case and rendered a verdict, the dissatisfied party is permitted to appeal his or her case. On appeal, an appellate court can affirm the trial court's decision, reverse the decision, or remand for further determinations. The appellate court's decision is recorded in an opinion that is published for all others to read and forms the basis of case law, one of the foundations of judicial interpretation.

 SKILLS YOU NEED IN THE REAL WORLD

How a Paralegal Can Do Some Basic Investigative Work

Most paralegals are not trained to carry out investigations. Many would be surprised to learn that knowing basic investigative techniques could be a real asset in the marketplace. When a firm needs basic information about a case, the most common method of obtaining it is for the attorney to investigate the basic details and then rely on discovery to ferret out additional details. However, there are times when this process is not efficient. Some cases do not have the financial resources to justify an attorney's time. In such a situation, the other alternative — a private detective — may also be too costly. Not all clients can afford the added expense of a private investigator. However, a paralegal who knows some basic investigative techniques can learn a great deal about a case, with less of a cost investment, and that paralegal will become even more indispensable to the firm in the process.

What Facts Do You Need?

Before a paralegal can begin to investigate a claim, he or she must first decide what facts are the most important to discover. For a plaintiff's firm, the most important facts are those that support the cause of action. Without that support, there can be no valid claim.

Using Public Records to Gather Information

Suppose your firm is investigating the defendant (or the person who will be the defendant if the lawsuit is actually filed). What public records can help a paralegal learn more information about this person? The best place to start is the local courthouse.

The Courthouse

The local courthouse is a gold mine of information, if you know where to look. Consider the following resources:

- **Clerk's Office**
  The local clerk's office maintains records about all civil and criminal cases in the county. Using the computer databases, a paralegal can learn whether someone has been sued, divorced, or convicted of a crime.
- **Deed Room or Registrar's Office**
  Sometimes called the registrar's office, or the land office, the deed room is where all records of real estate transactions are stored. In this office, a paralegal can find out what real estate a defendant owns (useful in evaluating the likelihood of enforcing a judgment against him).
- **Tax Office**
  The tax office is required to keep extensive records about real estate and other items. In some tax offices, you can even see a digital photo of the house. In larger counties, such as metropolitan areas, this information is available at public access terminals. A picture of the house and all of the details are just a mouse click away.

Internet

The Internet also offers some valuable research tools. There are numerous sites that allow you to search out a person's address, telephone number, e-mail address, and other information. However, there are also questionable sites that claim to provide you with a complete background on a person for a nominal fee. Unless the site is one that you recognize as a reputable company, you should avoid such sites. There is a great deal of free information available about persons, but if you plan on paying for research, the best bet is still a private detective.

Keep these sources in mind if you are ever called upon to do some basic investigative work in a case.

THE LIFE OF A PARALEGAL

Going to Court with the Attorney

When I go to court, I give the attorney my point of view and input with regard to jury selection. It can be very important. For one thing, it helps to keep all of the witnesses' information straight and keep up with their testimony. The attorneys often find that it's helpful to have another person in the courtroom who is listening for all sorts of things. [One] of the other things that I do is to keep the witnesses prepared and on standby, coordinating when they need to be called to come on in. I also keep the exhibits straight and the file in order so that I can put my hands on anything that the attorney might require without having to shuffle through an unorganized file.

Debra Holbrook, Paralegal

ETHICAL ISSUES FOR THE PARALEGAL: AN INTRODUCTION

Paralegals must have a finely developed sense of ethics. For one thing, a solid basis in ethical standards will keep a paralegal from violating an attorney's ethics. When a paralegal engages in unethical practices, this reflects on the attorney. The attorney may get sanctioned by the state bar and be sued for legal malpractice. In recent years, paralegals have also been named in such suits. Throughout this text, we explore ethical issues for paralegals involved in civil cases.

To begin with, a paralegal should read and understand the ethical obligations of the attorney. These rules can be found in the state bar's handbook, on the bar website, or in the published court rules. An hour or two spent with these rules can save a paralegal a great deal of heartache later on.

Relevant Cases

MILTON V. IIT RESEARCH INSTITUTE,
138 F.3D 519, 520-523 (C.A.4 (VA.),1998)

Opinion

WILKINSON, Chief Judge:

Donn Milton's wrongful discharge action against his former employer, IIT Research Institute (IITRI), raises [the] legal issue: the viability of his claim under that law. Maryland's cause of action for wrongful discharge is not available on these facts. We thus affirm the judgment of the district court dismissing Milton's claim.

I.

As the district court granted defendant's Fed.R.Civ.P. 12(b)(6) motion, we shall treat the allegations in the complaint as true. Martin Marietta Corp. v. International Telecomms. Satellite Org., 991 F.2d 94, 97 (4th Cir.1993).

IITRI is a not-for-profit scientific research organization that enjoys tax-exempt status under Section 501(c)(3) of the Internal Revenue Code. In 1993, IITRI hired Milton to supervise administration of a contract between the company and the federal government called the Tax Systems Modernization Institute (TSMI). In 1995, Milton became Vice President of IITRI's Advanced Technology Group, which included TSMI and several other projects. Throughout his tenure at IITRI, Milton's office was located at the IITRI facility in Lanham, Maryland.

During the course of his employment, Milton became convinced that IITRI was abusing its tax-exempt status by failing to report to the Internal Revenue Service taxable income generated by the substantial portion of IITRI's business that did not constitute scientific research in the public interest. Milton voiced his concerns to IITRI management, to no avail. In 1995, after similar allegations by a competitor, IITRI initiated an internal examination of the issue. In connection with this inquiry,

IITRI received an outside opinion letter concluding that the IRS could well deem some of IITRI's projects unrelated business activities and that the income from these activities was likely taxable. Milton urged the President of IITRI, John Scott, to take action in response to the letter, but Scott refused. Milton raised the issue with IITRI's Treasurer, who agreed that IITRI was improperly claiming unrelated business income as exempt income and promised to remedy the problem after Scott's then-imminent retirement. However, this retirement did not come to pass. Finally, in November 1996, when Scott falsely indicated to IITRI's board of governors that IITRI had no problem with unrelated business income, Milton reported the falsity of these statements to Lew Collens, Chairman of the Board of IITRI, and informed Collens of the opinion letter.

On January 1, 1997, Scott called Milton at home and informed him that he had been relieved of his Group Vice President title and demoted to his previous position as supervisor of TSMI. On February 12, 1997, Milton's attorney contacted IITRI about the demotion, alleging that it was unlawful retaliation for informing management of IITRI's unlawful practices. Two days later, at his office in Lanham, Maryland, Milton received a letter from Collens terminating his employment with IITRI.

Milton filed suit against IITRI in Virginia state court for wrongful discharge and breach of contract. The court found that Maryland law did not recognize a wrongful discharge claim on these facts, as Milton did not allege he was fired for refusing to engage in unlawful activities, and he could point to no statutory duty to disclose IITRI's wrongdoing. The district court also dismissed Milton's breach of contract action. Milton now appeals the dismissal of his wrongful discharge claim.

II.

"The word 'tort' has a settled meaning in Virginia. A tort is any civil wrong or injury; a wrongful act." Buchanan, 431 S.E.2d at 291 (citations omitted); see also Prosser and Keeton on Torts 2 (5th ed.1984). Thus Virginia's choice of law rule selects the law of the state in which the wrongful act took place, wherever the effects of that act are felt. Diaz Vicente itself illustrates this point. The plaintiffs in that case were citizens and residents of Mexico. They sued a former resident of Virginia for fraud arising out of a failed real estate investment in Virginia. Each of the plaintiffs lost a substantial amount of money, an impact presumably felt at home in Mexico. However the Diaz Vicente court, applying Virginia choice of law, held that Virginia law governed their tort actions for fraud, as Virginia was the place where the tortious conduct-the legal injury-occurred. 736 F.Supp. at 690.

III.

We now turn to the merits. Maryland has recognized a "narrow exception" to the general rule of at-will employment: "discharge may not contravene a clear mandate of public policy." Bagwell v. Peninsula Regional Med. Ctr., 106 Md.App. 470, 665 A.2d 297, 309 (1995), cert. denied, 341 Md. 172, 669 A.2d 1360 (1996). Maryland courts have found such a mandate only in limited circumstances: (1) "where an employee has been fired for refusing to violate the law or the legal rights of a third party," Thompson v. Memorial Hosp. at Easton, 925 F.Supp. 400, 406 (D.Md.1996), and (2) "where an employee has been terminated for exercising a specific legal right or duty," Thompson, 925 F.Supp. at 406. Because Milton does not fit in either category, his suit for wrongful discharge was properly dismissed.

Milton makes no claim that he was asked to break the law. He had no role in preparing IITRI's submissions to the IRS and no responsibility for their content. Instead, Milton claims he was fired for fulfilling his fiduciary duty as a corporate officer to inform IITRI's Board of activities injurious to the corporation's long-term interests. While we must accept this allegation as true, it does not support Milton's wrongful discharge claim.

Maryland law does provide a wrongful discharge cause of action for employees who are terminated because they perform their "statutorily prescribed duty." Adler v. American Standard Corp., 830 F.2d 1303, 1307 (4th Cir.1987). However, this exception to the norm of at-will employment has been construed narrowly by the Maryland courts and is not available in Milton's case. In Shapiro v. Massengill, the Maryland Court of Special Appeals refused to consider a claim of wrongful discharge "absent some clear mandate" or duty which the plaintiff himself "actually could be held responsible" for breaching. Likewise, in Thompson the district court applying Maryland law held that, because a hospital employee was not chargeable with the hospital's regulatory duty to report misadministration of radiation, he did not state a claim for wrongful discharge when he was fired for making such a report. 925 F.Supp. at 407-08. By contrast, the Bleich court recognized that an educator terminated for filing a report of child abuse and neglect, as she was explicitly required to do by Maryland law, did state a claim for wrongful discharge. These cases indicate that, for Milton to recover, it is not enough that someone at IITRI was responsible for correcting its tax filings or that the corporation may have been liable for tax fraud. This responsibility was never Milton's, nor did he face any potential liability for failing to discharge it, so his claim fails.

This search for a specific legal duty is no mere formality. Rather it limits judicial forays into the wilderness of discerning "public policy" without clear direction from a legislative or regulatory source. "The truth is that the theory of public policy embodies a doctrine of vague and variable quality, and, unless deducible in the given circumstances from constitutional or statutory provisions, should be accepted as the basis of a judicial determination, if at all, only with the utmost circumspection." Thus, in a recent case the Maryland Court of Special Appeals found that even a plaintiff who was subject to a statutorily prescribed duty nonetheless stated no cause of action for wrongful discharge because he could not "point to any declaration of policy in the statute on which he can rely." *Bagwell*, 665 A.2d at 310. In light of *Bagwell*, even if Milton was fulfilling a recognized fiduciary duty, his claim falls one critical analytical step short of the goal-he has not linked his duty to any explicit policy or "clear mandate" that was violated by his discharge. Maryland courts have been loath to create Maryland public policy without a clear legislative signal. It would be even less appropriate for a federal court to undertake this delicate task with no more guidance than we have here.

IV.

For the foregoing reasons, we affirm the judgment of the district court.

AFFIRMED.

IN RE ESTATE OF DESIR V. VERTUS,
418 N.J.Super. 310, 13 A.3d 428 (2011)

The opinion of the court was delivered by **GRALL, J.A.D.**

Cosme Novaly, a friend and neighbor of defendant Jean Robert Vertus, was shot in front of Vertus Financial Services by a robber leaving the premises. Novaly was there because he was lending assistance to Vertus, who had come to Novaly and told him that he thought "something was going on" in the apartment that he used as his residence and place of business. Novaly died from the gunshot wound, and his estate filed a complaint charging Vertus and his business with negligence.

The factual statement that follows is drawn from Vertus's deposition testimony. At the time of this incident, he operated a "financial services" business out of his second-floor apartment in a high-crime area of Irvington. In fact, Vertus had been robbed and stabbed while working there three years before the incident that led to Novaly's death. In Vertus's words, "in Irvington you have to be scared for your life."

The events at issue here started at around 5:00 p.m. on a September evening. Vertus had just finished doing business with a client at his dining room table. As the client walked toward the living room and the stairs to leave, Vertus saw her "step back." Although he did not see or hear anything else, he "knew inside" that something was wrong because "if you have to open the door and . . . you see something, you just . . . step back." He feared that "a robbery or something" was about to take place.

Vertus did not follow the client; he left by way of side stairs leading to the first-floor apartment to look for a telephone and call 911 because he thought "something happened." Vertus knocked, but his downstairs neighbor did not respond. He then sought help from Novaly and his roommate Mr. St. Louis, who lived three houses away. Both had done business with him, and they were very close to him — in his words, "like family." He did not stop at the first house because he knew those neighbors did not have a phone, and he did not stop at the second house because the residents were elderly.

When Vertus arrived, he told Novaly and St. Louis that "something" was going on in his apartment. He did not ask them to call 911 because he claimed to not know what was going on, but he did ask them to call his office to see if someone could pick up the phone. They complied, but the line was busy. Novaly and St. Louis left Vertus in their apartment because he was "scared," and they went outside to see what was happening.

Vertus acknowledged that he had not told his neighbors what he thought was happening. He just told them he saw the client "move back" and that "the way she moved it seemed like something was going on in his business."

When asked if he had requested help from Novaly and St. Louis, Vertus responded: "Well, they were helping me. I mean, I went downstairs, they gave me the telephone and they left." He also said that he thought Novaly and St. Louis were going in "the direction of his business" when they left, because he had "come to them to ask, you know, for help." There is no evidence that either Novaly or St. Louis had any law enforcement training or experience.

Soon after his neighbors left him, Vertus heard a gunshot and dialed 911. He stayed in Novaly's basement apartment until he heard sirens. When he went outside, he saw Novaly lying on his back on the ground suffering from a gunshot wound, and he applied pressure to the wound until an ambulance arrived. Novaly died from his injuries twenty-four days later. The parties agree that three intruders entered Vertus's business, assaulted several clients, shot Desir, demanded money and that Novaly was shot outside on the sidewalk.

The estate does not contend that Vertus violated a duty as a business proprietor to secure the premises from criminal attacks. Nor does the estate contend that Vertus's negligence was partially responsible for causing the robbery, which would provide a basis for concluding that Vertus owed Novaly a duty under the rescue doctrine. "That deterrent goal of the tort laws is effectuated through the recognition of a duty to exercise reasonable care and the imposition of liability for the breach of such a duty." This State's law governing the duties of occupiers of land and the rescue doctrine has been developed to effectuate that fundamental purpose. The duties of landowners should be consistent with the "fundamental purpose" of "deterring conduct that creates an unreasonable risk of injury to others."

The Supreme Court has applied the foregoing principles and held that a landowner has a duty to one injured off his premises by a dangerous condition on the site when an individual or identifiable class of individuals is foreseeably at risk of being harmed by the condition. On similar reasoning, this court has held that a person who negligently imperils himself and invites a foreseeable rescue owes a duty of reasonable care to the rescuer. Moreover, the Supreme Court has acknowledged "the existence of a duty predicated on foreseeability of an increased hazard" to bystanders created by one who contributes, by leaving her keys in a car parked at night in a high-crime area, to the theft and subsequent mishandling of an automobile.

This court has previously concluded that a wife confronted with the potential of her husband becoming violent because he had stopped taking medication he needed to control that behavior owed a duty to a nephew she exposed to the danger by requesting his assistance to get her husband to take his medicine. As in Hill, the duty imposed was based on conduct of the actor that resulted in exposure of the injured party to the foreseeably dangerous acts of another. In Hill, it was defendant's leaving of keys in her car that facilitated the car's theft and the thief's reckless driving that caused injury to an innocent plaintiff. In Arvanitis, it was the wife's requesting the "plaintiff's assistance in a potentially explosive situation and without warning him."

This conduct-based duty to refrain from exposing others to the foreseeable criminal or negligent acts of third parties is recognized elsewhere. For example, it has been said that when the "state puts a man in a position of danger from private persons and then fails to protect him, it will not be heard to say that its role was merely passive; it is as much an active tortfeasor as if it had thrown him into a snake pit."

Similarly, the Restatement recognizes that under certain circumstances an actor is negligent when his or her conduct leads another to a course of conduct that results in an unreasonable risk of injury. Restatement (Second) of Torts §303 (1965).

An act is negligent if the actor intends it to affect, or realizes or should realize it is likely to affect, the conduct of another, a third person, or an animal in such a manner as to create an unreasonable risk of harm to the other.

One illustration of the principle offered in the Restatement is that of a poor swimmer "who intentionally goes beyond his depth in a heavy surf" and thereby invites a rescue effort by one who then suffers exhaustion leading to illness. Casting this principle of negligence in terms of duty, an actor has a duty to refrain from conduct that he or she realizes or should realize is likely to evoke a response from another that creates a risk of injury to that person or others.

We acknowledge that this case is different than Arvanitis in that the plaintiff-nephew lent assistance and was injured by his violent uncle in the home of the defendant-aunt who summoned him to the danger. Thus, we primarily analyzed that case under the doctrines of premises liability. Here, Novaly was shot by one of the robbers outside the premises of Vertus Financial Services, making a straightforward premises-liability analysis inapplicable.

But the fact that the shooting occurred on the sidewalk rather than inside is immaterial. Our Supreme Court's "desire to maintain fairness and justness in our tort jurisprudence" has led it to conclude "that premises liability should no longer be limited by strict adherence to the traditional and rigid common law classifications." Instead, our courts focus on foreseeability in defining the scope of duty. Thus, in Olivo, the Court recognized that when a danger posed by a condition on property poses a foreseeable risk to an identifiable person off the premises, a duty to that person arises.

The facts in this case support the imposition of a duty of reasonable care based on Vertus's conduct that he knew or should have known would bring Novaly to the danger that caused his injury and death. Vertus acknowledges that he went to Novaly, a friend and neighbor, who was in the safety of his own home and not aware of or endangered by the events that led Vertus to flee from his apartment and seek assistance. While Vertus never acknowledged that he knew there was a robbery in progress, he admitted that from what he saw he was scared and thought that there was. Vertus passed by the house closest to his because that neighbor did not have a phone, and he passed by the second house because those neighbors were elderly and, one might infer, because he thought the elderly couple could or would not assist. Instead, he went to the home of Novaly and St. Louis who were his friends and clients. Vertus told them "something was going on" in his apartment and described what he saw, but he did not say that the something he feared was a robbery. Vertus asked Novaly and St. Louis to call his business to find out what was happening; he did not expressly ask them for additional help because they were already helping him. When the phone call to Vertus's apartment went unanswered, Novaly and St. Louis left to see what was happening. Vertus admits that he thought they were going to his business where he believed a robbery was underway yet he did nothing to warn or stop them, even though he had no reason to believe that either Novaly or St. Louis was better able to respond to the situation than he.

The factors most pertinent to duty — foreseeability of the harm, the relationship between the parties, and opportunity and ability to exercise care — warrant imposition of a duty here. Vertus had a relationship with Novaly and St. Louis that led him to expect they would help him, and he knew that by responding as they did they were leaving the safety of their home to help him and exposing themselves to what he thought was a robbery. As noted above, we held that Mrs. Arvanitis owed a duty to her nephew because she called him to assist her in getting her husband to take medication he needed to control his tendency to do violence to others. By her request for help, she caused him to become involved in a foreseeably dangerous situation with which he had no previous connection. We see no difference in the degree of foreseeability of harm or the relationships of the parties involved in this case and Arvanitis that would warrant a different result here. The principle is the same: where an imperiled person draws in another to his predicament, it is foreseeable that the person drawn in will be injured unless the victim exercises reasonable care.

The result might be different if the actor requested assistance from a trained professional with superior ability to exercise care under the circumstances, such as a police officer.

We briefly consider the scope of the duty of reasonable care owed here. In general, the scope of the duty is defined by what a reasonably prudent person would do under the same or similar circumstances. Here, the question is what the reasonably prudent person would do to avert a risk of harm to a person he asks for help. Certainly, obligating one who seeks assistance to alert the individual summoned to what he knows and should know about the nature of the danger is consistent with Arvanitis. A reasonably prudent person would also recognize other alternatives, such as suggesting placement of a 911 call from a place of safety or making it clear that the request was not for help that includes rushing to the danger.

Defendants argue that even if Vertus had a duty he did not breach it because he told Novaly what he knew and he had "no specific knowledge of what was happening in his apartment" as he did not see the intruders, their demeanor, or whether they were armed. We disagree. A reasonable jury could infer from Vertus's conduct and statements that he was aware that the "something" going on was what he admitted he thought was taking place—a robbery. At this point in the litigation, the estate is entitled to all favorable inferences. R. 4:46–2(c).

The orders under review are reversed and the case is remanded to the Law Division.

Websites

▪ **Lexis-Nexis**
   http://www.lexisnexis.com/

▪ **Tort Law legal definition of Tort Law**
   legal-dictionary.thefreedictionary.com/Tort+Law

▪ **Understanding mass personal injury litigation**
   http://www.rand.org/publications/RB/RB9021/RB9021.word.html

▪ **Personal Injury and Tort Law Cornell University**
   https://www.law.cornell.edu/wex/tort

▪ **Westlaw**
   http://www.westlaw.com

■ **Harassment/emotional distress links**
https://www.law.cornell.edu/uscode/text/47/223

■ **Law Resources by Category: Tort Law - Law Teacher**
www.lawteacher.net/category/tort-law

Forms and Court Documents

You will find this section at the conclusion of each chapter of this book. It is designed to provide you with examples of actual court documents, pleadings, and other relevant topics. Your first form consists of a basic negligence complaint. This complaint involves a car wreck — one of the most common forms of personal injury torts.

IN THE SUPERIOR COURT OF GANNETT COUNTY
STATE OF PLACID

John Doe,	)	CASE NO. CV 2013-0034
Plaintiff	)	
	)	
vs.	)	
	)	
Rhonda Roe,	)	
Defendant	)	

Complaint

COMES NOW, the plaintiff, John Doe, and complaining of the defendant alleges the following:

1.

The Plaintiff is a citizen and resident of Gannett County, Placid.

2.

The Defendant is, upon information and belief, a citizen and resident of Union County, Placid.

3.

On or about February 2, 2012, at approximately 10:30 A.M., the Plaintiff, John Doe, was operating a 1999 Honda Civic automobile, which was owned by the Plaintiff, in a general westerly direction along US Highway 22, within the County of Gannett in the state of Placid.

4.

At the time and place and on the occasion stated in paragraph #3, the defendant was operating a 1994 Ford pickup truck in a westerly direction along the same road as that being traveled by the Plaintiff, John Doe, approaching the location of the Plaintiff, John Doe.

5.

It is further alleged upon information and belief that at all times relevant hereto, the Defendant owned the 1994 Ford vehicle being driven by the Defendant.

6.

At the time and place stated above, the Plaintiff, John Doe, had slowed and stopped his 1999 Honda automobile in respect and in obedience to a traffic light emitting a signal compelling him to stop.

7.

At the time and place stated above, the 1994 Ford being operated by the Defendant did, without justification and without warning, drive into and collide with the rear of the vehicle operated by the Plaintiff, while the Plaintiff's automobile was at a complete stop in obedience and in conformity with the traffic signal.

8.

The defendant was negligent in that she:
a. Failed to keep reasonable and proper control of her vehicle;
b. Failed to keep and maintain a reasonably safe and proper lookout in her direction of travel; and
c. Drove her vehicle carelessly and in willful and wanton disregard of the rights and safety of others including the Plaintiff, John Doe.

9.

That as a proximate cause of the Defendant's negligence, the Plaintiff, John Doe, suffered severe and permanent injuries in excess of $10,000.00.

WHEREFORE, the Plaintiff prays that the Court:
1. That the Plaintiff, John Doe, have and recover a judgment against the Defendant in an amount in excess of $10,000.00 for personal injuries.
2. That the Plaintiff have and recover of the Defendant a sum to be determined at trial, but in any event, no less than $10,000.00 for damage to personal property.
3. That prejudgment interest be awarded as provided by law.
4. That the costs of this action be taxed against the Defendant.
5. That all issues raised be tried before a jury.
6. For such other and further relief as the Court may deem just and proper.

This the _____ day of May, 2013.

_____

Clarence D. Arrow
Attorney for Plaintiff, John Doe
State Bar No. 000-998

Key Terms

Affirm

Answer

Case law

Cause of action

Certiorari

Complaint

Damages

Defendant

Guilt

Indictment

Liable

Motion for directed
verdict

Plaintiff

Pleadings

Remand

Reverse

Stare decisis

Verdict

Voir dire

Review Questions

1   What is a cause of action?

2   How is tort law different from criminal law?

3   What are the names of the parties who bring a civil suit?

4   Explain the difference between a complaint and an answer.

5   Explain the difference between the burden of proof in a civil case and in a criminal case.

6   What is a litigation chart, and how does it help the parties prepare for trial?

7   What are some of the public records that can provide helpful information in investigating a case?

8   How is case law developed? Why is it important?

9   Explain stare decisis.

10 List and describe the basic steps of a civil trial.

Applying What You Have Learned

1   Search the Internet for general sources about tort law. How many sites can you find that provide guidance about the general law of torts, especially for such issues as the history of tort law, arbitration, and trials of civil cases?

2   Refer to your local newspaper for examples of recent automobile accidents or other actions that may result in a tort action. Summarize the facts involved, and identify the potential parties in a civil tort action.

3   How is your local courthouse organized? What types of public records are available there? What records could you use to investigate a potential defendant?

Endnotes

[1]Bureau of Justice Statistics, Department of Justice, Civil Justice Survey of State Courts, 1992, p. 2.

Crossword Puzzle

www.CrosswordWeaver.com

ACROSS

2 Official document issued by the grand jury, accusing the defendant of a criminal act

4 The power of a court to decide which cases it will hear and which it will not

5 Documents that describe the legal injuries and counterclaims raised by the parties in a civil case

8 Money that a court orders the losing side in a civil case to pay to the other side

9 The name of the document that the defendant serves on the plaintiff, outlining his defenses and any claims he may have against the plaintiff

14 The legal title of the person who brings a complaint

16 A motion brought by the defense at the end of the plaintiff's case, asking that the case be dismissed because the plaintiff has failed to prove the claims raised in the complaint

17 Document drafted by the plaintiff's attorney and served on the defendant. It details the personal or financial injury suffered by plaintiff.

18 to set the decision aside; an appellate court disagrees with the verdict, or some ruling, in the trial, and overturns that decision

DOWN

1 The principle that courts will reach results similar to those reached by courts in prior cases involving similar facts and legal issues

3 The jury's final decision in the case in which they decide questions of fact raised in the case

6 The appellate court requires additional information or an evidentiary hearing; it cannot conduct such a hearing itself, so it sends the case back to the trial court for the hearing, and then considers the appeal based on that hearing

7 A legal injury on which a lawsuit can be based

8 The legal title of the person who is served with the complaint

10 A finding that one of the parties in a civil case is obligated to pay damages to the other party

11 The appellate court agrees with the verdict, or some ruling, entered in the trial and votes to keep that decision in place

12 The jury's determination that the defendant in a criminal case is responsible for committing a crime

13 The body of cases decided by judges who have interpreted statutes and prior cases

15 "Look speak"; the process of questioning a juror to discover bias or prejudice, or who would make an acceptable juror to hear a case

Intentional Torts

Chapter Objectives

- Introduce the basic elements of intentional torts

- Show how intentional torts differ from torts involving negligence

- Point out the important types of information that a paralegal should obtain from a client

- Describe the elements of intentional torts to property

- Explain how an intentional tort is proved at trial

I. THE CHUMLEY CASE

Unlike almost every other chapter in this book, we do not begin this chapter with a discussion of the Chumley case. The simple reason is that the Chumley case does not involve an intentional tort. An **intentional tort** is one in which the defendant acted purposefully to injure the plaintiff. Most car wreck cases involve acts of negligence. As we see in later chapters, lawsuits involving negligence revolve around the issue of proper care and reasonable conduct, but not intentional actions. If a defendant intentionally runs over the plaintiff with his car, that is not a negligence case. That is a case involving an intentional tort. If a defendant fails to stop for a red light and by so doing causes a car wreck with the plaintiff, the result will be action for negligence. We spend several chapters discussing negligence cases, primarily because the

Intentional tort
A civil action based on a defendant's purposeful, intentional act that causes harm, as opposed to a defendant's act that causes harm through negligence.

vast majority of court cases involve negligence. But in this chapter, we discuss intentional torts.

THE PROBLEM WITH INTENTIONAL TORTS

Most civil lawsuits do not involve intentional torts. The vast majority of civil lawsuits involve car wreck cases, otherwise known as personal injury cases. On any given day in a courthouse anywhere in the United States, you are far more likely to see a civil trial that involves a car wreck or a divorce than a trial involving intentional torts. This is not because people do not intentionally injure each other. Unfortunately, people hurt, maim, and kill each other every day. The problem with intentional torts is that there is a large overlap between this area of law and criminal law. In fact, when you use the term *assault*, most people will jump to the conclusion that you are talking about the crime of assault, not the tort of assault.

Personal injury cases refer to lawsuits involving negligence, such as car wrecks, slip and fall cases, and product liability cases.

As we mentioned in the first chapter, there is a good deal of overlap in terminology and procedure between criminal cases and civil cases. This overlap is even more striking when we examine intentional torts. Not only is there a great deal of overlap in terminology, but when we discuss many intentional torts, the elements — the basic points of proof — are identical between crimes and intentional torts. As you can imagine, this often causes a great deal of confusion.

In the first chapter, we used the example of a person taking a swing at you while you are getting into your car. This is the crime of assault. It is also the tort of **assault.** The person who took a swing at you could be prosecuted for a crime, but you could also sue him civilly for the tort. The important difference in these two lawsuits involves the outcome of the case. A criminal prosecution could land the man in jail, while the civil case could compel him to pay you monetary damages. Before discussing these specific intentional torts, we should take a few moments to address some of the specific problems with intentional torts. One problem is that intentional torts often sound like crimes. For instance, there is the crime of battery, and there is the tort of **battery.** As we have already seen in Chapter 1, a civil case can proceed before, during, or after a criminal case has been brought. Intentional torts are all based on the premise that the defendant knowingly and intentionally caused the action that harmed the victim. See Figure 2-1.

Assault
When the defendant causes the plaintiff to have fear or apprehension of a harmful or offensive contact.

Battery
When the defendant causes harmful or offensive contact to the plaintiff.

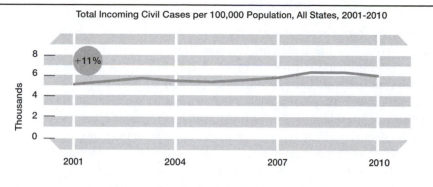

Total Incoming Civil Cases per 100,000 Population, All States, 2001-2010

FIGURE 2-1

Total Incoming Civil Cases per 100,000 Population, All States, 2001–2010

Civil caseloads declined in 2010 in both general and limited jurisdiction courts. Ninety-three percent of the total decrease of 545,000 cases occurred In limited jurisdiction courts, where small claims and other less complex civil cases are typically processed.

Source: **National Center for State Courts, Court Statistics Project, Publication: Examining the Work of State Courts: An Analysis of 2010 State Court Caseloads, 9/24/12**

 ## ASSAULT AND BATTERY

The torts of assault and battery are often intertwined and sometimes confused. However, it is important to keep the **elements** of each clearly delineated. We begin our discussion with the tort of assault.

A. THE ELEMENTS OF ASSAULT

In order to prove the tort of assault, the plaintiff must show:

- that the defendant intentionally caused the plaintiff to have
- fear or apprehension of a
- harmful or offensive contact.

Elements
The points raised by the plaintiff in his complaint that must also be proved at trial; failure to prove these points will often result in a dismissal of the plaintiff's case.

When we discuss the elements of a particular tort, we are really talking about what the plaintiff must prove in order to win a trial. For instance, in the tort of assault, the plaintiff must prove that the defendant did knowingly and intentionally cause fear or apprehension to the victim of a harmful or offensive contact. If we break these elements down and list them separately, we come up with a table that looks like the following:

Element	Proof
Defendant did knowingly and intentionally	Testimony that the defendant acted voluntarily
Cause apprehension	Plaintiff's testimony about his reaction to the defendant's actions
Of a harmful or offensive contact	Plaintiff's testimony about what contact defendant made

As you can see from the table, each of these elements stands separate and apart from the other elements. If the plaintiff presents evidence about each element, he has made a **prima facie**, or basic, case against the defendant. If the plaintiff fails to prove one of the essential elements, the case against the defendant will fail. The plaintiff must present sufficient evidence to prove each and every allegation against the defendant. By failing to prove that the defendant acted knowingly and intentionally, the plaintiff has failed to meet his burden. A plaintiff can present evidence or testimony to establish any of these elements. However, it is always up to the jury to decide whether the plaintiff has presented enough evidence. In cases where a judge acts as the jury, such as in a bench trial, it is the judge's responsibility to determine if the plaintiff has presented enough evidence. If the plaintiff fails to present sufficient evidence, the jury is authorized to find for the defendant. In other words, the jury will vote that the defendant is not liable. Later in this chapter, there is a checklist that you can use to help establish the basic facts for any intentional tort.

When a person assaults another person, he causes the victim to undergo fear or apprehension that he is about to receive a harmful or offensive contact. There is no touching in an assault. When a person swings a fist at the plaintiff and misses, this is an assault, and the plaintiff can bring a civil suit against the attacker. Let's examine the elements of the tort and explain how these elements become important during the trial.

1. THE DEFENDANT'S ACTIONS ARE INTENTIONAL

Although this sounds like an obvious point, it is worth mentioning that the defendant's action must be intentional. The word *intent* carries a specific meaning in law. When a person acts intentionally, it does not mean that he had a specific result in mind. A child will often say, "I didn't intend to hurt you," when he hits his friend with a stick. Although that defense may work on the playground, it won't work in the courtroom. The test of the defendant's intent is not what the ultimate result is; the test for intent is whether the defendant acted voluntarily and knowingly. Suppose you are in a crowded movie theater and the man next to you has an epileptic seizure. As he flails about, his hand strikes your face. Most people would agree that the man's actions are not intentional—that is, that he did not voluntarily and knowingly strike you—so he should not be held accountable for the damage he caused. This is the standard we use to determine intent.

2. FEAR OR APPREHENSION

In an assault, actual fear is not a requirement. The victim must simply be apprehensive of the contact. Because awareness is a requirement, a victim cannot be assaulted if he or she is unconscious. Unconscious people cannot be fearful or apprehensive, so an assault cannot be committed against them.

The defendant must have the apparent ability to carry through the threat of violence. If, for instance, a man is holding a baseball bat and screams at a woman passerby, "I'm going to hit you with this bat!" this may constitute an assault. If the man swings the bat and misses the woman, an assault has certainly occurred. However, if the man is standing on the other side of a tall fence, with no way to get to the woman, and he repeats the same threat, he now lacks the apparent ability to put the threat into action, and no assault has occurred.

The threat must be imminent and cannot be a future threat, such as, "I'll hit you with this bat at three o'clock!"

3. HARMFUL OR OFFENSIVE CONTACT

Assault involves the fear or apprehension of contact. However, the intended contact must be harmful or offensive. There is no requirement that the intended victim would have been seriously injured had the contact occurred. Because different people have different standards about what they consider "offensive" touching, most states approach this issue from the hypothetical reasonable person standard. The question becomes, would a reasonable person have considered this attempted contact to be harmful or offensive? If the answer is yes, an assault has occurred. The law does not take into account the subjective feelings of a particular victim.

The reasonable person standard is a guideline that courts use as an alternative to the subjective viewpoints of the parties involved.

B. THE ELEMENTS OF BATTERY

If an assault is an attempted battery, battery is a completed assault. In a lawsuit over battery, the plaintiff must prove that the defendant made knowing and voluntary, intentionally offensive, or harmful contact with the plaintiff.

To prove the tort of battery, the plaintiff must show:

- that the defendant intentionally
- made contact with the plaintiff which was
- harmful or offensive.

1. DEFENDANT ACTED INTENTIONALLY

In all intentional torts, the plaintiff must prove that the defendant acted voluntarily and knowingly. Just as we saw with assault, if the defendant inadvertently strikes another person, such as when someone bumps into you in a crowded restaurant, because the person did not act intentionally, there is no tort of battery.

2. WHAT DO WE MEAN BY "CONTACT"?

In battery, the term *contact* refers to any contact with the plaintiff, no matter how slight. This contact can consist of the defendant actually reaching out and touching the plaintiff with his hands. It can also be accomplished by other means. If a person throws a rock at you and strikes you on the head, that certainly qualifies as contact. Under the strict interpretation of the law, though, because the person who threw the rock is not holding it when it strikes you, can this qualify as a battery? Both law and common sense say yes. Battery can occur by physical touching, and it can occur through other means, too.

a. Making Contact with Weapons or Other Objects

The law recognizes that when a defendant uses a weapon to make contact with the plaintiff, this is as much a battery as when the defendant uses his own hands. The same rule applies to other objects. Harmful or offensive contact with the plaintiff through any object that the defendant uses qualifies as a battery, as long as the defendant acted intentionally.

b. The Connection Between the Defendant's Actions and Ultimate Harm

Proximate cause
Proof that the defendant's actions were the legal cause of the plaintiff's injuries (see Chapter 7).

This is a good place to discuss one other point that we return to in several other chapters: **proximate cause.** For example, let's suppose that two men get into an argument at their sons' hockey game. One man attacks the other and beats him severely. We will call the victim John and the attacker Steve. In this scenario, there is no question that a battery has occurred. An ambulance arrives and takes John to the hospital. On the way there, the ambulance driver, who is drunk, gets into a wreck, and John is injured even more severely. The issue becomes, is Steve liable for these new injuries to John? This is the concept of proximate cause. As we see in later chapters, proximate cause is a doctrine in tort law that requires a strong connection between the defendant's actions and the ultimate harm to the plaintiff. Closely tied to proximate cause is the issue of **foreseeability.** The law of proximate cause dictates that Steve will be liable for all foreseeable injuries to John but will not be liable for injuries that were not foreseeable. In this scenario, Steve will be liable for the injuries he caused to John but will probably not be liable for Steve's additional injuries caused by the car crash. We discuss proximate cause in much greater detail in Chapter 7.

Foreseeability
The legal requirement that the defendant can reasonably anticipate that his conduct would likely cause injury to the plaintiff.

The importance of proximate cause to society arises from the recognition that there should be an eventual termination of a person's liability. Here is another example: Marcy sees Barbara in the parking lot of a grocery store and shoves a shopping cart at her, hoping to knock her over. The shopping cart misses Barbara, but because the incident causes her some fear, she has an action for assault. The shopping cart continues to roll across the parking lot, and because it is on the side of a hill, it continues to roll into the street.

Several drivers swerve to miss the shopping cart, and one of the drivers hits a telephone pole. The shopping cart comes to rest in a vacant lot. Several years later, Rick is surveying the lot and trips over the shopping cart and breaks his leg. Under proximate cause, which of these people has an action against Marcy?

Let's take it one by one. First, Barbara certainly has an action against Marcy for assault, because the incident meets all of the elements for that tort. What about the driver who swerved to miss the shopping cart and struck the telephone pole? Because there is a strong connection between the harm to the driver and Marcy's actions, the law would probably allow an action by the driver against Marcy. What about Rick, the surveyor? There does not seem to be a close connection between Marcy's actions and Rick's broken leg. Proximate cause was developed to give some closure to a person's liability. We have all done things in the past that could come back to haunt us decades later. Under proximate cause, Rick's lawsuit against Marcy (assuming that he could even figure out who caused the shopping cart to be there in the first place) would probably be dismissed at trial because of the causation problem. After all, there should come a point in a chain of events when the original person is no longer responsible for what happens.

Proximate cause is the term for the legal standard courts use to determine the liability of the defendant's actions. Only if the defendant's act (or failure to act) is the proximate cause of the injuries to the plaintiff will he be liable.

TORT
BASICS
AT A
GLANCE

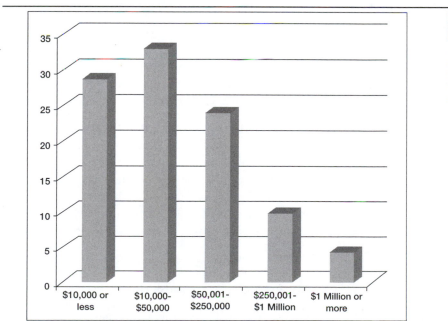

Figure 2-2

Jury Awards by Amount for Plaintiff Winners, State Courts, 2011

Tech Topic
DOCUMENTING INTENTIONAL INJURIES

Tort cases often involve intentional injury: injuries resulting from purposeful human actions, such as assault or battery. Consider two men in a bar. One accidentally bumps the other; there's no intent and no injury. But the second man reacts by punching the first man and breaking his jaw. Such a scenario could easily be the basis for an intentional tort. Intentional injury can also result from negligence, as in the case of a neighbor's dog running loose and attacking a pedestrian.

The challenge in intentional injury torts is documenting the extent of the injuries along with any long-term repercussions.

To achieve that documentation, technology plays an ever-increasing role in the invention of advanced medical equipment. The basic x-ray machine, invented in 1895 by William Roentgen, was the precursor to modern-day imaging devices and is still in wide use today. In addition to that basic device, physicians now have an array of equipment to help diagnose injuries:

- Ultrasound is used for visualizing body structures beneath the skin, including muscles, joints, tendons, and internal organs.
- Computed tomography (CT) scans produce a three-dimensional image of the inside of a body structure.
- Positron emission tomography (PET) is a nuclear imaging technique that produces three-dimensional pictures of body processes.
- Magnetic resonance imaging (MRI) offers a view of internal structures of the body in even greater detail.

With advanced medical equipment, injuries can be documented in a way that brings clarity and certainty to intentional injury torts, a goal that both parties aim for.

3. HARMFUL OR OFFENSIVE CONTACT

The last element of the tort of battery is that the contact must be harmful or offensive. Everyone has a different standard about what would be considered harmful or offensive. Because this standard shifts dramatically from one person to another, the law does not use a subjective standard to determine this element. Put another way, the determination of harmful or offensive contact is not based on the individual plaintiff. We don't ask the plaintiff if the contact was harmful or offensive to her. Instead, we use the reasonable person standard.

4. THE REASONABLE PERSON STANDARD

We return to this hypothetical reasonable person many times throughout this book. The reasonable person standard was developed as a way to address incidents where the parties could have very different interpretations about what happened. Here's an example: Andy is Carol's supervisor. One day, he walks into her office and while speaking with her about her job performance, he touches her in a place that she considers to be inappropriate. Andy doesn't think that his action is wrong; in fact, he thinks that Carol secretly wanted him to touch her. Carol brings a battery lawsuit against Andy. Will she win? If we relied on Andy's interpretation of the events, there would be no cause of action. On the other hand, Carol's interpretation of the events may not be conclusive either. For instance, if Andy touched Carol on the shoulder as a way of emphasizing a point he was making, Carol may find this contact offensive but would a hypothetical reasonable person? Probably not. However, change the facts, and you get a different result. Instead of touching her shoulder, Andy touches Carol's thigh or her breast. Would a hypothetical reasonable person find that to be offensive contact? The answer would almost certainly be yes.

IV. FALSE IMPRISONMENT

When a plaintiff brings a suit for false imprisonment, he is saying that he was intentionally, unlawfully restrained against his will by the use of force or the threat of force. Although this tort sounds as though it involves some form of incarceration, what the plaintiff is really saying is that he was restrained from moving about freely by the defendant.

Most false imprisonment lawsuits are brought by people who are detained in stores or malls under suspicion of committing shoplifting. A person who is wrongfully detained by store personnel can bring this suit against the people who restrained her and the store that employs them.

A. THE ELEMENTS OF FALSE IMPRISONMENT

The tort of false imprisonment must involve:

- intentional,
- unlawful
- restraint of a person
- by the use of force or threats.

1. RESTRAINT MUST BE INTENTIONAL

It is not false imprisonment if the defendant in the lawsuit did not realize that he or she was confining someone. Suppose that John is in a bathroom in the mall and comes out to find that the mall has closed and he is locked inside. Because the people who were locking up had no reason to know that John was inside, his lawsuit for false imprisonment will almost certainly fail.

2. RESTRAINT MUST BE UNLAWFUL

When a person acts without legal authority to detain someone, the detained person has a cause of action for false imprisonment. However, the reverse is also true. If a person acts with lawful authority, there is no suit for false imprisonment. How does someone acquire lawful authority to detain someone else? A police officer has such authority when he makes an arrest. But other people can also legally restrain a person. We have already mentioned shoplifting. Suppose that Mary is a security guard at a large retail store, and she sees Carl hiding merchandise inside his clothes. Carl walks toward the exit, looks around, and then walks out. Mary chases him, tackles him, and holds him until the police arrive. Can Carl sue Mary for false imprisonment? If Mary has acted unlawfully, the answer is yes. But has she? Does Mary have the right to detain a person who has committed a crime? Yes. In fact, a person can lawfully restrain another person for any of the following:

- To stop someone from injuring himself or others
- To stop someone from damaging property
- To prevent someone from committing a crime or to detain him if he has already committed a crime

In the scenario above, Mary has seen Carl commit the crime of shoplifting and therefore has the right to restrain him. Such a rule makes sense — merchants should be able to prevent people from stealing. However, suppose Mary is wrong. What if Carl wasn't the right person? This is an entirely different scenario. Now, Mary has unlawfully restrained a person. Her lawful right was based on the fact that the person she restrained had committed a crime. If he hasn't committed a crime, Mary has no lawful right to restrain him. Carl can bring a false imprisonment suit against her and will probably win.

3. BY THE USE OF FORCE OR THREATS

In the scenario we outlined above, Mary tackles Carl and holds him until the police arrive. False imprisonment can certainly be achieved through force. The force required does not have to be quite as spectacular as Mary's tackle. Simply putting a hand on a person's elbow and guiding him to the security office is sufficient. What if the person is never touched at all? Mary sees a young woman acting suspiciously and apparently stuffing items into a shopping bag. Mary approaches her, accuses her of shoplifting, and asks her to come to the security office. When the woman hesitates, Mary says, "If you don't come, I'll have to drag you there." Is this threat enough? Under the law, the answer is yes. Mary's threat of force is enough to justify a false imprisonment suit, assuming that the other elements of the tort are met.

4. HOLDING PERSONAL PROPERTY HOSTAGE

What if Mary simply takes the young woman's car keys and walks to the security office? She hasn't threatened the young woman and certainly hasn't used force on her either. Would this justify a suit for false imprisonment? Most jurisdictions would agree that it does. After all, without her car keys, the young woman is stranded at the store. Mary has effectively restrained the woman's movements but has not resorted to physical violence to do so.

B. DEFENSES TO FALSE IMPRISONMENT

Do Mary and her employer have any defenses to the claim of false imprisonment? We have already seen that so long as Mary acts in a lawful manner, a claim of false imprisonment is not justified. That is one defense, but there are several others.

1. CONSENT

If the plaintiff voluntarily accompanies Mary back to the security office to "clear the matter up," and agrees to remain in the office until the police arrive, she has consented to the restraint and has effectively waived her right to complain about it later. Consent is only a defense when the person does not act voluntarily. Consent cannot be the result of force, threats, or trickery. In Chapter 3, we discuss in greater depth the many other defenses available in a torts action. Consent is also a defense to assault and battery cases.

Case Excerpt

THOMPSON-EL V. BANK OF AMERICA
N.A., 327 Ga. App. 309, 759 S.E.2d 49 (2014)

ELLINGTON, **Presiding Judge.**
Emma Thompson-El filed this action in the Superior Court of DeKalb County against Bank of America, N.A. ("BANA"), Federal National Mortgage Association ("Fannie Mae"), McCalla Raymer, LLC ("McCalla"), Century 21 Bryant Realty ("Bryant Realty"), and William Braswell, asserting claims for wrongful foreclosure and intentional infliction of emotional distress. The defendants filed motions to dismiss the complaint for failure to state a claim upon which relief could be granted; the trial court granted the motions and dismissed all of Thompson-El's claims against the defendants. Thompson-El appeals. For the reasons explained below, we affirm.

   Thompson-El contends that there is a dispute of fact regarding whether she received advance notice of the foreclosure by certified mail as required by law. Specifically, she contends that, because the record does not contain a certified mail return receipt showing delivery to her, none of the defendants provided "[i]ndisputable proof" of statutory notice.

"In Georgia, a plaintiff asserting a claim of wrongful foreclosure must establish a legal duty owed to it by the foreclosing party, a breach of that duty, a causal connection between the breach of that duty and the injury it sustained, and damages." A lender owes a borrower a duty to exercise a power of sale in a security deed fairly, which includes complying with statutory and contractual notice requirements. Frank S. Alexander, Ga. Real Estate Finance and Foreclosure Law, §8:11 (updated September 2013). OCGA §44–14–162.2(a) provides, in pertinent part, that

> Notice of the initiation of proceedings to exercise a power of sale in a mortgage, security deed, or other lien contract shall be given to the debtor by the secured creditor no later than 30 days before the date of the proposed foreclosure. Such notice shall be in writing, shall include the name, address, and telephone number of the individual or entity who shall have full authority to negotiate, amend, and modify all terms of the mortgage with the debtor, and shall be sent by registered or certified mail or statutory overnight delivery, return receipt requested, to the property address or to such other address as the debtor may designate by written notice to the secured creditor.

In her complaint, Thompson-El alleged that she purchased a home in 2000 and that she granted BANA a deed to secure debt to secure the corresponding promissory note. She alleged that she defaulted in 2009 and that BANA foreclosed on the property on October 5, 2010, without providing notice by certified mail as required by OCGA §44–14–162.2. The defendants submitted evidence, however, that BANA's attorney mailed written notice of the initiation of foreclosure proceedings on September 1, 2010, by certified mail, return receipt requested, and by regular mail to the property address and to Thompson-El's post office box. Although there is no evidence that Thompson-El received any of the notices, where "the grantee in a security deed mails a notification of the sale under power correctly addressed to the grantor of the security deed in accordance with the provisions of OCGA §44–14–162.2, the actual receipt, or want of receipt, by the grantor is immaterial to the right of the grantee to sale under power." Here, the evidence that statutory notice was sent is undisputed. Accordingly, the trial court did not err in granting summary judgment on this basis in favor of BANA. Id.

Similarly, as to McCalla, Thompson-El cannot prevail on her claim for wrongful foreclosure because there is no evidence that the firm failed to follow statutory foreclosure procedures in representing BANA in the foreclosure. Finally, as to the remaining defendants, Fannie Mae, Bryant Realty, and Braswell, a claim for wrongful foreclosure will not lie because, in the framework of Thompson-El's complaint, none of them acted as a secured lender or was otherwise involved in foreclosing on her property.

Accordingly, the trial court did not err in granting summary judgment to the defendants' motions to dismiss.

Thompson-El contends that the trial court erred in dismissing her claim for intentional infliction of emotional distress.

Georgia has long recognized a cause of action for intentional infliction of emotional distress. However, the burden that the plaintiff must meet in order to prevail in this cause of action is a stringent one. To prevail, a plaintiff must demonstrate that (1) the conduct giving rise to the claim was intentional or reckless; (2) the conduct was extreme and outrageous; (3) the conduct caused emotional distress; and (4) the emotional distress was severe. The defendant's conduct must be so extreme in degree, as to go beyond all possible bounds of decency, and to be regarded as atrocious, and utterly intolerable in a civilized community. Whether a claim rises to the requisite level of outrageousness and egregiousness to sustain a claim for intentional infliction of emotional distress is a question of law.

In her complaint, Thompson-El alleged that the defendants failed to reverse the foreclosure after she complained that it had taken place without her knowledge, inundated her with court filings, used judicial proceedings to evict her, listed the property for sale and placed a "For Sale" sign in the yard, terminated her Georgia Power account, changed the locks, and obtained a warrant for her arrest for criminal trespass when she would not vacate the property. Taking the allegations of the complaint as true, the facts establish only that the defendants initiated foreclosure proceedings a year after Thompson-El entered default and then, after foreclosure, treated her as the owner of real property (or its agent) may treat a squatter on its property. The trial court did not err in concluding that Thompson-El's complaint failed to allege any acts by the defendants that were extreme and outrageous or that her emotional distress was so severe that no reasonable person could be expected to endure it. Therefore, within the framework of Thompson-El's complaint, there is no claim for intentional infliction of emotional distress that would allow her to recover.

Judgment affirmed.

DOYLE, P.J., and MILLER, J., concur.

Questions about the case:

1. What are the elements of "wrongful foreclosure"?
2. Did the plaintiff establish her claim of wrongful foreclosure?
3. What burden is the plaintiff required to meet in an action for intentional infliction of emotional distress?
4. Did the plaintiff meet the standard of intentional infliction of emotional distress in her action against the lender?

ALIENATION OF AFFECTIONS

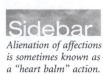

The tort of alienation of affections is based on a third party's interference with a marriage, usually by committing adultery with one of the spouses. In many states, this action is no longer authorized. Most parties prefer to handle the allegation as part of a divorce action and do not bring a separate action for alienation of affections. In some states, the tort has been merged with other torts and does not exist as a separate cause of action. At least one recent case has brought this tort back into nationwide prominence. In North Carolina, the wife of a man who had an affair brought suit against the mistress, basing her claim on alienation of affections. Her verdict for $1 million renewed interest in this tort.

The elements of alienation of affections are as follows:

- Interference with the marriage by the defendant
- Subsequent loss of affection by one spouse for another
- Loss of affection caused by this interference
- Interference motivated by malice

INTENTIONAL INFLICTION OF EMOTIONAL DISTRESS

Lawsuits involving the intentional infliction of emotional distress are far more common than claims for alienation of affections. In this tort, the injured party is claiming that either through intentional actions or recklessness, the defendant caused the plaintiff severe emotional distress through some outrageous behavior.

A. ELEMENTS OF INFLICTION OF EMOTIONAL DISTRESS

To prove the tort of intentional infliction of emotional distress, the plaintiff must prove that:

- intentional or reckless conduct
- caused the plaintiff severe emotional distress
- by defendant's outrageous conduct

Here's an example: Stan is a photographer who is down on his luck. If he can get a photograph of a celebrity, preferably an unflattering one, he knows he can sell it to a national tabloid. He gains access to the home of a famous actress by posing as a police officer. When the actress appears, Stan says, "I'm sorry to tell you this, but your son has been killed." He whips out his camera and takes her photograph just as she reacts to this news. Although he gets the photograph published in the tabloid, he also gets served with a complaint alleging intentional infliction of emotional distress. We use this example to discuss the elements of this tort.

1. INTENTIONAL OR RECKLESS CONDUCT

In order to be liable for this tort, the defendant must act with the specific intention of inflicting emotional distress on the plaintiff or act with such utter recklessness that emotional distress would naturally result. Stan's actions point to his intention of causing emotional distress. An example of recklessness is when someone reports a very damaging fact as true, without bothering to check it for accuracy. For instance, if Stan had announced the son's death on television without investigating whether it was true, his conduct would be reckless.

2. BYSTANDER EMOTIONAL DISTRESS

In some jurisdictions, a bystander or a witness to a horrific event may be entitled to bring a claim of "bystander emotional distress." For instance, a child might be permitted to bring a claim of bystander emotional distress if she witnesses injuries to her mother.[2]

3. CAUSATION

We have discussed the legal term *causation* before, but another word or two about it here is also required. The plaintiff has to prove that there is a direct connection between the emotional distress and the defendant's actions. If a plaintiff was already suffering from sleeplessness and anxiety, she couldn't allege that these conditions were caused by the defendant's actions, no matter how cruel they were.

B. EMOTIONAL DISTRESS: WHAT IS IT?

The biggest problem with this tort is the element of emotional distress. Like love, hate, pain, or joy, emotional distress is impossible to measure and varies considerably in intensity from one person to another. The fact that it is so difficult to define makes it very difficult to prove at trial. As in the case of assault and battery, the hypothetical reasonable person comes to our aid again.

In order to prove emotional distress, the plaintiff must show that the defendant's actions were such that a hypothetical reasonable person would have suffered emotional distress if he had been subjected to the same conduct. We do not look to the subjective reaction of the plaintiff. Instead we judge it by an objective standard. What about Stan's actions? Would a hypothetical reasonable person suffer emotional distress because of what Stan did? Most juries would probably answer yes. His actions would seem designed to cause anyone a great deal of emotional distress. However, there is still one requirement that the plaintiff must prove: outrageousness.

1. THE DEFENDANT'S ACTIONS WERE OUTRAGEOUS

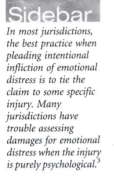

In most jurisdictions, the best practice when pleading intentional infliction of emotional distress is to tie the claim to some specific injury. Many jurisdictions have trouble assessing damages for emotional distress when the injury is purely psychological.[3]

Many would argue that the last element of the tort of intentional infliction of emotional distress is outrageousness. What do we mean by *outrageous?* Courts have defined this term in many ways, but the most common definition states that the defendant's actions must be "intolerable" or "beyond society's accepted standards of decency and morality." Why include this element at all? If the plaintiff can prove that the defendant's actions were intentional and that they were a direct cause of the plaintiff's emotional distress, isn't this enough? For most jurisdictions, the answer is no. See Figure 2-3 for examples of situations that do and do not meet the standard for intentional infliction of emotional distress.

The most common reason given for requiring the element of outrageousness is that it will help limit frivolous lawsuits. We must all suffer our fair share of emotional distress; there is no way to go through life without it. This tort is not intended to address the tragedies that affect everyone. Instead, this tort was created to give plaintiffs some redress against a person who goes out of his way to cause emotional distress to another person.

What about Stan, the photographer? If our hypothetical reasonable person considers Stan's actions to be outrageous, the actress has proved her case against him. Under these circumstances, Stan will probably lose this lawsuit. In Chapter 8, we discuss the kinds of damages (or monetary payments) the actress may be entitled to receive against Stan. He will probably end up losing a lot more money than he gained by taking the photograph.

FIGURE 2-3	
Examples of Emotional Distress Situations	Examples of situations that meet the standard for intentional infliction of emotional distress:

Examples of situations that meet the standard for intentional infliction of emotional distress:

- Plaintiff is 11 years old, and the defendant, a 40-year-old neighbor, harasses the child and continually tells him that a freckle on the back of his neck is cancer, that he's going to die very soon, and that his mother is planning on abandoning him.
- Plaintiff is particularly susceptible to loud noises; defendant knows this and sets off a firecracker in plaintiff's chair at work.

Examples of situations that do not meet the standard for intentional infliction of emotional distress:

- Defendant curses and insults the plaintiff.
- Plaintiff is particularly nervous or susceptible to loud noises; defendant sets off a firecracker during the Fourth of July celebration.

Intentional infliction of emotional distress is a cause of action asserted by plaintiffs who have suffered emotional or psychological damage because of the defendant's outrageous actions.

TORT
BASICS
AT A
GLANCE

VII MALICIOUS PROSECUTION

Malicious prosecution is a tort designed to punish people who use the court system as a way to harass or intimidate other people. When a person brings a baseless criminal charge against someone, or continues to press charges knowing that the person is innocent, the innocent party has the right to sue.

A. THE ELEMENTS OF MALICIOUS PROSECUTION

The elements of malicious prosecution include the following:

- The defendant brings or continues a criminal charge against the plaintiff.
- The case terminates in the plaintiff's favor.
- The defendant acted with malice in bringing the charge.
- There was no probable cause for the charge.

1. DEFENDANT BRINGS OR CONTINUES A CRIMINAL CHARGE AGAINST THE PLAINTIFF

Malicious prosecution is based on the idea that a private citizen is using the court system for unlawful purposes, such as harassment or intimidation. These cases normally originate when a private citizen appears before a magistrate, swears to certain facts, and as a result of this sworn testimony the magistrate issues a warrant for a person's arrest. If the sworn statement turns out to be false, the person who is arrested (whom we call the *plaintiff* from now on) has a cause of action against the other person (whom we call the *defendant*).

2. THE CASE TERMINATES IN THE PLAINTIFF'S FAVOR

Under malicious prosecution, it does not matter whether the allegation involved a misdemeanor or a felony. However, the plaintiff can only bring

Sidebar

*Can police or prosecutors be sued for malicious prosecution? Prosecutors, police, and judges cannot be sued for malicious prosecution as long as they are acting within their duties. This tort is only authorized against private individuals who try to use the criminal justice system for their own ends. If a prosecutor or a police officer brings charges against an individual, no matter what the ultimate outcome of the case, that government official is **immune** from suit. The rules of immunity were specifically designed to prevent people convicted of a crime from trying to sue government officials for doing their jobs. If the official is acting out of personal malice, however, the immunity may not apply. In a similar way, people who call in suspicious activities cannot be sued for malicious prosecution because they are not responsible for continuing the prosecution. That duty falls to the prosecutor.*

Immunity
A legal protection that prevents a person from being liable in a civil suit.

this suit when he can prove that the criminal action ended in his favor. If the prosecutor or judge dismisses the case against the plaintiff, he can prove this element. However, if his case goes to trial and the jury finds him not guilty, he cannot. What is the difference? In the first example, the case was dismissed for lack of probable cause (the basic requirement for any criminal charge). However, in the second example, the jury must find a person guilty of a crime beyond a reasonable doubt. Many juries have been convinced of a person's guilt but have failed to return a guilty verdict because they believed that the state had failed to meet its burden. By requiring that the case end favorably to the plaintiff before it goes to the jury, courts do not have to inquire into the jury's actions in the criminal case.

3. THE DEFENDANT ACTED WITH MALICE IN BRINGING THE CHARGE

Another requirement that the plaintiff must establish is that the defendant acted with malice in bringing the charge in the first place. How does the plaintiff prove malice? The plaintiff can present evidence that the defendant knew the criminal case was baseless but pressed for prosecution as a way of "getting even" with the plaintiff. The plaintiff can show that the defendant was biased against him or hated him.

4. THERE WAS NO PROBABLE CAUSE FOR THE CHARGE

The requirement that there was no probable cause for the criminal charge is a way of preventing frivolous lawsuits. If the plaintiff can prove that probable cause was lacking in the criminal case, he can prove his civil case. However, the requirement of lack of probable cause discourages many lawsuits from individuals who believe that they have been wronged by the criminal justice system but have either pled guilty to a charge or been convicted at trial.

TORT BASICS AT A GLANCE

Malicious prosecution is a civil suit authorized when the defendant uses the court system as a means of unwarranted, private retaliation against the plaintiff.

VIII TORT IMMUNITY FOR FAMILIES

We have already mentioned the concept of immunity in the context of a prosecutor's immunity from suit for malicious prosecution. There are many other forms of immunity (also known as privileges) that essentially prevent certain individuals from being sued for specific torts. We saw earlier that a police officer has the right to touch a suspect in order to arrest him. The suspect cannot sue the officer for this touching, even though technically it is a battery. The officer is protected by immunity (as long as he is acting within his official capacity). There is also something known as intrafamily tort immunity. Simply put, family members are protected from lawsuits filed by other family members. Although there are some important exceptions to this rule, children cannot, for example, sue their parents for a spanking. Although the spanking is again a technical battery, the law does not permit this suit, because to do so would contribute to disharmony inside the family. Imagine the legal hornets' nest that would open up if children could sue their parents for activities they think are unfair. In later chapters, we explore specific immunities as they arise in the context of the material discussed.

IX. INTENTIONAL TORTS INVOLVING PROPERTY: TRESPASS

We are all familiar with the term *trespass,* but we may not know the exact nature of the legal elements of this tort. At law, trespass consists of:

- the (intentional) unprivileged
- entry onto the plaintiff's real property
- without permission.

A. INTENT

Trespass is an unusual tort in that many states do not require intent on the defendant's part before he can be liable for the tort. Put another way, trespass can be viewed as a strict liability tort. A strict liability tort is one in which the intent of the defendant is irrelevant to the issue of liability. There are very few strict liability torts. Under the common law, trespass to another person's property, no matter what the reason, was actionable, even if the defendant had a very good reason for committing the tort. The common law rule opened up a wide range of problems. Consider the following scenario: It is a stormy night and John Doe loses control of his car and crashes through Jane's fence. Jane can sue him for trespass, simply because he entered onto her property without permission. You can see why many states have amended their trespass laws to require an intentional action on the defendant's part.

1. UNPRIVILEGED

If the trespass occurred through operation of law, or because of public safety concerns, a civil suit for trespass will fail. For example, a police officer is pursuing a fleeing suspect and chases him through Jane's backyard. Although this seems to meet the elements of trespass, Jane's suit against the officer will fail because the officer is protected at law by a privilege that allows him to use reasonable means to apprehend a fleeing suspect, even if this means that he carries out a trespass to do so.

B. ENTRY ONTO THE PLAINTIFF'S REAL PROPERTY

Real property refers to land. If you imagine an invisible wall that rises up along the boundaries of the property, then the defendant commits trespass when he breaks through this imaginary boundary.

1. PROVING "ENTRY"

Although "entry" would seem to be an easy element to prove, it can involve some very complicated issues. It's one thing to find someone on your property, and another to claim that a low-flying aircraft has trespassed on your property. Under the law, entry usually means the physical entry of the defendant onto the plaintiff's land. The defendant can also enter using some extension of his body, such as tools, or objects, such as thrown rocks or debris. However, the law is clear that it is not trespass if light or sound from the defendant's house filters over to the plaintiff's property. The same is true for odors. The plaintiff can sue for these unpleasant situations, but not because they are trespasses. (See "nuisance," next page.) What about air traffic? Surely every time that a plane flies overhead, it is crossing over the physical boundaries of hundreds, perhaps thousands, of individual pieces of property. Is this trespass? No. Under the law, entry onto the plaintiff's property occurs within the "immediate reaches" of the surface of the property. This can also mean the space above the surface of the property that the plaintiff can reasonably be expected to use. Above that, it is no trespass even when an airplane passes over the plaintiff's property lines.

C. WITHOUT PERMISSION

This is perhaps the easiest element of trespass to prove. If the defendant has permission from the property owner, he has the privileged right to enter the defendant's property. However, who exactly has permission may sometimes be more complicated than one would imagine. What about the men and women who read electric meters? When you first moved into your house, did someone from the local electric company come out and ask for permission to read your meter? Because they did not, why can't you sue them for coming onto your property? There are two problems: (1) The meter reader is privileged (they provide the service to your home, and it would go against public policy to allow them to be sued), and (2) you have given implied permission to allow them to come onto your property to maintain your service. You might be surprised to learn just how many different people, from water company representatives to the cable company, have access to your property.

X NUISANCE ACTIONS

Suppose a person does not actually trespass onto John's land, but the fumes, odors, or noises reaching his property make it impossible for him to enjoy his own property. John can bring a **nuisance** action against the person producing the fumes. This action alleges that a person is doing something off the property that is affecting a person's ability to enjoy or use features on the property. It is commonly seen in situations where fumes, liquids, or other substances are leaking from one person's property onto another's.[4]

Nuisance
A cause of action that is authorized when the defendant's behavior results in a loss of enjoyment or value in the plaintiff's property.

A. PUBLIC NUISANCE VERSUS PRIVATE NUISANCE

The law recognizes two different kinds of nuisances: public and private. A public nuisance is some condition that affects the rights of citizens in general. This condition could be a health risk or a general annoyance. When a condition is classified as a public nuisance, the local government must take a hand. Individuals are usually prevented from bringing a claim under public nuisance; such actions are generally reserved for the government. Placing such limitations on public nuisance lawsuits is a direct reflection of the fact that there are many things in life that we must all put up with and allowing a private person to bring a public nuisance suit for any of these things would cause the legal system to grind to a halt. However, these limitations disappear when the allegation is a private nuisance.

1. PRIVATE NUISANCE

John lives inside the city limits. His next-door neighbor, Sam, has recently acquired about 30 chickens and keeps them in his backyard, where he allows them to roam free. Sam doesn't clean up after the birds, and the resulting odors are overpowering. John has asked Sam to remove the birds, but Sam has refused. John can't sit in his backyard anymore because the prevailing winds come across Sam's backyard and onto John's property. Can John bring a private nuisance lawsuit against Sam? Let's take a look at the elements:

- The defendant maintains a condition that
- substantially interferes with the plaintiff's right
- to use and enjoy his property.

See Figure 2-4 for examples of situations that meet these criteria.

FIGURE 2-4

Examples of
Situations in
Which Courts
Have Found
Private
Nuisances

- Defendant's factory, located close to plaintiff's residence, produces terrible odors and fumes
- Defendant's business causes the ground to tremble constantly at plaintiff's residence
- Defendant's long-haul business involves trucks coming and going at all hours of the night and involves the use of heavy equipment, with loud noises and bright lights that keep the plaintiff up all night
- Defendant pumps untreated sewage across the plaintiff's property

Sam's chickens would seem to satisfy the elements for a private nuisance action. If John brings suit, what damages is he entitled to receive? John could receive monetary payments to compensate him for the decreased use of his property, but what John really wants is someone to force Sam to get rid of the chickens. Although we discuss damages in much greater detail in a later chapter, a quick word may help explain the situation.

2. DAMAGES AND INJUNCTIONS

Can a court order Sam to get rid of his chickens? Yes. The court can order Sam to remove the chickens through its power to issue injunctions. An injunction is a court order that tells a person to either stop carrying out a specific action or, in some cases, to do a specific thing. If the person refuses to follow the court's order, she can be held in contempt by the judge. A finding of contempt means that the judge could order a monetary fine assessed against the person or even order that she spend time in jail.

B. NEW LAWSUITS UNDER ENVIRONMENTAL THEORIES

New federal statutes have made the use of nuisance actions even more valuable to those claiming that large corporations are polluting groundwater or dumping hazardous waste. Working through the U.S. Environmental Protection Agency (EPA), many agencies use these various federal statutes to force companies to pay for the complete cost of cleaning up a site that has been designated as hazardous.

TORTS TO PERSONAL PROPERTY: TRESPASS TO CHATTELS

Chattel
Personal property, including animals.

So far our discussion has focused on real property. However, there is a wide range of other torts that involve personal property, or "things." The main category under this heading consists of trespass to **chattels.** A chattel is an ancient term for personal property. *Trespass to chattels* is a suit based on the defendant's interference with the owner's rights to his personal property. This interference could come in the form of theft (permanently removing the property from the plaintiff's possession), conversion (retaining someone's property without permission), and damage to property (depriving the plaintiff of the use of the property). Here are the general elements of trespass to chattels:

- intentional,
- unprivileged interference with the
- plaintiff's personal property
- that results in damages to or loss of the property.

Example: Rick sneaks onto Steve's property one night and pours sugar into Steve's car's fuel tank. What type of action does Steve have against Rick?

Actually, Steve may have two actions against Rick. Steve can sue Rick for trespass, because he entered onto Steve's property without permission. Steve can also sue Rick for trespass to personal property, because Rick's actions resulted in damage to Steve's car.

A trespass to chattels case can also be based on the theory of **conversion.** When a person converts property, it means that he initially had legal right to use or possess the property but then failed to return it. The unlawful detention amounts to theft, thus permanently depriving the owner of use of the property.

> **Conversion**
> The exercise of control over the property and removal of it from the possession of the rightful owner.

Chapter Summary

Intentional torts are a small and distinct category of tort law. As the name implies, intentional torts involve deliberate actions by the defendant. Assault, for instance, consists of causing fear or apprehension to the plaintiff. On the other hand, battery is intentional, harmful, physical contact between the defendant and the plaintiff. In both circumstances, the defendant has not acted in a negligent manner but in a deliberate and intentional manner. Intentional torts are judged from the reasonable person standard — that is, would a reasonable person believe that the defendant's actions were harmful or offensive? This objective standard prevents actions based on the subjective feelings of the plaintiff. Other intentional torts include false imprisonment, alienation of affections, and malicious prosecution. In each of these torts, the defendant is taking some action to affect the freedom, rights, or relationships of the plaintiff. Intentional torts can also consist of interfering with the plaintiff's rights to his property. Trespass to chattels involves the defendant's intentional actions to prevent the plaintiff from exercising control over his own property. This intentional interference with the plaintiff's property covers not only personal property (things), but real property (land) as well. When the defendant interferes with the plaintiff's use or enjoyment of his real estate, it is called a nuisance action.

 SKILLS YOU NEED IN THE REAL WORLD

Keeping Track of Your Time

Whether you are working for a plaintiff's firm or a defense firm, it is usually important for you to keep track of your billable hours. As we see in Chapter 5, plaintiffs' firms are generally only paid when the case settles. The amount of payment does not depend on the hours billed, so why would it be important to keep track of the hours you spend working on a particular case? The simple answer is that by keeping track of your hours, you can have a better idea of where you are spending the majority of your time and whether your activities ultimately benefit the firm. You may find, for example, that most of your time is spent dealing with clients on the telephone. Keeping track of your activities and the amount of time you spend on those activities gives you a better idea of how to streamline your workday and to eliminate some of the nonproductive periods. This helps you to be a better paralegal and consequently even more indispensable to the firm.

Billable Hours at Defense Firms

When a paralegal works for an insurance defense firm, keeping track of billable hours is often the only way to ensure that the firm is paid for its time. Insurance defense firms are not paid based on the ultimate settlement amount. Instead, most insurance defense firms bill their clients with an hourly charge. In such a situation, the attorneys working at the firm want to make sure that they bill for every possible activity. Some firms do this by requiring you to keep track of your activities and assigning not only how much time you spent on these particular activities but also for whom the activity was carried out. For instance, you may have spent a half hour writing a letter on the *Joe Doe v. Sue Doe* case. Most firms bill their clients on the basis of one-tenth of an hour. One-tenth of an hour equates to six minutes. Therefore, if you spend half an hour working on a letter, your time would appear as 0.5 hours. Insurance defense firms spend a great deal of time and energy making sure that all activities at the firm are billed to the appropriate client.

In the real world, attorneys realize that they cannot overbill their clients. For instance, billing three hours for a two-minute telephone call would not only be unethical, it might also be illegal. This is why it is important not to exaggerate the hours you spend on a particular task. In some firms, you hand in your worksheets at the end of each week. These days, it is far more common for paralegals to keep track of their time with software. Using software, a paralegal can bill each and every activity to the appropriate client as well as assign a time value depending on how long it took to complete that particular activity. Para-legals who routinely bill high amounts of hours are often the ones who receive bonuses and pay raises.

Dealing with Clients on the Telephone

When you are dealing with clients on the telephone, always keep a handy reference about the client nearby. This could be as simple as a three-by-five card listing the client's complete name and other important information. Your information card should contain the client's full name, address, and all relevant telephone numbers, as well as some personal information. For instance, you should keep track of the client's spouse's name. Also list the names of any children. When you are talking to a client, refer to this card. Work the child's name into the conversation. Your client will be favorably impressed that you remember, not realizing that you had the information on a card—a little detail that can mean a lot.

Returning Phone Calls

The biggest source of frustration for a client is when the client fails to get a return phone call from the attorney. Clients do not like leaving several phone messages without a return call. One way that you can deal with this problem is to return the client's call as soon as possible, even if you don't have any information for the client. You may have a natural tendency to hold off returning the phone call until you can tell the client something of interest. This is a mistake. Often a client will appreciate a telephone call even when you don't have any news to report. Sometimes the client will be reassured just by hearing another person's voice.

Talkative Clients

Everyone has had the experience of speaking with someone on the phone who simply won't stop talking. If you have a client who calls you frequently or doesn't stop talking after a reasonable amount of time, you have to develop some new strategies to get off the phone. For example, arrange a hand signal with a coworker to let the coworker know that he or she should call you and give you an excuse to hang up. Some people prearrange to have their cell phone ring after a certain period of time, which also gives them the excuse to pick up the other line.

In situations where the client has been particularly talkative, you may be able to arrange with the attorney a policy that dictates the client will be billed personally for all phone calls. This has a tendency to keep talkative clients off the telephone.

Billable Hour Software

There are numerous programs available these days that allow you to track your time. Billable hours are important for insurance defense firms, but they are also becoming increasingly important for plaintiffs' firms as well. (It helps the firm track how it spends its time and helps to improve overall efficiency.) Billable hour software comes in a vast array of forms, from standard programs that come bundled in office management software to individual programs that can be uploaded to a personal digital assistant or other mobile device. No matter what software you choose, there are some features that should be present. The program should be easy to use, both in entering information and assigning it to a particular client's file. It should be able to interface with other computer systems to allow you to print out the final version and e-mail to others in the firm. Finally, it should be flexible enough to allow for additional notes or other materials that you might need to enter about a particular activity.

THE LIFE OF A PARALEGAL

Having a Good Relationship with the Courthouse Personnel

A lot of paralegals don't realize how important it is to have a good relationship with the people at the courthouse. They're obligated to provide information and to do certain things whether you have a good rapport with them or not, but they're just so much more helpful if you've got a good relationship. I don't abuse that. Anything I can look up myself, I absolutely will. I only call on them when I need to know something now and don't have the time to run over to the courthouse and check it out.

There are even times when they'll provide information to you just to put you on notice of something that's happened. Sometimes the court schedule gets changed around or things have been delayed. A lot of times, a clerk will actually call you and fill you in on recent developments. The courthouse people have to deal with a lot of jerks; showing them some respect and kindness goes a long way with them.

Linda McCurry, Paralegal

ETHICAL ISSUES FOR THE PARALEGAL: STATUTES OF LIMITATION

When dealing with intentional torts, the most pressing issue is often the statute of limitations. Many people fail to realize that they often have a very short period during which they must bring their suit or have it barred forever. On your first meeting with the client, you should establish this date as precisely as possible. The more likely that the date is going to be an issue, that is, that the statute is going to run soon, the more you should do to make sure that the client understands the importance of that date. You should also let the attorney know that the statute may "run" shortly. How do you do this? Note it prominently in the file. Send a letter to the client noting this date as a major point in the letter. Send a memo to the attorney, again noting the importance of this date. That way, you've covered the legal point (and yourself) from every angle you can think of.

Relevant Cases

SPILLERS V. FIVE POINTS GUARANTY BANK
335 SO. 2D 851 (1976)

McCORD, Judge.
This action was brought in the court below by Five Points Guaranty Bank against Albert L. Spillers, etc., et ux., to foreclose a security agreement, pledge agreement and real estate mortgage. This is an interlocutory appeal from an order granting the bank's motion to strike the Spillers' affirmative defenses and to dismiss portions of the Spillers' counterclaim.

On April 1, 1975, the Spillers gave the bank a renewal note in the amount of $49,664.02 payable in 30 days. It was secured by a financing statement covering all equipment, furniture, fixtures and inventory of the Spillers' business, a life insurance policy, and a third mortgage on real estate. The bank's complaint sought foreclosure and the Spillers filed an answer admitting execution of a pledge agreement, a third mortgage, and an amended pledge agreement but setting up four affirmative defenses alleging invalidity of the instruments sued upon and a counterclaim. The first affirmative defense alleged that the Spillers proposed to the bank that the Spillers hold an art sale in the bank with the proceeds going to pay off the bank loan but that the bank president induced them to sign a pledge agreement to the effect that they could not remove their paintings from the bank until the indebtedness was paid in full; that he induced their agreement by threatening to put them out of business and by verbal abuse. The second affirmative defense alleged that the third mortgage on their home, given to obtain an extension on their loan, was obtained by the bank through verbal abuse and threats to close down their business; that these acts were committed when the bank president knew of Albert Spillers' poor physical and mental health. The third affirmative defense alleged that the bank induced the Spillers to sign the amended pledge agreement permitting the bank to sell the paintings held as collateral to anyone at any price through threats and verbal abuse. The fourth affirmative defense alleged that the amended pledge agreement was void under the provisions of s 679.501, Florida Statutes (a provision of the Uniform Commercial Code). The Spillers' counterclaim, seeking $500,000 damages, alleged that the bank had sold paintings under the original pledge agreement to preferred customers at discount prices and had induced the Spillers to sign the amended pledge agreement to legitimatize the violations and had intentionally inflicted emotional distress upon the Spillers. The court below granted the bank's motion to dismiss the four affirmative defenses and portions of the counterclaim.

The Spillers have raised three points on this appeal. First, they contend that threats to enforce rights through the institution of court proceedings render a contract void or viodable, depending upon the circumstances; that the allegations of their first, second and third affirmative defenses are sufficient defenses against the bank's foreclosure suit. While it is true that threats to enforce legal rights may constitute duress under certain circumstances, they do not constitute duress when the threat is to enforce existent legal rights. Duress would only occur when the threatened enforcement is to enforce rights which in fact are nonexistent. This would occur when the contract sought to be enforced is illegal. It appears that the Spillers simply borrowed money from the bank and signed various security documents to secure their obligation as it was renewed from time to time. They were 'coerced' into signing the various documents only in the sense that they had a choice of either signing them in return for renewals of their obligation or refusing to sign. A refusal could, of course, cause them to default on their obligation thereby putting the bank in position to accelerate the obligation and foreclose on their stock in trade, thus putting them out of business. While this was a type of coercion, it was not such coercion as gives rise to duress and undue influence because the bank had a legal right to follow the course of action it took. The affirmative defenses and counterclaim relying on duress and undue influence are devoid of allegations that the bank did anything which it did not have a legal right to do.

As a general rule, it is not duress to threaten to do what one has a legal right to do. Nor is it duress to threaten to take any measure authorized by law and the circumstances of the case.

Thus, it is the established rule that it is not duress to institute or threaten to institute civil suits, or take proceedings in court, or for any person to declare that he intends to use the courts wherein to insist upon what he believes to be his legal rights. . . . Under the foregoing principles, the fact that a threat was made to resort to legal proceedings to collect a claim which was at least valid in part constitutes neither duress nor fraud such as will avoid liability on a compromise agreement. A threat to resort to remedies given by a contract, or to sue on a past-due note and to foreclose the lien securing such a note, or to foreclose, or exercise the power of sale in a mortgage, . . . is not such duress as to justify rescission of a transaction induced thereby.

Business compulsion is not established merely by proof that consent was secured by the pressure of financial circumstances . . . The doctrine of business compulsion cannot be predicated upon a demand which is lawful, upon doing or threatening to do that which a party has a legal right to do.

The pressure must be wrongful, and not all pressure is wrongful. The law provided certain means for the enforcement of their claims by creditors. It is not duress to threaten to take these means.

As to the allegations of the Spillers relating to abusive and insulting language, the general law is stated in 74 Am.Jur.2d, Torts s 32 (1974), as follows:

'It is a general rule that a cause of action may not be predicated upon mere rudeness or lack of consideration of one person for another.'

It would follow that rudeness and lack of consideration for another does not constitute either a defense to an action for enforcement of a legal obligation or a cause of action in its own right. We find no error in the dismissal of the Spillers' first three affirmative defenses and their counterclaim.

Finding, pursuant to Florida Appellate Rule 4.2 c, that the interlocutory appeal is without substantial merit, it is dismissed.

BOYER, C.J., and RAWLS, J., concur.

KIRKLAND V. EARTH FARE, INC.
289 GA. APP. 819, 658 S.E. 2D 433 (2008)

MIKELL, Judge.

Dwain Lee Kirkland, acting pro se, filed the underlying action against Earth Fare, Inc., and its employee, Gere Warrick (called "Gere Doe" in the complaint), based on an incident that occurred in an Earth Fare store. Kirkland now brings this pro se appeal of the trial court's grant of summary judgment in favor of appellees. Finding no error, we affirm.

The record reveals that on July 7, 2003, Kirkland entered an Earth Fare grocery store in order to return an item. According to Kirkland, the manager of the store, Warrick, called Kirkland aside to an area immediately adjacent to the checkout lane and within earshot of the other customers, and asked him to leave the store. When Kirkland asked why, Warrick accused him of sexually harassing female employees of Earth Fare and of masturbating in the men's restroom. Kirkland denied these allegations. After their encounter, Kirkland was not ejected from the Earth Fare store nor was he asked not to return to the store; instead, according to Kirkland's verified complaint, "he was unmolested as he finished the refund and then his shopping and exited Earth Fare." Kirkland admitted that there was no physical contact between himself and any employee of Earth Fare.

Kirkland filed the underlying lawsuit against Earth Fare and Warrick on June 27, 2005, more than a year after the incident occurred, alleging damage to his reputation, "extreme emotional duress and irreversible mental damage," that the actions of appellees were "contributory to a near fatal event . . . that occurred in late 2003," "loss of companionship," "extreme unhappiness," and near loss of life, plus punitive damages and costs. Appellees moved to dismiss the complaint. After a hearing on November 29, 2005, the trial court converted appellees' motion to dismiss to a motion for summary judgment and subsequently granted summary judgment in favor of appellees. Kirkland appeals, asserting that the trial court erred, first, in failing to grant summary judgment in his favor and, second, in granting summary judgment to appellees as to Kirkland's claims for negligent infliction of emotional distress, intentional infliction of emotional distress, and tortious misconduct. Kirkland has not challenged the trial court's ruling that his claims for loss of reputation were time-barred.

In order to prevail on this claim, Kirkland must meet the requirements of the Georgia impact rule, which requires that he show that (1) he suffered a physical impact; (2) the physical impact caused him physical injury; and (3) the physical injury caused his mental suffering or emotional distress. It is undisputed that no physical impact occurred between Kirkland and any employee of Earth Fare; and there is no allegation or evidence of any physical injury to Kirkland.

Nor does Kirkland's claim come under the "pecuniary loss" exception to the impact rule. Kirkland failed to produce evidence showing that he suffered any pecuniary loss stemming from the July 7, 2003, incident at Earth Fare. Although Kirkland submitted an affidavit in which he averred that "all 31 counts of the original complaint . . . are true and correct to the best of my knowledge at this time," and his complaint alleged that Dwain Lee Kirkland believes he has suffered damages for Count 20 (relating to 'extreme emotional duress') in the amount of $20,000 per year for the past two years and $20,000 per year for the next seven years which he may be expected to survive totaling $180,000, or whatever amount the jury may award, these conclusory allegations do not provide evidence of pecuniary damage that would withstand summary judgment. We conclude that the trial court did not err in granting summary judgment to appellees on Kirkland's claim for negligent infliction of emotional distress.

In order to meet his burden as to the third required element, Kirkland must show that appellees' conduct was "so outrageous in character, and so extreme in degree, as to go beyond all possible bounds of decency, and to be regarded as atrocious, and utterly intolerable in a civilized community. Whether the alleged conduct is sufficiently extreme or outrageous is a question of law for the trial court."

Here, the undisputed facts show that Warrick, Earth Fare's store manager, confronted Kirkland concerning alleged misconduct on store property. Kirkland was allowed to explain his side of the story; and after this encounter, "he was unmolested as he finished the refund and then his shopping and exited Earth Fare." He was not expelled from the store at that time nor was he banned from the store for the future. Warrick's conduct was not, as a matter of law, sufficiently extreme or outrageous to support a claim for the intentional infliction of emotional distress. As this Court has recently reiterated, "outrageous conduct" sufficient to justify a claim of intentional infliction of emotional distress "does not include mere insults, indignities, threats, annoyances, petty oppressions, or other vicissitudes of daily living. Plaintiffs are expected to be hardened to a certain amount of rough language and to occasional acts that are definitely inconsiderate and unkind." Even if the store manager's manner in confronting Kirkland was annoying and insensitive, "there is no occasion for the law to intervene in every case where someone's feelings are hurt." Accordingly, the trial court did not err in granting summary judgment to appellees as to Kirkland's claim for intentional infliction of emotional distress.

Here, the store manager spoke to Kirkland about his supposed conduct in the store. There is no evidence or allegation that anyone else was in the store. Even if so, there is no evidence that anyone else in the store heard or was aware of the conversation, although Kirkland did allege that it took place "within earshot" of the checkout lanes. Further, as noted in Division 4 above, Kirkland continued with his business "unmolested" in the store after this confrontation. Although the store owner "has a duty to protect its customers from injury caused by the tortious misconduct of its employees," the incident of which Kirkland complains "does not rise to the level of unprovoked and unjustifiable opprobrious and insulting and abusive words by an employee tending to humiliate, mortify, and wound the feelings of the customer."

Judgment affirmed.

JOHNSON, P.J., BLACKBURN, P.J., SMITH, P.J., RUFFIN and BERNES, JJ., concur.

Websites

■ **National Center for State Courts**
http://www.ncsconline.org

■ **Time-Tracking Software**
http://www.timepanic.com

■ **Wikipedia — Intentional Torts**
http://en.wikipedia.org/wiki/Intentional_torts

■ **Mega Law**
http://www.megalaw.com

Forms and Court Documents

This complaint is for an allegation of battery in a bar fight.

IN THE SUPERIOR COURT OF GANNETT COUNTY
STATE OF PLACID

Richard Coe,	)	CASE NO. CV 2002-1101
Plaintiff	)	
vs.	)	
Terry Zoe,	)	
Defendant	)	

Complaint for Personal Injury

COMES NOW, the plaintiff, Richard Coe, and complaining of the defendant alleges the following:

1.

The Plaintiff is a citizen and resident of Gannett County, Placid.

2.

The Defendant is, upon information and belief, a citizen and resident of Gannett County, Placid.

3.

On or about August 13, 2000, at approximately 11:00 P.M., the Plaintiff, Richard Coe, was in an establishment known as Tilly's Tavern, 123 Highway 92, Florence City. The defendant, Terry Zoe, was also present in the same establishment.

4.

As the plaintiff was sitting quietly at the bar of the establishment, the Defendant, Terry Zoe, without warning and without any provocation, struck the Plaintiff with a bar stool. The Plaintiff had had no prior contact with the Defendant, and had neither instigated nor encouraged any physical altercation with the Defendant.

5.

Defendant's actions were an intentional, unjustified, unprovoked, and violent battery on the person of the Plaintiff, Richard Coe.

6.

After being struck by the Defendant, the Plaintiff lost consciousness and was later transported to the Memorial Mission Hospital for treatment.

7.

That as a proximate cause of the Defendant's intentional battery on the person of the Plaintiff, said Plaintiff suffered severe, debilitating, and permanent injuries in excess of $10,000.00.

WHEREFORE, the Plaintiff prays that the Court:
1. That the Plaintiff, Richard Coe, have and recover a judgment against the Defendant in an amount in excess of $10,000.00 for personal injuries.
2. That the Defendant be assessed with punitive damages as permitted by law.
3. That prejudgment interest be awarded as provided by law.
4. That the costs of this action be taxed against the Defendant.
5. That all issues raised be tried before a jury.
6. For such other and further relief as the Court may deem just and proper.

This the _____ day of June, 2002.

_____

Clarence D. Arrow
Attorney for Plaintiff, Richard Coe
State Bar No. 000-998

Key Terms

Assault	Elements	Nuisance
Battery	Foreseeability	Prima facie
Chattel	Immunity	Proximate cause
Conversion	Intentional tort	

Review Questions

1 How does assault differ from battery?
2 Explain what is meant by the term *elements of proof.*
3 Explain the reasonable person standard. Why is it used?
4 Why can't an unconscious person be assaulted?
5 What are the elements of false imprisonment?
6 What is the justification for continuing to allow lawsuits for interference with private property? Couldn't these situations simply be resolved through the criminal courts?
7 How does a "private nuisance" differ from a "public nuisance"?
8 Explain the elements of alienation of affections. Should such a civil injury continue to provide a cause of action for plaintiffs? Why or why not?
9 What are chattels? Why is there a tort for trespass to chattels?
10 What are some of the methods a paralegal can use to maintain good client relations?

Applying What You Have Learned

1 Rick is a fully competent adult who has decided that he doesn't want critical medical attention that would clearly save his life. His doctor decides to treat Rick anyway. Has the doctor committed the tort of battery?
2 Nora was originally admitted into Happy Dale Nursing Home without incident. However, after she'd been there for a day, she decided that she wanted to go home. The management of the nursing home facility refused to release her to her son when he arrived to take her home, because it was Nora's daughter who had arranged for Nora's admission to Happy Dale. Does Nora have a valid claim for false imprisonment?
3 Claudia's daughter, Rachel, goes out on a date one night with Ross. While they are driving, Ross loses control of the car and runs off the road. Rachel is killed. Ross drags her body several hundred feet from the scene of the accident and arranges Rachel's body to make it look like a car struck her while she was walking. The next morning, Ross calls Claudia and accuses Rachel of stealing his car and worries that something may have happened. Draft a complaint for intentional infliction of emotional distress based on these facts.

Endnotes

[1] Federal Tort Trial and Verdicts, 1994–1995. Bureau of Justice Statistics, U.S. Department of Justice.
[2] *Klein v. City of Stamford,* 669 A.2d 644 (1994).
[3] Am. Jur. 2d, Negligence.
[4] *Bousquet v. Com.,* 374 Mass. 824, 372 N.E.2d 257 (1978).

Crossword Puzzle

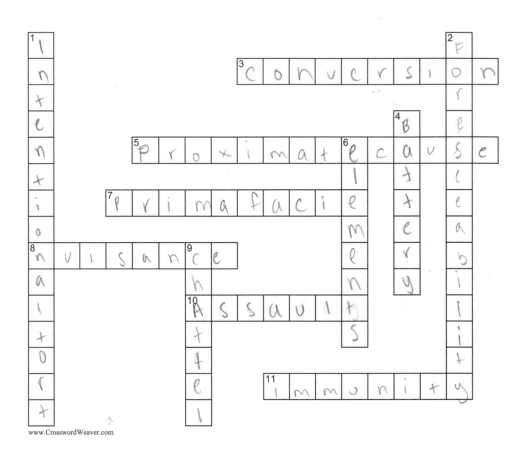

www.CrosswordWeaver.com

ACROSS

3 Exercising control over property and removing it from the possession of the rightful owner

5 The facts that show the defendant's legal responsibility for the injuries to the plaintiff, also known as legal cause

7 "at first sight"; the party has presented adequate evidence to prove a particular point

8 A cause of action that is authorized when the defendant's behavior results in a loss of enjoyment or value in the plaintiff's property

10 When the defendant causes the plaintiff to have fear or apprehension of a harmful or offensive contact

11 An exception or privilege granted by the law to an action that ordinarily would result in a cause of action

DOWN

1 A civil action based on a defendant's purposeful, intentional act that causes harm, as opposed to a defendant who causes harm through negligence

2 The legal requirement that the plaintiff be a person who would likely be injured by the defendant's conduct

4 When the defendant causes harmful or offensive contact to the plaintiff

6 The points raised by the plaintiff in his complaint that must also be proved at trial; failure to prove these points will often result in a dismissal of the plaintiff's case

9 Personal property, including animals

Defenses to Intentional Torts

- ■ Be able to explain the components of various defenses

- ■ Explain how and under what circumstances a defense is triggered

- ■ Describe how and under what circumstances self-defense is an available defense

- ■ Explain how age or mistake can affect liability analysis

- ■ Define the insanity defense

I. WHAT IS A DEFENSE?

We have already seen that when the plaintiff brings suit against the defendant, the plaintiff's complaint spells out in detail exactly what injury the defendant caused and why the plaintiff is entitled to recover damages from the defendant. When the defendant files an answer, he states that he is not responsible for the plaintiff's injuries and is not liable to pay damages. This is a simple denial. However, a defendant can also raise a defense. A defense seeks to mitigate, explain away, or completely remove liability. Some defenses are known as absolute defenses, meaning that if the jury or judge believes the defense, the defendant will not be liable to the plaintiff as a matter of law. Most defenses are designed to mitigate the defendant's responsibility. In civil law, these defenses often take the form of: "I did it, but . . ."

TORT
BASICS
AT A
GLANCE

A defense is a legal claim raised by a defendant that seeks to either mitigate or completely exonerate him from liability.

II SELF-DEFENSE

Self-defense
When a person uses force (sometimes deadly force) to protect himself from an attack.

In our first example, **self-defense,** the defendant is admitting that he used violence against the plaintiff but offers an explanation. The "but" in this example is the very core of the defense. The defendant is claiming that he used force only to protect himself or someone else.

Here's an example: Ron and Ramon are at a bar. Ron doesn't know Ramon, but as sometimes happens in a bar, Ron takes an immediate dislike to Ramon. After making a few insulting comments, Ron grabs a beer mug and rushes toward Ramon, swinging the mug over his head. Ramon, believing that he is about to be struck by the beer mug, kicks a chair in Ron's way. Ron falls over the chair and breaks his leg. Later, Ron sues Ramon for battery. Does Ramon have a legal defense? Yes, absolutely. Ramon, like anyone else, has the right to defend himself against physical attack. Ramon doesn't have to wait until someone actually strikes him before he has this right.

A. THE RESPONSE MUST BE EQUAL TO THE THREAT

Sidebar

In one case, a police officer fired his gun at and injured a motorist who was backing up his car in the officer's direction at two miles per hour. The court found that the use of deadly force was unreasonable, noting that the officer could have easily stepped out of the way of the car. The officer was found liable to the motorist for the torts of assault and battery.[1]

Can Ramon successfully raise self-defense if, instead of pushing a chair in Ron's way, he takes out a gun and shoots Ron? Put another way, just how far does self-defense go? Common sense alone would say that Ramon has overreacted. Shooting someone who is about to hit you with a beer mug doesn't seem to be a fair response. Interestingly enough, this is exactly what the law requires in self-defense. When you are defending yourself, you must use force that is approximately equal to the threat. If you are threatened with minimal force, you must respond with minimal force. On the other hand, if you are threatened with deadly force, you can respond with deadly force. Suppose that Ron had a knife in his hand instead of a beer mug. Could Ramon successfully claim self-defense if he shoots Ron? Under these circumstances, the answer would be yes. It would be silly to require Ramon to respond with exactly the same kind of force (a knife instead of a gun). Because a knife and a gun are both deadly weapons, Ramon can use deadly force to protect himself.

B. LIMITATIONS ON SELF-DEFENSE

The law also recognizes that there are certain situations in which a person is not permitted to use self-defense as a legal defense to a civil suit. We have already discussed one such example — when the victim of the attack responds with **excessive force.** But there are other situations as well.

1. NO SELF-DEFENSE FOR AGGRESSORS

Suppose in our example that Ramon had actually started the fight by attacking Ron. Ron then responds with the beer mug maneuver. Can Ramon still claim self-defense? As a general rule the answer would be no. People who start fights (called "aggressors" under tort law) do not have the legal defense of self-defense available to them.

a. Self-Defense Claim if Aggressor Voluntarily Stopped Fighting

However, this exception has its own exception. Ramon can successfully raise self-defense if he voluntarily stopped fighting, even though he was the aggressor, but Ron continues to fight.

2. NO SELF-DEFENSE FOR MARTIAL ARTISTS

We've all heard the expression "his hands were classified as deadly weapons." People with special training or abilities have a greater responsibility under the law and less opportunity to raise self-defense.

Excessive force
Force used in self-defense that is clearly disproportionate to the threat posed.

In some jurisdictions, a homeowner is required to warn a trespasser before resorting to force.[2]

At the time of the writing of the Declaration of Independence, the area of tort law was poorly developed and remained so for many years. The 1700s saw many legal treatises on criminal law, evidence, and other issues, but the first treatise on tort law did not appear until 1850, and it was a British publication.[3]

When Did the Biggest Changes in Civil Disposition and Trials Occur?			
	1984	**1992**	**2002**
Total Disposition	2,112,185	3,395382 ▲	3,087,857 ▼
Jury Trials	24,124	24,159	17,619 ▼
Bench Trials	629,572	688,517 ▲	469,547 ▼

FIGURE 3-1

Biggest Changes in Civil Trials

Source: National Center for State Courts, Data Source: Court Statistics Project, Publication: Examining the Work of State Courts: An Analysis of 2010 State Court Caseloads, 9/24/12.

Example: Ron threatens Ramon and they fight. Ramon is a black belt in a particularly lethal form of martial arts. He easily defeats Ron and causes him severe injuries. When Ron sues Ramon over his injuries, Ramon claims self-defense. The court rules against Ramon. Why? Ramon's special training essentially makes him a deadly weapon. We've already seen that responding with excessive force removes the claim of self-defense. When Ramon uses his hands, he is automatically responding with deadly force. Unlike most people, Ramon has stricter limits placed on him because of his training.

C. CLAIMING SELF-DEFENSE WHEN DEFENDING OTHERS

Can a person use self-defense as a legal defense when he uses violence against someone who is threatening a third person? The answer is yes, with some obvious limitations. Under the old common law rule, no longer applicable in most states, a person could only use violence to protect him- or herself and immediate family. The old rules did not extend this legal protection when a person used force to protect a stranger. That rule has been changed in almost every jurisdiction. These days, a person can use deadly force to protect a stranger, so long as the stranger is being threatened with deadly force.

The limitations on this defense are more practical than legal. In the first place, the person raising this defense has to show that the violence was necessary.

Example: Stan is walking through the park and he hears a man scream, "You devil! I'll fix you now!" He rounds a corner to see a man in flowing robes choking a woman while others look on and do nothing. Stan rushes forward, pulls out a gun, and shoots the man.

How would you analyze this situation from a legal perspective? Is the man using deadly force against the woman? Yes. Can Stan respond with deadly force when another person is being threatened with deadly force? Yes. The legal defense of self-defense should be available to Stan, but in this situation, it is not. Why? Because the man and the woman were actors, performing the last act of *Othello*. This is what we mean by the practical difficulties that are raised by defense of others. The person using force to save another has to be sure that he has a correct understanding of the situation.

D. OTHER LIMITATIONS ON SELF-DEFENSE: NO DEADLY FORCE TO PROTECT PROPERTY

A person cannot use self-defense when he uses deadly force to protect property. At law, "property" refers to anything that can be owned. Real property refers to land and the houses permanently attached to it; personal property refers to everything else: cars, candy, cannonballs, and so on. If a person is threatening to destroy personal property, the owner is not permitted to use deadly force to stop it.

Example: Around 2 A.M. one morning, Andy finally gives up trying to go to sleep and wanders around his house. He happens to look out his window, and he sees a man splashing gasoline inside Andy's car. Andy gets his gun and runs outside. The man lights a match and is just about to throw the match inside Andy's car and set it on fire. Andy shoots the man. When the man sues him for battery, Andy claims self-defense. Will he be successful?

No. Andy cannot use deadly force to protect his car.

(Note: Andy does have an action against the man for damaging his car, so even if the jury reaches a verdict favorable to the man Andy shot, they will probably also reach a verdict awarding damages to Andy for the damages the man caused to Andy's car.)

Example: Joanna is walking her beloved dog one evening when a man staggers out of his house, aims a gun at her dog, and shouts that he is going to kill it. Joanna pulls out a gun and shoots the man. Can she claim defense of others or self-defense?

No. Under the law, dogs are considered to be property, just like cars and jewelry and fountain pens. If Joanna cannot use deadly force to protect those items, she cannot use deadly force to protect her dog, either. A person is always entitled to use *reasonable* force to protect property, such as forcibly stopping someone from stealing a car, but a person cannot use deadly force in such a situation.

E. MUTUAL COMBAT

Closely related to self-defense, a claim of **mutual combat** is a defense that claims the plaintiff voluntarily entered into a fight with the defendant. If the plaintiff did agree to fight the defendant, he cannot then claim that the defendant battered him, especially while he was carrying out a battery himself. However, there are limitations on how far the defense of mutual combat goes. For instance, if the plaintiff voluntarily enters a fistfight with the defendant, and the defendant then escalates the violence by pulling out a gun, the defense of mutual combat will no longer be available to the defendant.

Mutual combat
When the parties to a fight voluntarily engage in violence.

 CONSENT

The defense of consent is based on the premise that the plaintiff agreed to whatever injury he received from the defendant. A plaintiff can consent to a wide range of injuries, including physical, emotional, and financial injuries. In order to prevail on a claim of consent, the defendant must show that the plaintiff voluntarily gave consent once he knew the possible consequences. This defense is not available when the defendant tricks the plaintiff into giving consent or when the plaintiff consents without knowing the full facts.

Not everyone is legally capable of giving consent. Children cannot give consent, because the law considers them to lack the maturity and knowledge necessary to understand what is happening. Other people who cannot give consent include people who have been declared mentally incompetent or who are acting under the influence of drugs or alcohol.

Sidebar

Informed consent is often raised as a defense in medical malpractice cases, discussed in Chapter 12.

IV. DURESS, NECESSITY, COMPULSION, AND COERCION

When a defendant raises any of the defenses of duress, necessity, compulsion, or coercion, the defendant is essentially admitting that he committed a particular action, but that he had no choice in the matter.

A. DURESS

Duress
When the defendant uses force, threat, or intimidation to overcome the plaintiff's will or to compel the plaintiff to do (or not to do) some action.

When a defendant pleads **duress** in his answer, he is saying that he was forced to carry out the act because someone was threatening his physical safety. Duress overcomes the person's will and unduly influences his behavior. This influence can come about through threats, intimidation, or other means. Whatever form it takes, the duress must be something that reasonable people would agree would cause someone to feel that he or she must commit a tort. It is not duress if the defendant "felt like" someone was pressuring him. The pressure brought to bear on the defendant must be something that an average person would consider to be compelling.[4]

Sidebar

Duress is based on the claim that the defendant was forced by someone else to carry out the intentional act.

B. COERCION

Sidebar

When a defendant intends to raise the defense of duress, he must plead it with specificity. His answer must clearly spell out all the elements of duress before the court will consider it.[5]

In most situations, duress and coercion are so closely related that there is no essential difference between them. When a person claims coercion, she is admitting that she committed the act but that she was forced to do so by physical or other type of threat. As is true with all of these defenses, the defendant must satisfy the jury that the facts support the defense. The jury is usually informed that the defendant must prove that she acted in a reasonable manner. Coercion, like duress, is judged from the standpoint of a reasonable person, not the subjective viewpoint of the defendant.

Sidebar

A claim of coercion is closely associated with the claim of duress; the defendant is claiming that he was forced to commit an intentional tort.

C. NECESSITY

Necessity is similar to duress. When a defendant claims necessity, he admits that he carried out the wrong to the plaintiff, but that he did so only to avoid some greater catastrophe.

Example: John is out in the woods when a sudden snowstorm strands him miles away from home. He trespasses onto Jim's land and breaks into his barn to seek shelter. Later, Jim brings suit against John for the damages he caused in breaking in. John can legally raise the defense of necessity as a defense to the allegation.

Sidebar

A claim of necessity is based on the claim that some natural force compelled the defendant to carry out an intentional tort.

Necessity is a defense in which the person claims that he committed one type of harm to avoid a more serious harm.

D. COMPULSION

The defense of **compulsion** actually goes to the mental state of the defendant at the time that he committed the tort. Mary sues Stan because Stan has stolen figurines she entrusted to him to clean. Stan claims that he has a compulsion called kleptomania. Whenever Stan sees figurines, he cannot help himself; he feels an overwhelming desire to take them. Compulsion is closely related to the defense of insanity, which we discuss later in this chapter.

Compulsion
An overwhelming or irresistible impulse to commit some action.

A claim of compulsion is a form of insanity plea; the defendant is essentially saying that he could not prevent himself from carrying out the intentional tort.

 **INTOXICATION**

When a person raises the claim of intoxication, he is essentially seeking to excuse his behavior on the grounds that he was not in his right mind. As such, intoxication is a form of insanity. At law, there are two types of intoxication: voluntary and involuntary.

A. VOLUNTARY INTOXICATION

When a person claims intoxication as a defense, he is actually saying that because of alcohol or some other drug, he lacked the ability to carry out intentional actions. However, a person can't use this defense if he voluntarily got intoxicated before carrying out the action.

Example: Stan wants to beat up Carl. Stan goes to a local bar, imbibes a lot of alcohol, and when Carl shows up, Stan attacks him. Carl sues Stan for battery, and Stan claims that he was so intoxicated that he didn't know what he was doing. However, because Stan's own actions created his intoxication, the judge refuses to allow Stan to use this defense.

Voluntary intoxication is not a valid, legal defense.

B. INVOLUNTARY INTOXICATION

Although a defendant is not permitted to use voluntary intoxication as a defense, the reverse situation can be a defense. If a person becomes intoxicated without her knowledge or intent, she may be allowed to use it as a defense. First of all, how does someone get "involuntarily intoxicated"? In the cases in which this defense has been used successfully, the defendant is usually exposed to chemicals or fumes that throw off her mental balance. That is the kind of involuntary intoxication the law recognizes as a valid defense.

 MISTAKE

Mistake can be a valid defense in which the defendant's actions would have been permissible but for his legitimate misunderstanding.

Example: A group of friends is playing a game of tackle football at the local park. Ron, who is not a member of the group and is not playing football, is wearing a jersey similar to one of the team members. Rick sees Ron out of the corner of his eye, and believing Ron to be carrying the ball, tackles him. Ron is badly bruised and brings a battery lawsuit against Rick. Rick raises the claim of mistake and has a good chance of winning the suit.

Mistake is a defense seen far more often in contract law cases or business torts than in intentional torts.

 **AGE**

In almost all jurisdictions, a child under the age of seven is not considered to be responsible for his actions. If the child commits a battery, or any other tort, the law will not permit an action against the child. The reason for this prohibition is simple: A child, especially a young child, often does not understand the consequences of his actions. The law works hard to protect children, including placing more responsibility on adults to take precautions when children are involved. Allowing lawsuits against children would fly in the face of that social policy. Later, we discuss some situations in which a suit is allowed against a child's parents for actions carried out by the child.

TORT BASICS AT A GLANCE

 **Children receive special protection under the law and are often barred from consenting to actions to which an adult could legally give consent.**

VIII   **INSANITY**

When a person raises the defense of insanity, he is saying that he is not legally responsible for his actions. The law will not allow a legally insane person to be found liable in a civil suit. Insane people do not have to pay judgments to plaintiffs. However, this raises the question: What is legal insanity? In most jurisdictions, the standard for determining legal insanity is that the defendant, at the time that he carried out his actions, did not know the difference between right and wrong. It should be noted that a person can be mentally disturbed to a great degree and still not be considered legally insane.

Why would the law protect an insane person by prohibiting suits against him? The idea behind the protection is that an insane person is no more able to control his actions than is a child. An insane person, like a child, does not understand the consequences of his actions. In such a situation there would be very little gained, and a good deal lost, if we permitted suits against those who are insane. Legally incompetent people receive special protection in our society. This is true for children and it is also true for the legally insane. The law of insanity is essentially a manifestation of public policy. However, this is not to say that we have always had the same approach to liability of the legally insane.

In previous decades, the standard for determining legal insanity has swung from one extreme to the other. In some periods, even marginal cases of mental disturbance were given the greatest protection, while in others, this protection was given only to the most disturbed of individuals.

A. THE INSANITY DEFENSE

A defendant in an intentional tort action may claim that he or she was insane at the time that the tort was committed. A defendant who claims insanity at the time of the action at one time might have been insulated from the effects of his or her actions in the same way that a criminal defendant who is legally insane cannot be convicted of a crime. However, the civil rule has changed across most of the United States to the effect that a legally insane person will be liable to another for an intentional tort whether the defendant was legally insane or not. State after state has adopted an approach that places the burden of the legally insane person's torts squarely on the shoulders of the person who committed it. In this way, legal insanity varies considerably between civil and criminal cases.

Some states have gone so far as to make a legally insane person liable for both intentional and negligent actions in the same way that a legally sane person would be. Although making a legally insane person liable for intentional torts has obvious societal implications, such as preventing potential fraud by those claiming insanity, there are different considerations for the insanity defense and negligence cases. As we see in the next chapter, a claim of negligence involves establishing that the defendant was aware of a duty to another and subsequently breached that duty. Proving these elements against a legally insane person can present practical difficulties. For instance, is it fair to ascribe fault to a person who is incapable of controlling himself?

"Where one of two innocent persons must suffer a loss, it should be borne by the one who occasioned it."[6]

When it comes to imposing damages for an insane person's actions, there are still some important differences that hold over from original case law stating that an insane person would not be liable. Punitive damages are designed both to punish an individual for actions that he or she knew were reckless or grossly negligent and to provide an example to society of behavior that will not be tolerated. However, because an insane person cannot by definition know, understand, or control his or her behavior, there would seem to be little point in imposing them. This is the rule followed in many jurisdictions: A legally insane person can be liable for intentional and even negligent actions but cannot have punitive damages imposed for those actions. Similarly, some jurisdictions also limit damages in cases where malice or specific intent is required, such as slander.

IMMUNITY

Immunity
An exception or privilege granted by the law to an action that ordinarily would result in a cause of action.

The claim of **immunity** is a defense that states that the plaintiff is legally barred from suing the defendant. When a person is immune from suit, it means that the lawsuit brought by the plaintiff must be dismissed. Immunity is reserved for people in specific professions or for specific circumstances.

Example: Last year, Judge South ruled against Ron in Ron's divorce action. The result was that Ron had to make high alimony payments to his ex-wife. Ron believes that the judge was wrong in her ruling and brings suit against her for intentional infliction of emotional distress, claiming that the high alimony payments have caused him to lose sleep and have left him generally irritable and cranky. Judge South's attorney, before addressing the questionable merits of Ron's lawsuit, files a motion to dismiss the suit, claiming judicial immunity. All jurisdictions have statutes that specifically bar suits against sitting judges when they act within the limits of their discretion in deciding cases before them. Ron has not alleged that Judge South exceeded her discretion or performed some action outside the scope and duties of her position. Without such an allegation, Ron has failed to show how the judge's actions are outside the protections of the immunity statute. Therefore, Judge South is immune from suit. The current judge will dismiss the lawsuit against Judge South.

The premise behind immunity is that government officials deserve protection from lawsuits for carrying out duties that are often unpopular with someone. Every time a police officer makes an arrest, at least one person (the arrestee) is upset with the officer's decision. When a judge makes a ruling in a case, it usually means that one side will lose. Protecting these officials with immunity allows these officials to act independently. Otherwise, they would be hampered by worrying about who would sue them for doing what they have been hired and trained to do. Immunities only apply when the official is acting in her professional capacity. When the person is "off duty," she has no greater protection against suit than anyone else.

Professions protected by immunity include police officers, judges, members of the legislature (for comments they make during debate), and others.

PRIVILEGE

When defendants raise the claim of **privilege,** they are agreeing that they did commit the act, but the act is protected from lawsuits by a statute or other law.

Example: Ron has a valid arrest warrant outstanding against him. Officer Steve, arresting Ron on this valid warrant, takes Ron's hands, puts them behind Ron's back, and then handcuffs him. Ron believes that he has been battered, and when he later makes bond on the arrest charge, he goes to his

Privilege
A protection or advantage given to a class of persons for actions taken by them.

Tech Topic
CLOUD COMPUTING

Many businesses are making the move to store their data offsite, or "in the cloud." The cloud is really nothing more than the Internet, and the idea has great appeal to business owners. Instead of having to invest in expensive in-house computer hardware and software, businesses can opt to pay a fee to upload and store their data on someone else's server—someone like Amazon, Microsoft, or Google.

In theory, it is a practical enterprise, but it presents some unique legal problems. For example, should Party A file a lawsuit against Company B and demand that the company produce documents, where do those documents legally reside?

In civil lawsuits, a company is usually required to produce relevant documents that are under its custody and control. What this usually means is that a company must produce its documents no matter where they are physically stored as long as the company has control over the records. But imagine that Company A in Cleveland stores its data with Cloud Company B in Atlanta, and Company B's servers are in Bangkok. This raises new questions.

For instance, what if the dispute is over ownership of the documents themselves? And if a company stores its records in the cloud, does it consent to jurisdiction in the cloud company's location? Is the company considered to be doing business in that location simply because its documents are there? These are issues that are being tested in courts, but currently there is little precedent for these matters.

attorney and asks that the attorney file a lawsuit against Officer Steve for battery.

After the complaint is filed and served on Officer Steve, the officer moves for a dismissal, raising the claim of privilege. He points out that police officers in his state are specifically protected under a statute that permits them to touch a suspect, even to use reasonable force, to make an arrest. The judge dismisses Ron's complaint. Others may enjoy a limited privilege, such as the limited privilege given to store employees to use reasonable force to subdue a shoplifter, as outlined in the case excerpt below.

Case Excerpt

CARTER V. SCOTT
320 Ga. App. 404, 750 S.E. 2d 679 (2013)

MILLER, Presiding Judge.

Christopher Scott sued Merrill Carter, as executor of the estate of Dr. Gordon W. Jackson, for injuries Scott allegedly sustained when Jackson kicked him in the knee. At the time of the alleged injury, Jackson was a resident of an advanced Alzheimer's unit at the assisted living facility where Scott worked as a security guard. Carter answered, raising several defenses, including lack of mental capacity. Scott moved for partial summary judgment on the issue of Jackson's lack of mental capacity. Carter filed a cross-motion for summary judgment. The trial court granted Scott's motion for partial summary judgment, and denied Carter's motion. This Court granted Carter's application for interlocutory appeal to review the trial court's decision. On appeal, Carter contends that Jackson, who was an institutionalized mental patient, owed no duty to Scott. Carter also contends that Scott assumed the risk of his injuries as a matter of law. For the following reasons, we affirm the grant of partial summary judgment to Scott on the issue of Jackson's lack of mental capacity. We also affirm the denial of summary judgment to Carter on that issue. However, we reverse the denial of summary judgment to Carter on the issue of whether Scott assumed the risk of his injuries. Accordingly, the trial court's decision is affirmed in part and reversed in part.

Summary judgment is proper when there is no genuine issue of material fact and the movant is entitled to judgment as a matter of law. A de novo standard of review applies to an appeal from a [grant or] denial of summary judgment, and we view the evidence, and all reasonable conclusions and inferences drawn from it, in the light most favorable to the nonmovant.

So viewed, the evidence shows that Jackson began residing at Carlyle Place (hereinafter "the facility") in 2003. Thereafter, Jackson suffered a dramatic decline in his mental capacity as a result of progressive Alzheimer's disease.

In September 2008, when Jackson exhibited agitation, aggression, and combative behavior, he was transferred to the facility's Alzheimer's unit.

On the night of December 23, 2008, Jackson was involved in a physical altercation. Scott, who worked as a security guard at the facility, received a call on his radio informing him of the fight. Upon arriving at the scene of the fight, Scott observed Jackson swinging and striking a nurse with his fists. Scott moved between Jackson and the nurse and separated them to break up the fight. Another resident then hit Scott in the head with her hand, and Jackson kicked Scott in the left knee, causing Scott's leg to buckle because of the pain.

Jackson died in November 2010, and his daughter, Carter, was appointed as executor of his estate. In August 2011, Scott brought suit against Jackson's estate seeking to recover for the injuries he allegedly suffered as a result of Jackson's actions. Carter answered, raising the affirmative defenses of lack of mental capacity and assumption of the risk.

Scott moved for partial summary judgment, asserting that, as a matter of law, Jackson's documented lack of mental capacity did not relieve him of liability. Carter filed a cross-motion for summary judgment, contending that Jackson, an institutionalized Alzheimer's patient, lacked capacity to control his conduct, and owed no duty of care to Scott, who was a paid employee of that institution. Carter also contended that Scott assumed the risk of his alleged injuries as a matter of law. The trial court granted Scott's motion for partial summary judgment. The trial court denied Carter's motion for summary judgment on the mental capacity defense, finding that "an insane person is liable for his torts the same as a sane person." The trial court also denied Carter's motion for summary judgment on the issue of whether Scott assumed the risk, finding that the factual record contained a material dispute that required jury resolution of that issue.

Carter contends that the trial court erred in granting Scott's motion for partial summary judgment, and denying her motion for summary judgment on the mental capacity defense. Specifically, Carter contends that the trial court should have adopted a rule that an institutionalized mental patient, who lacks capacity, owes no duty to an employee of the institution whose very duties contemplate dealing with patients who pose a risk of violent conduct. We disagree.

Carter acknowledges that Georgia law clearly provides that

> in a civil action for an injury done to the person or property of another, the intent is generally immaterial, and the rule is that an insane person is liable for his torts the same as a sane person, except for those torts in which malice, and therefore intention, is a necessary ingredient. In respect to this liability, there is no distinction between torts of nonfeasance and of misfeasance; and consequently an insane person is liable for his injuries caused by his tortious negligence. Insane persons are held to this liability on the principle that where a loss must be borne by one of two innocent persons, it shall be born by him who occasioned it.

Central of Ga. R. Co. v. Hall, 124 Ga. 322, 333, 52 S.E. 679 (1905) Applying this principle in a suit for compensatory damages arising from an assault, this Court has found that the fact that the defendant was in the throes of a condition of unsound mind, and was therefore incapable of forming or having any mental intent to injure, was not a defense. Moreover, this Court has held that insanity or lack of competence is a defense only to an intentional tort.

Although Carter argues that an exception to this rule should be made for an institutionalized mentally disabled person who injures a paid caregiver or other staff person, the cases Carter cites in support of her argument are not cases decided by Georgia's courts and have no binding precedential value. Georgia law provides that Jackson's mental deficiencies cannot relieve him of liability for his negligent acts. Therefore, we affirm the trial court's grant of partial summary judgment to Scott, and the trial court's denial of summary judgment to Carter on this ground.

Carter also contends that the trial court erred in denying her motion based upon her assumption of the risk defense. FN2 Carter argues that the undisputed evidence established without question that Scott assumed the risk of his injuries and was precluded from recovering as a matter of law. We agree.

> FN2. Carter argued in her appellate brief and in oral argument that Scott assumed the risk of his injuries because he was hired as a security guard to control the precise dangers he encountered. Carter further analogized this case to the Fireman's Rule, which provides that "a public safety officer cannot base a tort claim upon damage caused by the very risk that he is paid to encounter and with which he is trained to cope." We need not reach these contentions because we find that Scott assumed the risk as a matter of law.

Although Georgia law provides that Jackson can be held liable for his negligence, the crux of this case pertains to the application of assumption of risk principles. OCGA §51–11–2 provides the statutory basis for the assumption of risk defense, stating that "no tort can be committed against a person consenting thereto if that consent is free, is not obtained by fraud, and is the action of a sound mind." Moreover, it is well settled that an adult of ordinary intelligence assumes the risk of possible injury when he deliberately and voluntarily joins in a fight, or enters into a fight for the purpose of breaking it up.

Scott admitted in his affidavit in support of his motion for summary judgment that he intervened in the fight. Thus, the evidence clearly and palpably shows that Scott was injured when he attempted to break up the fight between Jackson and the nurse, and "only one conclusion is permissible here: that Scott deliberately interjected himself into the fight and assumed the risk of injury by voluntarily confronting those who had begun it." Accordingly, we find that based upon the facts and law Scott assumed the risk. Therefore, we reverse the trial court's denial of Carter's motion for summary judgment on this ground.

In sum, we affirm the partial grant of summary judgment to Scott because Jackson's mental deficiencies did not relieve him of liability for his negligent acts. For the same reason, we affirm the denial of summary judgment to Carter on the issue of Jackson's mental capacity. However, we reverse the denial of summary judgment to Carter on the defense of assumption of the risk, because Scott assumed the risk of his injuries as a matter of law and fact.

Judgment affirmed in part, and reversed in part.

RAY and BRANCH, JJ., concur.

Questions about the case:

1. What disease was Carter suffering from, and how did it affect his mental abilities?
2. How was Scott injured?
3. What is the standard of law in the state regarding the actions of people who are insane?
4. How did the "assumption of risk" argument factor into this case?

XI   STATUTES OF LIMITATION

All tort actions have statutes of limitation, that is, time limits in which the case must be brought or be forever barred. The limitation periods are usually set by the legislature and can be found in the various state and federal codes. For intentional torts, the time periods are usually short. For example, a battery action has a one-year statute of limitation in some jurisdictions. This means that if a battery suit is not brought within one year of the incident, the plaintiff cannot bring the action at all. Statutes of limitation are designed to provide some sense of closure to potential legal claims. Defendants can be secure that if a case is not brought within the applicable statute of limitation, it will not be brought at all. These statutes also encourage plaintiffs to bring actions as soon as possible, when witness memories are still clear and before the evidence is lost or destroyed.

Sidebar

In any intentional tort action, close attention should be paid to the statute of limitation.

XII   DEFENSES AVAILABLE TO CODEFENDANTS

Among the defenses available to a defendant is the right to apportion blame against a codefendant. In cases in which there is more than one defendant, each defendant has the right to assess the blame for the plaintiff's injuries against the other defendant. When there is more than one defendant, the plaintiff is often in the difficult position of assessing blame against both. How does a plaintiff specify which injuries were caused by which defendant?

Example: Ted is attacked and beaten by two men: Carl and Stanley. During the attack, Ted is knocked unconscious. When he regains consciousness, he has severe injuries but is unable to say which of the two men caused them. What does he do? He takes advantage of the legal principle of joint and several liability.

A. JOINT AND SEVERAL LIABILITY

The doctrine of joint and several liability was created for just such a situation as the one confronting Ted. Under this doctrine, a plaintiff who has been injured by more than one defendant is permitted to sue both and seek his total damages against them individually and as codefendants. Ted can sue Carl and Stanley and recover his entire damages from just one of them. Joint and several liability is based on the premise that between the plaintiff and the defendants in this scenario, the person who should be given the greatest consideration is the injured plaintiff. Ted can obtain judgments against both or against each man individually. If Carl ends up paying the full amount of Ted's injuries, Carl can seek reimbursement from Stanley in a separate legal action.

Sidebar

When two or more defendants are found liable to the plaintiff, the doctrine of contribution is triggered. Contribution is the process through which one defendant is reimbursed by other defendants when his payment exceeds his share of liability.

Joint and several liability has come under criticism in recent years by those who claim that plaintiffs use it as a way to sue everyone in sight, on the off chance that someone will have enough funds to pay for the plaintiff's injuries. There are some important limitations on joint and several liability. The plaintiff can only sue defendants who are potentially liable. A plaintiff is not allowed to sue anyone who might have "deep pockets," that is, someone who has financial resources. The person or corporation sued must be liable for some of the plaintiff's injuries. Another important limitation is that the plaintiff is not allowed to recover more than his claimed injuries. For instance, Ted can't recover twice the monetary damages he requests by having Stanley and Carl both pay him the total amount. See Figure 3-2 for a summary of some of the pros and cons of joint and several liability.

FIGURE 3-2	
Arguments for and Against the Joint and Several Liability Doctrine	**Pro:** Joint and several (J/S) liability is the only way to make sure the plaintiff receives a full monetary recovery and can return to something resembling a normal life. **Con:** J/S liability allows unscrupulous plaintiffs to sue everyone, hoping that someone will have the financial resources to enrich the plaintiff, even if a defendant isn't the main culprit. **Pro:** Of the people involved in the lawsuit, the plaintiff is the one who has been injured and is often in no shape to know which of the defendants actually injured him. **Con:** Defendants in J/S liability cases often settle cases before going to trial out of fear that the jury will assess huge verdicts against them.

TORT BASICS AT A GLANCE

In joint and several liability, when two or more defendants contribute to the plaintiff's injuries, they remain individually liable to the plaintiff for the total amount of the plaintiff's injuries.

B. VICARIOUS LIABILITY

We have seen that when there is more than one defendant, a plaintiff is permitted to sue all those who have injured him and can recover his entire damages against any one of them. Another principle closely associated with joint and several liability is vicarious liability. Under most situations, a person is solely responsible for her actions. However, there are times when the law allows suits against others, even people not present when the plaintiff's injuries occurred. In vicarious liability, one defendant is held liable for the actions of another. This is true even when the second defendant didn't actually do anything to injure the plaintiff. See Figure 3-4 for a summary of vicarious liability.

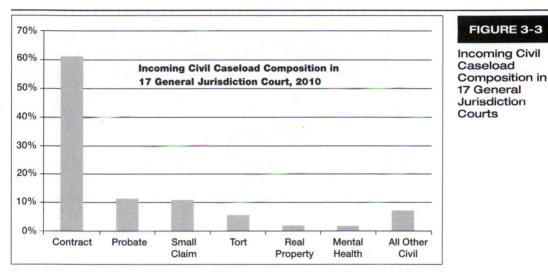

Incoming Civil Caseload Composition in 17 General Jurisdiction Court, 2010

FIGURE 3-3

Incoming Civil Caseload Composition in 17 General Jurisdiction Courts

Source: National Center for State Courts. National Center for State Courts, Data Source: Court Statistics Project, Publication: Examining the Work of State Courts: An Analysis of 2010 State Court Caseloads, Publication: Examining the Work of State Courts: An Analysis of 2010 State Court Caseloads, 9/24/12.

One person is found to be liable because someone else has acted unreasonably. The unreasonableness of one person is assessed against another, even though this other person didn't do anything wrong.

The most common examples of vicarious liability are

Employer/employee
Joint enterprise
Family purpose doctrine

FIGURE 3-4

A Summary of Vicarious Liability

Under the doctrine of vicarious liability, third parties can be liable for the actions of others. The most common example is when an employer is liable for the actions of her employee. This is also called *respondeat superior*.

TORT BASICS AT A GLANCE

1. EMPLOYER/EMPLOYEE LIABILITY (*RESPONDEAT SUPERIOR*)

The most common form of vicarious liability is the liability of an employer for the actions of an employee.

Example: Ron works for a local furniture store and is driving the delivery truck to deliver some furniture. He runs a red light and strikes Mary. Mary brings suit against Ron and Ron's employer, the furniture store. Her suit can proceed against Ron, as an individual, and against Ron's employer for Ron's actions.

The theory behind employer/employee liability is based on an ancient doctrine that said a slave's misdeeds could be assessed against his master. Under more modern interpretation, the principle continues to be used because the employee was acting within the scope of his employment at the time that he caused injury to the plaintiff. Since the defendant was working for a company, his negligence is imputed to his employer. This principle is also known as ***respondeat superior,*** a Latin term that translates, "Let the master respond."

Respondeat superior
(Latin) Liability imposed on an employer for the actions of the employee, when the employee is carrying out his duties for the employer.

a. Limitations on *Respondeat Superior*

Obviously, an employer is not liable for all actions carried out by an employee. For instance, Ron gets off work and goes home. As he is driving his own car, he runs another red light and hits Betty. Betty sues Ron and Ron's employer. The furniture store files a motion to be dismissed from the case, and the judge agrees. After all, Ron was not acting within the scope of his employment at the time of his accident.

Scope of Employment

As long as the employee is acting within the scope of his employment at the time that he injures the plaintiff, his employer will be liable for his actions. However, "scope of employment" has proved to be a difficult term to define. For instance, suppose that at the time that Ron is driving the delivery truck in his accident with Mary, he is actually running a personal errand. Because this errand has nothing to do with his job, his employer claims that she should not be liable under *respondeat superior.* Two clear exceptions have developed over time to protect employers from such situations.

Frolic and Detour

When an employee is out running a personal errand, or actually away from his job without permission, the employer will not be liable for his actions. When an employee is on a "frolic," he is no longer acting for his employer; he is carrying out personal business or simply having fun. When an employee deviates from his job duties to carry out personal business, this "detour" will also relieve his employer of liability for his actions. These two exceptions developed out of a need to restrict the doctrine of *respondeat superior* to the employee's actual job duties. Without such limitations, an employer would essentially be liable for all the employee's actions, even when the employee was not carrying out company business. Courts have consistently ruled that expanding the doctrine of *respondeat superior* to this extreme would place too high a burden on businesses. On the other hand, when the employee is acting within the scope of his duties, he is furthering the company's interests. In some cases, the employee's actions may actually have been caused by the company's policies.

Example: Mary works for a local pizza restaurant that guarantees a pizza delivery within 30 minutes of the time that the order is placed or the pizza is free. Local managers tell their drivers that any free pizzas will be deducted from the driver's paycheck. This has the natural effect of encouraging the drivers to deliver the pizzas as fast as possible. They often drive faster than the posted speed limit and even run traffic lights. Managers realize that the drivers are doing these things, but they do not change their policy. One evening, Mary is rushing to deliver a pizza before the 30-minute deadline and runs a red light. She crashes into another car driven by Amy. Amy is severely injured. She brings suit against Mary and the pizza restaurant. Her allegation is based on the fact that (1) Mary was working for the pizza restaurant at the time of the accident; (2) Mary was acting in furtherance of the restaurant's business; and (3) Mary's haste (and recklessness) was based on the restaurant's 30-minute policy, which encouraged the drivers to drive too fast.

When Amy's case is heard, her theory of *respondeat superior* is found to be valid, and her suit proceeds against both Mary and the restaurant.

Independent Contractor

When a person is classified as an independent contractor, he is not an employee and there is no *respondeat superior* claim. How does the law define an independent contractor? An independent contractor is a person who is usually some form of specialist. When a person is an independent contractor, he controls his day-to-day decisions and actions, as opposed to an employee who works under the direct supervision of a supervisor. An independent contractor might be someone like a software expert, who is called in to help debug new computer programs. This person will often work under his own initiative, decide how to proceed, and will ultimately declare when he has completed his task. In such a situation, this person is not an employee. The theory of *respondeat superior* has been specifically limited to employees. The principle behind *respondeat superior* is that the employee has very little discretion in what he does. The employee obeys the employer and is, at least in this regard, an extension of the employer. However, an independent contractor operates on his own, without supervision and direct control. Therefore, *respondeat superior* does not apply to him.

What makes an independent contractor?
Worker has control over job duties = IC
Worker has discretion in how the job is carried out = IC
Worker is hired to do a specific job = IC

2. FAMILY PURPOSE DOCTRINE

Sidebar

The family purpose doctrine cannot be used when there is no "family." For instance, when several people live together but are not related, the family purpose doctrine would most likely not apply.

The family purpose doctrine allows a plaintiff to sue the parents of a driver who causes injury, even though the parent wasn't present in the car at the time of the accident. Although this doctrine is not recognized in all jurisdictions, in the ones where it is, the doctrine essentially allows plaintiffs to sue parents for the actions of their children.

To bring a lawsuit under the family purpose doctrine, the plaintiff must show:

1. that the parent owns the car involved in the accident,
2. that the parent makes the car available to family members for family use,
3. that the driver is a member of the defendant's immediate family,
4. that the driver was using the car for a family purpose, and
5. that the driver had express or implied permission to use the car.

When the plaintiff can establish each of those elements, the plaintiff can recover damages from the car owner, even though the owner wasn't involved in the car wreck.

Example: Fred is injured in an accident in which Jimmy runs a stop sign and strikes Fred's car. Jimmy is 16 years old and is driving the family car. Fred brings suit against Jimmy and Jimmy's parents under the family purpose doctrine. Jimmy's parents file a motion to dismiss them from the suit. The judge rules against them, stating that the case clearly falls within the family purpose doctrine.

3. JOINT ENTERPRISE

The third situation in which a person may be liable for the actions of another is the joint enterprise doctrine. This doctrine allows a plaintiff to bring suit against one business partner for the actions of the other. However, to take advantage of this doctrine, the plaintiff must show:

1. that there was an express or implied agreement among the defendants to carry out a business,
2. that the defendants had a common purpose in carrying out the business, and
3. that the defendants each had the right to control the business (i.e., that one member wasn't an employee of the other).

Chapter Summary

When the plaintiff brings a claim of intentional tort against a defendant, the defendant is allowed to raise one or more defenses against the claim. The various defenses include self-defense, defense of others, or consent. These defenses essentially admit that the action occurred, but that it was excused, either because the defendant was protecting himself or protecting others, or because the plaintiff agreed to the action. Other defenses raise the specter of the defendant's will overcome by other forces. The defendant might claim duress — that is, that he committed the action because of pressure or undue influence of another. Similar defenses are necessity, compulsion, and coercion. Insanity is also a defense to a tort. In an insanity defense, the defendant is claiming that he did not know the difference between right and wrong at the time that he carried out the action. When more than one defendant is involved, both may be liable to the plaintiff under the theory of joint and several liability. The defendant's employer may also be liable under certain circumstances, under the theory of *respondeat superior.*

SKILLS YOU NEED IN THE REAL WORLD

Evaluating a Case

One of the most important skills a legal professional can acquire is the ability to evaluate a case objectively. Like any skill, getting good at evaluating a case takes time. Why should you invest this time? The simple answer is that the better you are at evaluating cases, the better you are at your job (and the more indispensable you become to the firm). An evaluation of any case takes into account the following factors:

- The nature of the claim
- The type of injuries
- The quality of the opposing counsel
- The judge's temperament and several other factors

Step One: Evaluate the Facts

The facts of the case are perhaps the single most important item in a case evaluation. This is true whether you are working for the plaintiff or the defendant. Before evaluating the plaintiff's injuries, there are some preliminary questions that must be answered. One of the questions that should be answered early on in the case evaluation process is "Just how liable is the defendant?" If the case against the defendant is shaky, this affects the rest of your evaluation. On the other hand, if the case against him is one of clear and obvious liability, you can feel much more secure in your evaluation. As such, the facts of the case are the most important aspect of the evaluation. Find out all the details and write them down. Make sure that you have a solid (and objective) view of the facts. Here is where having sympathy for the plaintiff could be your downfall. Take a cold, hard look at the case. If the answer to "Just how liable is the defendant?" is "not very," you don't have a strong case, no matter how many injuries the plaintiff has.

Step Two: Evaluate the Opposition

In theory, all attorneys know the rules and will do a good job in court. However, the reality is starkly different. Some attorneys are master trial advocates, and others are plainly terrible. A skilled adversary is obviously more of a challenge than a novice. Veteran attorneys can almost always justify a higher settlement in a case than recent law school graduates. One thing you can do is to find out how long the opposing attorney has been practicing. You could point out to your own attorney the skill level of the opposition (if he or she does not already know it). Find out what others in the legal community think about the opposition. What type of reputation does this attorney have? Is the attorney noted for excellent trial skills? If so, you can bet that this attorney will be a real challenge, and you must prepare accordingly.

Step Three: Evaluate the Likelihood of Recovery

The plaintiff always wants to know how much money he or she will get from the defendant. Frankly, there is no way to know that prior to the actual settlement. You should never promise a client that he is "guaranteed" to get at least x amount of dollars. There are times when the defendant's liability is not in question, but he has no assets. (In Chapter 8, we discuss the importance of asset searches.)

Step Four: Evaluate the Injuries

The plaintiff's injuries are a crucial part of any case evaluation. For instance, suppose that the defendant is clearly at fault, but the plaintiff has not been injured in any significant way. In such a case, the recovery amount will be low. Conversely, where the plaintiff's injuries are severe, and the defendant's liability is obvious, the recovery is likely to be large.

Step Five: Evaluate the Law

How does the applicable law affect the case? Some jurisdictions follow the rule of contributory negligence (see Chapter 9). This rule provides that the plaintiff is not entitled to any recovery if he can be shown to have contributed to his own injuries. Other jurisdictions follow a comparative negligence rule, in which the plaintiff's recovery is reduced by the amount of his own negligence. The rule followed in your jurisdiction has a profound impact on the evaluation of the case.

 THE LIFE OF A PARALEGAL

Assisting in Jury Selection

When I attend trials, I often take notes during jury selection. I will watch the people on the panel, looking at their facial expressions, their body language. Sometimes people will shake their heads or frown at something the lawyers say. I feverishly write down as many comments as I can. Usually, I'm looking for the people who aren't going to be sympathetic to our side. We dismiss those people.

I prepare a seating chart of the jury panel during jury selection, so we can remember who is sitting where. I'll write any important notes about the person right on the chart. It's good to have a woman's perspective during jury selection. I usually work with a male attorney, and once during jury selection on a case, the juror had answered the plaintiff's attorney's questions very sweetly, but then when my attorney started asking questions, she totally copped an attitude with him. When the attorney asked me what I thought, I said that he should get rid of her. "She doesn't like you," I told him. He said, "Really? I didn't pick up on that." He needed a woman's perspective on that juror.

Lisa Mazzonetto, Paralegal

ETHICAL ISSUES FOR THE PARALEGAL: AVOIDING A CLAIM OF UNAUTHORIZED PRACTICE OF LAW

Many times during your paralegal career, you will be asked by a client for advice about a legal topic. A client could, for example, ask you about the merits of the defense he is raising in his answer. A paralegal should always be careful to avoid any allegation of unauthorized practice of law (UPL). Paralegals who give legal advice are practicing law without a license. When they do, they run into two immediate problems. The first problem is that UPL is illegal in all states. Paralegals who give legal advice can end up in jail. The second problem is that paralegals who give legal advice can end up being named in legal malpractice suits brought against the attorney. If the attorney loses the suit, she could end up having to pay monetary damages to the former client.

Does giving an opinion about the client's legal defense constitute UPL? Probably. The safest course to follow is this: When in doubt, assume the worst. If you aren't sure if the answer you are about to give is legal advice, assume that it is. Pause for a moment and reflect. Perhaps this answer should come from someone else, such as the attorney? Perhaps it is time for a disclaimer? Gently remind the client that you're not an attorney and you can't give legal advice. Remember that the client who is smiling now could be an adversary in a lawsuit next year.

Relevant Cases

ESSHAKI V. MILLMAN
NOT REPORTED IN N.W.2D, 2009 WL 692451

PER CURIAM

In this suit to recover damages arising from an injury sustained during a soccer match, plain-tiff Basil Esshaki appeals as of right the trial court's order granting summary disposition in favor of defendant Scott Millman. On appeal, we must determine whether the trial court properly granted summary disposition of Esshaki's claims of battery, negligence, and intentional infliction of emotional distress. Because Esshaki presented sufficient evidence to establish a material question of fact on his battery and negligence claims, we conclude that the trial court erred when it granted summary disposition of those claims in favor of Millman. However, because Esshaki failed to establish that the alleged attack caused him to suffer severe emotional distress, we conclude that the trial court did not err when it dismissed Esshaki's intentional infliction of emotional distress claim. For these reasons, we affirm part, reverse in part and remand for further proceedings consistent with this opinion.

I. Basic Facts and Procedural History

Esshaki and Millman were players on different soccer teams in a league for men who are over age 30. At the time, Esshaki was 60 years old and Millman was 36. The teams played six-on-six matches at the Total Sports complex in Wixom, Michigan.

On February 4, 2007, Esshaki's team played Millman's team. At his deposition, Esshaki testified that at one point during the match Millman had the ball and began to approach Esshaki's goal. Esshaki stated that Millman lost control of the ball as another defender approached. Esshaki said he then ran up to Millman from behind and "hustled" the ball away from him. Esshaki testified that Millman became upset and walked right up to him. In response, Esshaki stated that he put his arms up and held Millman back at the shoulders. Esshaki testified that, after this, he began to walk by Millman when Millman punched him in the jaw with his fist. Esshaki admitted that, after being punched, he became angry with Millman and took a swing at him, but stated that he missed. Esshaki stated that, although his jaw hurt, he did not seek medical treatment until the next day.

At his deposition, Millman testified that the strike to Esshaki's jaw was accidental. Mill-man stated that, just prior to the incident, the ball play was going on to his front and left. He stated that he attempted to maintain his position in the middle of the field as the play moved from his left to his right. At that point, Esshaki moved up from behind and pushed him. Millman stated that he then turned abruptly to try to make a play on the ball when he inadvertently struck Esshaki with his elbow. Millman testified that after the incident, Esshaki tried to punch him and they were then both sent to the penalty box for two minutes. After serving their penalty time, Millman stated that they both returned and finished the game.

Esshaki testified that the next day his jaw did not feel right and he went to his doctor. Although an initial x-ray did not reveal a break, Esshaki continued to experience problems and eventually his doctor discovered that his jaw had been broken. Esshaki had to have his jaw wired shut for six to eight weeks and lost the bridge spanning four teeth. The bridge had been fractured and required implants to replace the missing teeth. Esshaki testified that his physicians expected his jaw to be fully healed in six months to a year.

In March 2007, Esshaki sued Millman for battery, negligence, and intentional infliction of emotional distress. Esshaki also asked for exemplary damages.

In November 2007, Millman moved for summary disposition. In his motion, Millman argued that Esshaki assumed the risk of injury when he elected to play soccer — including the risk that he would be injured during a "rule violation." Millman contended that, in order to be actionable, the conduct at issue had to be extreme or outrageous or amount to gross negligence. Because his actions were not extreme or outrageous and amounted to, at most, ordinary negligence, Millman further argued that summary disposition was appropriate.

In response, Esshaki argued that there was evidence that Millman's actions were not an attempt to make a play on the ball; rather, that Millman deliberately struck him out of anger and did so with the intent to injure.

This evidence, Esshaki contended, supported his claim for battery and intentional infliction of emotional distress. Esshaki further argued that the evidence suggested that, at a minimum, Millman's actions were reckless. For these reasons, Esshaki contended that summary disposition was inappropriate.

After holding a hearing on Millman's motion, the trial court concluded that Esshaki's claims should be dismissed. The court indicated that there was no evidence from "anyone other than Esshaki" that Millman's "conduct was reckless or anything other than in the normal course of playing soccer." Accordingly, in January 2008, the trial court dismissed Esshaki's claims against Millman.

This appeal followed.

The Standard of Care for Participants in Recreational Activities

When people engage in a recreational activity, they have voluntarily subjected themselves to certain risks inherent in that activity. For that reason, when a participant suffers an injury from a risk that is inherent in the recreational activity, he or she has no grounds for complaint unless the harm was the result of something more than mere carelessness or ordinary negligence. Thus, with regard to injuries unintentionally caused by a co-participant in the recreational activity, a plaintiff must demonstrate that the defendant's actions amounted to reckless misconduct. Id. at 89, 597 N.W.2d 517. In addition to unintentional acts that amount to reckless misconduct, a plaintiff may recover for a co-participant's "intentional act causing injury" if that act "goes beyond what is ordinarily permissible" within the game.

Application of the Legal Standards to the Facts

In the present case, Millman moved for summary disposition on the grounds that Esshaki had not demonstrated that Millman's conduct was an intentional act that went beyond what is ordinarily permissible in the game or otherwise amounted to reckless misconduct.

Because Esshaki had the burden of proof at trial on these issues, he had an obligation to "go beyond the pleadings to set forth specific facts showing that" Millman's conduct was a qualifying intentional or reckless act.

Battery

At his deposition, Esshaki testified that the incident at issue occurred after he "hustled" the ball from Millman. Esshaki stated that Millman was visibly upset and immediately approached him in a manner that caused Esshaki to raise his arms and hold Millman back by the shoulders. After holding Millman back for a time, Esshaki said he then tried to walk past Millman when Millman punched him in the face with his fist. This testimony clearly establishes a question of fact as to whether Millman intentionally committed an act that went beyond "what is ordinarily permissible" in soccer. Even assuming that soccer includes a degree of intentional—and potentially harmful—contact, we conclude that, as a matter of law, a participant's consent to the risks inherent to participating in a soccer match does not include consent to be attacked by a co-participant. In this case, when viewed in the light most favorable to him, Esshaki's testimony establishes that Millman's intentional contact was not part of the ordinary contacts that accompany playing soccer. Indeed, the testimony suggests that game play had actually stopped and that Millman simply lost his temper and punched Esshaki.

On appeal, Millman dismisses Esshaki's testimony as self-serving and concentrates on the fact that the other witnesses, including Millman, indicated that Millman did not punch Esshaki, but instead elbowed him. Although the trial court apparently elected to ignore Esshaki's testimony, courts are not permitted to weigh evidence or assess credibility on summary disposition. Thus, we are not at liberty to disregard this testimony—we must consider it and we must consider it in the light most favorable to Esshaki. For that reason, even though we acknowledge that a reasonable jury might find Millman's version of events to be more plausible, we must nevertheless conclude that summary disposition of the battery claim was inappropriate based on Esshaki's testimony alone; a jury must resolve the discrepancies between Esshaki's and Millman's versions of events. Moreover, even if we were to disregard Esshaki's testimony, we would still conclude that summary disposition was inappropriate based on the testimony of the referee who worked the match at issue.

Thomas Caranicolas testified that he was the referee who presided over the match between Esshaki's and Millman's teams. He stated that the incident occurred when Millman had the ball and was dribbling toward Esshaki's goal. He testified that Esshaki pushed Millman from behind, but that he did not blow the whistle. He explained that he did not call a foul because Millman did not lose possession of the ball. However, after a second push, he blew the whistle and gave Esshaki a two-minute penalty because Millman lost the ball. Caranicolas stated "that's when . . . Millman threw his elbow." When asked whether he thought the elbow was intentionally thrown, Caranicolas testified that it was his impression that Millman "threw the elbow because he was bothered by Esshaki." He explained that "an elbow thrown in somebody's face with a ball on the ground it's not accidental." Likewise, when asked whether Millman might only have accidentally struck Esshaki while trying to turn and make a move on the goal, Caranicolas stated that it "looked like more than just a turn. I think he was irritated and he threw the elbow to get rid of him."

Taken in the light most favorable to Esshaki, Caranicolas' testimony establishes that Millman deliberately struck Esshaki with his elbow. Further, the testimony indicated that the elbow was not part of a legitimate play on the ball but was done out of anger or frustration. Indeed, Caranicolas stated that Millman struck Esshaki with his elbow after he already blew the whistle and stopped play. Thus, this testimony established a question of fact as to whether Millman intentionally attacked Esshaki.

Finally, although a participant in a soccer match never consents to be outright attacked by a co-participant, we acknowledge that, in this case, a reasonable jury could find that Millman intentionally used his elbow during game play, but that it was part of a bona fide attempt to make a play on the ball. Thus, a reasonable jury could conclude that even though Millman intentionally threw his elbow, that action was nevertheless within the scope of what is ordinarily permissible in soccer. However, a reasonable jury could also conclude that Millman deliberately struck Esshaki with his fist or elbow and that he did so out of anger rather than out of any legitimate attempt to make a play on the ball. Thus, whether Millman attacked Esshaki with his fist or an elbow, or merely used his elbow in a way that is ordinarily permissible in a soccer match are questions that must be resolved by a jury. For that reason, the trial court erred when it granted summary disposition of Esshaki's claim premised on battery.

Reckless Misconduct

A participant in a recreational activity may also recover for injuries sustained as a result of a co-participant's reckless misconduct. Reckless misconduct is more than negligent conduct; it is conduct that places the actor in a "class with the wilful doer of wrong."

The only respect in which his attitude is less blameworthy than that of the intentional wrongdoer is that, instead of affirmatively wishing to injure another, he is merely willing to do so. The difference is that between him who casts a missile intending that it shall strike another and him who casts it where he has reason to believe it will strike another, being indifferent whether it does so or not.

Although Caranicolas' testimony clearly supports the conclusion that Millman deliberately threw his elbow in an outright attack, this same testimony could support a finding of reckless misconduct. Caranicolas opined that Millman deliberately threw his elbow at Esshaki based on Millman's demeanor and actions. Nevertheless, Caranicolas acknowledged that the entire incident occurred rapidly. That is, within seconds, Esshaki pushed Millman twice, Caranicolas blew the whistle, and then Millman threw out his elbow. A reasonable jury could conclude from this testimony that Millman threw out his elbow in frustration rather than with the intent to actually strike Esshaki. But the jury could also conclude that when Millman threw out his elbow in frustration, he had reason to believe that it would strike Esshaki, and he nevertheless did so out of indifference as to whether it would. Hence, there is also a question of fact as to whether Millman's conduct amounted to reckless misconduct.

General Conclusion

Given the parties' submissions, there was a question of fact as to whether Millman's conduct was intentional and, if it was, whether it was outside what is normally permissible in the game of soccer. Likewise, Esshaki presented sufficient evidence to establish a question of fact as to whether Millman's

conduct amounted to reckless misconduct. For these reasons, the trial court erred when it dismissed Esshaki's battery and negligence claims under MCR 2.116(C)(10). However, Esshaki failed to present sufficient evidence to create a question of fact as to whether Millman's conduct caused Esshaki severe emotional distress. Therefore, the trial court did not err in dismissing Esshaki's claim for intentional infliction of emotional distress. For these reasons, we affirm the trial court's decision to dismiss Esshaki's intentional infliction of emotional distress claim, but reverse the trial court's grant of summary disposition in favor of Millman on Esshaki's battery and negligence claims.

Affirmed in part, reversed in part, and remanded for further proceedings consistent with this opinion. We do not retain jurisdiction. As a prevailing party, Esshaki may tax costs under MCR 7.219(A).

TOUCHET V. HAMPTON
1 SO.3D 729 (LA.APP. 3 CIR., 2008)

PICKETT, Judge.
The plaintiff-appellant, Purvis Touchet, appeals a judgment of the trial court finding he failed to prove that Mark Hampton, the defendant, committed the intentional tort of battery against him.

Statement of the Case
This is the second time this case has been before this court on appeal. In the original appeal, the trial court granted Mr. Hampton's motion for an involuntary dismissal at the close of Mr. Touchet's presentation of evidence based on a finding that Mr. Hampton acted in self-defense. *Touchet v. Hampton*, 06–1120 (La.App. 3 Cir. 2/7/07), 950 So.2d 895. This court set forth the facts as follows:

The plaintiff, Purvis Touchet, was a sales manager at Hampton Mitsubishi, a car dealership owned by the defendant, Mark Hampton,

for approximately three years. Touchet testified that he briefly left his employment with the dealership but subsequently returned to his former job position. He testified that his employment was terminated during the summer of 2002.

According to Hampton, the parting was amicable. However, he testified that in October 2002, he received a telephone call from Touchet in which "he basically was sort of making fun of our business because our business had gone down." Hampton stated that he hung up the telephone and that Touchet called back later that day. Hampton did not speak with him. Hampton testified that when he spoke with Touchet again, Touchet cursed him, threatened him, and told him that he knew where he lived. According to Hampton, Touchet continued to call and when he did not answer, Touchet left him several threatening voicemail messages, three of which were left on October 13, 2002.

Hampton testified that on October 19, 2002, he went to Jackie Edgar RV Center, Touchet's place of employment, "because it was a public place, and I felt it was the safest place to talk to him." Touchet was not there. According to Hampton, he returned to Jackie Edgar RV Center on October 22, 2002 to "tell Touchet to quit harassing me and to ask him to stop calling me." Hampton asked if Touchet was in, and someone pointed him towards Touchet's office. Hampton testified that when he entered Touchet's office, Touchet, whose back was to Hampton, quickly turned around in his chair and yelled "F—k you, Hampton." Hampton stated that he was startled and scared because it appeared as if Touchet "was going to hit me, what he said he was going to do." Hampton testified that he defended himself by hitting Touchet. Although he did not know how many times he hit Touchet, Hampton surmised that the incident lasted approximately twenty seconds before Touchet's co-worker, David Raggette, intervened and pulled Hampton off Touchet. Hampton immediately left the premises.

This court found that the trial court committed manifest error by finding that Mr. Hampton acted in self-defense and remanded the case to allow the defendant to present evidence. On remand, Mr. Hampton submitted the deposition of Michael Reed, a friend of Mr. Hampton. Mr. Reed accompanied Mr. Hampton to Mr. Touchet's workplace three days before the incident occurred and spoke with him after the incident occurred. The defense then rested.

The trial court issued the following findings of fact and oral reasons for ruling in open court on January 29, 2008:

> This Court makes the following factual findings, and warns that these findings contain the offensive utterances of the plaintiff.
>
> On Sunday, 13 October 2002, Touchet called Hampton's home on three separate occasions and left threatening and offensive messages. The most significant portions of

those messages are: the first message that occurred on Sunday, October 13th at 2:41 P.M. contained a significant amount of information, but the most significant was the following language: "I am going to f—king murder your ass." Then there was a subsequent message on that same date at 2:45 P.M. which, again, contained lots of threatening and offensive language, the most significant of which was: "Anytime you want to f—k with me, let me know."

> Then there was another message that was recorded — all these messages were recorded on a voicemail recording system on Hampton's phone — this third message occurred, was delivered at 2:48 P.M., and, again, contains lots of offensive language, the most significant of which — the most significant because of his threat is: "Let me and you come meet me somewhere you f—king piece of shit."

> Then on Sunday, October 19, 2002, [sic] Hampton visited Touchet at his place of employment to tell Touchet to quit harassing Hampton and stop calling Hampton. Touchet's office within his place of employment has glass walls. When Hampton entered Touchet's office Touchet was seated in his chair with the back of his chair facing Hampton. Touchet rapidly turned his chair towards Hampton and yelled: "F—k you, Hampton." Then a consensual fistic encounter occurred between Touchet and Hampton. David Ragatta [sic] did not observe the events that immediately preceded this fistic encounter.

> So those are the factual findings. Now to the analysis of those facts coupled with the applicable law. Touchet's recorded phone messages to Hampton on the 13th of October 2002 constituted an offer from Touchet to Hampton to engage in mortal combat at a time and place to be chosen by either Touchet or Hampton. Touchet never recounted [sic] that offer, never terminated that offer. Touchet's assertion that this was a limited-time offer, limited in time specifically to the date of that offer, is incredulous and I do not believe it.

> Touchet's actions once Hampton entered Touchet's office on 19 October 2002 constituted consent to commence mortal combat at that time and place. Because Touchet consented to participate in a fight to the death, Hampton's actions during this fistic encounter were measured — were a measured response taken to prevent the significant harm of loss of life.

Given these findings of fact in this legal analysis this Court finds that Touchet failed to prove that Hampton committed a battery. Hampton, in fact, consented — I'm sorry. Touchet, in fact, consented to the harmful touching by Hampton who accepted Touchet's challenge and spared Touchet's life. Hampton's force application was appropriate given the circumstances and not excessive.

The trial court signed a judgment dismissing Mr. Touchet's suit on February 22, 2008. Mr. Touchet now appeals.

Assignments of Error

Mr. Touchet asserts two assignments of error:

1. The trial court's findings of fact are contrary to the prior findings of the appellate court and are manifestly erroneous.
2. The trial court's finding that Purvis Touchet consented to Mark Hampton's actions was manifestly erroneous.

Discussion

La.Civ.Code art. 2315, a person is liable for acts which cause damage to another. The intentional tort of battery is "a harmful or offensive contact with a person, resulting from an act intended to cause the plaintiff to suffer such a contact." In a suit for damages resulting from an intentional tort, the claimant must carry the burden of proving all prima facie elements of the tort, including lack of consent to the invasive conduct. Mere words will not justify a battery.

Here, we find the trial court erred in finding that the threats and insults made by Mr. Touchet on Mr. Hampton's voicemail constitute Mr. Touchet's consent to Mr. Hampton's actions nine days later. Mr. Hampton sought out Mr. Touchet at his place of employment, entered Mr. Touchet's office, and hit Mr. Touchet repeatedly until Mr. Raggette pulled Mr. Hampton away. Furthermore, nothing that Mr. Touchet did when Mr. Hampton entered his office can be considered consent. Turning around in his chair, yelling an expletive at Mr. Hampton, and beginning to stand up are not sufficient provocations to rise to the level of giving consent to a battery. The trial court's oral reasons are not an accurate statement of Louisiana law.

We find that Mr. Touchet proved that Mr. Hampton committed the intentional tort of battery. Therefore, we find that Mr. Hampton is liable for the damage suffered by Mr. Touchet.

At trial, Mr. Touchet claimed he suffered bruises and abrasion, neck pain, back pain, and severe headaches. Mr. Touchet submitted medical bills in the amount of $9,239.82. We award him that amount. Mr. Touchet also seeks damages for pain and suffering and for the embarrassment he suffered because this incident occurred at his workplace with co-workers and customers watching. We award Mr. Touchet $9,000.00 in general damages for his pain and suffering and $1,000.00 for his mental anguish and embarrassment.

Conclusion

We reverse the trial court's judgment in favor of Mark Hampton finding that Purvis Touchet did not prove lack of consent. We render judgment in favor of Purvis Touchet and find that Mark Hampton committed the intentional tort of battery upon the person of Purvis Touchet. We award medical damages of $9,239.82 and general damages in the amount of $9,000.00 for pain and suffering and $1,000.00 for mental anguish and embarrassment. Costs of this appeal are assessed to Mark Hampton.

REVERSED AND RENDERED.

Websites

■ **University of Minnesota Law School**
   http://www.law.umn.edu/library/tools/pathfinders/verdicts1.html

■ **Cornell Law**
   www.law.cornell.edu

■ **Hieros Gamos**
   http://www.hg.org

■ **Intimate Partner Violence, 1993–2001**
   www.bjs.gov/content/pub/pdf/ipv01.pdf

Forms and Court Documents

This form shows an answer to the complaint in Chapter 2.

IN THE SUPERIOR COURT OF GANNETT COUNTY
STATE OF PLACID

Richard Coe,	)	CASE NO. CV 202-1101
Plaintiff	)	
	)	
vs.	)	
	)	
Terry Zoe,	)	
Defendant		

Answer

The Defendant answers the Plaintiff's Complaint as follows:

1.

Admitted.

2.

Admitted.

3.

The Defendant admits that he was present in Tilly's Tavern on the evening of August 13, 2000. To the best of his knowledge, Plaintiff was also present.

4.

The Defendant admits that he struck the Plaintiff, but that he did so in self-defense to prevent the Plaintiff from severely injuring him with a weapon.

The remainder of the allegations contained in Plaintiff's Complaint Paragraph 4 are denied.

5.

Denied; Defendant acted in self-defense and his actions were, therefore, justified under the law to protect himself from a vicious, unwarranted, and unjustified violent attack by the Plaintiff.

6.

Defendant is without sufficient information to either deny or admit the allegations contained in Paragraph 6.

7.

Defendant is without sufficient information to either admit or deny the allegations contained in Paragraph 7, except to deny that he is responsible in any way for the Plaintiff's claimed damages.

First Defense

8.

The Defendant realleges and incorporates by reference his responses to Paragraphs 1 through 7 of the Complaint as if fully set forth.

9.

Defendant's actions on the evening of August 13, 2000, in striking the Plaintiff were motivated entirely by his desire to avoid Plaintiff's offer of violence and Plaintiff's unwarranted and unjustified threat of physical violence to the Defendant by use of a weapon, most likely a knife, which Plaintiff had in his possession at the time of the incident alleged in the Plaintiff's complaint.

Having fully answered each and every allegation of the complaint, the Defendant requests the court:

1. That Plaintiff have and recover nothing of the Defendant by way of this action.
2. That the costs of this action be taxed against the Plaintiff.
3. For a trial by jury of all triable issues of fact.
4. For such other and further relief as the court may deem just and proper.

This the _____ day of July 2002.

Respectfully submitted,

By: _____
Attorney for Defendant

Key Terms

Compulsion	Immunity	*Respondeat superior*
Duress	Mutual combat	Self-defense
Excessive force	Privilege	

Review Questions

1   When does a defendant lose the right to raise the defense of self-defense?
2   Explain "excessive force."
3   Under what circumstances can a person use deadly force to protect personal property?
4   Describe a situation in which the defendant's claim of consent would be legally invalid.
5   Explain the differences between duress, necessity, coercion, and compulsion.
6   When is a person permitted to raise the defense of "involuntary intoxication"?
7   What is the legal definition of insanity?
8   Give an example of a situation in which the defense of mistake would be appropriate.
9   Describe a class of persons who could be protected by immunity under tort law.
10   Explain joint and several liability.
11   What is vicarious liability?
12   When does a person qualify as an "independent contractor"?
13   What is the justification for *respondeat superior?*
14   What is the family purpose doctrine?
15   What are some of the important points to consider when evaluating a case?

Applying What You Have Learned

1   Ted is a police officer. One day, he pulls over a driver for speeding and begins writing a ticket. Stan, the driver, puts the car in reverse while Ted is writing the ticket and backs up toward Ted, who is standing between Stan's car and Ted's patrol car. Stan's car is moving about one mile per hour. Ted pulls his service revolver and shoots Stan though the back window, killing him. When Stan's relative brings a civil action against Ted, does Ted have a valid claim of self-defense?
2   A group of foreign guests at a local hotel decide that the service has not been acceptable. When the manager refuses to refund their money, they threaten him and the other staff members and then force them into the manager's office and refuse to allow them to leave. Does the doctrine of *respondeat superior* provide a claim for the manager and staff against the hotel for the guests' conduct?
3   John owes $10,000 to a local businessman. Jerry, the businessman, becomes angry when John fails to pay back the money. He sends John a letter that says, in part, "If you don't pay back the money, I'll release certain facts to the press and your friends and family that you won't find very flattering." Draft a complaint alleging duress based on these facts. Feel free to create your own dates for these specific actions, but make sure that your complaint meets the legal requirements for duress.

4 Does your state differentiate between defenses such as duress and coercion? If so, what are the elements of these defenses in your state?

5 Is "compulsion" recognized in your state? If so, is it a form of the insanity defense, or is it organized under some other defense?

Endnotes

[1] *Taran v. State,* 186 A.D.2d 794, 589 N.Y.S.2d 74 (1992).

[2] *Scheuermann v. Scharfenberg,* 163 Ala. 337, 50 So. 335 (1909); *Cornell v. Harris,* 60 Idaho 87, 88 P.2d 498 (1939).

[3] *A History of American Law* by Lawrence Friedman, Simon and Schuster, New York, p. 261 (1973).

[4] *Wilson v. Wilson,* 642 S.W.2d 132 (1982).

[5] *Bennett v. Auto. Ins. Co.,* 646 A.2d 806 (1994); *Imperial Refineries Corp. v. Morrissey,* 119 N.W.2d 872 (1963).

[6] *Seals v. Snow,* 123 Kan. 88, 254 P. 348, 349 (1927).

Crossword Puzzle

www.CrosswordWeaver.com

ACROSS

1 When a person uses force (sometimes deadly force) to protect himself from an attack

4 Liability imposed on an employer for the actions of the employee, when the employee is carrying out his duties for the employer

5 An exception or privilege granted by the law to an action that ordinarily would result in a cause of action

6 When the defendant uses force, threat, or intimidation to overcome the plaintiff's will or to compel the plaintiff to perform (or not to perform) some action

7 When the parties to a fight voluntarily engage in violence

8 A protection or advantage given to a class of persons for actions taken by them

DOWN

2 Force used in self-defense that is clearly disproportionate to the threat posed by another

3 An overwhelming or irresistible impulse to perform some action

Introduction to Negligence

- Explain the four elements of a negligence action
- Explain how negligence is different from other forms of torts
- Describe how a new file is created
- Explain the methods used to gather information from the client
- Identify the important features found in a negligence complaint

I. NEGLIGENCE: WHAT MAKES IT DIFFERENT?

A negligence case is very different from the intentional tort cases that we discussed in the previous chapter. In a negligence action, the plaintiff is not claiming that the defendant intentionally injured him. Instead, the plaintiff is claiming that his injuries are the result of the defendant's carelessness — his failure to pay attention or failure to take adequate measures to protect others. In an intentional torts case, the plaintiff must show that the defendant acted knowingly and voluntarily. In negligence cases, the elements of proof are very different.

THE HISTORY OF NEGLIGENCE

Although some commentators argue that the body of negligence law originated in the Middle Ages, others claim that the real impetus to treat negligence as a separate (and highly specialized) area of law arose in the twentieth century. That century saw huge social and economic upheavals and the development of vast new industries. These new chemical, industrial, and electronic developments had unseen potential dangers. And earlier, the dangers of the Industrial Revolution had a profound impact on the development of legal principles of negligence. We discuss the historical development of negligence in the chapters specifically devoted to each of the four basic elements.

In negligence cases, there are four elements that must be satisfied before the defendant can be found liable: the establishment of a legal duty, proof that the defendant breached that duty, a causal connection between the breach and the plaintiff's injuries, and damages suffered by the plaintiff that can be assessed against the defendant. For simplicity's sake, we abbreviate these four elements as duty, breach, causation, and damages.

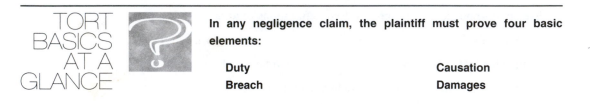

TORT BASICS AT A GLANCE

In any negligence claim, the plaintiff must prove four basic elements:

Duty	**Causation**
Breach	**Damages**

In this chapter, we explore the basic principles of each element, explaining them in general terms and providing examples. In the next four chapters, we examine each of these elements in depth. We also examine how a negligence case first reaches a firm and the important information that must be gathered early in the process. But first, we show how the elements of negligence factor into a discussion of the Chumley case.

THE CHUMLEY CASE

To remind you of the basic details of the Chumley case, Mr. and Mrs. Chumley were driving home when they were struck broadside by a train owned and operated by National Railroad Company. The engineer who was driving the train is a man named Stanley Blue. The basic contention that Mr. Chumley raises is that the intersection was dangerous. According to him, it was difficult, if not impossible, for a motorist stopping at the intersection to see down the railroad tracks because there were thick evergreen trees growing along the track. Because the track curved, these trees blocked the view of any oncoming train. Remember that Mr. Chumley was severely injured in the crash and his wife was killed. He wants to sue the railroad.

If our firm is going to take this case, we must first determine if the wreck falls into the category of a negligence case. In other words, we must go through each element of a negligence case and make sure there is enough evidence to support each element.

IV THE FOUR ELEMENTS OF NEGLIGENCE

As we discuss each of the four elements that must be proved by the defendant, consider why the courts would impose such elements in the first place.

A. DUTY

The first element of a negligence claim is **duty.** To prove a negligence claim, the plaintiff must prove that the defendant owed a duty to the plaintiff and that he failed to live up to that duty. How does a person come to owe a duty to another person? A duty can arise out of a relationship, such as the duty of a parent to a child. Duty can also arise out of legal obligation, such as the obligation of a police officer to take care of a suspect once he has been placed under arrest. In fact, the defendant doesn't even have to know the plaintiff to owe him a duty. People who drive on the public highways have a general duty to other drivers not to drive in a careless manner.

Duty
An outcome that a person should have known or been able to anticipate or predict based on certain facts.

In the chapter on duty, we discuss the issue of foreseeability. This term encompasses the concept that for the defendant to have a duty to the plaintiff, it must be foreseeable for the plaintiff to be a person who could be injured by the defendant's actions.

Duty can also be established through court-created doctrines. Courts frequently have created exceptions to the equation: duty + breach + proximate cause + damages = negligence. One such exception occurs because courts agreed that a duty could be created by a contractual agreement. Court doctrines can affect every step of the negligence equation, often supplying a missing or tenuous element.

We begin our overview of duty by taking a look at an excerpt from the Chumley complaint in Figure 4-1.

Notice that until paragraph 15, nothing in the complaint refers to the duty owed by the various defendants. A complaint must build its case by asserting facts. Once the facts are presented, the plaintiff can allege the defendants' duty. In later chapters, we examine this complaint and subsequent pleadings in detail, explaining how Mr. Chumley must set out each of the elements of negligence in his complaint and how the defendants in this case will attack those same elements.

Sidebar

Is negligence a question of fact or law? The answer is that it is both. A court can hold that a defendant is not negligent as a matter of law and dismiss the lawsuit, but only after finding that no reasonable jury could find negligence, based on the facts presented in the case.[1]

FIGURE 4-1

The Complaint in the Chumley Case

STATE OF NORTH CAROLINA
COUNTY OF HALEY

CHARLES CHUMLEY,

     Plaintiff,

     vs.

NATIONAL RAILWAY COMPANY
TOWN OF CLING,
and STANLEY W. BLUE,

     Defendant.

)
)
)
)
)
)
)

SUPERIOR COURT DIVISION
FILE NUMBER:

_____

COMPLAINT
JURY TRIAL DEMANDED

Plaintiff, by and through his attorneys, complains of the defendant as follows:

1. Plaintiff is, and all times hereafter was, a citizen and resident of the Town of CLING, County of HALEY, State of North Carolina.
2. Plaintiff alleges upon information and belief that the defendant National Railroad Company (Railroad) is, and at all times hereafter was, a corporation organized and existing under the laws of the State of Virginia, licensed to do business, and in fact doing business, in the State of North Carolina and having a registered agent for the service of process by the name of Richard Robin located at 1221 North Burke Ave., Suite 2000, Lakesboro, North Carolina, 27401.
3. Plaintiff alleges upon information and belief that the defendant Town of CLING (Town) is a duly chartered municipality in the County of HALEY and the State of North Carolina.
4. Plaintiff alleges upon information and belief that the defendant STANLEY W. BLUE is a citizen and resident of the County of Buncombe, State of North Carolina.
5. That at all times relevant to this Complaint the defendant STANLEY W. BLUE was an agent, servant, and employee of the defendant National Railroad Company (Railroad) and was acting within the course and scope of his employment with it.
6. The plaintiff is informed and believes and therefore alleges that the Town has waived any sovereign immunity that it otherwise might have through the purchase of liability insurance, thereby affording its residents and residents of other communities the right to sue for negligent acts that it might commit.
7. Railroad, at the time of the accident, owned, maintained, and used a set of railroad tracks laid in an east-west direction and passing through the Town.
8. Morgan Street is a public street in the Town that runs in a north-south direction crossing the tracks.
9. Plaintiff alleges, upon information and belief, that at the time of the accident, Railroad owned, maintained, and used the railroad tracks at railroad crossing number 728339E, which tracks cross and intersect with Morgan Street, in the Town of CLING, County of HALEY, North Carolina.

10. On August 23, 2010, at approximately 4:30 P.M., plaintiff was driving his automobile south on Morgan Street approaching the railroad crossing. A train belonging to and being operated by Railroad, its agents, servants, and employees, was approaching the crossing from an easterly direction.

11. At the crossing in question at the time of the accident, there were no mechanical devices to warn motorists of an approaching train; no blinking lights, automatic gates, bells or gongs, or stop bars were installed at the crossing.

12. The northeast quadrant of the grade crossing, at the time of the accident, contained vegetation and trees in such a position that they obstructed and/or severely restricted the view of the tracks or an approaching train by a motorist approaching the crossing. Upon information and belief, defendants, Railroad, Town, and STANLEY W. BLUE, were under a duty to maintain the area in question.

13. That as the plaintiff approached the crossing, he stopped and looked both ways; however, he was unable to see the train approaching because of the vegetation and overgrowth, which both the Town and the Railroad had negligently allowed to remain upon the right of way, until such time as he was on the tracks and a collision was inevitable.

14. Railroad's train struck plaintiff's automobile with great force as plaintiff attempted to cross the railroad track, knocked the car off the tracks in a southwesterly direction and dragged the car 100 yards from the point of impact, upon which the car rolled into a ditch.

15. The Town and Railroad owed to the plaintiff a duty of due care to reasonably and safely maintain the tracks and the area surrounding such tracks, particularly at crossings, in order to provide adequate sight distance for motorists operating automobiles on streets that intersect such crossings.

FIGURE 4-1

(continued)

B. BREACH

Once the plaintiff has established that the defendant owes a duty, the next step is to show how the defendant violated that duty. When a defendant **breaches** a duty, he violates a standard of care or acts in a careless or reckless way. Just as there are doctrines that affect the analysis of duty, so too there are similar doctrines that affect how we view breach of that duty.

One such court-created doctrine allows the plaintiff to establish a breach simply because the defendant violated a safety statute at the time that he injured the plaintiff. This doctrine of **negligence per se** allows the plaintiff to establish a presumption of negligence when the defendant violates a traffic law when he injures the plaintiff.

Breaches
When the defendant fails to live up to a legal standard, or violates a duty.

Negligence per se
Negligence in and of itself; the principle that the violation of a safety statute establishes a presumption of breach of duty in a negligence action.

The second element of a negligence claim is a showing that the defendant breached a duty to the plaintiff. Without proof of a breach, the other elements of a negligence case are meaningless.

TORT
BASICS
AT A
GLANCE

FIGURE 4-2

Excerpt from
the Chumley
Complaint:
Breach

16. The Town **breached** this duty of due care by the following acts of negligence (emphasis added):

  a. it failed to close the crossing pursuant to state law, when it knew, or in the exercise of due care should have known, that the crossing constituted an unreasonable hazard to vehicular or pedestrian traffic;

  b. it failed to require the installation, construction, erection, or improvement of warning signs, gates, lights, stop bars, or such other safety devices when it knew or should have known in the exercise of reasonable care that such devices were necessary;

  c. it allowed the crossing to remain in use with absolutely no safety devices with total, wanton, and reckless disregard for the safety of vehicular and pedestrian traffic;

  d. it allowed the vegetation and trees adjacent to the tracks to obstruct the view by motorists of the tracks and approaching trains when it knew, or in the exercise of due care should have known, that such vegetation and trees constituted an unreasonable hazard to vehicular and pedestrian traffic;

  e. it failed to keep the public street free from unnecessary obstructions in violation of State law.

Notice how the complaint in Figure 4-2 details the exact nature of the defendants' breach of the duty. In Chapter 6, we explore the legal concept of breach of duty in greater detail.

C. CAUSATION

Proximate causation
The facts that show the defendant's legal responsibility for the injuries to the plaintiff, also known as legal cause.

Once the plaintiff has proved that the defendant had a duty to him and the defendant breached that duty, the next step is that the plaintiff must prove that there is a factual connection between what the defendant did (or failed to do) and the resulting injuries to the plaintiff. This connection is referred to as **proximate causation.** This legal term requires a strong connection between the defendant's actions and the plaintiff's harm. Without this strong connection, the plaintiff cannot recover damages from the defendant. See Figure 4-3 for the section of the Chumley complaint regarding causation.

TORT
BASICS
AT A
GLANCE

Causation refers to the link between the defendant's actions (or failure to act) and the subsequent injury to the plaintiff.

D. DAMAGES

Damages
Monetary payments designed to compensate the plaintiff for an injury.

After the plaintiff proves duty, breach, and causation, he must still prove that he suffered some form of physical or financial loss. Without this final element, a negligence case will fail. **Damages** are awarded as a way to attempt to put the plaintiff back into the condition he was in before the injury (or as close as possible). There are several different categories of damages, including damages for pain and suffering, lost wages, future medical payments, and many others,

19. That the negligence of the defendants Town of CLING, National Railway, and STANLEY W. BLUE joined and concurred and combined in point of time and place ***proximately to cause*** the collision between plaintiff's vehicle and Railroad's train.

Excerpt from the Chumley Complaint: Causation

. . . plaintiff's resulting serious, painful, and permanent injuries and damages, all of which exceed the sum of Ten Thousand Dollars ($10,000.00), and which include, without limitation, the following: 1. bodily injury and resulting pain and suffering; 2. medical expenses, including the costs of therapy; 3. loss of earnings and earning capacity; 4. punitive damages as a result of the defendants' reckless and wanton conduct.

Excerpt from the Chumley Complaint: Damages

which we examine in greater depth in Chapter 8. See Figure 4-4 for the section of the Chumley complaint regarding damages.

To see a complete version of the Chumley complaint, please refer to Appendix C

***Damages* refer to the plaintiff's monetary losses, such as lost time from work and the medical expenses incurred due to the defendant's negligence.**

TORT BASICS AT A GLANCE

Here we see an example of how the various elements of a negligence case come together.

Case Excerpt

TRANSCARE MARYLAND, INC. V. MURRAY
431 Md. 225, 64 A.3d 887 (2013)

McDonald, J.

In the parable of the Good Samaritan, a man on the way from Jerusalem to Jericho is robbed, beaten, and left for dead. Two passers-by of significant social and religious status see the injured man, but choose to cross to the other side of the road. A third traveler of less repute, a Samaritan, comes to the man's aid, takes him to an inn, tends to him through the night, and then pays the innkeeper the next morning to continue the man's care.

We do not know from the parable whether the fear of civil liability discouraged the first two passers-by from intervening. In modern-day Maryland, a State law known as the Good Samaritan Act seeks to remove that disincentive, particularly for individuals who have the knowledge and skills to provide useful medical assistance at an emergency, by granting those individuals immunity from liability should something go awry. In some instances that immunity extends to an entity when its personnel provide emergency aid.

Background

The Transport of Bryson Murray

On November 15, 2007, Respondent Bryson Murray, a minor who was suffering from congestion and was having trouble breathing, was taken to Easton Memorial Hospital ("Easton Memorial") in Talbot County. At the hospital he was fitted with an endotracheal breathing tube. Because Easton Memorial was not equipped to handle intubated children, hospital officials sought to transfer him to the pediatric intensive care unit at the Medical Center of the University of Maryland Medical System ("UMMS") in Baltimore.

UMMS arranged for PHI Air Medical to carry out the transport by helicopter. Present on the helicopter was a flight paramedic team that included a UMMS pediatric intensive-care nurse, a PHI flight paramedic, and a PHI flight nurse. Also present was Chris Barbour, a paramedic employed by Petitioner TransCare who had been invited to ride along by the UMMS nurse (with PHI's permission) for orientation purposes. TransCare, a licensed commercial ground ambulance transport company, was under contract with UMMS to provide ground ambulance services for patients between the Medical Center and area hospitals. Mr. Barbour was a licensed emergency medical technician-paramedic.

After the helicopter arrived at Easton Memorial, Mr. Barbour set up equipment and the team placed Bryson on the aircraft. Shortly after take-off, however, Bryson's heart rate and oxygen blood level began to drop, because, according to the allegations in the complaint, the endotracheal tube had become dislodged and was blocking his airway. Members of the flight team searched for a pediatric air mask to restore Bryson's breathing, but were unable to locate it. The helicopter then landed at Bay Bridge Airport in Stevensville, where the flight paramedic retrieved the mask from its storage compartment and Bryson was reintubated. Bryson's cardiac activity returned to normal and the helicopter completed its trip to the Medical Center.

The Murrays' Negligence Action

Complaint

Bryson, by his mother, Karen Murray, subsequently filed a complaint against TransCare alleging medical malpractice on the basis that its employee, Mr. Barbour, had failed to provide the requisite standard of care and that TransCare was vicariously responsible under the principle of respondeat superior. According to the complaint, Bryson suffered hypoxic brain injury due to alleged acts and omissions of Mr. Barbour during the helicopter transport and, as a result, is blind, deaf, and mentally disabled. The complaint did not name Mr. Barbour individually as a defendant.

Summary Judgment Motion

TransCare moved for summary judgment, arguing that it was immune from liability under both the Good Samaritan Act and the Fire and Rescue Act. The Circuit Court for Talbot County was initially persuaded that there were disputes of material fact as to TransCare's corporate relationship with the other medical providers involved and as to whether it had received a "fee or compensation" that would preclude application of the Good Samaritan Act. The Circuit Court also tentatively concluded that the Fire and Rescue Act did not apply to a commercial ambulance company such as TransCare. Accordingly, the Circuit Court initially denied TransCare's motion for summary judgment based on those immunity provisions.

Appeal

TransCare petitioned this Court for certiorari. We granted the petition to determine whether either the Good Samaritan Act or the Fire and Rescue Act relieves a commercial ambulance company of civil liability for the alleged negligence of an employee committed when an emergency arises during a transfer of a patient between medical facilities.

Analysis

In order to assess TransCare's claims of immunity, we must construe two statutes — the Good Samaritan Act and the Fire and Rescue Act.

Whether TransCare Has Immunity under the Good Samaritan Act
Good Samaritan Laws

Under the common law, there is no general duty to provide assistance to those in peril. Moreover, under general principles of tort law, one who voluntarily chooses to aid another owes that person a duty of care; a failure to exercise such care may result in legal liability. This risk of potential liability led to the unsatisfactory result that health care professionals capable and willing to provide emergency medical services had (in theory, at least) a disincentive to do so.

Maryland Good Samaritan Act

Pertinent to this case, the Maryland Good Samaritan Act provides immunity to specified individuals and entities from liability for ordinary negligence that occurs in connection with assistance or medical care rendered without fee or other compensation at the scene of an emergency or in transit to a medical facility.

TransCare asserts that it has immunity directly under CJ §5–603(b)(3) as a "volunteer fire department or ambulance and rescue squad whose members have immunity." In addition, TransCare argues that, regardless of whether CJ §5–603(b)(3) directly confers immunity on it, it has immunity because its employee, Mr. Barbour, has immunity under the statute.

We agree with the Court of Special Appeals that TransCare, as a for-profit ambulance company, does not have immunity under CJ §5–603(b)(3) regardless of whether Mr. Barbour is personally covered by the Act.

Whether TransCare as Employer Necessarily Has Same Immunity as Its Employee

TransCare makes a broader argument for immunity under the Good Samaritan Act, untethered to any of the provisions that specifically confer immunity on corporations or other organizations. It asserts that, given that its liability is predicated on the actions of its employee, Mr. Barbour, it cannot be vicariously liable if Mr. Barbour is personally immune under the Good Samaritan Act.

TransCare's argument is contrary to the general rule on the relationship of employer immunity to that of an employee. As this Court recently stated: "The principal in an agency relationship is not entitled to receive immunity simply because the agent is entitled to receive immunity; the principal must establish an independent basis to receive the benefit of an immunity shield . . . Unless there is an independent source of immunity for the employer or principal, the cause of action premised on vicarious liability can be brought even if the employee or agent is entitled to immunity."

Conclusion

TransCare is not a volunteer ambulance and rescue squad and therefore does not qualify for immunity under CJ §5–603(b)(3). Nor is it shielded from liability under the Act for the alleged negligence of Mr. Barbour, regardless of whether he individually has immunity under the statute.

For the reasons stated above, a commercial ambulance company such as TransCare does not qualify for immunity under the Good Samaritan Act, regardless of whether the company's employee may qualify for immunity under the statute. Moreover, in the circumstances of this case, TransCare has not demonstrated it functioned as a "rescue company" that has the broad immunity from liability provided by the Fire and Rescue Act. Accordingly, TransCare was not entitled to summary judgment on the basis of statutory immunity.

Judgment of the Court of Special Appeals Affirmed. Costs to be paid by Petitioners.

Questions about the case:

1. What is the purpose of Maryland's Good Samaritan Act?
2. What is the basis of the complaint filed against TransCare?
3. What was the old common law rule about duty to provide assistance?
4. Was TransCare protected by the Good Samaritan Act?

THE LAWYERS WHO REPRESENT PLAINTIFFS AND DEFENDANTS

Any discussion of negligence cases should include the lawyers who actually represent either side in the action. Plaintiffs' lawyers and defendants' lawyers have different financial arrangements with their clients, have different strategies, and frequently have firms that are structured in dramatically different ways. Paralegals who work for these firms should understand the important differences between lawyers who regularly represent plaintiffs and those who regularly represent defendants.

A. BECOMING A LAWYER

Whether a lawyer eventually represents a plaintiff or a defendant in a particular case, the initial training is the same. To become a lawyer, a person must attend a law school and pass an examination called the bar exam. These days, to be allowed to take the bar exam, the future attorney must graduate from an American Bar Association–approved school. The ABA does not directly regulate attorneys. Instead, the ABA approves law schools by reviewing professors' qualifications, the quality of instruction, and even the law school's physical facility. The ABA stamp of approval is essential to a law school and helps maintain the high standard of legal education.

Once the law student completes what is almost always a three-year program of study, she graduates from law school and then takes the bar exam. (In some states, a third-year law student can take the bar exam shortly before graduation.) The bar exam is administered by the state bar. If a law student receives a passing grade on this exam, she can then be admitted to the bar. Admission to the bar means that a graduate now has a license to practice law and is entitled to give legal advice, receive compensation for services, and carry out any other action permitted of a fully licensed attorney.

To be admitted into law school, an applicant must have already earned a bachelor's degree. Law school curricula are designed to last for three years.

TORT
BASICS
AT A
GLANCE

B. THE ECONOMICS OF LAW FIRMS

It is important for any legal professional to understand the economics of a law firm. Attorneys who represent people in negligence cases almost always work in private firms. These firms may consist only of one attorney (called a sole practitioner) or of hundreds of attorneys in branch offices across the nation. In either situation, client fees pay an attorney's salary.

Our example is a 25-person firm that handles primarily defense work. This means that the firm represents people who have been sued by others. There is no prohibition against a firm handling both plaintiff and defense work — as long as the ethical rules are followed — but as a practical matter, most firms specialize in one or the other. Our hypothetical firm has six partners and nineteen associates. An associate is usually a relatively new lawyer who is hired to work for the firm. This associate earns a set salary, which, unlike what you often see on television, is not high. Even at big firms, the starting salary for an associate is often the same as the manager of a local retail store. Partners split the profits of the law firm once everyone else has been paid. Paying the associates, secretaries, and paralegals a fixed salary means that if the firm is particularly profitable, the partners will split these huge profits among themselves. It also means that when times are lean, the staff will continue to earn the same salary and the partners will have less to share among themselves.

If an associate does not make a large salary, why work for a large firm? The answer is simple. Associates know that if they work long hours, generating as much income as possible to impress the partners with their work ethic, they may be offered a partnership of their own. "Making partner" at a profitable firm is the ticket to wealth for an attorney.

An associate generates income by working on cases, hopefully bringing them to a successful conclusion, and then billing the client for the time spent on the case. The more that an associate bills, the more money he brings in for the firm. An associate who fails to generate income will eventually be fired.

C. PLAINTIFFS' FIRMS

Large plaintiffs' firms resemble their defense counterparts in many ways. The financial arrangements among associates and partners are often identical. However, while defense firms bill by the hour, often setting an hourly rate of $150 or more (for a large firm), plaintiffs' firms operate on an entirely different system. A plaintiffs' firm represents people who may have a claim for injuries against someone else. The most common type of personal injury claim is one arising from a car collision. Plaintiffs' firms generally do not bill by the hour. Instead, they work on a contingency fee.

TORT BASICS AT A GLANCE

Plaintiffs' firms **represent people who have been injured by others' negligence.** *Defense firms* **represent people who have been sued.**

Plaintiffs' firms are normally paid out of the ultimate settlement in the case. Many firms charge a standard rate (33 percent of the total recovery, for instance). This means that whatever amount the plaintiff ultimately gets in the case will be reduced by the firm's payment of one-third.

Example: Ron's case has finally settled, and the defense has agreed to pay him $100,000 to settle all claims. Ron ultimately receives $66,000, while the firm that represented him receives $33,000 (give or take a few hundred).

If the plaintiff ends up getting nothing because the jury entered a verdict in favor of the defendant, the firm gets no money. This often puts financial stress on plaintiffs' firms. They must decide not only if each case has merit, but also what the possibility of recovering any money is. No matter how great the case, if there is no possibility of recovering damages from the defendant, there is no incentive for the firm to take the case.

D. DEFENSE FIRMS

Insurance companies regularly pay the fees for firms that specialize in defense work. When a motorist is sued, his insurance policy often contains a provision that guarantees an attorney will represent him. Many firms have standing arrangements with insurance companies that they will represent all people in a geographic area who are sued. These attorneys normally charge an hourly rate, as opposed to the contingency fee arrangement followed by most plaintiffs' firms. The firm bills the insurance company at the end of each month, or in whatever interval the insurance company and the firm have decided on. In some cases, the insurance company will pay a flat fee to the firm to handle a certain kind of a case, for example, a basic car wreck case.

The two pay arrangements would seem to put the two types of firms in different philosophical approaches to a case. If the plaintiffs' firm gets paid only when the case is over, that firm would want to settle the case as soon as possible. On the other hand, the defense firm is paid by the hour and therefore would seem not to want to end the lawsuit quickly. Although this is somewhat of an oversimplification, it is an accurate picture of the different viewpoints these two firms bring to the case.

E. CONTRACTING WITH A LAW FIRM

When a client engages a law firm, whether to represent him as a plaintiff in a suit or to defend him in a suit, the firm enters into a contract with that client. In insurance defense cases, the contract is actually between the insurance company and the firm, but it accrues to the benefit of the insured party.

F. CONTRACT IN THE CHUMLEY CASE

For instance, suppose that a firm has decided to represent Mr. Chumley in his lawsuit against the railroad company. When it agrees to take the case, an attorney for the firm enters into a signed contract with Mr. Chumley. This contract of representation spells out the details of the arrangement between the plaintiff and the firm. One major item in the contract is the provision that

Sidebar

Practical suggestion: Give the client a copy of the contract to take home with her.

Sidebar

You should be very familiar with the firm's contract, so you can explain any particular item that the client may ask about. If the client has a legal question about the contract, you should refer him to the attorney.

authorizes the firm to receive one-third of the eventual settlement, if any. But the contract does more than simply deal with payment; it details what each party will do for the other, as shown in the sample contract form in Figure 4-5.

FIGURE 4-5

Contract of
Representation

THIS AGREEMENT, made this _____ day of _____, 20 _____ is between _____ the foregoing named person(s) being herein called Client, and Clarence D. Arrow, herein called "Attorney(s)." It is understood that litigation can be expensive, and that the Attorneys are prohibited by law from becoming liable for its costs, expenses, disbursements, and deposits. These may be advanced, but Attorneys cannot become ultimately liable for them. The Client and the Attorneys have agreed as follows:

WITNESSETH

1. The Client this day retains, employs, and authorizes the Attorneys:
    (a) To prosecute, administratively and judicially, if necessary in their judgment, each of the Client's claims; and
    (b) To prosecute or defend any and all appeals that may be taken in connection with the Client's claims; and
    (c) To receive and collect any final recovery that may be realized on the Client's claims and to satisfy the same upon the records of the appropriate agency or court. The words *final recovery* when used anywhere in this Agreement means the total gross amount of any and all monies, property, and compensation of any and every kind whatsoever realized or received by any Client for any claim, whether realized as the result of settlement or litigation or otherwise, and shall include, but not be limited to, any and all monies, funds, awards, verdicts, judgments, determinations, damages, principal, interest of every kind and nature, penalties, allowances, costs, and any and all compensation of every kind, nature, and description; and
    (d) To deduct and retain their Attorneys' fees out of the proceeds of the final recovery, and to remit the balance, less their costs, expenses, disbursements, and deposits, to the Client.
2. The Client agrees to pay the Attorneys, and the Attorneys agree to accept for all of the legal services rendered in accordance with this Agreement, the following fee:
    (a) A retainer, paid over and above the contingent fee and within ten (10) days of execution of this Agreement, as follows: $_____; or
    (b) *A contingent fee, paid within thirty (30) days of a final recovery or any portion thereof, computed as follows: percent (_____ %) of any final recovery obtained if the claim is settled without suit; or*
    (c) A contingent fee, paid within thirty (30) days of a final recovery or any portion thereof, computed as follows: percent (_____ %) of any final recovery obtained after commencement of suit; The final Attorneys' fees shall be due and shall be paid to the Attorneys at an earlier time if the Attorneys execute and tender delivery of their waiver of Attorneys' lien to the Client. In the event of an appeal to an Appellate Court from the Trial Court, an additional Attorneys' fee for such work shall be negotiated between the parties at the time a decision to pursue an appeal is made.
3. The Client agrees to pay, reimburse, and hold the Attorneys harmless from any and all costs, expenses, disbursements and deposits incurred and/or paid by the Attorneys, and same shall be due and paid to the Attorneys at any time when billed by the Attorneys. Examples of such costs, expenses, disbursements, and deposits are as follows: court and court reporter charges; document processing and copying costs; mail and delivery costs; telecommunications and research database expert fees and expenses; witness fees and expenses; computer costs; paralegal and consultant costs; photography, videotaping, and other visual aid costs; and investigation

charges and reports. In the event of a recovery, the Client agrees that the Attorneys may pay any unpaid bills from the Client's share of recovery. Should the Client recover nothing, it is understood that the Attorneys are not bound to pay any of the costs, disbursements, expenses, and deposits incurred or deemed necessary by the Attorneys handling the Client's case, and that the Client remains liable for their payment.

FIGURE 4-5

(continued)

A cost deposit of $ _____ is due and payable within ten (10) days after execution of this Agreement.

4. The Client hereby assigns to the Attorneys the portion of any final recovery realized or recovered by the Client which represents the Attorneys' fee computed in accordance with this Agreement, and an additional portion sufficient to cover all costs, expenses, disbursements, and deposits billed by Attorneys and unpaid by Client.

5. The Client reserves the absolute right to discharge the Attorneys at any time. Likewise, the Attorneys, in their absolute discretion, may withdraw at any time. If the Client discharges the Attorneys, or if the Attorneys withdraw for justifiable cause, all costs, expenses, disbursements, and deposits incurred by the Attorneys, as well as compensation to the Attorneys for the fair and reasonable value of services, to be determined as follows:

(a) If the Attorneys are discharged or justifiably withdraw before any settlement or similar understanding is effected or any verdict, award, determination, or judgment is rendered, the compensation of the Attorneys shall be paid within thirty (30) days of discharge and shall be computed on a time basis at the rate of One Hundred Fifty Dollars ($150.00) per hour, which rate the Client agrees is fair and reasonable for services rendered. The Attorneys, in the event of such discharge and upon the Client's request, shall furnish the Client with a statement of their services, which shall be binding on all parties. In lieu of payment pursuant to this similar understanding regarding Client's claims, or a verdict, award, determination, or judgment in Client's favor, at which point in time the Attorneys may select payment pursuant to either subparagraph 2(b) or 2(c);

(b) If the Attorneys are discharged by the Client or justifiably withdraw after a settlement or similar understanding is effected or after a verdict, award, determination, or judgment is rendered in favor of the Client, the compensation of the Attorneys shall be computed in accordance with the non-discharge provisions of this Agreement, just as if the settlement, verdict, award determination, or judgment had actually been collected in full hereunder for the Client;

(c) In case of discharge or justifiable withdrawal, the Attorneys shall not be obligated to return any of the Client's papers or property to the Client until the Attorneys' fees, computed as set forth in this paragraph, together with all costs, expenses, disbursements, and deposits, are fully paid to the Attorneys.

6. The Client agrees not to compromise the claim without the Attorneys' consent and the Attorneys are not authorized to do so without the Client's consent. It is mutually agreed that if the Client does settle his claim or cause of action without the consent of the Attorneys, the Client agrees to pay the Attorneys, within thirty (30) days of the settlement, all of the costs, expenses, disbursements, and deposits incurred and/or paid by him, together with their Attorneys' fee, computed in accordance with the terms of this Agreement, based upon the final recovery realized or received by the Client in such settlement, unless the Attorneys exercised their option hereby granted to be paid on that basis. If by the terms of such settlement it is agreed by the party making the same that he or she will also pay for the services of the Client's Attorneys, such percentage of the Attorneys' fee shall be computed on the amount of such Attorneys' fee agreed to be paid to the Client's attorney.

(continued)

FIGURE 4-5

(continued)

7. All monies due and payable to Attorneys by Client, which have been due and payable for at least thirty (30) days following the date a statement of the account is rendered by Attorneys to Client, will incur a finance charge of one and one-half percent (1.5%) per month calculated on the amount owed from the date upon which it became due and payable until paid.

8. The Client agrees to cooperate in the preparation and trial of the case, to appear on reasonable notice for conferences, medical examinations, videotaping, depositions and court appearances, and to comply with all reasonable requests made of Client in connection with this legal representation.

9. Client hereby gives Attorneys Client's power of attorney to execute all documents connected with the claim for the prosecution of which Attorneys are retained, including pleadings, contracts, commercial paper, settlement agreements, compromises and releases, verifications, dismissals, orders, settlement checks or drafts, and all other documents that Client could properly execute. The Client hereby authorizes the Attorneys to turn over all information, documentary and otherwise, to the defendant and others, as discretion of the Attorneys may dictate.

10. The Client agrees that the Attorneys have given no guarantees, promises, or representations regarding the successful termination of the Client's claim or cause of action relative to the Client's claim or reimbursement are only matters of their opinion given in good faith. No representation has been made as to what amounts, if any, the Client may be entitled to recover in this case.

11. The Attorneys shall have general, possessory, and retaining liens, and all special and charging liens known to the common law, in addition to any statuary lien, including upon the Client's cause of action, upon any recovery in the Client's favor, and to the proceeds thereof in whatever hands they may come. The Attorneys shall not be obligated to waive their Attorneys' lien until their Attorneys' fees and any and all of their costs, expenses, disbursements, and deposits hereunder have been fully paid. The Attorneys shall not be liable to the Client for any loss the Client may incur or suffer because of the Attorneys' exercising their Attorneys' lien in order to secure full payment of legal fees and costs, expenses, disbursements, and deposits under this Agreement.

12. The Attorneys shall receive no compensation in any manner or form in connection with this claim or cause of action other than that provided for in this Agreement, except by written modification of this Agreement.

13. The Attorneys, in their sole discretion, may employ or contract with other counsel in the prosecution of the Client's claims. The other counsel's fee will be covered by the Attorneys' fee herein for which Client is responsible, while the costs, expenses, disbursements, and deposits of the other counsel will be the Client's responsibility.

14. This Agreement shall be binding upon the heirs, executor, administrators, successors, and assigns of each of the parties hereto, and constitutes the entire Agreement between the parties hereto. Should any provision be rendered inoperative, the other provisions shall remain in full force and effect.

15. This Agreement is to be construed according to state law and all parties are agreed that the sole personal jurisdiction and venue for the resolution of any dispute hereunder shall be Anytown, New York, USA, and that any and all judgments rendered shall be enforceable in the jurisdictional residence of the Client.

     IN WITNESS WHEREOF, the parties have executed this Agreement the day and year first above written.

Sworn to and subscribed before me
this _____ day of _____, 20___

_____
Notary Public

My commission expires:

_____
Unofficial Witness

_____
CLIENT

FIGURE 4-5

(continued)

VI OBTAINING INFORMATION FROM THE CLIENT

Once the contract has been signed, there are some additional issues that should be addressed. One of them is the information that the firm should always get from the client. The Client Questionnaire in Figure 4-6 has an extensive list of questions that should be asked of clients, regardless of whether the firm represents plaintiffs or defendants.

As you can see in Figure 4-6, the firm requires a great deal of information from the client, including her full name, address, and all telephone numbers. You need all of this information so that you can contact your client, especially on short notice, so having access to this information can be crucial.

Sidebar

When getting information from your client, ask for all e-mail addresses and beeper and cell phone numbers.

A. AUTHORIZATIONS FROM THE CLIENT

In addition to signing a contract of representation, the firm will usually need a signed medical authorization from the client as well. A medical authorization is a legal document that allows the firm to get copies of the client's medical or other records. Because this material is confidential, most medical professionals will refuse to release the records without an authorization signed by the client. Many firms have the client sign several copies of authorizations. The authorization form provided in Figure 4-7 is for the release of medical records, but it could just as easily be directed to an employer or anyone else who keeps confidential records that the firm may need to prove its case.

B. OTHER INFORMATION FROM THE CLIENT: FACTS AND PHOTOS

In addition to a signed contract of representation and signed authorizations, you as the paralegal may also be called on to gather additional information from the client at the first meeting. What types of questions should you ask?

FIGURE 4-6

Client
Interview—
Personal Injury
Case

Client's Name:
    Address:
    Phone # Work:
    Phone # Home:
How long at present address?:
With whom does client live?:
    SPOUSE: _____   AGE: _____
    CHILDREN: _____   AGE: _____
    _____   AGE: _____

Other Prior Residences:

Persons Client Supports: _____   AGE: _____
    _____   AGE: _____

Client's Age:
Client's Date of Birth:
Client's Social Security Number:
Client's Place of Birth:
Client's Educational Background:
Client's Employment History:

Client's Current Employment:
    Employer:
    Address:
    Supervisor:
    Type of Work:
    Length of Employment:
    Present Job Still Available?:
    Pay:

Military History:

Client ever treated by psychiatrist or been in Mental Institution?:

Physical Ailments?:

Physical Ailments of Family Members?:

Other names by which client has been known?:

Brief explanation of what happened:

Prior Accidents/Lawsuits?:

YEAR	COURT	DISPOSITION	PARTY

FIGURE 4-7

Medical
Authorization
and Patient's
Request for
Confidential
Treatment of
Medical
Information

TO:

FROM:

You are hereby authorized and directed to permit the examination of, and the copying or reproduction in any manner, whether mechanical, photographic, or otherwise, by my attorney or such other person as my attorney may authorize, all or any portions requested by my attorney of the following:

1. Hospital records; X-rays; X-ray readings and reports; laboratory records and reports; all tests of any type and character and reports thereof; statement of charges; and any and all of my records pertaining to hospitalization, history, condition, treatment, diagnosis, prognosis, etiology, or expense;
2. Medical records, including patient's record cards; X-rays; X-ray readings and reports; laboratory records and reports; all tests of any type and character and reports thereof; statements of charges; and any and all of my records pertaining to medical care, history, condition, treatment, diagnosis, prognosis, etiology or expense.

You are further authorized and directed to furnish oral and written reports to my attorney, or his delegate, as requested by him for any of the foregoing matters.

By reason of the fact that such information you have acquired as my physician or surgeon is confidential to me, you are also requested to treat such information as confidential and requested not to furnish any of such information in any form to anyone without written authorization from me. I hereby revoke any previously dated medical authorization.

I also authorize my attorney(s) or their delegate(s) to photograph my person while I am present in any hospital.

I further authorize the sending of medical and hospital bills to my attorney, and in the event of recovery by trial or settlement to allow my attorney to withhold an amount sufficient to cover these bills and to make payment directly to you and to deduct the same from any recovery which may be due me. I agree that a photostatic copy of the authorization shall be considered as effective and valid as the original.

_____
Client

Sworn to and subscribed
before me this _____ day
of _____, 200_____

_____
Notary Public

You should not neglect obvious points. Does the client know of any witnesses to the collision? Has anyone taken photos of the car he was driving? Does he know if the local press did a story about the wreck? The only way you can find out this information is by asking. You should also acquire photographs of the plaintiff before the accident, preferably showing him smiling and happy, as in the Chumley case example in Figure 4-8.

FIGURE 4-8

Photos of
Mr. and
Mrs. Chumley

Chapter Summary

There are four elements to a negligence action: duty, breach, causation, and
damages. Each of these elements must be proved at trial before the plaintiff
can succeed on his claim. These elements build on one another. When you
evaluate the facts of a negligence case, you should proceed from one element
to the other in order. If the plaintiff fails to prove duty, for instance, there is no
point in proceeding to the other elements. The plaintiff's failure to prove one
of the elements brings the negligence action down like a house of cards.
A negligence complaint must state these four elements in clear language.

FIGURE 4-9

Civil Cases Terminated, by Nature of Suit and Action Taken, 2013

Nature of Suit	Total	No Court Action	Court Action						
			Total	Before Pretrial	During or After Pretrial	During or After Trial			Percent Reaching Trial
						Total	Nonjury	Jury	
Total Cases	254,427	54,032	200,395	172,338	24,887	3170	1,010	2,160	1.2
United States Cases	47.000	9.191	37,809	36,057	1.474	278	196	82	0.6
Contract Actions									
Franchise	1	1	-	-	-	-	-	-	-
Negotiable Instruments	39	11	28	22	6	-	-	-	-
Recovery of Overpayments and Enforcement of Judgments	2.693	1.466	1,227	1,184	39	4	4	-	0.1
Other Contracts	509	152	357	303	50	4	2	2	0.8
Real Property	1.138	233	905	832	71	2	2	-	0.2
Tort Actions									
Marine Personal Injury	35	4	31	16	12	3	3	-	8.6
Motor Vehicle Personal Injury	424	100	324	220	81	23	20	3	5.4
Heath Care/Pharma.	5	1	4	4	-	-	-	-	-
Other Personal Injury	3.459	232	3,227	2,956	223	48	40	8	1.4
Other Torts	279	73	206	178	27	1	-	1	0.4
Actions Under Statutes									
Consumer Credit	18	11	7	6	1	-	-	-	-
Cable/Satellite TV	-	-	-	-	-	-	-	-	-
Antitrust	13	3	10	9	1	-	-	-	-
Civil Rights									
ADA–Employment	92	13	79	59	17	3	1	2	3.3
ADA–Other	38	12	26	24	2	-	-	-	-
Employment	851	145	706	546	135	25	4	21	2.9
Education	-	-	-	-	-	-	-	-	-
Other Civil Rights	794	147	647	586	49	12	7	5	1.5

Tech Topic
FINDING WITNESSES ON THE INTERNET

Tracking down witnesses used to be a challenging endeavor. As recently as a couple of decades ago, if someone chose not to be found, finding him required a Herculean effort of ingenuity and persistence. Often, attorneys would engage the services of a private investigator to help locate witnesses.

Today it is much easier. A witness can try to keep a low profile, hoping to avoid being found, but the Internet has all but erased anonymity. Social media and networking sites such as Facebook, Twitter, LinkedIn, YouTube, and Google+ capture an indelible image of people that is difficult if not impossible to erase. Even if accounts are deleted, bits of information remain, scattered here and there, that can provide a breadcrumb trail directly to a witness.

Sometimes a simple Google search is all that's needed.

Likewise, many websites offer criminal history records. Law enforcement agencies in all levels of government maintain criminal histories in massive databases. Since they are public records, anyone is free to visit the local courthouse and examine criminal cases to compile a history. However, this can also be done on the Internet—not directly, but through a private company with access to databases nationwide. For a fee, these companies will provide a full criminal history, usually on a state-by-state basis.

Accuracy is a concern no matter what kind of search is being conducted, but the Internet has thrown open the gates for finding people and information.

In addition to understanding the elements of a negligence action, it is also important to understand the practical aspects of gathering information about the case and the people involved.

SKILLS YOU NEED IN THE REAL WORLD

Meeting with the New Client

When a person walks through the firm's front door, he or she is usually anxious and is often in trouble. People who have had no previous experience with lawyers and paralegals only know what they have seen on television—and that is often grossly inaccurate. What actually happens when a lawyer meets with a new client, and what procedure does the firm use to investigate the claim, accept the case, and open a new file?

The First Step: Getting the Information

When Mr. Chumley walks through the door, the lawyer and the paralegal meet with him and get the basic facts. He is able to tell you some of the details of the accident, but not very many, because he has amnesia concerning the actual event. He may have brought documentation with him, but most clients do not. What kind of documentation would you like to see at this point?

- The police report (helps determine any statute of limitations problem)
- Any investigative report
- Police accident-reconstructionist report (if any)
- Any correspondence between Mr. Chumley and the potential defendants and their insurance companies

Information About the Court Process

Information gathering is not a one-way street. Remember that the client may not have any experience with the court system and so may not understand many of the procedures. For instance, clients are often confused and frustrated by the length of time it takes from filing the complaint to actually trying the case. They don't understand why this process can take a year or more. Explaining it to them at this stage often prevents a lot of frustration later on.

Many times a client won't ask a question because he thinks it makes him sound stupid. Give the client a handout or brochure about the legal process to take home with him and read. This brochure should spell out in uncomplicated terms exactly what happens at each stage of the lawsuit. A well-written brochure can also serve as publicity for the firm. When the case ends successfully, Mr. Chumley may give the brochure to a friend who needs legal assistance.

Videotapes

Firms can now purchase professional-quality videotapes that discuss all phases of civil litigation. You might consider buying some of these tapes to show to clients at the initial meeting. They answer most of the common questions raised by new clients.

THE LIFE OF A PARALEGAL

Putting Together a Settlement Package

When I put together a settlement package that we intend to send to the claims adjuster or opposing counsel, I follow a set pattern. Once I've gotten in all of the medical bills and all medical records and the client has been released from his doctors, I type up a first-page cover sheet. It's usually called a "settlement packet for Client X." After the cover sheet, the first section is the police or accident report. The next section is the itemized statement of bills, which includes everything but our fee. These itemized charges could be things like copying costs for medical records, notes from physicians, and any other bills. Then, the next section is the medical bills.

I put copies of all of the medical bills in the settlement package. I confirm what bills have been paid by insurance and which ones remain unpaid. I make sure that the outstanding balances are correct. I do a summary on each one, stating whether or not this bill has been paid, or if there has been some reimbursement to the insurance company, things like that. After the medical bills, the next section is Discovery. Typically, this section contains witness statements, statements from anyone in the car with them at the time of the accident, and any other type of discovery (interrogatories, deposition transcripts, etc.). If it's a big case, there's usually a private investigator involved, and his report will go in this section. If the case involved a wrongful death, we would include any information about other pending lawsuits from the same action. After the Discovery section, I'll include photographs. Typically, I'll include photographs of the scene. If they ran off an embankment, for instance, I'll have photographs of the area, showing skid marks, obstructions, things like that. I usually take photographs of the scene. Then, I take photos of the car. Sometimes I have to go out to junkyards or body shops to find the car. In some cases, we include pictures of the client's injuries. I tell our clients, "If you haven't taken pictures of your injuries, do it immediately." We take photos of their injuries to show scarring or other injuries.

After the photo section, I include a copy of our representation letter, showing that we do, in fact, represent the client. Right next to that, I usually put in a copy of the medical releases, showing that we obtained the medical bills under the client's authority. The next section is the demand section (setting out the client's demand for settlement). Typically, in a demand letter we review the facts, list any serious bodily injuries and any permanent injuries, and then present our quote for demand. We always put what we demand, then we put in, "or best settlement offer." We always get closer to our demand if there is a lot of information. I believe that adjusters think, "Well, they've really done their homework; it's going to be worth our while to settle this case before taking it to trial."

                                                                    Wendy Seagle, Paralegal

 ## ETHICAL ISSUES FOR THE PARALEGAL: INITIAL CLIENT MEETING

One area that is filled with potential problems concerns the initial meeting with the client. We have already mentioned the dangers involved in unauthorized practice of law. This meeting is the most common time for a client to ask you a legal question, such as "Does my case look good?" There is almost no way to answer this question without getting into some form of legal advice. When this question comes up, the safest course is to simply say that you can't give legal advice and leave it at that. However, not all clients will let the issue go so easily. They ask what you think because they really want some assurance that things are going to work out all right. If you understand that the reason behind this question is to seek assurance, you can speak to the client's real concerns and still avoid giving legal advice.

Relevant Cases

HALBROOK V. HONDA MOTOR CO., LTD.
224 MICH.APP. 437, 569 N.W.2D 836 (1997).

MARILYN J. KELLY, Presiding Judge.

In this wrongful death action, plaintiff's appeal as of right from a grant of summary disposition to defendants pursuant to MCR 2.116(C)(8) and (C)(10). Plaintiffs argue that there were factual issues to be resolved by the jury. We affirm.

I

On March 21, 1990, plaintiff Patricia Loder was driving her automobile. Along with her as passengers were her two children, Stephanie and Stephen. While heading eastbound on Sleeth Road in Commerce Township, Loder stopped in preparation to turn left onto Half Penny Court. A motorcycle traveling westbound on Sleeth passed her at a high rate of speed. Loder then began to turn left. As she did, her automobile was struck in the right hand side by another westbound motorcycle driven by James Bondie. Upon impact, Stephen, Stephanie and Bondie were killed. Loder sustained serious injuries.

Patricia Loder and Wayne Loder, as personal representative of his two children, and Karen Halbrook, as personal representative of Bondie's estate, sued each other for negligence. Thereafter, the Loders sued defendants, claiming negligence in the design, manufacture, marketing and distribution of Bondie's motorcycle. The Loders claimed that defendants created and sold a vehicle that could travel and accelerate too fast. Neither the inexperienced rider nor other drivers on the road could appreciate its capabilities. Therefore, they claimed, the motorcycle was dangerous and unsuitable for public highways. The Loders also asserted that defendants deliberately marketed the motorcycle to young male riders with special emphasis on speed.

Halbrook filed a similar complaint. The cases were consolidated by the lower court which granted summary disposition for defendants. It found that defendants were not responsible for Bondie's reckless acts.

Duty is actually a question of whether the defendant is under any obligation for the benefit of the particular plaintiff and concerns "the problem of the relation between individuals which imposes upon one a legal obligation for the benefit of the other. 'Duty' is not sacrosanct in itself, but is only an expression of the sum total of those considerations of policy which lead the law to say that the plaintiff is entitled to protection."

The following policy considerations are often relevant: (1) the foreseeability of the harm, (2) the degree of certainty of injury, (3) the closeness of connection between the conduct and injury, (4) the moral blame attached to the conduct, (5) the public policy of preventing future harm, and (6) the burdens and consequences of imposing a duty and the resulting liability for breach. Whether defendants had a duty to protect the Loders depends on the relationship between the parties, the nature and foreseeability of the risk and any other considerations that may be relevant on the issue.

We find that it is foreseeable to manufacturers of motor vehicles that motorists speed and that excessive speed may cause accidents. This is especially true, as in this case, where it is alleged that defendants advertised the speed and acceleration capabilities of their motorcycle. However, the determination of whether a duty exists does not turn solely on foreseeability.

The second factor, degree of certainty of injury, weighs against the Loders. It is not certain that a motorcycle designed to travel in excess of the speed limit and accelerate quickly will cause injury to others. The risk of harm is dependent, in part, on the way the driver handles the vehicle. Even if vehicles were designed to travel no faster than the maximum highway speed limit, there is no certainty that injuries to others could be averted. For instance, in this case, we will assume that Bondie's motorcycle was traveling approximately 80 miles per hour in a 45 mile per hour zone. If it had been capable of traveling no faster than 70 miles per hour, there is no certainty that the injuries would have been avoided. Moreover an automobile traveling at 70 miles per hour in a 25 mile per hour zone could be just as deadly.

The third factor, closeness of connection between the conduct and the injury to the Loder plaintiffs, weighs in favor of defendants. The deaths were not closely connected to the fact that the vehicle could be driven in excess of the speed limit and could accelerate quickly. Rather, the accident was more closely connected to the failure of Patricia Loder to yield the right of way and Bondie's reckless driving.

The fourth factor, moral blame attached to the conduct, requires this Court to look at the participants to the tragedy and determine which were the most blameworthy. We find that defendants are the least blameworthy. They did not cause Bondie to disobey the law nor did they cause Patricia Loder to ignore the oncoming motorcycle. To shift the moral blame to the motor vehicle manufacturer merely because the accident involved automotive speed is a step we are not willing to take.

The policy of preventing future harm might be advanced by imposing a legal duty on motor vehicle manufacturers to design and market vehicles with limited speed and acceleration capabilities. However, the danger of a moving vehicle is heavily dependent on its driver. Moreover, in the highly regulated area of motor vehicles, it is preferable that the Legislature, not the courts, determine if speed limitations should be set for motor vehicles.

Finally, considering the burdens and consequences of imposing a duty and the resulting liability for breach, we find that automobile manufacturers should not be potentially liable to innocent persons in this type of case. If we impose a burden on motor vehicle manufacturers to protect persons who could be injured by the misuse of their products, the result would be a great increase in litigation. In some instances a product manufacturer is in a better position to assume the costs of litigation and redistribute them to the general public. However, in this case, we find it to be too great a burden. Automobile manufacturers are not insurers. We find they are not bound to guard against the careless misuse of their products by negligent drivers, as in the case before us.

Therefore, we hold that the trial court properly granted summary disposition to defendants with respect to the Loders' claims.

Affirmed.

DEAL V. BOWMAN
286 KAN. 853, 188 P.3D 941 (2008)

The opinion of the court was delivered by DAVIS, J.

This is a personal injury action arising from a collision at a controlled intersection. Trial evidence indicated that the defendant stopped at the stop sign and looked both directions before entering the intersection but neverthe-less collided with the plaintiff's car, which he did not see due to glare from the sun. In the district court, the jury found no fault/negligence by either party for the accident. The Court of Appeals reversed, concluding that defendant was negligent as a matter of law. *Deal v. Bowman*, No. 96,868, 167 P.3d

387, 2007 WL 2768037, unpublished opinion filed September 21, 2007. We granted the defendant's petition for review, reverse the Court of Appeals, and affirm the district court.

Underlying Facts and Jury Trial

On September 17, 2002, Bradley Deal was traveling eastbound on Main Street in Council Grove at approximately 5:50 P.M. Alan Bowman, who was traveling south on Adams Street, approached the intersection of Main and Adams. The traffic traveling on Main Street was not required to stop at this intersection, but vehicles on Adams Street had stop signs. After stopping and looking both directions, Bowman pulled into the intersection, where he collided with Deal's vehicle, injuring Deal.

Deal filed a negligence action against Bowman. Both parties agreed that Deal bore no fault for the accident. The questions to be determined at trial were whether Bowman was at fault and, if so, what damages should be awarded.

Because Deal had no recollection of the accident due to his injuries, Bowman provided the only testimony as to how the accident happened. Bowman testified that he came to a complete stop at the stop sign and looked both directions. He then pulled into the intersection and collided with Deal's vehicle, injuring Deal. Bowman testified that he did not see Deal's car because the sun hindered his vision when he looked west. On direct examination, the following exchange took place between Bowman and his attorney:

"Q. And what — tell the jury what happened when you looked to the west?

"A. When I looked to the west, I did not see any vehicles at all. There was a pretty good glare from the sun that day, but I did not see any vehicles.

"Q. Officer Furman wrote that vehicle two, which was you, stopped at the stop sign and looked to the west, and he did not see vehicle one, the plaintiff, due to the sun blinding him, so he pulled out. Is that what you told the officer?

"A. Yes.

"Q. Is that what you're telling us today?

"A. Yes.

"Q. When you pulled out, you were aware that it was your obligation to look, to be careful?

"A. Yes.

"Q. And were you trying to do that?

"A. Yes."

Deal's counsel conducted the following discussion with Bowman during cross-examination:

"Q. Well, you said that your vision was blocked to the west. At what point in time was it blocked to the west?

"A. I wouldn't necessarily say it was blocked, but I would say it was hindered by the sun.

"Q. Okay. And you knew it was hindered?

"A. Yes.

"Q. And you pulled out anyway?

"A. I very cautiously looked, then pulled out."

Police Officer Tom Furman, who arrived at the scene of the accident shortly after it occurred and filed the police report on the incident, also testified. According to Furman, Bowman told the officer immediately after the accident occurred that "he stopped at the stop sign and he looked, and due to the sun blinding him . . . he did not see the vehicle coming." Furman also testified that when he looked "to the west" after Bowman had provided his explanation, the officer noticed that "the sun was very blinding that day."

At the close of evidence, Deal moved for a directed verdict — i.e., for judgment as a matter of law, on the issue of Bowman's negligence/liability. The district court denied his motion, concluding that there was evidence that Bowman had stopped and had carefully looked both directions and that the only reason he did not see Deal was due to the sun. The case was given to the jury, which found that neither party was at fault for the accident.

Deal moved for a new trial on the issue of negligence/liability, arguing that the evidence conclusively indicated that Bowman had been negligent. The court denied the motion, relying primarily on *Diaz v. Duke*, 206 Kan. 650, 652, 482 P.2d 48 (1971), where this court reversed a directed verdict on the issue of liability in a negligence action when "it could have found that on account of being suddenly blinded by the sun, the driver did not negligently operate his automobile."

Court of Appeals Decision

Deal appealed the district court's denial of both his motions. A divided panel of the Court of Appeals reversed in an unpublished opinion. Although the majority recognized that determinations of negligence are normally left to the trier of fact, the court held that Bowman's actions in this case constituted negligence as a matter of law. The court therefore held that the district court erred when it denied Deal's motion for judgment as a matter of law, reversed the district court, and remanded the case for a determination of Deal's damages.

The majority reasoned that "Kansas courts have long recognized the general rule that a motorist must correlate his ability to stop his vehicle within the distance objects can be seen ahead." Recognizing the "blinding light rule" in Diaz, the majority explained that there is a distinction in Kansas case law between facts that involve a "sudden, unexpected, or surprising" change in conditions and situations as in the present case that involve "a constant condition which diminishes a motorist's ability to see." The majority found that otherwise-negligent acts are not excused where conditions are constant.

Because "reasonable minds could not differ as to the conclusion that the sunlight which impaired Bowman's vision was not a sudden, unexpected, or surprising condition . . . or that Bowman drove into the intersection knowing . . . that his vision was impaired by the sun," the majority held that Bowman was negligent as a matter of law.

Bowman filed a petition for review, claiming that the Court of Appeals opinion applied the incorrect legal standard, as the law requires drivers to exercise ordinary care, not to be "perfect." Bowman argued that the Court of Appeals majority substituted its opinion for that of the trial court and jury, both of which found that there was evidence in the record demonstrating that Bowman acted reasonably under the circumstances. Deal filed a response, claiming that the Court of Appeals majority correctly found that the blinding light rule "was never intended to provide the basis for a motorist to use the sun as a legal excuse to blindly continue driving or to enter into an intersection, road, or highway without knowing what was in his path."

Discussion

The question before us is whether Bowman's action of pulling into the intersection, after stopping, while aware that his vision was hindered by the glare from the western sun constitutes negligence as a matter of law. This question is resolved by considering whether there were facts in the record from which a jury could determine that Bowman exercised ordinary care when entering the intersection. For reasons set forth in this opinion, this court, like the district court, concludes that Bowman's testimony raised a factual question concerning the reasonableness of his actions and thus agrees with the decision to submit the question of negligence/liability to the jury.

Analysis

In a personal injury action based upon negligence, the plaintiff must prove "the existence of a duty, breach of that duty, injury, and a causal connection between the duty breached and the injury suffered." *Nero v. Kansas State University*, 253 Kan. 567, Syl. ¶1, 861 P.2d 768 (1993). The general rule is that "whether a duty exists is a question of law," while the question as to "whether the duty has been breached is a question of fact." 253 Kan. 567, Syl. ¶1, 861 P.2d 768.

"The policy of the law has relegated the determination of this reasonably careful person standard to the jury, to note the special circumstances of each particular case and then say whether the conduct is such as would be expected of a reasonably careful person under a similar state of affairs. Only when the facts are such that reasonable men must draw the same conclusion from them does the question of negligence become one of law for the court."

There is no dispute that Bowman's action of driving into the intersection proximately caused Deal's injuries. Moreover, it is established that Deal was not at fault. The only question we must resolve is whether there was evidence in the record raising a factual question as to Bowman's negligence — or, more specifically, whether reasonable minds could differ as to whether Bowman breached a duty of care when he pulled his vehicle into the intersection at the time of the accident.

Bowman testified at trial that he came to a complete stop at the stop sign at the intersection of Adams and Main, looked both directions, and — perceiving that the intersection was clear — entered the intersection. Bowman explained that there was "a pretty good glare from the sun" when he looked west, but he "did not see any vehicles." Bowman further testified that he was "aware that it was his obligation to look for other vehicles in the intersection, to be careful," and that he was "trying to do that."

The district court held that the evidence established a question of fact as to whether Bowman acted negligently, relying primarily on this court's decision in *Diaz*, 206 Kan. 650, 482 P.2d 48. Deal argues — and the Court of Appeals majority agreed — that it was inherently unreasonable to enter into the intersection when the sun prevented Bowman from seeing whether there were any approaching cars, so Bowman was guilty of negligence as a matter of law.

In *Diaz*, the plaintiff was driving west on a street in Junction City late on a summer afternoon when she came to a stop in order to turn left into a parking lot. The defendant, who was traveling in the same direction, rear-ended Diaz' vehicle, causing her injury. At trial, the defendant explained that "the sun suddenly flashed into his eyes, reflecting off the hood of his freshly washed and waxed automobile and blinded him so that he did not see the plaintiff's car." 206 Kan. at 651, 482 P.2d 48.

The district court granted the plaintiff's motion for a directed verdict on the issue of the defendant's negligence/liability, finding that the defendant was negligent as a matter of law. This court reversed, finding that "if the jury believed the defendant's testimony, it could have found that on account of being suddenly blinded by the sun, he did not negligently operate his automobile." 206 Kan. at 652, 482 P.2d 48.

In its explanation, the court explained that its conclusion was consistent with the "'blinding light' rule," which states that "ordinarily a motorist must correlate his ability to stop his vehicle within the distance objects can be seen ahead; but the rule is subject to qualification and exception where there is a sudden change in the motorist's situation not caused by his own failure or neglect, and that where he is suddenly blinded so that he has no opportunity to stop his vehicle or slacken his speed, he would not be guilty of negligence as a matter of law if he collides with something on the highway." 206 Kan. at 652, 482 P.2d 48.

The Court of Appeals majority disagreed that there was a factual question as to negligence/liability and discussed at length why the blinding light rule in Diaz should not apply to the present facts. The majority found that the holding in Diaz was premised on the fact that the "blinding light" was a sudden occurrence of which the defendant had no prior knowledge. The Court of Appeals distinguished the situation in Diaz from cases where a person continues to drive in constant conditions that knowingly block or impair the driver's vision. In cases involving the latter situation, the driver is liable for negligence as a matter of law.

In this case, Bowman's undisputed testimony was that he stopped at the stop sign at the intersection and carefully looked both directions. Although the western sun was causing quite a bit of glare from that direction, he perceived that the intersection was clear and began to proceed through the intersection at a speed of about 5 miles per hour. His vehicle then collided with the vehicle driven by Deal. Resolving all inferences in the light most favorable to Bowman, as this court must do in reviewing a motion for judgment as a matter of law under K.S.A. 60–250, Bowman did not violate a traffic law. The question was whether he behaved as a reasonably prudent driver would under similar circumstances.

Negligence is the lack of due care. The instances are relatively rare when the facts are such that the court should say that as a matter of law the negligence alleged had been established. Before the court should make such a holding the evidence should be so clear that reasonable minds considering it could have but one opinion; namely, that the party was negligent.

In this case, the district court correctly determined that the issue of whether Bowman acted reasonably by proceeding into the intersection—that is, whether he was negligent—was a question of fact to be determined by the jury in light of all of the surrounding circumstances.

Because we conclude that the district court correctly denied Deal's motion for a judgment as a matter of law, we similarly conclude that Deal's claims relating to the denial of his motion for a new trial—which was based on the same contention that Bowman's conduct was negligent as a matter of law—are without merit.

We affirm the district court's denial of Deal's motion for a judgment as a matter of law and the subsequent judgment in favor of Bowman. The decision by the Court of Appeals reversing the district court is reversed.

Websites

■ **Causation/Damages**
http://home.pon.net/wildrose/column4.htm

■ **Find Law**
http://www.findlaw.com

■ **Juris Dictionary: Law of Negligence**
http://www.jurisdictionary.com/SidePages/Samples/pLanguage.pdf

Forms and Court Documents

This form shows a typical automobile collision negligence complaint.

STATE OF PLACID	IN THE SUPERIOR COURT
COUNTY OF BARNES	FILE NUMBER: _____

Lisa Burnett,   )
)

Plaintiff   )
)

vs.   )
)

Marvin John Quartermain, and
Delia Xavier Quartermain,
Defendants

Complaint

COMES NOW THE PLAINTIFF, Lisa Burnett, and complaining of the defendants, alleges the following:

1.
That plaintiff Lisa Burnett (hereafter "plaintiff") is a citizen and resident of Barnes County, Placid.

2.
Upon information and belief, defendant Delia Xavier Quartermain (hereafter "defendant driver") is a citizen and resident of Barnes County, Placid.

3.
Upon information and belief, defendant Marvin John Quartermain (hereafter "defendant owner") is a citizen and resident of Barnes County, Placid.

a. Further, upon information and belief, defendant owner was the registered owner of the vehicle involved in the collision at issue in this case, said vehicle being a 2001 Ford, license plate number LZK 245.

b. That, at all times mentioned herein and upon information and belief, defendant driver was operating and using aforementioned vehicle with authority, consent, permission, and knowledge of defendant owner, and defendant driver's operation and use of the vehicle was under the direction and control of defendant owner.

c. Furthermore, at all times mentioned herein and upon information and belief, defendant driver was a member of the family or household of defendant owner and was living in such person's home; that the vehicle driven by defendant driver was owned, provided, and maintained for the general use, pleasure, and convenience of the family; and that the vehicle was being so used with the express or implied consent of defendant owner. Therefore, any negligence on the part of the defendant driver in causing the plaintiff's injuries should be imputed to defendant owner under the family purpose doctrine.

4.
That, on or about the 19th day of October, 2010, at approximately 9:40 A.M., plaintiff was operating a motor vehicle traveling west on East Union Street in Placid City, Barnes County, Placid.

5.
That, at the same time and place, defendant driver was operating the aforementioned 2001 Ford motor vehicle and traveling south on Kirk Drive in Placid City, Barnes County, Placid.

6.

That defendant driver entered plaintiff's lane of travel, thereby causing a collision with plaintiff's vehicle.

7.

That defendant driver at the scene stated that she did not see plaintiff's vehicle before pulling out into the intersection.

8.

That defendant driver was negligent in that she:
a. While operating a motor vehicle on the public streets and highways, failed to keep a reasonable and proper lookout in plaintiff's direction of travel.
b. Failed to maintain the vehicle that she was operating under proper control and drove the vehicle in such a manner so as to deprive the defendant driver of such control over the vehicle as a reasonable and prudent person would maintain under the circumstances then existing.

9.

That, as a direct and proximate cause of the negligent conduct of defendant driver, plaintiff was seriously injured, causing her great pain and suffering, medical expenses, lost wages, physical and mental anguish, and permanent injuries.

10.

That, as a direct and proximate result of the aforementioned negligence of defendant driver, plaintiff has sustained damage to her person in an amount in excess of Ten Thousand Dollars ($10,000.00), representing damage to plaintiff's person, medical bills, pain and suffering, lost wages, mental anguish, and permanent injuries.

WHEREFORE, the Plaintiff prays that the Court as follows:
1. That the Plaintiff have and recover a judgment against the Defendants in an amount in excess of $10,000.00 for personal injuries.
2. That the Defendants be assessed with punitive damages as permitted by law.
3. That prejudgment interest be awarded as provided by law.
4. That the costs of this action be taxed against the Defendants.
5. That all issues raised be tried before a jury.
6. For such other and further relief as the Court may deem just and proper.

This the _____ day of June, 2003.

_____

Clarence D. Arrow
Attorney for Plaintiffs
State Bar No. 000-998

Key Terms

Breach
Damages

Duty
Negligence per se

Proximate
causation

Review Questions

1 How are negligence cases different from intentional tort cases?
2 What are the four basic elements of a negligence case?
3 Under what circumstances does a person owe a duty to another?
4 When we use the term *causation,* what do we mean?
5 What are some of the differences between plaintiffs' firms and defense firms?
6 Is there a philosophical difference between plaintiffs' firms and defendants' firms?
7 What is a contingency fee?
8 What are the basic steps involved in investigating a new case?
9 List and explain some crucial information that you should obtain from a new client.
10 What is a medical authorization, and when would it be required?
11 List some ways of organizing a client's file.
12 Why is a settlement package necessary, and what is one way that it is put together?
13 What are some other methods for obtaining information about the cause of action?
14 When we discuss negligence, are we using this term as it is used in common parlance, or does it have a specific legal meaning? If so, define it.

Applying What You Have Learned

1   X, an 11-year-old boy, brings a suit against a priest alleging that the priest sexually assaulted him. His action is based on a claim of clergy malpractice and negligence. Does he have a valid negligence claim? Show how this claim would satisfy the basic elements of a negligence action.
2   Sally and Bill dated for several weeks. After they broke up, Sally discovered that Bill was HIV-positive and had failed to tell her. She has had herself tested, and although she doesn't test positive for AIDS or HIV, she brings a suit against Bill based on a negligence claim. Is this a valid claim under a negligence theory?
3   Bill and Ted are police officers. While they are chasing an escaped mental patient, they are both injured. They file a negligence claim against the hospital from which the mental patient escaped. Will their claim succeed?

4 Prepare a chart showing the significant differences between intentional tort law, criminal law, and negligence law.

5 How are firms in your area organized? Are there several large plaintiffs' firms, or many smaller firms?

Endnote

[1]*Cook v. Continental Casualty Co.*, 180 Wis. 2d 237, 509 N.W.2d 100 (1993).

Crossword Puzzle

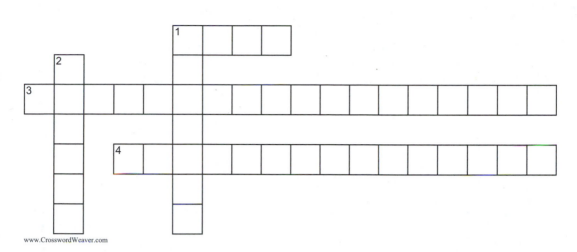

www.CrosswordWeaver.com

ACROSS

1 An obligation imposed by statute or common law
3 The facts that show the defendant's legal responsibility for the injuries to the plaintiff, also known as legal cause
4 Negligence in and of itself; the principle that the violation of a safety statute establishes a presumption of breach of duty in a negligence action

DOWN

1 Money that a court orders the losing side in a civil case to pay to the other side
2 When the defendant fails to live up to a legal standard, or violates a duty

Duty

Chapter Objectives

- **Describe how a duty arises and the legal consequences when it does**

- **Describe how certain special relationships give rise to a higher standard of care**

- **Explain the concept of "premises liability"**

- **Explain the different duties imposed on laypersons, professionals, and specialists**

- **Explain the "attractive nuisance" doctrine**

THE CHUMLEY CASE: A DANGEROUS INTERSECTION?

The train tracks that intersect with Morgan Street run through two other intersections in the town of Cling. Both of the other intersections have warning lights and gates that descend whenever a train is approaching. The Morgan Street intersection has only a sign. When a motorist approaches the intersection from one direction, he immediately notices that there are tall, thick evergreen trees growing along the track. These trees are so thick that they are impossible to see through. Mr. Chumley claims that in order to look past these trees and down the tracks for an oncoming train, he would have had to inch forward until the front of his car was almost on the tracks before he

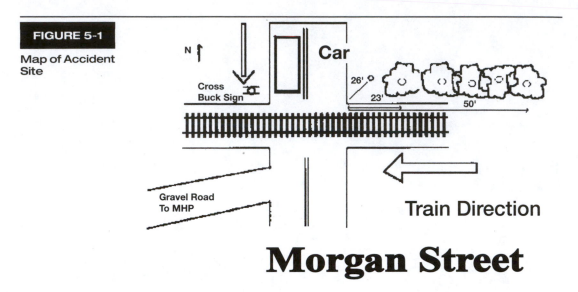

FIGURE 5-1

Map of Accident Site

N

Cross Buck Sign

Car

26' 23' 50'

Train Direction

Gravel Road To MHP

Morgan Street

could see far enough to tell if a train was coming. See Figure 5-1 for a map of the site.

In his suit, Mr. Chumley claims that National Railroad Company had a **duty** to keep the intersection safe and failed to meet that duty. Mr. Chumley claims that the intersection was dangerous and that the company failed to take any action to make it safe. He cannot be sure if the railroad company or the town had a duty to trim the trees, so he is suing both. Just to be safe, he is also suing the engineer, Stanley Blue, who was at the controls of the train that day.

As we have already seen, the first step in bringing a negligence suit is to show that there was a duty. If the defendant does not owe the plaintiff a duty, there can be no case. We explore the concept of duty throughout this chapter.

Duty
An obligation imposed by statute or common law.

THE LEGAL DEFINITION OF DUTY

Standard of care
The standard used to determine if a party has acted negligently in a particular case.

Courts have used a wide variety of terms to describe and define the term *duty*. At its simplest, duty refers to a person's obligation to conform his conduct to a particular **standard of care.** It is often defined as an obligation to protect someone else from an unreasonable risk of harm. In negligence cases, duty often simply means the obligation of a person to act in a reasonable manner. We often use the terms *standard of care* and *duty* interchangeably. The reason for this is that duty refers to the legal obligation and standard of care refers to how this obligation is put into practice. Put another way, duty is *why;* standard of care is *how.*

A. WHEN DOES A DUTY ARISE?

This simple question has been the focus of an amazing amount of litigation. In general terms, a duty arises when one person has the power to injure another and can only avoid injuring this other person by acting in a reasonable, prudent, and cautious way. The problem with that definition is its generality. In any given situation, how do we know if defendant B has a duty to plaintiff A? We must look to the facts of the case for an answer. Here is the most common question the courts ask to determine duty:

Was the injury to the plaintiff reasonably foreseeable?

Example: Jamal is driving his car and fails to stop at a red light. Is it reasonably foreseeable that by running the red light he could collide with another car? Most people would agree that it is. When Jamal does, in fact, collide with Rick's car, Rick can claim that Jamal had a duty and breached it by failing to act in a reasonable and prudent manner.

When we determine foreseeability, we are really asking: "Just how likely was it that the plaintiff would be injured?" Foreseeability does not mean a "mere possibility" but a clearly recognized danger.[2] By addressing the issue of foreseeability, the courts attempt to establish some clear guidelines to establish duty. If the injuries were foreseeable, it is more likely that the defendant owed a duty to the plaintiff to keep him from harm. In situations in which the plaintiff's injuries are not foreseeable, courts generally rule that the defendant had no duty.

Duty → Breach → Causation → Damages. Without duty, you cannot move on to the other three elements of a negligence claim.

TORT
BASICS
AT A
GLANCE

B. USING FORMULAS TO DETERMINE DUTY

In the past, some judges have attempted to come up with complex rules (some of them resembling algebraic formulas) to determine if a defendant in a case owed a duty to the plaintiff. However, most of these rules and formulas have disappeared over time. The reality of most cases does not lend itself to such rigidity, no matter how appealing such rules seem at first glance.

Examples of such rules include Judge Learned Hand's famous formula that he hoped would act as an infallible guide in negligence cases. Hand's formula is charmingly simplistic. In his equation, if the probability (P) of the defendant's harm multiplied by the loss (L) exceeded the burden (B) on the defendant, he had a duty to take precautions to prevent the harm. The equation is represented: $P \times L > B =$ duty. If, on the other hand, the burden on the defendant to prevent the harm was greater than the probability, there was no duty, or $P \times L < B =$ no duty.

The problem with using this equation to reach decisions in real cases is apparent almost immediately. For one thing, it is often difficult to quantify the probability of the defendant's harm. What numbers would you use to represent the likelihood of Jamal running a red light, and how this action would affect the probabilities for other drivers? Rather than continue to negotiate the tricky math of such formulas, we instead concentrate on the more pragmatic approaches adopted by most court systems.

C. DUTY DOES NOT DEPEND ON VICTIM'S IDENTITY

Accident versus negligence — what is the difference? At law, an "accident" refers to some event that did not involve human fault. When a bolt of lightning strikes a house, that is an accident. When a car rolls down a hill because the parking brake was not set and the car hits a pedestrian, that is not an accident; that is negligence.

Returning to our example of Jamal running a red light and crashing into Rick's car, notice that our discussion did not focus on Jamal's duty to Rick as a specific individual. In fact, there is no requirement that Jamal know who his eventual victim may be. The law of duty rests on the defendant and will be imposed to protect any eventual victim.[3] Jamal's duty to drive safely is a duty he owes to everyone on the road, not just Rick. Jamal has no legal defense by claiming that he did not know that Rick was coming in the opposite direction.[4] He had a duty, and he violated it. Anyone who was hurt by his actions could have brought suit; it just happened to be Rick.

D. DUTY AS A LEGAL OBLIGATION

The law of duty in civil injuries has some interesting twists and turns. First, for a particular person to have a duty, he must have some legal obligation. Jamal, as a driver, has a legal obligation to other drivers and pedestrians to drive responsibly. However, let's change the facts. Consider the following scenario:

Jamal is walking by a lake and sees Rick, a stranger, apparently drowning in a deep part of the lake. Rick, thrashing at the surface, yells out, "Help! I'm drowning!" Jamal, watching from the shore, does nothing to save Rick. Does Rick (or his heirs) have an action against Jamal? Or, put another way, does Jamal have a duty to save Rick?

Answer: No.

Why is the answer no? In our first scenario, Jamal was driving a car and failed to drive in a safe manner. Rick was injured by Jamal's negligence. Because Jamal had a duty to all other drivers and pedestrians, Rick can prove the first element of a negligence case against Jamal: duty. He can also prove a violation of that duty.

A small number of jurisdictions hold the view that under some circumstances, moral and humanitarian considerations may require one to render assistance to another who has been injured, even though the injury was not due to negligence on the former's part.[5]

But what about our second scenario? Remember, when you consider a civil injuries case, you must take each step in sequence. The natural tendency with such a factual situation is moral outrage at Jamal's inaction. But this skips over the question of duty. Does Jamal have a duty to save Rick? Does a stranger have a legal duty to save another person from certain death? No. The law does not impose that duty on strangers. We could certainly argue that Jamal had an ethical or a moral duty to try to save Rick, but that is a different question. The law of civil injuries is not a mirror image of society's morality. There are many moral obligations that cannot be enforced by law. If you think it through for a moment, you will realize that using the court system to enforce moral rules could never work. Under such a scenario, you could sue a friend for "not being a good person." The court system would have to spend time and energy trying to discern exactly what a good person is. Instead, courts stay away from the moral issues in most cases. They focus on the facts.

Does a stranger have a legal obligation to save another stranger from certain death? The answer is no. Notice that we keep saying "stranger." The situation can change dramatically if the relationship between Jamal and Rick in our scenario changes. We discuss duty arising from relationship later in this chapter.

E. DUTY DOES NOT ARISE FROM HABIT OR CUSTOM

The question of the defendant's duty to the plaintiff comes from the circumstances of the case — the relationship, if any, between the defendant and the plaintiff and the defendant's actions. It does not arise simply because there is a custom or a tradition.

Example: Most people would agree that holding the door for a person is polite. One day, Mary is carrying a large parcel, and as she approaches the door to the lobby of her apartment building, a man precedes her inside. He does not hold the door for her, even though he sees that she has a large package and that it would be nearly impossible for her to open the door for herself. He simply walks inside, letting the door close behind him. Mary slips on the wet pavement when she tries to open the door for herself. Does she have a cause of action against the man?

Answer: No. Just because holding the door for someone else is considered to be a polite action, there is no legal obligation (and no duty) for the man to hold the door for Mary. Without a duty, there is no action in negligence.

However, the rules change when the practice is deemed to be a behavior that all reasonable and prudent people would follow. For instance, in a later chapter, we discuss **custom** in regard to medical procedures. In those situations, if a majority of practitioners customarily perform the same action, such as taking a medical history from a new patient, that procedure can be seen as the baseline standard of care, and the failure to follow that custom can establish a breach of duty. The important distinction here is that in our first example, of the man not holding the door for Mary, there are several reasons why reasonable and prudent people would not hold the door for her. For one thing, the man simply might not have seen her. The man might have assumed that Mary would be offended by his assumption that she needed help. Using custom to establish duty is normally a procedure reserved for specific circumstances such as medical treatment, safety procedures in creating products, and so on. Failing to hold the door open does not qualify.

Is there a way to change the facts to create a duty? Suppose, for instance, that the man is the doorman at a hotel. Although nothing in his job description states that he must open doors for people carrying large packages, it is a custom followed by every doorman in the city. In this scenario, his failure to act might be considered a breach of duty. If Mary were to sue the hotel, how

Custom
A practice that has acquired a legal status over time such that failing to follow the practice would result in liability.

would Mary prove that this custom existed? She could simply present testimony from other doormen that they follow this practice. This might be enough to establish a custom and generate a duty.

F. DUTY ARISING FROM PROFESSIONAL STATUS

Nonprofessionals, or laypeople, do not have a duty that arises simply because of their education or training. However, there are many professionals who have a duty imposed on them by law because of their advanced training. Police officers, for instance, have a duty to assist people who are in trouble. Firefighters have the same duty. A firefighter could not, for instance, decide that today he doesn't feel like putting out fires. Stopping fires is his job, and because of this, he has a legally imposed duty to act. A bystander might not be under any legal duty to save someone from a burning building, but a firefighter is (which, of course, does not make the action any less heroic).

TORT BASICS AT A GLANCE

Professionals have a higher duty, or standard of care, simply because they are professionals and have more education and training than a layperson.

Medical professionals also have a duty to act. When a patient appears at the hospital with injuries, doctors and nurses are under a legal duty to act to treat him.

1. DIFFERENT LEVELS OF DUTY FOR SOME PROFESSIONALS

As we discuss in the malpractice section, some professionals have a different standard of care or a different duty. Medical doctors have one type of duty to a patient, while a specialist, someone like a heart surgeon, has a higher duty, often referred to as a higher standard of care. See Figure 5-2 for a partial list of professionals held to this higher standard of care.

2. WHAT IS THE STANDARD OF CARE FOR A PROFESSIONAL?

By way of an example, when a doctor treats a patient, what is his precise legal duty to that patient? Most jurisdictions define the legal duty as the reasonable degree of skill, knowledge, and training that other doctors under similar circumstances in the professional community would exercise. If the doctor fails to live up to that standard, then he has violated the standard of care and therefore has breached the legal duty owed to the patient.

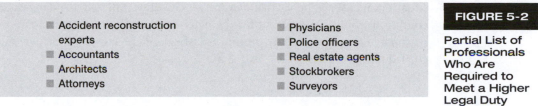

■ Accident reconstruction experts	■ Physicians
■ Accountants	■ Police officers
■ Architects	■ Real estate agents
■ Attorneys	■ Stockbrokers
	■ Surveyors

FIGURE 5-2

Partial List of Professionals Who Are Required to Meet a Higher Legal Duty to Others

3. SPECIALISTS

Some professionals have received intensive training in a very narrow field. This makes them **specialists.** With that greater training and specialization comes a greater legal duty to a patient or a client. The legal duty imposed on a specialist is what would be expected of a specialist with similar training under similar circumstances. Unlike the standard for a professional, the standard for a specialist is not tied to the geographic region where the specialist practices. A specialist is held to the highest standard, and this standard is nationwide (some would argue that it is worldwide).[6] We address the duty of medical (and legal) professionals in Chapter 12.

Specialist
One who has become an expert in a particular field through education, training, or both.

G. DUTY ARISING OUT OF OTHER FACTORS

When a person creates a dangerous condition, the law imposes a duty on him to take reasonable actions to prevent others from being injured by it. In this

Tech Topic
ELECTRONIC DISCOVERY

Electronic discovery, or e-discovery, is the process of identifying, preserving, collecting, filtering, and producing computer-based information for evidence in litigation.

Digital data lend themselves well to investigation. For one thing, unlike paper documents that must be reviewed manually, digital data can be electronically searched. Also, it's nearly impossible to completely destroy digital data. Even deleted digital files can be undeleted. Furthermore, if the data are on a computer that is part of a network, they will be preserved on many hard drives.

Many kinds of data can serve as evidence, including documents, photos, databases, social media postings, and websites, just to name a few. E-mail is particularly valuable as evidence in litigation.

Computer forensics is a specialized form of e-discovery. During a forensic examination, a specialist thoroughly examines all data on a computer system to locate any evidence and safely preserve it for use in litigation. An example of the kind of information that can be discovered during a forensic exam comes from the case of the BTK killer. A serial murderer, Dennis Rader, sent letters to the police on a floppy disk. Forensic examination of the disk revealed the name of the author to be "Dennis," and it also revealed "Christ Lutheran Church." This was enough evidence to lead police to Rader and arrest him for the crimes.

situation, it is social policy that determines the duty. After all, the dangerous condition would not exist but for the defendant's actions, so it would seem reasonable to impose a duty on him to safeguard the condition or face the consequences.

HOW THE COURTS DETERMINE DUTY

Courts have been presented with a wide variety of negligence cases, and from these cases they have established some basic ground rules for determining whether a duty exists. This determination is usually a balancing act between the interests of society and the interests of the injured plaintiff. To determine duty, courts might look to factors such as how difficult it would have been for the defendant to avoid injuring the plaintiff, the economics of the situation, and whether imposing such a duty would open up the possibility of a whole host of new lawsuits. See Figure 5-3 for a summary of the various factors used by courts to determine duty.

As you can see from Figure 5-3, duty is difficult to quantify and in many ways is a hodgepodge of many different factors, all weighted differently depending on the facts in a particular case. Duty is often difficult to establish, and in some cases, it is almost impossible. Is this a case, as a U.S. Supreme Court justice once said about a different topic, of "I know it when I see it"?

Example: Jamal loves to play golf, but he isn't very good. He tees up his golf ball and hits it. Unfortunately, it doesn't stay in the fairway. It veers well away from where he was aiming and into the adjacent fairway. Jamal yells "Fore!" The ball hits Matt in the head. Matt wants to sue Jamal. Can he prove that Jamal had a duty to him?

Answer: Probably not. You could argue that Matt had assumed the risk of getting hit with a golf ball (more about assumption of the risk in the next chapter), but there is another argument. At least one court has ruled that when a golfer yells "Fore!" he has satisfied his duty to other golfers.[7]

FIGURE 5-3

Factors That the Courts Use to Establish Duty

- Morality of the conduct as viewed by society
- Whether the courts should be involved in a particular relationship
- Social utility of the conduct
- How difficult it would be for the defendant to prevent the injury
- Can reasonable people agree on the practical means to prevent the injury?
- Proximate cause between defendant's actions and the harm to plaintiff
- Economic considerations
- Foreseeability
- Will allowing this case to go forward cause a flood of similar litigation?
- Will it encourage false claims or claims that are hard to establish?
- Will it prevent future harm?*

Valdez v. J. D. Diffenbaugh Co., 51 Cal. App. 3d 494, 124 Cal. Rptr. 467 (1975).

No duty = no negligence.

Example: Jamal and Carl are camping. Jamal falls asleep in front of the fire. During the night, Carl's sleeping bag catches on fire. Carl wants to bring a suit against Jamal for the damages to his sleeping bag. Can he prove duty?

Answer: Probably not. To have a duty, you must at least be aware of what is occurring. Because Jamal was asleep, Carl is going to have a hard time proving that Jamal acted negligently or failed to act, resulting in the damages to Carl's sleeping bag. Beyond that, Carl may have a hard time proving that Jamal had any duty, whether asleep or not.

A. RELATIONSHIP CAN DETERMINE DUTY

When we use the term *relationship,* we generally think of friends, family, or lovers. Relationship is not used in that context in civil injuries. Instead, relationship refers to the interaction between the parties. You may not know the other drivers on the road, but you have a relationship with them. In this case, it is the relationship of one driver with another. You owe a duty to other drivers to drive in a reasonable manner and exercise ordinary care, even if you don't know them.

B. SPECIAL RELATIONSHIPS

There are certain relationships that by their very nature impose an obligation on one person to the benefit of another. The prime example of this special relationship is parent to child. A parent owes a child a duty to protect her from foreseeable injury and to provide a safe environment. In this situation, the failure of a parent to act to safeguard a child is the violation of a duty. Unlike the previous example in which Jamal owed no duty to Rick, who was drowning in a lake, if we change the scenario and make it a child drowning in a lake, there is no question that the parent has a duty to act to save the child. However, this duty is not absolute. Like any relationship, the legal duty that one person owes to another changes over time. For instance, once the child grows up, does the parent still have the same level of duty to the child that he or she has when the child is a toddler? Obviously, the situation has changed. As the child grows up, most of us would agree that the parent's duty to the child decreases.

The parent-child duty is a direct result of the personal relationship between the parties. The parent is under no greater obligation to someone else's child than to any stranger. Generally, these special relationships involve only two people. See Figure 5-4 for more examples.

FIGURE 5-4

Special
Relationships
Giving Rise
to Duty

- Employer and employee
- Hotel/motel and guest
- Landlord and tenant*
- Carrier and passenger
- Student and teacher
- Parent and child

- Spouse and spouse
- Day care and child
- Person who created a danger and
  potential victim

*_Ventura v. Picicci,_ 227 Ill. App. 3d 865, 169 Ill. Dec. 881, 592 N.E.2d 368 (1992).

TORT
BASICS
AT A
GLANCE

**Whether a special relationship exists is a question of law. As such,
the judge, not the jury, determines it.**

Example: Martha had a child out of wedlock and decided to give the boy
up for adoption. The adoption agency ran routine medical checkups on the
baby boy and discovered that he had an inherited disease. Martha is a carrier
of this disease and will definitely pass it on to any male child she has in the
future. The adoption agency doesn't tell Martha about the disease.
Later, Martha has another boy, and he dies because of this disease. Martha
discovers that the adoption agency knew about the disease and failed to
notify her. She brings suit against the adoption agency, claiming that the
agency had a duty to tell her about the disease. Does the agency have such a
duty?

Answer: When you evaluate a case like this, you must confine yourself to
the facts and try to ignore the emotions. Most people's immediate reaction is
outrage that the adoption agency failed to inform Martha. But does the agency
have a legal duty? Is there a special relationship between Martha and the
adoption agency? No. (See Figure 5-4.) Is there some other legally recognized
obligation between Martha and the adoption agency that would make the
agency liable? No. The result in this case is clear: Martha's suit against the
adoption agency should be dismissed, because she has failed to prove the first
element of a negligence case—duty.[8]

DUTY FROM A SOCIAL RELATIONSHIP

A. ARE FRIENDS A SPECIAL RELATIONSHIP?

Do friends fall into the category of special relationships? Under most circumstances, the answer is no.

Example: Jamal is at a party with his friend, Terry. Jamal has too much to drink, and Terry begins to worry that Jamal will drive home. Terry asks Jamal if Jamal will permit Terry to drive him home. Jamal refuses and gets behind the wheel of his car and speeds off. Later, Jamal runs a red light and severely injures himself and Tiffany, who is in another car. Tiffany brings suit against Terry, alleging that Terry had a duty to keep Jamal from driving and that Terry did not work hard enough to keep Jamal from driving. Who will win this suit?

Answer: Terry. Under the facts as presented, Terry has no duty to Jamal and they are not in any special relationship; therefore, Terry has no duty to keep Jamal from driving. Jamal is responsible for his own drunken driving, and Tiffany cannot win a suit against Terry.

Let's change the facts of this case. This time, Jamal is at a party in Terry's home. Terry realizes that Jamal has had too much to drink but continues to ply him with liquor. Jamal leaves the party driving his own car, has an accident, and injures Tiffany. Does she now have a cause of action against Terry?

In many jurisdictions, the answer to this question is yes. Terry is liable under the theory of social host liability.

B. SOCIAL HOST LIABILITY

In some jurisdictions, a social host can be liable under the facts presented above. Tiffany is suing Terry, alleging that Terry had a duty to stop serving liquor to Jamal when a reasonable host would have realized that Jamal was impaired. When courts created the doctrine of social host liability, they were creating a duty where one had not previously existed. Prior to the creation of this doctrine, a host could claim that he had no duty and therefore could not be liable for serving drinks to an obviously intoxicated guest. With the adoption of this doctrine in many jurisdictions, the social policy of discouraging drunken driving by imposing legal liability on hosts has contributed to fewer situations such as the one we find in the hypothetical case.

However, many jurisdictions refuse to impose this duty on a host unless the host was acting in clearly unreasonable or careless manner. The problem with social host liability is that it sets a bad precedent. How far will a social host's liability go? Consider the following example:

Ted is a diabetic and attends a dinner party at Tom's house. Tom is famous for his desserts and serves up a multilayered chocolate confection that everyone, including Ted, finds irresistible. On the way home, Ted's blood sugar becomes elevated to the point that he loses consciousness. He crashes into another car and injures the occupants. Do the occupants have a cause of action against Tom?

Answer: Probably not. At some point, Ted's responsibility for his own actions will supersede Tom's carelessness in offering a sugary dessert to a diabetic. This example illustrates the difficulty that many jurisdictions have in imposing any form of social host liability.

PREMISES LIABILITY

Lawsuits involving injuries on land, such as "slip and fall" cases, have increased dramatically over the past few decades. People who sue under the theory of premises liability usually bring this case as a negligence suit. In fact, this area of law has increased so much that premises liability cases justify their own branch of negligence law.

People who possess land have a special duty to the people who visit their property. This duty arises out of the peculiar nature of land itself. Because it is fixed and immovable, a dangerous condition could exist on land and a visitor wouldn't necessarily know about it.

See Figure 5-5 for a list of what a complaint needs to say about duty. See Figures 5-6 and 5-7 for questions that should be answered in a premises liability case.

A. DUTY IS ON POSSESSOR, NOT OWNER

Notice that we use the term *possessor* of land when discussing premises liability. These duties are imposed by law on the person who is in possession of the land, not necessarily the owner. The reason the law imposes this duty on the current possessor is because this person is in the best position to know about potential problems and can take action to protect others from them. Consider the following scenario:

Jamal has lived in an apartment for four years. One day, Nancy pays him a visit and slips on a large pile of garbage that Jamal has allowed to accumulate inside his front door. Jamal claims that because he is not the owner of the property, he should not be liable for Nancy's injuries. The landlord claims that he should not be liable to Nancy because he had no way of knowing that Jamal would allow garbage to pile up inside his apartment. With each pointing the finger at the other, Nancy will be unable to get either to pay for her injuries.

Whose responsibility is it to keep the premises safe? In the scenario we have outlined above, it is Jamal's duty. After all, the apartment is his residence. If the harmful condition had arisen outside his apartment, Jamal might have a good argument that the landlord is at fault.

According to the Restatement of Torts, any person who takes control over the premises, whether as tenant, manager, or any other position, also takes on the duty to keep the premises safe. It is not a defense for this person to claim that he had no responsibility because he was not the actual owner.[9]

FIGURE 5-5	
What the Complaint Should Say About Duty	■ A complete description of the legal duty owed by the defendant to this plaintiff, setting out specific facts and allegations ■ A complete description of how the defendant's actions (or failure to act) breached this duty to the plaintiff or a description of the defendant's gross negligence, willful misconduct, or reckless disregard for the safety of others

Details of the incident:

- How and when did it occur? (Pin down the date as precisely as possible for statute of limitations problems.)
- Describe the location. What condition was the location in? Excellent? Good? Poor? Dangerous?
- Are there any photographs of the location showing the dangerous condition?
- What were the lighting conditions?
- Were there any witnesses to the incident? Get full names, addresses, telephone numbers (including cell and beepers), and e-mail addresses.
- Who was in charge of the premises? Is this person the owner of the property, or is someone else?
- What were the dangerous circumstances that should have put the possessor on notice?
- Were there any warning signs posted?
- Have there been similar incidents on the premises before?

Plaintiff's actions/health:

- Was the plaintiff at fault in any way?
- Did the plaintiff have permission to be on the premises?
- Was the plaintiff an invitee? A licensee? A trespasser? Was the plaintiff in an area where he did not have permission to be?
- Does the plaintiff suffer from vision problems? Does he wear glasses or corrective contact lenses?
- Does the plaintiff have any other prostheses, such as hearing aids, cane, etc.?
- Did the plaintiff have any pre-existing medical or physical problems that the incident aggravated?
- If so, give precise dates, complaints, and the names of the doctors who saw the plaintiff.
- What injuries did the plaintiff suffer as a result of this incident? Names of all medical professionals that plaintiff saw as a result of this incident.

B. CLASSIFYING VISITORS

People who come to the property fit into one of three possible categories: trespasser, licensee, and invitee. In examining the type of duty owed to each, we start with trespassers because their legal status is fairly straightforward.

When a person is injured on someone's property, the first task is to classify the person. Is he a trespasser, a licensee, or an invitee? The classification determines the duty.

TORT
BASICS
AT A
GLANCE

FIGURE 5-7

**Basic Contents
of Any Premises
Liability
Complaint**

- Defendant's residence (this helps to establish the court's jurisdiction)
- Venue
- Plaintiff's cause of action:
    - Defendant was the owner/possessor of the premises
    - Plaintiff had a right to be on the premises as a (licensee) (invitee)
- Defendant had a legal duty to the plaintiff
- Defendant acted in a negligent way, or failed to take reasonable care by the following: (list specific acts or omissions)
- Defendant had actual (or constructive) knowledge of the danger or the danger was foreseeable
- The date, time, and circumstances of the incident that resulted in plaintiff's injuries
- The facts that show the plaintiff did not contribute to his own injuries (in states where contributory negligence is a defense)
- The nature of the plaintiff's injuries
- How the defendant's action, or failure to act, was the proximate cause of the plaintiff's injuries
- The extent of the plaintiff's damages
- The plaintiff's request for relief from the court (the money it will take to compensate the plaintiff)

C. CLASSIFYING VISITORS: TRESPASSERS

Trespasser
A person who is on the property of another without permission.

The rule under the common law is that there is no duty to **trespassers.** Possessors of land have no obligation to make their property safe or to take reasonable action to ensure the safety of people who trespass on the land.

Example: Jamal's duty to Nancy might be different if she were in a different category of visitor. For instance, suppose that Nancy had not been invited to Jamal's apartment, but had instead broken in to burglarize it. She slips in Jamal's garbage and injures her knee. We have all heard about cases where burglars have sued homeowners because of the injuries they sustained in breaking in, but the news stories generally neglect to report the resolution of such cases. In this situation, Nancy is a trespasser. Possessors of land, like Jamal, have no duty to trespassers. Nancy's status as a trespasser will have a huge impact on her lawsuit.

A trespasser is someone who is on the property without permission. She does not have to be a burglar; she can simply be uninvited. If she injures herself while she is on the premises without permission, she will be unable to prove the first element of a negligence case. (Without duty, she cannot proceed to breach of duty.)

1. EXCEPTIONS TO THE GENERAL RULE OF NO DUTY TO TRESPASSERS

Over time, the rather harsh rule that a land possessor owed no duty to a trespasser was gradually modified. One of the biggest problems with the rule involved children. Under the law, children always receive special protection. Their inexperience with the world and their lack of maturity require adults to look after them. When a child trespasses on property and is injured, should the same "no duty" rule apply? What if the land possessor had good reason to know that children would attempt to trespass? What if the land possessor has a swimming pool or a junkyard or a closed playground? Shouldn't he be forced to take some precautions to protect children, even if he is under no obligation to protect adult trespassers?

a. The Attractive Nuisance Doctrine

The *attractive nuisance doctrine* was developed as a direct response to trespassing children. Courts developed this doctrine to specifically address dangerous conditions in areas that children would naturally find enticing. When the doctrine was originally developed, railroads were still the predominant mode of travel in the United States. Switching stations and railroad yards were often irresistible to young children, who were as fascinated by big machines then as they are now. When a child wandered into a railroad yard that had no fences or other protective devices, the child lacked any redress when he was injured. The courts felt that this was too drastic an outcome and carved out the attractive nuisance doctrine, which is really an exception to the rule that there is no duty to trespassers. When a plaintiff brings a suit and alleges the attractive nuisance doctrine to show that there was a duty to the injured child, the plaintiff must meet all the elements of the doctrine before the courts will impose a duty on the possessor.

Elements of the Attractive Nuisance Doctrine

To prove his case, a plaintiff who relies on the attractive nuisance doctrine must show:

- that the defendant has reason to know that there is a dangerous condition on his land (such as a railroad yard) and that children are likely to trespass there;
- that the defendant knows that this dangerous condition poses an unreasonable risk of injury to a child;
- that a young child, because of her lack of maturity and experience, would not realize how dangerous the condition actually was;
- that the financial burden of making the condition safer is slight in comparison with the danger posed to a child; and
- that the defendant failed to take reasonable precautions to prevent a trespassing child from being injured.

If the plaintiff can prove each of these elements, he can show that the defendant did owe a duty to the trespassing child, despite the general rule that no duty exists to trespassers.

b. Rescue Doctrine

Another exception to the general rule of no duty to trespassers involves rescuers. Like children, rescuers also receive special protection under the law.

Example: Timmy is playing and falls down a well on Rhonda's property. Rhonda has failed to properly cover the well. Rick is walking home and hears Timmy cry out. Rick rushes onto Rhonda's property to rescue Timmy, and in so doing, he is injured by the shards of metal that protrude from the top of the well. Can Rick bring an action against Rhonda?

Answer: Yes. Although Rick is technically a trespasser (he did not have permission to be on Rhonda's property), and Rhonda has no duty to trespassers, this case falls into an exception. Courts want to promote (and protect) people who seek to rescue others. We have already seen that when a person creates a dangerous condition, he must take steps to protect others from it. Here, we apply this idea to the possessor of real estate and impose a duty.

The courts created the rescue doctrine to address a public policy concern. The courts realized that not allowing a rescuer to be protected under the law might discourage people from rescuing one another.

D. CLASSIFYING VISITORS: LICENSEES

Licensee
A person who enters another person's premises for convenience, curiosity, or entertainment.

When someone is invited onto the property, that person is not a trespasser. In many jurisdictions, this invited person can fall into one of two categories: licensee or invitee. The defendant's duty to a licensee is different from his duty to an invitee.

The term **licensee** refers to a guest. This is a person who has come to the premises for personal or social reasons, not business. The duty of a possessor to a licensee is simply to warn of a dangerous condition.

TORT BASICS AT A GLANCE

Duty to licensee: warn of dangerous condition.

E. CLASSIFYING VISITORS: INVITEES

Invitee
A person who has a business purpose in coming onto the property.

An **invitee** is a customer or a client. This person has come to the premises for some business purpose and is not paying a social call. The possessor owes the highest duty to this person. He must not only warn of dangerous conditions but also take reasonable actions to make the premises safe.

Duty to invitee: warn of dangerous condition and make premises safe.

TORT
BASICS
AT A
GLANCE

1. "ECONOMIC BENEFIT" TEST

Sometimes the distinction between a licensee and an invitee is difficult to determine. Consider the following scenario:

Jamal and Rick have been friends since college. Jamal became a successful businessman, and Rick became an accountant. Rick has been handling all of Jamal's financial statements, accounts payable, and taxes since Jamal started out in business. They usually have lunch together every Friday, when they discuss business and also catch up on old college acquaintances. One day, when Jamal shows up at Rick's office to pick him up for their weekly lunch, he steps out on a balcony that Rick is in the process of remodeling. Rick tells Jamal to watch his step, since the balcony is not finished. While Jamal is standing on the balcony, it collapses. Jamal is severely injured. How do we classify Jamal—invitee or licensee?

Answer: One way of addressing this complicated situation is to apply a doctrine courts have developed in recent years, called the "economic benefit" test. Under this test, courts will consider a person to be an invitee if the primary reason for his presence is business with the defendant. Under that situation, Rick would be required not only to warn Jamal of the dangerous condition, but also to take reasonable actions to make the dangerous condition safe. If, on the other hand, Jamal's primary reason for being there is for nonbusiness reasons, the economic benefit test would dictate that Jamal must be classified as a licensee. Under that category, Rick must simply warn of a dangerous condition.

Under this test, is Jamal a licensee or an invitee? If the primary reason for the regular Friday luncheons is friendship and catching up, Jamal is a licensee and Rick would have satisfied his duty to Jamal when he warned him about the balcony.

2. ABNORMALLY DANGEROUS OR ULTRA-HAZARDOUS CONDITIONS

A defendant may be liable to all three categories of visitors when she has an abnormally dangerous condition on her premises. An abnormally dangerous condition would be keeping wild animals, storing dynamite or other explosives, or any other condition that is extremely dangerous. The term *ultra-hazardous* refers to situations that are very difficult to make safe and that pose an extreme risk to anyone nearby. The manufacture of radioactive materials is one such example. When an abnormally dangerous condition exists, the defendant must take precautions to protect all three classifications of visitors. Many of these dangerous conditions are often reclassified as *strict liability*

Sidebar

One of the fastest-growing areas of premises liability involves lawsuits based on criminal acts of others. Tenants, customers, and employees are bringing suits against owners and possessors based on the fact that they knew of a potential danger of criminal activity and failed to take action to prevent it. One example would be a poorly lit parking lot where a tenant is assaulted. In such an example, the property owner may be liable to the tenant for maintaining an unsafe condition that allowed a third party to commit a crime.

torts, meaning that any injury to a person will result in the defendant's liability, regardless of the safety procedures used. We discuss strict liability torts in a later chapter.

When dealing with dangerous conditions, the precautions must be equal to the danger.

F. ABOLISHING THE CATEGORIES (AND DISTINCTIONS) BETWEEN INVITEES AND LICENSEES

The problems with deciding who is, and who is not, an invitee and the harsh results that this classification sometimes entails have prompted several jurisdictions to revisit the entire scheme. Illinois and North Carolina are two jurisdictions that have abolished the distinction between invitees and licensees. In those jurisdictions, the occupant owes both the same duty, that of reasonable care under all the circumstances.

G. GUEST STATUTES

In some jurisdictions, an opposite approach has been taken — narrowing the definition of invitees and licensees. In these jurisdictions, *guest statutes* have been passed that limit the duty of a possessor when the person is a social guest or a trespasser. In these jurisdictions, the categories of invitee and licensee continue to exist, but a statute limits the type of action, or the amount of damages, that an injured social guest can bring against the host.

1. AUTOMOBILE GUEST STATUTES

Another type of guest statute has to do with guests in automobiles. In these situations, statutes make it more difficult for a guest in a car to sue the driver unless the guest can show gross negligence on the part of the driver, or that he or she acted with reckless disregard for the safety of others. The idea behind creating this limitation for automobile guests was to decrease the number of frivolous lawsuits filed by guests against drivers for relatively minor car crashes. The other reason was a fear that drivers and guests would collude to defraud insurance companies by creating scenarios where guests would sue the driver's automobile insurance liability company. However, most of the states that once embraced these auto-guest statutes have repealed them.

VI   DUTY TO THIRD PARTIES

The general rule about duty to third parties is that a person does not owe a third party any duty. The reason for this rule is that, unlike other situations, there is no direct contact between the defendant and a third party and therefore no special relationship. When we say "third party" in this discussion, we are referring to someone other than the plaintiff. For instance, in a typical car wreck case, we often see a negligent driver and an injured plaintiff. There is a direct connection between the defendant's negligence and the plaintiff's injuries. We would say that there is proximate cause between the defendant's actions and the resultant damages to the plaintiff. (We discuss proximate cause in greater detail in Chapter 7.) However, in this scenario, a third party would be someone who was neither present in the automobiles nor injured by the collision. Consider the following scenario:

Ted is walking down the sidewalk when a car crash occurs nearby. He is not injured, but the wreck upsets him. He wishes to bring an action against the negligent driver for causing him to be upset. He believes that he has a solid case of intentional infliction of emotional distress. Does he have a cause of action?

Answer: Barring any other facts, no. Ted has no physical injuries, and his mental upset at witnessing an accident does not provide a cause of action. If it did, car crash witnesses all over the nation would clog the court system with similar lawsuits. Ted is a third party, that is, someone who is not directly affected by the incident between the defendant and the plaintiff. In this situation, the defendant driver has no duty to Ted.

We could reach the same conclusion about Ted's third-party status by using the principle of foreseeability. Is it foreseeable that a pedestrian would suffer from intentional infliction of emotional distress because of the defendant's actions? In the pragmatic world of the law, the answer is no. If Ted could allege some special circumstance, such as the fact that the plaintiff was his child, he might then have a cause of action. But under these facts, he has none.

The general rule that there is no duty to third parties is slowly changing in many jurisdictions to a duty to third parties under certain, specific circumstances.

TORT
BASICS
AT A
GLANCE

What about a situation in which the defendant has reason to believe that the third party is in danger from someone? Consider the following scenario:

Dr. M diagnoses his patient, Danny, with a rare blood disease. The disease is not contagious but will substantially shorten Danny's life. Dr. M knows that Danny has recently married. Danny has no plans to tell his new wife about his condition. Does Dr. M owe any duty to Danny's wife to tell her about Danny's condition?

Answer: No. Why? For one thing, Dr. M's duty is to his patient, Danny, and Danny's wife is not Dr. M's patient. Dr. M also has an obligation of confidentiality about his patient's medical treatment. Dr. M has no obligation to Danny's new wife.

The rule seems very simple and straightforward. A person owes a duty to specific people, not *all* people. But this general statement begins to break down when we change some of the facts.

Example: Danny has been diagnosed with an extremely contagious disease. If Danny has any prolonged contact with anyone, that person will almost certainly become infected with the disease and will probably die. Dr. M knows that Danny is married. Does he now have a duty to inform Danny's wife about the disease?

Answer: Yes. In our example, the doctor may have not only an ethical duty to tell Danny's wife, he may have a legal duty. Because this scenario deals with a highly infectious disease, this may be enough to shift the focus from the doctor's duty to Danny to the doctor's duty to the general public. We can agree that there are situations in which a doctor's duty of confidentiality to his patient becomes secondary to the doctor's duty to the general public, or third parties. Having said that, however, many other professionals continue to have no legal duty to third parties for dangers that many people would consider to be obvious and serious.

Many jurisdictions have modified the general rule of no duty to third parties to address dangerous situations. In those jurisdictions, the courts have said that a person does have a duty to third parties when the danger is clear, the third party can easily be identified, and warning the third party would not cause any hardship. Once you have opened this door of duty to a third party, how far does it go? Consider the following scenario:

Dr. T is a psychologist with many clients. Fred is one of them. Fred has a history of violence, including some physical assaults. Dr. T has been counseling Fred for some time. In the past few months, Fred has been talking regularly about hurting Fred's ex-wife. Fred has described exactly how he plans on abducting his ex-wife, how he will kill her, and how he plans on disposing of her body. Fred has even set a date for this killing: next Tuesday. Does Dr. T have a legal duty to warn Fred's ex-wife?

Answer: Although most of us would agree that Dr. T seems to have a moral duty to warn Fred's ex-wife, the situation for Dr. T is actually very difficult. Dr. T is bound by law to keep her patient's conversations confidential. Fred may also simply be "blowing off steam" by talking about the murder as a way of fantasizing about something he would never do. Do the specifics of Fred's plan give some guidance? After all, it's one thing to say, "I'm going to kill that person," as opposed to "I'm going to kidnap her next Tuesday when she gets off at work at 3 P.M., kill her with a knife, and dump her body in a secluded area." The specifics of the threat really go to the question of foreseeability. If an action is foreseeable, the situation may impose a duty on Dr. T.

A. FORESEEABILITY OF INJURY TO THIRD PARTY

Perhaps the most famous case dealing with an obligation to third parties and how this rule can (and perhaps should) be modified is *Tarasoff v. Regents of University of California.*[10]

Case Excerpt

TARASOFF v. REGENTS OF UNIVERSITY OF CALIFORNIA
17 Cal. 3d 425, 551 P.2d 334, 131 Cal. Rptr. 14 (1976)

On October 27, 1969, Prosenjit Poddar killed Tatiana Tarasoff. Plaintiffs, Tatiana's parents, allege that two months earlier Poddar confided his intention to kill Tatiana to Dr. Lawrence Moore, a psychologist employed by the Cowell Memorial Hospital at the University of California at Berkeley. They allege that on Moore's request, the campus police briefly detained Poddar, but released him when he appeared rational. They further claim that Dr. Harvey Powelson, Moore's superior, then directed that no further action be taken to detain Poddar. No one warned plaintiffs of Tatiana's peril.

Plaintiffs' complaints predicate liability on . . . defendants' failure to warn plaintiffs of the impending danger. Defendants, in turn, assert that they owed no duty of reasonable care to Tatiana and that they are immune from suit under the California Tort Claims Act of 1963 (Gov. Code, 810ff).

We shall explain that defendant therapists cannot escape liability merely because Tatiana herself was not their patient. When a therapist determines, or pursuant to the standards of his profession should determine, that his patient presents a serious danger of violence to another, he incurs an obligation to use reasonable care to protect the intended victim against such danger. The discharge of this duty may require the therapist to take one or more of various steps, depending upon the nature of the case. Thus it may call for him to warn the intended victim or others likely to apprise the victim of the danger, to notify the police, or to take whatever other steps are reasonably necessary under the circumstances. In the case at bar, plaintiffs admit that defendant therapists notified the police, but argue on appeal that the therapists failed to exercise reasonable care to protect Tatiana in that they did not confine Poddar and did not warn Tatiana or others likely to apprise her of the danger. Defendant therapists, however, are public employees. Consequently, to the extent that plaintiffs seek to predicate liability upon the therapists' failure to bring about Poddar's confinement, the therapists can claim immunity under Government Code section 856.

No specific statutory provision, however, shields them from liability based upon failure to warn Tatiana or others likely to apprise her of the danger, and Government Code section 820.2 does not protect such failure as an exercise of discretion. "The assertion that liability must . . . be denied because defendant bears no 'duty' to plaintiff begs the essential question—whether the plaintiff's interests are entitled to legal protection against the defendant's conduct. . . . (Duty) is not sacrosanct in itself, but only an expression of the sum total of those considerations of policy which lead the law to say that the particular plaintiff is entitled to protection." (Prosser, Law of Torts (3d ed. 1964)). Liability should be imposed for an injury occasioned to another by his want of ordinary care or skill. Whenever one person is by circumstances placed in such a position with regard to another . . . that if he did not use ordinary care and skill in his own conduct . . . he would cause danger of injury to the person or property of the other, a duty arises to use ordinary care and skill to avoid such danger.

We depart from "this fundamental principle" only upon the "balancing of a number of considerations"; major ones "are the foreseeability of harm to the plaintiff, the degree of certainty that the plaintiff suffered injury, the closeness of the connection between the defendant's conduct and the injury suffered, the moral blame attached to the defendant's conduct, the policy of preventing future harm, the extent of the burden to the defendant and consequences to the community of imposing a duty to exercise care with resulting liability for breach, and the availability, cost and prevalence of insurance for the risk involved."

The most important of these considerations in establishing duty is foreseeability. As a general principle, a "defendant owes a duty of care to all persons who are foreseeably endangered by his conduct, with respect to all risks which make the conduct unreasonably dangerous." As we shall explain, however, when the avoidance of foreseeable harm requires a defendant to control the conduct of another person, or to warn of such conduct, the common law has traditionally imposed liability only if the defendant bears some special relationship to the dangerous person or to the potential victim. Since the relationship between a therapist and his patient satisfies this requirement, we need not here decide whether foreseeability alone is sufficient to create a duty to exercise reasonable care to protect a potential victim of another's conduct. Although, as we have stated above, under the common law, as a general rule, one person owed no duty to control the conduct of another, nor to warn those endangered by such conduct, the courts have carved out an exception to this rule in cases in which the defendant stands in some special relationship to either the person whose conduct needs to be controlled or in a relationship to the foreseeable victim of that conduct. Applying this exception to the present case, we note that a relationship of defendant therapists to either Tatiana or Poddar will suffice to establish a duty of care; as explained in section 315 of the Restatement Second of Torts, a duty of care may arise from either "(a) a special relation . . . between the actor and the third person which imposes a duty upon the actor to control the third person's conduct, or (b) a special relation . . . between the actor and the other which gives to the other a right of protection."

Although plaintiffs' pleadings assert no special relation between Tatiana and defendant therapists, they establish as between Poddar and defendant therapists the special relation that arises between a patient and his doctor or psychotherapist. Such a relationship may support affirmative duties for the benefit of third persons. Thus, for example, a hospital must exercise reasonable care to control the behavior of a patient which may endanger other persons. A doctor must also warn a patient if the patient's condition or medication renders certain conduct, such as driving a car, dangerous to others.

Although the California decisions that recognize this duty have involved cases in which the defendant stood in a special relationship both to the victim and to the person whose conduct created the danger, we do not think that the duty should logically be constricted to such situations. Decisions of other jurisdictions hold that the single relationship of a doctor to his patient is sufficient to support the duty to exercise reasonable care to protect others against dangers emanating from the patient's illness. The courts hold that a doctor is liable to persons infected by his patient if he negligently fails to diagnose a contagious disease or, having diagnosed the illness, fails to warn members of the patient's family.

Defendants contend, however, that imposition of a duty to exercise reasonable care to protect third persons is unworkable because therapists cannot accurately predict whether or not a patient will resort to violence. In support of this argument amicus representing the American Psychiatric Association and other professional societies cites numerous articles which indicate that therapists, in the present state of the art, are unable reliably to predict violent acts; their forecasts, amicus claims, tend consistently to overpredict violence, and indeed are more often wrong than right. Since predictions of violence are often erroneous, amicus concludes, the courts should not render rulings that predicate the liability of therapists upon the validity of such predictions.

The role of the psychiatrist, who is indeed a practitioner of medicine, and that of the psychologist who performs an allied function, are like that of the physician who must conform to the standards of the profession and who must often make diagnoses and predictions based upon such evaluations. Thus the judgment of the therapist in diagnosing emotional disorders and in predicting whether a patient presents a serious danger of violence is comparable to the judgment which doctors and professionals must regularly render under accepted rules of responsibility.

We recognize the difficulty that a therapist encounters in attempting to forecast whether a patient presents a serious danger of violence. Obviously we do not require that the therapist, in making that determination, render a perfect performance; the therapist need only exercise "that reasonable degree of skill, knowledge, and care ordinarily possessed and exercised by members of (that professional specialty) under similar circumstances." Within the broad range of reasonable practice and treatment in which professional opinion and judgment may differ, the therapist is free to exercise his or her own best judgment without liability; proof, aided by hindsight, that he or she judged wrongly is insufficient to establish negligence.

In the instant case, however, the pleadings do not raise any question as to failure of defendant therapists to predict that Poddar presented a serious danger of violence. On the contrary, the present complaints allege that defendant therapists did in fact predict that Poddar would kill, but were negligent in failing to warn. In each instance the adequacy of the therapist's conduct must be measured against the traditional negligence standard of the rendition of reasonable care under the circumstances. In sum, the therapist owes a legal duty not only to his patient, but also to his patient's would-be victim and is subject in both respects to scrutiny by judge and jury.

Our current crowded and computerized society compels the interdependence of its members. In this risk-infested society we can hardly tolerate the further exposure to danger that would result from a concealed knowledge of the therapist that his patient was lethal. If the exercise of reasonable care to protect the threatened victim requires the therapist to warn the endangered party or those who can reasonably be expected to notify him, we see no sufficient societal interest that would protect and justify concealment. The containment of such risks lies in the public interest. For the foregoing reasons, we find that plaintiffs' complaints can be amended to state a cause of action against defendants for breach of a duty to exercise reasonable care to protect Tatiana. We conclude that defendant therapists in the present case are not immune from liability for their failure to warn of Tatiana's peril. We conclude, therefore, that the therapist defendants' failure to warn Tatiana or those who reasonably could have been expected to notify her of her peril does not fall within the absolute protection afforded by section 820.2 of the Government Code.

The judgment of the superior court in favor of defendants is reversed, and the cause remanded for further proceedings consistent with the views expressed herein.

Questions about the case:

1. What is the plaintiff's theory about the liability of Dr. Moore?
2. Are therapists always free from liability when the person who is injured is not their patient?
3. What test does the court create to determine when a therapist should be liable to a third party?
4. What balancing of principles does the court engage in to determine liability in these cases?
5. How does the court explain foreseeability in this case?

B. CAN A DEFENDANT WAIVE HIS DUTY?

Under certain circumstances, a defendant can legally waive his duty to another. A waiver usually takes the form of a written contract between the defendant and some other party. It often includes language to the effect that the plaintiff, by engaging in some dangerous practice, is waiving all rights to sue the defendant for negligence. However, these contracts are subject to strict interpretation because they often encourage a lax attitude toward the standard of care for another. This means that when there is any ambiguity in the contract, it will be held against the defendant.

Waivers are not legally valid in some situations, such as the duty arising from a special relationship. Many jurisdictions have also said that it is not legal to attempt to contract against your own negligence. Waivers will also not be enforced when they run counter to public policy.

Example: John is suffering from severe chest pain and drives himself to the local emergency room. At the front triage desk, he tells the nurse on duty about his symptoms. The nurse hands him a form and tells him that he cannot be seen by a doctor until he signs the form. John sees a paragraph at the bottom of the form that states, "Patient, by receiving treatment, hereby waives any claim against the attending physician, nurse, or nurse practitioner that may arise due to medical malpractice." John signs the form. Doctors discover that he needs emergency surgery, and during the surgery, one of the surgeons forgets to remove a sponge. It remains inside John's chest cavity, where it causes a severe infection. Can John sue the doctor for malpractice, even though he waived his right when he came to the hospital?

Answer: Yes. Most jurisdictions would label such a clause a violation of public policy and refuse to enforce it. There is also the issue that John signed the waiver under duress, because he was suffering from severe chest pain and was in dire need of medical treatment.

Chapter Summary

The first element in a negligence action is duty. A plaintiff must clearly establish that the defendant owed a duty before the plaintiff can present further evidence of how and when the defendant breached that duty, and how that breach was a legal cause of the plaintiff's subsequent injuries. Duty can arise out of specific situations, such as a motorist's duty to the other drivers on the road. Duty can also be established by the special relationship existing between the parties. The defendant's status as a professional, or specialist, subjects him to a higher duty than someone who is considered to be a layperson. Duty may also be established by the fact that the defendant was in possession of the premises and was in a better position to know about potential dangers than anyone else. Finally, some plaintiffs receive a higher level of protection under the law. Children, for instance, are protected in situations in which adults might not receive similar treatment under the law.

SKILLS YOU NEED IN THE REAL WORLD

Beginning Your Legal Research

When you get your first research assignment, your impulse will be to grab a book (or click on an Internet site) and get started. That's not where you should begin. Before you tackle any legal research assignment, think it through. Thinking about your assignment doesn't sound like as much fun as doing something, but it can save you lots of time (and anxiety). Let's take a legal research assignment and break it down into steps.

Step One: Key Words

Before you begin your research, take a long, hard look at your question, and then begin writing down key words. Here's an example:

Attorney: We've got a case involving a collision at a railroad intersection. Shortly after the accident, the railroad company went out to the site and cut off all the tree limbs that were blocking the view. This sounds like subsequent remedial measures. Normally, that evidence is not admissible in the trial. See if you can find some way to make it admissible.
Paralegal: No problem. When do you need this?
Attorney: Oh, no rush. Before lunch will do.

Before you rush off to the statutes trying to find something dealing with subsequent remedial measures, think about your assignment. What is the issue here? If you don't know what the term *subsequent remedial measures* means, look it up in a legal dictionary. You'll see that it refers to the basic idea that anything done after the accident to make the premises safer can't be used in the trial to show that the premises were unsafe before the accident. (Otherwise, people would be discouraged from repairing dangerous conditions.) Right away, we can jot down some key words: repair, subsequent remedial measures, evidence. If you think about it, you will realize that this is an evidentiary question dealing with what kinds of evidence can, and cannot, be admitted at trial.

Step Two: Research from the General to the Specific

In a perfect world, you can turn to the correct answer every time. That occasionally does happen, but most of the time you have to move from the general to the specific. Where should you begin? Start with the most general term on your list and see where that takes you. The most general term on the list is . . . *evidence.* That's about as general as you can get. Start with any good book, digest, or treatise, and see where that takes you.

Step Three: Use Your Common Sense

Paralegals sometimes make the mistake of not using their common sense. Let's say that you have researched your topic to the point that you have discovered that evidence of subsequent remedial measures can be admissible to show ownership of the premises in question, under certain conditions. Are you done? What's the most obvious question that follows this result? "What do they mean by 'certain conditions'?" If you anticipate some of the more obvious questions that your research raises, you will be far more effective.

Step Four: Use Free Internet Legal Research Sites

Finally, you should take advantage of the many different free legal research sites currently available online. Not all of these sites have the same depth of coverage, but they can help get you started, especially if the research topic is one with which you are unfamiliar. Any Internet search engine will return numerous hits with the search string "free legal research sites."

THE LIFE OF A PARALEGAL

Getting and Maintaining Complete Information on a Client

When a client comes in, we'll have them fill out an information sheet. It asks a lot of questions about their addresses and telephone numbers. You'd be surprised how many clients don't want to completely fill it out. They'll quibble and say this part doesn't apply, or say that they don't want to fill in the complete form. Sometimes, they're not certain about some information. They don't understand, until I explain it to them, that all of this information comes in handy later on when we're trying to contact them about interrogatories or trial or even settlement. Once I have this information, I'll enter it into our database. We have a commercial database that was specifically designed for law offices. It keeps track of clients' names, addresses, adverse parties, opposing attorneys, you name it. A lot of times while I'm creating a computer file on the client, I'm also creating a physical file, too. I'll generate a client number and paste it on a manila file folder while I'm also entering all of this information on the computer. You have to be able to juggle several different jobs at the same time. A lot of times, I'm entering computer information, putting together a physical file, and answering phone calls all at the same time.

Christina Lynn, Paralegal

ETHICAL ISSUES FOR THE PARALEGAL: KEEPING UP WITH DEVELOPMENTS IN THE LAW

One of the most important things you can do as a legal professional is to keep up with the law on a particular topic. Suppose that your firm handles a lot of personal injury cases. It makes sense for you to stay current on the law in this area. You can do this by reading legal newspapers and legal magazines, but the best way is to read the most recent decisions of the courts in your jurisdiction. There is nothing more embarrassing, and a better justification for a claim of legal malpractice, than relying on a case that has been overruled by a higher court. Your knowledge about recent trends in the law can be extremely valuable to an attorney who might not have taken the time to stay as current on the law as she should have. Those kinds of little reminders of your helpfulness will only make you that much more indispensable to the firm.

Relevant Cases

CARTER V. ABBYAD
299 S.W.3D 892 (2009)

Opinion

G. Alan Waldrop, Justice.

This is an appeal from the dismissal of appellants' negligence suit. Appellants Jennifer Carter and Eleanor Draughn were stabbed at a party by Dustin McManus, a companion of appellees Ramzi Abbyad, Jason Nuckolls, and Travis McLemore. The stabbing victims and their parents—Bonnie Carter, Scott Carter, Andrew Draughn, and Susan Draughn—argue that they have alleged facts that, if proven, would demonstrate that appellees owed them a duty of care to have prevented the drug-addled and threatening McManus from coming into contact with unsuspecting guests at a party that the appellees attended. Appellees contend that the trial court correctly determined that the companions of an individual under the influence of behavior-altering drugs had no duty, based on the circumstances as alleged in this case, to protect others from that individual. Guided by case law constraining the recognition of legal duties to control the actions of others, we affirm.

This case was dismissed based on the pleadings. Consequently, the following description of events underlying this case is drawn from appellants' allegations in their petition. While at the home of former codefendant Tyler Hunkin, appellees provided McManus with and/or watched him consume excessive amounts of illegal drugs including marijuana and hallucinogenic mushrooms in celebration of McManus's completion of a probation term. It is alleged that appellees knew that McManus consumed more than three times the "normal dose" of hallucinogenic mushrooms and knew that he had a knife. Appellants also assert that appellees knew that McManus's behavior grew more bizarre, threatening, and unpredictable as

time passed, that he was having a "bad trip," and that he was a danger to himself and others. Appellants also allege that appellees were under the influence of illegal drugs and alcohol as well.

Appellants claim that appellees decided to take McManus in this condition to a party on Halloween night to expose him to ridicule for their own amusement. They also allege that appellees did this despite knowing that these circumstances would expose McManus and other partygoers to danger. On the way to the party, appellants stopped at a convenience store to evaluate McManus's increasingly bizarre behavior. According to the petition, he was behaving "insanely" with a wild look in his eyes, was completely incoherent, and lacked the ability to communicate effectively. Nevertheless, appellees went on to the party with McManus.

At the party, McManus's behavior allegedly grew still more bizarre and threatening toward himself and others. Eventually, appellants allege, McManus stabbed Abbyad, after which appellees fled. McManus then stabbed appellants Eleanor Draughn and Jennifer Carter, and others.

Appellants filed an original petition and at least five amended petitions. Appellees filed motions to dismiss and for special exceptions. After appellants repleaded, appellees filed motions to dismiss on the basis that they did not have a legal duty to control McManus. The trial court dismissed the case.

In determining whether the defendant was under a duty, the court will consider several interrelated factors, including the risk, foreseeability, and likelihood of injury weighed against the social utility of the actor's conduct, the magnitude of the burden of guarding against the injury, and the consequences of placing the burden on the defendant. Courts have also considered whether one party has superior knowledge of the risk, and whether a right to control the actor whose conduct precipitated the harm exists. Appellants do not cite any authority establishing a legal duty by individuals to control the actions of a companion who is under the influence of drugs or similar behavior-altering substances. Therefore, to hold that there is a duty in this case, we must interpret an existing duty to include the behavior described in the plaintiffs' pleadings or recognize a new duty under Texas law.

Appellants urge that, because appellees enabled McManus's intoxication and transported him to the party knowing he was a danger to himself and others, they created a dangerous situation from which they had a duty to protect others. Appellants also contend that appellees' conduct constituted an undertaking to render services that were necessary for the protection of third parties, the negligent performance of which resulted in liability to those third persons.

Although one does not generally have the duty to control another person or to aid a person in distress, one who chooses to exercise that control or provide the aid must do so responsibly and not make the circumstances worse. *Otis Eng'g Corp. v. Clark*, 668 S.W.2d 307, 312 (Tex.1983). In *Otis*, upon learning that an employee was intoxicated while on the job, the employer suggested that the employee go home. The employee drove away from work and caused a collision that killed other motorists. Id. The court held that "when, because of an employee's incapacity, an employer exercises control over the employee, the employer has a duty to take such action as a reasonably prudent employer under the same or similar circumstances would take to prevent the employee from causing an unreasonable risk of harm to others."

Providers of alcoholic beverages can owe a duty to protect third parties under certain circumstances. In *El Chico v. Poole*, a pre-Dram Shop Act case, the supreme court recognized a duty for bars not to serve obviously intoxicated persons, and that the duty existed for the protection of third parties as well as the drinker. 732 S.W.2d 306, 312 (Tex.1987). The court imposed the duty because "the risk and likelihood of injury from serving alcohol to an intoxicated person whom the licensee knows will probably drive a car is as readily foreseen as injury resulting from setting loose a live rattlesnake in a shopping mall." Id. at 311. In *Venetoulias v. O'Brien*, a bar patron limited her drinking until assured by a co-owner of the corporation that owned the bar that he would ensure that she had a ride home. Venetoulias, the co-owner, took the patron's keys and money to make sure she did not try to drive herself home, and she proceeded to become so intoxicated that she needed support to walk out of the bar when it closed. Id. When she declined to accompany Venetoulias to a party, he put her in her car, returned her money, and put her keys in the ignition. Id. Although she did not remember what happened next, she attempted to drive home and was injured in a one-car accident. Id. The bar was held liable under the Dram Shop Act for serving alcohol to an obviously intoxicated person. The court held that, although the owner had no general duty to ensure that the patron did not attempt to drive home, his promise that he would do so created a duty. The court held that the owner "negligently created the situation and failed to act reasonably by leaving O'Brien in her car with the keys in the ignition."

Courts have described the bounds of a duty to protect persons from the actions of others in situations apart from intoxicated individuals who injure themselves and others. For example, the supreme court held that a regional boy scout council had a duty to scouts not to knowingly appoint a child molester as a scoutmaster. The Tyler court of appeals held that a physician may owe a duty to the motoring public to warn a patient of drug side effects. By contrast, the supreme court held that, although a physician owed his patient a duty to properly diagnose and treat the patient, he did not owe that duty to others. Consequently, the doctor could not be held liable for the injuries and death inflicted by the patient after the doctor released him from restraint and intense supervision. The court reasoned that the doctor-patient relationship does not give the doctors the right or duty to control their patients.

Each of these cases has distinguishing characteristics from this case. An obvious distinction is that none of them involves a tortfeasor who voluntarily ingested hallucinogens. Further, the supreme court's decision not to impose a duty to warn in Thapar was based in part on the statutory confidentiality of doctor-patient communications. Id. Otis hinges on a power to control under an employer-employee relationship that is absent here.

The arguments for recognizing a duty in this case have force. McManus foolishly chose to consume the hallucinogenic substances he did, particularly in excess. Appellees' actions as described by the petition, if proven, are reprehensible. They were allegedly aware that McManus's consumption of drugs had put him in a precarious mental state. The consequences to appellants of appellees' actions in transporting McManus to the party and failing to alert others to his condition, if proven as alleged, contributed to a chain of events that caused significant damage to a number of people. McManus himself was convicted of eight counts of aggravated assault with a deadly weapon, and sentenced to terms ranging from five to fifteen years in prison. Appellants allege that none of this would have happened had appellees not taken McManus to the party. Our role, however, is not to determine whether appellants have alleged reprehensible behavior or even behavior that can be characterized as part of the cause of the events at issue. Rather, our role is to determine whether appellants have pleaded a breach of a legal duty owed to them by appellees.

Regarding the risk, foreseeability, and likelihood of injury, appellants allege the following.

- Appellees provided and/or observed McManus consume an excessive amount of illegal drugs, including marijuana and more than three times the normal dose of hallucinogenic mushrooms. At one point, appellants describe McManus's ingestion of the excessive amount of mushrooms as "accidental."
- Appellees knew McManus had a knife.
- McManus's behavior turned "more bizarre, threatening, and unpredictable" before they went to the party. "It was apparent at the Hunkin home to the defendants Abbyad, Nuckolls, McLemore and Hunkin that the defendant McManus was a danger to himself and others."
- Appellees took McManus to the party despite observing that he "had already begun to hallucinate, and that he was having a bad trip."
- Appellees took McManus to the party despite knowing that strangers would ridicule him. Taking McManus to the party exposed him "to a situation that would certainly result in danger to defendant McManus or those to whom the defendant McManus was exposed."
- En route to the party, McManus's behavior became "increasingly bizarre," as he behaved "insanely with a wild look in his eyes," was "completely incoherent and lacked the ability to communicate," and acted "threateningly to himself and others."
- At the party, McManus's behavior "became increasingly bizarre and threatening toward himself and others."

◼ "At all times material hereto, Defendant McManus relied on these Defendants who had full control of him to take care of him and the others he was exposed to."

A problem with these allegations is that they are not specific about the nature of the risk posed, the foreseeability of the result, and the likelihood of injury. Unlike in Venetoulias, there is no allegation that McManus took the drugs while relying on appellees' promise that they would ensure his safety. While there is an allegation that McManus had a knife, appellants do not allege that appellees had reason to believe that McManus would use the knife to attack someone or that he was threatening to do so. For instance, there is no allegation that McManus was threatening to use the knife to hurt himself or others. Beyond general assertions of "threat" and "danger," the allegations do not set out what danger McManus posed to others that appellees should have reasonably been aware of and taken action to prevent before he actually started attacking party guests. There are not sufficient facts pleaded to support the imposition of a duty based on the foreseeability of McManus's ultimate actions and the perception of the likelihood of injury to others.

The argument for recognizing a duty in this case becomes more problematic when we consider the countervailing elements of the social utility of the actor's conduct, the magnitude of the burden of guarding against the injury, and the consequences of placing the burden on the defendant. The social utility of McManus's consumption of drugs is zero. The utility of appellees taking McManus to the party is negligible, and nonexistent beyond not abandoning him at Hunkin's house. Beyond that, however, the undefined nature of the duty appellants would impose makes assessing its existence difficult. There is no showing that appellees had any right to control McManus. The magnitude of the burden of guarding against injury depends on the trigger and scope of the duty. Did the duty arise when appellees provided McManus with illegal drugs, when they saw him ingest them, when they recognized that he had consumed an inordinate amount, when they began to witness the results, when they chose to take him to the party, or when they elected not to monitor or attempt to control his conduct? Does the duty attach only if the observers provide him with the drugs, or when they transport a drug-addled person to a location where he will come into contact with others? Did they have a duty to keep him in the location where he consumed the drugs, or could they move him? When does the duty end? A potential consequence of imposing a duty on appellees at any of these points is that it might encourage future observers of drug intoxication to abandon intoxicated or drug-addled persons before a duty attaches lest they be held responsible for the intoxicated or drug-addled person's actions despite the fact that such a person's potential behavior is, by its nature, unpredictable.

Ultimately, we conclude that appellants have not alleged facts sufficient to demonstrate that appellees owed them a duty to have attempted to control McManus's behavior or not transport him to the party under Texas law. Texas common law is fundamentally premised on individuals' responsibility for their own actions. The exceptions to that rule — e.g. employer-employee, parent-child, all involve situations where the defendant either had a recognized legal obligation to control the other person's conduct or the right to do so. These important factors are not present here. Although appellants argue for application of the duties described by the Restatement of Torts sections 321(1) and 324A and adopted by Texas courts, we find the duty described in section 319 more relevant to the facts in this case. While appellants do not expressly argue here for application of the duty described by section 319, that section more plainly and directly states the duty that appellants seek to impose through sections 321 and 324A. The

Restatement (Second) of Torts section 319 describes the duty that is the essence of appellants' case:

> One who takes charge of a third person whom he knows or should know to be likely to cause bodily harm to others if not controlled is under a duty to exercise reasonable care to control the third person to prevent him from doing such harm.

Appellants' allegations that appellees created the danger by transporting a drug-addled person exhibiting bizarre behavior to a party are disturbing. The relevant authority, however, sets out the rule that, absent some sort of special relationship recognized in the law or voluntarily taking control of another with the other's reliance on that control, a person is not responsible for the tortious acts of another. Under existing Texas law, we conclude that plaintiff's allegations outline a case that McManus created a dangerous situation by consuming large quantities of illegal, behavior-altering drugs, but fail to show that appellees owed appellants a legal duty to control or prevent McManus's subsequent actions.

Affirmed.

CAVIN V. KASSER
820 S.W.2D 647 (1991)

REINHARD, Presiding Judge.

Plaintiff sought damages alleging negligence of defendants. The trial court entered summary judgment for defendant Thomas Kasser. Plaintiff appeals; we affirm.

On September 5, 1987, plaintiff was waiting to tee off on the No. 2 hole of the Creve Coeur Golf Club. Plaintiff heard a shouted warning of "fore" and moved to protect himself too late to avoid being struck by a ball hit from the No. 3 tee by defendant Kasser. Plaintiff was struck on the left cheek and fell to the ground on his right shoulder. He required an operation and continues to experience constant ringing in his ears, insomnia, stiffness in the right shoulder, and swelling of his right hand when he wakes up in the morning. Plaintiff can still play golf but his swing has been affected.

Plaintiff brought an action against defendant Kasser and 90136 Fairview, Inc., d/b/a Creve Coeur Golf Club (golf club). Defendant Kasser moved for summary judgment alleging that there was no issue of fact remaining. He contended that he was under no duty to give a warning before he teed off and that when it became apparent that his drive was going errant he gave a warning. Plaintiff filed a cross-motion for summary judgment and golf club filed a motion for summary judgment.

The court sustained defendant Kasser's motion and denied the motions of plaintiff and defendant golf club. It designated the judgment in favor of defendant Kasser as final for purposes of appeal under Rule 74.01(b). This appeal followed.

In ruling on the motions, the trial court had before it the pleadings; the depositions of plaintiff, defendant Kasser, a member of defendant's foursome, and the marshal who was standing by plaintiff at the time of the accident; and an exhibit showing the layout of the golf course along with the distances of the holes.

From these documents it appears that plaintiff was familiar with the Creve Coeur golf course. He had played there numerous times and had regularly played golf for 12 years. Defendant had played golf for many years, was familiar with the Creve Coeur golf course and considered it a "tight" course. He usually drove the ball 175 to 200 yards.

The length of the No. 2 fairway was 156 yards. The length of the No. 3 fairway was 385 yards. The two fairways were parallel to each other and played in opposite directions. The No. 3 tee was directly across from the No. 2 green. The No. 2 and No. 3 fairways were separated by trees but a person teeing off of the No. 3 tee had an unobstructed view of the No. 2 tee and a person at the No. 2 tee had a similar view of the No. 3 tee.

Plaintiff and three others were waiting to tee off on the No. 2 tee. The club marshal was standing with this foursome. They were waiting for golfers to clear the No. 2 green.

According to defendant, he did not yell "fore" prior to striking the ball. However, as soon as he saw it was going to the left he yelled "fore," as did others in his group. Plaintiff did not notice defendant tee off but did hear the "fore" before he was struck and was in the process of responding by turning when he was hit on the cheek with the ball.

J.B. Taylor, one of the employed marshals of the golf course, said he was standing with plaintiff's group as they prepared to tee off. He was watching defendant tee off and as soon as he heard the "fore" warning he also yelled "fore." The marshal's exclamation was made prior to the ball hitting plaintiff. In driving off the No. 3 tee, according to the marshal, the intended flight of the ball would be "down the No. 3 fairway . . . if the fairway is open they tee off. They don't hold up because someone is standing on the 2 tee."

Plaintiff first claims that defendant had a duty to warn him prior to hitting his tee shot. Both parties cite *Hoffman v. Polsky*, 386 S.W.2d 376 (Mo.1965) on this issue.

In Hoffman, the Missouri Supreme Court reviewed cases from jurisdictions throughout the United States, including the Missouri case of *Page v. Unterreiner*, 130 S.W.2d 970 (Mo.App.1939) relied upon by plaintiff. The court affirmed a directed verdict in favor of the defendant, whose shot from the fairway of the No. 1 hole had struck the plaintiff while walking in the rough alongside that hole towards the No. 10 tee. The court held that a golfer does not have an absolute duty

to warn everyone in the area of his play before making each shot. *Hoffman v. Polsky*, 386 S.W.2d at 378. Rather, its review concluded that the cases stand for the proposition that one about to strike a golf ball must exercise ordinary care to warn those within the range of intended flight of the ball or general direction of the drive, and the existence of such a duty to warn must be determined from the facts of each case.

The court's application of the law in that case relied upon the fact that the defendant had intended to hit her shot to the southeast, down a clear fairway. Id. The plaintiff had been standing to the northeast and was not in danger until after the defendant hit her ball and it hooked in his direction. Id. The court held that that was when the duty to warn attached. Id.

Similarly, in the present case, it is agreed that defendant did not intend to hit the ball towards the No. 2 tee. His duty to warn therefore attached only when it became apparent the shot was errant and plaintiff was in danger. This view is buttressed by the Hoffman court's specific reliance upon the cases of *Benjamin v. Nernberg*, 102 Pa.Super. 471, 157 A. 10 (1931); and *Houston v. Escott*, 85 F.Supp. 59 (D.C.Del.1949).

In Benjamin, plaintiff was struck by a shot from the No. 7 tee while putting on the No. 6 green. The green in question was located 120 feet to the left and about 100 feet in front of the No. 7 tee. The court affirmed the trial court's entry of judgment notwithstanding the verdict in favor of defendant, stating:

> . . . the entire No. 7 fairway was clear before the defendant; plaintiff was not in the line of defendant's play; he was not where anyone could reasonably believe that he was in danger of being struck by a drive from No. 7 tee; it was not until after the ball was driven and it appeared that defendant had made a bad shot, and when the ball was going directly towards plaintiff, that anyone thought it necessary to shout a warning. There was no duty, under the facts of this case, on defendant to warn plaintiff of his intention to play. We cannot see that

defendant was at fault or that he disregarded any rule or custom of the game. The warning in Benjamin, like the warning here, was "not sufficiently timely to save plaintiff." *Hoffman* at 379.

Houston, 85 F.Supp. 59, is even more directly on point. Plaintiff and defendant were playing holes with parallel fairways, as here.

Plaintiff was not more than 125 feet forward of and 50 yards south of and in full view of defendant as he addressed his ball and hit it from the 18th tee. The point where plaintiff was standing was approximately 19 degrees left (or to the south) of the intended flight of defendant's ball. The court granted summary judgment in favor of defendant, relying on the holding in *Benjamin v. Nernberg*, supra.

Thus we perceive Hoffman to stand for the general proposition that a golfer has a duty to give a timely warning to other persons within the foreseeable ambit of danger, and that there is generally no duty to warn persons not in the intended line of flight on another tee or fairway of an intention to strike the ball. This view is supported not only in the cases cited in the Hoffman opinion but in the more recent case of *Noe v. Park Country Club of Buffalo*, 115 A.D.2d 230, 495 N.Y.S.2d 846 (1985).

The facts of each case determine whether or not a warning is required before striking the ball. Here we find nothing that was before the trial court on its ruling for summary judgment that would fit defendant's conduct within an exception to the rule that there is no duty to warn a person not in the intended line of flight on another tee.

Plaintiff also contends that factual issues remain as to the timeliness of the warning that was made. We disagree. It appears to be an accepted rule of golf that, if no duty to warn exists prior to the striking of a ball, one does exist when it becomes apparent the ball is errant. However, there is absolutely no evidence here that this duty was not met. Defendant testified that he and others yelled "fore" as soon as it was apparent that the drive was heading toward the second tee. A marshal heard the warning and repeated it before plaintiff was struck. Plaintiff admits he heard it before he was struck and attempted to react to it. Plaintiff does not reveal any evidence that this warning could have been made sooner and thereby prevented the injury.

Thus it is apparent as a matter of law that defendant had no duty to warn prior to striking of the ball and all the evidence indicates that he warned as soon as the ball went astray. The entry of summary judgment in favor of defendant Kasser is affirmed.

Websites

■ **Hieros Gamos Law**
http://www.hg.org/torts.html

■ **FindLaw**
http://www.findlaw.com/01topics/22tort/index.html

■ **Negligence**
lawschoolhelp.com
www.west.net/~smith/negligence.htm

■ **Wikipedia — Duty of Care**
http://en.wikipedia.org/wiki/Duty_of_care

Forms and Court Documents

This form is a typical motion to dismiss the plaintiff's claim, filed by the defendant on the grounds of "failure to state a claim on which relief may be granted." Such a motion might be filed when the defendant wishes to dismiss the plaintiff's claim for failure to prove duty.

Sidebar

In many jurisdictions, this is referred to as a "12(b)(6) motion," based on the rule of civil procedure that authorizes it.

IN THE SUPERIOR COURT OF GANNETT COUNTY
STATE OF PLACID

John Jones,	)	CASE NO. 8790CR
Plaintiff	)	
	)	
	)	
vs.	)	
	)	
Mary Wilson,	)	
Defendant		

Motion to Dismiss

Defendant, by counsel, pursuant to Placid State Rules of Civil Procedure 12(b), moves the court to enter its order of dismissal of this action on the grounds that the plaintiff's complaint fails to state a claim on which relief can be granted, warranting dismissal pursuant to P.S.R.C.P 12(b)(6).

(a) Plaintiff fails to state a legally cognizable cause of action, which is a prerequisite to the relief he requests.

This the _____ day of July 2012.

Respectfully submitted,

By: _____
Attorney for Defendant

Certificate of Service

This is to certify that the undersigned has this date served this document in the above-captioned action on all other parties to this cause by depositing a copy hereof, postage prepaid, in the United States Mail, properly addressed to the attorney for each party as follows:

This the _____ day of July 2012.

Respectfully submitted,

By: _____

Attorney for Defendant

Key Terms

Custom   Licensee   Standard of care
Duty   Specialist   Trespasser
Invitee

Review Questions

1   What is a legal duty?
2   How would you describe the relationship between the terms *duty* and *foreseeability*?
3   What duty is owed by one stranger to another?
4   X Company has adopted the custom of always double-checking its packaging before sending out its patented fruitcakes. One day, an inspector fails to notice that a piece of sharp metal has fallen into a fruitcake. Does X Company have a duty to inspect its product simply because it adopted the custom of always doing so?
5   List at least five professions that have a higher standard of care or duty than that of a layperson. Now explain why these professions have a higher duty.
6   How is the legal duty of a professional different from that of a specialist?
7   Explain what is meant by a "special relationship" under negligence law. How do special relationships affect duty?
8   What is the duty owed by the possessor of premises to a trespasser? Are there any exceptions to this rule?
9   What is the attractive nuisance doctrine? Why was this doctrine created?
10 What is the difference between an invitee and a licensee? Give an example of both.
11 What is an "abnormally dangerous" or "ultra-hazardous" condition, and how does this affect the analysis of the defendant's duty?
12 Why was the court in the *Tarasoff* case willing to extend the doctor's liability to a third party?
13 Can a defendant waive her duty to a plaintiff? If so, under what circumstances would a waiver be valid? Under what circumstances would a waiver be considered invalid?
14 What is a "12(b)(6) motion"?

Applying What You Have Learned

1   "True to Our Word" Burglar Alarm Company installed a state-of-the-art burglar system in High Art Galleries last year. Two nights ago, a burglar broke into the gallery by climbing through a skylight. He stole 20 paintings valued at over $100,000. The skylight was not wired to the burglar alarm system. The gallery owners have found a safety expert who will

testify that any professional would have wired the skylight and that failure to do so is a breach of the standard of care. Is this enough to show that the alarm company had a duty?

2   Same facts as above, but with one slight change. When the alarm company installed the system, they had the gallery sign a contract that stated that they would not be liable for any break-ins or thefts that occurred because of unprotected "windows, doors, or skylights." Is this a valid waiver of their duty? If the gallery owners signed this contract, are they now barred from suing the alarm company?

3   ABC Sign Company is in the business of designing billboards. They do not make the actual signs; they simply design what will go on them. They also do not install the signs. A different company is responsible for that. Sandy is a nurse at the local hospital and one evening, when she is leaving work, a large sign falls on her and breaks both of her legs. Sandy sues ABC Sign Company for negligence, specifically alleging that ABC failed to inspect its sign. If the company had inspected the sign, they would have seen that several of the supporting bolts had rusted through. Sandy must establish that ABC had a duty to her. Can she prove it?

4   Does your state recognize the doctrine of social host liability? If so, what are the elements?

5   Has your state abolished the distinction between licensee and invitee, or is it still in use? Does your state's definition of licensee and/or invitee differ in some ways from the definition provided in the text? If so, how?

6   What are some of the factors the court considered in finding the psychiatrist owed a duty to third parties in *Tarasoff v. Regents of University of California?*

Endnotes

[1] *Becker v. Schwartz,* 46 N.Y.2d 401, 413 N.Y.S.2d 895, 386 N.E.2d 807 (1978).

[2] *Ortiz v. Chicago,* 79 Ill. App. 3d 902, 398 N.E.2d 1007 (1979), overruled on other grounds, *Johnson v. Colley,* 128 Ill.App.3d 849, 471 N.E.2d 587 (1984).

[3] *Rockweit by Donohue v. Senecal,* 187 Wis. 2d 170, 522 N.W.2d 575 (1994); overruled on other grounds, *Estate of Burgess v. Peterson,* 196 Wis.2d 55, 537 N.W.2d 115 Wis.App. (1995).

[4] *Hertelendy v. Agway Ins. Co.,* 177 Wis. 2d 329, 501 N.W.2d 903 (1993).

[5] *Tubbs v. Argus,* 140 Ind. App. 695, 225 N.E.2d 841 (1967).

[6] *Pesantes v. United States,* 621 F.2d 175 (5th Cir. 1980).

[7] *Cavin v. Kasser,* 820 S.W.2d 647 (1991).

[8] *Olson v. Children's Home Society,* 204 Cal. App. 3d 1362, 252 Cal. Rptr. 11 (1988).

[9] Restatement (Second) of Torts, §360.

[10] *Tarasoff v. Regents of University of California,* 17 Cal. 3d 425, 551 P.2d 334, 131 Cal. Rptr. 14 (1976).

Crossword Puzzle

ACROSS

1 Person who enters another person's premises for convenience, curiosity, or entertainment

6 The standard used to determine if a party has acted negligently in a particular case

DOWN

2 One who has become an expert in a particular field through education, training, or both

3 A practice that has acquired a legal status over time such that failing to follow the practice would result in liability

4 A person who is on the property of another without permission

5 A person who has a business purpose in coming onto the property

7 An obligation imposed by statute or common law

Breach of Duty Under Negligence Law

- Determine when a breach of duty has occurred

- Describe how a defendant's actions (or failure to act) violate the standard of reasonableness under tort law

- Be able to explain the difference between the objective and subjective standards of care

- Define *res ipsa loquitur* and negligence per se

- Describe how to locate expert witnesses

INTRODUCTION

In this chapter, we address the concept of breach of duty. This is the second element of the four (duty, breach, causation, and damages) that must be proved in any negligence case. We assume as we discuss the various topics related to breach that the existence of the duty has already been proved. Now that we have made that determination, we must next explore whether the defendant's actions (or his failure to act) is a breach of duty under negligence law.

WHO BREACHED A DUTY IN THE CHUMLEY CASE?

As we continue to explore the details of the Chumley case, we must answer the question of who, if anyone, breached a duty to Mr. and Mrs. Chumley. If we have established that someone had a duty to maintain the intersection in a safe manner, our next question must be, whose duty was it? There are two obvious choices. If our theory is that the railroad tracks are owned and operated by the railroad company and these tracks are dangerous, it would seem to be a straightforward proposition to say that the railroad company breached its duty. However, we could just as easily make the same claim against the town government. After all, it is responsible for maintaining all the roads inside the town limits. If the intersection was unsafe, the town's employees must shoulder some responsibility. Rather than choose between these two possible defendants, most plaintiffs would opt to sue them both. Just to be on the safe side, the plaintiff in the Chumley case will also list the railroad engineer as a defendant, under the theory that he may have also acted in a negligent manner. (Suppose, for instance, that he could have stopped his train in time to avoid the collision if he had been paying attention.)

Now that we have some idea about who will be sued, we must also address the question of how to prove negligence. The plaintiff's attorney (like the defendants' attorneys) will focus on proof throughout the lawsuit. How will the plaintiff prove that the intersection was dangerous? Put another way, how will the plaintiff prove that the three defendants breached their legal duty?

The plaintiff's team will present evidence and witness testimony that attempts to conclusively show that the intersection was not safe at the time that Mr. Chumley drove across it and was hit by the locomotive. One way of presenting this evidence is to have the plaintiff testify about the conditions that day. However, we do not have that option in this case. Mr. Chumley had traumatic head wounds and suffers from amnesia. He can't remember anything about the collision. Is there some other way of presenting this evidence? One method that many plaintiffs' attorneys use is expert testimony. The plaintiff in this case could hire a safety expert and ask him or her to evaluate the intersection and give an expert opinion about the conditions. We discuss expert testimony later in this chapter.

Tech Topic
ELECTRONIC DATA RECORDERS

The most valuable piece of equipment that can be recovered from an airplane crash is its black box, which contains data about the last moments just prior to the crash. These data allow investigators to help pinpoint the cause of the crash.

It is estimated that more than 85 percent of automobiles are equipped with a similar device, called an electronic data recorder, or EDR. The National Highway Traffic Safety Administration would like to see all vehicles equipped with EDRs, but since the trend is already heading in that direction, it has not yet mandated it. Nevertheless, the NHTSA does mandate a minimum standard for the 15 types of data

EDRs collect, including precrash speed, brake use, engine throttle, safety belt use, warning lamp status, and airbag deployment times.

What this means for tort cases involving automobile accidents is that attorneys have a powerful tool to support a client's account of the facts of an accident (or, conversely, refute the opposition's claims). Data from EDRs are routinely admitted as evidence in every state, although it is up to the judge to make the determination on the data's admissibility. Such evidence is particularly valuable because it is not subject to the vagaries or inconsistencies of memory, as is the case with human witnesses.

BREACH OF DUTY

Simply because the plaintiff was injured does not establish that the defendant violated a duty. To satisfy a cause of action for negligence, the plaintiff must show not only that he was injured, but also that the injury was directly tied to the defendant's breach of a duty to him.[1] One of the ways of answering that question is to determine whether the defendant failed to use reasonable care in his actions.

Example: Joe is driving his car and fails to stop for a stop sign. When he runs the stop sign, he causes a car accident with Barbara. Does Joe owe a duty to Barbara? Yes. Joe owes a duty to all other motorists, and because Barbara is a motorist, he owes a duty to her. Has Joe breached his duty? If the standard that we use is whether Joe caused an unreasonable risk of harm, the answer to that question must be yes. (However, a defendant is not required to exercise greater care than what the plaintiff is required to exercise for her own safety.)[2]

TORT
BASICS
AT A
GLANCE

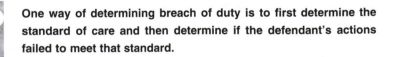

The plaintiff must prove not only that the defendant breached a duty, but also that this breach was closely connected to her injuries.

Reasonable person standard
The standard used by the court as a yardstick by which it can evaluate the defendant's actions in a particular case.

Sidebar

Once a legally recognized duty has been established, the next point, the breach of that duty, must be clearly shown. To determine a breach of duty, the parameters of that duty must be determined. Precisely what actions create the standard of care? Only when the standard of care has been determined can the defendant's actions be evaluated to see if he has violated it. Under most situations, the standard of care is what a reasonably prudent person would have done under the same circumstances as the defendant.[3]

In this example, determining a breach of duty is rather simple. However, there are many other situations in which determining a breach can be quite difficult. Courts have created various doctrines and tests to help determine when a breach of duty has occurred. One such test is the **reasonable person standard.** To determine if a breach of duty has occurred, courts will often ask the question, what would a reasonable person have done under the same circumstances? If this hypothetical reasonable person would not have acted the way the defendant did, the court can feel justified in its determination that the defendant has breached a duty.

Obviously, the court is basing its decision on the fact that a hypothetical reasonable person would not take any action that would cause an unreasonable risk of harm to other people. However, there have been many situations in which the hypothetical reasonable person standard has been difficult if not impossible to apply. In novel situations, for example, the hypothetical standard may not be the best approach. In the last chapter, we discussed another method used to evaluate the defendant's duty: economic benefit analysis. The idea of using a cost-benefit analysis to determine breach of duty has great appeal, as we see in the discussion of product liability cases. However, cost-benefit analysis will not work in every situation. We must therefore examine breach of duty at its most basic level and build up an understanding of the ramifications as we go.

TORT
BASICS
AT A
GLANCE

One way of determining breach of duty is to first determine the standard of care and then determine if the defendant's actions failed to meet that standard.

Sidebar

Some commentators have suggested that the reasonable person standard is one that can — and should — take into account the fact that people are fallible and should therefore include a consideration for those potential faults.[5]

A. THE OBJECTIVE STANDARD

Every person is required by law to use a basic level of common sense and care in his actions.[4] Having said that, however, it is usually up to the jury, not the individuals involved, to determine just what that common sense and caring action should have been. When evaluating the defendant's actions, we do not look at them from his viewpoint. A defendant could justify his actions subjectively on almost any grounds. We look instead at what objectively occurred. We are permitted to take into account unusual or stressful events that occurred around the actions, but we only take those into account as they might have affected a reasonable person. We do not take into account, in most situations, the subjective characteristics of the defendant. For instance, if one driver does not drive with the same level of proficiency as another driver, we do not give this first driver any special advantage. To do so would open up a world of problems in every civil case. A defendant would claim that he should receive special treatment because of a mental or physical characteristic that is somehow different from the population at large. Instead, we generally hold all defendants to the same standard of care. This means that people with special characteristics, whether they are emotional or mental, are treated the same as people who do not have such characteristics. (Later we discuss how this rule has some limited exceptions when dealing with certain physical characteristics.)

Example: Ron has a low IQ. While he is driving to work one day, he sees a new sign that he does not understand and as a result he crashes into a highway crew who are working on the road. Ron claims that because of his low IQ, he should not be held to the same standard of care as people with a higher IQ. The court will not allow a special standard of care for Ron. People with lower intelligence or people who suffer from certain forms of mental problems are held to the same standard as people who have normal intelligence and normal mental processes. The defendant's actions are not judged by whether he carried out a specific act, but by whether he exercised that degree of care that a reasonable person would have exercised under the facts of the case.[6]

When evaluating the reasonableness of the defendant's actions, the jury compares the defendant's actions with those of a hypothetical reasonable person. The jury must answer the question: What would this person have done under similar circumstances?

TORT
BASICS
AT A
GLANCE

This principle of holding defendants to the same standard also applies to people who are intoxicated. When persons are acting under the influence of alcohol or some other drug, they cannot claim a special privilege under the law when they cause an unreasonable risk of harm to other people. They are held to the standard of what a reasonable, sober person would do. Put another way, intoxication does not create a special category under the law.

The same rule applies to people who are legally insane. When we have a situation involving a person who is claiming that at the time of the incident he was legally insane, his conduct will be judged by the standard of what a sane person would have done under the same circumstances. An insane person is held to the same standard as a sane person.[8]

B. THE JURY DETERMINES THE STANDARD OF CARE

Ultimately, the people who determine the standard of care are the jurors. Who better to determine the standard of care than these representatives of the community? With their varied backgrounds and experiences, jurors can bring a sense of what the community at large considers to be reasonable actions. Most jurisdictions agree and make the question of violation of the standard of care a fact question and therefore one that the jury must resolve in deliberations.[9] However, when the jury clearly ignores the applicable laws or makes an unreasonable determination, the trial judge is authorized to overturn that verdict.[10] In evaluating the defendant's actions in a case calling for a basic standard of care, the jury must consider what an average person would do, not what someone with special abilities could do. There have been instances of people taking amazingly difficult or brave actions. Simply because someone, somewhere was able to perform an amazing act (such as wrenching a car door off its hinges in an act of desperation), this singular act does not raise the standard for everyone else. Those acts of superhuman strength occupy a place of their own and are not factored into the jury's consideration of what an average person's standard of care should be.[11]

C. PHYSICAL CHARACTERISTICS

We have said that a defendant cannot claim a special privilege or a different standard under the law because of certain characteristics. However, there is an exception to this rule. There are times when a defendant can claim a different standard when a physical characteristic is involved. Let's take the defendant's age as an example. Children are not held to the same standard as adults. We do not expect the same level of maturity and judgment to be exercised by a child as by an adult. Therefore, if a child is involved in a negligence action, the duty will change. The standard becomes what a child of the same age and background would do when placed in a similar situation. If age is one such physical characteristic that will result in a shift in the standard of care, are there other physical characteristics that will do the same? In fact, there are. A physically handicapped person is not held to the same standard as a fully able person. For instance, a person who is paralyzed from the waist down is held to the standard of a hypothetical reasonable and similarly paralyzed person. The law does not expect that a paralyzed person can respond in the same way as a person who isn't paralyzed. Another example would be disabilities such as blindness.

Notice that mental characteristics such as intelligence or emotional disturbance usually do not affect the defendant's standard of care while physical characteristics do. Tort law seems to have a bias toward characteristics that are more easily defined. It is easy to tell if a person is paralyzed or not. It is much harder to determine if someone is suffering from an emotional or psychological problem. Mental characteristics are much harder to determine, and in such cases, courts usually opt for a uniform standard. However, when a

Sidebar

How is the evaluation of standard of care affected when the defendant is confronted with two equally unpleasant alternatives? For instance, suppose the defendant is attempting to flee from a fire and can either jump through a window or knock over another person to get to an open door? Either alternative is unappealing. Suppose that the defendant chooses to knock over the plaintiff instead of jumping through the window and receiving numerous cuts and bruises? In this case, the jury is called upon to evaluate the situation and to answer the question: Did the defendant choose a reasonable course of action? There are times when the defendant's actions in injuring someone else might actually be reasonable under the circumstances.[12]

characteristic is easily defined, such as the fact that the defendant is a child, courts will usually take that characteristic as the basis to modify the defendant's standard of care.

As a general rule, the defendant's physical characteristics, such as disabilities, can be taken into account when evaluating his actions. As a general rule, his mental characteristics will not.

TORT
BASICS
AT A
GLANCE

D. EMERGENCIES

There are other circumstances that can affect the defendant's standard of care and thus the determination of whether she has breached a duty to the plaintiff. Emergencies are a prime example. In an emergency situation, people are not expected to act with the same level of care and consideration as they would in a more relaxed setting. Courts have consistently recognized that emergency situations change the nature of one person's duty to another. What would be a breach under a normal situation might not be considered a breach in an emergency.

Example: Rhonda is a firefighter who responds to a call at a burning apartment building. During her frantic efforts to free two children who are trapped on the fourth floor of the apartment building, she breaks the window, reaches through, and seizes both children. She inadvertently breaks one child's wrist. Under a normal situation, her actions would probably be considered a breach of duty. However, because of the fire and imminent threat, most jurisdictions would rule that she has not breached a duty.

E. CUSTOM OR TRADITION TO ESTABLISH BREACH OF DUTY?

Can we establish a standard of care based on custom or tradition? For instance, in certain parts of the country it is a custom of motorists who are driving in the right lane on interstate highways to move over to the left lane to allow motorists on the entrance ramp some room to get on the road. There is no law that requires this lane change to accommodate a driver entering the highway. One day, Jean is attempting to get onto a highway from an entrance ramp. As she begins to merge into the right lane, she is cut off by a man driving in the right lane who has refused to move over to the left lane. Jean runs off the roadway, and her car is damaged. She sues the other driver, claiming that he violated a standard of care. She claims that the custom of changing lanes has essentially become the standard of care that a hypothetical reasonable person would follow under similar circumstances. However, courts have been very reluctant to use traditions or customs in this way. In this situation, Jean will most likely lose her suit. Consider the opposite side of this argument. If a custom or tradition established a standard of care, anyone who followed the custom would be immune from suit, even if the custom were faulty. Plaintiffs would be unable to bring a suit against anyone who claimed that he was following a local custom or tradition. When we discuss product liability cases, we consider a modification of this rule, but for general purposes, tradition will not establish a duty (or a subsequent breach).

PROFESSIONALS HAVE A HIGHER STANDARD OF CARE

Professional
Someone who through education, training, or a combination of both, possesses skills that an average person does not.

In the last chapter, we explained the duty owed by someone who is a **professional.** A professional has a higher standard of care than a nonprofessional. Doctors and lawyers, among others, have a higher standard of care to their patients and clients than someone who does not hold that designation. The reason for a higher standard of care should be obvious. Professionals have received extensive training in their chosen fields (and charge higher fees) because of their expertise. Along with that higher status comes a higher standard of care that is often stated as what another professional, in good standing, would do under similar circumstances.

TORT
BASICS
AT A
GLANCE

Professionals are entitled to greater financial rewards for attaining their positions. However, they also must shoulder a higher standard of care.

Specialist
A professional who has achieved the highest level of training and expertise in a given field.

There are some professionals who are classified as **specialists.** A specialist is someone who has an intensive educational background and expertise in a specific area. A specialist is held to an even higher standard than is a professional. The standard for a specialist is what any other specialist with similar training and background would have done under similar circumstances.

The standard of care for a doctor is the degree of care, skill, and proficiency that would be exercised by a similar physician faced with the same or similar circumstances.[13]

COURT DOCTRINES THAT HELP TO DETERMINE BREACH OF DUTY

In some cases, the standard of care has been fixed by statute or some other enactment. For instance, the standard of care for possessors of land is usually set out in a statute. In medical malpractice cases, the standard has been set by case law. In other cases, such as when a defendant is handling particularly dangerous materials, the standard may be set by a combination of statutes and case law. Later, we discuss safety statutes and how they play a crucial role in setting the standard of care for motorists.

Just as we have seen with duty, courts have created several different doctrines to help determine when a breach of duty has occurred. Two of the best-known examples of these doctrines are *res ipsa loquitur* and negligence per se.

A. *RES IPSA LOQUITUR*

As we have seen in the previous chapter, courts have created doctrines over the centuries to address specific problems in negligence cases. We know that in any negligence case, there must be proof of the four elements: duty, breach of that duty, causation linked to the breach, and damages. In some instances, court doctrines have been developed to deal with inadequacies in one or more of these elements.

Res ipsa loquitur literally means, "The thing speaks for itself." It was created to assist plaintiffs in helping to prove the element of breach of duty in certain kinds of cases.

Res ipsa loquitur (Latin) "The thing speaks for itself"; the principle that under certain circumstances, such as the type of accident that would not ordinarily occur without some form of negligence, the defendant's negligence can be presumed.

Example: Ron is caught in traffic one day on a bridge just outside Washington, DC. He hears a loud roar and turns just in time to see a 747 jetliner screaming toward the bridge. The plane hits the bridge and Ron's car. Ron is severely injured. The plane's fuselage breaks into thousands of pieces, and a large portion of the plane ends up in the river. Can Ron sue the airline company for negligence?

Consider the elements of a negligence case. Can Ron prove duty? Do the airline company and the pilot have a duty to Ron? We can establish that element without too much effort. Airlines certainly must have a duty to passengers and others to protect them from air disasters. Has the company and/or pilot breached that duty? Now we have a slight problem. One of the elements that Ron would have to prove in a traditional negligence case is *how* the breach occurred. Ron is no expert on airplane crashes, and when he approaches people who are considered experts, they tell him that there could be several reasons why the plane crashed and that no one will ever know for sure which reason is the right one. The plane itself has broken into thousands of fragments, and piecing together exactly what happened might well be impossible.

If Ron pursues a traditional negligence action, he will not be able to prove his case against the airline company. What evidence can he present to show that the airline company or the pilot was negligent? He does not know what happened on the airplane; he can't prove specific acts of negligence. Here is where the doctrine of *res ipsa loquitur* comes to his rescue.

Under *res ipsa,* a defendant is presumed to have acted negligently (or breached his duty) when certain actions occur. To take advantage of *res ipsa,* the plaintiff must show:

- that the event is one that ordinarily would not occur without someone acting negligently;

■ that the event was caused by some instrumentality exclusively in the defendant's control; and

■ that the event was not caused, even in part, by the plaintiff's actions or failure to act.

When Ron brings his lawsuit against the airline company, can he prove each of these elements? Was the event one that ordinarily would not occur without someone acting negligently? Airplanes do not normally fall out of the sky, so the answer to this question is yes. Was the instrumentality that caused the event exclusively in the defendant's control? The airline company owned and operated the airplane; it was serviced, maintained, and operated by airline personnel, so this step is also proved. Did Ron contribute to his own injuries? Remember that Ron was simply caught in traffic on a bridge. He did not contribute to his own injuries, and therefore he has satisfied every element of a *res ipsa* claim. That being the case, Ron can now bring his lawsuit and will probably win, as well.

ISSUE AT A GLANCE

Res ipsa loquitur **claims allow a plaintiff to bring an action even when he cannot prove what precisely happened to cause his injury.**

1. THE COMMONSENSE ELEMENT OF *RES IPSA LOQUITUR*

Almost all jurisdictions follow some form of *res ipsa* doctrine. (The exceptions are Michigan, Pennsylvania, and South Carolina.) *Res ipsa* is sometimes referred to as the "commonsense" negligence claim. It is often used in cases like airplane crashes and other catastrophes in which the plaintiff has no ability to determine what the defendant did wrong, except to say, "There just had to be negligence." This sounds more like common sense than any intensive legal analysis. The plaintiff is not even required to prove that the only explanation for the incident is negligence; he simply has to show that this kind of incident normally does not happen without negligence. In many ways, a negligence claim based on *res ipsa* makes the plaintiff's jobs at trial much easier than they ordinarily would be.

2. DEFENSES TO A *RES IPSA* CLAIM

Sidebar

Sometimes the only way to pin down exactly what happened in a particular case is to present expert testimony to explain the sequence of events, and the technicalities involved, to the jury.

Although we examine defenses to negligence cases in a later chapter, a word about defenses to *res ipsa* claims is included here. A defendant's best defense against such a claim is to attack the individual elements of the *res ipsa loquitur* doctrine. A defendant could show, for instance, that he was not in the exclusive control of the instrumentality or that the plaintiff in some way contributed to his own injuries. Attacking the first element of *res ipsa* (the event is one that ordinarily does not occur without negligence) is hard to do. How does a defendant prove a negative? Given that the first element relies almost completely on common sense, a defendant would have better luck attacking the second and third elements instead. *Res ipsa* claims are also subject to the contributory negligence defenses in states that still recognize that concept. (See Chapter 9, "Defenses to Negligence.")

3. PLEADING *RES IPSA LOQUITUR:* WHAT THE COMPLAINT SHOULD ALLEGE

When pleading *res ipsa,* the complaint should use language that invokes the doctrine in your jurisdiction. At a minimum, a *res ipsa loquitur* complaint should contain language that states:

- that the instrumentality that caused the plaintiff's injury was under the exclusive control of the defendant;
- that the event that occurred is one that would not normally occur without negligence; and
- that the plaintiff was not responsible for and in fact did not exercise any control over the instrumentality.

See Figure 6-1 for examples of *res ipsa* complaints and Figure 6-2 for examples of cases in which *res ipsa* has been used.

- (Unattended railroad car rolls down track, strikes plaintiff) "[T]he collision would not have occurred, and defendant's train car would not have struck the plaintiff if the defendant had exercised due care in controlling, maintaining and using said railroad car, the details of such control being exclusively within the knowledge of the defendant and not within the knowledge of the plaintiff."

- (Construction crane suddenly swings out of control, strikes plaintiffs while they are walking through parking lot) "[T]he operation and control of the construction crane was wholly and exclusively within the control of the defendant, and the plaintiffs having no control or responsibility for said crane, were struck by said crane, an event that would not normally occur without negligence on the part of the defendant."

FIGURE 6-1

Excerpts from Real Complaints Alleging *Res Ipsa Loquitur*

- Plane crashes
- Railroad derailments

- "Exploding" soda bottles
- Building collapses

FIGURE 6-2

Incidents in Which *Res Ipsa Loquitur* Has Been Used Successfully

B. NEGLIGENCE PER SE

Another court-created doctrine that is useful to plaintiffs is **negligence per se.** Here, the plaintiff can prove a breach of duty by showing that the defendant violated a statute. As far as the law is concerned, violation of certain types of

Negligence per se
Negligence in and of itself; the principle that the violation of a safety statute establishes a presumption of breach of duty in a negligence action.

statutes equates to violation of the duty of care. Negligence per se means "negligence by itself." This is a doctrine that states that the court can infer (or even presume) breach of duty when the defendant violated a statute at the time that he injured the plaintiff. To take advantage of negligence per se, the plaintiff must show:

- that the statute was, in fact, violated;
- that the statute was designed with safety in mind;
- that the defendant's violation of the statute was a major factor in the plaintiff's injuries; and
- that the plaintiff was in a "class" of people the statute was intended to protect.

ISSUE AT A GLANCE

In negligence per se, reasonable conduct is dictated by statute, not the reasonable person standard.

Example: Rick is driving at 90 mph and loses control of his car. He runs off the road and crashes into Joan's car. At the time, Joan was at the wheel of her car, waiting for a light to turn green. Joan brings a suit against Rick, basing her claim on negligence per se. Can she prove the elements? See Figure 6-3 for a list of the elements.

FIGURE 6-3

Evaluating the Defendant's Breach

- The defendant knew or should have known that his action/inaction would cause a potential hazard.
- The defendant knew or should have known that an injury to someone was foreseeable.
- The defendant's action/inaction was a proximate cause of the plaintiff's injury.

Let's take each element of negligence per se and apply it to the facts of this scenario. The first element is proof that the statute was violated. Proving that the statute was in fact violated is usually quite simple. Testimony from a police officer that he issued a ticket to Rick for driving too fast would be enough evidence to prove this element.

What about the second element — that the statute was designed with safety in mind? Before we answer this question, perhaps we should take a moment to address why this element is required. Suppose that instead of being charged with speeding and reckless driving, Rick instead had crashed into Joan's car at a normal speed. When the police arrive, they discover that Rick's license is expired. Can Joan use this as evidence of negligence per se? No. The doctrine was created as a way of helping plaintiffs prove breach of duty. Rick's driver's license status, at least under these facts, has nothing to do with Joan's injuries. Put another way, could Rick reasonably foresee that having an expired driver's license would put other drivers at risk? Probably not. Could Rick reasonably foresee that driving at excessive speed would put other drivers at risk? Absolutely. So the answer to why the statute involves safety goes back to our prior analysis of foreseeability. In fact, throughout negligence law, we rarely stray from the issue of foreseeability. Joan can prove the second element of her claim because speeding statutes were designed primarily as a safety precaution.

What about the third element? Many jurisdictions have inserted this element (a causal link between the statute violation and the plaintiff's injuries) for the same reason given in the previous paragraph. Presuming negligence in a case where the statutory violation had nothing to do with the accident seems a bit unfair. However, we do not have that problem in Joan's suit. She can easily prove that Rick's excessive speed had a direct link to her injuries.

Finally, we reach the fourth element. Was Joan in a "class" of persons designed to be protected by the statute? Why was this statute created in the first place? Speed limit statutes are created to punish people who drive at excessive speeds, because those people often pose a threat to other motorists. Again we come back to the issue of foreseeability. Was it foreseeable that another motorist could be hurt by Rick's negligent driving? Yes. Joan is a motorist; therefore, she falls into the class of people that the statute was designed to protect.

Joan has now proved all four elements of her negligence per se allegation, which means that she has also proved breach of duty. Assuming that she can also prove causation and damages, she should be successful in her action against Rick. See Figure 6-4 for a list of other common acts of negligence and Figure 6-5 for unintentional death statistics.

▪ Failure to drive safely	▪ Failure to warn of dangerous
▪ Excessive speed	conditions
▪ Failure to keep a proper	▪ Unsafe work conditions
lookout	▪ Unsafe premises
▪ Following too closely	▪ Failure to maintain equipment
▪ Driving under the influence of	
alcohol or some other drug	

FIGURE 6-4

The Most Common Acts of Negligence

1. WHAT THE COMPLAINT SHOULD SAY ABOUT NEGLIGENCE PER SE

Most authorities agree that some or all of the following language should be used when drafting a complaint based on negligence per se:

- There was a safety statute in effect at the time of the plaintiff's injury.
- The defendant violated that safety statute in the following, specific ways: (list each way that the defendant violated the safety statute).
- The defendant's violation of the statute was a proximate cause of the plaintiff's injuries.
- The statute was specifically designed with safety in mind.
- The plaintiff was clearly in the class of persons for whom the statute was created.

Figure 6-5

10 Leading Causes of Death by Age Group, United States—2012

Rank	<1	1-4	5-9	10-14	15-24	25-34	35-44	45-54	55-64	65+	Total
					Age Groups						
1	Congenital Anomalies 4,939	Unintentional Injury 1,353	Unintentional Injury 743	Unintentional Injury 807	Unintentional Injury 11,908	Unintentional Injury 15,851	Unintentional Injury 15,034	Malignant Neoplasms 48,028	Malignant Neoplasms 113,130	Heart Disease 477,840	Heart Disease 599,711
2	Short Gestation 4,202	Congenital Anomalies 501	Malignant Neoplasms 440	Malignant Neoplasms 472	Suicide 4,872	Suicide 6,216	Malignant Neoplasms 11,337	Heart Disease 35,265	Heart Disease 71,228	Malignant Neoplasms 403,497	Malignant Neoplasms 582,623
3	SIDS 1,679	Malignant Neoplasms 392	Congenital Anomalies 167	Suicide 306	Homicide 4,614	Homicide 4,342	Heart Disease 10,489	Unintentional Injury 20,394	Unintentional Injury 15,822	Chronic Low. Respiratory Disease 122,375	Chronic Low. Respiratory Disease 143,489
4	Maternal Pregnancy Comp. 1,507	Homicide 339	Homicide 138	Homicide 173	Malignant Neoplasms 1,574	Malignant Neoplasms 3,674	Suicide 6,758	Liver Disease 8,877	Chronic Low. Respiratory Disease 15,212	Cerebro-vascular 109,127	Cerebro-vascular 128,546
5	Unintentional Injury 1,169	Heart Disease 154	Heart Disease 67	Congenital Anomalies 160	Heart Disease 956	Heart Disease 3,231	Homicide 2,705	Suicide 8,862	Diabetes Mellitus 12,553	Alzheimer's Disease 82,690	Unintentional Injury 127,792
6	Placenta Cord. Membranes 1,018	Influenza & Pneumonia 93	Chronic Low. Respiratory Disease 63	Heart Disease 108	Congenital Anomalies 423	HIV 652	Liver Disease 2,469	Diabetes Mellitus 5,747	Liver Disease 11,230	Diabetes Mellitus 52,881	Alzheimer's Disease 83,637
7	Bacterial Sepsis 566	Septicemia 62	Benign Neoplasms 47	Chronic Low Respiratory Disease 56	Diabetes Mellitus 196	Diabetes Mellitus 646	Diabetes Mellitus 1,867	Cerebro-vascular 5,654	Cerebro-vascular 11,070	Unintentional Injury 44,698	Diabetes Mellitus 73,932
8	Respiratory Distress 504	Cerebro-vascular 56	Influenza & Pneumonia 44	Cerebro-vascular 51	Cerebro-vascular 183	Liver Disease 597	Cerebro-vascular 1,730	Chronic Low. Respiratory Disease 4,533	Suicide 6,929	Influenza & Pneumonia 43,355	Influenza & Pneumonia 50,636
9	Circulatory System Disease 492	Benign Neoplasms 55	Cerebro-vascular 34	Influenza & Pneumonia 41	Complicated Pregnancy 169	Cerebro-vascular 535	HIV 1,345	HIV 2,582	Septicemia 4,982	Nephritis 37,740	Nephritis 45,622
10	Neonatal Hemorrhage 422	Chronic Low Respiratory Disease 51	Septicemia 26	Benign Neoplasms 40	Influenza & Pneumonia 147	Congenital Anomalies 401	Septicemia 757	Septicemia 2,340	Nephritis 4,765	Septicemia 27,022	Suicide 40,600

Centers for Disease Control and Prevention
National Center for Injury Prevention and Control

CDC

Source: National Vital Statistics System, National Center for Health Statistics, CDC

Produced by: National Center for Injury Prevention and Control, CDC using WISQARS™.

Case Excerpt

YOUNG-GIBSON V. PATEL
957 F.Supp. 2d 269 (W.D.N.Y., 2013)

Background

Defendant Pravin Patel is a citizen of New York and owns the Best Western Dunkirk and Fredonia, a hotel located in Dunkirk, New York. Plaintiff is a citizen of Glouster, Massachusetts.

From August 1 to August 6, 2004, Plaintiff was a guest at Defendant's hotel while attending a business seminar. Plaintiff's stay was unremarkable until August 4, when she alleges that she began to suffer from "migraine-like symptoms." When these symptoms worsened, Plaintiff contacted her physician, Dr. Edward Foley, who prescribed her medication.

Since Plaintiff was far from home, Dr. Foley told her that he would send the prescription to a pharmacy near her. Dr. Foley did not tell Plaintiff to which pharmacy he planned to send her prescription, but he told her that he would provide that information.

Plaintiff did not hear from Dr. Foley again until two days later, on August 6, 2004. This delay was allegedly not for Dr. Foley's lack of effort. Plaintiff claims that Dr. Foley attempted to reach her by telephone at the hotel 20 times, each time allowing the telephone to ring 10 times. Plaintiff alleges that Defendant failed to answer the telephone, which prevented her from learning the location of her prescription. Plaintiff states that she suffered a number of ills while waiting to hear from Dr. Foley, including an eye infection that developed into glaucoma. These afflictions required numerous doctor visits, surgeries, and expensive medications.

Discussion

When determining whether a complaint states a claim, the court must construe it liberally, accept all factual allegations as true, and draw all reasonable inferences in the plaintiff's favor. Legal conclusions, however, are not afforded the same presumption of truthfulness.

Courts therefore use a two-pronged approach to examine the sufficiency of a complaint, which includes "any documents that are either incorporated into the complaint by reference or attached to the complaint as exhibits." This examination is context specific and requires that the court draw on its judicial experience and common sense. First, statements that are not entitled to the presumption of truth—such as conclusory allegations, labels, and legal conclusions—are identified and stripped away. Second, well-pleaded, non-conclusory factual allegations are presumed true and examined to determine whether they "plausibly give rise to an entitlement to relief.... Where the well-pleaded facts do not permit the court to infer more than the mere possibility of misconduct," the complaint fails to state a claim.

Plaintiff's Negligence Claim

To establish a claim of negligence, a plaintiff must demonstrate that (1) a duty exists, owed by the defendant to the plaintiff; (2) defendants breached that duty; and (3) an injury to the plaintiff proximately resulted from the defendant's breach.

"Proof of negligence in the air, so to speak, will not do." *Palsgraf v. Long Island R.R. Co.*, 248 N.Y. 339, 162 N.E. 99, 99 (1928). Ignoring a ringing telephone can constitute actionable negligence only if this Court decides, as a matter of law, that the defendant innkeeper owed a duty to the guest to answer.

Innkeepers are bound by a duty to exercise reasonable care for the convenience, comfort, and safety of their guests, which includes a right to respectful and decent treatment, protecting guests from harm and providing the inn as a safe harbor. New York courts have imposed liability upon innkeepers for failing to remedy dangerous conditions on the premises, failing to protect guests during emergencies, failing to protect guests from criminal attacks, and failing to respect guests' privacy and comfort. In addition, an innkeeper's duty of reasonable care depends in part on "the grade of the inn and the character of the accommodation which it is designed to afford."

The scope of an innkeeper's duty expands no further than to encompass foreseeable risks. Chief Judge Cardozo's maxim that "the risk reasonably to be perceived defines the duty to be obeyed" still resonates in New York, as does his conception of an "orbit," or zone, of danger, created by a defendant's conduct, within which a plaintiff must be located.

Modern New York courts graft an additional requirement onto the duty inquiry: liability will attach only if the plaintiff is harmed as the result of "an occurrence that is within the class of foreseeable hazards that the duty exists to prevent."

Moreover, even if the defendant had a duty to the plaintiff to take precisely the action that would have avoided the plaintiff's injury, such duty does not extend to occurrences caused by hazards falling outside of this class of hazards. But the mere fact that the plaintiff was harmed in an unexpected manner does not relieve the defendant from liability. In re Sept. 11 Litig., 280 F.Supp.2d at 296 (concluding that defendants could be liable for negligently performed airport security screening even though the precise manner by which air crashes were inflicted was unprecedented).

This district is one of few to have considered a claim involving facts similar to the ones presented here. In *Dean*, the court considered whether a hotel owner and operator could be held liable for failing to keep the front desk of the hotel staffed or otherwise ensure that a hotel employee would answer telephone calls originating from a guest's room. The plaintiff-guests alleged that they were unable to communicate with hotel employees to confirm the identity of persons demanding entry to their room, which caused them to deny entry to those persons. These persons were in fact police officers, who allegedly assaulted the guests after eventually forcing the guests out of their room.

Upon a motion for summary judgment, applying New York law, the court found that the innkeeper's duty to protect guests from harm would apply to such circumstances. The court characterized the hotel's failure to "answer every call to the front desk" as a possible breach of the hotel's duty to protect guests with reasonable safety precautions, akin to a failure to provide working door locks or peepholes. But in *Dean*, the court did not reach the issue of whether a hotel owner has a duty to ensure that the staff answers all calls. Thus, *Dean* does not establish a duty of a hotel owner to ensure that every call is answered.

Other courts have contemplated whether an inn's failure to allow a guest to communicate could be a source of liability. Others still have considered whether innkeepers can be liable for failing to maintain particular staff positions or provide particular services.

This Court need not resolve whether an innkeeper's duty could ever require the innkeeper to guard against unanswered telephones, as proposed by *Dean* and *Wassell*. Assuming arguendo that an innkeeper's failure to answer the hotel telephone does create some risk, reasonably to be perceived, that is sufficient to invoke such innkeeper's duty of care, the "class of foreseeable hazards" prong of the New York duty inquiry excludes Plaintiff's particular claim.

The guests in *Dean* and *Wassell* were unable to request assistance when faced with threats, real or perceived, by third party assailants. Similarly, the guest in *Lewis* was unable to summon help when threatened by illness. Though the court in *Lewis* ultimately concluded that the innkeeper was under no duty to provide the guest with telephone service, the guest's predicament illustrates the particular type of hazard which flowed from that inoperable telephone. If an innkeeper's failure to answer the telephone creates a risk sufficient to invoke such innkeeper's duty to protect, these three cases help define the class of foreseeable hazards that would be associated with that risk. This class of hazards comprises scenarios where guests are threatened with some type of harm but are unable to communicate their plight or request assistance. Thus, the innkeeper's purported duty would exist for the purpose of preventing guests from finding themselves in peril with no chance of outside assistance. Plaintiff would surely be within the zone of that danger.

Thus, Defendant's conduct may have created a risk and an associated class of hazards that posed a threat to Plaintiff. If Defendant ignored the hotel telephone, guests who needed help could have been left to languish in their rooms, unable to summon aid. Had Plaintiff, as her health deteriorated, attempted to call the front desk for help and received no answer, Defendant's duty to protect Plaintiff from harm might have applied. That scenario is much like *Dean*, and illustrates the type of hazard that could naturally flow from Defendant's failure to answer the telephone. Thus, that hazard would be part of the class of foreseeable risks.

But that is not what happened here. The hazard Defendant allegedly created in this case is quite different. Plaintiff alleges that Defendant's conduct placed her in danger, and that such danger caused her harm. That "danger," or hazard, that Defendant's conduct allegedly created was the risk that a guest could suffer harm by failing to receive outside communication. This purported hazard is of a much different class than the hazards found in *Dean*, *Wassell*, and *Lewis*, and is not part of the class of foreseeable hazards that an innkeeper's failure to answer the telephone could be said to create. In other words, if an innkeeper has a duty to answer the hotel telephone, that duty would not exist to prevent the type of hazard that Plaintiff alleges led to her harm. "In danger" is a peculiar way to describe a hotel guest who is unable to receive an incoming telephone call, and further demonstrates why Defendant's duty as an innkeeper to protect Plaintiff does not extend to Plaintiff's circumstances. Even if Defendant had a duty to answer the telephone to avoid certain foreseeable hazards, and thus take precisely the action that Plaintiff alleges would have averted her injuries, as in Di Ponzio, Hanna, and Mei Cai Chen, Defendant's duty falls short because Plaintiff's injury was not the result of one of those hazards.

New York courts recognize the familiar principle that liability in negligence cannot be defeated simply because harm is inflicted in an unforeseeable manner. But as Di Ponzio warns, this tenet should not be confused with the class of foreseeable hazards requirement. A defendant can be liable for a harm-producing occurrence of an unusual or unpredictable manner, but the source of such an occurrence still must be traced to a hazard that was within the class of foreseeable hazards created by the defendant's risky behavior.

In re September 11 Litigation illustrates the important difference between these two principles. There, the court recognized that the harm-producing occurrence—the use of commercial aircraft as guided missiles—was unusual and perhaps unforeseeable. But the hazard—the potential for hijacked aircraft to crash and cause injuries and property damage—was within the class of hazards naturally associated with unreasonably deficient airport security screening. Id. Thus, liability for that unpredictable occurrence could still attach to the defendant's performance of the security screening procedure.

Here, the harm-producing occurrence—Plaintiff growing increasingly ill while waiting to learn of the location of her prescription—also seems unusual. Pivotally, in contrast to In re September 11 Litigation, the hazard responsible for this occurrence—Plaintiff's inability to receive messages—was not within the class of hazards that would be associated with Defendant's purported duty to answer the hotel telephone. Thus, the somewhat unusual nature of the harm-producing occurrence is not the reason why Plaintiff's claim fails. Rather, Plaintiff's claim is outside of Defendant's scope of duty, because the hazard at play is outside the limited class of hazards for which Defendants could be responsible for creating.

An innkeeper's duty is to provide a safe harbor. Even if Defendant's duty to Plaintiff should have compelled Defendant to answer the hotel telephone, the hazard that allegedly ensnared Plaintiff is not within the class of hazards that such a duty would exist to prevent. Because this Court finds that Plaintiff's harm was brought about by an occurrence outside the scope of Defendant's duty as an innkeeper, Plaintiff's complaint fails to state a claim upon which relief can be granted and must be dismissed.

IV. Conclusion

The law of New York State establishes that duty is limited by a class of foreseeable hazards. If the alleged harm is outside that class, then a defendant does not have a duty to prevent such harm from occurring. Plaintiff's injuries allegedly resulted from her inability to receive outside communication while at Defendant's inn, which is not within the class of foreseeable hazards that an innkeeper might create by failing to answer the inn's telephone. Therefore, Defendant's motion is granted.

V. Orders

IT HEREBY IS ORDERED, that Defendant's Motion for Judgment on the Pleadings (Docket No. 47) is GRANTED.

FURTHER, that the Clerk of Court shall close this case.

SO ORDERED.

Questions about the case:

1. What negligence is the innkeeper alleged to have committed in this case?
2. What are the traditional duties that innkeepers owe to their guests?
3. What duty does the plaintiff allege the innkeeper failed to meet in this case?
4. How does the court rule regarding the plaintiff's contentions against the innkeeper?

VI EXPERT EVIDENCE AND BREACH OF DUTY

Many times the only way to establish that the defendant breached his duty to the plaintiff is through the presentation of expert testimony. Was the defendant speeding at the time of the collision? Naturally enough, the defendant claims that he was not. The plaintiff believes that he was. Is there any way to settle this issue? One way is to locate an expert in accident reconstruction. This expert can calculate the defendant's speed based on the conditions: the skid marks, the impact point, the spread pattern of broken glass, and so on.

An expert witness is someone who, either through training or education, has acquired specialized knowledge that most people don't have. Because of this specialized knowledge, an expert witness is permitted to do the one thing that no other witness is allowed to do — testify about a conclusion in the case. Lay witnesses are not allowed to offer any opinion about what happened in the case or who was at fault. Expert witnesses can. Because this opinion can have a big impact on the jury, there are several requirements the attorney must meet before the witness will be allowed to offer this opinion. The attorney will have to establish the qualifications of the expert and show how this person has specialized knowledge about an area and how this testimony would assist the jury in reaching a verdict. See Figure 6-6 for a checklist of information to gather about an expert.

| **FIGURE 6-6**

Expert
Checklist | Name, address, fax, beeper, cell
    phone and telephone numbers,
    and e-mail address
What's the best and
    fastest way to contact
    this person?
Training and background
    (be thorough)
       Academics | Degrees
Schools attended
Publications
Honors, awards
Association memberships,
    positions held
Testified as an expert witness before?
    How often? Primarily for one side or
    the other? |

Chapter Summary

Once the legal duty of the defendant has been established, the plaintiff must then prove that the defendant breached this duty. Proving breach of duty involves not only evidence and testimony, but also an analysis of the law. Court doctrines have been created over time to assist with this analysis. *Res ipsa loquitur* is a doctrine that courts created to assist plaintiffs in proving negligence when a more traditional legal analysis left them without a possibility of recovery. To prove a *res ipsa* claim, the plaintiff must show several factors, including that the instrument that caused the plaintiff's injury was under the control of the defendant; the injury that occurred was something that does not normally occur unless negligence is present; the plaintiff did not contribute to her own injuries; and that of the two parties, the defendant is in a better position to explain what happened than the plaintiff. Another doctrine that was created to help establish breach of duty is negligence per se. Under negligence per se, if the plaintiff can show that the defendant was violating a safety statute at the time of the plaintiff's injuries, that the plaintiff was in a class of persons designed to be protected by the safety statute, and that the defendant's violation of this statute was a proximate cause of the plaintiff's injuries, the court is allowed to infer that the defendant did, in fact, breach his duty.

 SKILLS YOU NEED IN THE REAL WORLD

Locating Expert Witnesses

How do you locate an expert witness? In the past, the process was hit or miss. But in these days of advanced technology and a new openness among the professions, finding an expert is much easier. Need an expert who will testify that excessive sugar intake causes blackouts? You can probably find one in the legal classifieds. Experts realized years ago that being in the business of testifying is lucrative. Some experts even advertise on the Internet.

Here are some methods for finding an expert witness:

- Word of mouth
- The pro who beat you last time
- Listings maintained by the bar
- Other prominent cases
- Associations
- Advertisements
- The Internet

Word of Mouth

One of the best ways to find an expert is by talking with other firms and other paralegals who have used experts in the past. This kind of personal experience with a witness is invaluable. For instance, the other paralegal may tell you that although this witness has an impressive resume (the term *curriculum vitae* is often used with experts), he is arrogant and difficult to work with. If you're going through the trouble of hiring an expert to work on a case, you need to find someone you can work with. It doesn't matter how impressive a person's credentials are if he doesn't return phone calls or, even worse, makes a bad impression on the jury.

The Pro Who Beat You Last Time

Surprisingly enough, many attorneys will hire the expert who beat them last time. Keep a list of all of the expert witnesses who have testified for the other side in prior cases and complete the checklist (Figure 6-7) on each one. Is this a person you'd rather have working with you than against you? If the answer is yes, retain this expert on your next big case.

Listings Maintained by the Bar

Local and state bar associations often have lists of people who are qualified to testify as expert witnesses on a wide variety of topics. Although this will help you get started, once you locate a likely candidate, you should always try to find people who have worked with this person in the past. Ask the expert for references, such as other firms who have used her in the past. If she refuses this reasonable request, that alone has told you plenty about her and means you should move on to the next person on your list.

Other Prominent Cases

Many paralegals maintain files of prominent cases and the names of the expert witnesses who testified in those cases. This file not only is helpful in locating experts for future cases but may also provide the basis for cross-examination of the other

FIGURE 6-7	Expert witness name: _____

The Pro from Last Time Scoring Sheet

Expert witness name: _____
Case testified in: _____
Overall ranking (on a scale of five): _____

Testimony on the witness stand

Very Good		Not much impact			Terrible
5	4	3	2	1	0

Personality: impact with the jury

Very Good		Not much impact			Terrible
5	4	3	2	1	0

Ability to explain complex issues

Very Good		Not much impact			Terrible
5	4	3	2	1	0

Use of charts, diagrams, and other aids

Very Good		Not much impact			Terrible
5	4	3	2	1	0

How well did the witness do on cross-examination?

Very Good		Not much impact			Terrible
5	4	3	2	1	0

How much did he or she contribute to the other side's win?

Very Good		Not much			Not at all
5	4	3	2	1	0

Notes:

side's expert. For instance, if you can show that in the past five years this witness has only testified for the defense, this could show a possible bias against plaintiffs.

Associations

Some professional associations maintain lists of people who have testified or could testify about particular topics. Your next case might involve the American Numismatist Association (coin experts). Contact the association and find out if they have a list of qualified experts.

Advertisements and the Internet

The least successful techniques for finding good experts are advertisements and the Internet. Both of these media have the same problem: inability to double-check facts. Just because someone advertises in the back of a legal magazine or has a nice Web page does not make her an expert witness. What makes a person an expert witness is training and education, not a nice ad. However, if you can't locate a witness any other way, start with the Web page or back-page ad and then thoroughly interview this person. Ask for references. Double-check the resume or curriculum vitae. Talk to other people who've worked with her. Remember, this person could make or break your case, so the more you know about her the better.

There are some Internet sites that can provide you with valuable information. TASA is one such site (Technical Advice for Attorneys, www.tasanet.com). At this site, you can search for a dizzying variety of expert witnesses, arbitrators, mediators, and other consultants.

THE LIFE OF A PARALEGAL

"Red Flagging" Records

As the case gets closer to trial, I help get the file organized and prepare trial note-books. I go through the entire file and red flag anything that could be of concern. I look at the client's prior medical histories, whether they've had previous personal injury cases, what their work history has been like, anything that the other side might focus on. You look at every aspect of the clients themselves. Are they a credible witness? You try to get a feel for and screen the client to see if they are a good person to take to trial. Some clients, you can tell right away that they wouldn't make a good witness, either because they're anxious or crying all the time or for some other reason. You go through different documents, seeing if anything conflicts. You compare dates and make sure that they all match up. If they don't, you red flag them. This check-through is really helpful. You don't ever want to take even the simplest things for granted. In one case that I was involved with, in looking over the accident report and the photos of the car that were provided, I realized that the car in the photos wasn't the same vehicle that was listed in the accident report. The insurance carrier had taken a picture of the wrong car, one that was involved in another accident not related to our case. No one else had caught it and we used it to our advantage. You should always check the basic information to make sure that you've got your facts right. You don't want to assume anything. I go through the case step by step and look at everything. When you're putting a trial notebook together, or just reviewing records, as a rule, more information is always better. The attorney might not ever use it, but it's there if they do.

Gwyn Huffman, Paralegal

ETHICAL ISSUES FOR THE PARALEGAL: CONFIDENTIALITY

A client's communications with his attorney are as confidential as those made to a doctor or a pastor. Unless it falls into a narrow exception, an attorney cannot be compelled to testify about what the client has told him. Although paralegals are not protected by this same evidentiary privilege, they should always act as though they are. Revealing sensitive or even mundane information about a client can have disastrous consequences. When a paralegal reveals confidential information about a client, the client may decide to take action. This action could be as simple as firing the lawyer, bringing a complaint before the bar, or even a legal malpractice claim naming not only the lawyer but also the paralegal as defendants. Confidentiality extends not only to the facts and issues of the client's case, but could even extend to the client's identity. There are times when the client does not wish anyone else to know that he is represented by an attorney. Any questions about this or any other potentially confidential matter should be handled with the blanket statement, "I'm not allowed to discuss the firm's business." By taking that simple precaution, you keep the client's trust and avoid a potential legal entanglement later on.

Relevant Cases

GOULD V. AMERICAN FAMILY MUT. INS. CO.
198 WIS. 2D 450, 543 N.W. 2D 282 (1996)

BRADLEY, Justice.

Both the plaintiffs, Sheri and Scott Gould, and the defendant, American Family Mutual Insurance Company, seek review of a court of appeals' decision which reversed and remanded a judgment of the Circuit Court of St. Croix County, Eric J. Lundell, Judge. The judgment imposed liability against American Family for personal injuries caused by its insured, Roland Monicken, who was institutionalized suffering from Alzheimer's disease. The Goulds assert that the court of appeals erred by abandoning the objective reasonable person standard and adopting a subjective mental incapacity defense in negligence cases. American Family challenges the need for a remand.

While we affirm the court of appeals' reversal of the judgment, we do so on other grounds. We hold that an individual institutionalized, as here, with a mental disability, and who does not have the capacity to control or appreciate his or her conduct cannot be liable for injuries caused to caretakers who are employed for financial compensation. Because the Goulds, in essence, admit that it would be impossible to rebut the evidence of Monicken's incapacity, we reverse the part of the court of appeals' decision remanding the case to the trial court for a determination of Monicken's capacity.

Monicken was diagnosed with Alzheimer's disease after displaying bizarre and irrational behavior. As a result of his deteriorating condition, his family was later forced to admit him to the St. Croix Health Care Center. Sheri Gould was the head nurse of the center's dementia unit and took care of him on several occasions.

Monicken's records from St. Croix indicate that he was often disoriented, resistant to care, and occasionally combative. When not physically restrained, he often went into other patients' rooms and sometimes resisted being removed by staff. On one such occasion, Gould attempted to redirect Monicken to his own room by touching him on the elbow. She sustained personal injuries when Monicken responded by knocking her to the floor.

Gould and her husband brought suit against Monicken and his insurer, American Family. American Family admitted coverage and filed a motion for summary judgment, arguing that Monicken was incapable of negligence as a matter of law due to his lack of mental capacity. An affidavit of Monicken's treating psychiatrist filed in support of the motion stated that Monicken was unable to appreciate the consequences of his acts or to control his behavior. The trial court denied American Family's summary judgment motion and the liability portion of the bifurcated trial was tried to a jury.

After presenting its case, American Family proposed giving instructions and a special verdict that directed the jury to decide, as a threshold question of law, whether Monicken had the mental capacity to understand and appreciate the duty to act with reasonable care at the time of the incident based on his Alzheimer's disease. The trial court denied this request. Pursuant to Wis JI-Civil 1021, the court instructed the jury to disregard any evidence related to Monicken's mental condition and to determine his negligence under the objective reasonable person standard. The jury found Monicken totally negligent and a judgment of liability was entered against American Family.

The court of appeals granted American Family's interlocutory appeal and reversed the judgment, holding that "a person may not be held civilly liable where a mental condition deprives that person of the ability to control his or her conduct." *Gould v. American Family Mut. Ins. Co.*, 187 Wis.2d 671, 673, 523 N.W.2d 295 (Ct.App. 1994). The court remanded the case "for a determination of whether there is a disputed issue of material fact as to whether Monicken's mental condition prevented him from controlling or appreciating the consequences of his conduct." Id. at 680, 523 N.W.2d 295.

Both the Goulds and American Family petitioned this court for review. The Goulds argue that the court of appeals abandoned clear, long-standing precedent in determining that mental disability may constitute a defense to negligence. American Family agrees with the court of appeals' holding, but petitioned for cross review to reverse the court's remand mandate. American Family asserts that a remand is unnecessary because Monicken's mental incapacity was virtually conceded at trial.

It is a widely accepted rule in most American jurisdictions that mentally disabled adults are held responsible for the torts they commit regardless of their capacity to comprehend their actions; they are held to an objective reasonable person standard. See generally, Restatement (Second) of Torts §283B (1965); W. Page Keeton et al., Prosser and Keeton on the Law of Torts, §135 (1984). Legal scholars trace the origins of this rule to an English trespass case decided in 1616, at a time when strict liability controlled.

When fault-based liability replaced strict liability, American courts in common law jurisdictions identified the matter as a question of public policy and maintained the rule imposing liability on the mentally disabled. Although early case law suggested that Wisconsin followed this trend, this court specifically adopted the common law rule and the public policy justifications behind it in *German Mut. Fire Ins. Soc'y v. Meyer*, 218 Wis. 381, 385, 261 N.W. 211 (1935).

In *Meyer*, the defendant was criminally charged with arson to a barn but was committed to a mental hospital after he was found to be insane. In the civil claim filed by the insurer who covered the loss, the defendant pled his insanity as a defense. *Meyer*, 218 Wis. at 382-85, 261 N.W. 211. The court primarily relied on cases from other jurisdictions to conclude that insanity was not a defense for tort liability.

In doing so the court quoted with approval the following statement of the general rule and public policy rationale behind it:

> It is the well settled rule that a person non compos mentis is liable in damages to one injured by reason of a tort committed by him unless evil intent or express malice constitutes an essential element in the plaintiff's recovery. This rule is usually considered to be based on the principle that where a loss must be borne by one of two innocent persons, it shall be borne by him who occasioned it, and it has also been held that public policy requires the enforcement of the liability in order that those interested in the estate of the insane person, as relatives or otherwise, may be under inducement to restrain him and that tort-feasors may not simulate or pretend insanity to defend their wrongful acts causing damage to others. . . .

This court did not have occasion to address the issue again until *Breunig v. American Family Ins. Co.*, 45 Wis.2d 536, 173 N.W.2d 619 (1970). In *Breunig*, Erma Veith was overcome with a mental delusion while driving and crossed the center line of a roadway, striking the plaintiff's vehicle. The plaintiff sued Veith's automobile liability insurer, and a jury returned a verdict finding her causally negligent on the theory that she had knowledge or forewarning of her mental delusions.

On appeal, the insurer argued that Veith could not be negligent as a matter of law because she was unable to drive with a conscious mind based on the sudden mental delusion. This court created a limited exception to the common law rule, holding that insanity could be a defense in the rare case "where the person is suddenly overcome without forewarning by a mental disability or disorder which incapacitates him from conforming his conduct to the standards of a reasonable man under like circumstances." However, because this court concluded that there was sufficient evidence for the jury to find that Veith had forewarning of the mental delusions, she was not entitled to use her condition as a defense.

The court of appeals in the present case relied on expansive dicta in *Breunig* to hold that *Breunig* overruled *Meyer*. It interpreted *Breunig* as a turning point in the law. See *Gould*, 187 Wis.2d at 677-78, 523 N.W.2d 295. We disagree. In contrast to the broad dicta found in *Breunig*, the actual holding was very limited:

> All we hold is that a sudden mental incapacity equivalent in its effect to such physical causes as a sudden heart attack, epileptic seizure, stroke, or fainting should be treated alike and not under the general rule of insanity.

The court of appeals erroneously perceived the underlying premise of *Breunig* to be that a person should not be held negligent where a mental disability prevents that person from controlling his or her conduct. *Gould*, 187 Wis.2d at 678, 523 N.W.2d 295. By limiting its holding to cases of sudden mental disability, the *Breunig* court chose not to adopt that broad premise. We also decline to do so.

We are concerned that the adoption of the premise, as set forth by the court of appeals, would entail serious administrative difficulties. Mental impairments and emotional disorders come in infinite types and degrees. As the American Law Institute recognized in its Restatement of Torts, a legitimate concern in formulating a test for mentally disabled persons in negligence cases is "the difficulty of drawing any satisfactory line between mental deficiency and those variations of temperament, intellect and emotional balance which cannot, as a practical matter, be taken into account in imposing liability for damage done." Restatement (Second) of Torts, §283B, cmt. b.1.

The difficulties encountered by the trier of fact in determining the existence, nature, degree, and effect of a mental disability may introduce into the civil law some of the issues that currently exist in the insanity defense in criminal law. We are wary of establishing a defense to negligence based on indeterminate standards of mental disability given the complexities of the various mental illnesses and the increasing rate at which new illnesses are discovered to explain behavior.

Further, while the traditional public policy rationale relied on by this court in *Meyer* in support of the common law rule are subject to criticism, we remain hesitant to abandon the long-standing rule in favor of a broad rule adopting the subjective standard for all mentally disabled persons. Generally, the public policy rationale, in varying degrees, remain legitimate concerns. Accordingly, we turn our discussion to how those rationale apply to the facts before us.

American Family does not dispute that Monicken committed an act that was a substantial factor in causing Gould's injury. Rather, it asserts that Monicken cannot be held liable for his alleged negligence as a matter of law based on his lack of mental capacity.

Even though the jury determined that Monicken was negligent and that his negligence was a cause of the plaintiff's injuries, liability does not necessarily follow. Public policy considerations may preclude liability.

One recognized public policy reason for not imposing liability despite a finding of negligence is that allowance of recovery would place an unreasonable burden on the negligent tortfeasor. As explained in detail below, this court concludes that the circumstances of this case totally negate the rationale behind the *Meyer* rule imposing liability on the mentally disabled, and therefore application of the rule would place an unreasonable burden on the institutionalized mentally disabled tortfeasor.

The first rationale set forth in *Meyer* is that "where a loss must be borne by one of two innocent persons, it shall be borne by him who occasioned it." *Meyer*, 218 Wis. at 385, 261 N.W. 211. The record reveals that Gould was not an innocent member of the public unable to anticipate or safeguard against the harm when encountered. Rather, she was employed as a caretaker specifically for dementia patients and knowingly encountered the dangers associated with such employment. It is undisputed that Gould, as head nurse of the dementia unit, knew Monicken was diagnosed with Alzheimer's disease and was aware of his disorientation and his potential for violent outbursts. Her own notes indicate that Monicken was angry and resisted being removed from another patient's room on the day of her injury.

By analogy, this court in *Hass v. Chicago & N.W. Ry.*, 48 Wis.2d 321, 326-27, 179 N.W.2d 885 (1970), relied on public policy considerations to exonerate negligent fire-starters or homeowners from liability for injuries suffered by the firefighters called to extinguish the fire. This court held that to make one who negligently starts a fire respond in damages to a firefighter who is injured placed too great a burden on the homeowner because the hazardous situation is the very reason the fireman's aid was enlisted.

Likewise, Gould, as the head nurse in the secured dementia unit and Monicken's caretaker, had express knowledge of the potential danger inherent in dealing with Alzheimer's patients in general and Monicken in particular. Holding Monicken negligent under these circumstances places too great a burden on him because his disorientation and potential for violence is the very reason he was institutionalized and needed the aid of employed caretakers. Accordingly, we conclude that the first *Meyer* rationale does not apply in this case.

The second rationale used to justify the rule is that "those interested in the estate of the insane person, as relatives or otherwise, may be under inducement to restrain him. . . ." *Meyer*, 218 Wis. at 385, 261 N.W. 211. This rationale also has little application to the present case. Monicken's relatives did everything they could to restrain him when they placed him in a secured dementia unit of a restricted health care center. When a mentally disabled person is placed in a nursing home, long-term care facility, health care center, or similar restrictive institution for the mentally disabled, those "interested in the estate" of that person are not likely in need of such further inducement.

The third reason for the common law rule set forth in *Meyer* is to prevent tortfeasors from "simulating or pretending insanity to defend their wrongful acts. . . . " Id. This rationale is likewise inapplicable under the facts of this case. To suggest that Mr. Monicken would "simulate or pretend" the symptoms of Alzheimer's disease over a period of years in order to avoid a future tort liability is incredible. It is likewise difficult to imagine circumstances under which persons would feign the symptoms of a mental disability and subject themselves to commitment in an institution in order to avoid some future civil liability.

In sum, we agree with the Goulds that ordinarily a mentally disabled person is responsible for his or her torts. However, we conclude that this rule does not apply in this case because the circumstances totally negate the rationale behind the rule and would place an unreasonable burden on the negligent institutionalized mentally disabled. When a mentally disabled person injures an employed caretaker, the injured party can reasonably foresee the danger and is not "innocent" of the risk involved. By placing a mentally disabled person in an institution or similar restrictive setting, "those interested in the estate" of that person are not likely to be in need of an inducement for greater restraint. It is incredible to assert that a tortfeasor would "simulate or pretend insanity" over a prolonged period of time and even be institutionalized in order to avoid being held liable for damages for some future civil act. Therefore, we hold that a person institutionalized, as here, with a mental disability, and who does not have the capacity to control or appreciate his or her conduct cannot be liable for injuries caused to caretakers who are employed for financial compensation.

Accordingly, we reverse that part of the decision of the court of appeals remanding the case to the trial court for a determination on the issue of Monicken's mental capacity. We remand to the trial court with directions to enter judgment for American Family in accordance with this decision.

The decision of the court of appeals is affirmed in part and reversed in part; the cause is remanded to the circuit court with directions to enter judgment in accordance with this decision.

ESTATE OF MULLIS BY DIXON V. MONROE OIL CO., INC.
349 N.C. 196, 505 S.E. 2D 131 (1998)

ORR, Justice.

This case arises out of a drunk-driving accident in which four young people were tragically killed. On 30 April 1993, the four persons involved, Otis Blount, twenty; Dwaine Darby, nineteen; Melissa Mullis, fifteen; and Patricia Teel, eighteen, decided to meet several other individuals at a local teen nightclub in Monroe between 7:00 and 8:00 P.M. Before meeting at the Monroe club, Blount bought some liquor for himself and two other individuals from a store operated by defendant City of Monroe Board of Alcoholic Beverage Control ("Monroe ABC"). Blount returned to the same Monroe ABC store later that evening and bought some more liquor for himself and the other individuals. Later, Blount left the club again and this time bought beer from a convenience store owned by defendant Monroe Oil Company, Inc. ("Monroe Oil").

At about 11:00 P.M., Blount, Darby, Mullis, and Teel decided to go to a party at a friend's house. The four got into Darby's Volkswagen Jetta: Darby in the driver's seat; Blount in the front passenger seat; and the two girls, Mullis and Teel, in the back passenger seat. Prior to leaving the club, Blount was given money which had been collected at the club to buy beer for the party, and on the way to the party, Darby stopped at the convenience store owned by Monroe Oil so that Blount could buy the beer. Two other carloads of teenagers in the group also stopped at the store.

After Blount bought the beer, he returned to Darby's car and got behind the wheel to drive. Darby sat in the front passenger seat, and the two girls remained in the backseat. After consuming alcohol in the parking lot, Blount drove the car out of the parking lot and headed towards the location of the party. Moments later, at approximately midnight, Blount drove the car off the road into a tree. The car caught fire, killing all four occupants. An officer responding to the scene concluded that Blount's alcohol use contributed to the accident. Blount's autopsy report also revealed that his blood-alcohol content was 0.13 at the time of the accident, an amount exceeding the then-legal limit of 0.10 alcohol content under our impaired-driving statute, N.C.G.S. §20-138.1 (1989) (amendment for offenses committed on or after 1 October 1993 substituted "0.08" for "0.10").

Based on the above, the administrator of the estate of Melissa Mullis, one of the passengers, filed suit alleging that defendants Monroe ABC and Monroe Oil were negligent for selling alcohol to an underage person under the Dram Shop Act, N.C.G.S. §§18B-120 to -129 (1995). Plaintiff brought the action under N.C.G.S. §§28A-18-1 to -18-8, dealing with the survival of actions and wrongful-death provisions. Defendants answered the complaint and moved to dismiss it for failure to state a claim upon which relief could be granted, pursuant to Rule 12(b)(6) of the North Carolina Rules of Civil Procedure. In their 12(b)(6) motions, defendants contended that the Dram Shop action should be dismissed because plaintiff had failed to file the complaint within the statute of limitations period under the Act. Plaintiff then filed a motion to amend the complaint, which was granted on 11 April 1995. In the amended complaint, plaintiff withdrew the Dram Shop action and asserted a negligence per se claim alleging that defendants' acts were in violation of N.C.G.S. §18B-102, which prohibits the illegal sale of alcohol, and, more specifically, were in violation of N.C.G.S. §18B-302, which prohibits the sale of alcohol to underage persons. In addition to the negligence per se claim, plaintiff also alleged that defendants were liable for the negligent sale of alcohol to an underage person under common law negligence.

Defendants renewed the 12(b)(6) motions to dismiss the complaint, and both motions were denied. Defendants subsequently moved for summary judgment pursuant to Rule 56 of the North Carolina Rules of Civil Procedure, arguing that there was no genuine issue as to any material fact as shown by the pleadings, depositions, and responses, and that defendants were entitled to judgment as a matter of law. The trial court granted the summary judgment motions for defendants on 10 May 1996, and plaintiff appealed.

The Court of Appeals affirmed the trial court's decision and held that plaintiff's sole and exclusive remedy was under the Dram Shop Act. The Court of Appeals explained that to maintain a wrongful-death suit, plaintiff/estate had to show that the deceased,

Melissa Mullis, could have maintained a negligence action against defendants if she had lived. The Court of Appeals concluded that, here, a negligence per se or common law negligence claim could not be so maintained based on this Court's decision in *Hart v. Ivey*, 332 N.C. 299, 420 S.E.2d 174 (1992). The Court of Appeals stated that a negligence per se action could not be maintained because this Court held in Hart that a violation of N.C.G.S. §18B-302 is not negligence per se. Plaintiff, therefore, could not establish that defendants' violation of N.C.G.S. §18B-302 in this case was negligence per se.

The Court of Appeals also held that plaintiff could not maintain a common law negligence claim against defendants for selling alcohol to an underage person. The Court of Appeals explained that in *Hart*, this Court held that a common law negligence suit could be maintained against a social host for furnishing alcohol to an underage guest if it was shown that the social host served alcohol to the guest when the host knew or should have known that the guest was intoxicated and was going to drive a car. The Court of Appeals noted that, here, plaintiff did not allege that defendants knew or should have known that Otis Blount was intoxicated when defendants sold him the alcohol on 30 April 1993. Emphasizing plaintiff's failure to allege knowledge of intoxication, the Court of Appeals concluded that a common law negligence action could not be maintained and that the Dram Shop Act provided the sole cause of action available to plaintiff. The Court of Appeals stated that since plaintiff failed to timely file an action under the Dram Shop Act, the trial court's grant of summary judgment was proper. For reasons set forth below, we affirm the Court of Appeals' decision affirming the trial court's orders of summary judgment for defendants.

The issues in this case are whether plaintiff may maintain negligence claims against defendant commercial vendors for selling alcohol to an underage person on two grounds:

(1) negligence per se, based on a violation of N.C.G.S. §18B-302; and (2) common law negligence. First, the Court of Appeals correctly determined that plaintiff may not maintain a negligence per se action based on a violation of N.C.G.S. §18B-302. In *Hart v. Ivey*, 332 N.C. 299, 420 S.E.2d 174, this Court reversed the Court of Appeals and held that a violation of N.C.G.S. §18B-302 is not negligence per se. Under N.C.G.S. §18B-302, it is a misdemeanor to give or sell alcoholic beverages to anyone less than twenty-one years old. Id. at 306, 420 S.E.2d at 178. In a divided opinion, this Court held that a violation of N.C.G.S. §18B-302 was not negligence per se because the statute was not a public safety statute which imposed a duty for the protection of the public. Id. at 303-04, 420 S.E.2d at 177. The majority in *Hart* concluded that the purpose of N.C.G.S. §18B-302 was to restrict minors' consumption of alcohol, that it was therefore not a public-safety statute, and that it could not be the basis for a negligence per se claim. In light of the majority decision in *Hart*, we are bound in this case to conclude that plaintiff may not maintain a negligence per se action based on a violation of N.C.G.S. §18B-302.

The next issue we must address is whether plaintiff may maintain a common law negligence action against defendant commercial vendors arising out of the sale of alcohol to an underage person. Presently, commercial vendors are subject to liability for the negligent sale of alcohol to an underage person under the North Carolina Dram Shop Act. N.C.G.S. §§18B-120 to -129. Any effect that the Dram Shop Act may have on the existence of a common law negligence suit must be addressed first since the Act was specifically created to impose liability for the conduct upon which plaintiff's suit is based.

Under the Dram Shop Act, an aggrieved party has a claim against a "permittee or local Alcoholic Beverage Control Board" if the party shows that the seller "negligently sold or furnished an alcoholic beverage to an underage person," that consumption of the beverage caused or contributed to the underage driver's impairment, and that the injury which resulted was "proximately caused by the underage driver's negligent operation of a vehicle while so impaired." N.C.G.S. §18B-121. The legislature has also provided that "the creation of any claim for relief by this Article may not be interpreted to abrogate or abridge any claims for relief under the common law." N.C.G.S. §18B-128. Under this section, the legislature has made clear that previously existing common law rights are preserved. We may conclude, therefore, that the Dram Shop cause of action was not intended to be the exclusive remedy available to a third party who wishes to assert a negligence suit against a seller based on the sale of alcohol to an underage person.

In addition to the Dram Shop Act's not excluding common law remedies, this Court held in *Hart v. Ivey*, 332 N.C. 299, 420 S.E.2d 174, that a common law negligence claim could exist for the negligent provision of alcohol by a social host. There, we held that a common law negligence claim could be maintained where the plaintiff alleged that the social host provided alcohol to an underage guest when the host knew or should have known that the guest was intoxicated and was going to drive a car shortly after consuming the alcohol. In acknowledging this common law claim in *Hart*, we stated that we were not creating a new cause of action but were instead merely allowing "established negligence principles" to be applied to the facts alleged. Id. at 306, 420 S.E.2d at 178. We stated that, under established common law negligence principles, a plaintiff must offer evidence of four essential elements in order to prevail: duty, breach of duty, proximate cause, and damages. In *Hart*, we further explained that

> actionable negligence is the failure to exercise that degree of care which a reasonable and prudent person would exercise under similar conditions. A defendant is liable for his negligence if the negligence is the proximate cause of injury to a person to whom the defendant is under a duty to use

reasonable care. *Hart*, 332 N.C. at 305, 420 S.E.2d at 177-78.

Applying these long-standing negligence rules to the plaintiff's allegations in *Hart*, we concluded that the plaintiff's factual averments were sufficient to satisfy all common law negligence elements. First, the defendants had a "duty to the people who travel on the public highways not to serve alcohol to an intoxicated individual who was known to be driving." Id. at 305, 420 S.E.2d at 178. Furnishing alcohol to a noticeably intoxicated person who is going to drive would constitute a breach of that duty, and a jury could determine that this breach proximately caused harm.

The Court next addressed social-host liability in *Camalier v. Jeffries*, 340 N.C. 699, 460 S.E.2d 133 (1995). In *Camalier*, Charles Jeffries attended a party at the home of defendant Frank Daniels and consumed several gin and tonics over a three-hour period. Jeffries then left the party in his car and collided into a car driven by Caleb Camalier. Camalier died from injuries received in the accident, and his estate asserted a common law negligence claim against the social hosts of the party. The trial court later granted summary judgment for the defendants, and the Court of Appeals affirmed. We subsequently affirmed the Court of Appeals' decision, finding that summary judgment for the defendants was proper. We determined that evidence presented by the plaintiffs established that the hosts had served Jeffries alcohol and that the hosts knew that Jeffries was going to drive a car shortly after consuming the alcohol. The plaintiffs' evidence failed, however, to show whether the social hosts knew or should have known that Jeffries was intoxicated when they served him the alcohol. While the plaintiffs' evidence did show that Jeffries had a blood-alcohol concentration of 0.191 and that he was visibly intoxicated after the accident, it failed to show that he was visibly intoxicated while at the party or that anyone at the party should have known that he was intoxicated. No one at the party said that Jeffries appeared intoxicated, and fifty-three people who were present at the party expressly stated that he did not appear intoxicated. Thus, we held that the plaintiffs in Camalier failed to produce sufficient evidence to establish a common law negligence claim against the social host.

Applying the foregoing principles developed in Hart and Camalier to the present case, we conclude that a common law negligence suit may be maintained against a commercial vendor, based on a sale of alcohol to an underage person, provided that the plaintiff in such a case presents sufficient evidence to satisfy all elements of a common law negligence suit, that is, duty, breach of duty, proximate cause, and damages. As was the case in *Hart*, we do not recognize a new cause of action but merely allow "established negligence principles" to be applied to the facts of plaintiff's case.

Having determined that a common law cause of action may be maintained for the negligent sale of alcohol to an underage person if all common law negligence elements are satisfied, we must now determine whether plaintiff's forecast of evidence was sufficient to establish a prima facie case of common law negligence. Pursuant to Rule 56(c) of the North Carolina Rules of Civil Procedure, dealing with summary judgment motions, "the motion shall be allowed and judgment entered when such evidence reveals no genuine issue as to any material fact, and when the moving party is entitled to a judgment as a matter of law." The party moving for summary judgment meets its burden "by proving that an essential element of the opposing party's claim is non-existent, or by showing through discovery that the opposing party cannot produce evidence to support an essential element of his claim." To survive a motion for summary judgment, the nonmoving party must therefore "'forecast sufficient evidence of all essential elements of his claim' to make a prima facie case at trial."

Plaintiff's forecast of evidence showed the following: On the night of 30 April 1993, Otis Blount, who was twenty years old and under the legal age to buy alcohol, purchased alcohol twice from defendant Monroe ABC and twice from defendant Monroe Oil. Melissa Baucom stated in her deposition that she drove Blount to the Monroe ABC store twice that evening to buy liquor for himself and two other individuals; she also stated that she later drove Blount to an Amoco station convenience store owned by Monroe Oil, where he bought beer. Several other teenagers stated that shortly after 11:00 P.M., Blount went back to the Amoco station owned by Monroe Oil with Darby in Darby's car and purchased more beer. Witnesses present stated that Melissa Mullis and Patty Teel were with Blount in Darby's car when Darby and Blount drove to the Amoco station to buy the beer. Aaron Tedder and Christopher Mullis, two teenagers present that night, stated that they saw Blount walk out of the Amoco station with beer and drink a portion of it in the parking lot. Blount then drove Darby's Volkswagen from the Amoco station; a short time later, he drove the car off the road and into a tree, killing himself and the other car occupants, Melissa Mullis, Patty Teel, and Dwaine Darby.

Other evidence tended to show that, although Blount was intoxicated, he did not readily appear so. Blount's autopsy report revealed that he had a blood-alcohol content of at least 0.13 and was therefore driving while impaired; an officer who responded to the scene also concluded that Blount's alcohol use caused the accident. Melissa Baucom, however, stated that she did not notice anything unusual about Blount's eyes or speech to indicate that he had been drinking, adding that it was usually difficult to tell if Blount had been drinking alcohol. Several other teenagers stated that Blount's speech was normal that evening, that he was walking straight and had control over his body motions, and that he did not smell of alcohol.

Tommy Quick, another teenager present that night, stated that he had not seen Blount drink that evening, but that the only way to tell if Blount was intoxicated was "if you knew him." Quick stated that "Otis Blount usually when he drinks, he gets in a cheery mood. . . . If you didn't know him, he would be sober to you." Several other witnesses also stated that Blount was not noticeably intoxicated and that it would be difficult to know when he was because he did not typically show outward signs of intoxication.

While plaintiff's evidence tends to show that defendants Monroe Oil and Monroe ABC illegally sold alcohol to Blount on 30 April 1993 and that Blount shortly thereafter drove a car while impaired and caused irrevocable harm, it fails to forecast sufficient evidence to make a prima facie case for common law negligence. Plaintiff has not established that defendants owed a duty based on a forecast of evidence showing only that defendants sold alcohol to an individual who was later found to be an underage person. As we have explained, a duty is "an obligation, to which the law will give recognition and effect, to conform to a particular standard of conduct toward another." A legal duty is owed "whenever one person is by circumstances placed in such a position towards another that every one of ordinary sense who did think would at once recognize that if he did not use ordinary care and skill in his own conduct with regard to those circumstances he would cause danger of injury to the person or property of the other." "Every man is in general bound to use care and skill in his conduct wherever the reasonably prudent person in his shoes would recognize unreasonable risk to others from failure to use such care." Risk-creation behavior thus triggers duty where the risk is both unreasonable and foreseeable. As explained by Justice Cardozo in his classic analysis of duty in Palsgraf:

> We are told that one who drives at reckless speed through a crowded city street is guilty of a negligent

act and therefore of a wrongful one, irrespective of the consequences. Negligent the act is, and wrongful in the sense that it is unsocial, but wrongful and unsocial in relation to other travelers, only because the eye of vigilance perceives the risk of damage. . . . The risk reasonably to be perceived defines the duty to be obeyed, and risk imports relation; it is risk to another or to others within the range of apprehension. *Palsgraf v. Long Island R. Co.*, 248 N.Y. 339, 344, 162 N.E. 99, 100 (1928). "The orbit of the danger as disclosed to the eye of reasonable vigilance is the orbit of the duty." Id. at 343, 162 N.E. at 100.

In this case, there is no evidence showing that the defendant commercial vendors should have recognized that Mullis, or anyone similarly situated might be injured by their conduct, and thus there was no duty. Plaintiff's evidence tends to show that defendants sold alcohol to Blount on 30 April 1993 and that Blount consumed some of the alcohol prior to driving Darby's car. Although the evidence tends to show that a sale was made, plaintiff's evidence fails to show that defendants should have perceived that the sale of alcohol to Blount was going to create an unreasonable risk of harm to third persons. The evidence in fact fails to indicate that the sellers should have been aware that anything but an ordinary transaction was occurring when selling the alcohol to Blount. Blount did not appear inebriated that evening according to observers, and there is no evidence in the record showing that Blount was noticeably intoxicated when buying the alcohol from defendants. Plaintiff's evidence tends to show the contrary: that although Blount may have been intoxicated, he appeared sober throughout the evening when buying liquor from Monroe ABC and when buying beer from the Amoco station owned by Monroe Oil.

There was also no evidence tending to show that the defendant commercial vendors should have known that Blount was going to drive a car even if he had appeared inebriated. The evidence tended to show instead that, as previously stated, Blount did not appear intoxicated and that every time he purchased alcohol from defendants, he was driven to the store by other persons and was not driving a car. Thus, from the perspective of the vendors, this was an ordinary transaction for the sale of alcohol to a person who was driven to the store by another. Thus, there was no indication that foreseeable harm would occur from the sale of alcohol to Blount.

Such a scenario is quite different from that which occurred in Hart where the facts alleged were sufficient to establish foreseeability and the duty element. The plaintiff's allegations in Hart that the host served alcohol to an underage person who the host knew or should have known was intoxicated and was going to shortly drive a car were sufficient to show that the host should have perceived a risk of harm. There, we stated that a jury could find that "a man of ordinary prudence would have known that such or some similar injurious result was reasonably foreseeable from this negligent conduct." *Hart*, 332 N.C. at 305, 420 S.E.2d at 178. Furnishing alcohol to an intoxicated driver was conduct creating an unreasonable risk of harm to others. In such a situation, the host could also perceive the risk: Serving alcohol to an inebriated individual who is going to drive is a foreseeable risk "clear to the ordinarily prudent eye."

Such is not the case here. No evidence tended to show that defendants should have been aware that selling alcohol to Blount could produce foreseeable harm and subject other drivers or passengers to an unreasonable risk of harm. Evidence offered by plaintiff indicated merely that defendants sold alcohol to an individual who was later discovered to be underage. Evidence of this alone, without an offer of some additional factor or factors which would put the vendor on notice that harm was foreseeable, is insufficient to establish the duty element and thus maintain a common law negligence suit. It was necessary, in other words, for plaintiff's forecast of evidence to point to some additional factor or factors that would alert the defendant commercial vendors that the act of selling the alcohol would likely produce some foreseeable injury. Whether harm is foreseeable simply depends on the circumstances of each case and is not determined according to any predetermined set of factors. However, since plaintiff's forecast of evidence failed to have such an additional factor or factors which would have enabled the vendors to foresee that harm was, in all likelihood, going to occur, the duty element is not satisfied, and plaintiff's prima facie case must fail.

Thus, based on the foregoing, plaintiff has not produced a sufficient forecast of evidence to maintain a common law negligence claim against defendants based on the sale of alcohol to Otis Blount. Accordingly, we affirm the Court of Appeals' decision affirming the trial court's grant of summary judgment for defendants.

AFFIRMED.

Websites

■ *Jensen v. White Star Line*
http://www.andersonkill.com/titanic/negl.htm

■ **University of Washington Law School, tort law PowerPoint presentation**
http://www.law.washington.edu/Streetlaw/lessons/Torts_Negligence_Pres.ppt

■ **Essortment — Defining Breach of Duty**
http://ar.essortment.com/breachoffidu_rkwv.htm

Forms and Court Doctrines

In this section, we examine an excerpt from the complaint in the Chumley case. This excerpt focuses on the allegations of the various defendants' breach of duty.

STATE OF PLACID   IN THE SUPERIOR COURT OF HALEY COUNTY
                                                            SUPERIOR COURT DIVISION
COUNTY OF HALEY   FILE NUMBER: _____

CHARLES CHUMLEY,   )
)
Plaintiff   )
)
vs.   )   COMPLAINT
)   JURY TRIAL DEMANDED
)

NATIONAL RAILWAY COMPANY,   )
TOWN OF CLING,   )
and STANLEY W. BLUE   )
)
Defendant   )
)

Notice in 16(b) how precise the allegations are.

Paragraphs 1 through 15 are omitted for this discussion. Please see Appendix C for the entire Chumley complaint.

16.

The Town breached this duty of due care by the following acts of negligence:

a. it failed to close the crossing pursuant to state law, when it knew, or in the exercise of due care should have known, that the crossing constituted an unreasonable hazard to vehicular or pedestrian traffic;

b. it failed to require the installation, construction, erection, or improvement, of warning signs, gates, lights, stop bars, or such other safety devices when it knew or should have known in the exercise of reasonable care that such devices were necessary;

c. it allowed the crossing to remain in use with absolutely no safety devices with total, wanton, and reckless disregard for the safety of vehicular and pedestrian traffic;

d. it allowed the vegetation and trees adjacent to the tracks to obstruct the view by motorists of the tracks and approaching trains when it knew, or in the exercise of due care should have known, that such vegetation and trees constituted an unreasonable hazard to vehicular and pedestrian traffic;

e. it failed to keep the public street free from unnecessary obstructions in violation of State law.

Although the strongest part of the case would seem to be an allegation of vegetation growing along the track that obscured the oncoming train [16(d)], this is not the only allegation brought in the complaint. Why? One answer is that by making several allegations, the plaintiff is improving his chances of a recovery if the jury decides against him on the vegetation issue.

Key Terms

Negligence per se   *Res ipsa loquitur*
Professional   Specialist
Reasonable person standard

Review Questions

1 Can we use *res ipsa* or negligence per se doctrines in the Chumley case? Explain why or why not.

2 In any given situation, once you have determined that a duty was owed, how do you determine if a breach of that duty has occurred?

3   What is the reasonable person standard, and how does it help determine breach of duty?

4   How does "standard of care" apply to breach of duty?

5   In determining a breach of duty, you must look at the facts objectively. Why?

6   Mental characteristics of tortfeasors are not taken into account, but physical characteristics, such as blindness, often are. Why does the law make this distinction?

7   Should a judge determine the standard of care instead of a jury? Why or why not?

8   Can custom establish a breach of duty? Why or why not?

9   A professional is held to a higher standard of care than a layperson. What is that standard? How is that standard different for specialists?

10   When we hold a specialist to a higher standard of care, does that mean that proving a negligence case against a specialist is easier than proving one against a professional? Why or why not?

11   Explain *res ipsa loquitur*. Why was this doctrine created?

12   What are some of the defenses available to a claim of *res ipsa loquitur*?

13   What is the doctrine of negligence per se? Why was this doctrine created?

14   How is *res ipsa loquitur* different from negligence per se?

Applying What You Have Learned

1   Using the following facts, draft a complaint alleging *res ipsa loquitur*:

Our firm represents the estate of a passenger who was killed in a plane crash. The plane crashed into the sea, and very little evidence has been recovered, especially in regard to what caused the crash.

2   Using the following facts, draft a complaint alleging negligence per se:

In the Chumley case, assume that the train engineer was exceeding the posted speed limits for trains by traveling 30 mph when 25 mph was the restricted speed limit.

3   Tom is home one afternoon and notices that the local telephone company is replacing a telephone pole on the corner of Tom's lot. Two hours after the workers complete the installation of the new telephone pole, it falls, crushing Tom's roof and injuring Tom. Does Tom have a negligence per se claim? Go through each element of negligence per se and prove or disprove the elements.

4   How does your state define negligence per se?

5   Does your state follow the doctrine of *res ipsa loquitur*? If so, does your state's approach differ from the general one presented in the text?

Endnotes

[1] *Fields v. Napa Milling Co.,* 164 Cal. App. 2d 442, 330 P.2d 459 (1958).

[2] *Handley v. Halladay,* 92 N.M. 76, 582 P.2d 1289 (1978).

[3] *Denver & R.G.R. Co. v. Norgate,* 141 F. 247 (8th Cir.), *cert. denied,* 202 U.S. 616, 50 L. Ed. 1172, 24 S. Ct. 764 (1905).

[4] *Estate of Mullis by Dixon v. Monroe Oil Co.,* 349 N.C. 196, 505 S.E.2d 131 (1998).

[5] Restatement (Second) of Torts §283, comment b.

[6] *Gould v. American Family Mut. Ins. Co.,* 198 Wis. 2d 450, 543 N.W.2d 282 (1996).

[7] *Gould v. American Family Mut. Ins. Co.,* 198 Wis. 2d 450, 543 N.W.2d 282 (1996).

[8] *Garafola v. Rosecliff Realty Co.,* 24 N.J. Super. 28, 93 A.2d 608 (1953).

[9] *Palombizio v. Murphy,* 146 Conn. 352, 150 A.2d 825 (1959).

[10] Restatement (Second) of Torts §285, comment f.

[11] Restatement (Second) of Torts §298, comment d.

[12] Restatement (Second) of Torts §295.

[13] *Vergara v. Doan,* 593 N.E.2d 185 (1992).

Crossword Puzzle

www.CrosswordWeaver.com

ACROSS

2 One who has become an expert in a particular field through education, training, or both

3 Someone who either through education, training, or a combination of both, possesses skills that an average person does not

4 "the thing speaks for itself"; the principle that under certain circumstances, such as when the type of accident is one that would not ordinarily occur without some form of negligence, the defendant's negligence can be presumed

5 The standard used by the court to provide a yardstick by which it can evaluate the defendant's actions in a particular case

DOWN

1 Negligence in and of itself; the principle that the violation of a safety statute establishes a presumption of breach of duty in a negligence action

Proximate
Cause

- Determine when a defendant's actions (or omissions) are the proximate cause of a plaintiff's injuries

- Explain the various court tests used to establish the existence of proximate cause

- Explain the concept of foreseeability

- Describe the significance of *Palsgraf v. New York*

- Apply your knowledge of proximate cause in preparing pleadings

- Define the concepts of intervening and superseding causes

PROXIMATE CAUSE IN THE CHUMLEY CASE

Mr. Chumley was severely injured and Mrs. Chumley was killed when their car was struck broadside by a locomotive. In earlier chapters, we examined how Mr. Chumley's attorney would have to prove duty and breach of duty in order to bring a negligence claim against the railroad company. In this chapter, we explore the concept of causation or the degree of the defendants' responsibility for the injuries to Mr. and Mrs. Chumley. In the Chumley case, the analysis for proximate cause is relatively straightforward. If the railroad company's employees were at fault, there can be no question of the direct responsibility of those employees for the injuries to the plaintiffs. However, suppose that after the collision, Mr. Chumley received substandard care at the hospital. Or suppose that Mr. Chumley had pre-existing injuries. Should the railroad company also be liable for those injuries? We address these issues in addition to exploring the concepts of intervening and superseding causes as they apply to the issue of proximate causation.

INTRODUCTION

Proximate causation
The facts that show the defendant's legal responsibility for the injuries to the plaintiff, also known as legal cause.

In this chapter, we explore the third element of a negligence claim: **proximate causation.** Before a plaintiff can succeed in a negligence action, she must prove that there was a direct link between the defendant's breach of duty and the resulting injuries to her.

A. PROVING PROXIMATE CAUSE

Sidebar

Duty → Breach → Causation → Damages

Proof of proximate cause actually involves a two-step analysis: There must be a determination that (1) the defendant breached the duty of care, and (2) the breach was the cause of the injury.

1. BREACH OF DUTY OF CARE

We discussed breach of duty in Chapter 6. That element must be satisfied before any analysis of causation can begin. It is important to reiterate that the basic elements of a negligence case are sequential. A plaintiff must prove each of the elements, beginning with duty and concluding with damages. The plaintiff is not permitted to skip over any element. This concept is crucial to an understanding of negligence in general and proximate cause in particular.

2. BREACH WAS THE CAUSE

The second element of proof for proximate cause is that the breach of duty was the proximate cause of the injury. Without this proof, the element of causation is not proved and the plaintiff's negligence case collapses. We spend the remainder of this chapter addressing the question of how the plaintiff proves causation and the various court-created tests and doctrines that have developed over the centuries to address this issue.

B. THE LAW ON PROXIMATE CAUSE TENDS TO BE VAGUE

Although it is the third specified element of a negligence claim, the issue of proximate cause is not as clear or as settled as any of the other elements of negligence. Experts have been arguing over the term since it was created. What is and is not proximate cause often depends on the facts of a particular case. Another problem with proximate cause has to do with public policy. This element of negligence is the one most easily assailed by public policy concerns. Just how far should a defendant's liability to the plaintiff extend? That sounds more like a philosophical question than a strictly factual one. Consider the following scenario:

> John drives negligently and crashes his car into another car driven by Tara. Tara, a professional athlete, breaks her leg in the wreck. She sues John for her injuries. When Tara is taken to the hospital, she receives substandard care from the physician on duty. The doctor does a poor job of treating her broken leg. As a result, an infection sets in. Tara becomes very ill, and eventually the infection in her leg becomes so bad that her leg must be amputated. Is John liable for all of Tara's injuries or just some of her injuries? If he is liable for only some of the injuries, which ones are they?

Some would argue that John should be liable for everything that happened after he acted negligently. Although this argument has a certain appeal, there are some obvious problems in applying it. Because of Tara's injury, she is cut from the college track team, where she had been a major competitor. She then loses her scholarship. Should Tara be allowed to recover the cost of her remaining education from John? Tara also had plans to try out for the U.S. Olympic team and believed that she was a solid contender to make that team. Should Tara be allowed to sue John for the millions of dollars she would have made in endorsements after becoming a medal winner in the next Olympics? Should Tara's future children be allowed to bring suit against John because their mother was an amputee for the rest of her life and was not able to provide the same level of interaction with them that other mothers provided?

As you can see, the argument for the defendant's continued responsibility for his negligence could be spun out to ridiculous lengths. The further removed from the defendant's actual negligence, the more tenuous the connection (and the more difficult it becomes to prove). A different argument suggests that John should only be liable for the injuries that are closely connected with his negligence. Any other negligence (such as the malpractice by the doctor) should be assessed against that person. Creating a theory of causation that makes a defendant liable only for those actions closely and obviously resulting from his negligence is certainly easier to prove in a courtroom than the never-ending and far-reaching causation theory proposed earlier. However, this theory also means that there will be times when a plaintiff will not be satisfied with the amount of her recovery or the scope of the defendant's responsibility. Faced with these two conflicting theories, the courts have opted for the second. They have chosen, time and again, a more limited scope of the defendant's responsibility.

FIGURE 7-1

Arguments in
Support of
Proximate
Cause

- Protracted defendant responsibility would be difficult, if not impossible, to enforce. For instance, when would the defendant's liability be cut off? Surely his liability must terminate at some point.
- By making the defendant liable only for his actions closely

connected to his negligence, there is a deterrent effect on negligent conduct.
- The legal system would eventually bog down under the litigation involved in making a defendant liable for all remote consequences of his negligence.

There is a benefit to society in eventually terminating defendants' responsibilities in cases. Even negligent people need to know when all possible claims against them are exhausted. More than simply letting negligent people off the hook, however, a more limited theory of causation and responsibility allows the rest of society some assurance that a particular case can and will end. The various witnesses and others involved can be secure in the knowledge that, regardless of the particular parties' level of satisfaction, no additional claims will be forthcoming from a specific incident of negligence. We have seen other examples of this desire to close off the claims in particular cases. Statutes of limitation are a good example. Those statutes provide a time limit in which a claim must be brought or it is barred forever. The concept of proximate cause was created as a way for courts to determine the parameters of a defendant's responsibility. See Figure 7-1 for arguments in favor of the concept of proximate cause.

DEVELOPING THE CONCEPT OF PROXIMATE CAUSE

Sidebar

Proximate causation involves proof of responsibility.

Proximate cause analysis varies depending on the nature of the civil injury. For instance, the analysis is often very different between negligence cases and intentional tort cases. A defendant who acts with intent or in wanton, willful, or reckless disregard for the safety of others may be legally responsible for all the ramifications of his actions, however remote. Many jurisdictions also follow this rule when the defendant's actions are criminal in nature. However, when the claim is based on negligence, different rules apply. Most jurisdictions apply the proximate cause rule to negligence cases. These jurisdictions make a defendant liable only for the logical or foreseeable results of his actions.[1]

Sidebar

The term proximate cause *was first suggested by an English jurist, Lord Bacon, who wrote, "in jure non remota causa, sed proxima, spectatur" (in law, not the remote cause, but the proximate cause is sought).*[2]

A. HISTORICAL DEVELOPMENT OF PROXIMATE CAUSE

The concept of proximate cause has been a bone of contention in jurisprudence for centuries. Different societies have applied different standards to how far the defendant's liability should extend. The English standard, which eventually found its way to the United States, has a stated preference for factually closer connections to the plaintiff's injuries than more remote causes.

B. PROBLEMS DEFINING PROXIMATE CAUSE

No jurisdiction has come up with a test for proximate cause that works in all cases. The very concept is often difficult to define. There may be a subtle purpose here. Some experts believe that this vagueness is actually helpful. It gives the court a more fluid approach to the issue, unlike the other elements of negligence, which only allow for a fairly straightforward analysis.

Proximate cause has long been recognized as a confusing concept because the term makes it sound as if the defendant's negligence has to be closest in time to the plaintiff's injury. However, that is not true. A plaintiff can be injured by Defendant A, then subsequently injured by Defendant B, and Defendant A may still be liable to the plaintiff. Because nearness in time is not the primary consideration when deciding proximate cause, courts have developed various tests to help them determine proximate cause. The working definition for proximate cause used by many jurisdictions is one that states, "a cause without which the accident could not have happened."[4] It has also been described as the "primary moving cause," or the "predominating cause" of the plaintiff's injuries.[5] With so many definitions of proximate cause, we need a working definition to frame the rest of our discussion.

C. WORKING DEFINITION OF PROXIMATE CAUSE

The most widely accepted definition of proximate cause (and the one we use for the remainder of the chapter) involves the following:

- proof of an injury caused by the defendant
- that occurred in a natural, unbroken, and continuous sequence
- that was uninterrupted by any intervening causes
- that produced the plaintiff's injury
- without which the result would not have occurred.[8]

1. ELEMENTS OF THE WORKING DEFINITION

In the next few paragraphs, we expand on the concepts raised in the working definition.

a. Proof of an Injury Caused by the Defendant

The first element of the working definition of proximate cause is the plaintiff's proof that the injuries were caused by the defendant. Without that proof, there

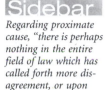

Sidebar

Regarding proximate cause, "there is perhaps nothing in the entire field of law which has called forth more disagreement, or upon which the opinions are in such a welter of confusion."[3]

Sidebar

Other commentators have gone even further in denouncing the term proximate cause. Prosser, for instance, in his well-known treatise, Prosser and Keeton on the Law of Torts,[6] states: "The term 'proximate cause' is applied by the courts to those more or less undefined considerations which limit liability even where the fact of causation is clearly established. The word 'proximate' is a legacy of Lord Chancellor Bacon, who in his time committed other sins. The word means nothing more than near or immediate; and when it was first taken up by the courts it had connotations of proximity in time and space which have long since disappeared. It is an unfortunate word, which places an entirely wrong emphasis upon the factor of physical or mechanical closeness. For this reason 'legal cause' or perhaps even 'responsible cause' would be a more appropriate term."[7]

Lord Bacon was also responsible for a few other legal maxims that are somewhat confusing. Consider: "[I]t were infinite for the law to judge causes of causes, and their impulsions one of another; therefore it is contenteth itself that the immediate cause, and judgeth of acts by that, without looking to any further degree."

can be no case against the defendant and the remainder of the working definition, indeed of the entire case, would be useless.

b. In a Natural, Unbroken, and Continuous Sequence

This element of the working definition requires that the series of events beginning with the defendant's negligence and ending with the plaintiff's injuries all involved a natural sequence. There were no intervening actions; it was an unbroken chain of events. If there is a disruption in the sequence between the defendant's actions and the ultimate injuries, it could well be that the defendant was not the cause of the injuries.

c. Uninterrupted by Any Intervening Causes

We discuss intervening and superseding causes later in this chapter. A word about them here, however, helps to establish the reason for this requirement in the working definition. If some other defendant, or some other force of nature, intervened between the original defendant's negligence and the plaintiff's ultimate injuries, the original defendant may be released from liability. (Consider the scenario discussed earlier, concerning Tara's injuries and the malpractice by her attending physician.)

d. Produced the Plaintiff's Injuries

Although it sounds like a basic point, it must be established that the defendant's actions actually did cause the plaintiff's injuries.

Example: John runs a red light and causes a minor collision with Barbara's car. Fortunately, Barbara is not hurt. There is no question of John's negligence, but Barbara has not received any physical injuries. Later, at work, a colleague bumps into Barbara and she falls, injuring her knee. John is not the cause of Barbara's knee injury, despite the fact that she was in an accident earlier that day.

e. Without Which the Result Would Not Have Occurred

Proximate cause is sometimes defined as the natural, foreseeable, and probable consequence of an act of negligence.

This is often the pivotal issue in any negligence case. Most jurisdictions have some form of this test as part of their working definitions of proximate cause. The defendant's actions must be such that had it not been for his negligence, the result (the plaintiff's injuries) would not have occurred. Later, we discuss the various court-created "tests" or doctrines used to determine this particular point, including the substantial factor test and the "but for" test.

2. RESTATEMENT'S POSITION ON DEFINING PROXIMATE CAUSE

The Restatement of Torts takes a slightly different approach to defining proximate cause. According to the Restatement, under proximate cause a defendant may be liable for the harm to the plaintiff from his conduct, as long as he is the legal cause of the harm.[10] The Restatement's position on "legal cause" is similar to the elements we have set out above.

D. PROXIMATE CAUSE REQUIRES A CLOSE CONNECTION BETWEEN THE DEFENDANT'S ACTIONS AND THE PLAINTIFF'S INJURIES

Under proximate cause theory, it is easier to decide which events are too remote in time to be considered the direct cause of the plaintiff's injuries than it is to determine which events are close enough. Generally, the more tenuous the connection between the defendant's actions and the plaintiff's injuries, the less likely that proximate cause will be found. This is often referred to as "remoteness." However, the reverse situation is often confusing. Given the facts of the Chumley case, for instance, can we say with any degree of certainty what the proximate cause is?

We know that Mr. Chumley was driving his car south on Morgan Street and that he crossed the railroad tracks. We also know that his car was struck on the driver's side by the locomotive owned and operated by National Railway Company. Those facts are not in dispute. Can we, from this simple factual scenario, determine that the defendant railway company was the proximate cause of his injuries?

Actually, we cannot. The first problem with the factual outline is that it fails to establish the first two elements of a negligence case: duty and the breach of a duty. For the sake of argument, we will assume that these questions have been answered. Defendant railway company had a duty to Mr. Chumley and subsequently breached it, either by some action taken shortly before the collision or by failing to maintain the tracks in such a way that motorists could see an oncoming train. If those two elements are satisfied, can we then determine proximate cause?

Actually, we still need some additional information. What, for instance, were Mr. Chumley's injuries? (For a complete overview of the Chumley case, see Appendices A, B, and C.) We know that Mr. Chumley was severely injured and that Mrs. Chumley died in the collision. His injuries seem to be closely connected both in time and sequential events to the collision with the train. Is that enough? Do we need to know about his medical treatment? Do we need to know if his car was struck by another car shortly after the accident? Do we need to know, in fact, everything that happened both immediately before and immediately after the collision? The answer to all these questions is yes. In later chapters, we discuss how a paralegal can learn all this information (and a great deal more) through discovery. We still need some additional information before we can complete our analysis of proximate cause in the Chumley case. For instance, we need to know what the law considers to be a remote cause.

1. REMOTE CAUSES ARE LESS LIKELY TO BE CONSIDERED PROXIMATE CAUSE

In the pragmatic world of civil lawsuits, a plaintiff who can show a direct factual connection between his injuries and the defendant's negligence has a much greater chance of prevailing at trial than a plaintiff who can only show a remote connection. Direct factual connections (proximate causes) lend themselves to greater precision and easier methods of proof at trial. In a courtroom, if the plaintiff's proof is uncertain, this will almost always accrue to the defendant's favor.

2. REMOTE CAUSES ARE HARDER TO PROVE

Sidebar

The plaintiff must show not only a negligent act, but also that this act was the legal cause of his injuries. Some jurisdictions simplify this analysis by requiring a "reasonably close" connection between the defendant's actions and the plaintiff's injuries.[11]

Sidebar

Some jurisdictions define probable cause as that first act that produces an injury immediately or sets other events in motion.

Sidebar

The term legal cause *was created in part to deal with the confusion surrounding the term* proximate cause. *"Legal cause," "direct cause," "efficient cause," and "proximate cause" all refer to the same doctrine.*

The more remote the cause of the plaintiff's injuries, the more difficult it is for the plaintiff to prove who actually caused the harm. Remember that the plaintiff must prove her case to the satisfaction of the jury and to a preponderance of the evidence. If the jurors are not convinced of a factual connection between the defendant's actions and the plaintiff's injuries, the jury will not find the defendant liable.

When dealing with remote events, it is also more likely that some other event either contributed to or even superseded defendant's negligence in causing the plaintiff's injuries.

Finally, although it is hardly the predominant factor, it is ultimately unfair to a defendant to find him liable for actions that are remote in time and fact from the plaintiff's injuries.

3. PROXIMATE CAUSE DEPENDS ON THE FACTS IN THE CASE

Determining proximate cause involves following a chain of events back, like a detective, to uncover the original event that brought about the plaintiff's injuries and then to decide if that event should be ascribed to the defendant.[12] Because determining probable cause depends so much on the facts of the case, a paralegal must know these facts as well as anyone else involved in the case. What was the sequence of events that ended with the plaintiff's injuries? Who, precisely, was involved, and what part did each person play? Later, we discuss investigative methods that can be used to determine these facts, but there is no substitute for having a solid understanding of the facts of a case.

4. EVALUATING A CASE FOR PROXIMATE CAUSE

John is driving his car one afternoon and fails to stop for a stop sign. John's car crashes into the side of Barbara's car, and Barbara is severely injured. John is also injured in the collision. These are the facts of a simple — and all too common — car collision case. How can we analyze this case for proximate cause?

FIGURE 7-2

Factual Proof
Under the
Restatement

For a defendant to be found liable for the plaintiff's injuries, the plaintiff must prove that (1) the defendant acted in a negligent way and (2) this negligence is the legal cause of the plaintiff's injuries.*

Source: Restatement (Second) of Torts §430.

Under a factual analysis of this case, Barbara's injuries appear to be a direct result of the collision with John's car. John appears to be the sole and proximate cause for Barbara's injuries. On the other hand, John was also injured. John's injuries are a result of the collision with Barbara's car. Strictly speaking, each has been injured by the other's car. If we were to approach this case from a purely factual scenario, free from any determination of wrongdoing, our analysis would end here. Each has been injured by contact with the other's car. However, proximate cause is concerned with more than the basic facts. Proximate cause addresses how the facts ultimately determine liability. See Figure 7-2 for a statement of how the facts relate to an assignment of liability.

When Barbara later brings a suit against John for negligent driving, she must prove that John was the proximate cause of her injuries. In this case, she should not have any trouble doing so. Notice that the analysis in this case focuses on John's negligence, not simply on the series of events that ended with Barbara's injuries. Proximate causation involves the proof of John's actions, or failure to act, and how those actions were a direct cause of Barbara's injuries. However, in many cases, proving proximate causation is not as clear-cut as this example. Consider this next scenario:

John has borrowed a car from his friend, Ted. Ted has not maintained the car very well and has noticed recently that the brakes do not seem to be working well. He does not tell John about the brake problem. As John is approaching a stop sign, he applies the brakes and nothing happens. John fails to stop at the stop sign and crashes into Barbara's car. Does this scenario change the analysis for proximate causation?

In the first example, John was the proximate cause of Barbara's injuries. Looking at the second case from a factual viewpoint, John is still the driver of a car that injures Barbara, but is it John's negligence that causes the collision? Many juries would likely assign the negligence not to John, but to Ted. At what point does the negligence of one party overcome the responsibility of another party? Suppose in the most recent example that Ted had informed John about the brake problem, but John decided to drive the car anyway. Who is the proximate cause of Barbara's injuries now? As you can see, proximate cause often involves a balancing of the various factors and responsibilities of the parties involved.

E. PROXIMATE CAUSE MUST SHOW THAT THE DEFENDANT IS RESPONSIBLE

As part of this element of proving causation, the facts must point to the defendant's responsibility for the actions that ultimately led to the plaintiff's

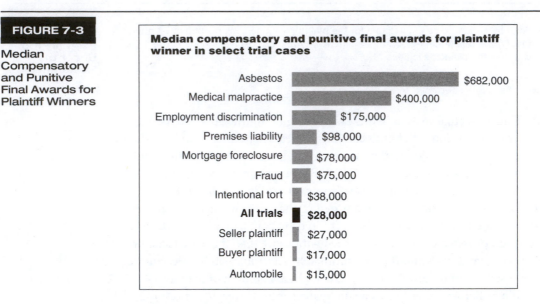

FIGURE 7-3

Median Compensatory and Punitive Final Awards for Plaintiff Winners

Median compensatory and punitive final awards for plaintiff winner in select trial cases

Asbestos	$682,000
Medical malpractice	$400,000
Employment discrimination	$175,000
Premises liability	$98,000
Mortgage foreclosure	$78,000
Fraud	$75,000
Intentional tort	$38,000
All trials	**$28,000**
Seller plaintiff	$27,000
Buyer plaintiff	$17,000
Automobile	$15,000

Civil Bench and Jury Trials in State Courts, revised 2009, Bureau of Justice Statistics

injuries. Put another way, the defendant is responsible for all consequences that are reasonably foreseeable based on his conduct. In the example above, in which John is driving Ted's car unaware that the brakes are faulty, he may well avoid any liability for Barbara's injuries. In such a case, liability would most likely shift to Ted (Figure 7-3).

F. FORESEEABILITY

Foreseeability
The extent to which the defendant should have anticipated that her actions could cause possible injuries to another.

Courts in this country have wrestled with the concept of proximate cause for decades. In the famous *Palsgraf* case, the concept of **foreseeability** was brought into greater prominence as a method to determine when a defendant's actions were the legal cause of the plaintiff's injuries. The concept of foreseeability encompasses the view that a defendant should only be liable for a plaintiff's injuries when the defendant's actions (or failure to act) would likely result in the kinds of injuries that the plaintiff sustained. Using foreseeability as the test for proximate cause provided at least a workable test that courts could apply to various suits and provided some measure of predictability from case to case.

TORT BASICS AT A GLANCE

The jury must determine if it was foreseeable that the defendant's conduct created a risk of harm to the plaintiff.

1. THE *PALSGRAF* CASE

The *Palsgraf* case was one of the first — and some would argue the best — court-created doctrines to examine and analyze foreseeability in proximate cause. The *Palsgraf* case continues to be taught in law schools around the country, even though it is over 90 years old.

Sidebar

Pay particular attention to the concise wording used by Justice Cardozo as he lays out the basic facts of the Palsgraf case.

Case Excerpt

PALSGRAF V. LONG ISLAND R.R. CO.
162 N.E. 99 (1928)
HELEN PALSGRAF, Respondent,
v.
THE LONG ISLAND RAILROAD COMPANY, Appellant.

CARDOZO, C.J.

Plaintiff was standing on a platform of defendant's railroad after buying a ticket to go to Rockaway Beach. A train stopped at the station, bound for another place. Two men ran forward to catch it. One of the men reached the platform of the car without mishap, though the train was already moving. The other man, carrying a package, jumped aboard the car, but seemed unsteady as if about to fall. A guard on the car, who had held the door open, reached forward to help him in, and another guard on the platform pushed him from behind. In this act, the package was dislodged, and fell upon the rails. It was a package of small size, about fifteen inches long, and was covered by a newspaper. In fact it contained fireworks, but there was nothing in its appearance to give notice of its contents. The fireworks when they fell exploded. The shock of the explosion threw down some scales at the other end of the platform, many feet away. The scales struck the plaintiff, causing injuries for which she sues. The conduct of the defendant's guard, if a wrong in its relation to the holder of the package, was not a wrong in its relation to the plaintiff, standing far away. Relatively to her it was not negligence at all. Nothing in the situation gave notice that the falling package had in it the potency of peril to persons thus removed. Negligence is not actionable unless it involves the invasion of a legally protected interest, the violation of a right. "Proof of negligence in the air, so to speak, will not do." (Pollock, Torts). "Negligence is the absence of care, according to the circumstances." 1 Beven, Negligence (4th ed.) The plaintiff as she stood upon the platform of the station might claim to be protected against intentional invasion of her bodily security. Such invasion is not charged. She might claim to be protected against unintentional invasion by conduct involving in the thought of reasonable men an unreasonable hazard that such invasion would ensue. These, from the point of view of the law, were the bounds of her immunity, with perhaps some rare exceptions, survivals for the most part of ancient forms of liability, where conduct is held to be at the peril of the actor. If no hazard was apparent to the eye of ordinary vigilance, an act innocent and harmless, at least to outward seeming, with reference to her, did not take to itself the quality of a tort because it happened to be a wrong, though apparently not one involving the risk of bodily insecurity, with reference to some one else. In every instance, before negligence can be predicated of a given act, back of the act must be sought and found a duty to the individual complaining, the observance of which would have averted or avoided the injury. The ideas of negligence and duty are strictly correlative. The plaintiff sues in her own right for a wrong personal to her, and not as the vicarious beneficiary of a breach of duty to another. A different conclusion will involve us, and swiftly too, in a maze of contradictions. A guard stumbles over a package which has been left upon a platform. It seems to be a bundle of newspapers. It turns out to be a can of dynamite. To the eye of ordinary vigilance, the bundle is abandoned waste, which may be kicked or trod on with impunity. Is a passenger at the other end of the platform protected by the law against the unsuspected hazard concealed beneath the waste? If not, is the result to be any different, so far as the distant passenger is concerned, when the guard stumbles over a valise which a truck man or a porter has left upon the walk? The passenger far away, if the victim of a wrong at all, has a cause of action, not derivative, but original and primary. His claim to be protected against invasion of his bodily security is neither greater nor less because the act resulting in the invasion is a wrong to another far removed. In this case, the rights that are said to have been violated, the interests said to have been invaded, are not even of the same order. The man was not injured in his person nor even put in danger. The purpose of the act, as well as its effect, was to make his person safe. If there was a wrong to him at all, which may very well be doubted, it was a wrong to a property interest only, the safety of his package. Out of this wrong to property, which threatened injury to nothing else, there has passed, we are told, to the plaintiff by derivation or succession a right of action for the invasion of an interest of another order, the right to bodily security. The diversity of interests emphasizes the futility of the effort to build the plaintiff's right upon the basis of a wrong to some one else. The gain is one of emphasis, for a like result would follow if the interests were the same. Even then, the orbit of the danger as disclosed to the eye of reasonable vigilance would be the orbit of the duty. One who jostles one's neighbor in a crowd does not invade the rights of others standing at the outer fringe when the unintended contact casts a bomb upon the ground. The wrongdoer as to them is the man who carries the bomb, not the one who explodes it without suspicion of the danger. Life will have to be made over, and human nature transformed, before prevision so extravagant can be accepted as the norm of conduct, the customary standard to which behavior must conform. The argument for the plaintiff is built upon the shifting meanings of such words as "wrong" and "wrongful," and shares their instability. What the plaintiff must show is "a wrong" to herself, i.e., a violation of her own right, and not merely a wrong to some one else, nor conduct "wrongful" because unsocial, but not "a wrong" to any one. We are told that one who drives at reckless speed through a crowded city street is guilty of a negligent act and, therefore, of a wrongful one irrespective of the consequences. Negligent the act is, and wrongful in the sense that it is unsocial, but wrongful and unsocial in relation to other travelers, only because the eye of vigilance perceives the risk of damage. If the same act were to be committed on a speedway or a racecourse, it would lose its wrongful quality. The risk reasonably to be perceived defines the duty to be obeyed, and risk imports relation; it is risk to another or to others within the range of apprehension. This does not mean, of course, that one who launches a destructive force is always relieved of liability if the force, though known to be destructive, pursues an unexpected path. It was not necessary that the defendant should have had notice of the particular method in which an accident would occur, if the possibility of an accident was clear to the ordinarily prudent eye. Some acts, such as shooting, are so imminently dangerous to any one who may come within reach of the missile, however unexpectedly, as to impose a duty of prevision not far from that of an insurer. Even today, and much oftener in earlier stages of the law, one acts sometimes at one's peril. Under this head, it may be, fall certain cases of what is known as transferred intent, an act willfully dangerous to A resulting by misadventure in injury to B. These cases aside, wrong is defined in terms of the natural or probable, at least when unintentional. The range of reasonable apprehension is at times a question for the court, and at times, if varying inferences are possible, a question for the jury. Here, by concession, there was nothing in the situation to suggest to the most cautious mind that the parcel wrapped in newspaper would spread wreckage through the station. If the guard had thrown it down knowingly and willfully, he would not have threatened the plaintiff's safety, so far as appearances could warn him. His conduct would not have involved, even then, an unreasonable probability of invasion of her bodily security. Liability can be no greater where the act is inadvertent. Negligence, like risk, is thus a term of relation. Negligence in the abstract, apart from things related, is surely not a tort, if indeed it is understandable at all. Negligence is not a tort unless it results in the commission of a wrong, and the commission of a wrong imports the violation of a right, in this case, we are told, the right to be protected against interference with one's bodily security. But bodily security is protected, not against all forms of interference or aggression, but only against some. One who seeks redress at law does not make out a cause of action by showing without more that there has been damage to his person. If the harm was not willful, he must show that the act as to him had possibilities of danger so many and apparent as to entitle him to be protected against the doing of it though the harm was unintended. Affront to personality is still the keynote of the wrong. Confirmation of this view will be found in the history and development of the action on the case. Negligence as a basis of civil liability was unknown to mediaeval law. For damage to the person, the sole remedy was trespass, and trespass did not lie in the absence of aggression, and that direct and personal. Liability for other damage, as where a servant without orders from the master does or omits something to the damage of another, is a plant of later growth. When it emerged out of the legal soil, it was thought of as a variant of trespass, an offshoot of the parent stock. This appears in the form of action, which was known as trespass on the case. The victim does not sue derivatively, or by right of subrogation, to vindicate an interest invaded in the person of another. Thus to view his cause of action is to ignore the fundamental difference between tort and crime. He sues for breach of a duty owing to himself. The law of causation, remote or proximate, is thus foreign to the case before us. The question of liability is always anterior to the question of the measure of the consequences that go with liability. If there is no tort to be redressed, there is no occasion to consider what damage might be recovered if there were a finding of a tort. We may assume, without deciding, that negligence, not at large or in the abstract, but in relation to the plaintiff, would entail liability for any and all consequences, however novel or extraordinary. There is room for argument that a distinction is to be drawn according to the diversity of interests invaded by the act, as where conduct negligent in that it threatens an insignificant invasion of an interest in property results in an unforeseeable invasion of an interest of another order, as, e.g., one of bodily security. Perhaps other distinctions may be necessary. We do not go into the question now. The consequences to be followed must first be rooted in a wrong. The judgment of the Appellate Division and that of the Trial Term should be reversed, and the complaint dismissed, with costs in all courts.

Judgment reversed.

2. AN ANALYSIS OF *PALSGRAF:* "ORBIT OF THE RISK" DOCTRINE (FORESEEABILITY)

What makes the *Palsgraf* case so important, decades after it was decided? First, the case stands as a model of a well-written and well-reasoned legal decision. Second, it clearly establishes a legal principle that has proved to be important ever since: foreseeability. Finally, the case has often served as an example of how courts can create other new legal concepts.

The "zone of foreseeability" (also known as the "orbit of risk" doctrine) developed by Chief Justice Cardozo in the *Palsgraf* case holds that a person is only liable to others when his actions could foreseeably result in injuries to others. Essentially, a defendant is only liable when the plaintiff falls inside the "orbit of risk" of his actions. If his actions result in an injury that is clearly not foreseeable (such as someone helping another onto a train and triggering an explosion that causes scales to fall and injure the plaintiff), there is no proximate cause and therefore no liability.

Under the foreseeability doctrine, harms can be categorized by those that could reasonably be expected to occur and those that could not. This provides the court with a workable model to assess liability. If the jury determines that the defendant's action could foreseeably have injured the plaintiff, the court can find the defendant liable. On the other hand, if the jury finds that the actions were not foreseeable, the verdict would go in the defendant's favor. However, in practice, this neat theory tends to break down on the issue of defining exactly what foreseeability is.

3. DEFINING FORESEEABILITY AFTER *PALSGRAF*

Foreseeability can be defined as:

1. a natural and continuous sequence, unbroken by any new and independent cause, that produces plaintiff's injury;
2. without which the injury would not have occurred; and
3. from which a person of ordinary prudence could have reasonably foreseen that such a result, or some similar result, was likely or even probable under the facts as they existed at that time.[13]

"In one sense, almost nothing is quite unforeseeable, since there is a very slight mathematical chance, recognizable in advance, that even the most freakish accident will occur. In another, nothing is entirely foreseeable, since the exact details of a sequence of events never can be predicted with complete omniscience."[16] — Prosser and Keeton on the Law of Torts.

Put another way, the "foreseeability" element of proximate cause is satisfied at law when the defendant could have anticipated the danger that his negligence would create for others.[14] There is no requirement that the defendant must anticipate the precise nature of the threat, or even to whom the danger is posed, as long as a reasonably prudent person would have foreseen the possibility.[15] Using the reasonable person standard as a way of determining foreseeability would seem to be a positive solution to the quandary of defining the term, but in the practical world of civil injury litigation, this standard often becomes vague and highly dependent on the facts of the particular case.

COURT-CREATED TESTS FOR PROXIMATE CAUSE

Courts have wrestled with the definition of proximate cause almost from the instant that the term was first used. Over time, at least two major court doctrines have been created as a way of assessing proximate cause and thus the defendant's liability. The two most popular tests are the "but for" test and the "substantial factor" test.

Under the "but for" test, a defendant's actions will be the proximate cause when the plaintiff's injuries would not have occurred but for the defendant's negligence.

TORT BASICS AT A GLANCE

A. "BUT FOR" TEST

The "but for" test states that but for someone's negligence, the plaintiff would not have been injured. This test applies a very rigid standard to the facts of a case. The jury must reach a conclusion that but for the defendant's actions, the plaintiff would not have suffered the injuries in the case. Although the test sounds simple to apply, jurors often find themselves caught in a dilemma in how to apply the test. Essentially, this test requires that the plaintiff prove that had it not been for the defendant's actions, the plaintiff would not have been injured. In the often uncertain actions surrounding car crashes, slip and fall cases, and the myriad other negligence actions, this simple cause and effect is often hard to prove.

Sidebar

There is no mathematical formula that will help determine the defendant's liability; it is a question of facts and of the jury's interpretation of those facts.

In the Chumley case, for instance, can we say that but for the defendant railway's actions, the plaintiff would not have been injured? We have one obvious problem with that question: What if the plaintiff himself was negligent? What if Mr. Chumley failed to stop at the intersection as he is required to do by law? His failure to exercise due care would mean that Mr. Chumley cannot conclusively say that, but for the defendant railway's failure to maintain a safe intersection, he would not have been injured. (We discuss defenses to negligence in Chapter 9.) The rigidity of this test has forced some jurisdictions to adopt a different approach — the substantial factor test.

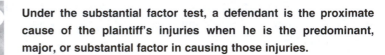

TORT BASICS AT A GLANCE

Under the substantial factor test, a defendant is the proximate cause of the plaintiff's injuries when he is the predominant, major, or substantial factor in causing those injuries.

B. "SUBSTANTIAL FACTOR" TEST

Another test that is used in many jurisdictions is the "substantial factor" test. This test mandates that a defendant will be liable to the plaintiff if the defendant's actions were a primary factor in the plaintiff's injuries.[17] This is the test advocated by the Restatement of Torts. Many argue that the substantial factor test is more forgiving than the but for test, because the substantial factor test only requires that the defendant play a significant role in injuring the plaintiff, while the but for test requires that the defendant play a predominant role. Some jurisdictions use both tests; some use one or the other. The important feature to keep in mind about these tests is that they are designed as guides for the courts and juries. They do not take the place of the fact-finder. There is nothing foolproof about either test. Each case must be taken on its own merits.

To better explain the difference between the substantial factor test and the but for test, let's examine the facts of an actual case.

Case Excerpt

WILLIAMS V. ROSNER
7 N.E.3d 57 (2014)

Opinion

Justice PUCINSKI delivered the judgment of the court, with opinion.

Plaintiffs Cynthia Williams and Kenneth Williams, individually, and as parents and next friends of Kennadi Williams, a minor, filed a complaint advancing claims of negligence and wrongful pregnancy against defendants Byron Rosner, M.D., and Reproductive Health Associates (Reproductive Health). Among the damages that plaintiffs sought to recover were the extraordinary expenses that they would incur in raising their daughter, who was born with sickle cell disease following an unsuccessful sterilization procedure. Defendants filed a motion to dismiss the wrongful pregnancy action filed by plaintiffs, arguing their claim failed as a matter of law because there was no authority permitting plaintiff parents who file wrongful pregnancy actions in Illinois to recover the extraordinary expenses they would incur in raising a child who is born with a genetic abnormality. The circuit court denied defendants' motion to dismiss; however, it recognized that the case involved an issue of law as to which there were substantial grounds for differing opinions and certified a question for appellate review. For the reasons explained herein, we answer the certified question in the affirmative.

I. Background

Cynthia and Kenneth Williams are both carriers of the sickle cell trait, and their first child, a son, was born with sickle cell disease. In January 2001, after the birth of the couple's son, Cynthia began receiving obstetrics and gynecology services from various physicians, including Doctor Rosner, who were employed by Reproductive Health, and practiced various birth control options prescribed by the doctors. On November 28, 2005, Cynthia elected to undergo a tubal ligation in an effort to achieve permanent sterility. The procedure was subsequently canceled, however, when complications arose with respect to the anesthesia.

Thereafter, on December 8, 2008, Cynthia had another consultation with Doctor Rosner to further discuss birth control options. At the conclusion of the consultation, Cynthia elected to undergo a mini-laparotomy FN3 and tubal ligation procedure, to be performed by Doctor Rosner. Cynthia underwent the procedure on December 30, 2008. Unbeknownst to her, Doctor Rosner left one of her fallopian tubes and one of her ovaries intact.

Subsequently, on June 24, 2009, Cynthia learned that she was pregnant. Cynthia gave birth to a daughter, Kennadi, on February 1, 2010, via cesarean section. At this time, Cynthia learned that her left fallopian tube and ovary had not been removed during the December 2008 procedure. Kennadi was subsequently diagnosed with sickle cell disease.

Complaint

Following Kennadi's birth and diagnosis, the Williamses filed a complaint against Doctor Rosner and Reproductive Health advancing claims of medical negligence and wrongful pregnancy. The complaint was amended twice. In the second amended complaint, the complaint at issue here, plaintiffs alleged that Cynthia had a consultation with Doctor Rosner, during which she communicated the following relevant information: that she and her husband were carriers of the sickle cell trait; that they had a son afflicted with sickle cell disease; and that they desired permanent sterility to avoid conceiving another child with sickle cell disease. Doctor Rosner scheduled a bilateral tubal ligation procedure following their discussion. Thereafter, plaintiffs made the following allegations with respect to their wrongful pregnancy claim:

36. In providing medical care to CYNTHIA WILLIAMS, Defendants BYRON ROS-NER, M.D., and REPRODUCTIVE HEALTH ASSOCIATES, S.C., had a duty to possess and apply the knowledge and use the skill and care which a reasonably well-qualified physician would use in cases like that of CYNTHIA WILLIAMS.

37. Defendants, BYRON ROSNER, M.D., and REPRODUCTIVE HEALTH ASSOCIATES, S.C., breached that duty and were negligent in the care and treatment of Plaintiff CYNTHIA WILLIAMS in one or more of the following respects:

(a) Failed to review Cynthia Williams' prior medical records including, but not limited to, her previous operative notes.
(b) Failed to perform an ultrasound or other tests to determine and evaluate Cynthia Williams' reproductive organs prior to surgery.
(c) Failed to perform an adequate or appropriate tubal ligation on Cynthia Williams on December 30, 2008.

38. That as a direct and proximate result of one or more of the foregoing wrongful acts and/or omissions Defendants BYRON ROSNER, MD and REPRODUCTIVE HEALTH ASSOCIATES, S.C., proximately caused injury to plaintiffs CYNTHIA WILLIAMS and KENNETH WILLIAMS in that CYNTHIA WILLIAMS had an unplanned pregnancy and undesired fertility and gave birth to a child afflicted with Sickle Cell Disease, KENNADI WILLIAMS.

39. The birth of a child with Sickle Cell Disease — to wit, KENNADI WILLIAMS — was a foreseeable consequence of the negligence of Defendants BYRON ROSNER, M.D., and REPRODUCTIVE HEALTH ASSOCIATES, S.C., because Defendants BYRON ROSNER, M.D., had actual knowledge that Plaintiffs CYNTHIA WILLIAMS and KENNETH WILLIAMS were carriers of the Sickle Cell Trait, and that the birth of a child afflicted with Sickle Cell Disease would be a likely consequence of a failed tubal ligation.

40. That as a direct and proximate result of one of more of the foregoing wrongful acts and/or omissions of Defendants, BYRON ROSNER, M.D., and REPRODUCTIVE HEALTH ASSOCIATES, S.C., Plaintiffs CYNTHIA WILLIAMS and KENNETH WILLIAMS have become obligated for large sums of money for medical treatment for KENNADI WILLIAMS and will become obligated for large sums of money for further medical treatment as a result of CYNTHIA WILLIAMS' pregnancy, and the extraordinary expenses they will incur in raising KENNADI WILLIAMS to the age of majority.

* * *

WHEREFORE Plaintiffs CYNTHIA WILLIAMS and KENNETH WILLIAMS, individually, and as parents and next friends of KENNADI WILLIAMS, a minor, demand judgment against Defendants BYRON ROSNER, MD, and REPRODUCTIVE HEALTH ASSOCIATES, S.C., in the amount of money necessary to fully and thoroughly compensate CYNTHIA WILLIAMS for personal injury to her, emotional distress, and for lost wages, that far exceeds the jurisdictional minimum for this Court, and for the extraordinary expenses that Plaintiffs CYNTHIA WILLIAMS and KENNETH WILLIAMS will incur in raising KENNADI WILLIAMS to the age of majority.

Motion to Dismiss

Defendants responded with a motion to dismiss. In the motion, defendants urged the court to dismiss, with prejudice, plaintiffs' claim for wrongful pregnancy, or in the alternative, to "certify issues related to count I for interlocutory appeal pursuant to Supreme Court Rule 308." In support of their motion to dismiss the wrongful pregnancy count, defendants observed that there was no Illinois authority expressly permitting parents who file wrongful pregnancy actions to recover extraordinary expenses associated with raising a child born with a genetic defect or abnormality following an unsuccessful sterilization procedure. Instead, defendants maintained that, based on current prevailing legal authority, "wrongful pregnancy plaintiffs who allege a cause of action based on an unsuccessful sterilization procedure, generally are limited to recovering damages for the cost of the unsuccessful operation, pain and suffering, any medical complications caused by the pregnancy, the cost of the child's delivery, lost wages, and loss of consortium." Defendants further argued that plaintiffs were not entitled to recovery because they could not satisfy the element of proximate cause. Although a negligently performed sterilization procedure was undeniably the cause of Cynthia's pregnancy, defendants argued that it was not the cause of Kennadi's genetic defect. Accordingly, defendants maintained that plaintiffs' wrongful pregnancy claim failed as a matter of law.

Circuit Court Ruling

In a written order, the circuit court denied defendants' motion to dismiss, finding:

> After the unsuccessful operation, Plaintiff, Cynthia Williams, conceived and gave birth to a child afflicted with sickle-cell disease. Plaintiffs allege that Defendant, Dr. Rosner, knew that Plaintiffs were carriers of the sickle-cell trait, were already raising one child with sickle-cell disease, and desired sterilization to avoid conceiving another child with the affliction. Count I seeks recovery, inter alia of the extraordinary expenses of raising a child with sickle-cell disease.
>
> * * *
>
> Illinois courts have yet to determine whether plaintiffs in a wrongful pregnancy action may recover the extraordinary expenses associated with raising a child afflicted with a congenital disease where the child's disease was reasonably foreseeable by the defendant physician who negligently performed the sterilization procedure. Absent authority barring Plaintiffs' prayer to recover extraordinary expenses, the court must resolve this motion in the light most favorable to Plaintiffs.

Certified Question

After denying defendants' motion to dismiss, the court subsequently entered a supplemental order nunc pro tunc and certified the following question for interlocutory review pursuant to Supreme Court Rule 308 (Ill. S.Ct. R. 308 (eff. Feb. 26, 2010)):

> Whether a plaintiff in an action for wrongful pregnancy may recover the extraordinary expenses of raising a child afflicted with sickle cell disease when the defendant physician knew (1) that the plaintiff and her husband were carriers of the sickle-cell trait, and (2) that the plaintiffs had previously conceived a child with sickle-cell disease, and (3) that the plaintiffs desired sterilization to avoid giving birth to another child afflicted with sickle-cell disease.

The court expressly found that the matter contained in the certified question "involved a question of law as to which there is a substantial ground for a difference of opinion and, that an immediate appeal from the Order would materially advance the ultimate termination of the litigation."

This court allowed defendants' petition for interlocutory appeal and accepted the certified question for review.

II. Analysis

On appeal, defendants argue that there is no authority in Illinois allowing plaintiff parents who file wrongful pregnancy actions to recover extraordinary damages. Specifically, defendants contend that neither the current body of Illinois case law pertaining to birth-related torts nor the traditional proximate cause framework allows expansion of the scope of damages in wrongful pregnancy actions to include such damages.

Plaintiffs, in turn, urge this court to reject defendants' invitation to impose an artificial limit on the damages available in wrongful pregnancy actions. They argue that "where, as here, the foreseeable consequences of the defendant's negligence is the birth of a child with a serious hereditary disease, and where that consequence in fact results, the defendant should be held liable for the extraordinary medical expenses that the parents will incur in raising the child to the age of majority because those damages proximately flow from the defendant's negligence."

When reviewing a certified question pursuant to Supreme Court Rule 308, an appellate court is generally limited to answering the question certified by the trial court and will not determine the propriety of the underlying order. Given the procedural posture of this case, we note that the question presented for review is not whether the plaintiffs should, or would, prevail in this litigation; rather, the issue before this court is simply whether their complaint states a legally cognizable cause of action. Accordingly, to resolve this question we must accept as true all of the well-pleaded facts contained in plaintiffs' complaint without expressing any opinion as to defendants' liability.

We begin our analysis by providing a brief overview of the three different birth-related medical negligence tort claims recognized in Illinois. "Wrongful birth" actions are suits brought by parents who allege that they would not have conceived a child or carried their child to term but for the negligence of the doctor who administered neonatal testing or genetic testing and failed to counsel them of the likelihood of giving birth to a physically or mentally impaired child. The premise underlying wrongful birth actions is that "prudent medical care would have detected the risk of a congenital or hereditary genetic disorder either prior to conception or during pregnancy" and that "as a proximate result of this negligently performed or omitted genetic counseling or prenatal testing, the parents were foreclosed from making an informed decision whether to conceive a potentially handicapped child or, in the event of a pregnancy, to terminate the same."

Plaintiffs who succeed in wrongful birth claims are entitled to recover extraordinary damages, including the medical, institutional and educational expenses that are necessary to properly manage and treat their child's congenital or genetic disorder.

"Wrongful life" claims, in turn, are corresponding actions brought by a parent or guardian on behalf of a minor child who suffers from a genetic or congenital disorder. The basis for such claims is that the defendant medical provider either failed to accurately perform genetic screening tests and inform the child's parents about the hereditary nature of certain disorders, failed to accurately advise the child's parents about the genetic risks associated with childbirth, or failed to perform a surgical procedure intended to prevent the birth of a genetically disordered child. Siemieniec, "In a wrongful life case, the child does not assert that the negligence of the defendants caused his inherited or congenital abnormality, that the defendants could have done anything that would have decreased the possibility that he would be born with such defects, or that he ever had a chance to be normal. The essence of the child's claim is that the medical professional's breach of the applicable standard of care precluded an informed parental decision to avoid his conception or birth. But for this negligence, the child allegedly would not have been born to experience the pain and suffering attributable to his affliction."

Courts in this state have repeatedly rejected wrongful life actions on public policy grounds. See *Siemieniec*, 117 Ill.2d at 239–40, 111 Ill.Dec. 302, 512 N.E.2d 691 ("Resting on the belief that human life, no matter how burdened, is, as a matter of law, always preferable to nonlife, the courts have been reluctant to find that the infant has suffered a legally cognizable injury by being born with a congenital or genetic impairment as opposed to not being born at all."). Given the public policy favoring life over nonlife, as well as the inherent difficulties associated with calculating damages in wrongful life actions, plaintiffs who have filed such actions have been precluded from recovering both general and extraordinary damages.

Finally, "wrongful pregnancy" or "wrongful conception" claims, the cause of action at issue in the instant appeal, are claims brought by parents of a child who is born following a negligently performed sterilization procedure. Parents who file such actions seek to recover compensation for a pregnancy that they had sought to avoid.

Historically, plaintiffs in wrongful pregnancy actions have been limited to general damages, including costs associated with the "unsuccessful operation, the pain and suffering involved, any medical complications caused by the pregnancy, the costs of delivery, lost wages, and loss of consortium." For example, in *Cockrum*, our supreme court declined to expand the scope of damages permitted in wrongful pregnancy actions to include the costs of raising an unexpected, but otherwise healthy child, who was born following a negligently performed sterilization procedure. In doing so, the court expressed an "unwillingness to hold that the birth of a normal healthy child can be judged to be an injury to the parents" because such a notion "offends fundamental values attached to human life." Id. at 198, 69 Ill.Dec. 168, 447 N.E.2d 385. The court thus limited the plaintiffs' recovery to general damages.

Following its decision in Cockrum, the court was again called upon to address the permissible scope of damages in wrongful pregnancy actions in *Williams v. University of Chicago Hospitals*, 179 Ill.2d 80, 84, 227 Ill.Dec. 793, 688 N.E.2d 130 (1997). In Williams, the plaintiffs were parents of a child diagnosed with attention deficit hyperactivity disorder (ADHD), who was born following a negligently performed tubal ligation procedure. In the complaint that the parents filed against the defendant doctor, the plaintiffs alleged that the doctor was aware that they were already the parents of another child who was hyperactive and learning disabled. The parents sought to recover general damages as well as the extraordinary expenses that they would incur in raising their special needs child to the age of majority, including expenses for psychological treatment and special education.

The supreme court, however, relying on "familiar principles of tort law, as well as considerations of public policy," rejected the plaintiffs' claim for extraordinary damages. Williams, 179 Ill.2d at 86, 227 Ill.Dec. 793, 688 N.E.2d 130. Observing that plaintiffs in wrongful pregnancy actions must satisfy the elements of duty, breach and proximate cause to be entitled to damages, the court concluded that the allegations contained in the plaintiffs' complaint were insufficient to establish that their medical care provider proximately caused their injury, stating:

> "There are no allegations in the present case that the defendants caused the child's condition or misled the parents about the likelihood that a child born to them would be defective. Indeed, the plaintiffs acknowledge in their briefs before this court that they do not contend that the defendants caused their son's condition or that the defendants could have detected the condition before the child was born. Nor do the plaintiffs allege that the defendants knew that Mrs. Williams sought sterilization as a means of avoiding the conception of a child with the particular defect involved here. Without determining in this case whether such an allegation would be sufficient to sustain recovery under a wrongful-pregnancy theory, we do not believe that proximate cause can be established in the absence of allegations forging a closer link between the defendants' negligence and the eventual birth of the defective child." Williams, 179 Ill.2d at 87, 227 Ill.Dec. 793, 688 N.E.2d 130.

Emphasizing that a key element of proximate cause is foreseeability, the court explicitly rejected the plaintiffs' argument that the doctor's knowledge that their first child suffered from the same affliction was enough, in itself, to make the birth of another child with ADHD a foreseeable consequence of medical negligence. The court reasoned:

> "Under the allegations in this case the plaintiffs' injury cannot be said to be of such a character that an ordinarily prudent person should have foreseen it as a likely consequence of the alleged negligence.*67 **641 The plaintiffs do not allege that any act or omission by the defendants caused the child's condition, that the defendants knew of the possibility that a child conceived in the wake of a failed operation would suffer from a particular defect, or even that the parents were seeking to avoid a specific risk and that the defendants were aware of that, assuming that

allegations of that nature would be a sufficient basis for liability." *Williams*, 179 Ill.2d at 87–88, 227 Ill.Dec. 793, 688 N.E.2d 130.

Accordingly, given that the birth of the plaintiffs' ADHD-afflicted child was an unforeseeable consequence of the defendants' negligence, the court concluded that the parents were not entitled to recover the extraordinary expenses that they would incur in raising their child to the age of majority.

Both parties rely on Williams in support of their respective arguments. Defendants argue that plaintiffs in this case, just like the parents in Williams, cannot satisfy the requisite element of proximate cause that is necessary to justify expanding the scope of recoverable damages in wrongful pregnancy actions to include extraordinary expenses. Specifically, defendants contend that Dr. Rosner's knowledge that plaintiffs already had a child diagnosed with sickle cell disease did not make it reasonably foreseeable that a negligently performed tubal ligation procedure would result in the birth of another child with the same congenital disorder.

Plaintiffs, in turn, maintain that Williams merely "stands for the uncontroversial proposition that a plaintiff in a negligence action may only recover those damages which are foreseeable as a likely consequence of the defendant's negligence." Thus, where the pleadings establish that the birth of a diseased child is a foreseeable consequence of a negligently performed sterilization procedure, then wrongful pregnancy plaintiffs should be able to obtain an award of extraordinary damages. We agree with plaintiffs.

In *Williams*, the court did not create a per se ban on extraordinary damages available to wrongful pregnancy plaintiffs. Rather, the Williams decision was decided on the narrow grounds of proximate cause and the deficiencies of the allegations contained in that complaint. Notably, the court specifically declined to resolve the question at issue in the instant case: whether parents "with a particular need to avoid conception of a child, and who communicate that need to the defendant who performs the sterilization procedure, may recover as damages the extraordinary expenses of raising a child born in the wake of an unsuccessful and negligently performed operation." Williams, 179 Ill.2d at 89, 227 Ill.Dec. 793, 688 N.E.2d 130. Unlike the parents in Williams, plaintiffs here have set forth allegations that if, taken as true, establish the requisite link between Dr. Rosner's negligence and Kennadi's condition. Specifically, plaintiffs alleged that they had a special need to avoid conception of additional children, as both were carriers of the sickle cell trait and were parents of a son born with sickle cell disease, and that they communicated their need to avoid conception of additional children with the same affliction to Dr. Rosner. As the court explained in Williams, to justify a finding that a defendant proximately caused a plaintiff's injury: "The injury must be the natural and probable result of the negligent act or omission and be of such a character as an ordinarily prudent person ought to have foreseen as likely to occur as a result of the negligence, although it is not essential that the person charged with negligence should have foreseen the precise injury which resulted from his act." *Williams*, 179 Ill.2d at 87, 227 Ill.Dec. 793, 688 N.E.2d 130. Here, based on the allegations in plaintiffs' complaint, one can conclude that plaintiffs' injury, the birth of a second child afflicted with sickle cell disease, was of such a character that an ordinarily prudent person should have foreseen it to be a likely consequence of a negligently performed tubal ligation procedure.

Defendants, however, argue that even if the allegations contained in plaintiffs' complaint are true and the birth of a child with sickle cell disease was a foreseeable consequence, the element of proximate cause is still not satisfied because Dr. Rosner's negligence in performing the tubal ligation did not actually cause Kennadi to develop sickle cell disease as her condition was determined at conception; rather, his actions merely created a condition under which a child with sickle cell disease could be born. Defendants' argument, however, is based upon a misunderstanding and oversimplification of the element of proximate cause.

Proximate cause encompasses both "cause in fact" and "legal cause." "Legal cause" encompasses the aforementioned issue of foreseeability. Actual cause or "cause in fact," however, is satisfied only if there is evidence that the plaintiff's injury could not have occurred "but for" the defendant's conduct or if it can be determined that the defendant's conduct was a "substantial factor" or material element in creating the injury. Here, although Dr. Rosner did not actually cause Kennadi's sickle cell disease, one can conclude that her birth and affliction was not only foreseeable, but that it would not have occurred "but for" the negligently performed tubal ligation procedure. Accordingly, we reject defendants' argument that plaintiffs' wrongful pregnancy claim fails on proximate cause grounds.

Accordingly, for the aforementioned reasons, we decline to impose a rigid arbitrary limitation on damages available to wrongful pregnancy plaintiffs. Rather, we conclude that whereas here, the birth of a child with a genetic abnormality is a foreseeable consequence of a negligently performed sterilization procedure and where the parents' desire to avoid contraception precisely for that reason has been communicated to the doctor performing the procedure, parents may assert a claim for the extraordinary costs that they will incur in raising their child to the age of majority. We emphasize that our disposition is limited to propriety of extraordinary damages in this case and we render no opinion regarding the other types of damages sought by plaintiffs in their complaint.

III. Conclusion

Certified question answered in the affirmative.

Justices NEVILLE and MASON concurred in the judgment and opinion.

Questions about the case:

1. Why did the parents in this case file a claim for wrongful pregnancy?
2. What negligence resulted in the mother's pregnancy?
3. What claim do the defendants raise concerning extraordinary damages in regard to wrongful pregnancy cases?
4. How does the court address the defendants' issues?

V. PLEADING PROXIMATE CAUSE

On a practical level, attorneys have long since realized that the more tenuous the connection between the plaintiff's injuries and the defendant's actions, the more the plaintiff should focus on the facts of the case to establish proximate cause. After all, failure to prove this element negates the rest of the case. Another complicating factor is that, in many ways, proximate cause is determined on a case-by-case basis. Given the almost infinite variety of ways that negligent actions (or inactions) can result in injuries to others, each case must be considered on its merits and the theories and court tests applied to the specific facts of the pending case.

As such, when pleading proximate cause, the best practice is to break the facts of the case down into the smallest discernible units possible to explain each phase of the case and to help relate the defendant's actions to the plaintiff's injuries. (For an example of how to phrase proximate cause language, see "Forms and Court Documents" at the end of this chapter.)

The plaintiff must always prove that the defendant was the legal cause of the plaintiff's injuries. The plaintiff will lose the case on a directed verdict for the defendant if the plaintiff fails to prove causation.

A. IS PROXIMATE CAUSE A DEFENSE?

A defendant does not have to raise the failure to prove proximate cause as a defense. Proximate cause is an essential element of the plaintiff's case, and failure to prove it demands a verdict for the defendant.[18] A general denial is sufficient to attack the issue of proximate cause.

B. IN THE END, PROXIMATE CAUSE IS A JURY QUESTION

Whether the defendant's actions rise to the level of proximate cause of the plaintiff's injuries is a question for the jury. The underlying principle behind proximate cause is a question of public policy — that is, how far the law will extend the defendant's responsibility for negligent conduct.[19]

Some commentators suggest that proximate cause is both a factual question (which the jury determines) and a question of law (which the judge decides).

Proximate cause is a jury question.

FIGURE 7-4

Sample Jury In-
struction on
Proximate
Cause

Ladies and gentlemen of the jury, I charge you that the plaintiff bears the burden of proving proximate cause in this case. I hereby charge you that a proximate cause of an injury is a cause which, in natural and continuous sequence, produces the injury, and without which the injury would not have occurred.

Bolen v. Woo, 96 Cal. App. 3d 944, 158 Cal. Rptr. 454 (1979).

Sidebar

Practical suggestion: For sample jury instructions on proximate cause, see 18A Am. Jur. Pleading and Practice Forms (rev.), Negligence, Form 223, 224. This would make a good addition to the jury instructions subfile in one of your pending cases.

Because the plaintiff will present evidence attempting to prove that the defendant was the proximate cause of the plaintiff's injuries, the jurors must receive some direction about how they make this decision. The judge can, and often does, give the jurors a jury charge (often called a jury instruction) that explains what proximate cause is. The jurors will actually receive numerous jury charges before they retire to consider their verdict, and in a negligence case the issue of proximate cause is likely to be an important one.

According to the Restatement of Torts, the jury's function is to determine: (1) if the defendant's breach of duty was a substantial factor in causing the plaintiff's injuries and (2) how to apportion responsibility (and damages) if there are two or more defendants.[20] See Figure 7-4 for a jury charge example.

1. HOW MUCH EVIDENCE DOES THE PLAINTIFF HAVE TO PRODUCE TO MAKE PROXIMATE CAUSE A JURY QUESTION?

Plaintiffs are not required to prove proximate cause to an absolute certainty. As long as the plaintiff presents substantial evidence tending to show proximate cause, it then becomes the jury's function to decide if it exists. In some jurisdictions, even if the plaintiff presents a "scintilla" of proof of proximate cause, it must be presented to the jury for a determination.

2. ON APPEAL, COURTS WILL LEAVE THE JURY'S DETERMINATION INTACT, UNLESS CLEARLY WRONG

Appellate courts are bound by the jury's determination of proximate cause (because it is largely a factual determination) except where the jury's conclusion is clearly wrong.[21] When the jury clearly disregards the facts of a case and decides that proximate cause exists when there are no supporting facts, an appellate court could overturn the verdict and find for the defendant.

Tech Topic
RE-CREATING AUTO ACCIDENTS WITH CAD

Computer-aided design, or CAD, has long been a tool for creating technical and engineering documents. But CAD is finding a new application in the process of re-creating automobile accidents. It is critical for juries to be able to visualize what happened during a car crash, but often all they have is a verbal description, perhaps some rudimentary drawings, and photos of the aftermath. With CAD software, every element of the accident can be drawn to scale, and the events can even be animated.

Quick Scene is a CAD program that allows users to draw a detailed crash-scene diagram, complete with lines, rectangles, circles, arcs, and curves. The scene itself can be drawn with turn lanes, medians, street names, trees, shrubs, and more. Intersections of up to 20 lanes on each street can be easily rendered. Another feature allows for the importing of digital photographs, satellite images, and aerial images for use as background.

Another software program is MapScenes Forensic CAD. This program also produces diagrams for use in court. Users input evidence collected from the crash scene to create accurate and detailed diagrams, including driving conditions at the time of the accident. MapScenes Capture, an add-on to MapScenes Forensic, helps users create an animation to visually enact the entire accident from beginning to end.

VI   MULTIPLE DEFENDANTS AND PROXIMATE CAUSE

Our discussion so far has focused on the actions of one defendant. What happens to the analysis when more than one defendant is involved? We have already seen that liability for two negligent defendants will usually be apportioned between them according to their degree of negligence. However, suppose the facts clearly show that only *one* defendant could have been negligent?

Example: Tara is sitting in her backyard, which borders on a wooded section. Two hunters, one on each side of Tara's property, fire their rifles at the same time, mistakenly believing that Tara is a deer. Tara is hit by one bullet, but it is impossible to tell which hunter fired the shot. How does the court decide proximate cause?

When the plaintiff is injured by the negligence of Defendant A and then receives additional injuries because of Defendant B's negligence, Defendant A is not absolved of liability. In such a case, both defendants may be liable to the plaintiff, each for the injuries his negligence proximately caused (Figure 7-5).

FIGURE 7-5

Median Compensatory and Punitive Final Awards for Plaintiff Winners. Civil Bench and Jury Trials in State Courts, revised 2009

Case type	Total trials		Percent disposed through jury trial
	Number	Percent of total trials	
All cases	**26,948**	**100.0%**	**68.3%**
Tort cases	**16,397**	**60.8%**	**90.0%**
Motor vehicle	9,431	35.0	92.1
Medical malpractice	2,449	9.1	98.7
Premises liability	1,863	6.9	93.8
Intentional tort	725	2.7	78.3
Other or unknown tort	664	2.5	71.6
Conversion	378	1.4	46.3
Product liability	354	1.3	93.5
Asbestos	87	0.3	95.5
Other	268	1.0	92.7
Slander/libel	187	0.7	64.2
Professional malpractice	150	0.6	59.9
Animal attack	138	0.5	80.6
False arrest, imprisonment	58	0.2	63.9
Contract cases	**8,917**	**33.1%**	**36.0%**
Seller plaintiff	2,883	10.7	16.6
Buyer plaintiff	2,591	9.6	44.1
Fraud	1,114	4.1	50.2
Rental/lease	605	2.2	19.2
Other employment dispute	558	2.1	62.9
Employment discrimination	319	1.2	91.2
Mortgage foreclosure	249	0.9	3.5
Other or unknown contract	245	0.9	52.2
Tortious interference	152	0.6	61.7
Partnership dispute	119	0.4	32.3
Subrogation	82	0.3	7.4
Real property cases	**1,633**	**6.1%**	**26.4%**
Title or boundary dispute	963	3.6	15.0
Eminent domain	542	2.0	50.7
Other or unknown real property	129	0.5	9.0

Source: Bureau of Justice Statistics

When liability cannot be determined between two negligent defendants, both are held liable, despite the fact that only one could have actually caused the injuries. The reasoning behind this apparent exception to assessing responsibility against the negligent party is a public policy concern. Presented with this problem, the court is faced with either finding both defendants liable, or finding neither liable. The second option leaves an innocent plaintiff without any possibility of recovery. Because both defendants were acting negligently, both will pay, even if only one could have proximately caused the plaintiff's injuries.

VII   INTERVENING CAUSES

An **intervening cause** contributes to the plaintiff's injuries. When two or more defendants act negligently, both can be liable to the plaintiff. Only when the intervening cause rises to the level of creating an independent proximate cause is it classified as a **superseding cause.** A superseding cause relieves the original defendant's liability by substituting the negligence of the next defendant.

What makes a negligent act an intervening cause or a superseding cause? This is usually a factual question that must be determined by the jury (or, in a bench trial, the judge). Classifying causes as intervening and superseding often becomes very confusing, especially because so many jurisdictions have different rules about these terms. In some jurisdictions, for example, the original defendant remains liable for any foreseeable negligence by another party. In other jurisdictions, the original defendant is not liable for intervening negligence by another which could not have been reasonably foreseen.

An intervening cause can expand the pool of defendants from the original defendant to the one who caused the additional injuries to the plaintiff. Some jurisdictions follow a rule that is easier to implement: A superseding cause must come from some source not associated with the original defendant. If the source of the additional injuries is somehow associated with the original defendant, the original defendant remains liable.[22]

Intervening cause
Any event that occurs after the initial plaintiff's injury that contributes to or aggravates those injuries.

Superseding cause
Any event that occurs after the initial plaintiff's injury that replaces one act of negligence with another.

Sidebar

According to the Restatement (Second) of Torts, an intervening force is one that operates to produce harm to the plaintiff after the original defendant's negligent act or omission has occurred.

When two or more defendants combine to injure the plaintiff, each may be considered intervening causes and all will be liable to the plaintiff.

TORT
BASICS
AT A
GLANCE

A. SUPERSEDING CAUSES

A superseding cause eliminates the original defendant's negligence by replacing it with the negligence of another. To be classified as a superseding cause, the new negligent act must be one that exceeds the original defendant's negligence to such an extent as to render it nearly meaningless. Put another way, a superseding cause is one that takes precedence over the original negligent act and makes that original negligent act legally "remote."[23]

Example: Tom is driving his car on the freeway during rush hour and in a moment of distraction, he allows his front bumper to tap the back bumper of

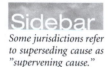

Not all jurisdictions draw a clear distinction between intervening and superseding causes. Some jurisdictions follow the rule that the original defendant is responsible for the plaintiff's injuries, even when some new force contributes or cooperates in the plaintiff's injuries, whether this new force was foreseeable or not.[24]

the car in front of him. He puts on his warning flashers and climbs out. Elizabeth, the other driver, also gets out of her car. While they are inspecting the minor damage, Ron, who is speeding and driving recklessly in the breakdown lane, crashes into both cars, pinning Elizabeth between both cars and severely injuring her. Ron's liability for Elizabeth's injuries will likely be considered a superseding act to Tom's original negligence in bumping into Elizabeth's car.

Some jurisdictions have done away with the distinctions between intervening and superseding causes, considering them unworkable. Instead, they have substituted a foreseeability analysis. Those jurisdictions ask the question: Was the injury to the plaintiff foreseeable, no matter what the source? If the answer is yes, the defendant is liable.[25]

The basic policy behind superseding causation is that there are times when it is unreasonable or unjust to make the original defendant liable for negligence that was so obviously exceeded by the actions of a second defendant.[26]

Some jurisdictions refer to superseding cause as "supervening cause."

Example: Ted and Marsha were invited to a wedding held at a friend's house. The invitations included the following language: "The ceremony will take place beside the family pool (weather permitting); please arrange for child care as seating is limited and we cannot provide supervision for children." Ted and Marsha decide to bring their three-year-old daughter, Tiffany, to the ceremony. During the nuptials, neither parent supervises Tiffany, who is playing in the backyard near the unfenced pool. Tiffany falls into the pool and suffers brain damage when she nearly drowns. Ted and Marsha sue the friend for failing to properly fence the pool. The court rules that Ted and Marsha's negligence in failing to properly supervise Tiffany supersedes any negligence of the homeowner in failing to fence off the pool.[27]

TORT
BASICS
AT A
GLANCE

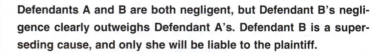

Defendants A and B are both negligent, but Defendant B's negligence clearly outweighs Defendant A's. Defendant B is a superseding cause, and only she will be liable to the plaintiff.

B. ACTS OF GOD OR ACTS OF NATURE

Finally, there is a category of events that fall outside the classifications of proximate cause, intervening cause, or even superseding cause. These are "acts of God," also sometimes referred to as "acts of nature." Plaintiffs are barred from bringing suit against individual defendants for natural catastrophes. For example, when the plaintiff is injured in a tornado or earthquake, the plaintiff cannot sue any specific person for his injuries. In effect, acts of nature fall outside the realm of tort law.

However, there are some exceptions to this general rule. A plaintiff may be permitted to bring an action against a defendant who failed to follow routine and normal precautions against expected natural forces, such as building a retaining wall to hold in dirt from a recent excavation in an area where rainfall is often heavy or sudden. In such a case, the defendant's actions have increased the likelihood of injury from an act of nature, and therefore he can be liable.

Chapter Summary

Courts have been wrestling with the concept of proximate cause since its origins in the early 1600s. As the third element of a negligence action, the plaintiff must prove that the defendant's action (or inaction) brought about the plaintiff's injuries. However, proving that connection is often difficult, given the vague way that proximate cause is often defined by courts. An early attempt to bring more consistency to the application of proximate cause analysis is the famous *Palsgraf* case, which held that a defendant would not be the proximate cause (and thus not liable) for the plaintiff's injuries when it was not foreseeable that the defendant's negligent act would result in the plaintiff's injuries. However, the test of foreseeability continues to be difficult to apply in some cases. Additional court doctrines have been created to deal with the proof required in proximate cause cases. For instance, some jurisdictions have adopted the "but for" test, meaning that the defendant will only be liable when the plaintiff would not have been injured but for the defendant's actions. Other jurisdictions have opted for the "substantial factor" test. Under that test, a defendant will be considered the proximate cause of the plaintiff's injuries when he is the predominant or major cause of those injuries. Finally, courts must also apportion blame when more than one defendant is involved. In some cases, two or more defendants will be negligent, and this liability must be divided among them. In other cases, such as superseding negligence, one defendant's negligence will so outweigh another defendant's negligence as to remove all of the other defendant's liability to the plaintiff.

SKILLS YOU NEED IN THE REAL WORLD

Internet Legal Research

The days of curling up in a law library to spend hours poring over books on arcane legal topics are long over. These days, you need fast answers and even faster research methods. In the past few years, the Internet resources available to legal researchers have increased dramatically. With this huge increase, there has been a growing misconception about Internet legal resources. One of the biggest problems with Internet legal research is that many of these sites limit their coverage. If the legal database only covers cases from the past ten years, any valuable case that is more than a decade old will not be listed, even if it is the most important case for your research. Having stated that caveat, however, there are some valuable legal research sites available on the Internet, and they can dramatically lessen your research time.

Strategies for Online Legal Research

Before you begin researching any topic on the Internet, you must decide what you want to know and what you do *not* want to know. Some sites will cycle you through endless links until you have lost the thread of your research. You should come up with a list of key words and terms before you begin researching. After that, you should confirm what sources you need. For instance, are you researching federal law or state law? This will help you focus on websites that concentrate on those areas.

All Websites Are Not Created Equal

As you conduct your research, you should concentrate on the pedigree of the site, which refers to the URL. If you are researching U.S. Supreme Court cases, for instance, and you have a choice between *http://www.RonniehatestheSupreme-court.org* and *http://www.supremecourtus.gov/* (which is the actual link to the Supreme Court of the United States), you would probably have more success at the second site than the first. Besides getting to your primary sources more quickly, the first site sounds like a site that would not provide the same depth of coverage or accuracy in sources that could be found at the second. As you visit legal research sites, evaluate the URL to determine where this information is coming from. For legal research purposes, you are safest with government, law school, and university websites.

Free Sites

Rather than provide a list of the available free legal research websites here (that would probably have expired or become inactive by the time you read this section), I have provided a list of Internet search engines. Your best bet to find free legal research sites is to visit a major Internet search engine and enter a search term such as "legal research sites." General Internet search engines include:

www.yahoo.com
www.excite.com
www.dogpile.com
www.google.com
http://bing.com
http://Ask.com

Pay Sites

Just about everyone has either heard of or worked with Westlaw (*www.westlaw.-com*). However, there are other sites, such as Lexis-Nexis (*www.lexis-nexis.com*), that also provide in-depth coverage. Free sites cannot compete with the pay sites in terms of scope, timeliness, and comprehensiveness. Pay sites provide access to all state and federal court decisions, state and federal codes, and other sources too numerous to list. Lexis-Nexis also provides access to the invaluable Shepard's service so that you can "shepardize" your cases online.

THE LIFE OF A PARALEGAL

Balancing Work and School

When I decided to get a paralegal degree, I was already working full time. I knew that I'd have to do some of my homework during lunch breaks, so the first thing I did was run it by my boss. Both of the bosses that I've had while I've been in the paralegal program have been totally supportive. Their approach was, "Well, this will only make you better at what you're doing."

I take Internet courses through a local community college. During lunch, I'll log on to my course website to take care of an assignment. If I have to do a paper or a project, I'll stay at work late to type it up, or to use our library for research. Our library has statutes and other books, and that's very helpful. I also asked an attorney across the street if I could borrow his library. He was very kind and told me that I could come over anytime that I needed to. One semester, I spent nearly every lunch hour over there, reading and researching. It's amazing how friendly most people will be, if you explain your situation to them. They have just opened up their resources to me. It makes you realize how nice most of the people in the legal community are.

I've always been interested in the law. When I worked for the city's legal department, the city attorney asked me if I was interested in going back to school. The city had a tuition reimbursement policy. I really hadn't given it that much thought until he mentioned it to me. I thought, *I'd be stupid not to do it. Now is my chance.* I thought that at least I'd try it and if I couldn't do it, I'd stop. So far, it's worked out really well.

My advice to anyone trying to balance school and work: don't put anything off until the last minute because everything will go wrong. Try to stay ahead of the game; try to get your assignments done ahead of time. When I have a doctor's appointment or a dentist's appointment, I take my books with me. As I'm sitting in the waiting room for an hour, I read. Use every spare minute of your time to stay ahead. After a while, you get in the habit of doing that. Then it's a relief when you've got something due and you've already done it.

Pamela Tallent, Paralegal

ETHICAL ISSUES FOR THE PARALEGAL: ATTORNEY-CLIENT PRIVILEGE

Often considered to be one of the most sacred tenets of law, the attorney-client privilege protects communications between clients and attorneys from being revealed to others. An attorney who is called to the stand and asked to testify about a conversation with a client can legally refuse to answer these questions. The attorney cannot be held in contempt or otherwise penalized for failure to answer such questions. Is a paralegal protected by a similar privilege? No. There are some jurisdictions that have held that the presence of the paralegal during an attorney-client discussion may actually waive or eliminate the privilege. That being true, a paralegal cannot refuse to answer questions about conversations with a client. However, the paralegal should ensure that the attorney-client privilege is not waived under other circumstances. Because the conversations between the attorney and the client are supposed to be private, the paralegal should make sure that they remain so. The best way to do this is not to discuss any client business away from the office. Unless given permission to do so, it is a good idea to refuse to state that a particular person is even represented by the attorney.

Relevant Cases

ORTIZ V. CITY OF CHICAGO
79 ILL. APP. 3D 902, 398 N.E. 2D 1007 (1979)

MEJDA, Justice.

Jamin Ortiz, a minor (plaintiff), and his mother brought this action for personal injuries and medical expenses allegedly caused by the negligence of the City of Chicago (defendant) in failing to remove an abandoned van from an alley. A jury awarded plaintiff $22,500 and the trial court entered judgment on the verdict. It is from that judgment that defendant appeals.

On June 29, 1972, plaintiff was burned on his left arm and his upper torso when the gas tank of a van which had been abandoned in an alley burst into flames. He brought this action against the defendant alleging that it carelessly and negligently failed to remove the van from the alley and that this failure was the proximate cause of his injuries. The following pertinent testimony was adduced at trial.

Mrs. Rivera, plaintiff's neighbor, testified that the van had been parked in the alley for approximately two months before the accident. The wheels were gone, the doors and windows were broken, and the van was stripped. She considered it dangerous because some children played around it. She called the police about four times and told them about the van and its danger to the children.

On the day of the accident, children were playing ball in the alley and Mrs. Rivera heard a loud noise and saw a flash of light. She saw plaintiff standing in the alley with his clothes

afire. The next day the van was removed. There was a police station about 1 1/2 blocks from her house.

Carmen Rios, another of plaintiff's neighbors, testified that the van had been in the alley for about 2 to 2 1/2 months. She had called the police two or three times to tell them about the van. She had also stopped squad cars to complain about the van. On the day of the accident she did not hear any firecrackers exploding. The van was towed from the alley on the following day.

Mrs. Whittle, who lived near plaintiff, testified that the van had been in the alley for several months and had two tow tickets on it. She had also called the police several times to inquire why the van had not been towed. She did not hear any firecrackers on the day of the accident.

Gilbert Ortiz, plaintiff's older brother, testified that the van had been in the alley for 2 1/2 to 3 months and was stripped.

Plaintiff testified that he was born on August 13, 1961. On June 29, 1972, he had just finished delivering papers on his daily route and was on his way home when the accident occurred. He stopped in the alley to play catch with some friends and then walked past the van. As he was walking next to the van he heard an explosion and he caught fire. He ran until a woman put a cover over him to smother the fire.

He could not remember if any of the boys in the alley were playing with firecrackers before the accident but stated that he was not. In response to defense counsel's question if plaintiff knew what caused the fire that burned him, plaintiff answered, "They sat (sic) it was a firecracker." Plaintiff's counsel objected and the answer was stricken as hearsay and the jury was instructed to disregard it.

David Ortiz, plaintiff's brother, testified that before the explosion he was playing catch with plaintiff and his friends. About ten minutes after plaintiff left to go home, there was an explosion and he saw that his brother was afire. He also stated that the van had been parked in the alley for three to four months. He denied speaking to any police officers after the accident and specifically to Officer Cristia. He denied that he, plaintiff, or any other boy had been playing with firecrackers before the accident.

For the Defense

Chicago police officer Newman of the Auto Pound Section testified that cars to be towed are classified as immediate or abandoned tows. Immediate tows include stolen cars and cars involved in accidents which are immediate traffic hazards. Each police district has men assigned to locate abandoned cars, write tow reports, and give them to a foreman who assigns trucks to tow the cars to a city auto pound. In 1972, there were 2,786 abandoned vehicles and 1,964 immediate tows in plaintiff's police district. At that time the district had one or two trucks to tow abandoned cars and were aided by private trucks and trucks from the Department of Streets and Sanitation. Officer Newman acknowledged that according to police policy, the ordinance and statutes authorizing the towing of vehicles were vigorously enforced. He agreed that the Police Department defines a "hazard" as a vehicle located on a public way in such a manner as to constitute a clear and present danger to the safety of the community or an obstruction to the normal thoroughfare of traffic. He

also agreed that an "abandoned tow" is a vehicle unused or unmoved for a period of seven days.

Chicago police officer Fleming testified. At the time of the accident he was an abandoned auto officer in plaintiff's district. His duties included locating abandoned cars, writing a tow report, and seeing that the cars were towed. In June 1972, there were two abandoned auto officers in the district. He stated that he had no knowledge of the towing of a Ford van from the scene of the accident on June 29, 1972, and that any tow report would have been destroyed within a year of the tow. In 1972 the number of trucks in the district varied from two to five. Since the police department had no trucks of their own, private trucks and trucks from the Bureau of Streets and Sanitation are used for towing purposes.

Chicago police officer Cristia testified that he investigated plaintiff's accident but did not have an independent recollection of his investigation. By referring to his report of the incident, he stated that he spoke with David Ortiz following the accident. At this point plaintiff's counsel objected to questions regarding the substance of the conversation on hearsay grounds. At the sidebar, defendant's counsel stated that Officer Cristia would testify that David Ortiz told him that "they" were playing with firecrackers on the day of the accident and that this would impeach David's credibility. The court felt that "they" was ambiguous and refused to speculate whether it included David and plaintiff. He therefore refused to allow impeachment by this evidence. Defense counsel sought to ask Cristia if he remembered to whom "they" referred, but the court denied the request since the officer had already shown that he had no independent recollection of the investigation. Cristia was allowed to testify that David told him that he had removed the gasoline from the van's tank on the day before the accident. An offer of proof was made outside the presence of the jury. Officer Cristia testified that David Ortiz told him that shortly before the fire, he and several friends, including plaintiff, were playing by a van and that someone put a firecracker into the van's gas tank and that he saw fire coming from the van's gas tank. Plaintiff's attorney again objected to the offer on hearsay grounds. The court declined the offer of proof.

The jury found for plaintiff and set damages at $22,500. A special interrogatory asking "Do you find that the plaintiff immediately before and at the time of the occurrence in question was guilty of negligence which proximately caused or contributed to the accident?" was answered "No."

Opinion

On appeal defendant contends that: (1) the plaintiff's failure to plead or prove wilful and wanton negligence bars recovery; (2) defendant had no duty to remove the van from the alley; (3) defendant could not have foreseen the possibility that the van might explode spontaneously; and (4) the court erred in refusing to permit impeachment of David Ortiz regarding the use of firecrackers. At oral argument, counsel for defendant informed this court that the fourth issue had been abandoned as grounds for reversal. Because of the disposition of this appeal, it is only necessary to address defendant's third contention.

A complaint for negligence must set out the existence of a duty to the injured party, a breach of that duty and an injury proximately resulting from the breach. A local public entity has a duty to exercise ordinary care to maintain its property in a reasonably safe condition. The duty requires that a city keep its streets and alleys in a reasonably safe condition for the use of persons who are in the exercise of ordinary care for their own safety. In the instant case, the evidence presented at trial did not establish a breach of that duty or that plaintiff's injuries were proximately caused by any act or omission of the defendant.

Defendant initially contended that it should have been allowed to impeach David Ortiz regarding the possible use of firecrackers by the boys. Because defendant no longer urges this claim, evidence of their possible use will not be considered on appeal. There is no evidence in the record to show that an external force or agency caused the gas tank to explode. Therefore, it must be assumed that the tank exploded spontaneously. Defendant argues that such an occurrence is so unforeseeable that it is not liable as a matter of law.

Plaintiff presented no evidence at trial to show the possibility that an abandoned vehicle could explode spontaneously. Nor is that event a common one or of such a nature that a juror would be aware of its likelihood from his own observation and experience in the affairs of life. While it may be foreseeable that a child could place a lighted match into the gas tank of an abandoned vehicle, thereby causing his injury, it is not reasonably foreseeable that a vehicle will spontaneously explode causing injury to a passerby.

Because the explosion of the van was not reasonably foreseeable, defendant cannot be held liable in negligence for plaintiff's injuries. Foreseeability is considered as a factor in determining the existence of a legal duty and also is considered in deciding whether a certain negligent act is the proximate or legal cause of an injury. Although foreseeability may enter into the analysis of both elements, the question of the existence of a legal duty is a question of law to be determined by the trial court, while the issue of proximate cause is ordinarily a question for the jury. In this case the unforeseeability of the explosion requires that defendant is not liable either because it owed no duty to plaintiff or because any negligence on the part of defendant was not the proximate cause of plaintiff's injuries.

The supreme court has made it clear that in determining whether a legal duty exists, the occurrence must have been reasonably foreseeable; more than a mere possibility of occurrence is required. "No man can be expected to guard against harm from events which are not reasonably to be anticipated at all, or are so unlikely to occur that the risk, although recognizable, would commonly be disregarded." (Prosser, Torts s 31, at 146 (4th ed. 1971).) The existence of a legal duty is not dependent on the factor of foreseeability alone but includes consideration of public policy and social requirements. Aside from the unforeseeability of the explosion, other considerations require that no duty be imposed on defendant under the facts of this case. The likelihood of injury, the magnitude of the burden of guarding against it and the consequences of placing that burden upon the defendant, must also be taken into account. As already noted, the likelihood of injury here is extremely remote, if it exists. The burden of guarding against spontaneously exploding gas tanks would be great, as all abandoned vehicles would have to be towed immediately since each would be equally susceptible to explosion. Considering the number of these vehicles in plaintiff's district alone, this would place an undue burden on defendant. The consequence of such a duty would be that defendant would have to acquire additional tow trucks and manpower, which would place an undue economic burden on defendant.

A duty is an obligation imposed by law which requires one to conform to a certain standard of conduct for the protection of another against an unreasonable risk. Considering all of the factors detailed above, we conclude that the risk in this case was not unreasonable or foreseeable and that defendant owed no duty to protect plaintiff from the injuries he suffered as a result of the explosion. "A municipality is not expected to anticipate unusual or extraordinary happenings." The facts in the record present just that sort of an extraordinary happening.

Even if defendant had breached a duty to plaintiff in this case, we do not find that the alleged negligent failure to tow the van was the proximate cause of plaintiff's injuries. To be proximately caused by a defendant's negligence, an "injury must be the natural and probable result of the negligent act or omission and be of such a character as an ordinarily prudent person ought to have foreseen as likely to occur as a result of the negligence, although it is not essential that the person charged with negligence should have foreseen the precise injury which resulted from his act." As already concluded, an ordinarily prudent person would not foresee that failure to tow an abandoned vehicle would result in its spontaneous explosion causing injury to a passerby. The injury suffered here is not the natural and probable consequence of permitting a van to remain in an alley.

There was no proof introduced at trial to show that a vehicle could spontaneously explode or that the likelihood of such an occurrence increased in proportion to the length of time the vehicle remained derelict. In short, there was no proof that the failure to remove the van caused its explosion and the resulting injuries. Liability cannot be based on surmise or conjecture as to the cause of the injury; proximate cause can only be established when there is a reasonable certainty that defendant's acts caused the injury. A jury cannot be allowed to predicate a verdict on mere conjecture or surmise. Because of the lack of proof at trial that defendant's failure to tow the van was the proximate cause of his injury, and because he did not prove a breach of duty by the defendant, plaintiff did not sustain his burden of proof to establish a cause of action in negligence, and the jury's verdict may not stand.

Accordingly, the judgment of the circuit court is reversed.

Reversed.

COLEMAN V. EQUITABLE REAL ESTATE INVESTMENT MANAGEMENT, INC.
971 S.W.2D 611 (1998)

Opinion
ROACH, Justice.

In this premises liability case, appellants Joan Lindsey Coleman and Gerald and Nanci Armstrong appeal the trial court's summary judgment in favor of appellees Equitable Real Estate Investment Management Inc. and United Commercial Management, Inc. In two points of error on appeal, appellants complain the trial court erred in concluding, as a matter of law, that (i) appellees owed no duty in this case and (ii) appellees' conduct was not a proximate cause of the injuries suffered. For the reasons set forth below, we overrule both points of error and affirm the trial court's judgment.

Factual Background

On Sunday, April 4, 1994, Brad Vale Lindsey and James Armstrong were working at Blockbuster Video in Casa Linda Shopping Center. Armstrong was the store's assistant manager; Lindsey was a customer service representative. The store, which had been open about one week, closed at midnight. When Lindsey failed to return home after work, his mother went to the store to check on him. The store's lights were on, but the entrance door was locked. Hours later, the police gained entry into the store and found both employees fatally shot. The police impounded a videotape from the store's surveillance cameras that depicted what occurred that night. The videotape had no audio.

The videotape showed that Armstrong, as required by Blockbuster policy, locked the store's doors at midnight. About five minutes later, he checked out the last two customers. After completing the transaction, Armstrong unlocked the exit door, let the customers out, and relocked the exit door. No customers remained in the store. Armstrong then walked around the counter to the door of the entrance vestibule. The door did not have an inside handle, and Armstrong pried it open and unlocked the exterior entrance door. In violation of Blockbuster policy, Armstrong then let in an unidentified man and relocked the door. Armstrong, who "appeared comfortable" with the man, walked with him to the cash register. Both men appeared to take something from the cash register. Lindsey, who had been working in another area of the store when Armstrong let the man in, walked up to the counter where Armstrong and the man were standing. Armstrong and the man stepped out of the diamond-shaped counter into the exit corridor. Lindsey "raised his hands" and then removed something from his pocket and handed it to the assailant. The object appeared to be an envelope.

After that, the man placed Armstrong and Lindsey in front of him and followed them to the back office, where the tape showed the man with a gun for the first time. Armstrong went to the safe, rattled the handle, and shrugged his shoulders, as if he were unable to open the safe. At that point, the tape showed the gunman shoot Armstrong. The tape does not show Lindsey being shot.

The gunman left the office and attempted to leave the store through the entry vestibule. He noticed the door had no handle, circled the diamond-shaped counter, and left the store through the exit door. The gunman was "moving at a very calm, normal pace as if you just paid for a video and walked out of the store." It was determined that about $300 was missing. Some Blockbuster employees speculated that Armstrong knew the assailant.

An earlier portion of the videotape showed that the gunman had been in the store about thirty minutes before closing that night. Armstrong had an armful of tapes and was putting them back on the shelves. The assailant selected a tape and approached Lindsey, who was behind the counter. After an interaction with Lindsey, the assailant put the tape on the counter.

At the time of the incident, Blockbuster did not have in-store security officers and appellees Equitable and United (the shopping center's asset and property managers) provided no security officers in the common areas on Sunday nights. Appellees' security contract provided for one uniformed, unarmed guard to patrol on foot from noon to 7 A.M. Monday through Saturday and from noon to 6 P.M. on Sunday. The guard was to report daily to the shopping center manager, assist customers with problems such as a stalled car, assist tenants and employees to and from their cars if requested, and watch for any type of safety hazards, mischief, or other activity in the common areas.

The parents of the employees (appellants) sued appellees for negligence, alleging they failed to provide adequate security when they knew or should have known of several prior incidents of criminal activity in the area. Thereafter, appellees moved for summary judgment on the grounds that (i) they owed no duty to the Blockbuster employees because they had no right of control over Blockbuster's operation, i.e, the security of the leased premises and (ii) no acts or omissions by them proximately caused the deaths of the Blockbuster employees. The trial court granted summary judgment in appellees' favor without specifying the basis for its ruling. This appeal ensued.

Duty

In the first point of error, appellants complain the trial court erred in granting summary judgment on the basis that appellees owed no duty to provide security to the Blockbuster employees killed inside the store. In particular, appellants argue summary judgment was improper because the summary judgment evidence showed that appellees knew or should have known of prior criminal activity, including violent crime, in the shopping center area.

Appellants argue that appellees nevertheless failed to provide any security in the common areas on the night of the murder and thus breached their duty.

Appellees counter they had no duty to protect Blockbuster's employees from criminal acts occurring inside the Blockbuster store. They urge any duty they may have had was dependent on control of security of the premises where the crime was committed. Specifically, they contend any duty they may have had to provide security extended only to the common areas of the shopping center. Because they had no control over the security of the Blockbuster premises, they argue they had no duty to prevent the murders in this case. We agree.

The threshold inquiry in a negligence case is whether the defendant owes a legal duty to the plaintiff. The plaintiff must establish both the existence and the violation of a duty owed to the plaintiff by the defendant to establish liability in tort. Id. The existence of a duty is a question of law for the court to decide from the facts surrounding the occurrence in question.

As a general rule, a person has no legal duty to protect another from the criminal acts of third parties or to control the conduct of another. Walker, 924 S.W.2d at 377; Centeq, 899 S.W.2d at 197. Similarly, a lessor generally has no duty to tenants or their invitees for dangerous conditions on the leased premises. This general rule stems from the notion that a lessor relinquishes possession or occupancy of the premises to the lessee.

This general rule, however, is not absolute. One who controls the premises does have a duty to use ordinary care to protect invitees from criminal acts of third parties if he knows or has reason to know of an unreasonable and foreseeable risk of harm to the invitee. But, as the Texas Supreme Court has emphasized, this duty is commensurate with the right of control over the property. Thus, a lessor who retains control over premises used in common by different occupants of his property has a duty to keep those common areas reasonably safe for the tenants and their guests. Likewise, a tenant is responsible for so much of the property as he controls pursuant to his lease.

Control is the dispositive factor in determining whether a legal duty should be imposed on appellees in this case. Specifically, we focus on "who had specific control over the safety and security of the premises, rather than on the more general right of control over operations." Centeq, 899 S.W.2d at 199; Exxon, 867 S.W.2d at 23. Before we will impose a duty against appellees to protect against the criminal acts of third parties, we must find appellees had specific control over the security of the premises where the criminal act took place.

Included in appellees' summary judgment evidence was the shopping center lease. Although the lease does not specifically address "security," it does set forth the rights and obligations of each party with respect to the demised premises and common areas. Under the lease, the Casa Linda owners relinquished possession of and control over the Blockbuster premises to Blockbuster for the purpose of selling and renting prerecorded audio and/or video products. With respect to those leased premises, appellees, as property managers, had only a limited right of access. Specifically, article 21 of the lease provided:

> Upon reasonable prior notice, but in no event less than twenty-four hours (24) (except in the case of an emergency), Landlord may enter the Demised Premises during Tenant's business hours for purposes of inspection, to show the Demised Premises to prospective purchasers and lenders, or to perform maintenance and repair obligations imposed upon the Landlord by this Lease. . . .

In contrast, appellees retained control over the common areas and were obligated to maintain those areas "in good order and repair." LaRee Stein, director of property management for United, testified that tenants were responsible for the security of their own premises and she stressed that appellees did not maintain keys to its tenants' premises, including Blockbuster.

We conclude this evidence established that appellees had no control over security decisions of the leased premises where the murders occurred. The burden, therefore, shifted to appellants to present some evidence raising a fact issue. Although appellants presented hundreds of pages of deposition testimony and affidavits as summary judgment proof, none of this evidence even remotely suggests that appellees retained any control over the security of the leased Blockbuster store. Instead, appellants rely on appellees' control over the common areas to establish a duty to protect the Blockbuster employees inside the store. We cannot agree. If appellees did not have any right to control the security of the Blockbuster premises, they cannot have any duty to provide the same.

The murders in this case did not occur on the portion of the premises over which appellees retained control of security decisions, i.e., the common areas. Rather, the criminal conduct occurred inside the locked Blockbuster store, an area over which Blockbuster had specific control of security. Under such circumstances, we cannot conclude appellees had a duty to protect Blockbuster employees from criminal acts occurring inside the store once it was closed and locked. Accordingly, we overrule the first point of error.

Proximate Cause

Even assuming appellees owed a duty to appellants and breached that duty, we would nevertheless conclude summary judgment was proper because there was no proximate cause in this case. In Texas, proximate cause involves two distinct elements: cause-in-fact and foreseeability. The term "cause-in-fact" contemplates that the defendant's negligent act or omission was a substantial factor in bringing about the plaintiff's injury and without it no harm would have occurred. Foreseeability means that the actor, as a person of ordinary intelligence, should have anticipated the dangers his negligent act created for others. Foreseeability does not require the actor to anticipate the precise manner in which an injury will occur; it only requires that (i) the injury be of such a general character as might reasonably have been anticipated, and (ii) the injured party be so situated with relation to the wrongful act that injury to him or to one similarly situated might reasonably have been foreseen.

There can be more than one proximate cause of an injury, and all persons whose negligent conduct contributed to the injury are responsible for it. Although proximate cause is typically a question of fact, the lack of it may be established as a matter of law where the circumstances are such that reasonable minds cannot arrive at a different conclusion.

In their summary judgment motion, appellees argued Armstrong's security breach was an unforeseeable act that destroyed any causal connection between their negligence and the employees' deaths. We agree.

Texas courts distinguish between a new and independent cause, which destroys the causal connection between the original negligent act or omission and the complained-of injury, and a "concurrent act," which cooperates with the still-persisting original act in proximately causing the injury and is itself a proximate cause of the injury. In determining whether the later negligent act is, in fact, a new and independent cause, Texas courts focus on the foreseeability of the intervening party's actions. If the cause could have been foreseen, it does not "break" the chain of causation and relieve the original tortfeasor of liability.

In applying the test of foreseeability to situations where a negligently created pre-existing condition combines with a later act of negligence causing an injury, there is a distinction between a situation in which one has created a dangerous condition and a later actor observes, or by the circumstances should have observed, the existence of the dangerous condition and a situation in which the dangerous condition is not apparent and cannot be observed by the actor. In regard to the first situation, the intervening act interrupts the natural sequence of the events and cuts off the legal effect of the negligence of the initial actor. This is based upon the premise that it is not reasonable to foresee or expect that one who actually becomes cognizant of a dangerous condition in ample time to avert the injury will fail to do so.

We conclude Armstrong's act was an unforeseeable event that was of such a nature as to break the natural sequence of events and create a new and independent cause in this case. According to James McCoy, the Blockbuster store manager at the time of the murders, the Blockbuster entrance and exit doors were to be locked at midnight. If there were customers remaining in the store, McCoy testified that an employee would check them out, unlock the door so the customers could leave, and then relock the door. Additionally, Blockbuster policy prohibited allowing anyone to be let into the store once the doors were locked. Armstrong had been trained with respect to this policy. Further, according to McCoy, he and Armstrong had discussed that very policy earlier on the day of the murder, and McCoy reiterated that no one was allowed in the store after midnight.

In this case, the evidence shows that Armstrong followed policy and locked the Blockbuster doors at midnight. After that, however, Armstrong went around the vestibule, pried open the interior entrance door, unlocked the exterior entrance door, and opened it to allow an unidentified man to enter the store. This deliberate violation of safety policy is simply extraordinary in light of the fact that Armstrong had been told that same day not to open the doors after midnight. In essence, Armstrong opened the doors to a locked store late at night, after hours, knowing that an undetermined amount of cash was on hand. In so doing, he defeated the very purpose of the policy put in place for his and other employees' safety. If Armstrong had followed prescribed safety policy, the assailant would not have been able to gain access to the store and the murders inside the store would not have occurred. Under these circumstances, we conclude Armstrong's actions were not foreseeable to appellees and were of such a character as to break the natural sequence of events, thereby creating a new and independent cause. We conclude the trial court properly granted summary judgment to appellees.

We affirm the trial court's judgment.

Websites

▪ **Wikipedia — Proximate Cause**
   http://en.wikipedia.org/wiki/Proximate_cause

▪ **Law.com — Proximate Cause**
   www.law.com (click in search box for proximate cause issues)

▪ **Free Legal Dictionary**
   http://legal-dictionary.thefreedictionary.com (click in search box for articles about proximate cause)

Forms and Court Documents

Here is an excerpt from a complaint filed in a real case (although the names of the parties have been changed). Notice how the language in paragraph 9 sets out proximate cause.

STATE OF PLACID		IN THE SUPERIOR COURT
COUNTY OF BARNES		FILE NUMBER: _____

Jane Smith,	)	ANSWER
Plaintiff	)	
	)	
vs.	)	
	)	
John Doe,	)	
Martha Doe,		

Defendants

The plaintiff, Jane Smith, complaining of the defendants, alleges and says the following:

1.

That plaintiff Jane Smith is a citizen and resident of Barnes County, Placid.

2.

That, upon information and belief, defendant Martha Doe (hereinafter "defendant driver") is a citizen and resident of Barnes County, Placid.

3.

That, upon information and belief, defendant John Doe (hereinafter "defendant owner") is a citizen and resident of Barnes County, Placid.

a. Further, upon information and belief, defendant owner was the registered owner of the vehicle involved in the collision at issue in this case, said vehicle being a 1999 Ford, license plate number FAB 9925.

b. That, at all times mentioned herein and upon information and belief, defendant driver was operating and using the aforementioned vehicle with the authority, consent, permission, and knowledge of defendant owner, and defendant's driver's operation and use of the vehicle was under the direction and control of defendant owner.

c. Furthermore, at all times mentioned herein and upon information and belief, defendant driver was a member of the family or household of defendant owner and was living in such person's home; that the vehicle driven by defendant driver was owned, provided, and maintained for the general use, pleasure, and convenience of the family; and that the vehicle was being so used with the express or implied consent of defendant owner.

d. Therefore, any negligence on the part of defendant driver in causing plaintiff's injuries should be imputed to defendant owner under the family purpose doctrine.

4.

That, on or about the 19th day of October, 2000, at approximately 9:40 A.M., plaintiff was operating a motor vehicle traveling North on Union Street in Rock Pleasant, Barnes County, Placid.

5.

That, at the same time and place, defendant driver was operating the aforementioned 1999 Ford motor vehicle and was traveling South on Brown Drive in Barnes County, Placid.

6.

That defendant driver entered plaintiff's lane of travel, thereby causing a collision with plaintiff's vehicle.

7.

That defendant driver admitted at the scene that she did not see plaintiff's vehicle before pulling out into the intersection.

8.

That defendant driver was negligent in that she:

a. While operating a motor vehicle on the public streets and highways, failed to keep a reasonable and proper outlook in plaintiff's direction of travel.

b. Failed to maintain the vehicle that she was operating and drove the vehicle in such a manner so as to deprive the defendant of such control over the vehicle as a reasonable and prudent person would maintain under all the circumstances then existing.

c. Drove a motor vehicle upon the public streets and highways at a speed greater than was reasonable and prudent under the conditions then existing in violation of P.G.S. 20-141 (a).

d. Drove her vehicle at a speed greater than that which was posted for the particular street or highway upon which said automobile was being operated in violation of P.G.S. 20-141 (b).

e. Failed to yield the right of way to the plaintiff's automobile, which was lawfully proceeding in a straight line of travel.

9.

That, as a direct and proximate cause of the negligent conduct of the defendant driver, plaintiff was seriously injured, causing her great pain and suffering, medical expenses, lost wages, physical and mental anguish, and permanent injuries.

10.

That, as a direct and proximate result of the aforementioned negligence of defendant driver, plaintiff has sustained damage to her person in an amount in excess of Ten Thousand Dollars ($10,000.00), representing damage to plaintiff's person, medical bills, pain and suffering, lost wages, mental anguish, and permanent injuries.

WHEREFORE, plaintiff demands judgment against the defendants as follows:

1. That plaintiff have and recover of defendants, jointly and severally, a sum in excess of Ten Thousand Dollars ($10,000.00) for compensatory damages, plus interest as allowed by law, including prejudgment interest.

2. That a jury trial be had on all issues of fact.

3. That the costs of this action be taxed against the defendants, including a reasonable attorney's fee for plaintiffs' attorneys as provided by P.G.S. 6-21.1.

4. For such other, further, and different relief as the Court deems just, reasonable and proper.

This the _____ day of _____, 20 _____.

_____
Attorney for Plaintiff

Key Terms

Foreseeability	Proximate causation
Intervening cause	Superseding cause

Review Questions

1 What is proximate cause?
2 How does proximate cause differ from the proof of the series of events in the case?

3   Some commentators suggest that the law on proximate cause is deliberately vague. Why would this be so?

4   What are three arguments in support of proximate cause?

5   Why should a defendant's liability be limited only to proximate causes?

6   Some authors refuse to use the term *proximate cause* and prefer to use the terms *legal cause* or *responsible cause.* Are these labels more descriptive? Why or why not?

7   Why would one of the requirements of a working definition of proximate cause involve the proof of a "natural, unbroken, and continuous sequence" of events?

8   Explain foreseeability.

9   Why is the *Palsgraf* case considered to be so important?

10 Explain the "orbit of the risk" doctrine from *Palsgraf.*

11 Would the analysis of the *Palsgraf* case have been different if the man attempting to board the train had carried a box labeled "Dangerous Explosives: Do Not Drop"? Explain.

12 Explain the difference between the "but for" test and the "substantial factor" test.

13 Describe how the defendants in the Chumley case are the proximate cause of the plaintiff's injuries by detailing the precise facts that give rise to their liability.

14 Is there a justification for altering the rules of proximate cause to limit them to the immediate injuries caused by the defendant? If so, justify this position based on the concepts in this chapter.

15 How is the Restatement's position on proximate cause different from the approach used in some jurisdictions?

16 Explain proximate cause analysis when two or more defendants are implicated, but only one could have been negligent.

17 Explain intervening causes.

18 How is an intervening cause different from a superseding cause?

19 How does an act of nature affect the proximate cause analysis?

20 Explain the attorney-client privilege.

Applying What You Have Learned

1   Assuming that we can prove that Mr. Chumley stopped at the railroad crossing, looked, but could not see the oncoming train because of obscuring vegetation, draft a paragraph explaining how the railway company is the proximate cause of his injuries.

2   June is driving home on January 10 of this year and comes to a stop at a red light at an intersection in the Town of Lucy, Barnes County, State of Placid. She is on State Street. The intersecting road is called Dellinger Boulevard. As she waits for the light to turn green, a 2002 Ford Explorer SUV driven by Randy Reckless approaches from the east on Dellinger Boulevard and runs the red light. June, who sees that the light in her

direction has turned green, begins to accelerate and reaches the intersection just as Randy Reckless runs the red light. Randy's vehicle slams into June's car on the driver's side. June is pinned inside the car, and it takes over two hours to get her out. When the local fire department finally frees her, they discover that June has numerous broken bones and internal injuries. Police cite Randy for failing to stop at the red light, failure to yield, and reckless driving.

Draft a complaint based on these facts and pay particular attention to your allegation of proximate cause. How do you allege proximate cause under these facts?

3 How does your state define foreseeability?

4 Does your state follow the basic holding in *Palsgraf,* or has it developed a different definition of proximate cause?

Endnotes

[1] *Oklahoma Gas & Electric Co. v. Hofrichter,* 196 Ark. 1, 116 S.W.2d 599 (1938); *Hunter v. Horton,* 80 Idaho 475, 333 P.2d 459 (1958).

[2] *Hentschel v. Baby Bathinette Corp.,* 215 F.2d 102 (2d Cir. 1954).

[3] *Chism v. White Oak Feed Co.,* 612 S.W.2d 873 (1981).

[4] *Malo v. Willis,* 126 Cal. App. 3d 543, 178 Cal. Rptr. 774 (1981).

[5] *Maryland Steel Co. v. Marney,* 88 Md. 482 (1898).

[6] Prosser and Keeton on the Law of Torts, 5th ed., West Wadsworth (1984).

[7] Quoted in *Beilke v. Coryell,* 524 N.W.2d 607 (1994).

[8] *Collins v. American Optometric Assn.,* 693 F.2d 636 (7th Cir. 1982); *Sosa v. Coleman,* 646 F.2d 991 (5th Cir. 1981).

[9] *Hentschel v. Baby Bathinette Corp.,* 215 F.2d 102 (2d Cir. 1954).

[10] Restatement (Second) of Torts §430, comment d.

[11] *Livingston v. Gribetz,* 549 F. Supp. 238 (D.C.N.Y. 1982).

[12] *Bole v. Pittsburgh Athletic Co.,* 205 F. 468 (3d Cir. 1913).

[13] *Goode v. Harrison,* 45 N.C. App. 547, 263 S.E.2d 33 (1980).

[14] *Coleman v. Equitable Real Estate Investment Management, Inc.,* 971 S.W.2d 611 (1998).

[15] Id.

[16] *Prosser and Keeton on the Law of To* rts, 5th ed., West Wadsworth (1984) §48.

[17] *Coleman v. Equitable Real Estate Investment Management, Inc.,* 971 S.W.2d 611 (1998).

[18] *Clement v. Rousselle Corp.,* 372 So. 2d 1156, *cert. denied,* 383 So. 2d 1191 (1979).

[19] *Bell v. Irace,* 619 A.2d 365 (1993).

[20] Restatement (Second) of Torts §434.

[21] *Stahl v. Metropolitan Dade County,* 438 So. 2d 14 (1983).

[22] *Chambers v. Bunker,* 598 S.W.2d 204 (1980).

[23] *Crull v. Platt,* 471 N.E.2d 1211 (1984).

[24] *Northwest Mall, Inc. v. Lubri-Lon International, Inc.,* 681 S.W.2d 797 (1984).

[25] *Becker v. Barbur Blvd. Equipment Rentals, Inc.,* 81 Or. App. 648, 726 P.2d 967 (1986).

[26] *Rockweit by Donohue v. Senecal,* 187 Wis. 2d 170, 522 N.W.2d 575 (1994).

[27] *Perotta v. Tri-State Ins. Co.,* 317 So. 2d 104, *cert. denied,* (Fla.) 330 So. 2d 20 (1976).

Crossword Puzzle

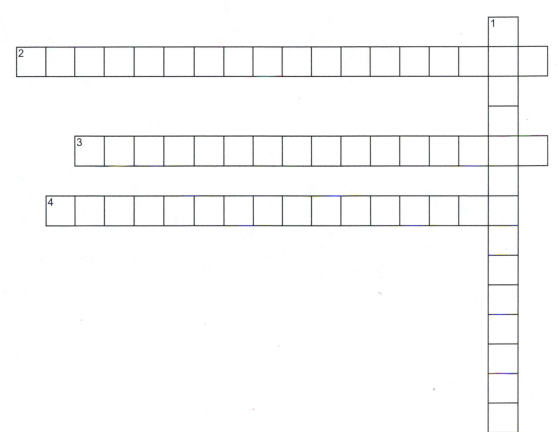

ACROSS

2 The facts that show the defendant's legal responsibility for the injuries to the plaintiff, also known as legal cause

3 An event that occurs after the initial plaintiff's injury that replaces one act of negligence with another

4 Any event that occurs after the initial plaintiff's injury that contributes to or aggravates those injuries

DOWN

1 The legal requirement that the plaintiff be a person who would likely be injured by the defendant's conduct

Damages

Chapter Objectives

- Describe the basic differences between compensatory, punitive, and nominal damages
- Explain the difference between general and special damages
- Explain how a plaintiff proves damages at trial
- Describe the basic steps involved in an asset search
- Explain the difference between a loss of consortium claim and a pain and suffering claim

I   DAMAGES IN THE CHUMLEY CASE

Mr. Chumley's health prior to the crash was excellent, with only occasional ulcer trouble and some infrequent thyroid problems. In the five years before the crash, he had missed only three days from work. However, after the collision, his health took a drastic turn for the worse. The injuries he received have had a dramatic impact on his life. In addition to his physical injuries, there are also out-of-pocket expenses and the pain and suffering he has endured.

In this chapter, we address the fourth and final element of a negligence case: damages. Just as we have seen with the other three elements of a negligence claim, proof of damages involves its own set of problems.

The plaintiff's legal team must calculate the total financial loss suffered by the plaintiff. This calculation must include not only the plaintiff's medical bills, but also any other financial loss directly attributable to the collision. In addition to these damages, the plaintiff must put a dollar amount on such intangibles as pain and suffering. In this chapter, we discuss how these damages are calculated and how this fourth and final element of a negligence case is proved. (For a sample of the medical records involved in the Chumley case, please see Appendix E.)

Mr. Chumley's injuries included a closed head injury; fractured left tibia; internal hemorrhaging; hemo-pneumothorax (blood-filled, collapsed lung); and severe abdominal trauma. In addition, he had five broken ribs and a left hip fracture. Mr. Chumley has had extensive surgery on several occasions and suffered from severe infections. For three months following the collision, Mr. Chumley languished in a coma, his breathing controlled by a ventilator. When he finally revived, doctors noted that Mr. Chumley suffered from short-term memory loss. For example, he cannot remember anything about the collision. Several months later, he was diagnosed with diabetes mellitus. Significantly, there is no family history of diabetes. Mr. Chumley's doctors have determined that the severe trauma he received to his head and abdomen, and the resultant injuries to both his brain and his pancreas, are the most likely cause of the diabetes mellitus.

The outlook for Mr. Chumley is bleak. He has suffered extensive brain damage and internal injuries and is now suffering from severe diabetes. His doctors believe that he may only have one or two years of life left. Before the wreck occurred, Mr. Chumley had a good chance of living well into his 70s.

We have contacted an expert in economic analysis and asked him to take a look at the long-term financial impact of Mr. Chumley's injuries and the medical bills associated with Mr. Chumley's recovery and maintenance. The medical bills alone are $344,554.06 (as shown in Figure 8-1). However, the expert points out that Mr. Chumley also has lost time from work and has a decreased life span, pain and suffering, and future medical needs. The figure the expert has come up with is $1,230,119.00. (For a complete copy of this report, see Appendix A.)

FIGURE 8-1

Charles Chumley: Medical Bill Summary

EMS	$ 365.50
Bolstridge Memorial Hospital	$219,380.01
Haley County Hospital	$ 2,677.94
Morningside Surgical Residence Associates	$ 12,935.00
Springfield Radiological Associates	$ 4,561.00
Carr-Headley Rehabilitation	$ 83,494.41
Turlow Bone and Joint: Sean Turlow & Carla Moyers, M.D.	$ 6,151.20
Morrisville Associates	$ 760.00
Option Care Infusion Therapy	$ 11,875.00
Home Health Visits	$ 2,354.00
Total	$344,554.06

II INTRODUCTION TO DAMAGES

The final step in our analysis of negligence actions involves the element of damages. Damages refer to the monetary, property, or personal losses suffered by the plaintiff. The point of an award of damages is to restore the plaintiff to the condition he was in prior to the injury, if that is possible. A second consideration is to punish the defendant for his negligence and send a message to others that similar negligent actions will result in monetary losses.

Paying the victim for his injuries is not a new concept. Early Hebrew law provided that a person who injured another must pay a set fee for an injured hand, an injured eye, and so on. This idea of apportioning a strict monetary amount for parts of the body was later revived in the schedule seen in workers' compensation statutes.[1]

Damages come in at least three broad categories, although some jurisdictions break them down in other ways. These broad categories include the following:

- Compensatory damages
- Punitive damages
- Nominal damages

Every society has created a scheme for providing damages to injured persons. There are even examples in the Bible: "When a man causes a disfigurement in his neighbor, as he has done it shall be done to him, fracture for fracture, eye for eye, tooth for tooth; as he has disfigured a man, he shall be disfigured."[2]

The Restatement of Torts defines damages as "a sum of money awarded to a person injured by a tort of another."[3]

A. COMPENSATORY DAMAGES

Compensatory damages are designed to do exactly what their title suggests — compensate the victim for losses caused by the defendant's negligent conduct. The stated purpose of compensatory damages is to place the plaintiff in the condition she was in prior to the injury. Of course, that is often impossible. In situations where it is impossible to return the plaintiff to her original condition, compensatory damages are designed to compensate her for the change in her condition. Some jurisdictions define compensatory damages as the monetary assessments paid by the defendant to "make the plaintiff whole" again. These assessments usually take the form of monetary payments made by the defendant to the plaintiff to compensate the plaintiff for injury and property and other losses. Compensatory damages are usually divided into two separate categories: general and special damages.

When the plaintiff's injuries are financial, the jury's award of money is designed to put the plaintiff back in the situation he was in before the defendant's negligence. When the plaintiff's injuries are physical, money is seen as a form of compensation for aggravation, pain, and suffering, even though these conditions do not lend themselves to monetary calculation. The plaintiff can recover for all harm past, present, and future. See Figure 8-2 for a list of possible past and future damages.

Compensatory damages
An award by a judge or jury designed to compensate the plaintiff for physical or financial losses.

There are two types of compensatory damages: general (nonspecific) and special (specific).

1. GENERAL DAMAGES

General damages
Those awards that are closely tied to the defendant's negligence.[4]

General damages are those payments by the defendant to the plaintiff that are most closely associated with the defendant's negligent act. One example of a general damage is pain and suffering. General damages are usually harder to quantify. For instance, how much is pain and suffering actually worth? The jurors must often rely on their own feelings and life experiences to come up with a figure that they believe will compensate the plaintiff for his disfigurement, paralysis, or constant pain. The result is often unpredictable. The jury awards in two similar cases can have wildly different amounts of general damages. In most jurisdictions, the plaintiff is not required to state a specific amount that he is seeking to recover in general damages; the plaintiff usually leaves this determination to the jury.

The Restatement uses a slightly different definition of general damages. According to the Restatement, general damages are those injuries that result so frequently from most negligence and other tort actions that their existence can be assumed and their amount can be proved at trial. See Figure 8-3 for a list of general damages that the jury may award.

FIGURE 8-2

Past and Future Damages

A plaintiff can recover for past and future damages if they fall into one of the following categories:

- Bodily harm
- Loss of or reduction in earning capacity
- Medical expenses
- Damage to personal property
- Emotional distress

FIGURE 8-3

General, Compensatory Damages That the Jury May Award Without Proof of Financial Loss by the Plaintiff

- Bodily harm
- Pain and suffering

- Emotional distress

a. Pain and Suffering

How much should a jury award for the plaintiff's "pain and suffering"? The jury might turn to the judge for an instruction on this point. Unfortunately, the law here is vague. The jury is allowed to award an amount that a "reasonable person" would believe was just compensation for the plaintiff's injury. This standard allows a great deal of freedom to juries to determine what is reasonable in any particular case.

b. Presenting an Argument to the Jury for Pain and Suffering and Other General Damages

Because general damages are often difficult to quantify, an attorney will often resort to practical arguments in asking the jury to award money to his client. For instance, an attorney might present a **per diem** argument by asking the jury if it is "worth" $2 a day not to have the pain that his client suffers. The attorney might then point out that experts believe that his client will live another 20 years at a minimum. Two dollars a day, 365 days a year, for 20 years amounts to $14,600. When the plaintiff's pain is severe, or when the plaintiff has a disfiguring scar, this daily amount could easily climb to $50 a day, or even $100. These simple equations give the jury solid figures to work with. On the other hand, the defendant's attorney might argue that any large amount of money is simply a windfall to a plaintiff who is either exaggerating his pain or actively deceiving the jury.

Per diem
By the day, or daily.

There is no mandated mathematical formula that a jury must follow when determining general damages.

Lost earnings are usually classified as special damages, lost future earning capacity as general damages. If a complaint alleges both losses, each must be proved separately. See Figure 8-4 for a list of factors in determining lost earnings.

FIGURE 8-4

Calculating Lost Future Income

The following are some of the factors that an expert will use to determine lost future income:

- What is the highest and best career the plaintiff could possibly have had?
- How many more productive years was the plaintiff likely to have?
- What is the plaintiff's life expectancy based on actuarial tables?
- How does the plaintiff's current disability affect his possibility for future employment?
- What are the plaintiff's future costs for medical treatments, rehabilitation, etc.?
- Will the plaintiff require retraining or reeducation?
- What is the best possible income the plaintiff can anticipate following this injury?
- What is the total amount of all of these calculations?
- What is the "present value" of this amount?

The plaintiff is entitled to request reimbursement for past losses and any future losses tied to the defendant's negligent conduct.

2. SPECIAL DAMAGES

Special damages
Those damages, such as medical bills, closely tied to the plaintiff's injuries and for which a specific amount can usually be calculated.

Special damages are those damages that are usually easier to quantify because they have specific amounts. Examples of special damages are items such as the plaintiff's total medical bill for the injuries sustained in the accident, or the total time lost from work. Similarly, the plaintiff is also entitled to recover for payments to doctors and other medical providers for treatment received as a direct result of the defendant's actions. The plaintiff must present proof of the amount of his special damages and, in most jurisdictions, he must state an exact amount of special damages he is seeking to recover. See Figure 8-5 for some examples of special damages.

a. Lost Wages

To prove the plaintiff's lost wages, something more than testimony is required. A bald assertion, such as "I would have made over $100,000 this year if it hadn't been for the accident," is not legally sufficient. How does the plaintiff prove actual lost wages? She must present tax returns, pay stubs, affidavits from employers or clients, IRS 1099 forms, and similar items. The paralegal is often the person directly responsible for gathering, storing, and organizing this information for trial.

b. Medical Bills

Plaintiffs are often anxious about paying their medical bills. They have received the treatment and have been billed for this service long before the case ever comes to trial. The hospital may have even attempted collection actions against the client. Usually, the plaintiff's attorney will intercede with the medical providers and at least inform them that the plaintiff's case is in litigation. However, the plaintiff often remains concerned about the payment of what are often enormous medical bills. Certainly, these bills should be summarized and pleaded in the complaint as special damages,

---

FIGURE 8-5	
Examples of Special Damages	■ Prescription costs ■ Special equipment ■ Damage to automobile ■ Professional nursing day care

■ Travel expenses (to and from medical appointments) ■ Costs of doctor, psychiatrist, chiropractor, etc.

payable by the defendant because of his negligence. The plaintiff is entitled to recovery for all medical treatments tied to the injuries she received from the defendant.

Special damages can usually be determined to a reasonable certainty.

c. Future Losses

A plaintiff is permitted to seek recovery for future medical services that are reasonably certain to be required. The award is supposed to take into account all reasonable expenses relating to medical care, including charges for doctors, nurses, therapists, and medical supplies. The plaintiff is also entitled to compensation for having to hire someone else to perform her job while she is incapacitated. However, a plaintiff is not legally entitled to compensation for lost "time" — that is, the time lost from leisure activities while recuperating from the injuries.

Measuring Future Lost Income

At the end of the trial, the jurors will be instructed that before they can determine an amount of future lost income, they must determine the difference between what the plaintiff's future income would have been before he was injured and what it will be now that he has been injured. Proving lost future income usually involves expert testimony. The expert will calculate future lost income, based on complicated formulas involving the plaintiff's past income, his education, his likelihood of promotion, and a wide range of other factors. (For an example of such a calculation, see Appendix A.)

Some authorities state that general damages are tied to the defendant's actions while special damages are tied to the plaintiff's losses.

3. PROVING DAMAGES

What is the standard that the plaintiff must meet in proving his damages? Generally, the plaintiff must meet the same standard with regard to damages as he had to meet for proving the other elements of his action. In most jurisdictions, this standard is preponderance of the evidence. There is no relaxation of proof for this final element. The nature and extent of the damages and the defendant's responsibility for them must all be proved at trial before the jury is authorized to award any amount to the plaintiff. Having said this, however, there is a recognized practical limitation on this theory. If the jury is convinced of the defendant's liability for the first three elements of the negligence claim, it is impractical to think that the jurors will require the same level of proof for the plaintiff's medical and other bills.

Courts require a certain level of certainty in calculating damages. Although no court has ever developed a precise mathematical formula for doing so, most jurisdictions are in agreement that the amount of damages must be based on testimony and evidence, not mere conjecture or the emotions of the jurors.[5]

a. Why Is the Distinction Between General and Special Damages Important?

How damages are classified in a particular case is important to the plaintiff when it comes to presenting proof. General damages are often harder to prove than special damages. General damages involve intangibles such as pain and suffering and loss of emotional support. Proving these damages often involves testimony from the plaintiff's friends and family about the effect that the accident has had on her. This testimony is, by its very nature, purely subjective. On the other hand, special damages involve presentations of bills and other hard evidence. They are not subjective, and they present the jury with a straightforward proposition. If the jurors believe that the defendant is responsible for the plaintiff's damages, they will usually award special damages with little demur. Another reason why the classification is important is that if the case should go up on appeal, general damages are easier for the defendant to appeal than special damages.

b. Day-in-the-Life Video

One method of proving damages in a dramatic fashion is the "day-in-the-life" video. This presentation has become almost routine in cases involving severe injuries. For instance, when a plaintiff has been left permanently disabled, the plaintiff's attorney may hire a video producer to videotape the plaintiff going through normal daily activities. These videos can be extremely effective when the jurors see just how difficult it is for a disabled plaintiff to get out of bed in the morning, or to make breakfast. The video will also show the plaintiff interacting with others, such as home health care nurses. As a visual aid, they are unsurpassed for giving the jury an accurate, and often unforgettable, peek into the plaintiff's life. The extra expense is often justified by larger jury awards for disabled plaintiffs.

c. Proving Property Losses

Different types of evidence are required to prove the existence of different types of damages. Property losses, for example, are handled differently than the evidence presented to prove pain and suffering.

Fair market value
The amount that a willing buyer would pay and that a willing seller would accept for an item.

When the plaintiff claims damage to or reduction in value for his property, he must present some evidence showing what the value of the property was before the defendant's actions and what the value of the property is after the defendant's negligence. This often involves calculations of the **fair market value** of the property. Fair market value is usually determined by an appraiser—someone who is an expert in the field and can give an accurate estimate of the property's value.

Tech Topic
DAY-IN-THE-LIFE VIDEOS

Trying to document how a plaintiff's injuries affect day-to-day life can be a difficult enterprise. Often, the injured plaintiff makes a poor witness because it is human nature to downplay one's own suffering. A videotaped documentary goes far beyond a verbal description in that it can objectively portray a plaintiff's altered lifestyle and how it affects the entire family. So-called day-in-the-life videos allow the jury to fully understand the routine obstacles the plaintiff deals with every day. If the plaintiff's attorney can make the jurors understand the extent of the injury, they can more easily place a value on the injury.

Day-in-the-life videos must follow strict guidelines in how they are created, so it is not as simple as having Uncle Elmer follow the client around with his video camera. In fact, producing day-in-the-life videos has become a professional legal service.

The video documents the plaintiff from the moment she awakes and continues documenting her activities until the end of the day. Condensed into 15 to 30 minutes, the video presents an objective view of what her daily life is like as a result of the injury.

A day-in-the-life video is powerful and effective. Conversely, it can be disastrous if the goal is to create something untrue by not being objective or trying to manipulate the facts in any way. This is yet another reason to work with a professional, certified legal video producer.

d. Collateral Source Rule

When a jurisdiction has a **collateral source rule,** it means that the jury cannot be told that the plaintiff has received compensation from other sources. Most people have insurance of some form, and after a person is injured, several different insurance policies will reimburse the plaintiff for medical treatment or property damage. In jurisdictions that follow the collateral source rule, the jury cannot be informed that the plaintiff has already received compensation for some of the injuries claimed in the complaint. The reasoning behind the collateral source rule is that if the jury were permitted to hear about the plaintiff's other sources of compensation, they might be inclined to lower the amount awarded to the plaintiff at the conclusion of the trial. In essence, this would penalize persons who did the right thing: obtained insurance coverage for medical treatment and property damage. A plaintiff who has fully insured himself against potential losses will end up with a smaller award than a plaintiff who failed to take such reasonable precautions. Thus, the collateral source rule prohibits the defense from introducing evidence showing that the plaintiff had other insurance coverage that has already been paid out for some of the plaintiff's injuries. See Figure 8-6 for a list of compensatory sources that may be introduced when the collateral source rule is in place.

Although the jury will not be informed of the plaintiff's other sources of compensation during their deliberations, the jury's final award will be reduced

Collateral source rule
An evidentiary rule that prohibits the jury from being told about the plaintiff's other sources of compensation, such as insurance, workers' compensation, and so on.

Mitigation of damages
The responsibility of the plaintiff to lessen her potential injuries or losses by taking reasonable actions to seek medical treatment or take other precautions when a reasonable person in the same situation would have done so.

Mitigation of damages is often seen in contract disputes as well. A vendor has an obligation to sell perishable merchandise to another when the original customer refuses to purchase it. The vendor can then sue the original purchaser for the difference between what he would have received on the sale and what he actually received from another purchaser.[7]

by the judge to reflect the amounts that the plaintiff has already received. A jurisdiction that follows the collateral source rule does not allow a plaintiff to receive awards for injuries that have already been compensated. In the end, the judge will review the jury's award and make appropriate reductions for medical bills that have already been paid on the plaintiff's behalf.

e. Mitigation of Damages

A plaintiff is obligated to **mitigate** or lessen her damages whenever reasonably possible. This means that the plaintiff is not permitted to refuse medical treatment for the injuries caused by the defendant's negligence and then later bring an action when the injuries worsen.

For instance, in the Chumley case, Mr. Chumley's obligation to mitigate could have arisen if he had chosen not to undergo certain medical procedures, or if he failed to follow up medical attention with the proper care. Certainly, a failure to take his insulin medication would raise a mitigation of damages issue.

Example: John is an independent contractor who installs roofs. One day, as he is climbing up some scaffolding that has been improperly placed by Dave Defendant, he falls and injures his shoulder. John's doctor recommends that John receive immediate surgery to tighten his shoulder muscles. John refuses. Later, John suffers from frequent subluxations, that is, his shoulder pops out of joint. The pain from this is excruciating. John brings suit against Dave for the expensive procedure involved to build up John's shoulder joint. The court rules against John, stating that John had a responsibility to mitigate his damages when doing so was reasonable.[6]

4. EMOTIONAL DISTRESS

In many jurisdictions, a plaintiff is not allowed to recover for injuries that are psychological only. In those jurisdictions, the emotional impact must be coupled with some physical impact. For instance, in these jurisdictions, a plaintiff

---

FIGURE 8-6

Other Compensatory Sources That the Jury May Be Told About in Jurisdictions That Follow the Collateral Source Disclosure Rule

▪ disability income	▪ public assistance
▪ workers' compensation	

cannot request damages when the defendant's actions cause the plaintiff to lose sleep or to feel anxious, but there is no other physical injury. In many other jurisdictions, this requirement of physical trauma has either slowly eroded or been replaced entirely with actions allowing recovery for purely emotional or psychological injuries.[8]

5. LOSS OF CONSORTIUM

Another type of damage that falls into a special category is a **loss of consortium** claim. This is a claim raised not by the injured plaintiff, but by his or her spouse. This claim states that when the plaintiff was injured, the marital relations between the plaintiff and spouse were also injured. In all jurisdictions, the spouse is entitled to file some form of loss of consortium claim. The spouse is entitled to damages for the loss of companionship, affection, sexual relations, and other losses that frequently occur when one spouse has been injured. At trial, the plaintiff's legal team must present additional testimony and evidence to prove this claim. Often, the affected spouse will take the stand and give testimony about the marital relationship prior to the plaintiff's injuries and how that relationship has been affected since the accident.

6. PRIOR INJURIES

One of the best attacks that the defendant's attorney can mount against the plaintiff is a claim that the plaintiff was actually injured in a prior accident and this prior accident is what caused his pain, not the collision he had with the defendant. A paralegal should always ask the plaintiff about any prior medical problems, including prior accidents or collisions. Any prior injury that is even vaguely like the current injury should be closely documented. At trial, the plaintiff's attorney will have to address this issue of prior injuries, to make sure that the jury understands that this prior injury has nothing to do with the current claim and to deflate any attempt by the defense to make a dramatic presentation during its case. See Figure 8-7 for a list of methods for obtaining prior injury information.

An award of damages for emotional distress or mental anguish can include not only the plaintiff's sufferings in the past, but also any mental distress the plaintiff is likely to endure in the future.[9]

Loss of consortium
A claim filed by the spouse of an injured party for the loss of companionship in the marriage caused by the injuries.

---

1 *Ask the client.* The best way to learn about prior injuries and accidents is to simply ask the client. Most clients will be honest and forthright about prior injuries, but there are always some who try to conceal these facts.
2 *Review the medical records carefully.* You should always carefully review the medical records provided by the client and returned by medical offices through discovery. Occasionally, you will see a reference to a "prior complaint." This, or similar language, indicates that the client has been injured before.
3 *Review prior lawsuits.* Even if the client claims that she has never been involved in a prior lawsuit, a quick check of the local docket is always a good idea. Sometimes clients genuinely forget prior suits. Other times, a client may be actively deceiving his legal team. Better to know this before the defense attorney produces it — with a dramatic flourish — in the middle of the trial.

FIGURE 8-7

Learning About Prior Injuries: Three Proven Methods

FIGURE 8-8

Actions That Could Justify a Claim of Bad Faith

- Claim has no basis in fact or law
- Suit involves a matter that is clearly frivolous
- Attorney makes threats against opposition witnesses
- Attorney or party harasses opposition
- Attorney or party engages in unnecessary delaying tactics

7. BAD FAITH DAMAGES

Often confused with punitive damages (discussed later), bad faith damages generally do not involve the facts of the case but involve instead a party's conduct during the litigation. For instance, if a plaintiff brings a lawsuit solely for the purpose of harassing the defendant, the plaintiff may be subject to bad faith damages. In such a situation, the court might order that the plaintiff pay the costs of the action and the defendant's attorney's fee. Normally, the losing party in a suit is not required to pay the fees of the opposing attorney. However, when a party files frivolous claims or has engaged in unethical or unfair tactics, a judge is authorized to make such an award.[10] See Figure 8-8 for a list of actions that could constitute bad faith.

Case Excerpt

RACHAL V. BROUILLETTE
111 So.3d 1137 (2013).

THIBODEAUX, Chief Judge.

Plaintiff, Victor Rachal, filed this suit on behalf of his minor son, Nicholas, against Justin Brouillette and State Farm Mutual Automobile Insurance Company for the wrongful death of Nicholas's mother, Joann Isaac. Mr. Brouillette, driving a large sports utility vehicle, crashed into Ms. Isaac and her two daughters as they walked along a highway in Alexandria, Louisiana. All three individuals were killed. Defendants admitted liability before trial, leaving only the issue of damages for the jury. The jury awarded Nicholas $2,800,000 in compensatory and $100,000 in exemplary damages. Defendants appeal the amount of compensatory damages, and Plaintiff appeals the amount of exemplary damages. For the following reasons, we affirm the compensatory damages and increase the exemplary damages to $500,000.

I. Issues

We will consider:

- whether the jury awarded an excessive amount of general damages;

- whether the jury erroneously awarded damages for loss of financial support; and
- whether the jury awarded an insufficient amount of exemplary damages.

II. Facts and Procedural History

Mr. Brouillette was driving erratically at a high speed when he inexplicably left the highway and headed toward the right-hand shoulder. He immediately struck Ms. Isaac and her two minor daughters as they walked side-by-side on the shoulder near the grass. Mr. Brouillette continued driving past the shoulder, with Ms. Isaac and one of her daughters still on the hood of his car, until he struck one culvert, flew in the air, and crashed into a second culvert. Ms. Isaac and her two daughters were killed. Authorities discovered marijuana and hydrocodone in Mr. Brouillette's system immediately after the accident. He was driving at ninety-one miles per hour when he hit the victims.

Mr. Brouillette was convicted of three counts of vehicular homicide and sentenced to five years in prison for each count. After Mr. Rachal sued on behalf of Nicholas, State Farm and Mr. Brouillette admitted liability before the jury trial started, leaving only the issue of damages for the jury's consideration. After a three-day trial, the jury awarded Nicholas $2,500,000 in general damages, $300,000 in loss of financial support damages, and $100,000 in exemplary damages for his mother's wrongful death. Defendants appeal the judgment and assert the following issues: (1) the award of general damages is excessive; (2) the jury erroneously determined that Mr. Brouillette was impaired during the accident and that his impairment caused the accident. Mr. Rachal appeals the amount of exemplary damages as insufficient.

III. Law and Discussion

A jury's award of damages is a finding of fact. We review the award for abuse of discretion. The discretion vested in the trier of fact is so great that a court of appeal should rarely disturb an award of damages.

Discussion

General Damage Award Review

Defendants assert that the award of $2,500,000 in general damages was excessive. We disagree. We will review the damage award for abuse of discretion. Only if no reasonable trier of fact could award Nicholas $2,500,000 will we disturb the award.

Nicholas enjoyed a close, loving relationship with his mother. Although his parents were separated and Nicholas lived primarily with his father, he spent most weekends with his mother. Ms. Isaac and Mr. Rachal went to great lengths to ensure their son was in the best environment for him considering his struggles with Attention Deficit Hyperactivity Disorder (ADHD). This thoughtfulness and attention shows Ms. Isaac was extremely involved in her son's life. Defendants try to minimize the effects of Ms. Isaac's death on Nicholas; however, the evidence suggests that Nicholas has endured severe physical and mental trauma as a result of this tragedy. Following his mother's death, Nicholas suffered from hallucinations and suicidal thoughts and gained an extraordinary amount of weight. Nicholas's father described how Nicholas has left school on more than one occasion to visit his mother's grave and cry. The jury was apparently convinced that Ms. Isaac's death had a profound effect on Nicholas. This finding is not clearly wrong; therefore, the jury did not abuse its discretion by awarding $2,500,000 in general damages.

Loss of Financial Support

Defendants contend that the jury erroneously awarded Nicholas loss of financial support damages. We find no merit in this contention. The factors considered for an award of loss of financial support include the decedent's present earnings; age and life expectancy; the minor's age at the time of decedent's death; the decedent's work life expectancy; the possibility of a decrease or increase in earnings with age; and any other factors relevant to the premature demise of the decedent. Although Ms. Isaac's income of $14,322 the year she died was not dramatically high, it steadily increased each year, suggesting she would have continued to strive to improve her financial situation had she lived. Ms. Isaac clothed Nicholas, fed him, and took care of him. Defendant argues that because Mr. Rachal did not present testimony regarding exactly how much money Ms. Isaac contributed to raising her son, we should presume she did not contribute anything. Common sense, however, dictates that since Ms. Isaac and Mr. Rachal maintained joint custody of Nicholas, Ms. Isaac financially contributed to her son's upbringing. Further, the jury evidently believed that Ms. Isaac would have provided for her son until she reached the limits of her work life expectancy, some thirty years in the future. Although $300,000 may be on the higher end of the scale, it was not abusively high.

Exemplary Damages: Amount

Plaintiff argues that the award of exemplary damages, $100,000, was unreasonably low. We agree and increase the award to $500,000. The purpose of exemplary damages is to punish the defendant and deter future similar behavior. These damages are regarded as a fine or penalty for the protection of the public interest. The following factors are considered in determining whether the award is too high or low: (1) the nature and extent of the harm to the plaintiff; (2) the wealth or financial situation of the defendant; (3) the character of the conduct involved; (4) the extent to which such conduct offends a sense of justice and propriety; and (5) the amount necessary to deter similar conduct in the future. Id. The amount of exemplary damages is the result of a fact-intensive inquiry into the case. These awards should only be disturbed if the damages are such that "all mankind at first blush would find [them] outrageous."

The circumstances of this case illustrate the need to increase the exemplary damages. Ms. Isaac is not merely injured, she is deceased; therefore, the injury to this plaintiff is great. Defendants suggest that because Mr. Brouillette had only "a small amount" of drugs in his system, his behavior was not as reprehensible as Mr. Rachal asserts. This "small amount" of drugs was apparently enough to cause Mr. Brouillette to drive erratically at a high speed, kill three people, and not remember any of it. We find this behavior sufficiently reprehensible.

Defendants also argue that Mr. Brouillette's ten years in prison is punishment enough to deter this conduct in the future. The court notes, however, that Mr. Brouillette will actually spend only five years in prison since two of his five-year sentences were ordered to run concurrently (the other five year sentence was suspended). Five years in prison for killing three people is not as punitive as Defendants contend. Mr. Brouillette was previously convicted of driving while intoxicated, and he was in another car accident prior to this one. Moreover, he showed very little remorse at trial by consistently denying that he ingested marijuana or hydrocodone, despite scientific evidence of the drugs in his system. Mr. Brouillette clearly has no regard for the safety of others while he is driving a vehicle and continually refuses to obey the law. As further evidence of Mr. Brouillette's disregard for the law, he was disciplined for possessing synthetic marijuana while in prison. Likewise, on a separate occasion a month later, he admitted to using marijuana and an opiate substance when ordered to undergo a random drug test. We cannot emphasize enough the need to deter this conduct.

Defendants suggest that we should refrain from increasing the award of exemplary damages because Mr. Brouillette will never be able to pay such a high award. The defendant's financial situation, however, is only one factor to consider and is not dispositive.

We find the jury abused its discretion by awarding an unreasonably low amount of exemplary damages. Accordingly, we have determined that $500,000 is an amount sufficient to punish Mr. Brouillette's behavior and protect the public interest.

V. Conclusion

For the reasons above, we affirm the award of general damages and increase the award of exemplary damages. Costs of this appeal are assigned to Defendants, Justin Brouillette and State Farm Mutual Automobile Insurance Company.

AFFIRMED AND AFFIRMED AS AMENDED.

Questions about the case:

1. What is the basis of this lawsuit?
2. Did the court consider the award of $2,500,000 in exemplary damages to be excessive? Why or why not?
3. The jury awarded $300,000 to Nicholas for the loss of financial support from his mother, but she only made $14,322 per year. How did the court justify this award?
4. The jury awarded $100,000 in exemplary damages, but the appellate court increased the amount to $500,000. What justification did the court give for this action?

FIGURE 8-9				

Punitive Damage Awards in State Courts, 2005, Updated 2011

Case type	All civil trials		Civil trials with plaintiff winners	
	Number	Punitive damages sought	Number	Punitive damages sought
All cases	**24,929**	**12%**	**14,550**	**13%**
Tort	**16,057**	**10%**	**8,645**	**10%**
Slander/libel	186	33	--	--
Conversion	377	31	--	--
Intentional tort	724	29	429	33
Other or unknown tort	642	24	305	27
Product liability	350	12	101	4
Professional malpractice	143	15	--	--
Medical malpractice	2,448	8	591	10
Automobile accident	9,173	7	6,062	7
Premise liability	1,815	5	718	4
Contract	**8,874**	**16%**	**5,904**	**17%**
Tortious interference	151	42	--	--
Fraud	1,108	32	665	39
Employment	873	32	491	36
Other or unknown contract	242	21	137	23
Buyer plaintiff	2,574	17	1,642	23
Seller plaintiff	2,871	6	2,184	4
Rental/lease	605	4	342	4

Source: U.S. Bureau of Justice Statistics, U.S. Department of Justice

B. PUNITIVE DAMAGES

An award of punitive damages against a defendant is the jury's way of punishing the defendant for particular actions. Punitive damages are awarded in addition to compensatory damages. When the jury awards punitive damages, the jurors are essentially sending a message to the defendant that his conduct was particularly reprehensible and deserves to be punished. The jury in a civil case is not empowered to request jail time for the defendant, so the only real punitive action the jury can take is financial. See Figure 8-9 for statistics on punitive damage awards in state courts.

1. TORT REFORM AND PUNITIVE DAMAGES

Many jurisdictions have passed statutes that limit the jury's total amount of punitive damages in any case to an amount that is three times the total amount of compensatory damages. These statutes were passed out of a perception of runaway juries awarding millions of dollars to plaintiffs in punitive damages for relatively minor lawsuits. Whether this perception is true is a matter of some debate.

Punitive damages are relatively rare in negligence actions because, by the very nature of the claim, the plaintiff's injuries were caused by inattention, not out of malice. However, punitive damages can be awarded in negligence cases where the defendant's actions reveal a wanton disregard for the safety of others. Punitive damages can be awarded against a corporation or an employer.[11]

In some jurisdictions, punitive damages are not permitted against a deceased defendant. Because punitive damages are designed to punish, the fact of the defendant's death precludes this application. In many jurisdictions, a person who has been declared legally insane cannot be forced to pay punitive damages.

Punitive damages are designed to punish the defendant for his actions; they can be tailored to his actions and his income.

TORT
BASICS
AT A
GLANCE

1930s	Researchers begin to link smoking with health problems.	**FIGURE 8-10**
1940s	Major movie stars smoke cigarettes in their movies; cigarettes seen as "cool."	**The Changing Social and Legal Attitudes Toward Nicotine**
1964	U.S. Surgeon General links smoking with lung cancer.	
1964+	Lawsuits based partly on the Surgeon General's report are almost all unsuccessful. Courts rule that smokers do not have a cause of action when they voluntarily take up the smoking habit.	
1966	New federal statute requires health warnings on all cigarette packages.	
1971	All cigarette advertisements on television and radio are banned.	
1973	Arizona becomes the first state to restrict smoking in public buildings. Over the next few years, most states follow suit.	
1988	Surgeon General C. Everett Koop states that tobacco is as addictive as cocaine or heroin.	
1994	Top cigarette executives testify before Congress that cigarettes are not addictive.	
1994	Minnesota and Mississippi bring the first successful lawsuit against the tobacco industry, under the theory of being reimbursed for their payments to Medicaid for medical bills of people who had died from smoking-induced health problems. Other states quickly follow suit.	
1995	FDA places tighter advertising restrictions on tobacco products, especially those aimed at underage smokers.	
1995	FDA makes the controversial ruling that nicotine can be regulated like any other drug; tobacco companies sue, and eventually that determination is overturned.	
1996	Former tobacco executive admits that his company knew that nicotine was addictive, and had studies confirming that fact going back to the 1950s.	
1998	Tobacco industry settles lawsuits with 46 states for $206 billion, making it the largest civil settlement in U.S. history.	

2. TOBACCO COMPANIES AND PUNITIVE DAMAGES

In 2001, a Florida jury awarded a staggering $144 billion in punitive damages against the tobacco industry. After deliberating only four hours, the jury announced its verdict, which easily surpassed the largest punitive damages award ever assessed in that state. The case involved a class action lawsuit against several tobacco companies, including Philip Morris U.S.A. Inc. See Figure 8-10 for a time line of the shifting attitudes toward tobacco.

C. NOMINAL DAMAGES

A brief word should be said here about nominal damages. A nominal damage is the jury's award of a small amount of money to the plaintiff. In some cases, the plaintiff may have received a legal injury, but the jury does not believe that a large payment is either warranted or justified. In such a case, the jury may award the plaintiff the amount of $1 to show that, although the plaintiff presented a technically proficient case, as far as the jury is concerned, the plaintiff's actual injuries are nonexistent. Generally, nominal damages are not seen in typical negligence cases because the plaintiff must prove loss as part of his case.

D. EQUITABLE REMEDIES

There are times when a plaintiff's demand cannot be satisfied by monetary damages. For example, suppose that Gail has a large, 300-year-old oak tree in front of her home. One day, the local telephone company informs her that they are planning to cut the tree down to make room for a new telephone pole. Gail brings suit to stop the telephone company. In this case, she is not seeking monetary damages for the removal of the tree; she is asking the court to order the telephone company not to cut the tree down. Her suit invokes the court's equity powers. **Equity** refers to a court's power to enforce justice.

Equity
The court's authority to order individuals and corporations to do (or not do) certain activities because they are unjust.

Injunction
A court order that demands a certain action or that prohibits a certain action.

Declaratory judgment
A court order that specifies the duties and obligations of a party.

When a plaintiff brings suit requesting an **injunction,** as Gail is doing in this case, the plaintiff is asking the court for an order specifically directing someone to stop performing a specific action. In this case, the court could order that the telephone company cease and desist in its plans to cut down the tree. Simply because Gail has requested an injunction doesn't mean that the court will grant it. In fact, the court will have a hearing in which the judge decides whether to grant the injunction. Once the court enters an order, if a person ignores the order, the court can punish the party through its contempt powers.

A court's equity power can be exercised alongside its normal powers. For example, it is common for the parties in a personal injury suit to seek a **declaratory judgment** about a particular issue in the case. An insurance company might file such an action to determine if it is legally bound to provide (and pay for) a legal defense in a situation in which their insured is sued. (For further discussion about these issues, see Chapter 13.)

Another example of an equitable remedy is a temporary restraining order. This order specifically directs a person to stop performing a specific action and sets a date for a full-court hearing on the plaintiff's request. Temporary restraining orders are usually seen in situations where immediate action is required and there is no time to set a later court date. Gail might file for a temporary restraining order if the telephone company employees show up and begin preparing to cut down the tree. Temporary restraining orders are often seen in cases of domestic violence as well.

EVALUATING A CASE FOR POTENTIAL DAMAGES

One of the first questions that a plaintiff usually asks her attorney once the lawsuit is under way is, "How much money am I going to get from this case?" The defendant might ask, "How much am I likely to lose?" Unfortunately, there is no reference book that can provide the answer to either question. Each case is unique, and any experienced lawyer will probably answer both questions the same way: "It depends." The final verdict in any lawsuit depends on many different factors: the nature of the claim, the type of injuries, the quality of the opposing counsel, the judge's rulings, and the ultimate makeup of the jury. Whether you are affiliated with the plaintiff or the defense, it makes sense to understand some of the factors that go into evaluating a case.

A. EVALUATING A CASE

Case evaluations are not an exact science. They rely on both objective facts and an intuitive understanding of judges and juries. The most important starting point for any case evaluation involves an objective and hard-nosed review of the facts.

B. REVIEWING THE FACTS OF A CASE

Even before you review the plaintiff's injuries, careful attention must first be paid to the defendant's liability. Here is where a firm understanding of the four elements of a negligence action is absolutely essential. Once you have gone through the four-step analysis of duty, breach of duty, causation, and damages that we have outlined in the past four chapters, there is one other consideration that usually goes into any case evaluation: the likelihood of recovery.

There are times when the case against the defendant is easy to prove, but he has no assets. Pursuing such a claim would only be an exercise in futility. No matter how good the case against the defendant, if he has no financial resources it is ultimately going to be a waste of time to bring a lawsuit against him. These are the brutal lessons of legal finances. Moral victories may vindicate the soul, but they do not pay salaries.

FIGURE 8-11	■ To determine if a lawsuit will result in a likely recovery	■ To locate hidden assets
Reasons for Conducting an Asset Search	■ To collect on a judgment	■ To locate assets in a probate matter

FIGURE 8-12	*Hot coffee:*
Some of the More Famous (or Infamous) Jury Verdict Awards	In 1992, a woman in New Mexico was awarded $3 million in punitive damages when she was scalded by a cup of hot coffee. However, she never received that amount. In a settlement after trial, she was awarded a much smaller (and confidential) amount to avoid a lengthy appeals process.
	O.J. Simpson:
	In 1997, a civil jury awarded the families of Ronald Goldman and Nicole Brown Simpson $8.5 million in compensatory damages and $12.5 million in punitive damages against former football star O.J. Simpson in a wrongful death action.
	Exxon Valdez:
	In 2002, the U.S. Supreme Court refused to overturn a jury award of $5 billion against Exxon Oil Company for the Exxon *Valdez* oil spill off the coast of Alaska in 1989 — still the worst oil spill in U.S. history.

C. ASSET SEARCHES

In many situations, the law firm may conduct an asset search of a defendant before deciding to accept a case. It is always important to assess the defendant's ability to pay damages long before the actual complaint is filed. If the defendant is covered by an insurance policy, knowing the policy limits is an important consideration (if they can be learned prior to filing the complaint).

In the practical world that attorneys must inhabit, a great case might become one to pass up for the simple reason that the defendant is "judgment proof." Such a defendant has no assets, no insurance coverage, and no other way of paying any damages assessed against him by the jury. In such a case, an asset search prior to filing would be an excellent precaution. See Figure 8-11 for a list of reasons to conduct an asset search.

D. JURY'S FUNCTION IS ASSESSING DAMAGES

When a party seeks damages, it is usually up to the jury to decide what amount, if any, should be awarded. In cases in which the case is tried before a judge without a jury, the judge assumes that role. Once the jury has heard all of the evidence and the judge has instructed the jury on the law of damages, it is up to the jury to determine the final amount. In complex cases, the jury will often be given a verdict form to help in deciding the issues. See Figure 8-12 for a list of famous jury awards and Figure 8-13 for a sample verdict form.

FIGURE 8-13

Verdict Form

We the jury find, as to Count One of the Complaint

For the Plaintiff
For the Defendant

(Only when the jury has found for the Plaintiff) we further find that defendant is liable to the plaintiff in the amount of $ _____.

FIGURE 8-14

Plaintiff Award Winners in Civil Trials in State Courts, by Case Type

Case type	Number of trials with plaintiff winner[a]	Median final award amount[b]	Percent of plaintiff winners with final awards				
			<$10,000	$10,001–$50,000	$50,001–$250,000	$250,001–$1 million	>$1 million
All cases	14,170	$28,000	28.7%	33.0%	24.1%	9.9%	4.4%
Tort cases	8,455	$24,000	32.7%	30.6%	21.3%	10.4%	5.0%
Product liability	99	567,000	4.0	17.2	13.1	35.4	30.3
Asbestos	47	682,000	2.1	0.0	19.1	53.2	25.5
Other	52	500,000	5.8	32.7	7.7	17.3	36.5
Medical malpractice	584	400,000	0.7	5.3	29.1	43.8	21.1
False arrest, imprisonment	8	259,000	37.5	0.0	12.5	12.5	37.5
Professional malpractice	63	129,000	3.2	31.7	22.2	28.6	14.3
Premises liability	666	98,000	5.6	30.9	32.9	23.3	7.4
Other or unknown tort	305	83,000	36.1	8.9	27.2	12.5	15.4
Intentional tort	429	38,000	28.7	23.8	36.1	7.0	4.4
Conversion	148	27,000	24.3	31.8	37.2	4.1	2.7
Slander/libel	80	24,000	22.5	40.0	2.5	22.5	12.5
Animal attack	107	21,000	37.4	32.7	29.0	0.9	0.0
Motor vehicle	5,964	15,000	40.0	34.8	17.7	5.4	2.1

Source: Bureau of Justice Statistics, Federal Tort Trials and Verdicts, 2006

FIGURE 8-15

Final Awards for Plaintiff Winners

Over 60% of plaintiff winners were granted final awards of $50,000 or less

Plaintiff winners in civil bench and jury trials were awarded an estimated sum of $6 billion in compensatory and punitive damages in 2005. Among the 14,000 plaintiffs awarded monetary damages, the median final award amount was $28,000. Contract cases in general had higher median awards ($35,000) than tort cases ($24,000).

Almost two-thirds (62%) of all plaintiff award winners were awarded $50,000 or less. A small percentage (about 4%) of all plaintiff award winners were awarded $1 million or more. Plaintiff winners in asbestos cases tended to win the highest award amounts. The median final award in asbestos cases was almost $700,000. More than three-quarters of all award amounts in asbestos cases were greater than $250,000.

Cases with median final awards over $150,000 included other product liability ($500,000), medical malpractice ($400,000), false arrest or imprisonment ($259,000), employment discrimination ($175,000), and tortious interference ($169,000).

Motor vehicle accident cases accounted for more than 40% of all plaintiff award winners in 2005. The median award in motor vehicle accident cases was $15,000. Forty percent of plaintiff winners in motor vehicle accident trials were awarded $10,000 or less.

Civil Bench and Jury Trials in State Courts, 2005, Bureau of Justice Statistics, U.S. Department of Justice.

E. JURY INSTRUCTIONS

Before the jurors retire to consider the verdict, the judge will inform them about the law in the case. This is called a jury charge, or jury instruction. In a jury charge, the judge reads the applicable law to the jurors to help guide them in their deliberations. For instance, in a case involving punitive damages, the judge might read the following jury charge:

> Ladies and gentlemen of the jury, I hereby instruct you that you may award punitive damages only if you find by a preponderance of the evidence that the conduct of the defendant in this case was malicious or taken in reckless disregard of plaintiffs' rights.

When the jurors retire to consider the facts of the case and how they should finally decide the case, they are supposed to be guided by the jury instructions. The jury charge in a negligence case could easily run to dozens of pages. In these days of copy machines and computers, many judges give a written copy of the charge to the jurors to aid them in their deliberations.

Chapter Summary

The final element in a negligence case is the plaintiff's proof of loss, or damages. A plaintiff's request for damages can fall into three broad categories: compensatory, punitive, and nominal damages. Compensatory damages are the plaintiff's out-of-pocket losses and losses for pain and suffering. Compensatory damages can be divided into general damages and special damages. General damages consist of the plaintiff's losses that are difficult to quantify. How much is it worth to the plaintiff to endure the pain associated with his injuries? This question is answered by the jury in its award of damage amounts. Special damages refer to those damages that can be stated with specificity, for example, medical bills and lost wages. Punitive damages are those jury awards that are designed to punish the defendant for his actions. They are often called exemplary damages. A jury awards punitive damages as a way of discouraging others from committing the same actions as the defendant. Nominal damages refer to minor awards that have little significance. To prove this fourth and final element of a negligence action, the plaintiff must present evidence of his losses.

 SKILLS YOU NEED IN THE REAL WORLD

Keeping Track of Medical Records

It is surprising how many clients fail to keep an accurate record of their medical bills. The paralegal must often work with the client for days or even weeks to get copies of all the different medical bills. Clients often forget about treatments they have received, who gave them, and when they received them. In addition to the doctors' bills, the client should be reminded to keep track of receipts for items such as:

- prosthetic devices: walkers, canes, crutches, and so on;
- over-the-counter medication purchases: aspirin, and so on; and
- comfort aids such as special headrests, cushions, or mattresses.

Once all the medical providers have been documented, a complete and accurate list should be developed for the amounts owed. Thoroughness is absolutely essential at this stage. If the plaintiff fails to request sufficient special damages before the case is resolved, she cannot go back and request additional compensation from the defendant. When the case is resolved, the defendant is only obligated to pay the amount in the jury verdict or the agreed-upon settlement. Any undiscovered charges become the plaintiff's responsibility.

THE LIFE OF A PARALEGAL

Paperwork and Phones

My biggest surprise about working for a lawyer is that there is nothing magical about paperwork. For instance, when you need to file a motion, you type it up, have the attorney sign it, and take it over to the courthouse or call a courier to take it for you. It's no big deal. That absolutely shocked me. I had visions of every court document requiring triple signatures and service guys who had to formally accept it from you. It's like that with certificates of service. You prove that you served a document by saying that you did it. That's it. I almost had a heart attack the first time that I had to file a motion at the courthouse. When I handed it to the clerk, she didn't even look at it. She just stamped it, and that was it. I always thought that this stuff was very formal and required all kinds of technicalities.

The hardest part of my job is juggling all of the different tasks. You are doing all of this work, and you still have to answer the telephone. The phone has to be the top priority because that's how clients contact you, and you have to be available. When a judge calls, you have to drop everything and give it your total attention. In between phone calls, you are trying to figure out what priority to give to other tasks. I don't guess; I ask the attorney for some direction. I make her prioritize. I'll say, "Which of these is the most important to you?" It isn't always what I think. Sometimes it's more important that a letter get mailed than that a motion get filed. I wouldn't have thought that before I started working here. I would have thought that a court document always gets higher priority than a letter, but it all depends on what's going on in a particular case.

Celeste Jenks, Paralegal

ETHICAL ISSUES FOR THE PARALEGAL: NATIONAL PARALEGAL ASSOCIATIONS

There are two major national paralegal associations: the National Federation of Paralegal Associations (NFPA) and the National Association of Legal Assistants. Practicing paralegals and paralegal students are eligible to join either or both of these organizations. Benefits of membership include newsletters, annual conventions, and a ready-made network of friendly professionals who can often assist a paralegal with difficult or unusual legal matters. Both organizations have created model rules of ethical behavior for paralegals. The websites for both are provided below.

In addition to these national organizations, almost all states have some form of local paralegal association. These smaller chapters meet regularly to discuss important issues and practice concerns. You can often locate a local paralegal association by contacting the bar association or by asking practicing paralegals.

Relevant Cases

GRAY BROWN-SERVICE MORTUARY, INC. V. LLOYD
729 SO.2D 280 (1999.)

KENNEDY, Justice.

In 1990, Fred Lloyd and his wife, Faye Lloyd, entered into an installment contract with Gray Brown-Service Mortuary, Inc. ("Gray Brown-Service"), for the purchase of a double-crypt space in the chapel section of the Forestlawn Mausoleum, which is owned and operated by Gray Brown-Service. Lloyd and his wife chose Forestlawn so that they could be entombed near Faye Lloyd's mother and sister. The purchase price of the space was $3,390. The contract provided for a 15% per annum interest rate, and, after a $100 down payment, the Lloyds were required to make 60 monthly payments of $78.27. The contract also provided that no entombment would be permitted until payment in full had been made for the crypt space.

The contract, written by Gray Brown-Service, also provided:

> Section 10.3. That this agreement and the parties hereto shall be subject to the Rules and Regulations and provisions now or hereafter enacted by company concerning said cemetery pertaining to the operation of said cemetery.
> ***
> Section 11.3. PERPETUAL CARE: The company hereby binds itself to maintain the burial spaces or other interment facilities herein described, and to deposit from the purchase price of said burial spaces to a Care and Maintenance Fund created for the continual maintenance of all

developed cemetery property without assessment to the Purchaser. Said deposit of the Perpetual Care Fund to be made upon final payment of interment or entombment spaces purchased herein. The sum of said deposit to equal no less than ten percent (10%) of purchase price of said spaces as shown above. THIS AGREEMENT PROVIDES FOR PERPETUAL CARE. (Emphasis in original.)

Gray Brown-Service's rules and regulations, adopted before the Lloyds entered their contract, provided:

> Section 3. CASKET NOT TO BE DISTURBED. Once a casket containing a body is within the confines of the cemetery, no funeral director, employee, or agent shall be permitted to open the casket or touch the body without the consent of the person or persons having legal control of the disposition of the remains, all heirs at law, and next of kin.
> Section 4. SUBJECT TO LAWS, RULES AND REGULATIONS. Besides being subject to these Rules and Regulations, plots, crypts, property, property rights and matters covered herein, and all interments, disinterments and removals are made subject to the orders and laws of the properly constituted authorities of the City of Anniston, County of Calhoun and State of Alabama, and to the Certificate of Incorporation and By-Laws of the Corporation.

In 1991, Faye Lloyd died unexpectedly from a heart attack, at the age of 49. Fred Lloyd contacted Chapel Hill Funeral Home, Inc.

("Chapel Hill"), and requested it to provide funeral services for his wife. The total price of the services was $4,398.00, which included embalming his wife's body to sanitize and preserve the remains. The casket, which was included as one of the items covered by the price of the funeral services, was designed to preserve human remains in an air-tight and liquid-tight state. Before entombment at Forestlawn, the casket was locked and sealed. Unless the casket was damaged while it was being placed in the above-ground crypt, which was located in an air-conditioned building, the casket should have preserved the remains of Faye Lloyd.

Following the funeral service, Chapel Hill entrusted the casket to Gray Brown-Service for entombment in the Lloyd crypt space. The Lloyd crypt is located on the top level of the mausoleum, with five crypts below it. The space itself is slightly taller, wider, and longer than a casket.

Employees of Gray Brown-Service used a scissor lift to raise the casket to the space. One of the employees then placed a handful of BBs throughout the space so that the casket could be placed in position and moved around easier. Once the casket was in position, the crypt was sealed with a fiberglass sealing plate and silicone caulk. A decorative stone face was then attached over the plate.

Jane Hill worked for Gray Brown-Service as the manager of the cemetery and mausoleum. She was in charge of operating and maintaining the mausoleum. Hill was a licensed funeral director, but did not know how the crypt spaces were drained or how they were ventilated. Franklin McGee, vice president of Gray Brown-Service, was in charge of business operations of Gray Brown-Service properties and interests.

In the summer of 1992, Harolyn Williams, whose father was entombed near the Lloyd crypt, telephoned Jane Hill and told her that the mausoleum had an odor smelling of decaying human remains. Hill told Ms. Williams that the odor was due to a sewage problem. In the fall of 1992, Ms. Williams again complained about the noxious odor in the mausoleum. Hill told Ms. Williams that the smell was due to the burial in a crypt at the mausoleum of a woman who had been dead in her driveway for three days before her body was discovered.

In the spring of 1993, Nathan Hall, an employee of Gray Brown-Service was asked to find the source of the odor. Hall traced the odor to the vicinity of the Lloyd crypt. He removed the decorative plate from the empty crypt underneath the Lloyd crypt and found a long crack through which fluids of a decomposing body were seeping and pooling on the floor of the vacant crypt. Because the Lloyd crypt was the only crypt above the vacant one, it had to be the source of the fluids. The only action taken at that time was to seal the vacant crypt. Gray Brown-Service did not repair the crack in the Lloyd crypt, and no effort was made to contact Fred Lloyd.

The odor became worse in the summer of 1993. Following a funeral service on Father's Day, at which many of the attendees held their noses during the service or left the mausoleum, Gray Brown-Service attempted to address the odor. Fluids from the Lloyd crypt had by then seeped through a crack in the vacant crypt to another vacant crypt below that one. Because the second vacant crypt was not sealed, the odor seeped into the public areas of the mausoleum.

Jane Hill, without permission of the Lloyd family and without the required permit from the Department of Public Health, disinterred the remains of Faye Lloyd. Present at the disinterment were Gray Brown-Service employees Jane Hill, Nathan Hall, James Nail, and Paul Starr. Larry Hill, the husband of Jane Hill, was also present. Everyone at the disinterment was asked to keep the matter a secret. Jane Hill falsely told Nathan Hall that she had permission to open the crypt. Because of the odor coming from the casket, the casket was placed in the breezeway of the mausoleum.

An examination of the casket revealed many "pin-sized" rust spots and perforations over the entire length of its bottom. The rust and/or perforations were caused by the BBs that had been placed on the bottom of the crypt. Body fluids were escaping through the many pin-sized holes. Jane Hill directed that Faye Lloyd's casket be opened. Shortly before midnight, the lock on the casket was sawed off with a hacksaw and the lid was pried open with a crowbar.

Once the casket was open, Faye Lloyd's remains were exposed. Jane Hill directed Nathan Hall to distribute a caustic chemical called Viserock throughout the casket and on the remains of Faye Lloyd. Viserock is designed to absorb fluid, and it dries to a plaster-like cast. Nathan Hall testified that he tossed the Viserock "by the cupful" onto Faye Lloyd's chest, thoracic area, face, and neck.

The casket had been damaged so badly when it was opened that it could not be resealed. Duct tape was applied to hold the lid in place. Viserock was put on the body fluids that had pooled in the Lloyd crypt. The crypt space was not cleaned or sealed or repaired.

Jane Hill did not tell Gray Brown-Service's vice president, Franklin McGee, about the disinterment until after it had taken place. After learning of the disinterment, McGee made no effort to contact the Lloyd family. McGee testified that he "strongly suspected" that the BBs had caused the perforations in the casket. Instead of contacting the Lloyd family, McGee, several weeks later, ordered a second invasion of the Lloyd crypt. Again, the Lloyd family was not contacted, nor was the required permit obtained from the Department of Public Health. Employees of Gray Brown-Service opened the casket and physically removed the remains of Faye Lloyd and placed them in a plastic body bag. Body tissues and fluids were left behind in the original casket. A few pounds of Viserock was placed in the body bag with Faye Lloyd's remains. The remains in the body bag were then placed in a different casket, which was then reentombed in the Lloyd crypt. Again, the crypt was not cleaned and the crack was not repaired.

Following the reentombment, the original casket Fred Lloyd had purchased, which contained some fluids and tissues, was dumped near a wooded area adjacent to the cemetery. Days later, the casket was buried in an unmarked location. No photographs were taken of the casket, and Fred Lloyd and Chapel Hill employees were not allowed to inspect it before it was buried.

When Fred Lloyd was contacted by Gray Brown-Service, he was told only that there had been a minor problem with a leak in the crypt and that it had been taken care of by professionals. Mr. Lloyd was not told until later that his wife's crypt had been opened or that his wife's remains had been desecrated. Nathan Hall was fired for talking about the disinterment, along with another Gray Brown-Service employee who had helped to locate the members of the Lloyd family.

Fred Lloyd sued Gray Brown-Service, alleging the tort of outrage; trespass to the remains of Faye Lloyd; unlawful and unwarranted interference with the entombed remains of Faye Lloyd; unlawful and illegal disinterment of the remains of Faye Lloyd; wanton and willful desecration, injury, invasion, and mutilation of the remains of Faye Lloyd; abuse of a corpse; breach of contract; suppression; and failure to provide perpetual care for the tomb of Faye Lloyd. Fred Lloyd also sued Chapel Hill.

Before the judge charged the jury, the following occurred outside the presence of the jury:

> COURT: All right. Now, I want to make sure that I understand everyone's position so far as the verdict forms that the Court would submit in this

case. And I want to get everybody bound to this and make sure there's not going to be any objection made after the fact.

On the record, it's my understanding from our precharge conference last evening that it's the desire of counsel for the defendants that I submit to the jury what we would call a general-verdict form. I'm going to submit verdict forms for each of the defendants in the claims against them. This is, a separate verdict form, one in favor of the defendants and, of course, one against each defendant. But it is simply going to be then the jury finding in favor of the plaintiff and against that particular defendant and assessing blank damages.

GRAY BROWN-SERVICE'S COUNSEL: That's correct.

COURT: Without any delineation as to particular cause of action. And without any delineation as to compensatory damages or punitive damages.

Is that correct on behalf of Chapel Hill, Mr. Bloom?

CHAPEL HILL'S COUNSEL: Yes, sir, Your Honor.

COURT: And, Mr. Fite, is that correct on behalf of your defendant, Gray Brown-Service?

GRAY BROWN-SERVICE'S COUNSEL: It is.

COURT: Is that satisfactory with the plaintiff?

PLAINTIFF'S COUNSEL: If that's what the defendants want, it's satisfactory with the plaintiff.

COURT: So there will be no objection to the Court's using those charges; is that correct?

GRAY BROWN-SERVICE'S COUNSEL: That's correct.

CHAPEL HILL'S COUNSEL: That's correct."

The jury returned a verdict in favor of Chapel Hill, but returned a general verdict against Gray Brown-Service in the amount of $2 million. Gray Brown-Service filed a motion for a remittitur of damages, which was denied. The court entered a judgment on the verdict. Gray Brown-Service appeals, but only from the trial court's denial of a remittitur. Lloyd does not appeal from the judgment in favor of Chapel Hill.

Gray Brown-Service argues that where the only claim for compensatory damages is based on an allegation of mental anguish, the court should apply a strict-scrutiny standard to determine whether the amount of the award is excessive, particularly where the evidence of mental anguish is relatively scant. Gray Brown-Service further argues that, assuming the amount this Court would consider the most the jury could properly have awarded as compensatory damages would be substantially less than the total amount awarded, then the balance of the award should be considered punitive and that that amount would be excessive.

We note that Gray Brown-Service is appealing from the trial court's order denying its motion for a remittitur. Section 6-11-1, Ala.Code 1975, provides that in tort actions, except wrongful-death actions, parties are entitled to have the fact-finder itemize its award as "past damages," "future damages," and "punitive damages." However, Gray Brown-Service expressly asked for a general-verdict form, which did not distinguish between compensatory and punitive damages.

This Court has been able to review a possible ratio of compensatory damages to punitive damages when a general verdict was used. In *Union Sec. Life Ins. Co. v. Crocker*, 709 So.2d 1118 (Ala.1997), cert. denied, 523 U.S. 1074, 118 S.Ct. 1515, 140 L.Ed.2d 668 (1998), a general-verdict form was used. *Crocker* involved fraud based upon the intentional misconduct of a credit-life-insurance policy. With regard to the general verdict of $2 million against the insurance company, we stated that we could not determine with certainty the ratio of punitive damages to compensatory damages.

"Certainly we do not consider the compensatory damages award to be based solely upon economic loss, as Justice See suggests in his dissent. Rather, we have thoroughly reviewed the compelling evidence of the plaintiff's emotional and mental distress over the insurance company's misconduct, as well as her economic loss, in determining the possible ratio of punitive damages to compensatory damages." *Crocker*, 709 So.2d at 1121.

In this present case, we do not need to determine a possible ratio of compensatory damages to punitive damages, because the particular facts of this case would support an award of compensatory damages for mental anguish and would support an award high enough that, taking the remainder of the jury's award as punitive damages, the ratio of punitive to compensatory damages would not be unreasonable. It has long been the law of Alabama that mistreatment of burial places and human remains will support the recovery of damages for mental suffering.

In *Whitt v. Hulsey*, 519 So.2d 901, 906 (Ala.1987), the defendant/contractor owned land adjacent to an old family cemetery. After the defendant had been bulldozing near the cemetery, some gravestones were found broken. We held that the punitive damages award was proper:

> We realize that there may be differences of opinion regarding the dividing line between merely offensive conduct and conduct that is atrocious and intolerable in a civilized society. Great respect is afforded the resting place of the dead. This sentiment is repeated in *Holder v. Elmwood Corp.*, 231 Ala. 411, 413, 165 So. 235, 237 (1936): "Our decisions lay much stress upon the sacredness of the resting ground of the dead . . . , and the exclusive right of interment and possession being shown, guard the spot against unlawful invasion and give a right of action for any illegal interference. . . ." Under the particular facts of this case, and in view of the deep human feelings involved, we find the evidence sufficient to support the claim of outrageous conduct, where the alleged act was the desecration and destruction of a portion of a family burial ground. 519 So.2d at 906.

Gray Brown-Service knew in 1992 that there was an odor problem in the mausoleum and chose to do nothing about it. When it became unbearable for mourners to be inside the mausoleum, Gray Brown-Service, acting under the cover of night, swearing those present to secrecy, acting without permission of the family, and acting without the proper legal permits, pried open Faye Lloyd's casket with a crowbar. An employee of Gray Brown-Service then tossed a caustic chemical on the remains of Faye Lloyd. Binding the casket with duct tape, Gray Brown-Service reentombed Faye Lloyd's body. Shortly thereafter, Gray Brown-Service again entered the Lloyd crypt, actually removed most of the remains of Faye Lloyd, and placed them into a body bag, while leaving some of the remains in the original casket, which it tossed into some woods and later buried in another location.

As to Gray Brown-Service's contention that there was scant evidence of mental anguish, we disagree. There was testimony that when Fred Lloyd learned of what had happened to his wife's remains, he was angry and upset. He testified that if, when he talked to Franklin McGee, he had known the details of what happened to his wife, he would have "hurt" McGee. Lloyd testified that he had "been miserable since 1994," when he found out what had actually happened. He testified that he had had nightmares about his wife's remains being in a body bag and about the chemical being thrown on her face. He also stated that he was concerned as to whether his wife's remains were still in the crypt. He said he has not moved her remains because she had desired be buried near her sister and mother and because he did not want to disturb her remains again. He testified that when he thinks of good memories with his wife, he then recalls how her remains were mistreated by Gray Brown-Service.

Given these facts, it is hard to question that Fred Lloyd suffered severe emotional distress. Suffice it to say there was ample evidence to support the jury's award, based on the undignified and disrespectful manner in which Gray Brown-Service treated the remains of Faye Lloyd.

AFFIRMED.

WARDLAW V. IVEY
297 GA.APP. 240, 676 S.E.2D 858 (2009.)

JOHNSON, **Presiding Judge.**

Andrew Wardlaw and his landscaping company, ACW Lawn & Landscape Management, Inc. (collectively "Wardlaw"), sued Greg Ivey, Ivey Management Corporation, and Wayne Baxter (collectively "the defendants") for personal injuries and property damage after a tree cut by Baxter fell on Wardlaw's truck. The defendants moved for summary judgment, which the trial court granted in part and denied in part.

So viewed, the record shows that Ivey owns Ivey Management Corporation, a building and land management company. In November 2005, Ivey asked Baxter, a company employee, to cut down a dead tree in front of his residence on Cold Harbor Drive in Roswell. Baxter had eight years of experience in tree removal and managed various developments and office parks for the company.

Ivey checked the weather forecast on the day of the tree removal and believed the weather would be calm. Baxter also testified that winds were calm as he began the project. Based on the weather conditions, the lean of the tree, its size, and shape, Baxter determined how to cut the tree. Although the tree was located just 20 feet from Cold Harbor Drive, Baxter believed that he could cut it safely without endangering anyone on the road.

Using a large chainsaw and an anchor rope, Baxter and two assistants began to cut the tree, intending to make it fall away from Cold Harbor Drive into Ivey's yard. Baxter had made several cuts in the tree when he noticed gusty winds in the area. As he continued cutting, the tree twisted with the wind and fell toward the road.

At that time, Wardlaw was driving his company-owned pickup truck down Cold Harbor Drive. As he passed the Ivey residence, the tree fell on his truck, crushing part of the cab and totaling the vehicle. Wardlaw managed to avoid serious injury, but he sustained muscle soreness and minor scratches.

Wardlaw sued the defendants for, among other things, personal injuries, emotional distress, and destruction of the truck. He also sought punitive damages based on their recklessness in "attempting to cut and remove the subject tree in a manner that so clearly endangered unsuspecting members of the community and innocent motorists." The defendants moved for summary judgment on Wardlaw's claims for punitive damages, emotional distress, and property damage. The trial court granted the motion with respect to the punitive damage and emotional distress claims, but denied it as to Wardlaw's claim for the damaged truck.

In this appeal, Wardlaw challenges the trial court's summary judgment ruling on his punitive damage and emotional distress claims. We find no error.

"Punitive damages may only be awarded in tort actions where it is proven by clear and convincing evidence that the defendant's actions showed wilful misconduct, wantonness, oppression, or that entire want of care raising the presumption of conscious indifference to consequences." Neither negligence nor gross negligence alone can support a punitive damages claim. As we have explained, "something more than the mere commission of a tort is always required for punitive damages. There must be circumstances of aggravation or outrage."

Asserting that issues of material fact remain as to punitive damages, Wardlaw points to evidence that Baxter did not use proper methods or techniques in removing the tree, particularly given the windy conditions that day. He argues that Baxter's improper techniques revealed wantonness or a conscious disregard for the safety of others.

We disagree. Under Georgia law, "wanton conduct is that which is so reckless or so charged with indifference to the consequences as to be the equivalent in spirit to actual intent." Conscious indifference to consequences involves "an intentional disregard of the rights of another, knowingly or wilfully disregarding such rights."

Nothing in the record demonstrates the required recklessness or indifference here. On the contrary, Baxter considered various factors as he prepared to take down the tree, including the weather and the tree's size, location, and shape. Based on his eight years of experience removing trees, he believed that he could cut the tree so that it would fall away from the road. He also used an anchor rope to control its descent. Given these circumstances, no rational trier of fact could find by clear and convincing evidence that Baxter was indifferent to the consequences or disregarded the rights of others.

Wardlaw further argues that the defendants "flaunted" a local ordinance by failing to obtain a city permit before removing the tree and violated traffic laws by blocking Cold Harbor Drive with the fallen tree. In his view, these violations create an issue of fact as to whether the defendants acted wantonly or with conscious indifference.

The tree ordinance Wardlaw cites, however, is specifically intended "to promote the preservation of trees." Wardlaw has not shown—or argued—that it has any relevance to safety or proper tree removal. And he has pointed to no evidence that the alleged ordinance violation proximately caused or had any connection to his damages. We fail to see how this violation—or the fact that the tree blocked the road after it hit Wardlaw's truck—demonstrates wanton or consciously indifferent conduct.

Wardlaw's evidence undoubtedly raises questions of fact as to negligence. But he did not present the type of proof necessary to create a jury issue on punitive damages. The trial court, therefore, properly granted the defendants summary judgment on this claim.

Wardlaw also challenges the trial court's emotional distress ruling, advancing two theories on appeal. First, he asserts that the physical injuries he suffered when the tree fell bring his claim within Georgia's impact rule. Second, he argues that the defendants' wilful and wanton behavior authorizes recovery for emotional distress. Neither theory has merit.

Under Georgia's impact rule, a claimant seeking damages for emotional distress must demonstrate that: (1) he suffered a physical impact; (2) the impact caused him physical injury; and (3) the injury caused his mental suffering or emotional distress. Failure to satisfy any one element is fatal to recovery. In this case, Wardlaw cannot meet the third requirement.

The evidence shows that Wardlaw sustained minor physical injuries when the tree fell on his truck, and he subsequently experienced mental stress. Nothing in his testimony, however, connected his stress to the physical injuries. Instead, Wardlaw asserted that the stress resulted because his business stagnated. And he attributed his business problems not to his physical injuries, but to issues with replacing his truck and his preoccupation with the thought that he could have been killed by the tree. Under these circumstances, he cannot bring his emotional distress claim within the impact rule.

Alternatively, Wardlaw argues that he can recover for emotional distress based on the defendants' wilful and wanton conduct. As discussed in Division 1, however, Wardlaw offered no evidence that the defendants acted wilfully, wantonly, or with conscious indifference to consequences. The trial court, therefore, properly granted summary judgment on this claim.

In these appeals, the defendants challenge the denial of their motion for summary judgment on Wardlaw's claim for damage to his truck. The record shows that following the incident, Wardlaw's insurance company totaled the truck and paid him the value. The defendants now argue that, given this insurance recovery, Wardlaw cannot seek further damage for the loss of his truck. They also argue that the insurance payment conclusively establishes the truck's value.

We disagree. The collateral source rule bars a tortfeasor from offering evidence that a claimant has received payment from a third party — such as an insurer — for damage caused by the tortfeasor's conduct. "This is because a tortfeasor is not allowed to benefit by its wrongful conduct or to mitigate its liability by collateral sources provided by others." Generally, therefore, a claimant may sue a tortfeasor and seek recovery for damages caused by tortious conduct, even if the claimant has been reimbursed by his insurer.

An exception arises when the claimant assigns his cause of action to the insurer, at which point any suit must be brought in the insurer's name. But the defendants have not pointed to evidence of an assignment in this case. And although they argue vigorously that Wardlaw should not benefit from a double recovery, the insurance payment was not made on their behalf. Accordingly, a verdict for Wardlaw would not result in a "double recovery" from the defendants.

Simply put, the defendants cannot reduce their liability based on payments made by Wardlaw's insurer. They also cannot establish the value of the truck through these payments. To hold otherwise would directly violate the collateral source rule and allow the defendants to take credit for sums tendered by a third party. A jury must decide whether the defendants are liable for the damage to Wardlaw's truck and, if so, in what amount. The trial court, therefore, properly denied the defendants' motion for summary judgment on the property damage claim.

Judgments affirmed.

Websites

- **National Association of Legal Assistants**
  http://www.nala.org

- **National Federation of Paralegal Associations**
  http://www.paralegals.org

- **'Lectric Law Library**
  http://www.lectlaw.com (click on the search box for damage issues)

- **Gonzaga Law Review — Use Search box, "calculating tort damages"**
  https://www.law.gonzaga.edu/law-review/ **Cornell Law School — Damages (Wex)**
  http://www.law.cornell.edu/wex/index.php/Damages

- **Wikipedia — Tort Reform**
  http://en.wikipedia.org/wiki/Tort_reform

Forms and Court Documents

Notice the loss of consortium claim alleged in paragraph 9.

STATE OF PLACID   IN THE SUPERIOR COURT
COUNTY OF BARNES   FILE NUMBER:_____

Joseph Josephson and   )
Marie Josephson,   )
Plaintiffs   )
)
vs.   )
)
Darryl Dangerous,   )
Defendant

Complaint

Now comes the plaintiffs in the above-styled action and complaining of the defendant do hereby allege:

1.

Plaintiffs are both citizens and residents of Barnes County, State of Placid.

2.

Defendant is a citizen and resident of Barnes County, State of Placid.

3.

On December 20, 2002, plaintiff Joseph Josephson was driving a 2001 Honda Viper, northbound on Starnes Cove Road in the City of Bevanston, State of Placid.

4.

Defendant, Darryl Dangerous, was driving his car, a 1976 Mercury Impala, on the same road, driving in a southbound direction.

5.

As the two cars approached one another on Starnes Cove Road, Defendant Dangerous crossed the centerline of the road and entered the plaintiff's lane of traffic, striking the plaintiff's car in a head-on collision. At all times prior to the collision, plaintiff was operating within his lane of traffic and did not depart from his lane until his automobile was struck by the defendant's automobile.

6.

Defendant was negligent in that defendant:
a. Failed to maintain a proper lookout.
b. Failed to keep his car within his own lane of traffic.

c. Drove at excessive and dangerous speeds.

d. Failed to keep his vehicle under proper control.

7.

As a result of the collision, plaintiff received serious and painful bodily injuries causing medical and other expenses, lost earnings, and other damages, in an amount in excess of $10,000.

8.

Plaintiffs incorporate each and every allegation as set forth hereinabove and repeat and re-allege each such averment hereinafter with the same force and effect.

9.

As a direct and proximate result of the injuries sustained by Plaintiff Joseph Josephson, the husband of Plaintiff Marie Josephson, resulting from the collision herein complained of and by the Defendant's negligence as alleged, Plaintiff Marie Josephson has been caused to be deprived of love, companionship, society, relations, and normally expected and rendered household duties and chores performed and rendered by Plaintiff Joseph Josephson prior to the collision herein complained of. Plaintiff Marie Josephson's spouse, Joseph, was able to and in fact did perform and render such services prior to the collision complained of herein, and such loss of consortium is a direct and proximate result of the negligence of the Defendant and the resulting injuries to Plaintiff's spouse.

WHEREFORE, the Plaintiffs pray that the Court as follows:

1. That the Plaintiffs have and recover a judgment against the Defendant in an amount in excess of $10,000.00 for personal injuries.
2. That the Defendant be assessed with punitive damages as permitted by law.
3. That prejudgment interest be awarded as provided by law.
4. That the costs of this action be taxed against the Defendant.
5. That all issues raised be tried before a jury.
6. For such other and further relief as the Court may deem just and proper.

This the _____ day of June, 2012.

_____
Clarence D. Arrow
Attorney for Plaintiffs
State Bar No. 000-998

Certificate of Service

This is to certify that the undersigned has this date served this document in the above-captioned action on all other parties to this cause by depositing a copy hereof, postage prepaid, in the United States Mail, properly addressed to the attorney for each party as follows:

This the _____ day of June, 2012.

Respectfully submitted,

By: _____
Attorney for Plaintiffs

Key Terms

Collateral source rule	Fair market value	Mitigation of damages
Compensatory damages	General damages	Per diem
Declaratory judgment	Injunction	Special damages
Equity	Loss of consortium	

Review Questions

1   What are the three categories of damages?
2   Why do courts make a distinction between general and special damages?
3   Describe how the plaintiff would go about proving property losses.
4   Explain fair market value.
5   What is the collateral source rule, and what significance does it have for the plaintiff?
6   Why is a plaintiff required to mitigate his damages, when possible?
7   Explain loss of consortium claims.
8   Why should you ask about prior existing injuries?
9   Under what circumstances would a claim of bad faith be justified?
10   When and under what circumstances is a plaintiff entitled to receive punitive damages?
11   How has tort reform affected the award of punitive damages in many jurisdictions?
12   What are nominal damages?
13   What are three important factors to consider when evaluating a case for damages?
14   Why would a plaintiff conduct an asset search of a defendant prior to bringing suit?
15   What is a verdict form? When is it used?

Applying What You Have Learned

1   Larry's wife of 47 years died last year and was sent to a local crematorium for processing. After the body was purportedly cremated, Larry received a decorative jar that was supposed to contain his wife's ashes. Several months later, Larry saw news reports that the crematorium in question had been seized by the local authorities and dozens of corpses had been recovered that had been scheduled to be cremated, but had never actually been processed. Instead, the bodies were simply left outside or stacked in a shed. Larry decides to sue the crematorium. What kind of damages, if any, can Larry seek?[12]

2   Linda is involved in a car collision. The driver of the other car ran a red light and struck Linda's car on the driver's side. Linda was severely bruised. She was taken to the hospital and discharged the next day. Her hospital bill was $2,456. Because she was in terrible pain, she lost almost eight days from work. When she returned, she found that she had trouble concentrating. She kept reliving the collision in her mind. Her work suffered, and her employer eventually fired her. She worked as an advertising salesperson, which means that she spent most of her day driving from one client to another. Because of the accident, she suffers from terrible anxiety whenever she gets behind the wheel of a car. What type of damages can Linda seek against the other driver, and how would you classify these damages: compensatory-general, compensatory-special, punitive, or nominal?

3   Draft an answer to the complaint in the Forms and Documents section. How should the defendant respond to the loss of consortium complaint?

4   What types of compensatory damages are permissible in your state? Can a plaintiff recover for a "psychic" injury, or must the injury be tied to a physical injury?

Endnotes

[1] *Origin and History of Hebrew Law*, John M.P. Smith, Hyperion Press, 1990.

[2] Leviticus, 24:17–20.

[3] Restatement (Second) of Torts, §902.

[4] Restatement (Second) of Torts, §621 (1977).

[5] *Walston v. Greene*, 246 N.C. 617, 99 S.E.2d 805 (1957).

[6] *Fuches v. S.E.S. Co.*, 459 N.W.2d 642 (1990).

[7] *International Correspondence School, Inc. v. Crabtree*, 162 Tenn. 70, 34 S.W.2d 447 (1931).

[8] *Tancredi v. Dive Makai Charters*, 823 F. Supp. 778 (D.C. Haw. 1993).

[9] *Davis v. Green*, 188 F. Supp. 808 (W.D. Ark. 1960).

[10] *Edwards-Warren Tire Co. v. Coble*, 102 Ga. App. 106, 115 S.E.2d 852 (1960).

[11] Restatement (Second) of Torts, §909.

[12] *Gray Brown-Service Mortuary, Inc. v. Lloyd*, 729 So. 2d 280 (1999).

Crossword Puzzle

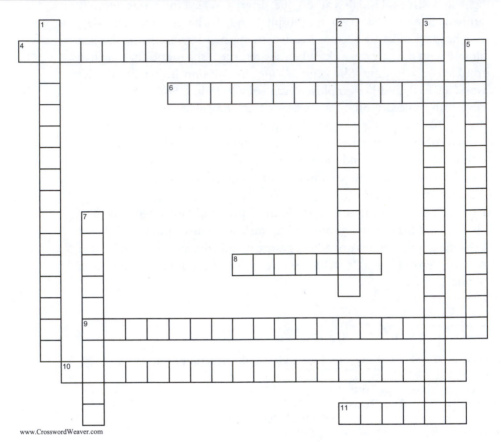

www.CrosswordWeaver.com

ACROSS

4 An evidentiary rule that permits the jury to be told about the plaintiff's other sources of compensation, such as insurance, worker's compensation, etc.

6 The amount that a willing buyer would pay for an item that a willing seller would be willing to accept

8 By the day or daily

9 An award by a judge or jury designed to compensate the plaintiff for his physical or financial losses

10 The responsibility of the plaintiff to lessen his potential injuries or losses by taking reasonable actions to seek medical treatment or take other precautions when a reasonable person in the same situation would have done so

11 The court's authority to order individuals and corporations to perform (or not to perform) certain activities because they are unjust

DOWN

1 A claim filed by the spouse of an injured party for the loss of companionship in the marriage caused by the injuries

2 Those awards that are closely tied to the defendant's negligence

3 A court order that specifies the duties and obligations of a party

5 Those damages, such as medical bills, closely tied to the plaintiff's injuries and for which a specific amount can usually be calculated

7 A court order that demands a certain action, or that prohibits a certain action

Defenses to Negligence

- Explain the difference between contributory negligence and comparative negligence

- List and explain some of the exceptions to contributory negligence, such as the last clear chance doctrine and the rescuer doctrine

- Describe the various types of comparative negligence systems in place in the United States

- Be able to draft a comparative negligence defense in an answer

- Explain the continued significance of contributory negligence law in the United States

THE RAILROAD'S DEFENSE IN THE CHUMLEY CASE

This chapter focuses on defenses peculiar to negligence actions. One of the more important questions to be answered in the Chumley case is which model of negligence the jurisdiction follows. If the Chumley case is tried in a jurisdiction that follows the contributory negligence model, the analysis of the case will be very different than it would be in a comparative negligence jurisdiction. If the case is tried in one of the few remaining contributory negligence jurisdictions, the outcome for Mr. Chumley is in doubt. The reason for this is that there is no evidence, and Mr. Chumley cannot provide any, that he stopped at the railroad crossing (as required by law) before proceeding across the tracks and colliding with the train. In a contributory negligence state, Mr. Chumley's failure to stop could remove any possibility of recovery in this case. However, if the Chumley case is filed in a comparative negligence jurisdiction, Mr. Chumley's possible negligence is only one of many factors to consider and probably will not cause any major problems for the legal team representing him. Before we can further analyze the legal implications of Mr. Chumley's case, we must first discuss exactly what contributory and comparative negligence are.

INTRODUCTION TO CONTRIBUTORY NEGLIGENCE

Contributory negligence
A defense available in only a few jurisdictions that provides that a plaintiff who is even partially at fault is barred from any recovery.

The doctrine of **contributory negligence** was once followed in almost all jurisdictions. Contributory negligence is a court-created doctrine that prevents any award to plaintiffs when they contribute to their own injuries. Under the most draconian application of contributory negligence, a defendant who is 99 percent at fault will not pay any damages to a plaintiff who is 1 percent at fault in the accident. In the last few decades of the twentieth century, many jurisdictions abandoned contributory negligence in favor of a more flexible — and some would argue more just — system called comparative negligence. Under that system, the plaintiff's negligence is measured against the defendant's negligence, and the plaintiff's ultimate recovery is reduced by the percentage of his fault.

Most other countries that have a legal system similar to that in the United States have long since abandoned contributory negligence. For instance, all of the following countries follow some form of comparative negligence scheme:

- All European Union countries, including Great Britain
- Canada
- New Zealand
- Australia[1]

The doctrine of contributory negligence has been called one of the harshest doctrines in law.[2]

See Figure 9-1 for a list of which states use a contributory negligence scheme and which use a comparative negligence scheme.

A. HISTORICAL REASONS FOR THE DEVELOPMENT OF CONTRIBUTORY NEGLIGENCE

Why would such a harsh rule ever be developed? Over the decades, several justifications have been offered. Some commentators have suggested that

Alabama	**Contributory Negligence**
Alaska	Comparative Negligence: adopted by legislature in 1986
Arizona	Comparative Negligence: adopted in 1984
Arkansas	Comparative Negligence: adopted "pure" comparative negligence in 1954; later amended to plaintiff's negligence must be less than defendant's
California	Comparative Negligence
Colorado	Comparative Negligence: statute passed in 1971; plaintiff's negligence must be less than 50%
Connecticut	Comparative Negligence: statute passed in 1973, amended in 1986; plaintiff who is 50% at fault can still recover
Delaware	Comparative Negligence
Florida	Comparative Negligence: first state to judicially adopt comparative negligence
Georgia	Comparative Negligence: plaintiff must be less than 50% at fault to recover
Hawaii	Comparative Negligence: adopted in 1969
Idaho	Comparative Negligence: adopted the Georgia plan of comparative negligence in 1971. It requires that plaintiff's negligence be less than 50%
Illinois	Comparative Negligence: adopted in 1986
Indiana	Comparative Negligence: adopted in 1983; plaintiff who is 50% negligent may still recover
Iowa	Comparative Negligence: adopted in 1984; plaintiff is denied recovery when more than 50% at fault
Kansas	Comparative Negligence: adopted in 1974; plaintiff can recover only when less than 50% at fault
Kentucky	Comparative Negligence: adopted in 1984; "pure" comparative fault
Louisiana	Comparative Negligence: adopted in 1979; "pure" comparative fault
Maine	Comparative Negligence: adopted in 1965
Maryland	**Contributory Negligence**
Massachusetts	Comparative Negligence: plaintiff must be less than 50% at fault to recover
Michigan	Comparative Negligence: adopted in 1979; "pure" comparative fault
Minnesota	Comparative Negligence: adopted in 1969; plaintiff must be less than 50% at fault to recover
Mississippi	Comparative Negligence: adopted in 1910
Missouri	Comparative Negligence: adopted in 1983; "pure" comparative fault
Montana	Comparative Negligence: adopted in 1975
Nebraska	Comparative Negligence: adopted in 1913
Nevada	Comparative Negligence: plaintiff can be up to 50% at fault
New Hampshire	Comparative Negligence: plaintiff who is 50% at fault can still recover
New Jersey	Comparative Negligence: adopted in 1973; plaintiff can be up to 50% at fault and still recover
New Mexico	Comparative Negligence: adopted in 1980; "pure" comparative fault
New York	Comparative Negligence: "pure" comparative negligence

(continued)

FIGURE 9-1

A State-by-State Breakdown Showing Contributory Negligence States and Comparative Negligence States

FIGURE 9-1
(continued)

North Carolina	**Contributory Negligence**
North Dakota	Comparative Negligence: adopted in 1973; plaintiff's negligence must be less than defendant's
Ohio	Comparative Negligence: plaintiff may be up to 50% at fault and still recover
Oklahoma	Comparative Negligence: adopted in 1979; plaintiff may be up to 50% at fault and still recover
Oregon	Comparative Negligence: plaintiff may be up to 50% at fault and still recover
Pennsylvania	Comparative Negligence: adopted by statute in 1976; plaintiff may be up to 50% at fault and still recover
Rhode Island	Comparative Negligence: "pure" comparative negligence
South Carolina	Comparative negligence, modified 51% rule
South Dakota	Comparative Negligence: plaintiff's negligence must be "slight"
Tennessee	Comparative Negligence: modified comparative negligence; remote contributory negligence will mitigate damages, not bar recovery
Texas	Comparative Negligence: follows New Hampshire plan
Utah	Comparative Negligence: defendant's negligence must exceed plaintiff's
Vermont	Comparative Negligence: plaintiff can be up to 50% negligent and still recover
Virginia	**Contributory Negligence**
Washington	Comparative Negligence: adopted in 1981; "pure" comparative negligence
West Virginia	Comparative Negligence: modified system of comparative negligence
Wisconsin	Comparative Negligence: plaintiff may be up to 50% at fault and still recover
Wyoming	Comparative Negligence: legislature adopted in 1973; plaintiff may be up to 50% at fault and still recover
Washington, D.C.	Although not a state, the District does follow the contributory negligence rule

contributory negligence is actually a component of proximate cause analysis. That argument runs something like this: To prove that the defendant is liable to the plaintiff, the plaintiff must prove that the defendant had a duty, that he violated that duty, and that the violation of that duty was the proximate cause of the injuries to the plaintiff. When the plaintiff has actually contributed in some way to his own injuries, the causal connection between the defendant's actions and the resulting harm is disrupted and should therefore absolve the defendant of any liability. However, this argument fails to take into account many of the other doctrines that have developed over time that have modified proximate cause analysis.

Another justification for contributory negligence is that a plaintiff should enter the court with *clean hands*. This term is usually reserved for actions by plaintiffs who seek injunctive relief from the courts. In injunctive relief, the plaintiff requests a court order preventing the defendant from taking some action, such as bulldozing a tree or selling corporate bonds. The court is permitted to deny the request when it is obvious that the plaintiff has been acting improperly. Similarly, supporters of contributory negligence claim that this rule should apply in negligence actions. If the plaintiff can be shown to be at least partially at fault for his own injuries, the clean hands doctrine should operate to bar his recovery. However, the doctrine of clean hands in injunctive cases is not a complete bar to a plaintiff's request; it is simply a factor that the court can consider in deciding what action, if any, to take.[3] Another argument against the clean hands doctrine is "last clear chance," discussed later in this chapter.

A more cynical reason for contributory negligence can be found in its historical roots. The doctrine of contributory negligence arrived on the legal scene at the same time as the Industrial Revolution was sweeping through the United States and Great Britain. This newfound wealth and the prosperity that it generated were considered vital to our national interest. Anything that might slow, or even disrupt, this development was seen as bad. Contributory negligence was a doctrine ready-made for the industrial mishaps, maimings, and deaths that occurred through industrial accidents. By eliminating recovery against a major railroad or other corporation when the plaintiff was in some way at fault for his own injuries, these business sectors were protected from a deluge of lawsuits, which allowed the industries to prosper and develop.[4]

Contributory negligence is also an excellent way for a judge to keep control of "runaway juries" — that is, juries that might be swayed by the facts of a case to award large damages to a sympathetic plaintiff against a huge corporation.

B. DEFINING CONTRIBUTORY NEGLIGENCE

According to the Restatement of Torts, contributory negligence is defined as the plaintiff's failure to take reasonable care for his own safety.[5] Put another way, contributory negligence is the plaintiff's lack of ordinary care that merges with the defendant's negligence to bring about the plaintiff's injuries. Under the theory of contributory negligence, the plaintiff is held to a standard of care for his own actions at the same time that the defendant is held to a standard of care for his actions toward the plaintiff.[6] In practice, this standard of care is often different for the two parties. Many jurisdictions apply a more rigid standard of care toward the defendant in a contributory negligence action than is applied to the plaintiff. The reason for this is that by holding the plaintiff to a lower standard, there is less chance of the harsh result that sometimes results in contributory negligence cases.[7]

One commentator has referred to contributory negligence as the "all-or-nothing lottery."[8]

If a plaintiff is found to be contributorily negligent, she will receive nothing, no matter how severe her damages.

TORT BASICS AT A GLANCE

Sidebar

*Some commentators
have suggested that a
better name for con-
tributory negligence
would be "contributory
fault" or "contributory
misconduct."[9]*

Negligence and contributory negligence are not flip sides of the same coin. In a negligence action, the defendant can be liable to the plaintiff for breaching a duty to the plaintiff that results in the plaintiff's injuries. In contributory negligence, we do not see the reverse — that is, that the plaintiff breached a duty to the defendant. Instead, contributory negligence is a theory that states that the plaintiff breached a duty of care to herself, and this breach merged with the negligence of the defendant to bring about the plaintiff's injuries.

TORT
BASICS
AT A
GLANCE

A defense of contributory negligence presumes negligence on the part of the defendant.

The basic premise behind contributory negligence is that a plaintiff should not be permitted to recover damages from someone else's negligence when she failed to exercise reasonable care herself. To take advantage of contributory negligence, there is no requirement that the defendant knew about the plaintiff's negligence prior to the incident. See Figure 9-2 for the elements of contributory negligence.

Although this theory sounds practical enough, in practice it often has drastic results. In states where contributory negligence is still the law of the land, a defendant who is clearly at fault can be absolved of all liability by a showing that the plaintiff was at fault in a minor way. Dissatisfaction with the sometimes unjust results in these cases has led many jurisdictions to abandon the concept entirely and opt for a more reasonable and judicious approach: comparative negligence (discussed later in this chapter).

TORT
BASICS
AT A
GLANCE

Contributory negligence is a complete bar to recovery; comparative negligence will lessen the plaintiff's recovery in proportion to his own negligence in bringing about his injuries.

1. WHY STUDY CONTRIBUTORY NEGLIGENCE?

Unless you live in one of the few states that continues to follow contributory negligence, why should you bother to study the concept? The reason is simple: Even in states that have adopted some form of comparative negligence, contributory negligence continues to have an important impact. Because most jurisdictions once followed contributory negligence theories, the case law that developed under those theories provides an important underpinning to

A plaintiff is considered to be contributorily negligent if:

1 he breaches the duty imposed upon him by law to protect himself from injury;

2 his actions concur and cooperate with actionable negligence of the defendant; and

3 his actions contribute to the injuries as a proximate cause.*

FIGURE 9-2

The Elements of Contributory Negligence

*Steinauer v. Sarpy County, 217 Neb. 830, 353 N.W.2d 715 (1984).

current cases. In addition, comparative negligence developed as a direct response to contributory negligence, and it is difficult to understand comparative negligence principles without referring to the doctrine of contributory negligence.

2. WHY DOES THE DOCTRINE CONTINUE TO EXIST?

Although only a handful of states still follow contributory negligence, the question arises: Why would any state continue to apply a doctrine that almost all legal commentators consider to be overly harsh and sometimes unjust? There are several possible reasons. These states may continue to follow more conservative legal views on a wide variety of topics that include an adherence to contributory negligence. In states in which contributory negligence has been eliminated, the judiciary has often taken the lead by abolishing the doctrine. Later, the state legislature makes the change official by enacting a statute that changes the law from contributory negligence to comparative negligence. In many states, such as Delaware, the judiciary has taken the time-honored position that the courts do not have the power to create law, only to interpret it. In these states, the judiciary may favor a move from contributory negligence to comparative negligence, but feels obligated to leave this decision to the state legislature. Another reason could be simple inertia. Society changes rapidly; the legal community does not. In the states in which contributory negligence continues to remain in effect, there may be a simple reluctance to abandon a century or more of legal precedents for the dramatically different concept of comparative negligence.

Sidebar

Contributory negligence is based on the premise that justice is served best when the courts stay out of the business of apportioning degrees of fault among the parties.[10]

Sidebar

"Plaintiff may be contributorily negligent if his conduct ignores unreasonable risks or dangers which would have been apparent to a prudent person exercising ordinary care for his own safety."[11]

C. THE DOCTRINE OF "AVOIDABLE CONSEQUENCES"

Although sometimes confused with contributory negligence, the doctrine of avoidable consequences is actually a completely separate doctrine. It focuses on what happened after the accident, not the plaintiff's actions before the accident. Under this doctrine, the plaintiff must take reasonable steps to obtain proper medical treatment for his injuries or to protect damaged property. Under the doctrine of avoidable consequences, the plaintiff is not entitled to recover damages from his failure to take these steps.

Example: Carl is injured in a collision. He refuses medical treatment, and as a result his minor injury becomes aggravated to the point that he requires major surgery and prolonged rehabilitation. Carl sues the driver who caused the collision. The jury awards damages to Carl, but only for the medical treatments and expenses that he would have required after the wreck, not for his exacerbated injuries due to his own failure to look after himself.[12] It is similar to the principle of mitigation of damages discussed in Chapter 8.

D. HOW MUCH AT FAULT MUST PLAINTIFF BE?

Different states follow different rules on this point. Under the basic theory of contributory negligence, a plaintiff can be barred from recovery for any amount of negligence, no matter how slight. However, some states have modified that approach, requiring that the defendant prove the plaintiff's contributory negligence was more than a small amount.[13]

TORT BASICS AT A GLANCE

The basic issue in contributory negligence is whether the plaintiff knew of the danger he was in, whether he failed to exercise ordinary care to protect himself, and whether his failure to exercise such care contributed in some way to his own injuries.[14]

Example: Tom visits Claire at her family farm. She offers to give Tom a ride on the family tractor. She admits that she has had very little experience driving the tractor, but Tom climbs on the back anyway. While they are traveling to the pond, Claire loses control of the tractor and Tom falls off, severely injuring his back. This occurred in a contributory negligence state. Will Tom be prevented from recovering under the theory of contributory negligence?

Answer: Yes.[15]

E. IS THERE SUCH A THING AS "CONTRIBUTORY NEGLIGENCE PER SE"?

In some jurisdictions, the defendant's violation of a safety statute (negligence per se) bars the use of contributory negligence as a defense.[16]

What if the plaintiff is violating a safety statute at the time of the accident? Under contributory negligence, would this mean that she has committed "contributory negligence per se"? (See negligence per se in Chapter 6.) Most jurisdictions do not follow such a hard-and-fast rule. If the plaintiff is violating some statute at the time of her injuries, her violation is one more element that the defendant may use to show contributory negligence. However, the plaintiff's violation must be a proximate cause of her own injuries. For example, Marsha is driving a car that has a broken taillight. As she proceeds through a green light, Ted's car broadsides her. Ted has failed to stop at the red light. At trial, Ted raises the defense of contributory negligence by claiming that at the time of the accident, Marsha was driving in violation of a safety equipment statute (that is, nonfunctioning taillight). This fact alone will not justify a defense of contributory negligence, because there is no causal connection between the broken taillight and the subsequent collision.

F. THE "ALL OR NOTHING" ELEMENT OF CONTRIBUTORY NEGLIGENCE

Much of the criticism about contributory negligence has to do with its "all or nothing" approach to a negligence action. If the plaintiff has not contributed in any way to her own injuries, she is permitted to recover all the damages the jury has awarded. However, if she has contributed, even in a minor way, to her own injuries, she is not entitled to any of the jury's award. In this modern era, many question the continued wisdom of such a system.

G. IS CONTRIBUTORY NEGLIGENCE DOOMED?

Some commentators argue that the doctrine of contributory negligence will eventually disappear from the U.S. legal system. In support, they point to the many jurisdictions that have abandoned the concept over the past 30 years.[17] However, there are many legal concepts that have been modified or eliminated in some jurisdictions that continue to have full legal effect in others. Whether contributory negligence will eventually disappear as a civil injuries doctrine is still an open question.

H. EXCEPTIONS TO CONTRIBUTORY NEGLIGENCE

Almost as soon as the concept of contributory negligence was developed, courts began carving out exceptions by stipulating certain types of cases, or certain factual scenarios, that would preclude the use of contributory negligence. Among the most famous, and certainly the most discussed, is the last clear chance doctrine.

1. LAST CLEAR CHANCE

Under the **last clear chance doctrine,** a plaintiff's contributory negligence will be excused if the defendant had the last opportunity of avoiding the accident and failed to do so.

The application of the last clear chance doctrine is highly dependent on the facts of the case. As such, it is often considered a malleable doctrine — that is, one that can fit many different situations.[19] It was developed as a way of allowing a partially negligent plaintiff to avoid the strict and often harsh application of contributory negligence. If contributory negligence is a doctrine that helps a negligent defendant avoid liability, last clear chance is a doctrine that helps a negligent plaintiff avoid a finding of contributory negligence.[20]

Last clear chance
A claim by a plaintiff in a contributory negligence allegation that the defendant was the person who had the last opportunity to avoid the event that caused the plaintiff's injuries, and therefore, the defendant should remain liable for the injuries, despite any negligence by the plaintiff.

Sidebar

Last clear chance is also known as the doctrine of discovered peril, the doctrine of supervening negligence, the humanitarian doctrine, the doctrine of gross negligence, and the doctrine of subsequent negligence.[18]

FIGURE 9-3 Proving Last Clear Chance	The plaintiff must present evidence showing: ■ That he or she was in a dangerous position ■ That he or she was unable to escape the danger through ordinary care ■ That the defendant either knew or should have known that the plaintiff was in danger	■ That the defendant had the ability to avoid the accident ■ That the defendant failed to exercise ordinary care to prevent the injuries to the plaintiff ■ That there was proximate cause between the defendant's failure to act and the resultant injuries to the plaintiff

a. Proving Last Clear Chance

In many jurisdictions, the plaintiff is allowed to raise the issue of last clear chance as a routine matter when the defendant raises the defense of contributory negligence. Just as the burden of proving contributory negligence is on the defendant, the burden of proving last clear chance is on the plaintiff. Ultimately, it is the jury's decision whether the doctrine applies to the facts of a particular case.

b. Pleading Last Clear Chance

Depending on the jurisdiction, the plaintiff may be able to raise evidence of last clear chance at trial or may be required to raise it as a contention in her complaint. Check the applicable case law to be sure of the procedure in your state. The elements of last clear chance are set out in Figure 9-3.

TORT BASICS AT A GLANCE

Last clear chance is usually only available to plaintiffs in contributory negligence actions. It is invoked by the person who is injured as a way of refuting a claim of contributory negligence.[21]

2. SUDDEN EMERGENCY

Sudden emergency
A doctrine that relieves a person of the normal standard of care because of a swiftly developing and dangerous event.

Another exception to contributory negligence is the **sudden emergency** doctrine. Under this doctrine, when a plaintiff is confronted with a sudden emergency, something that requires a quick response, he will not be held to the same standard as would a plaintiff who had more time to consider his actions. This situation is also seen in traditional negligence analysis. In an emergency, a person is not expected to exercise the same standard of care, whether the person is a defendant in a negligence action or a plaintiff in a contributory negligence counterclaim.[22] This doctrine was originally created to avoid some of the difficult situations that can develop under contributory negligence. Holding the plaintiff to a lower standard of care in an emergency makes it easier for the plaintiff to avoid a claim of contributory negligence.[23] See

Figure 9-4 for a list of factors to help determine if the sudden emergency doctrine applies to a given situation.

3. ASSUMPTION OF THE RISK

We have discussed assumption of the risk in regard to intentional torts, but it is also an important defense in negligence cases. Essentially, a defense of assumption of the risk is the defendant's assertion that the plaintiff should be barred from recovering any damages because the plaintiff knowingly placed himself in a dangerous situation (a defense that admittedly sounds a great deal like contributory negligence). Despite the similarity to contributory negligence, many jurisdictions continue to apply the defense of assumption of the risk to comparative negligence cases as well. Other comparative negligence jurisdictions have abolished the defense. The assumption of the risk defense is based on the idea that the plaintiff knew the danger he was getting into and voluntarily assumed the risk. In such a situation, the plaintiff waives the right to sue for damages. Whenever a defendant raises a claim of the assumption of the risk, the defendant must prove that the plaintiff knew a particular action was dangerous and voluntarily engaged in it. Without that proof, the jury cannot find that the plaintiff knowingly undertook a risky action.

Example: Ron likes to ride "mechanical bulls." One evening, he hears about a new club that has opened in town and has a brand-new mechanical bull that the owners claim is more powerful than any other in the state. Ron goes to the club and waits his turn to ride the bull. A club employee hands Ron a waiver form that reads, in part, "By agreeing to ride the mechanical bull, you acknowledge that you are engaging in a dangerous activity that can cause serious injury or even death. You agree that you assume the risk of this activity and absolve this club for any negligence in the operation of this bull." Ron signs and gets on the bull, but unfortunately for him, the bull has not been properly maintained and three seconds into his ride the main drive pulley breaks and throws Ron 20 feet. Ron is severely injured and wants to bring suit against the club. The club owners counter with the defense of assumption of the risk. Who will win?

Sudden emergency applies when the following are true:

- There is competent or compelling evidence that a sudden emergency existed.
- The plaintiff's apprehension must be a response to what a reasonable person would consider to be a life-threatening situation.
- That danger could not have been anticipated.
- The emergency was caused by the defendant.
- The plaintiff was the person in danger. (If the plaintiff was rescuing another person, this doctrine does not apply; instead the rescuer doctrine applies.)

FIGURE 9-4

Factors to Consider When Determining If Sudden Emergency Applies

Source: *Katcher v. Heidenwirth*, 254 Iowa 454, 118 N.W.2d 52 (1962).

Answer: Ron may lose. Although there are several other potential issues raised here, assumption of the risk is a good defense for the club owners. After all, if they can prove that Ron knew the danger involved and voluntarily assumed the risk, he may lose at trial. However, this issue may be complicated by the fact that Ron did not knowingly and voluntarily assume the risk of the club's negligence, only the dangers associated with riding a properly functioning mechanical bull.

4. OTHER EXCEPTIONS TO CONTRIBUTORY NEGLIGENCE

a. Plaintiff's Age and Physical Factors

We have already discussed the reasonable person standard in other contexts related to negligence, so it should not be any surprise that it also factors into exceptions to the rule of contributory negligence. For instance, what standard applies to a claim of contributory negligence involving a child or a visually impaired person? The general rule is that a child is held to the standard of a similarly situated child and an impaired person is held to the standard of a hypothetical reasonable person with the same disability.[25]

However, the same limitations of the reasonable person standard in other contexts also apply here. For instance, although a plaintiff can claim age or some other physical factor as justification for a lower standard of care, she is not allowed to plead intoxication or mental deficiency as a means of lowering the standard of care in contributory negligence. When a contributory negligence claim involves intoxication, for example, the plaintiff's inebriation does not lessen her standard of care any more in a contributory negligence action than it does for the defendant's standard of care in the main negligence action.

Under contributory negligence, a plaintiff is required to use her senses in a normal way to "maintain a lookout" and to take whatever other steps a reasonable person would to keep herself safe.[26]

b. Mental Incompetence

In almost all jurisdictions, a legally insane person cannot be liable under contributory negligence.[27] The reasoning behind this exception is the same as that for not finding legally incompetent people liable in other contexts. Such people are incapable of assessing their responsibilities or conforming their conduct to society's standards and deserve special protection under the law.

5. THE RESCUER DOCTRINE

When a person is attempting to save the life of another, the doctrine of contributory negligence does not apply.[28] Of course, this assumes that the rescuer did not put the person in jeopardy in the first place. This doctrine has been applied when people engage in actions that would otherwise be

Contributory negligence is not a defense to		**FIGURE 9-5**

Contributory negligence is not a defense to

- Breach of contract
- Intentional torts[i]
- Willful, wanton, or reckless conduct[ii]
- Strict liability (in some jurisdictions)[iii]

- Ultra-hazardous activities[iv]
- Product liability (in some jurisdictions)[v]

FIGURE 9-5

Types of Cases in Which Contributory Negligence Is Not a Factor

[i]*Brown v. Chapman*, 304 F.2d 149 (9th Cir. 1962).
[ii]*Reynolds v. Guthrie*, 145 Kan. 315, 65 P.2d 272 (1937).
[iii]*Mahoney v. Corralejo*, 36 Cal. App. 3d 966, 112 Cal. Rptr. 61 (1974).
[iv]*Carlson v. Glanville*, 170 Cal. App. 2d 246, 338 P.2d 580 (1959).
[v]*Davenport v. Walker*, 280 S.C. 588, 313 S.E.2d 354 (1984).

considered contributory negligence, such as running into a fiery building to save another person or jumping into icy water to save a drowning man. The reasons for this doctrine are obvious: Society does not wish to penalize people who rescue others. This doctrine applies even when the rescuer takes desperate and extremely dangerous chances in rescuing another.[29]

I. SITUATIONS IN WHICH CONTRIBUTORY NEGLIGENCE DOES NOT APPLY

There are many types of situations in which the defense of contributory negligence does not apply, even in jurisdictions that continue to follow the doctrine. See Figure 9-5 for a list of situations in which contributory negligence cannot be applied.

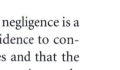

Sidebar

Another term used for willful, wanton, or reckless negligence is gross negligence.[30]

J. CONTRIBUTORY NEGLIGENCE IS A JURY QUESTION

All jurisdictions provide that the determination of contributory negligence is a question for the jury.[31] The defense must present sufficient evidence to convince the jury that the plaintiff contributed to his own injuries and that the jurors must follow the law in awarding no damages. The court can intercede on the defendant's behalf only in rare cases. For instance, one jurisdiction allows directed verdicts of contributory negligence against the plaintiff only when the facts are "very clear" that the plaintiff was at fault.[32]

The defendant must prove the plaintiff's contributory negligence. It is usually raised in the context of an affirmative defense in the[33] defendant's answer.

TORT BASICS AT A GLANCE

In jurisdictions where contributory negligence is followed, the jury is often instructed that the plaintiff must take reasonable actions to protect

Tech Topic
DOCUMENTING PERSONAL INJURY FRAUD

All too often, dishonest people fake personal injury in order to sue or get compensation from others. For example, a Philadelphia man who was employed by a home-improvement store claimed he had injured his back and neck and was unable to work. Nevertheless, it was proved that during the time he claimed he was injured, he played a game of stick ball, danced, and did push-ups. His claim not only was denied, but he also was charged with fraud. How did these facts come to light? Through video surveillance of his activities.

It is legal to shoot video, record audio, or take still photographs of an injured person anytime he is in a public setting. This includes going out to dinner, going for a walk in a park or on a public street, or engaging in any public activity. Also, if a person's job involves being in the public, his activities can be recorded while at work. Sophisticated, high-tech video equipment and cameras can produce high-resolution images that leave no doubt if someone is overstating or even faking an injury. There are limits, though. Phones cannot be tapped, and videos cannot be taken through a window of the person's home.

GPS technology is another useful tool in tracking personal injury fraud, as it can track a person's movements, say, to the gym when an injury supposedly prevents a workout.

One sophisticated, albeit low-tech, system for spotting fraudsters is a written test that can expose those who are faking their pain. People lying about their injuries score significantly higher—by more than 10 points—than those who have real injuries.

himself, and the jury must decide if he failed to do so. Along these lines, the court might instruct the jury as follows:

> Ladies and Gentlemen of the jury, I charge you that the plaintiff's risk must be unreasonable at the time that he took it.[34] I further charge you that is not contributory negligence if the plaintiff was placed in the position of being forced to take a risky action by the negligence of the defendant.[35]

COMPARATIVE NEGLIGENCE

Comparative negligence
An approach to negligence cases that balances the negligence of the defendant against the negligence of the plaintiff and permits a reduced recovery for the plaintiff in proportion to the plaintiff's negligence.

The doctrine of **comparative negligence** was developed as a way of circumventing the frequently harsh rulings in contributory negligence cases. Whether adopted by state legislatures or by judicial decree, comparative negligence has swept away contributory negligence in all but a handful of states.

The underlying principles of the various comparative negligence theories may be different, but the general approach is the same. Instead of forfeiting any recovery, a plaintiff who is negligent will have his ultimate recovery reduced by the proportion of his negligence.

The ghost of contributory negligence still haunts many of the comparative negligence jurisdictions, either because the common law principles that developed under that theory still form an important part of the new law, or because the comparative negligence statutes are simply a form of modified contributory negligence.[36]

A. HISTORICAL DEVELOPMENT OF COMPARATIVE NEGLIGENCE

The concept of comparative negligence is as old as Roman law and has been adopted by most countries that follow the Roman model. In the U.S. law system, contributory negligence was the model adopted by almost all jurisdictions, and comparative negligence is a relatively recent phenomenon. That is not to say that comparative negligence was not considered by various states, even as early as the nineteenth century. Georgia, for example, experimented with the concept in the mid-1800s. However, most states began adopting comparative negligence statutes and case law in the mid- to late twentieth century. In fact, the latter part of the twentieth century saw a growing momentum of states turning away from contributory negligence in favor of comparative negligence.[37]

States that have adopted comparative negligence through judicial action have generally opted for the "pure" form, while states that have adopted the concept through legislation have usually opted for the modified form. This difference could be explained by the prominence of the insurance industry lobby. The modified form of comparative negligence is much more insurance friendly than the pure form. From 1969 onward, several states have adopted some form of modified comparative negligence scheme. The different schemes are shown in Figure 9-1.

Under comparative negligence, a plaintiff is not barred from recovery if he is negligent; however, his ultimate award will be reduced in proportion to his negligence.

TORT
BASICS
AT A
GLANCE

B. THE UNIFORM COMPARATIVE FAULT ACT

The Uniform Comparative Fault Act was proposed as a way of creating a more uniform approach to comparative negligence in the various states. However, it has never been enacted in its entirety in any jurisdiction. Instead, portions of the act have been incorporated into statutes or comparative negligence schemes. Some states use the act as a guideline for judicial interpretations.[38]

C. THE THREE MODELS OF COMPARATIVE NEGLIGENCE

Different types of comparative negligence approaches are taken by different jurisdictions. Some have adopted the pure form of comparative negligence, while the vast majority of others have adopted a modified form. Tennessee may be the only state to adopt the "slight-gross" model of comparative negligence.

There are three different forms of comparative negligence:

▪ **Pure**   ▪ **Slight-Gross**

▪ **Modified**

---

1. PURE COMPARATIVE NEGLIGENCE

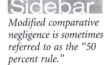

Pure comparative negligence has been adopted in three of the most populous states: New York, California, and Florida. As a consequence, more litigants are involved with pure comparative negligence than any other form.[39]

Under pure comparative negligence schemes, a plaintiff is entitled to receive an award of damages no matter how great her fault, assuming that the defendant is also found to be at fault. In pure comparative negligence states, a determination that the plaintiff is 75 percent at fault and the defendant is 25 percent at fault would have the following result: The plaintiff would be entitled to receive only 25 percent of her total damages.

Under the "New Hampshire" plan, a plaintiff can recover if she is 50 percent negligent or less. If she is more than 50 percent negligent, she is barred from recovery, echoing the provisions of contributory negligence.

Under the "Georgia" plan, a plaintiff must be less than 50 percent negligent before she can recover.

2. MODIFIED COMPARATIVE NEGLIGENCE

Modified comparative negligence is sometimes referred to as the "50 percent rule."

Under the modified comparative negligence rules, a plaintiff's recovery could be limited in at least two ways. In some jurisdictions, a plaintiff's negligence must be less than 50 percent. In those states, like Georgia, if the plaintiff's negligence is greater than 50 percent or greater than the defendant's negligence, she will receive no recovery, mirroring the result in a contributory negligence jurisdiction. In other states that follow a form of modified comparative negligence, the plaintiff's negligence can be equal to the defendant's negligence. In those states, the plaintiff's recovery will be reduced by the amount of her percentage of fault. If the plaintiff is 50 percent at fault, she will receive only half of her damages. However, even in these states, a plaintiff is not entitled to any recovery if her negligence exceeds that of the defendant.

3. SLIGHT-GROSS COMPARATIVE NEGLIGENCE

This rule is followed in only a small percentage of jurisdictions. Under the "slight-gross" comparative negligence scheme, a plaintiff is entitled to recover if her negligence is slight and the defendant's negligence is great. However, if the plaintiff's negligence is more than what a jury would consider to be slight, she is not entitled to any recovery. Tennessee, for example, allows a plaintiff to recover when her negligence is a "remote" cause but not when her negligence is a proximate cause.

4. COMBINATIONS OF APPROACHES

In some jurisdictions, different forms of comparative negligence are followed depending on the issues in the case. For instance, a state could follow modified comparative negligence in personal injury cases and pure comparative negligence in product liability cases.

The New Hampshire plan is the most popular form of comparative negligence, having been adopted in more states than any other comparative negligence scheme (18 in all). Most jurisdictions have enacted some form of statute officially making comparative negligence the law of the land. The Georgia plan is the next most popular. Under the Georgia rule, a plaintiff must be less negligent than the defendant before he will be allowed to recover.

Review your state's statutes on contributory negligence or comparative negligence to verify the rules governing negligence actions.

D. TYPES OF CASES IN WHICH COMPARATIVE NEGLIGENCE APPLIES

Comparative negligence generally applies only to actions involving physical or property damage. In many jurisdictions, actions based on other torts (intentional torts, product liability torts, strict liability torts, etc.) will often follow entirely different rules.

In states that follow a modified form of comparative negligence, the judge is permitted to rule that the plaintiff is not entitled to any recovery when his negligence "clearly exceeds" that of the defendant. In such a situation, the case will not be submitted to the jury and the judge will enter a judgment in favor of the defendant. See Figure 9-6 for the types of cases in which comparative negligence might apply.

E. COMPARATIVE NEGLIGENCE AND PUNITIVE DAMAGES

Generally, the adoption of comparative negligence doctrines does not affect a plaintiff's right to seek punitive damages. However, on a practical level, if a plaintiff is negligent in a case in which he claims negligence by the defendant, his own fault may weigh against the award of punitive damages.[40]

F. HOW COMPARATIVE NEGLIGENCE AFFECTS PROXIMATE CAUSE ANALYSIS

Generally, the principles of proximate cause (discussed in Chapter 7) are not affected by a jurisdiction's switch from contributory negligence to comparative negligence. However, there are some important points to raise about proximate cause analysis under comparative negligence. Some

FIGURE 9-6	Comparative negligence would apply in cases involving:	■ Malpractice actions (discussed in Chapter 12)[i]
Types of Cases in Which Comparative Negligence Would Apply	■ General negligence claim involving damage to persons or property ■ Nuisance actions	■ Negligent misrepresentation ■ Negligence of common carrier[ii]

[i]*Newell v. Corres, 125 Ill. App. 3d 1087 (1984).*
[ii]*Floyd v. Albany, 105 Ga. App. 31, 123 S.E.2d 446 (1961); Roberts v. Yellow Cab Co., 240 A.2d 733 (1968).*

jurisdictions have adopted a rule commonly referred to as the "sole proximate cause" rule. Under this rule, if the plaintiff is the sole proximate cause of his injuries, he is not entitled to recover any damages from a negligent defendant. This ruling, which sounds like a revival of contributory negligence, has more to do with proximate causation. A plaintiff who cannot prove that the defendant was the proximate cause of his injuries, even in a comparative negligence state, has failed to establish the third element of a negligence action (causation), and therefore his claim must fail.[41] The jury is responsible for making the determination of sole proximate cause.

G. DEFENSES TO COMPARATIVE NEGLIGENCE

As a general rule, the defenses available under contributory negligence are not available under comparative negligence. The simple reason for this is that defenses such as assumption of the risk, last clear chance, and others are not needed when the jury is permitted to weigh the actions of both parties and award damages even if both are negligent. However, this approach is not followed in all jurisdictions. Some states adhere to the view that assumption of the risk is a defense that is independent of comparative negligence, while others have abolished the defense as inconsistent with comparative negligence. Similarly, some jurisdictions have also abolished the "sudden emergency" or "sudden peril" doctrines because they tend to confuse the issues involved in a comparative negligence case.[42]

1. THE RESCUER DOCTRINE

Many jurisdictions have retained this defense only to the extent that the rescuer's behavior can factor into comparative negligence when the rescuer acts recklessly.[44]

2. MENTALLY INCOMPETENT PERSONS

Under comparative negligence, a mentally ill person's actions are evaluated in much the same way that they were evaluated under contributory negligence. If the mentally ill person has enough mental capacity to recognize that his actions are negligent, his ultimate recovery can be reduced by his percentage of fault. However, when a person is held to be mentally incompetent, his degree of fault often will not be a consideration in trial.

H. PLEADING COMPARATIVE NEGLIGENCE

We have previously seen that contributory negligence is an affirmative defense that must usually be raised in the defendant's answer before he will be allowed to take advantage of it. When a jurisdiction follows a comparative negligence model, does that same rule apply? Jurisdictions seem to be split on this issue. Most attorneys opt for the safe course and make some allegation in the complaint that the plaintiff's negligence "equaled or exceeded" any negligence of the defendant. That way, even if their jurisdictions do not require an affirmative statement in the answer alleging comparative negligence, the attorney has raised the issue anyway. (See the Contributory Negligence and Comparative Negligence Answers at the end of this chapter.)

I. SETTLEMENT ISSUES IN COMPARATIVE NEGLIGENCE CASES

In comparative negligence jurisdictions, a claims adjuster no longer has the option of refusing to settle a case when the plaintiff could be found negligent. Obviously, the settlement discussions in a comparative negligence state will be more involved and more complicated than in a state that follows contributory negligence. For example, the insurance company knows that the plaintiff may receive some form of recovery, even when she is at fault. Under this scenario, it may make more sense to settle such a case prior to trial. On the other hand, in a contributory negligence state, this pressure to settle a close case may often be considerably less.

J. MULTIPLE DEFENDANTS AND COMPARATIVE NEGLIGENCE

Although some commentators claim that multiple defendants in comparative negligence jurisdictions are more antagonistic than multiple defendants in contributory negligence states, the truth is probably that co-defendants are just as adversarial in all states. It is common practice for co-defendants to file cross-claims against one another, whether they are in contributory negligence states or comparative negligence states. In either event, they will seek to prove that the plaintiff was negligent and that some other co-defendant was primarily responsible for the injuries.

K. MOTIONS FOR DIRECTED VERDICT IN COMPARATIVE NEGLIGENCE CASES

We have seen in Chapter 1 that a motion for directed verdict is a common occurrence in a contributory negligence case, and it is not uncommon for such

FIGURE 9-7 A Jury Interrogatory Form in a Comparative Negligence Case	If you find that the plaintiff was negligent in this case, state the percentage of the plaintiff's overall fault. If you find that the defendant was negligent in this case, state the percentage of the defendant's overall fault.

a motion to be granted. However, in comparative negligence jurisdictions, a directed verdict for the defendant would be rare, because the jury must determine the percentage of fault of both parties. Some states provide that a judge can only grant such a motion when the evidence of the plaintiff's negligence is clear and convincing and is greater than 50 percent.[45]

L. THE JURY'S VERDICT

In some jurisdictions, the jury is asked a series of questions to help determine the percentage of fault of all parties. The jury might, for instance, be sent back to deliberate with a set of interrogatories, asking them specific questions. (See Figure 9-7.) On appeal, an appellate court will normally leave the jury's finding of percentages intact and will only alter the findings when they are obviously against the weight of the evidence.[46]

Case Excerpt

AYALA V. LEE
215 Md.App. 457, 81 A.3d 584 (2013)

ZARNOCH, J.

Can a driver be found negligent if an accident occurs when his truck crashes into a parked vehicle but the apparently healthy driver has no memory of the accident?

Appellants Rigoberto E. Domingos Ayala and Jose R. Rodas Santacruz were working for Ebb Tide Tents and Party Rentals ("Ebb Tide") when they were involved in a motor vehicle accident. The truck driven by appellee Robert F. Lee, holder of a commercial driver's license, on behalf of his employer Bay State Pool Supplies of Baltimore, Inc. ("Bay State"), collided with Ebb Tide's parked truck, resulting in severe injuries to Ayala and Santacruz. Ayala, Santacruz, and Imelda Carolina Chavez Ventura, Ayala's wife, sued Lee and Bay State for negligence. A six-day jury trial resulted in a jury verdict for Lee and Bay State, which appellants now ask us to reverse. We agree with appellants and therefore we reverse the judgment and remand for further proceedings.

Facts and Legal Proceedings

Ayala and Santacruz were working for William Edward Comegys, Jr., then the owner of Ebb Tide, on September 27, 2010. Comegys was driving the three of them from the company headquarters to a job site in Annapolis and was traveling westbound on Route 50. It was raining, and the truck's windshield wipers stopped working at some point during the drive. After crossing the Bay Bridge, Comegys stopped the truck and pulled over to the right hand shoulder of Route 50. The vehicle was fully out of the travel lanes, with the two right wheels on the grass and the two left wheels on the paved part of the shoulder. The emergency flashers were also on. Comegys, Ayala, and Santacruz all exited the truck and went to work on the windshield wipers. They had just fixed the wipers and were standing in front of the vehicle when suddenly their truck was struck from behind by the truck owned by Bay State and operated by Lee. Comegys was killed as a result of the impact. Ayala and Santacruz survived, but suffered serious and permanent injuries to their lower extremities.

Ayala, Santacruz, and Ventura filed a complaint against Lee and Bay State in the Circuit Court for Anne Arundel County on November 3, 2010.FN2 Ayala and Santacruz each alleged counts of negligence against Lee and Bay State (Counts I and II) and counts of negligent entrustment and hiring against Bay State (Counts III and IV). Ayala and Ventura also claimed loss of consortium against Lee and Bay State (Count V). The damages sought included past and future medical expenses, loss of income, and loss of earning capacity.

Ayala and Santacruz also testified about their injuries as a result of the accident and how those injuries had affected their ability to work. They called expert witnesses to corroborate their testimony, including the orthopedist who treated them, a rehabilitation specialist, and an economist. The Maryland State Troopers who had responded to the accident also testified. They described the work they did to reconstruct the accident scene, which showed that the front right corner of the Bay State truck hit the back left corner of the Ebb Tide truck. There was no damage to any other part of the Bay State truck. The officers also testified that the conditions that day included some rain but no obstructions to vision or any construction along that portion of Route 50.

Lee and Bay State relied on testimony from their own medical expert, who testified that Ayala and Santacruz's injuries were less severe than they claimed, and video evidence from an investigator who had recorded Ayala and Santacruz performing various day-to-day activities. Absent from the trial, however, was Lee himself. Because Lee was hospitalized, his deposition was read to the jury and served as his testimony. Accordingly, the jury heard that Lee was driving about fifty miles per hour in the right travel lane of Route 50. He saw a vehicle in his left side mirror and thought "Buddy, you're getting too close. You're coming into my lane." Lee's next memory was of crashing through the brush on the right side of the highway. He did not remember striking the Ebb Tide truck, nor did he remember seeing the truck. When asked how his vehicle moved to the right shoulder, Lee stated that "I must have just turned the wheel to the right, slightly." When asked if he was guessing, Lee said "I don't remember turning the wheel, but I could have — but it could have been a reaction as I was looking, you know."

Appellants moved for "judgment on the issue of liability" at the close of Lee and Bay State's case, which the circuit court denied. The case was submitted to the jury, which found that Lee and Bay State were not negligent. Ayala and Santacruz timely appealed.

Questions Presented

I. Did the circuit court err when it denied appellants' motion for judgment?

II. Did the circuit court abuse its discretion when it denied appellants' motion in limine to exclude evidence of appellants' immigration status at trial?

III. Did the circuit court abuse its discretion when it permitted a de bene esse deposition of a witness who was legally issued the Social Security Number Ayala used?

IV. Did circuit court err when it refused to give appellants' requested jury instructions?

Because we conclude that the circuit court erred when it denied appellants' motion for judgment, we do not reach the third and fourth questions. We therefore reverse the denial of the motion for judgment and remand for trial on the issue of damages. Given that appellants' immigration status may again appear relevant at that stage, however, we also consider appellants' second question and address the propriety of evidence of immigration status.

Discussion

I. Motion for Judgment

Background

Appellants argue that the facts of the accident "create a presumption of negligence" because Lee failed to maintain control of his vehicle. They assert that Lee violated two Maryland state laws when he crashed into the Ebb Tide vehicle: (1) Md.Code (1977, 2012 Repl.Vol.), Transportation Article ("Trans."), §21–309(b), which states that a "vehicle shall be driven as nearly as practicable entirely within a single lane"; and (2) Trans. §21–312(b), which states that a "person may not drive a vehicle from any controlled access highway except at the entrances and exits established by public authority." They contend that these violations are prima facie evidence of negligence. They therefore ask us to reverse the circuit court's denial of their motion for judgment. By contrast, appellees argue that Lee did not violate any state laws because restrictions on lane changes and access to and from a highway do not apply to travel to and from the shoulder of a highway. Appellees argue in the alternative that even if the laws apply, they create only an inference of negligence, not a presumption, making the court's denial of the motion for judgment and submission of the case to the jury appropriate.

Negligence as a Matter of Law

Finding negligence as a matter of law requires finding "in the evidence some prominent and decisive act, or failure to act, which permits of but one interpretation and in regard to which there is no room for reasonable minds to differ." *Weishaar v. Canestrale*, 241 Md. 676, 681, 217 A.2d 525 (1966). Appellants bear the burden of proof of showing that Lee and Bay State were "guilty of negligence which directly contributed to the accident, since the happening of the accident does not of itself constitute negligence, and evidence of negligence does not give rise to liability unless the negligence was the cause of the injury." We believe that appellants have met their burden, as the evidence shows both that Lee was negligent as a matter of law in two significant ways and that his negligence was the cause of appellants' injuries. Lee was negligent as a matter of law because he (1) moved the Bay State truck from a travel lane to the shoulder when it was not safe to do so, and (2) failed to maintain a proper lookout.

Lee would gain nothing by couching the events that led to the collision as an "unavoidable accident." In *Fry v. Carter*, 375 Md. 341, 825 A.2d 1042 (2003), the Court of Appeals concluded that an unavoidable accident is not a separate defense and that an instruction on unavoidable accident should no longer be given in negligence actions because it allows the jury "to speculate about last minute happenings." In so doing, the Court "recounted earlier cases discounting the notion that automobile accidents occur without negligence." And the Court found that there was ample evidence of negligence on the part of a tractor-trailer driver who struck and killed a traffic control manager standing in the gore off the road. Although the driver said he did not see the victim, blamed the accident on the State Highway Administration for narrowing the lanes, and argued that he could not have moved left to avoid the accident because of the presence of another vehicle, the Court rejected his contention that the accident was unavoidable and not negligent. The driver "could have slowed his speed further and continued to sound his horn," but did not. In this case, Lee did even less to prevent the collision.

We pause to address two other points Lee raises in arguing that he was not negligent as a matter of law. Lee characterizes the evidence as "merely establishing that he was not speeding, was watching for vehicles around him, and reacted to a motorist drifting into his lane of traffic." This view misstates the evidence before the trial court and the inferences that can logically be drawn from that evidence. First, the fact that Lee did not recall seeing the Ebb Tide truck demonstrates that he was not in fact watching for vehicles around him, despite his duty to keep a lookout. Second, Lee's own testimony established that his "reaction" to seeing a vehicle on his left was both unintentional and unexplained. In his deposition, Lee stated that he "must have just turned the wheel to the right, slightly," though he did not remember doing so. Whether or not Lee made the less negligent choice in the moment is irrelevant because he did not in fact make a choice at all: he saw a vehicle on his left but did not "remember turning the wheel" or crashing into the Ebb Tide truck on his right.

To hold that this "I–didn't–see–it–and–I–don't–remember" defense without any real proof of justification is enough to force a negligence question to the jury would only encourage irresponsible behavior and foster bad tort law. We therefore vacate the jury verdict and reverse the denial of appellants' motion for judgment on the issue of liability.

If the court determines that evidence of a party's immigration status is not unfairly prejudicial, its relevance typically relates to whether a party is entitled to lost wages at a United States pay rate or at the home country rate. The question of whether a party is entitled to United States earnings or home country earnings is a question of fact, because it necessarily depends on the jury determining the likelihood of whether or not the party will remain in the United States for the duration of the awarded compensation. In other words, if it is unlikely that a plaintiff will be deported or if he shows a long history of working in the United States, a United States pay rate is more appropriate. If there is evidence that the plaintiff is likely to return to his home country, whether by choice or by deportation, a country of origin pay rate is more appropriate.

Immigration status alone does not reflect upon an individual's character and is thus not admissible for impeachment purposes. Immigration violations that involve false statements, such as false employment papers, are more likely to be relevant, but are still subject to an intensive inquiry into the likelihood of prejudice, as discussed above. Further, the relevance of an immigration-related false statement, standing on its own, is limited if the party against whom it is offered is not charged with an immigration-related.

For all these reasons we reverse the judgment of the circuit court and remand for further proceedings.

Questions about the case:

1. Why had the three men stopped by the side of the road, and what happened after they did?
2. Was there a "presumption of negligence" in this case, and if so, why?
3. Does the court favor jury instructions concerning "unavoidable accidents"? Why or why not?
4. Is the "I-didn't-see-it-and-I-don't-remember" defense considered valid by the court?

SMITH V. CIANELLI
2006 WL 697479, *5 (Conn. Super. 2006)

MARK H. TAYLOR, Judge.

I. Background

These actions were commenced by Gregory Smith, who was the unfortunate victim of two automobile accidents during the same month; the first on April 9, 1999, and the second on April 29, 1999. These matters were consolidated for trial on June 13, 2002 (Gilardi, J.). John Barboza, now deceased, is represented in these proceedings by the administrator of his estate, Norman Fishbein. General liability and damages are not contested in either of these combined files, except to the extent that they should be apportioned between the parties.

II. Facts

The first accident occurred on Interstate 91 in New Haven, and there is no dispute as to the following facts. At or about 7:42 A.M. on the morning of April 9, 1999, three automobiles were heading in a northerly direction in three contiguous lanes near Exit 3. The plaintiff, Gregory Smith was in the right lane. The defendant, Julie Cianelli, was in the center lane, and an unknown driver and automobile were in the left-hand lane. Cianelli's automobile collided with the left-rear side of Smith's automobile causing him to lose control, spin 180 degrees around across the road and hit the barrier on the left-hand side of the highway causing approximately $4,000.00 in damages to his 1993 Volvo sedan. Smith testified that he was driving in the right lane at a speed of 55-60 miles per hour. Immediately prior to the collision, Smith heard the squeal of wheels and saw Cianelli's vehicle lose control. He then saw her strike the back of his vehicle. He has no recollection of seeing the third unknown vehicle.

Cianelli testified that as she was driving in the center lane at approximately 55 miles per hour, she noticed that the unknown vehicle had a "dealer plate" and that the driver was conversing on his cellular telephone. She also testified that she took some interest, along with her husband who was also in the car, in identifying the individual driving the unknown vehicle because her husband is an automobile dealer. At or about the time she was discussing these matters with her husband, Cianelli testified that the unknown driver suddenly and without warning changed lanes from the left lane to the center lane. At the time of this sudden and unanticipated lane change, her automobile was positioned in a manner that some portion of the front left side of her vehicle was in close proximity to some portion of the back right side of the unknown vehicle. She testified that this required her to immediately apply her brakes to avoid a collision. She also testified that she shut her eyes, panicked and lost control of her vehicle. Her husband similarly testified that she panicked.

Immediately after this incident, Smith sought medical treatment from the following medical providers: Dr. Arthur Siegel, neurologist, Dr. Anthony Lavorgna, chiropractor, and Dr. Donald Austria, a general practitioner.

The second accident occurred approximately three weeks later on April 29 at 8:02 A.M., when Smith was traveling in a southerly direction on Hemingway Avenue in East Haven. There is no dispute between the parties that as Smith approached Tyler Street at approximately 40 miles per hour, John Barboza negligently made a left-hand turn in front of Smith's on-coming vehicle. Smith applied his brakes but was unable to stop before colliding head-on with the side of Barboza's vehicle, causing approximately $900 in damage to Smith's 1984 Audi sedan.

On the same day and thereafter, Smith continued to seek regularly scheduled treatment from the same medical providers that he had seen in connection with the first accident. As the result of either or both of these accidents, Smith suffered injuries to the lumbar, dorsal and cervical areas of his spine. In the opinions of various medical professionals, he has sustained permanent partial impairment to each of these areas. In a report of April 28, 2000, Dr. Siegel ascribes a 5% permanency to the dorsal spine attributable to injuries caused by the second accident with Barboza. In the same report, Dr. Siegel also ascribes a 2.5% permanency to Smith's cervical spine and 7.5% permanency to his lumbar spine, both attributable to injuries caused by the first accident with Cianelli. He also reported an injury to his left knee.

However, Dr. Siegel's medical records are inconsistent with regard to the cause of the injury to Smith's cervical spine. In a report dated April 16, 1999, Dr. Siegel indicates that Smith's neck is "asymptomatic." Yet on April 30, 1999, Dr. Siegel discusses "persistence of symptoms" and refers to neck discomfort among others in this category. He then goes on to discuss the April 29 accident as the cause of injury to Smith's dorsal spine.

To add further confusion to the issue of the permanent partial injuries to various portions of Smith's spine, Dr. Lavorgna's notes and reports are entirely inconsistent. Dr. Lavorgna's notes do not seem to discuss injuries to Smith's dorsal or cervical spine. In fact, his notes from the date of the second accident April 29, 1999, specifically state "there have been no significant events since the last report." The notes then consistently refer to the treatment of L5 and S1 areas of the lumbar region. In a report from Dr. Lavorgna to Dr. Siegel dated April 11, 2000, Lavorgna ascribes a 7% permanent partial injury to Smith's lumbar spine attributable to the first accident and makes no other findings. Yet in a letter to Attorney Michael F. O'Connor dated May 6, 2004, Lavorgna states that Smith's cervical and dorsal ailments are attributable to the second accident on April 29, 1999. This is thoroughly inconsistent with his notes and his previous report to Dr. Siegel.

Several years thereafter, Smith sought treatment from Doctors Mangieri, an orthopedic surgeon, and Opalak, a neurosurgeon. This medical treatment was for continued significant neck pain and for knee pain that has received no permanency rating, but which appears to have some foundation in the medical record for attribution to the first accident. Despite the more significant disability ratings for Smith's lumbar and dorsal areas, Doctors Mangieri and Opalak have focused their efforts on a significant problem with Smith's cervical spine, which is considered significant enough to seriously consider surgical treatment.

The parties have submitted two issues for consideration to the court. The first issue is to determine the degree of fault between Cianelli and the "unknown driver" in the first accident. The second issue is for the court to determine the relative causes of Smith's injuries attributable to the first compared with the second accident.

III. Discussion

A. Cianelli Vis-à-Vis the "Unknown Driver"

The court will first address the degree of fault attributable to the "unknown driver" in the first accident that occurred on April 9, 1999. At the hearing in this matter, it was suggested that the court consider two legal principles; first, the assumption that others will obey the law, and second, the principle of sudden emergency.

As driver of an automobile in Connecticut, Ms. Cianelli was entitled to assume that other drivers would obey the law. Therefore, Cianelli had the right to assume that the "unknown driver" would obey all statutes governing the operation of motor vehicles in this state and that he would use the care that a reasonably prudent person would use in the same circumstances. Cianelli was allowed to make this assumption until she knew or in the exercise of reasonable care should have known that the assumption has become unwarranted. See *Turbert v. Mather Motors, Inc.,* 165 Conn. 422, 429, 334 A.2d 903 (1973). Based upon a preponderance of credible evidence, the "unknown driver" changed lanes suddenly and without sufficient warning. Therefore, the court finds that the "unknown driver" committed an act of statutory negligence, in violation of General Statutes §14-236(1), by moving from one lane to another on a multiple lane highway without ascertaining whether the lane change could be accomplished with reasonable safety.

Ms. Cianelli urges the court to consider the existence of a sudden emergency in the court's evaluation of whether she acted as a reasonable person under the circumstances. "The sudden emergency doctrine applies only in cases in which the operator is suddenly confronted by a situation not of his own making and has the opportunity of deciding rapidly between alternative courses of action." *Mei v. Alterman Transport Lines, Inc.,* 159 Conn. 307, 312, 268 A.2d 639 (1970). However, a person choosing a course of action in an emergency is nonetheless required to exercise the care of an ordinarily prudent person acting in such an emergency.

The court finds that Cianelli was, indeed, faced with an emergency situation. The court further finds, however, that she failed to exercise the care of an ordinary prudent person acting in such an emergency. There are two factors that the court takes into consideration in this regard. First, there was testimony from Cianelli that she panicked, applied the brakes and shut her eyes. Second, she also testified that her attention was focused on the dealer plate and the identity of the "unknown driver," instead of keeping a proper lookout. A driver is required to keep a reasonable lookout for any persons and traffic likely to encounter. She is chargeable with notice of dangers or conditions that she could become aware through a reasonable exercise of her faculties. *McDonald v. Connecticut Co.,* 151 Conn. 14, 17, 193 A.2d 490 (1963).

Had Cianelli been more focused on the location of Smith's car in advance of the sudden emergency, and had she kept her eyes open throughout the emergency situation, she would have had the opportunity to keep her vehicle in proper control. Nonetheless, the court finds the negligence of the "unknown driver" to be the primary and more significant cause of the accident. As Cianelli approached the right-rear side of his automobile, the "unknown driver" failed to keep a proper lookout for her vehicle, which set in motion the chain of events that caused the accident. The court therefore assigns liability as follows: seventy-five percent to the "unknown driver" and twenty-five percent to Cianelli.

B. The Cause of Smith's Injuries

As the parties acknowledge and the court also finds, the medical records are less than perfectly clear and consistent concerning the cause of Smith's injuries to his lumbar, dorsal and cervical spine. Dr. Siegel's opinions appear to be far more consistent than Dr. Lavorgna's opinions, and they also appear to relate to and be based upon more contemporaneous observations of Mr. Smith's conditions. Despite the inconsistencies in these reports, the court sees no reason to dramatically depart from Dr. Siegel's opinion that the lumbar and cervical injuries occurred as the result of the first accident on April 9, 1999. It is also relatively clear from the record that Smith's knee injury was due to the first accident as well.

The plaintiff cites the case of *Card v. State,* 57 Conn. App. 134, 747 A.2d 32 (2000) to support an apportionment of the vast majority of damages to the first accident. In *Card,* the Appellate Court approved the apportionment instructions of the trial court, wherein there were three different defendants, each of whom was involved in different automobile accidents with the same plaintiff within a relatively short period of time. In *Card,* the plaintiff was unable to differentiate the extent to which each accident caused her damages within reasonable medical certainty. The court therefore approved an instruction that allowed the jury to equally apportion damages among the three defendants.

In *Card,* the Appellate Court reasoned that "the trier of fact's responsibility in cases involving injuries sustained in successive accidents is to apportion the damages among the parties whose negligence caused the plaintiff's injuries. We hold that the trial court should instruct the jury that if it is unable to determine how much of the plaintiff's damages is attributable to each tortfeasor, the jury may make a rough apportionment. The absence of conclusive evidence concerning allocation of damages will not preclude apportionment by the jury, but will necessarily result in a less precise allocation than that afforded by a clearer record." (Internal quotation marks omitted.) Id., at 145, 747 A.2d 32.

Given the lack of clarity in the expert opinions of the medical professionals involved in the treatment of Smith, the court will apply the rule in *Card* to apportion some of his cervical injuries to the second accident. There is some indication, based upon Dr. Siegel's records, that Smith's injury to his cervical spine from the first accident was aggravated by the second accident as it became symptomatic, or more symptomatic after the accident that occurred on April 29, 1999.

IV. Conclusion

The injuries to Smith's dorsal spine related to the second accident were relatively minor compared with the long-lasting treatment of his lumbar spine and the continuing treatment of his cervical spine and knee. In fact, there was very little treatment for Smith's dorsal spine, if any at all. Therefore, the court apportions damages as follows: 90% attributable to the first accident and 10% to the second.

The court has previously concluded that the "unknown driver" was responsible for three-quarters of the first accident, compared with Cianelli's responsibility for one-quarter of Smith's injuries. Accordingly, in the case of *Smith v. Barboza,* the defendant is liable for $4,500.00 of the stipulated damages of $45,000.00 for both cases. In the case of *Smith v. Cianelli,* the defendant is liable for damages in the amount of $10,125.00 of the remaining $40,500.00. The "unknown driver" is responsible for the remaining $30,375.00 in damages.

Questions about the case:

1. How was the plaintiff involved in two separate accidents?
2. Why did the court find that Cianelli was 25 percent liable for the plaintiff's injuries?
3. What role did the "unknown driver" play in the first accident?
4. How does the court resolve the issues concerning the confusing medical notes and treatment received by the plaintiff?

Chapter Summary

Contributory negligence is a defense to negligence actions in only a handful of jurisdictions, yet this principle remains an important doctrine in tort law. Under contributory negligence, a plaintiff who is partially at fault is barred from any recovery. This rather drastic finding was originally justified under the theory that the plaintiff's own negligence affected the proximate cause analysis. However, over time several important exceptions developed to contributory negligence to help soften its application. Among these exceptions, the doctrine of last clear chance has proven to be the most widely used, and the most controversial. Under last clear chance, a negligent plaintiff will not be barred from recovery when the defendant had the last opportunity of avoiding the accident and failed to do so. Other exceptions to the contributory negligence defense include the sudden emergency doctrine and the rescuer doctrine.

A growing dissatisfaction with contributory negligence encouraged many jurisdictions to adopt a new system: comparative negligence. Under comparative negligence, a plaintiff's negligence will not bar his recovery but will simply reduce the amount of his award. Over time, at least three different approaches to comparative negligence have developed. Under pure comparative negligence, a plaintiff's negligence is compared to the defendant's, no matter how negligent the plaintiff's actions were. A plaintiff who is 99 percent at fault can still recover from a defendant who is 1 percent at fault. However, his award will be reduced by the amount of his negligence. Modified comparative negligence is the system adopted by most jurisdictions. There are two approaches to modified comparative negligence. Under one plan, a plaintiff can recover when he is up to 50 percent at fault. If at greater than 50 percent at fault, he cannot recover. Under the other plan, the plaintiff's negligence must always be less than the defendant's. The third approach to comparative negligence is the "slight-gross" model, in which the plaintiff can recover only when his negligence is slight in comparison with that of the defendant.

Comparative negligence is the predominant form of defense to negligence actions, having been adopted in one form or another in all but a few states.

 SKILLS YOU NEED IN THE REAL WORLD

Preparing a Trial Notebook

A trial notebook is a handy reference guide that is filled with all the legal topics and questions that an attorney will need at trial. We use the term *notebook* broadly here. Some attorneys use a system of file folders containing all the information that they will need for trial, while others actually use a three-ring binder. The benefit of a binder is that the pages can be securely fastened inside the cover, while folders have a tendency to disappear, usually at the most inopportune moment. Trial notebooks are used by attorneys to help them stay organized during the course of a trial. A good trial notebook should contain the following:

- Voir dire questions
- Motions in limine
- Trial briefs
- Notes for opening statements
- Witness list
- Direct or cross-examination points to be raised with specific witnesses
- Evidence to be admitted during the direct examination of specific witnesses
- Any foundation questions required for specific evidence
- Evidence list
- Exhibit list
- Foundation questions for specific types of evidence
- Relevant pleadings, including the complaint, answer, counterclaim, and cross-claim
- Witness deposition excerpts and summaries

■ Medical summaries and crucial medical records

■ Relevant case law, usually about issues that the attorney anticipates will arise during trial

Many attorneys have a standard format for a trial notebook. This format may be unique to the particular attorney, so you should learn his or her system.

It is usually helpful to have all the items contained in a single notebook. Large documents, such as lengthy depositions, can be held in separate files. The crucial points of a deposition transcript can be copied off as single pages and placed under the heading for that witness.

Paralegal Trial Notebook

In addition to the attorney's notebook, a paralegal should have a trial notebook. What types of information should you have in your trial notebook? If you are attending the trial with the attorney, your focus will be slightly different from the attorney's. You are there to support the attorney and to anticipate problems. Trying a case is a stressful event, and it often brings out the worst (and sometimes the best) in an attorney. Anything that you can do to eliminate complications helps alleviate that stress (and makes you that much more valuable to the attorney).

A paralegal trial notebook is built on the premise of avoiding problems at trial or being able to handle them as expeditiously as possible. Your notebook should contain the following:

■ Basic information about the case: case file number; important filing dates; copies of the complaint and answer (unmarked), as well as your own highlighted copy of both documents

■ Evidence checklist, cross-referenced by witness and foundation questions

■ Jury charts, juror questions, and a section listing improper questions that may be asked by the opposing counsel with the cases that clearly state such questions are improper

■ Order of witnesses who will testify, and the evidence that should be admitted during each witness's testimony

■ Contact information: witness telephone and cell phone numbers (for those occasions when you must contact that witness immediately)

■ Telephone and cell phone numbers and e-mail addresses of the following:

1 Opposing counsel

2 Opposing counsel's paralegal/legal assistant/legal secretary (they usually know how to get in contact with the attorney better than anyone else)

3 Name of the judge's secretary, law clerk, and other staff and their direct dial numbers (sometimes it is easier to contact these people with a cell phone call in the courthouse hallway than to try to talk to them personally)

4 Client's work, home, cell, and any other telephone number where he or she can be reached, including e-mail address and contact numbers for friends and relatives (you never know whom you may have to speak with to track down a missing client)

- Home telephone numbers of all trial team members, including attorneys, paralegals, runners, and anyone else who might be useful
- Names, addresses, and telephone numbers for special witnesses, such as expert witnesses, investigators, and so on
- Names and contact information for any support personnel, such as FedEx, UPS, court reporters, computer technicians, network administrator, and even the attorney's laptop manufacturer (remember Murphy's Law: Anything that can go wrong will go wrong, and at the worst possible moment)
- Complete list of all equipment needed for the trial, as well as a checklist showing that each piece of equipment has been tested and confirmed working; backup lightbulbs for projectors; dark-colored duct tape (for emergency patches and to hold down pesky wires and electrical cords)
- Diagram of the courthouse, showing the location of bathrooms, vending machines, and water fountains (and designated smoking areas for clients who smoke)

A paralegal notebook with all this information will make trial work a much smoother and less stressful experience.

 ## THE LIFE OF A PARALEGAL

Working with Insurance Adjusters

We do a lot of plaintiff work, and that means working with insurance adjusters. Adjusters are odd creatures. We have them from all ends of the spectrum. Some of them are very nice and pleasant people, but others will go out of their way to make your life miserable — and they can really succeed in doing that. Overall, I think we have a good rapport with most of the ones that we deal with. Some insurance companies are just harder to deal with. I don't know if they've been trained to be that way or not, but there are some companies that, when you get the case, you just know that you are going to have a harder time because it's X Insurance Company. You can prove that their insured was at fault a hundred times over, and they still don't want to pay. We settle most of our cases, just like everybody else, but there are some companies that force you to go to the limit before they will settle.

We will contact the adjuster pretty early on in the case. Usually, by the time the client comes to us, they have already had contact with the adjuster themselves. The first thing that we do is send the adjuster a letter of representation telling them that we represent the client now and that the adjuster should deal with our firm from now on. The attorney will also tell the client not to speak with the adjuster anymore. We communicate with adjusters through faxes, phone, mail, you name it. What's interesting is that I've never actually met a single adjuster in person.

Elizabeth Adams, Paralegal

ETHICAL ISSUES FOR THE PARALEGAL: PARALEGALS WHO CAN APPEAR IN COURT

As we have seen in previous chapters, a paralegal must avoid the unauthorized practice of law. This not only includes avoiding giving legal advice but also appearing in court to represent a client. However, it is important to note that a paralegal can appear in court to represent clients in some hearings. For instance, there are proceedings involving Social Security benefits and other administrative hearings in which a paralegal can represent another person. A paralegal may accompany the attorney to court and may often act as an indispensable assistant to the attorney, but the paralegal is not allowed to conduct direct or cross-examination during the trial, or to perform any of the other duties normally associated with attorneys.

Relevant Cases

OUELLETTE V. CARDE
612 A.2D 687 (1992)

Opinion
MURRAY, Justice.

This civil action in negligence is before the court on the defendants' appeal from a judgment entered in favor of the plaintiff. We affirm.

On March 18, 1986, defendant Orin V. Carde attempted to change the muffler and tailpipe of his 1979 Mercury Cougar. The defendant parked his car in the closed garage connected to his home and elevated the back of the car with a hydraulic jack. He placed two stanchion jacks underneath the rear axle and removed the hydraulic jack so that the car's rear axle rested on the stanchion jacks. He blocked the front wheels of the car and unloosened the bolts connecting the tailpipe and muffler to the chassis. He was unable to remove the tailpipe, however, because the car chassis pressed too closely to the rear axle resting on the stanchion jacks to allow him to pull it free. To provide an adequate opening defendant placed a bumper jack underneath the right rear bumper and jacked the car up so that the right side of the rear axle was no longer resting on a stanchion jack. This

position tilted the car at a precarious angle but created a space through which the tailpipe could pass.

The defendant again tried to remove the tailpipe, but it was rusted to the exhaust pipe and would not slide off. He began pulling on the muffler and exerted such pressure in attempting to wiggle it free that the right side of the car fell off the bumper jack onto the stanchion jack and trapped defendant underneath the car. Because of the angle at which the car fell, the gas tank landed on the right stanchion jack puncturing the tank and releasing approximately ten gallons of gas onto the garage floor. The defendant remained trapped under the car in a semiconscious state for an unknown period. He eventually recovered and worked himself free, and called the plaintiff, Beverly Ouellette, from the garage telephone. In the middle of the conversation he passed out, and plaintiff, a long-time friend and neighbor, immediately drove to defendant's house. She entered the front door of the home and made her way to the garage through the laundry room. She nearly slipped in a puddle of gasoline on the garage floor as she entered the garage and found defendant lying on the ground beneath the dangling phone. She attempted to call a rescue squad but was unable to get a dial tone, and defendant became agitated. He told plaintiff that they should leave through the garage door and directed her to press the electric door opener. When the door was one-half to three-quarters open, the gas ignited in an explosion. Both plaintiff and defendant escaped but were severely burned. The plaintiff was taken directly to the emergency room where she was treated for third-degree burns to her left ankle and to both feet. She was released later that day but was readmitted one week later. She stayed in the hospital for fifteen days during which time she had a series of operations and a skin graft. She was subsequently released and entered a home-care program through which a nurse would visit and change her bandages three times a day. In addition to the physical injuries, plaintiff experienced extreme anxiety and panic attacks. She received treatment for anxiety over a three-year period and was still taking medication at the time of the trial.

The plaintiff filed a civil action in negligence in Kent County Superior Court on February 25, 1987. The complaint requested money damages for personal injuries sustained in the fire at defendant's home on March 18, 1986. A five-day jury trial commenced on March 27, 1990, during which defendant filed two motions for directed verdict. The trial justice denied the first motion and reserved decision on the second motion filed at the end of the presentation of evidence. The case was submitted to the jury on April 2, 1990, and the following day the jury returned a verdict in favor of plaintiff for $85,000 plus interest and costs. The court thereafter reconsidered and denied defendant's second motion for directed verdict. The defendant subsequently filed a motion for a new trial, which was also denied. On appeal defendant raises six issues. We address each issue separately.

I

The defendant's first claim is that the trial justice erred in prohibiting the defendant from arguing comparative negligence to the jury and in instructing the jury on the rescue doctrine. The defendant argues that Rhode Island's comparative-negligence statute incorporates the public-policy principles of the rescue doctrine and that the jury should have been instructed to apply standards of comparative negligence to plaintiff's case. The plaintiff responds that the rescue doctrine survives the adoption of comparative negligence because comparative negligence inadequately promotes the public policy of encouraging a person under no duty to rescue to save the life of a human being in peril.

The rescue doctrine is a rule of law holding that one who sees a person in imminent danger caused by the negligence of another cannot be charged with contributory negligence in a non-reckless attempt to rescue the imperiled person. The doctrine was developed to encourage rescue and to correct the harsh inequity of barring relief under principles of contributory negligence to a person who is injured in a rescue attempt which the injured person was under no duty to undertake. In practice the doctrine may be used either to establish a plaintiff's claim that the defendant was guilty of actionable negligence in creating the peril which induced the rescue attempt or to eliminate the defenses of contributory negligence and assumption of risk. The instant case, however, raises the question of whether Rhode Island's adoption of the comparative-negligence doctrine, G.L.1956 (1985 Reenactment) §9-20-4, requires that rescue-doctrine cases be adjudicated under standards of comparative negligence.

Comparative fault removes the harsh consequences of contributory negligence because a rescuer is not barred completely from recovery for negligently performing a rescue. Under a comparative-negligence standard the trier of fact apportions fault among responsible parties, and the negligent rescuer is entitled to recover only that percentage of total damages for which the party creating the peril is responsible. The comparative-negligence doctrine, therefore, arguably incorporates this policy consideration of the rescue doctrine, but there is a split in authority whether the doctrine of comparative negligence fully addresses the other policy considerations of the rescue doctrine. Most courts addressing this issue focus on the fact that comparative negligence removes the harsh consequences of contributory negligence and have ruled that a plaintiff who is negligent in performing a rescue should recover only a pro rata share of the damages sustained attributable to the defendant.

We are of the opinion, however, that the comparative-negligence doctrine does not fully protect the rescue doctrine's underlying policy of promoting rescue. No common-law duties changed as a result of the enactment of Rhode Island's comparative-negligence statute, and there is nothing other than an individual's moral conscience to induce a person under no legal duty to undertake a rescue attempt. The law places a premium on human life, and one who voluntarily attempts to save a life of another should not be barred from complete recovery. Only if a person is rash or reckless in the rescue attempt should recovery be limited; accordingly we hold that the rescue doctrine survives the adoption of the comparative-negligence statute and that principles of comparative negligence apply only if a defendant establishes that the rescuer's actions were rash or reckless. In adopting this reasoning we recognize that the oft quoted words of Justice Cardozo apply now as they did in 1921:

> Danger invites rescue. The cry of distress is the summons to relief. The law does not ignore these reactions of the mind in tracing conduct to its consequences. It recognizes them as normal. The risk of rescue, if only it be not wanton, is born of the occasion. The emergency begets the man. The wrongdoer may not have foreseen the coming of a deliverer. He is accountable as if he had.

Wagner v. International Railway, Co., 232 N.Y. 176, 180, 133 N.E. 437, 437-38 (1921).

In the instant case, defendant was not entitled to a jury instruction on comparative negligence unless plaintiff's rescue was rash or reckless. Because defendant did not assert that plaintiff acted recklessly, the trial justice did not err in denying defendant's requested jury instruction on comparative negligence.

II

The defendant next asserts that the trial justice erred in charging the jury with only "but for" causation. The defendant claims that because the trial justice failed to give an instruction on foreseeability, the issue of proximate cause and foreseeability was never properly submitted to the jury. As error defendant argues that a foreseeability instruction in accordance with *Palsgraff v. Long Island Railroad*, 248 N.Y. 339, 162 N.E. 99 (1928), as adopted by this court in *Radigan v. W.J. Halloran*, 97 R.I. 122, 128, 196 A.2d 160, 163 (1963), should have been charged to the jury. The plaintiff responds that the trial justice did instruct the jury on foreseeability.

Absent a showing otherwise, this court assumes that the jury followed and understood the instructions of the trial justice. Moreover, when a jury requests reinstruction on a specific charge, the jury is presumed to understand all other charges for which it did not request reinstruction.

Applying these principles to the instant case, we find that the trial justice did not err. The trial justice's initial instructions adequately explained foreseeability. Specifically the trial justice stated:

> There has been discussion during the course of arguments with you with respect to something called foreseeability. Foreseeability relates to the natural and probable consequences of an act. To be held liable the defendant need only reasonably foresee that an injury or some type of injury

may result from a dangerous condition on the premises. The particular kind of injury need not have been foreseen. Although a defendant is not, of course, expected to foresee the unforeseeable, he is charged with a duty to foresee that which a prudent person in like circumstances would have reasonably foreseen. The mere fact that an accident happened standing alone, ordinarily does not permit the jury to draw the inference that the accident was caused by the defendant's negligence. The plaintiff has the burden to demonstrate by a preponderance of the evidence that the defendant was negligent, and that such negligence was a proximate cause of the event in question.

After the jury retired to deliberate, the jury foreman requested reinstruction from the court on proximate cause and on the rescue doctrine. The court repeated these two charges only, and defendant claims error on the basis of the court's failure to reinstruct the jury with respect to foreseeability.

The claim is without merit. The jury did not request a reinstruction on foreseeability; therefore, the jury is presumed to have understood the initial foreseeability instruction and defendant was not entitled to have it repeated.

III

The defendant's third claim is that the trial justice erred in admitting certain medical bills into evidence. The defendant claims that the affidavits used to enter medical bills from Kent County Memorial Hospital and from Dr. Klaus Haas failed to comply with G.L.1956 (1985 Reenactment) §9-19-27 and that plaintiff was therefore precluded from entering the documents into evidence. The plaintiff contends that the bills were properly admitted under Rule 803(6) of the Rhode Island Rules of Evidence.

At trial plaintiff attempted to introduce medical records and bills from plaintiff's treatment for burns sustained in the accident. The plaintiff first attempted to introduce the records under §9-19-27, but the supporting affidavits prepared by Dr. Haas did not comply

with the statute and Dr. Haas was unavailable to testify. The trial justice excluded the documents, and in the alternative, plaintiff requested that the bills and records be admitted under Rule 803(6), the business-records exception to hearsay. The trial justice initially denied this request and ruled to exclude all medical affidavits. The following day, however, the trial justice reversed his decision in part and admitted the bills, but not the medical records, under Rule 803(6). The defendant objected, asserting that the bills failed to comply with §9-19-27 and this court's decisions in *Parrillo v. F.W. Woolworth Co.*, 518 A.2d 354 (R.I.1986). The defendant argued that §9-19-27 controls the admissibility of medical affidavits and that the bills as medical affidavits could not be entered under any other evidentiary rule. The defendant further argued that the bills were inadmissible because there was no testimony or supporting affidavit offered to establish a causal relationship between defendant's act and plaintiff's injury.

A review of the record shows that the trial justice correctly refused to admit Dr. Haas's medical records and bills under §9-19-27 because the supporting affidavits did not satisfy the statute's requirements. The trial justice did, however, correctly admit the medical bills, but not the records, into evidence under Rule 803(6). The plaintiff satisfied the foundation requirements of Rule 803(6) and properly authenticated the documents through testimony of the custodian of records for Kent County Hospital. The bills were thereafter admitted to show only the measure of damages sustained by plaintiff, and plaintiff was not allowed to use the bills to show the proximate cause between the fire and her injury. This admission of the bills under Rule 803(6) did not circumvent the requirement of §9-19-27, as explained in Parrillo, that medical affidavits purporting to establish proximate cause be supported by properly documented affidavits or by direct testimony of the physician rendering the opinion.

Accordingly the trial justice did not err in admitting the bills under Rule 803(6) as evidence of the measure of damages claimed by plaintiff.

IV

The defendant's final claim is that the trial justice erred in refusing to direct a verdict for

defendant and in refusing to grant defendant's motion for a new trial. In support of this claim defendant asserts that plaintiff's injury was not foreseeable and that defendant was therefore not negligent as a matter of law. The plaintiff responds that this is a classic "rescue doctrine" case and that plaintiff's rescue attempt was a foreseeable consequence of defendant's negligence in creating a dangerous situation.

The rescue doctrine assigns the party who negligently creates a dangerous situation with responsibility for any rescuer injured in a reasonable rescue attempt. The party creating the danger is by law charged with foreseeing all nonreckless rescue attempts; therefore, the trial justice did not err in denying the defendant's motions for directed verdict and the defendant's motion for new trial.

HUNTOON V. TCI CABLEVISION OF COLORADO, INC.
969 P.2D 681 (1998)

JUSTICE MARTINEZ delivered the Opinion of the Court.

In this personal injury action brought by Sharon Huntoon against TCI Cablevision of Colorado, Inc. ("TCI") for injuries sustained in a rear-end automobile collision, we discuss the appropriate standards to resolve a motion for directed verdict and to admit specialized neuropsychologist testimony. The court of appeals reversed a directed verdict for Huntoon on issues of liability because it found some evidence of comparative negligence. The court of appeals also found that the admission of neuropsychologist testimony regarding the cause of Huntoon's organic brain injury was erroneous, and ordered that similar testimony be prohibited at a new trial.

In our view, the trial court properly directed a verdict on liability. Considering the evidentiary context, we find that the inference the court of appeals would have the jury indulge is not supported by the record. In addition, the court of appeals' opinion might be read to unjustifiably subject neuropsychologists to a level of scrutiny different than that applied to all other experts under CRE

702. Colorado law supports no such distinction. We therefore reverse the decision of the court of appeals.

I.

On October 15, 1992, Sharon Huntoon was stopped on University Avenue in Boulder when a truck owned by TCI and driven by a TCI employee struck her 1982 Subaru from behind. The impact caused Huntoon's Subaru to be pushed forward, where it came into contact with a Cadillac Seville driven by Diana Kahn, who had apparently stopped to wait for a car in front of her that was impeding the flow of traffic. While Kahn stated that the car before her was slowly pulling into a diagonal parking place to the right, the TCI employee testified that he remembered seeing reverse lights and believed the car was backing out. Huntoon testified that she did not remember whether the car in front of Kahn was pulling in or out.

Huntoon did testify, however, that she was aware of activity taking place in the roadway and stopped her Subaru when she saw Kahn's Cadillac Seville stop in front of her. Huntoon originally thought it could have been as long as a minute from the moment she stopped until the TCI truck struck her vehicle. However, she conceded she may have been mistaken in light of Kahn's testimony that only five to ten seconds elapsed before the impact.

The TCI driver gave testimony to the effect that he first noticed the back-up lights of the car in front of Kahn, followed by both Kahn and Huntoon's brake lights. He explained that he saw the rear of Huntoon's Subaru "hunch up" and forcefully applied his brakes, but was unable to stop in time to avert a collision. The TCI employee testified that he was partly at fault because he failed to avoid the accident, and that Kahn was also at fault for stopping suddenly. He acknowledged that there was nothing Huntoon could have done to avoid being hit.

Police officers investigating the accident found some thirteen feet of skid marks attributable to the TCI vehicle. No marks were left by either the Huntoon or Kahn automobiles. Testimony indicated TCI's internal investigation found its driver to have been at fault, and this employee was placed on probation at work as a result. Witnesses also confirmed that TCI paid for the damage to both the Huntoon and Kahn vehicles.

Although Huntoon told an investigating officer that she was experiencing pain, she initially refused medical assistance. However, she continued to experience physical discomfort and subsequently began having difficulties with short-term memory and other cognitive abilities. Huntoon was eventually diagnosed with cognitive dysfunction, including difficulties with completion of tasks, attention to detail, and interaction with others.

Dennis McCarthy, Ph.D., a neuropsychologist involved in Huntoon's post-accident treatment regimen, was one of several professionals called to testify during her case in chief. He explained that neuropsychologists perform the "study of brain behavior relationships and

use a battery of psychological and neuropsychological tests that are standardized in order to elicit observations of relevancy of various aspects of the brain in terms of cognitive and intellectual function." Dr. McCarthy also related his educational history, which consisted of three degrees in psychology, a master's and doctoral degree, and post-doctoral training — including coursework and understudy — in the field of neuropsychology.

Dr. McCarthy stated that he gave Huntoon an extensive series of neuropsychological tests and analyzed the results. The eight to ten hour assessment included an extensive clinical interview designed to provide a detailed life history.

When Dr. McCarthy was asked for his opinion on the relation between Huntoon's injuries and the accident, TCI objected, arguing:

> This witness has not been qualified as a medical doctor and to the extent that counsel is asking him to render an opinion as to brain injury, which is a physical manifestation, which is a result of neuropsychological testing, so we would object.

The trial court initially sustained the objection on the basis of insufficient foundation. Huntoon's counsel then asked a series of questions which allowed Dr. McCarthy to relate the extent to which test results allow neuropsychologists to diagnose and treat organic brain injury. He was again asked to discuss his findings with regard to the brain injuries Huntoon suffered from the October 15 accident. TCI renewed its objection, insisting "this expert is not qualified to testify as to the causation of brain injury as opposed to, for example, cognitive impairment as related to neuropsychological testing." The trial court overruled the objection, and Dr. McCarthy was allowed to answer. He testified that there was injury to the brain and he identified several areas of the brain where there was continuing impairment.

At the close of the evidence, the trial court directed a verdict in favor of Huntoon on the issue of liability, finding the TCI employee negligent, and the evidence introduced at trial insufficient to establish negligence on the part of Huntoon or Kahn. The jury awarded damages.

The court of appeals reversed. It found that the trial court erred by directing the verdict on liability because the evidence, viewed in the light most favorable to TCI, was such that "a jury could find that a portion of fault lay with Huntoon." It therefore remanded the case for a new trial.

The court of appeals also addressed TCI's assertion that Dr. McCarthy, the neuropsychologist, should not have been allowed to testify as to the causation of Huntoon's organic brain injury. Finding the "clear import" of the testimony to touch upon the issue of causation, the court stated, "no authority in Colorado allows a neuropsychologist to testify to the physical cause of organic brain injury."

Because we agree with the trial court that the evidence was insufficient to submit a theory of comparative negligence to the jury, and because we find no abuse of discretion in the admission of neuropsychologist testimony on issues of causation, we now reverse the judgment of the court of appeals.

II.

Huntoon argues that the court of appeals applied the wrong standard in its analysis of the directed verdict in this case, and that the evidence before the trial court was simply insufficient to support an inference of comparative negligence. TCI contends that the court of appeals employed an appropriate standard, and that the record contains facts sufficient to allow a jury to entertain a theory of comparative negligence. We are of the view that the court of appeals should have let the directed verdict stand.

Colorado's comparative negligence statute, see §13–21–111, 5 C.R.S (1998), requires a jury to apportion the relative percentages of fault attributable to the plaintiff and the defendant in cases where there is evidence the plaintiff was responsible, in some part, for the injuries sustained. However, where there is no evidence in the record that could support a finding of negligence on the part of the plaintiff, it is reversible error to submit the question of comparative negligence to the jury.

In a rear-end collision, the driver who overtakes and collides with a car stopped ahead on the roadway is presumed negligent. This presumption may be rebutted by evidence tending to show that the negligence of the driver in front caused the damages.

Where the theory of comparative negligence is that the driver in front stopped suddenly, the law also requires evidence that the stop was unwarranted. As such, it is not enough to merely show that the stop in question may have been sudden.

A sudden stop may be unwarranted if the evidence suggests it was made without reason, or in an unexpected and uncalled-for location. Thus, even if the evidence before the trial court in the instant case supported an inference Huntoon stopped suddenly, TCI's theory of comparative negligence could not go to the jury unless the evidence would also allow a jury to rationally and legitimately conclude the stop was unwarranted.

The court of appeals found an inference of comparative negligence based on (1) testimony that the rear of Huntoon's Subaru "hunched up"; (2) the inconsistency between Huntoon and Kahn's testimony as to the length of time that had elapsed before the impact from the TCI vehicle; and (3) testimony by Huntoon to the effect that she was "not really paying attention." Huntoon insists these points cannot establish comparative negligence in the context of the presumption fashioned by the law governing rear-end collisions. We agree.

While testimony by the TCI driver that the Huntoon automobile appeared to "hunch up" supports an inference the stop was in some part sudden, it does not address whether the stop was unwarranted under the circumstances. As noted, evidence that a stop was sudden, standing alone, will not justify sending the issue of comparative negligence to the jury.

We also find that reliance upon the different intervals stated by Kahn and Huntoon with respect to the time between their stops and the impact by the TCI vehicle is misplaced. Directed verdict analysis presumes that the jury would disregard all testimony contrary to the position advocated by TCI. But Kahn's testimony that only five to ten seconds elapsed from the time she stopped until the TCI truck pushed Huntoon's Subaru into her vehicle is not evidence from which one can conclude that Huntoon's stop was unwarranted.

Finally, we disagree with the court of appeals' characterization of the record when it states "plaintiff Huntoon testified she was 'not really paying attention' to the activity on the street at the time of the accident." Apparently, the court of appeals is referring to the following exchange:

Q: Do you know why Ms. Kahn came to a stop?

A: I remember she was stopping because there was some activity because I wasn't paying attention because it was a normal day. So I wasn't thinking I would have to remember what was going on, so I stopped because something was happening in front of — someone was going in or out, but I don't remember which way.

For the purposes of directed verdict analysis, we do not consider Huntoon's further testimony that she saw "activity" in front of Kahn, knew it had something to do with a vehicle pulling in or out of a parking space, and brought her own vehicle to a gradual stop. We also ignore the testimony of the TCI employee admitting he was at least partially at fault, and his concession that Huntoon could have done nothing to avoid the accident, as such admissions do not conclusively eliminate the possibility of negligence on the part of the preceding driver.

Even when viewing the evidence in this light, we are persuaded the trial court was correct when it ruled that the testimony could support only a legitimate inference that Huntoon was not paying attention to whether the driver in front of Kahn was pulling in or out of the parking space in question. Although a driver ignoring the roadway while preoccupied by some other distraction and stopping suddenly at the last possible moment might be comparatively negligent, the record does not support such a finding here. If the testimony could potentially lead to that conclusion, the issue would have to be submitted to the jury for a determination of whether the stop was unwarranted given those circumstances. In this case, however, Huntoon's testimony failed to raise the inference that she was inattentive as to anything beyond whether the vehicle in front of Kahn was pulling in or out.

It was not necessary to submit a theory of comparative negligence to the jury based on the points highlighted by the court of appeals. In our view, the evidence viewed in the light most favorable to TCI supports an inference that Huntoon's stop might have been sudden, but not that it was unwarranted. Accordingly, we conclude the trial court did not err by directing a verdict for Huntoon on issues of liability.

III.

We hold that the trial court properly directed a verdict on the issue of liability in this case. We also hold that the trial court did not abuse its discretion by admitting the testimony of the neuropsychologist. Accordingly, we reverse the judgment of the court of appeals and remand this case with directions to reinstate the trial court's judgment and the jury's award of damages.

Websites

■ **Contributory Negligence – Defined**
http://dictionary.law.com/Default.aspx?selected=341

■ **Washington Law School**
http://www.washlaw.edu/subject/torts.html

■ **Wikipedia — Contributory Negligence**
http://en.wikipedia.org/wiki/Contributory__negligence

■ **'Lectric Law Library — Comparative Negligence**
http://www.lectlaw.com/def/c076.htm

Forms and Court Documents

Following is an excerpt from the defendant's answer in a contributory negligence jurisdiction:

STATE OF PLACID	IN THE SUPERIOR COURT
COUNTY OF BARNES	FILE NUMBER: _____
JOHN SMITH,)	ANSWER
Plaintiff)	
)	
vs.)	
)	
JANE DOE,)	
Defendant)	

Defendant denies the allegations contained in paragraph 3 of the plaintiff's complaint and further alleges that the sole and proximate cause of the collision between the defendant's automobile and the plaintiff's automobile was the negligence of the plaintiff in:

■ failing to maintain a proper lookout;
■ failing to stop at a posted stop sign as required by statute; and
■ driving at excessive speeds.

WHEREFORE, defendant, having fully answered the complaint of the plaintiff, prays as follows:
1. That this action be dismissed as to this Defendant;
2. That Plaintiff have and recover nothing of this Defendant;
3. That there be a trial by jury;

4. That the Defendant recover his costs, including reasonable attorney's fees, as provided by law; and

5. That this Defendant have and recover such other and further relief as this Court may deem appropriate.

Respectfully submitted, this the _____ day of _____, 20 _____.

_____

Clarence D. Arrow

Attorney for the Defendant

Answer excerpt in a state that follows a modified comparative negligence model:

		IN THE SUPERIOR COURT
		FILE NUMBER: _____
JANE SMITH,	)	ANSWER
Plaintiff	)	
	)	
vs.	)	
	)	
JOHN DOE,	)	
MARTHA DOE	)	
Defendants		

Defendants deny the allegations contained in paragraph 3 of the plaintiff's complaint and further allege that the sole and proximate cause of the collision between the defendants' automobile and the plaintiff's automobile was the negligence of the plaintiff in:

- failing to maintain a proper lookout;
- failing to stop at a posted stop sign as required by statute; and
- driving at excessive speeds.

As a result of the above negligence, plaintiff's negligence equaled or exceeded that of the defendants, and consequently the plaintiff should take nothing by his complaint.

WHEREFORE, Defendants, having fully answered the Complaint of the Plaintiff, pray as follows:

1. That this action be dismissed as to these Defendants;

2. That Plaintiff have and recover nothing of these Defendants;

3. That there be a trial by jury;

4. That the Defendants recover their costs, including reasonable attorney's fees, as provided by law; and

5. That these Defendants have and recover such other and further relief as this Court may deem appropriate.

Respectfully submitted, this the _____ day of _____, 20_____.

_____

Clarence D. Arrow
Attorney for the Defendants

Key Terms

Comparative negligence
Contributory negligence

Last clear chance
Sudden emergency

Review Questions

1   Most of the states that have adopted "pure" comparative negligence did it through judicial action; most of the states that enacted comparative negligence through legislation opted for a more limited form of comparative negligence. What is the reason for this discrepancy?

2   Why would such a harsh concept as contributory negligence be developed in the first place?

3   It is said that comparative negligence developed as a reaction to contributory negligence. In what way?

4   Is comparative negligence an improvement over contributory negligence? If so, how?

5   In recent years, there have been claims of runaway juries and huge awards in personal injury cases brought to plaintiffs with purportedly marginal cases. Does this situation call for the reinstitution of contributory negligence? Why or why not?

6   What are the three elements of a contributory negligence claim that a defendant must prove?

7   Explain the last clear chance doctrine. When does it apply? When is this defense not available in a negligence action?

8   What is a "sudden emergency," and what effect does it have on a contributory negligence case?

9   Why is contributory negligence not a defense to intentional torts?

10   Explain the difference between the various types of comparative negligence.

11   How is "pure" comparative negligence different from "modified" comparative negligence?

12   Some commentators have suggested that comparative negligence is inconsistent with traditional proximate cause analysis. Draft an argument in support of this view.

Applying What You Have Learned

1   Joe is driving his motorcycle in a state in which helmet use is required by statute. Joe is not wearing his helmet because it flattens his hair and he thinks he looks sexy without it. As Joe is driving down the highway, a car driven by Amanda pulls out directly in front of Joe. Joe runs into Amanda's car and receives severe head injuries. Joe sues Amanda in a state that follows the "Georgia" plan on comparative negligence. You are on the jury in Joe's case. What is your verdict?

2   If Mr. Chumley's case is filed in a state that still follows contributory negligence, is he likely to lose? Why or why not?

3   John buys a ticket for a Ferris wheel ride at a traveling carnival. The back of the ticket has language that states, "Ferris wheels are a dangerous form of entertainment. The purchaser assumes all risks in the operation and function of the Ferris wheel and waives any claims against the Carnival Company for any negligence that might occur in the operation of said Ferris wheel or for any damages or injuries he may receive as a result of this ride." While John is sitting in one of the seats, the operator wanders away from his post and doesn't see that several bolts attaching the seat to the wheel have come loose. John's seat falls and he is injured. Can he sue the carnival company? If your answer is yes, what defenses are available to the carnival company? Does your answer change if the entire incident occurred in a contributory negligence state?

4   It's the annual office picnic, and Steve has arrived late. He is supposed to be running one of the large grills. He rushes to the grill and spills in an immense amount of lighter fluid, thinking that it will get the grill hot in a short period of time. He doesn't realize that the can of lighter fluid has several leaks and when he lights the grill, fire shoots from the grill and catches Steve's clothing on fire, causing severe burns. Draft a complaint based on these facts and then an answer using contributory negligence as a defense. What key points must you raise in your answer?

5   John was injured in a crash with another car driven by Martha. At the end of the trial, the jury determines that John and Martha are both 50 percent at fault in the accident. This states follows the "New Hampshire" rule. What is the result in this case?

6   Using the same facts as the previous question, evaluate the case under the "Georgia" rule. Is the result in the case different? If so, how?

Endnotes

[1] *Maki v. Frelk,* 85 Ill. App. 2d 439, 229 N.E.2d 284 (1967).
[2] Turk, Comparative Negligence on the March, 28 Chi.-Kent L. Rev. 189 (1950).
[3] The Law of Torts §22.1; Prosser, Torts (4th ed.).
[4] *Sun Oil Co. v. Seamon,* 349 Mich. 387, 84 N.W.2d 840 (1957).
[5] Restatement (Second) of Torts §463.

[6] *O'Connor v. G.R. Packing Co.,* 74 App. Div. 2d 37, 426 N.Y.S.2d 557, *aff'd,* 53 N.Y.2d 278, 440 N.Y.S.2d 920, 423 N.E.2d 397 (1980).

[7] Restatement (Second) of Torts §468, comment c.

[8] Using Comparative Fault to Replace the All-or-Nothing Lottery Imposed Intentional Torts, 46 Vand. L. Rev. 121 (1993).

[9] *Hoelter v. Mohawk Service, Inc.,* 170 Conn. 495, 365 A.2d 1064 (1975).

[10] *Commercial Union Assur. Cos. v. Western Farm Bureau Ins. Cos.,* 93 N.M. 507, 601 P.2d 1203 (1979) (*Scott v. Rizzo,* 96 N.M. 682, 634 P.2d 1234 [1981]).

[11] *Smith v. Fiber Controls Corp.,* 300 N.C. 669, 673, 268 S.E.2d 504, 507 (1980).

[12] Restatement (Second) of Torts §918 (1); *Bailey v. J. L. Roebuck Co.,* 135 Okla. 216, 275 P. 329 (1929).

[13] *Benton v. Hillcrest Foods, Inc.,* 524 S.E.2d 53 (1999).

[14] *Willis v. Stauffer Chemical Co.,* 348 So. 2d 158, *on reh'g,* 349 So. 2d 1390, *cert. denied,* 352 So. 2d 1047 (1977).

[15] *Willis v. Stauffer Chemical Co.,* 348 So. 2d 158, *on reh'g,* 349 So. 2d 1390, *cert. denied,* 352 So. 2d 1047 (1977).

[16] *Byrne v. Kansas City, Ft. S. & M. R. Co.,* 61 F. 605 (6th Cir. 1894).

[17] Malone, Some Ruminations on Contributory Negligence, 65 Utah L. Rev. 91 (1981).

[18] *Kirby v. Larson,* 400 Mich. 585, 256 N.W.2d 400 (1977).

[19] *Exum v. Boyles,* 272 N.C. 567, 158 S.E.2d 845 (1968).

[20] *Sanders v. State Farm Ins. Cos.,* 354 So. 2d 663, *cert. denied,* 356 So. 2d 436 (1977).

[21] *Maricle v. Spiegel,* 213 Neb. 223, 329 N.W.2d 80 (1983).

[22] *Hrivnak v. Perrone,* 472 Pa. 348, 372 A.2d 730 (1977).

[23] *Bruggeman v. Illinois C. R. Co.,* 147 Iowa 187, 123 N.W. 1007 (1909).

[24] *Ruffo v. Schwegmann Bros. Giant Supermarkets, Inc.,* 424 So. 2d 470 (1982).

[25] *Andre v. Allynn,* 84 Cal. App. 2d 347 (1948).

[26] *Safeco Ins. Co. v. Watertown,* 529 F. Supp. 1220 (1981).

[27] *Noel v. McCaig,* 174 Kan. 677 (1953).

[28] *Norris v. Atlantic C. L. R. Co.,* 152 N.C. 505, 67 S.E. 1017 (1910).

[29] *Wilford v. Salvucci,* 117 Vt. 495, 95 A.2d 37 (1953).

[30] *Jacobs v. General Accident Fire Life Assur. Corp.,* 14 Wis. 2d 1, 109 N.W.2d 462 (1961).

[31] *Lindenberg v. Needles,* 203 Md. 8, 97 A.2d 901 (1953).

[32] *Jaworski v. Great Scott Supermarkets,* 71 Mich. App. 235, 247 N.W.2d 363 (1976).

[33] *Holiday Inns, Inc. v. Drew,* 276 Ark. 390, 635 S.W.2d 252 (1982).

[34] *Papagni v. Purdue,* 74 Nev. 32, 321 P.2d 252 (1958).

[35] Restatement (Second) of Torts §473.

[36] Am. Jur. 2d, Negligence §1160.

[37] Prosser, Comparative Negligence, 51 Mich. L. Rev. 465 (1953).

[38] Miller, Adoption of the Uniform Comparative Fault Act, 14 Pac. L.J. 835 (1983).

[39] Am. Jur. Negligence §1140 (2003).

[40] *Pedernales Electric Cooperative, Inc. v. Schulz,* 583 S.W.2d 882 (1979).

[41] *Finninger v. Johnson,* 692 S.W.2d 390 (1985).

[42] *Knapp v. Stanford,* 392 So. 2d 196 (1980).

[43] Conn. Gen. Stat. Ann. §52-572h(m); Or. Rev. Stats. §8.475.

[44] *Ouellette v. Carde,* 612 A.2d 687 (1992).

[45] *Lillemoen v. Gregorich,* 256 N.W.2d 628 (1977).

[46] *Martin v. Bussert,* 292 Minn. 29, 193 N.W.2d 134 (1971).

Crossword Puzzle

www.CrosswordWeaver.com

ACROSS

1 An approach to negligence cases that balances the negligence of the defendant against the negligence of the plaintiff and permits a reduced recovery for the plaintiff in proportion to the plaintiff's negligence

3 A doctrine that relieves a person of the normal standard of care because of a swiftly developing and dangerous event

4 A defense available in only a few jurisdictions that provides that a plaintiff who is even partially at fault is barred from any recovery

DOWN

2 A claim by a plaintiff in a contributory negligence allegation that the defendant was the person who had the last opportunity to avoid the event that caused the plaintiff's injuries and therefore the defendant should remain liable for the injuries, despite any negligence by the plaintiff

Strict Liability and Products Liability

- Explain the difference between strict liability and other negligence actions

- Define the basic characteristics of a products liability lawsuit

- Explain how the case law of strict liability shifted from pro-business to pro-consumer

- Explain the three theories on which a products liability case can be based

- Describe the significance of cases such as *Rylands v. Fletcher* and *MacPherson v. Buick Co.*

INTRODUCTION

Although we usually begin each chapter with a discussion of the Chumley case, because that case did not involve a claim of strict liability or products liability, we examine the facts of a different case here.

A PRODUCTS LIABILITY CASE: TIRE BLOWOUT

Susan is driving her car one day when the left front tire suddenly blows out. Susan's car overturns, and she is seriously injured. During her hospital stay, Susan learns that her model of car and the type of tires that she had on her car have been involved in numerous lawsuits across the country. Apparently, this brand of tires has a history of blowouts. Many people across the United States have been injured or killed when these tires blew out at high speeds. Susan, who has severe injuries and huge medical bills, is strongly considering bringing a products liability lawsuit against the tire manufacturer. Does Susan have a case? As we explore the issues in this chapter, we analyze the facts of her case and decide if she can actually bring a products liability lawsuit.

We begin by addressing the issue of strict liability, then move to the issue directly involved in Susan's case: product liability.

STRICT LIABILITY

Strict liability
A finding of liability regardless of fault.

The theory behind **strict liability** is that there are some activities that are so dangerous that a person is liable for any harm caused by them, whether or not he was negligent. This theory runs counter to the theory of negligence we have explored in previous chapters. Under the traditional analysis, a defendant first must have a duty to the plaintiff, he must breach that duty, the breach must be the proximate cause of the plaintiff's injuries, and the plaintiff must have sustained legally recognizable damages. However, in strict liability, the courts short-circuit the first two elements. Instead of requiring proof of the defendant's breach, the court now assumes that the defendant's actions were the cause of the plaintiff's injuries. This assumption was a substantial departure from previous negligence law and created a stir in the legal community when it was first created.

Before a defendant can be held liable under strict liability, he must be engaged in some activity that the court deems to be "ultra-hazardous" or "abnormally dangerous." These activities are usually limited to the manufacture of explosives, poisons, or firearms and similar high-risk activities.[1]

A. ULTRA-HAZARDOUS ACTIVITY

Ultra-hazardous
A condition of special or unusual dangerousness.

Under the theory of strict liability, the defendant is liable for all the injuries that result when he engages in **ultra-hazardous** or abnormally dangerous activity. This is true even if the defendant was not at fault, and even though he exercised all the normal precautions that should have been taken. Suppose that the defendant is in the business of manufacturing dynamite. During the manufacturing process, the dynamite explodes and injures the plaintiff. The dynamite company would be liable for the plaintiff's injuries, even though

FIGURE 10-1

Examples of Ultra-hazardous Activities

■ Transport of dangerous substances through populated areas
■ Blasting
■ Explosives (in use and in storage)
■ Nuclear power plants
■ Livestock
■ Keeping dangerous or wild animals
■ Storage of poison

Examples of items that can become ultra-hazardous under certain conditions:

■ Electricity
■ Natural gas
■ Steam

the company followed all the safety precautions that were required by law, and even if it could not have anticipated that the dynamite would explode under those conditions. Many other types of activities have been labeled as ultra-hazardous (see Figure 10-1).

Under strict liability, a defendant is liable for the injuries caused by his activities whether or not he was negligent.

TORT BASICS AT A GLANCE

B. A SHORT HISTORY OF STRICT LIABILITY

1. BACKGROUND

Prior to the late 1800s, a plaintiff who was injured by a defendant who was engaged in dangerous activity had no recourse if he could not prove that the defendant was negligent. Although proof of negligence was seemingly a reasonable requirement, in practice it often produced harsh results. For one thing, in cases of industrial accidents, the plaintiff was often in no position to prove how the defendant corporation was negligent. Often, the evidence was destroyed along with everything else. When a dynamite factory explodes and injures nearby villagers, how can they prove that the company was negligent? Another problem with applying traditional negligence theory to such cases is that the courts often required a rigorous standard on the question of duty. In the early 1800s, there was virtually no industry, and consumers dealt directly with craftspeople. Consumers ordered specific products and had definitive contractual relationships with the producers. However, by the 1860s, this model, although still a feature of case law, was no longer the economic reality. Consumers no longer dealt directly with producers. Instead, they dealt with retailers, such as Sears and Roebuck, or local general stores that provided a wide range of products on store shelves. However, as it often is, the

Sidebar

In ruling that natural gas is an ultra-hazardous instrumentality, a Wyoming federal court stated, "Because of the dangerous characteristics and properties of natural gas, a utility engaged in the business of transmitting and distributing natural gas has a duty to the public of exercising the high degree of care and diligence proportionate to the danger presented that was known or should have been known by the utility in building, emplacing and maintaining its gas mains and service lines."[2]

legal community was slow to grasp this change in society. Instead, it clung to the outmoded belief that the parties could negotiate risks and costs directly with one another, and cases involving defective products were still considered more a contract case than a torts case.

When plaintiffs brought suit against a defendant engaged in dangerous activities, more often than not they were turned away with no compensation. The courts began to realize that their approach was causing widespread injustice, and they began casting about for some other legal theory. Fortunately, a new case holding appeared to clear a path out of this morass.

No discussion of the concept of strict liability would be complete without reference to the case of *Rylands v. Fletcher*. Decided in England in 1868, this was one of the first cases to establish the principle of strict liability for abnormally dangerous situations. The ruling in *Rylands* was that if a person maintained an abnormally dangerous condition on his property, he would be liable for any damages that resulted from that condition whether he was negligent or not. This case was applied to situations in which people kept dangerous animals, carried out dangerous manufacturing processes, and a wide range of other inherently dangerous activities. Later, this principle was embodied in the Restatement of Torts. (See Figure 10-2.)

Although the decision in *Rylands* seems modest by today's standards, it was the equivalent of a legal earthquake. All across Britain and the United States, commentators were swift to condemn or hail the decision. Some judges applied the decision in their own cases; many others refused to ever follow such a radical notion.

2. DEVELOPING STRICT LIABILITY IN THE UNITED STATES

The *Rylands* principle was adopted slowly in the United States. The courts in this country were very generous toward businesses in the 1800s. Throughout the century, courts consistently ruled in favor of large corporations, such as railroads, and against consumers and others injured by these corporations. The rationale behind these rulings was that any decision that would have a negative impact on the company might have a corresponding negative impact on the developing economy. The Industrial Revolution had only recently begun, and jurists were often of the opinion that these companies should be given as much freedom as possible.

Sidebar

Strict liability is also known as absolute liability.

Sidebar

The Rylands *case involved an action by the owners of a mine against a mill owner. The mill owner had a large pond built above a working mine. The contractor who built the reservoir failed to properly support it, and the pond collapsed and flooded the mine.*

Sidebar

"The principle of the [Rylands] *case, some-what fuzzy to be sure, was that a person who sets in motion some extraordinary or dangerous process must take the consequences; it would be no excuse to show that he was as careful as he could be, or as careful as the reasonable man.*"[3]

FIGURE 10-2	
Justifying a Ruling of Strict Liability Under the Restatement of Torts*	There are six different conditions that will lead to a ruling of strict liability: **1** The existence of a high degree of risk to some person or to property; **2** The likelihood that some harm will result from this condition is great; **3** The inability of the owner to eliminate the risk by reasonable care; **4** The extent to which the activity is uncommon; **5** The activity is inappropriate in the place where it is carried out; and **6** The value of the activity is outweighed by the risk in carrying it out.

*Restatement (Second) of Torts, §520.

However, over time the principle in *Rylands* was slowly applied to one situation after another. Blasting was ruled an ultra-hazardous activity, if for no other reason than to encourage railroads and road builders to be extremely careful in this very dangerous activity. Later, poison manufacturing was added to the list. Keeping wild animals was also ruled to be an ultra-hazardous activity. Since the 1860s, the list has grown considerably.

C. STRICT LIABILITY FOR ANIMAL BEHAVIOR

Strict liability lawsuits can be based not only on abnormally dangerous conditions, but also on other situations. For instance, when a person keeps a wild animal on his premises, such as a lion or a tiger, and that animal injures the plaintiff, the animal's owner can be sued on the basis of strict liability in tort. If the animal is wild, the owner is considered to be on notice that the animal is dangerous and that he will therefore be responsible for any injuries that the animal causes. The rule changes slightly when we discuss domestic animals. Normally, a pet owner will not be strictly liable when his dog bites another person, unless the owner had reason to believe that the dog was dangerous. Under the law, the owner is put on notice that his animal is dangerous when the pet has acted aggressively in the past. Many states have a rule that essentially gives every dog one free bite. What that rule means is that an owner is not put on notice that the dog is aggressive until it has actually bitten someone. After that point, the owner will then be liable if the dog attacks anyone else. Many states have modified that rule. For instance, some states have adopted a rule that creates a presumption of dangerousness in certain breeds of dog. Pit bulls, for example, have been ruled to be dangerous dogs in some jurisdictions, even when individual dogs have not demonstrated any aggressive behavior before their first attack.

D. STRICT LIABILITY HAS NOT BEEN ADOPTED IN ALL JURISDICTIONS

The concept of strict liability for ultra-hazardous activities has not been adopted in all jurisdictions. In the jurisdictions in which it has not been made the law of the land, other theories, such as modified negligence theory, have been put into service.

E. STATUTE OF LIMITATIONS CONCERNS IN STRICT LIABILITY LAWSUITS

Whenever a strict liability lawsuit is contemplated, it is important to note the applicable statutes of limitations. As we have discussed in prior chapters, a statute of limitations is a time limit placed on a lawsuit that sets a deadline by which a plaintiff must bring a case or the case is waived. Other statutes may also cause concern in these cases.

Some states, such as North Carolina, have complicated products liability statutes. Under these statutes, it is very difficult for a person to prove that a defective product injured her. Not only is the standard of proof higher in these states, but in many situations the statute of limitations is shorter.

INTRODUCTION TO PRODUCTS LIABILITY

Products liability
Also known as "product liability," the liability assessed against a manufacturer, seller, wholesaler, and so on, for placing a dangerous or defective product on the market which causes injury or damage.

When we discuss **products liability,** we're talking about a relatively recent legal innovation. A lawyer from the early 1900s would not have been familiar with the term. Only in the last few decades has the law progressed to such an extent as to allow consumers to bring lawsuits against manufacturers who create defective products. Prior to the creation of products liability as a separate category of tort law, these types of cases, if they were permitted at all, were generally handled under the broad umbrella of negligence cases.

The typical products liability case involves a defective product purchased by the plaintiff, who was subsequently injured by the product. The injury is generally the result of a defective design or a product that has been manufactured in a dangerous way. Products liability cases are firmly rooted in public policy concerns. In situations in which a consumer is injured by the negligence of a multinational corporation, the law has begun to favor the consumer with her limited resources over the corporation with its vast resources.

The public policy behind products liability theory is based on the idea that by discouraging corporations from producing faulty products, the law can provide financial incentive to corporations to create safer products.

TORT
BASICS
AT A
GLANCE

We use the term *products liability* to refer to almost any type of case that involves an action against a manufacturer or seller of a product that subsequently injures an individual.

A. PRODUCTS LIABILITY IN THE UNITED STATES

In the 1800s, if a consumer was injured by a defective product, she had very little legal recourse. These suits, if allowed at all, had the requirement of **privity.**

Privity
A direct financial relationship between the parties. For example, when a home seller signs a contract for the sale of his home to a buyer, the parties are in privity with one another.

1. PRIVITY OF CONTRACT REQUIREMENT

Under nineteenth-century analysis, if there was no privity of contract between the consumer and the manufacturer, there could be no cause of action for negligence. This was the rule of law in this country for decades even though modern business transactions usually involve a consumer purchasing products from a middleman (i.e., a retailer) rather than the manufacturer. This limited view was first espoused in *Winterbottom v. Wright,* an 1842 English case that was enthusiastically adopted in the United States as a means of preventing strict liability and products liability actions by consumers injured by defective products.

Exceptions to the harsh results of the *Winterbottom* rule were created within a few years of its adoption in the United States. For instance, one court created an exception when the product was "inherently dangerous," such as a handgun or an explosive. This exception sounds very much like what other courts had done in creating strict liability in the first place.

2. THE THEORY UNDERLYING THE PRIVITY REQUIREMENT

The idea behind the privity requirement, although not directly expressed in the case law, is that both parties had certain expectations in a contract and that each had some power over the other to affect the appearance and safety of the ultimate product. There were at least three problems with this approach:

1. It gave no relief to third parties, people not in privity, for injuries sustained by a dangerous product.
2. It failed to recognize an important change in society, that is, a move away from direct contact between manufacturer and consumer by the creation of intermediaries, such as retailers in the chain of commerce from raw materials and production through the retail and the resale of products.
3. It also permitted corporations to be, if not careless about safety, at least to put it as a secondary consideration.

The original judicial approach had favored the corporation under the theory that fledgling manufacturers needed time and resources to develop their products. The theory was that this "breathing space" would help the United States develop economically, and this increase in overall economic health would essentially work its way down to every member of society.

In practice, exactly the opposite occurred. The manufacturers and corporations, like spoiled children, indulged themselves and failed to apply their profits toward improved safety and better design of products. In an environment in which profits are the only yardstick, all other considerations, even those concerning injuries to consumers, take a back seat.

B. A NEW JUDICIAL APPROACH

The problems with the judicial approach to product liability cases became obvious even to the most conservative and pro-business members of the judiciary. The corporations were clearly not going to take action to protect consumers unless forced to do so. Legislatures around the country, with some important exceptions, were reluctant to enact any laws that might be restrictive of business. Events seemed bogged down in a stalemate primarily of the courts' creation.

Then a new judicial interpretation changed the status quo. New York Appellate Justice Benjamin Cardozo, in a case that would eventually have national importance, wrote a decision about a faulty automobile tire and opened up an entirely new branch of law.

Sidebar

In creating the rule that privity must exist between the injured consumer and the manufacturer, the judge ruled, "I am clearly of the opinion that the defendant is entitled to our judgment. We ought not to permit a doubt to rest upon this subject, for our doing so might be the means of letting in upon us an infinity of actions. . . . There is no privity of contract between these parties; and if the plaintiff can sue, every passenger, or even any person passing along the road, who was injured by the upsetting of the coach, might bring a similar action. Unless we confine the operation of such contracts as this to the parties who entered into them, the most absurd and outrageous consequences, to which I can see no limit, would ensue." Winterbottom v. Wright, 10 M. & W. 109, 152 Eng. Rep. 402 (Ex. 1842).

1. THE *MacPHERSON* CASE AND A CHANGE IN JUDICIAL ATTITUDES

The *MacPherson* case is significant because it signaled the beginning of the end of the pro-business court rulings in strict liability and products liability cases.

Case Excerpt

MacPHERSON v. BUICK MOTOR CO.
217 N.Y. 382, 111 N.E. 1050, 1055 (1916)

CARDOZO, J.

The defendant is a manufacturer of automobiles. It sold an automobile to a retail dealer. The retail dealer resold to the plaintiff. While the plaintiff was in the car, it suddenly collapsed. He was thrown out and injured. One of the wheels was made of defective wood, and its spokes crumbled into fragments. The wheel was not made by the defendant; it was bought from another manufacturer. There is evidence, however, that its defects could have been discovered by reasonable inspection, and that inspection was omitted. There is no claim that the defendant knew of the defect and willfully concealed it. The charge is one, not of fraud, but of negligence. The question to be determined is whether the defendant owed a duty of care and vigilance to any one but the immediate purchaser.

The foundations of this branch of the law, at least in this state, were laid in *Thomas v. Winchester.* A poison was falsely labeled. The sale was made to a druggist, who in turn sold to a customer. The customer recovered damages from the seller who affixed the label. "The defendant's negligence," it was said, "put human life in imminent danger." A poison falsely labeled is likely to injure any one who gets it. Because the danger is to be foreseen, there is a duty to avoid the injury. Cases were cited by way of illustration in which manufacturers were not subject to any duty irrespective of contract. The distinction was said to be that their conduct, though negligent, was not likely to result in injury to any one except the purchaser. We are not required to say whether the chance of injury was always as remote as the distinction assumes. Some of the illustrations might be rejected today. The principle of the distinction is for present purposes the important thing.

The defendant argues that things imminently dangerous to life are poisons, explosives, deadly weapons—things whose normal function it is to injure or destroy. We find in the opinion of Brett, M. R., afterwards Lord Esher (p. 510), the same conception of a duty, irrespective of contract, imposed upon the manufacturer by the law itself: "Whenever one person supplies goods, or machinery, or the like, for the purpose of their being used by another person under such circumstances that every one of ordinary sense would, if he thought, recognize at once that unless he used ordinary care and skill with regard to the condition of the thing supplied or the mode of supplying it, there will be danger of injury to the person or property of him for whose use the thing is supplied, and who is to use it, a duty arises to use ordinary care and skill as the condition or manner of supplying such thing."

We hold, then, that the principle of *Thomas v. Winchester* is not limited to poisons, explosives, and things of like nature, to things which in their normal operation are implements of destruction. If the nature of a thing is such that it is reasonably certain to place and limb in peril when negligently made, it is then a thing of danger. Its nature gives warning of the consequences to be expected. If to the element of danger there is added knowledge that the thing will be used by persons other than the purchaser, and used without new tests then, irrespective of contract, the manufacturer of this thing of danger is under a duty to make it carefully. That is as far as we are required to go for the decision of this case. There must be knowledge of a danger, not merely possible, but probable. It is possible to use almost anything in a way that will make it dangerous if defective. That is not enough to charge the manufacturer with a duty independent of his contract. Whether a given thing is dangerous may be sometimes a question for the court and sometimes a question for the jury. There must also be knowledge that in the usual course of events the danger will be shared by others than the buyer. Such knowledge may often be inferred from the nature of the transaction. But it is possible that even knowledge of the danger and of the use will not always be enough. The proximity or remoteness of the relation is a factor to be considered. We are dealing now with the liability of the manufacturer of the finished product, who puts it on the market to be used without inspection by his customers. If he is negligent, where danger is to be foreseen, a liability will follow. We are not required at this time to say that it is legitimate to go back to the manufacturer of the finished products and hold the manufacturers of the component parts. To make their negligence a cause of imminent danger, an independent cause must often intervene; the manufacturer of the finished products must also fail in his duty of inspection.

This automobile was designed to go fifty miles an hour. Unless its wheels were sound and strong, injury was almost certain. It was as much a thing of danger as a defective engine for a railroad. The defendant knew the danger. It knew also that the car would be used by persons other than the buyer. This was apparent from its size; there were seats for three persons. It was apparent also from the fact that the buyer was a dealer in cars, who bought to resell. The maker of this car supplied it for the use of purchasers from the dealer.

We think the defendant was not absolved from a duty of inspection because it bought the wheels from a reputable manufacturer. It was not merely a dealer in automobiles. It was a manufacturer of automobiles. It was responsible for the finished product. It was not at liberty to put the finished products on the market without subjecting the component parts to ordinary and simple tests.

The obligation to inspect must vary with the nature of the thing to be inspected. The more probable the danger, the greater the need of caution.

Other rulings complained of have been considered, but no error has been found on them.

The judgment should be affirmed.

2. THE SIGNIFICANCE OF THE *MACPHERSON* CASE

Because the *MacPherson* case was such a departure from previous court rulings, it was slow to catch on in other jurisdictions. But by the 1950s, nearly every state had adopted the *MacPherson* approach. It is interesting to note that Justice Cardozo himself seemed uncomfortable with the consequences of his own reasoning. In 1931, he pulled back from the trend that he had helped to set in motion. In one case, he stated, "[T]he hazards of a business conducted on these terms are so extreme as to enkindle doubt whether a flaw may not exist in the implication of a duty that exposes to these consequences."[4]

TORT
BASICS
AT A
GLANCE

The "MacPherson rule" has been extended far beyond the original issues involved in that case. It was eventually applied to situations involving third parties, companies that were not in the business of manufacturing, and even to bystanders.

Tech Topic
WHEN TECHNOLOGY BECOMES THE ENEMY

Technology has enriched nearly every facet of daily life, and its reach has enhanced the practice of law as well. However, although the benefits of technology are many, it has its downside. For example, repetitive-strain injuries have been well documented for years, afflicting those who use computers for many hours during the day. Other injuries are surfacing, too:

- According to medical experts, young users of iPads, cell phones, and tech toys are complaining of repetitive-strain injuries, stiff necks, headaches, and sore shoulders. Such injuries are particularly widespread among teens, who send literally hundreds of text messages on a daily basis.
- The maximum volume of devices such as MP3 players, headphones, and Bluetooth headsets is the same as a jet plane taking off nearby. The potential damage includes the destruction of sensory cells that transmit auditory information to the brain, producing a permanent hearing loss.
- Cell phone use lasting longer than four hours a day can increase the risk of sperm damage because of electromagnetic radiation. In addition, scientists claim that the prolonged use of a laptop heats the testicles, further impairing normal sperm production.
- A major area of concern is whether cell phone use causes brain cancer or noncancerous tumors in the brain and neck. No definitive link has yet been established, but the concern persists.

When technology begins harming quality of life in a demonstrable way, tort cases will follow.

A consumer who is injured by a faulty product ought to have the right to seek compensation from the manufacturer who created the defective product.

Traditionally, such a case would fall under negligence law. However, at that time, such actions required privity. Plaintiffs found it difficult, if not impossible, to establish privity.

Result: Abolish privity as a requirement.

FIGURE 10-3

The Reasoning Behind Creating Products Liability Theory

C. THE BASIC ELEMENTS OF A PRODUCTS LIABILITY CASE

With the holding in the *MacPherson* case, the era of products liability suits had begun. We now examine the details of these claims and the basic requirements. The first, and most obvious, requirement is that the plaintiff must sustain some form of personal injury. No matter how defective the product, if it fails to injure the plaintiff, there is no cause of action. The loss suffered in a products liability case can also include property damage. Another requirement is that the injury originate either from a defective design or a dangerous application of the product.

Products liability cases are really a hybrid between lawsuits on the basis of a contractual relationship between the parties and losses based on personal injuries incurred by one of the parties. See Figure 10-3 for an explanation of the reasoning behind products liability theory.

Sidebar

Some commentators have said that the holding in MacPherson *(written by a future U.S. Supreme Court Justice) actually began the modern era of products liability lawsuits.*

D. PRODUCTS LIABILITY CASES DO NOT INVOLVE CONSUMER DISSATISFACTION

Products liability lawsuits do not involve cases in which a product fails to live up to consumers' expectations. When the consumer is dissatisfied with the product's performance, he can bring a different type of civil action, but he is not permitted to bring a products liability claim. Products liability cases have as one of their most important ingredients an injury to the plaintiff. This injury can be physical, financial, psychological, or property based.

For instance, when the consumer is sold a defective item — one that does not work properly — such a suit is usually handled as a contractual dispute. Products liability litigation focuses on dangerous and harmful products.

In states in which strict liability in tort had already been accepted, the courts fixed on this as the principle to use in products liability cases. First, they removed the requirement of privity of contract, and then they made the manufacturer liable for any injuries from a defective product, under the theory that allowed others to be held liable for defective or dangerous conditions in ultra-hazardous situations. In strict liability, people who kept wild animals or companies that manufactured poisons or explosives were liable for any injuries that occurred whether the plaintiff could prove that they were negligent or not.

This theory would now be applied to consumer products. Cases in which a manufacturer created a product that eventually injured a person were analogous to a company that manufactured dynamite; the company had put a dangerous product into the stream of commerce, and the responsibility for the eventual injury would be laid at the feet of the manufacturer in strict liability.

In states that had never adopted strict liability in tort, there was a different approach. Privity of contract was also removed as a requirement of recovery, but these states based suits on a different theory. Strict liability was not an option, so these jurisdictions opted for a variation of contractual law. Although privity had been removed, the courts continued to impose other contractual obligations as though the end-consumer and the manufacturer were still contractual parties. Specifically, courts imposed warranties on the manufacturers and allowed plaintiffs to recover for breaches of those warranties.

In permitting such suits, courts relied on express warranties—that is, those promises stated by the manufacturer and other parties in the stream of commerce. End-users were given the benefit of these express warranties even though they technically may not have been contractual parties, at least not with the original manufacturer.

TORT BASICS AT A GLANCE

Products liability cases can be based on negligence, strict liability, or breach of warranty.

Courts also created "implied" warranties—that is, promises and conditions that any reasonable person would assume that a manufacturer gives when it creates a product.

Warranty
A pledge, assurance, or guarantee that a particular fact is true.

E. WARRANTIES

One of the most important areas of products liability lawsuits deals with express and implied **warranties.** There are several warranties that are now either presumed under the law or required for manufacturers and suppliers when they sell products.

Some states have never completely adopted the theory of strict liability in tort, or have not recognized it in the context of products liability cases. Those states are Delaware, Massachusetts, Michigan, North Carolina, and Virginia. In those states, a products liability case must be based on some alternative theory, such as breach of warranty.[6]

1. WARRANTY OF MERCHANTABILITY

The warranty of merchantability is the implied promise that the product will perform normally and safely. When a product is actually dangerous, it violates this warranty, and this can provide the basis for an action against the manufacturer. See Figure 10-4 for a statement of the U.C.C.'s position on implied warranties.

2. WARRANTY OF FITNESS FOR PURPOSE

Like the warranty of merchantability, the warranty of fitness for particular purpose is an implied promise that the product will perform the duty for which it has been advertised. The seller is essentially promising the buyer that the product will satisfy the buyer's needs. Although implied, it often has a factual basis in statements and representations made by the seller. The implied warranty of fitness for purpose is different from the implied warranty of merchantability in the following critical way: The implied warranty of fitness for purpose is based on the representations, statements, and negotiations between the buyer and seller and is therefore highly dependent on the type of proof that can be had about these representations.

Example: David goes to his local computer supplier and asks for a single computer that will handle two different, and usually incompatible, computer systems. After a few minutes' thought, the salesman takes him to the model Odyssey Compu-3000 and says, "This is the one for you." David pays for the computer and takes it home. When he starts the computer, he discovers that the computer is not configured to run either computer operating system. Does he have an action against the computer store for breach of an implied warranty of fitness for purpose?

Sidebar

Proof of a breach of warranty requires no showing of fault and is therefore a "strict liability" tort.[7]

FIGURE 10-4

U.C.C. Position on Implied Warranties

U.C.C. §2-314. Implied Warranty: Merchantability; Usage of Trade
　　(1) Unless excluded or modified (Section 2-316), a warranty that the goods shall be merchantable is implied in a contract for their sale if the seller is a merchant with respect to goods of that kind. Under this section the serving for value of food or drink to be consumed either on the premises or elsewhere is a sale.
　　(2) Goods to be merchantable must be at least such as:
　　　　(a) pass without objection in the trade under the contract description; and
　　　　(b) in the case of fungible goods, are of fair average quality within the description; and
　　　　(c) are fit for the ordinary purposes for which such goods are used; and
　　　　(d) run, within the variations permitted by the agreement, of even kind, quality and quantity within each unit and among all units involved; and
　　　　(e) are adequately contained, packaged, and labeled as the agreement may require; and
　　　　(f) conform to the promises or affirmations of fact made on the container or label if any.
　　(3) Unless excluded or modified (Section 2-316), other implied warranties may arise from course of dealing or usage of trade.

FIGURE 10-5

A Plaintiff Must Prove the Following Elements Under an Express Warranty Theory

1　An express warranty was given.
2　The product failed to conform to the warranty.
3　The plaintiff suffered damages because of this failure.
4　The plaintiff notified the manufacturer of the breach.

Answer: Yes. When the salesman directed David to that particular computer, he was essentially saying that that computer is the one that can meet David's needs. Although he didn't specifically make that statement, it is certainly a reasonable interpretation of his actions and an implied promise that the computer would fit David's needs.

3. EXPRESS WARRANTIES

Sidebar

Although most products liability cases seem firmly rooted in tort law applications, there is a side branch of these cases that actually bases the plaintiff's case in breach of warranty. Some have argued that this smaller offshoot of warranty-based products liability arose because some states (such as Delaware, Massachusetts, Michigan, and Virginia) never adopted the concept of strict liability in tort for defective products. Basing a products liability case on a broken promise involves proof of contractual relationship between the parties. Cases in this vein often rely on the Uniform Commercial Code for both the types of warranties given for a product and the types of damages that can be recovered. Because most states have adopted the U.C.C. in virtually identical language, this does create more uniformity across court decisions.

In addition to implied warranties, any warranties actually stated by the manufacturer will also be applied. "Express warranties" could cover a wide range of activities, such as guarantees about how and under what conditions the product will perform, statements about safety and inspection, or even health hazards associated with use. See Figure 10-5 for a list of the elements a plaintiff must prove under express warranty theory and Figure 10-6 for a statement of the U.C.C.'s position on express warranties.

F. LIABILITY WITHOUT FAULT UNDER PRODUCTS LIABILITY

Just as we saw in our discussions on strict liability cases, products liability lawsuits do not focus on the intent of the parties. A plaintiff is not required to show that the manufacturer deliberately set out to create a defective design. Such proof would be almost impossible. Instead, products liability cases are firmly rooted in strict liability theory or warranty theories. However, products liability cases go one step further than most strict liability suits. In a negligence action, one of the primary elements that the plaintiff must prove is that the defendant was at fault. In states that follow a comparative negligence model, the plaintiff is not required to prove that the defendant was completely at fault, but proof of fault is still a requirement. This is not true of strict liability cases in general and products liability cases specifically. A plaintiff can bring a successful products liability lawsuit against a manufacturer without proving that the manufacturer was at fault. In fact, it is not a defense in a products liability lawsuit that the manufacturer followed all the safety requirements.

FIGURE 10-6	
Express Warranties Under the Uniform Commercial Code	U.C.C. §2-313 Express Warranties by Affirmation, Promise, Description, Sample (1) Express warranties by the seller are created as follows: (a) Any affirmation of fact or promise made by the seller to the buyer which relates to the goods and becomes part of the basis of the bargain creates an express warranty that the goods shall conform to the affirmation or promise. (b) Any description of the goods which is made part of the basis of the bargain creates an express warranty that the goods shall conform to the description. (c) Any sample or model which is made part of the basis of the bargain creates an express warranty that the whole of the goods shall conform to the sample or model. (2) It is not necessary to the creation of an express warranty that the seller use formal words such as "warrant" or "guarantee" or that he have a specific intention to make a warranty, but an affirmation merely of the value of the goods or a statement purporting to be merely the seller's opinion or commendation of the goods does not create a warranty.

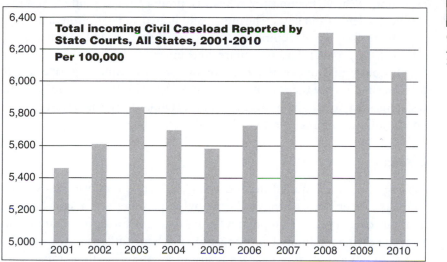

FIGURE 10-7

Civil Caseloads,
All States, 2001–
2010

G. THE STANDARD OF CARE
IN PRODUCTS LIABILITY CASES

Given that a products liability case can be brought under several different types of theories, when the case is based on negligence, an important issue arises: What is the standard of care? Is the standard of care that a manufacturer must follow different from what a retailer must follow? Unfortunately, courts have been vague in spelling out the standard of care in products liability cases. Instead of using precise terms, they often simply state that the manufacturer's duty is "reasonable care." Usually this is interpreted in the same way that the standard of care is applied in any negligence case: The standard of care is what a reasonable person, under the same circumstances, would have used. Because the conduct in question is that of a manufacturer instead of an actual human being, the courts create a hypothetical "reasonable manufacturer" and ask a similar question: What would this hypothetical reasonable manufacturer have done under similar circumstances? If this hypothetical manufacturer would have tested and inspected its products before shipping them out to consumers, the failure of the defendant company to do the same is a breach of the standard of care. Of course, determining what is reasonable under the circumstances is often a hotly contested issue.

1. MANUFACTURER'S DUTY TO TEST AND INSPECT PRODUCTS

The law places a burden on the manufacturer to both test and inspect its products to ensure that they are not dangerous.[8] How far does this obligation extend? A manufacturer is required to test and inspect during the manufacturing process and to test the finished product, but it is not required to have detected a latent defect that would not appear in normal testing or

Sidebar

Some of the most common products liability cases involve common objects such as kitchen appliances, automobile tires, and pharmaceutical drugs.

Sidebar

One of the first consumer movements in the United States concerned food, specifically meat. In the early 1900s, journalist Upton Sinclair published The Jungle, *which described, in nauseating detail, how meat was processed in this country. By revealing that meat-processing plants routinely had rats falling into the meat grinders and that putrefying meat was often sold to the public, Sinclair sparked a national movement. Meat sales were cut in half almost overnight. The meat packing industry and other industries began quite literally to clean up their acts. In 1906, this cleanup was formalized in one of the first federal food and drug acts.*

inspection.[9] When a manufacturer creates a product, it has a duty to test that product for defects and flaws. The more complicated and dangerous a product is, the more likely it will require greater testing, inspection, and design analysis to ensure the product does not injure consumers.

Obviously, machines with more moving parts will require a greater degree of testing and review than would a simple object. This view is echoed in the Restatement of Torts, which suggests that the standard to be used should be an amount of care commensurate with the dangerousness of the object.

a. Food

The degree of care required in food is higher than is found in many other products (for obvious reasons). For many years, there was a split between "natural" contaminants in food and "unnatural" (or foreign) contaminants. A consumer who was injured by biting into a fish bone while eating canned fish would, under most situations, have no cause of action against the company, but if the same fish contained a piece of metal, the consumer would have a cause of action. This distinction has gradually faded over the years. Courts have come to realize that natural substances can be just as damaging as foreign ones, so they have instead focused on what a reasonable person would expect from the food. If bones or any other contaminants would not reasonably be expected in the food, the person injured would have a cause of action.[10]

b. Compliance with Safety and/or Health Regulations

Suppose that the manufacturer can show that it followed all applicable safety and health regulations. How will this compliance affect the manufacturer's liability? Some courts have held that such compliance is at least a rebuttable presumption of proper testing and inspection; some have ruled that it is conclusive proof of proper testing and inspection.[11]

H. PRODUCTS LIABILITY PER SE?

If a products liability case is based on negligence, does this also mean that other negligence principles, such as negligence per se, will operate in this area as well?

Example: Furry Foods put out a food product called furry beef jerky. Consumers who ate this modified beef jerky became seriously ill. Upon investigation, it turned out that part of the "furry" texture of the beef jerky came from the presence of mold, which had caused the consumers to become ill. Several plaintiffs have filed suit against Furry Foods and as part of their allegations have shown that Furry failed to have the new jerky inspected by the state food and drug agency. This is a clear violation of an existing statute. As we have already seen, violation of a safety statute in a negligence case can justify the use of negligence per se (a rebuttable presumption that the defendant has committed negligence). Can the same theory be used here?

Answer: In most jurisdictions, yes. So long as the plaintiffs can meet the requirements of a negligence per se action (the purpose of the statute was designed to protect a class of persons; the plaintiff was a member of the class to be protected; etc.), the plaintiffs are entitled to use negligence per se theory against Furry Foods.

I. PUBLIC POLICY ARGUMENTS FOR PRODUCTS LIABILITY CASES

Products liability litigation is based on the premise that of the two parties involved, the individual consumer and the company that created the product, the company is in a better position to remedy the danger than is the consumer. The theory underpinning these cases is that if a company is sued successfully for a dangerous product, the company will have a financial incentive to change the product to make it safer. Over time, this natural tendency toward creating better products will ultimately result in most products being made better, stronger, and safer. One could certainly argue that with the extent of products liability lawsuits brought in the United States, this reasoning has shown to be correct. After all, the United States has one of the world's strongest economies while at the same time creating products that are generally far safer than products produced 50 or 100 years ago. Although detractors would point out that products liability suits have damaged the U.S. economy, America is the world's remaining superpower, with an enormously strong and vibrant economy, even in the face of products liability verdicts that far exceed amounts seen in most other countries. In the United States, products are continually refined and made safer and more effective for the consumer. Many argue that this is a direct result of products liability litigation placing the burden on the manufacturers to create safer products. Others might argue that safer products are the result of other forces and that the U.S. economy perseveres despite huge jury awards. This issue is hotly debated.

J. PROVING A PRODUCTS LIABILITY CASE

To prove a products liability case, the plaintiff must show that the product was defective in some way. Under the law of products liability, there are three categories of defects. These include design defects, manufacturing defects, and defects in marketing. See Figure 10-8 for a list of general elements that must be proven in a products liability case under a negligence theory.

The plaintiff must present proof that:

1 The manufacturer owed the plaintiff a duty.
2 The manufacturer subsequently breached that duty.
3 The manufacturer's breach was the proximate cause of the plaintiff's injury.
4 The plaintiff has legally compensable injuries.

FIGURE 10-8

Proving Products Liability Under a Negligence Theory

1. DESIGN DEFECTS

A design defect is an inherent problem with the product. Something in the manufacturing or design has created a product that can cause damage. This damage could come in the form of personal injury or property damage. A design defect includes objects that, although designed to suit a particular use, can be unreasonably dangerous in that use.

An example of a design defect would be a game called lawn dart. In this game, players threw one-foot-long, steel-tipped darts at a target laid on the ground. The steel-tipped arrows were sharp enough to pierce through skin, and it was not uncommon during play for one of the darts to strike one of the players. Although lawn darts were manufactured correctly, in their use their design was potentially dangerous.

2. MANUFACTURING DEFECTS

A manufacturing defect is a defect in the product that is caused by faulty manufacturing processes or through the use of inadequate base materials. Relatively few lawsuits are based on manufacturing defects.

Example: Tom is shopping at a local grocery store and picks up a bottle of soda. As soon as his hand touches it, the bottle explodes. Tom's hand is injured, and he brings a products liability lawsuit against the soda manufacturer. Does he have a products liability case?

In this example, the products liability lawsuit would probably be based on a manufacturing design defect. Normally, soda bottles do not explode on contact. Tom's lawsuit will be based on a manufacturing defect, alleging that something in the manufacturing process caused the bottle to be unnaturally prone to explode. This could be caused by the fact that the bottle material was too thin to support the pressurized liquid inside it, or it could be because of some other manufacturing defect. What is important is that Tom can base his products liability lawsuit on the fact that a manufacturing process has resulted in a dangerous product.

3. DEFECTS IN MARKETING

When a products liability lawsuit is based on a marketing defect, this usually means that the lawsuit is based on faulty instructions or the company's failure to warn the consumer of a potential danger of the product. For example, manufacturers of upright refrigerators and freezers now routinely include warnings about the dangers of children playing inside unattended refrigerators. This is because children, once inside the closed refrigerator, do not have sufficient strength to open the door. When the door is sealed, they quickly run out of oxygen. Manufacturers of large plastic bags include similar warnings on their products about the dangers of smothering.

4. PLEADING PRODUCTS LIABILITY CASES

When we say that a products liability suit is a strict liability action, what we are really saying is that a products liability suit can be brought even when the defendant can demonstrate a high degree of caution and strict adherence to safety rules and regulations. A strict liability offense, such as a products liability suit, is not dependent on fault. The plaintiff must simply show that the product was defective in some way and that the defect caused an injury. The plaintiff is not required to show that the manufacturer was at fault.

What is interesting about these theories of recovery is that they are not mutually exclusive. A plaintiff is allowed to plead these theories in the alternative in his complaint. This means, on a practical level, that the plaintiff is allowed to sue for breach of warranty, sue on the basis of a contractual relationship, sue on the basis of negligence, and sue on the basis of a products liability claim, even though some of the elements of each of these claims are contrary to one another. For example, a suit alleging negligence must involve proof that the defendant acted in an unreasonable way. On the other hand, a products liability case has no requirement of negligence whatsoever. Regardless of these seeming contradictions, a plaintiff in a products liability lawsuit is entitled to plead all the theories that are available. The plaintiff is not required to choose the theory on which he bases his case. The jurors are permitted to make up their own minds about which theory is the most likely. If this seems to you as though a products liability suit would be much easier to prove, your observation would be correct. However, this does not necessarily mean that everyone who sues a manufacturer for defective products will win. Winning a products liability lawsuit is still a difficult proposition and is often based on the facts of the particular case.

See Figure 10-9 for the Restatement's position on products liability.

FIGURE 10-9

Restatement Position on Products Liability — Liability for the Sale or Distribution of Defective Products

(a) One engaged in the business of selling used products who sells a used product in a defective condition is, with the exceptions set forth in Subsection (c), subject to liability for harm to persons or property caused by the product's defect.

(b) A used product is defective for the purposes of this Section if, at the time of commercial sale, it contains a manufacturing defect, is defective in design, or is defective because of inadequate instructions or warnings, as defined in §2.

(c) Used products sellers are not subject to liability under this Section if:

(1) the sale of the used products is accompanied by clear and conspicuous language informing the buyer in writing that the seller disclaims all legal responsibility for products defects that might cause harm, provided that the seller makes no material representations or warranties with regard to products safety or performance relating to the time period, or component part of the products that caused harm, to which the disclaimer purports to apply; or

(2) the circumstances surrounding the sale, including the age and condition of the product, would have caused a reasonable person in the buyer's position to expect the products to be accompanied by the risk that caused the plaintiff's harm.

K. MODEL UNIFORM PRODUCTS LIABILITY ACT

Although the U.S. Department of Commerce created the Model Uniform Products Liability Act as a guideline for the various states, there is no federal products liability law. Many states have created their own products liability statutes, based in whole or in part on the Model Uniform Products Liability Act.

L. DISCOVERY IN PRODUCTS LIABILITY CASES

Frequently, products liability cases are brought in the context of class action lawsuits (see Figure 10-10). In such cases, the discovery can be enormous. Documents and other materials produced through discovery requests can fill entire rooms. In such huge cases, it is common for the lawyers involved to use special software to help them sift through the huge quantity of material. Often the attorneys will scan every document and then save these digital documents on a computer hard drive or a CD. Once saved, the software can be used to cross-reference the documents with pleadings, deposition transcripts, and other discovery materials.

TORT BASICS AT A GLANCE

The idea behind products liability is that a manufacturer can be liable for producing a defective product even though the manufacturer followed all the safety precautions and manufacturing processes that were customary at the time the product was created. Courts reason that the cost and burden of improving the product is more sensibly placed on the shoulders of the manufacturer than on the consumer.

Can a product liability case be based on a product that does not appear to be dangerous at all, until it is misused and turned into a bomb?

FIGURE 10-10

Class Action Lawsuits

A class action lawsuit requires that (1) the number of persons be so numerous that it would be impractical to bring them all before the court, (2) the named representatives can fairly represent all of the members of the class, and (3) the class members have a well-defined common interest in the questions of law or fact to be resolved (*Black's Law Dictionary*).

Of the 11,908 civil trials litigated in 2001, only one could be classified as a class action. This lawsuit, "Bell v. Farmers Insurance Exchange," resulted from the decision of Farmers Insurance Exchange to classify their claims' representatives as administrative personnel, which exempted the insurance company from having to pay overtime. The suit was certified as a class action because it involved over 2,400 California claims adjustors. The jury trial took place in Oakland, California, and a finding was entered for the plaintiffs. The award totaled $124.5 million, of which $90 million was for uncompensated overtime, $1.2 million for double time, and $34.5 million for prejudgment interest. The case took almost five years from filing to verdict to litigate.

Source for additional case details: *The National Law Journal* (February 2002) Vol. 24, No. 22 (Col. 3).

Source: Civil Trial Cases and Verdicts in Large Counties, 2001, Bureau of Justice Statistics, U.S. Department of Justice.

Case Excerpt

ONTIVEROS V. 24 HOUR FITNESS CORP.
169 Cal.App.4th 424, 86 Cal.Rptr.3d 767 (2008)

Mosk, J.

Introduction

Plaintiff and appellant Susana Ontiveros (plaintiff) sustained personal injuries while exercising on a stair step machine at a fitness center owned and operated by defendant and respondent 24 Hour Fitness USA, Inc. (defendant). She sued defendant, asserting, inter alia, a claim for strict product liability. The trial court granted defendant's summary judgment motion as to that claim on the grounds that plaintiff acknowledged in her membership agreement that defendant could not be held liable for defective exercise equipment and that defendant provided "recreational services."

On appeal, plaintiff contends that there are triable issues of fact concerning whether the dominant purpose of plaintiff's transaction with defendant was for the use of defendant's exercise machines or for the provision of fitness services. We hold that the undisputed evidence shows that the dominant purpose of plaintiff's membership agreement with defendant was for the provision of fitness services and that as a result, defendant is not strictly liable to plaintiff under a product liability theory of recovery. We therefore affirm the judgment.

Factual Background

A. Defendant's Facts

At the premises where plaintiff was injured, defendant operated a fitness center at which members could utilize various exercise equipment and participate in aerobic exercise classes, among other activities, pursuant to the terms of a membership agreement between defendant and the member. According to defendant's risk management analyst, each of defendant's exercise facilities offered the following equipment, services, and amenities: free weights; cardio-vascular conditioning machines and other specialized fitness equipment; group exercises such as aerobics, dance classes, and yoga; testing centers to record certain physical characteristics such as blood pressure and weight; an optional introductory membership program that included three sessions with staff trainers; and locker rooms. For additional fees, a member could obtain personal training and nutritional counseling.

Plaintiff entered into a membership agreement with defendant, which was thereafter modified to provide an upgraded membership. Both her original agreement and upgraded agreement contained liability release provisions that included the following language: "You understand and acknowledge that [defendant] is providing recreational services and may not be held liable for defective products. By signing below, you acknowledge and agree that you have read the foregoing and know of the nature of the activities at [defendant's facilities] and you agree to all the terms of the front and back pages of this agreement and acknowledge you have received a copy of it and the membership policies."

The upgraded membership agreement entitled plaintiff to use defendant's facilities, described as "Active," "Express," and "Sport." An "Active" facility referred to a facility that is less than 25,000 square feet, offering fitness amenities such as group exercise classes, weight training, cardiovascular equipment, and locker rooms. A "Sport" facility referred to a facility generally 25,000 to 50,000 square feet, offering the same amenities as the other facilities, as well as further amenities.

As to the incident in question, defendant referred to plaintiff's allegations that she was injured while exercising on stair step equipment at defendant's facility in Panorama City. According to plaintiff's allegations, due to the failure of a component part, both "steps" of the machine lost all resistance as she was using it, causing plaintiff to fall backwards off the machine onto the floor.

B. Plaintiff's Evidence

Plaintiff did not dispute defendant's facts set forth above or argue that there were conflicting inferences that could be drawn from those facts. Instead, she provided the additional facts set forth in this section.

Plaintiff purchased a membership with defendant because she wanted to lose weight and believed that exercising using defendant's exercise equipment would help her achieve that goal. Plaintiff could not afford to purchase exercise equipment on her own and believed that using defendant's equipment would be the most cost effective means of obtaining the exercise she wanted.

Because plaintiff was familiar with exercise machines, which she described as simple to use, she did not need instruction, training, or assistance from defendant concerning the use of its exercise machines, and no such instruction, training, or assistance was provided to her by defendant. Although all of defendant's trainers were certified, defendant's staff members that worked in the area where members used exercise equipment were not certified trainers.

Plaintiff could have purchased from defendant, at an additional cost, the services of a trainer and nutritional counseling, but she chose not to do so. Plaintiff did not become a member of defendant to take aerobic classes, to check her blood pressure, to determine her body fat, or to use the sauna and steam room. She purchased her membership with defendant for the sole purpose of using exercise equipment.

Procedural Background

Plaintiff sued defendant, asserting causes of action for premises liability and strict product liability. The trial court heard and granted defendant's summary adjudication motion on the premises liability cause of action, a ruling that plaintiff does not challenge on appeal. Defendant then filed a motion for summary judgment as to the remaining strict product liability cause of action on the ground that the claim "was not actionable against defendant as defendant was not in the chain of distribution of the allegedly defective exercise equipment which caused her injury." Defendant also relied on the waiver or release language in plaintiff's agreement acknowledging that defendant was providing "recreational services" and could not be held liable for a defective product.

Plaintiff opposed the motion on the ground that defendant was in the chain of distribution; plaintiff's product liability claim could not be waived; and the dominant purpose of plaintiff's membership agreement with defendant was the use of defendant's exercise machines, not the performance of fitness services.

After hearing argument, the trial court granted defendant's motion and entered judgment. According to the trial court, "Defendant's motion is granted because there exist no triable issues of material fact, and moving party is entitled to judgment as a matter of law. Plaintiff has acknowledged in the Club Membership Agreement that Defendant 'does not manufacture fitness or other equipment' and that it provides 'recreational services.'"

Plaintiff filed a timely appeal from the judgment of dismissal following the order granting defendant's motion for summary judgment.

Discussion

Strict Product Liability Claim

Plaintiff acknowledges that if the dominant purpose of her agreement was to provide fitness services, and not just the use of exercise equipment, she cannot prevail on her strict product liability claim because defendant would not be in the chain of distribution of the equipment. She contends, however, that there are triable issues of fact concerning the dominant purpose of her transaction with defendant, citing to *Murphy v. E.R. Squibb & Sons, Inc.* (1985) 40 Cal.3d 672, 221 Cal.Rptr. 447, 710 P.2d 247 (*Murphy*). According to plaintiff, her evidence shows that she purchased her membership with defendant for the sole purpose of using the exercise equipment that defendant made available at its fitness facility. She claims she did not need any of the fitness services available to her under the agreement, and defendant did not provide any such services to her. Thus, under plaintiff's view of the evidence, defendant is strictly liable for defects in its equipment.

Defendant agrees that for purposes of the product liability analysis, the key distinction is whether defendant provided a service, in which case it would not be strictly liable for defective equipment, or whether defendant just made equipment available for use, in which case defendant would be strictly liable for defective equipment because defendant would, in effect, be in the chain of distribution. According to defendant, the dominant purpose of its transaction with plaintiff was to provide the various fitness services that were available to plaintiff under her agreement.

The general principles of California's product liability law have been summarized in *Bay Summit Community Assn. v. Shell Oil Co.* (1996) 51 Cal.App.4th 762, 772-773, 59 Cal.Rptr.2d 322 (*Bay Summit*).

Our high court first adopted the strict liability doctrine in *Greenman v. Yuba Power Products, Inc.* (1963) 59 Cal.2d 57, 62 [27 Cal.Rptr. 697, 377 P.2d 897, 13 A.L.R.3d 1049], holding "a manufacturer is strictly liable to consumers when an article it places on the market, knowing that it is to be used without inspection for defects, proves to have a defect that causes injury to a human being." *Greenman* reasoned the doctrine would "insure that the costs of injuries resulting from defective products are borne by the manufacturers that put such products on the market rather than by the injured persons who are powerless to protect themselves." The court recognized imposing strict liability would discourage the marketing of unsafe products and was necessary to "protect consumers in an increasingly complex and mechanized society." One year later, the court extended the strict liability doctrine to retailers because retailers "are an integral part of the overall producing and marketing enterprise that should bear the cost of injuries resulting from defective products." (*Vandermark v. Ford Motor Co.* (1964) 61 Cal.2d 256, 262 [37 Cal.Rptr. 896, 391 P.2d 168].) *Vandermark* explained that holding retailers strictly liable would (1) enhance product safety since retailers are in a position to exert pressure on manufacturers; (2) increase the opportunity for an injured consumer to recover since the retailer may be the only entity "reasonably available" to the consumer; and (3) ensure fair apportionment of risk since retailers may "adjust the costs of such protection between them in the course of their continuing business relationship."

The courts have since applied the doctrine to others similarly involved in the vertical distribution of consumer goods, including lessors of personal property, developers of mass-produced homes, wholesale and retail distributors. Although these defendants were not necessarily involved in the manufacture or design of the final product, each was responsible for passing the product down the line to the consumer. Thus, the parties were "able to bear the cost of compensating for injuries" and "played a substantial part in insuring that the product was safe or were in a position to exert pressure on the manufacturer to that end."

Plaintiff relies on the decision in *Murphy, supra,* 40 Cal.3d 672, 221 Cal.Rptr. 447, 710 P.2d 247. In that case, the plaintiff filed a personal injury claim against a retail pharmacy and a drug manufacturer alleging injuries from her mother's use of the prescription drug DES during pregnancy. As to the plaintiff's products liability claim, the court held that the trial court had correctly granted the pharmacy's motion for judgment on the pleadings. In doing so, the Court of Appeal observed, "It is critical to the issue posed to determine if the dominant role of a pharmacist in supplying a prescription drug should be characterized as the performance of a service or the sale of a product." Quoting with approval from the Court of Appeal decision in *Carmichael v. Reitz* (1971) 17 Cal.App.3d 958, 978, 95 Cal.Rptr. 381, the court in *Murphy* stated that the distinction for purposes of the products liability analysis was "'between a transaction where the primary objective is the acquisition of ownership or use of a product and one where the dominant purpose is to obtain services.'" The court in *Murphy* also quoted with approval from the decision in *Magrine v. Krasnica* (1967) 94 N.J.Super. 228, 227 A.2d 539, 544, stating, "'the *essence* of the transaction between the retail seller and the consumer relates to the *article sold.* The seller is *in the business* of supplying the product to the consumer. It is that, and that alone, for which he is paid. A dentist or physician offers, and is paid for, his professional services and skill. That is the *essence* of the relationship between him and his patient.'" Based on its analysis of the role of a pharmacist, the court in *Murphy* held that a pharmacy in dispensing prescription drugs is performing a service and therefore is not strictly liable for an inherent defect in a drug.

Although the decision in *Murphy, supra,* 40 Cal.3d 672, 221 Cal.Rptr. 447, 710 P.2d 247 is instructive as to the distinction under the strict liability doctrine between providing a product for use by a consumer and providing a service, it is factually different from this case because *Murphy* involved an actual sale of a product by a professionally licensed defendant. Here, there was no sale and no evidence of services by a licensed professional.

This case is more analogous to the decision relied upon by defendant, *Ferrari v. Grand Canyon Dories* (1995) 32 Cal.App.4th 248, 38 Cal.Rptr.2d 65 (*Ferrari*). In that case, the plaintiff was a customer injured on a whitewater rafting trip sponsored and conducted by the defendant. She sued the defendant under, inter alia, a product liability theory of recovery. The trial court granted summary judgment on the plaintiff's product liability claim and the Court of Appeal affirmed that ruling.

In determining whether the defendant's river rafting company was strictly liable for the injuries plaintiff suffered as a result of an allegedly defective raft, the court in *Ferrari, supra,* 32 Cal.App.4th 248, 38 Cal.Rptr.2d 65 analyzed the application of the product liability doctrine in cases where the transaction involved both a product and a service.

> Plaintiff contends the raft is a product as contemplated by the doctrine of strict product liability, and defendants are therefore subject to strict liability as licensors of the raft. In a given transaction involving both products and services, liability will often depend upon the defendant's role. For example, an airline passenger injured because of a defect in the craft would have a strict liability claim against the manufacturer. The manufacturer's role is that of a provider of a product, the airplane. On the other hand, the airline operating the plane would be primarily involved in providing a service, i.e., transportation. The airline is itself the end user of the product and imposition of strict liability would be inappropriate.

Although the facts in the instant case concerning the provision of services are not as compelling as those at issue in *Ferrari, supra,* 32 Cal.App.4th 248, 38 Cal.Rptr.2d 65, they do support the conclusion that the dominant purpose of plaintiff's membership agreement was to provide fitness services. In addition to entitling her to use exercise equipment, plaintiff's agreement entitled her to engage in aerobics, dance classes, and yoga, among others activities. It also allowed her to take advantage of testing centers where she could check her blood pressure and weight. Thus, unlike in *Garcia, supra,* 3 Cal.App.3d 319, 82 Cal.Rptr. 420, in which the defendant laundromat owner provided washers and dryers for use by customers, and apparently nothing more, there is undisputed evidence here that defendant provided more to members than just the use of exercise machines. That evidence shows that defendant was in the business of providing fitness services and made exercise machines available to members as an incident to those services. Thus, the law of strict product liability does not apply to defendant under the facts of this case, and defendant was therefore entitled to summary judgment on the product liability claim.

That plaintiff chose not to avail herself of the services provided under her membership agreement does not change the essential nature and purpose of that agreement because it is the terms of her agreement, rather than her subjective intentions, that define the dominant purpose of her transaction with defendant. There is no evidence that plaintiff ever explained to defendant that she only wanted to use its exercise machines, not its services, or that the mutual intention of the parties was to exclude such services. Her uncommunicated subjective intent in that regard is therefore irrelevant. From the language of her agreement and defendant's uncontradicted evidence, we conclude that the dominant purpose of plaintiff's membership agreement was to make available fitness services; accordingly, plaintiff has no valid claim under the strict product liability doctrine.

Disposition

The judgment of the trial court is affirmed. Defendant is awarded its costs on appeal.

We concur: TURNER, P.J., and ARMSTRONG, J.

Questions about the case:

1. Did the waiver that the plaintiff signed when she joined the gym prevent her from bringing the lawsuit in this case? Why or why not?
2. How was the plaintiff injured in this case?
3. What is the plaintiff's argument that the defendant's fitness center is strictly liable for her injuries?
4. What was the purpose in creating California's strict liability approach to manufacturers?
5. Explain the court's reasoning in preventing the plaintiff from bringing her product liability case.

M. RETAILERS AND "MERE CONDUITS"

Approximately 200 products are recalled every year due to safety concerns.

When the plaintiff brings an action against a retailer, the plaintiff must show that the product was dangerous and that the retailer had reason to know that the product was dangerous. When the retailer acts as a mere conduit, that is, someone who forwards products from one location to another, the plaintiff will have a more difficult time proving his products liability suit.

When a retailer acts in some capacity that is greater than a mere conduit, the retailer's obligations include a requirement to test and inspect. Some jurisdictions require that a retailer who assembles parts or takes any other proactive role in the distribution of the project has a correspondingly greater role in testing and inspecting the products for defects.

Example: Haphazard Company buys and resells all types of merchandise at wholesale prices. When Haphazard makes out a receipt to a customer, the following information appears at the bottom: "By purchasing this product, you and reseller, purchaser or other person who later comes into possession of this product in the stream of commerce, disclaims and waives any action in products liability or negligence against Haphazard Co., Inc., for any failure to properly inspect, test or examine any products sold by us."

Toby purchases a safety harness from Haphazard. Later, the harness, which was made from poor-quality materials, breaks while Toby is using it to climb a tree to cut off a limb. Toby falls and is severely injured. Can he bring a suit against Haphazard Co.? Put another way, did Toby waive any possible lawsuit against the company by accepting the receipt?

Answer: Toby did not waive his rights to sue. Sidestepping the question of whether the "waiver" was validly created between Toby and Haphazard Co., there is a more basic question involved here: Can a company disclaim its own negligence? Courts have ruled that when a retailer, seller, or manufacturer places a defective product into the "stream of commerce," it cannot disclaim liability from its own negligence.[12]

N. INHERENTLY DANGEROUS OBJECTS

There are some objects that have been specifically designed to be dangerous. These objects, such as handguns, are considered to be inherently dangerous. In fact, their dangerousness forms the basis of their function. There is no way to make a handgun safe without essentially destroying its function. For instance, if you remove the trigger to prevent the gun from firing, the gun ceases to function. Because a consumer purchases a handgun desiring it to function, there is very little that a manufacturer can do to minimize the danger inherent in the design.

O. DEFENSES TO PRODUCTS LIABILITY ACTIONS

Defendants have many of the same defenses to a products liability case that they have in other tort actions. These include:

- contributory negligence/comparative negligence;
- assumption of the risk; and
- obvious hazard (a manufacturer will not be liable for failure to warn about an open and obvious danger or one that is a matter of common knowledge).

Sidebar

"The manufacturer of a knife cannot be charged with strict liability when the knife is used as a toothpick and the user complains because the sharp edge cuts."[13]

Sidebar

In recent years, some jurisdictions have experimented with the idea of requiring trigger locks on handguns as a way of making them safer. While it is in place, a trigger lock prevents the gun from being fired. However, a trigger lock also prevents the gun from being used. Once the trigger lock has been removed, the gun is as dangerous as it was before. Other technological approaches to handgun safety require the handgun user to wear a special ring. When someone who does not wear the ring handles the gun, the gun will not fire.

THE TIRE BLOWOUT HYPOTHETICAL

Now that you have reviewed this chapter, we return to Susan's tire blowout case. Can she bring a products liability action against the tire manufacturer? In most jurisdictions, the answer would be an unequivocal yes. Whether Susan proceeds on a negligence theory or a breach of warranty theory, she should have no trouble in making out a case of products liability. Whether she convinces the jury to award her damages is another matter entirely, but she should certainly survive a pretrial motion to dismiss the case.

Chapter Summary

In this chapter, we learned that there are some classes of injuries that fall into the category of strict liability. When the plaintiff is injured by a defective product, or by actions that the court considers to be abnormally dangerous, the defendant's proof of adherence to safety rules and regulations, and his testimony about how careful he was carrying out the procedures, are considered irrelevant. Strict liability is liability without regard to the defendant's fault. Therefore, a strict liability case can be successfully brought against the defendant even when he is not technically negligent or at fault. A form of strict liability lawsuit is a products liability action. Under a products liability action, a person who has been injured by a defective product is permitted to sue the manufacturer or the seller of the product, even though she is not able to prove exactly how the defect came about. In most cases, the mere fact that the product was defective and dangerous and that it injured someone is enough to sustain the minimal requirements of a products liability lawsuit.

SKILLS YOU NEED IN THE REAL WORLD

Maintaining the Chain of Custody for Evidence

Evidence is important in all cases, but it is often critical in products liability cases. In one case, a client reported that when she handled a sealed can of cat food, the can exploded, severely injuring her hand. Her hand became infected with some rare form of bacteria and required several operations. The client eventually lost some of the use of her hand. What started out as a clear-cut case of products liability swiftly became no case at all when the client reported that she threw away the can of cat food. Without that crucial piece of evidence, there was really no solid case. After all, how could the attorney prove that the can was defective if he could not produce the actual can?

Securing and storing evidence is an important skill for any paralegal. However, simply obtaining the evidence is not enough. In many cases, the chain of custody is also important. The chain of custody refers to all the people who come into contact with the evidence. Whoever handles the evidence should be recorded, by name, in case there is any question later about tampering. In the best situation, the evidence should be handled by as few people as possible. If you obtain evidence from the client, note the date and time that you receive it. Note the appearance of the evidence. Put it in a secure place and leave it there. On television shows, detectives always put evidence in sealed plastic bags. They don't do this to preserve fingerprints; they do it to keep anyone from tampering with the evidence. In a criminal case, the prosecution must present testimony from everyone who handled the evidence in order to prove the chain. You should adopt the same standards in a civil case. The less contact you have with the evidence, the better. If features of the evidence are important, such as expiration dates, warranty notices, or other information, photograph the evidence and work from the photographs. When you work with evidence that is perishable, such as the contents of an exploded cat food can, wrap it in plastic and store it in a freezer. Later, if tests are required, the contents can be thawed and examined. If they are left out to spoil, valuable evidence, such as the presence of harmful bacteria, will be lost.

THE LIFE OF A PARALEGAL

Becoming a Paralegal

I had been thinking about taking paralegal courses for some time. After speaking with a friend of mine who works as a paralegal, I decided to start taking some classes. Almost as soon as I started my classes, my friend called me and said that the attorney who she was working with needed an office manager. I interviewed for the job and was hired. Although I was hired as an office manager, the attorney began giving me more and more paralegal work to do. He also encouraged me to continue my courses at the Community College. At first, I was preparing motions and other basic legal work. However, before long, I was handling very complicated civil cases.

One of the things that surprised me the most about the law was how nice the attorneys were. The attorneys that I work with, and even the opposing attorneys, were always very polite to one another. I thought that they would argue and fight with each other at every opportunity. In fact, it was just the opposite. Most attorneys are very nice people and very ethical. I think that movies and television have given attorneys a bad name. Most of the ones that I know are good and decent people.

When I started working for the firm, the attorney who I worked with did have a computer on his desk, but he never touched it. He had me draft all of the complaints and answers on my own computer and then give them to him for proofing. I learned a lot about drafting legal documents that way.

Before long, I was drafting discovery documents, preparing settlement packages, helping to interview clients, and helping prepare the case for trial. It is fascinating work.

Renae Elam, Legal Assistant

ETHICAL ISSUES FOR THE PARALEGAL: FRIVOLOUS LAWSUITS

In situations involving strict liability lawsuits in general and products liability lawsuits in particular, there is a certain temptation to bend or break the rules. After all, most of these suits are brought against large corporations that are considered to be wealthy and faceless. Some frivolous lawsuits have been brought against manufacturers simply on the premise that the company will probably be more likely to pay to settle the case rather than risk negative media coverage. With this potential for fraudulent claims, the paralegal and the attorney should always be on the lookout for a client who appears to be manufacturing a claim just to make some money. Indications that a claim is fraudulent can come from a variety of sources.

For instance, the client's story does not stand up under close scrutiny. The client gives conflicting versions of how he was injured. There is no direct connection between the plaintiff's reported injuries and the supposed design defect of the product. Another indication of a fraudulent claim comes when you investigate the client's background and discover that he has brought other frivolous claims against other manufacturers. You should always be on the lookout for any indication that the client is not being truthful with you. A frivolous lawsuit can be the basis of a bad faith claim later in the litigation. A groundless lawsuit will also reflect badly on the law firm itself. Firms, and attorneys, have been sanctioned for bringing frivolous lawsuits. If a paralegal discovers any information that would tend to indicate that the claim is fraudulent, she should bring this to the attorney's attention immediately.

Relevant Cases

SPLENDORIO V. BILRAY DEMOLITION CO., INC.
682 A.2D 461 (1996)

Opinion
BOURCIER, Justice.
This case comes before us on appeal after summary judgment and entry of final judgment in favor of Certified Engineering and Testing Co., Inc. (Certified), one of three named defendants in a pending Superior Court civil action for damages. Plaintiffs' claims against the remaining defendants are pending trial in the Superior Court.

Facts and Travel
On September 2, 1988, Certified entered into a contract with the Providence Housing Authority (PHA) whereby Certified was required to inspect for the presence of asbestos in three buildings located in a public-housing development, Hartford Park that were scheduled for demolition. If asbestos was discovered, Certified was then required by its contract to develop a plan for the abatement of the asbestos and, after its removal, to certify its absence in the three buildings. Asbestos was found in the three buildings, and Certified thereafter developed an abatement plan. As part of that plan, the PHA contracted with D. Dixon Donovan Co. to remove the asbestos. After D. Dixon Donovan Co. removed the asbestos, Certified again inspected the three buildings, and determined from its examination that no

asbestos remained. Certified then issued its certification. Shortly thereafter, the PHA contracted with Bilray Demolition Co., Inc. (Bilray), another of the defendants, to demolish the buildings. That demolition contract required Bilray to transport the debris from the demolition site. General Laws 1956 §23–18.9–5 required Bilray to deliver the debris to a licensed solid waste facility. Bilray, however, in the course of its demolition work transported some of the debris from the buildings to its own wrecking yard, located in the town of Johnston, so that it could crush the debris and resell it as fill. That action was in clear violation of §23–18.9–5.

In 1990, while the third and final building included in the contract between the PHA and Certified was being demolished by Bilray, Certified, during the course of an inspection being conducted pursuant to a different and separate contract with the PHA, discovered a thin coat of asbestos on some walls it was examining in some different buildings located in the Hartford Park housing development. Certified then decided to reexamine the debris from the three buildings demolished by Bilray, both at the demolition yard and at Bilray's wrecking yard in Johnston, to determine if any of that debris contained any similar thin coats of asbestos. A small amount of asbestos was in fact found. As a result, the debris at both sites was then moistened so as to prevent the dispersal of any asbestos fibers into the air, and the debris that had been transported to the Bilray wrecking yard was then removed to a special waste facility in Indiana. Its having been placed at Bilray's wrecking yard in the first instance is the catalyst of this litigation.

Frances M. and Anthony J. Splendorio (the Splendorios) live in the vicinity of the Bilray wrecking yard in Johnston. They filed a civil action in the Superior Court against Bilray, Certified, and R & T Realty, Inc., the last being the owners of the property on which Bilray's wrecking yard is located. Although the Splendorios' complaint was filed as a class-action complaint, it has never been certified as a class action as required by Rule 23 of the Superior Court Rules of Civil Procedure.

In their complaint, the Splendorios allege, inter alia, that the value of their property has been diminished as a result of the defendants' actions. They contend that they must now disclose to any prospective buyers of their property the possible release of asbestos from Bilray's wrecking yard located in the vicinity of their property. Although the Splendorios have never attempted to market their property, they rely upon an affidavit from Robert Colieci (Colieci), a neighboring homeowner in the vicinity of the wrecking yard who is a licensed realtor, for proof of their diminution of property value claim. In his affidavit Colieci asserts that the potential release of asbestos from Bilray's wrecking yard site has reduced property values in the area and has dissuaded local homeowners from marketing their properties because of their fear of having to disclose to any prospective purchasers the possible presence of asbestos in or about their properties. He asserts further that the one house that was actually sold following the discovery of the asbestos at the Bilray wrecking yard was sold at a "25% reduction," from the seller's asking price, and that he "reasonably believe was attributed to the potential presence of asbestos in the neighborhood." That fact however was not disclosed prior to the sale. Moreover, according to Colieci, the one other house that is listed for sale in the neighborhood of Bilray's wrecking yard has not sold for a full year, a condition that he again attributes to the asbestos fear situation. The Splendorios' claim for damages is based solely upon Colieci's affidavit.

In responding to the Splendorios' complaint, Certified, one of the three named defendants in the civil action, moved for summary judgment on counts 1 and 4 in the Splendorios' complaint. Those counts allege absolute liability and negligence on the part of all defendants, including Certified. The trial justice after hearing on Certified's summary judgment motion found that the Splendorios had no cause of action against Certified. He found, specifically, that Certified was not subject to absolute liability pursuant to *Rose v. Socony–Vacuum Corp.*, 54 R.I. 411, 173 A. 627 (1934). He also found that Certified could not be held liable on the negligence theory advanced by the Splendorios because Certified owed no legal duty to the Splendorios and that in order for a duty to exist, the risk of harm to the Splendorios had to be foreseeable to them. The trial justice concluded that the risk of any harm coming to the Splendorios' property from any actions taken by Certified from which any duty flowed to the plaintiffs was not foreseeable. We affirm the trial justice's decision.

Under any theory of absolute liability for ultrahazardous or abnormally dangerous activities, Certified could not be found liable to the plaintiffs under the particular facts present in this case. Those facts mandate affirmance of the trial justice's grant of summary judgment under either Rose or the application of an absolute liability theory.

The Absolute Liability Count

The question of whether a defendant should be held strictly liable for ultrahazardous or abnormally dangerous activities is a question of law. Absolute liability attaches only to ultrahazardous or abnormally dangerous activities and not to ultrahazardous or abnormally dangerous materials. In such an analysis properties of the particular substance are not determinative, rather the defendant's activity as a whole is analyzed. If the rule were otherwise, virtually any commercial activity involving substances which are dangerous in the abstract automatically would be deemed as abnormally dangerous. This result would be intolerable.

Although asbestos is understandably an ultrahazardous or abnormally dangerous material, Certified's activities in this case were not ultrahazardous or abnormally dangerous. An analysis of whether an activity is ultrahazardous or abnormally dangerous requires a consideration of the following factors, as set forth in the Restatement (Second) Torts §520 (1977):

(a) existence of high degree of risk of some harm to the person, land or chattels of others;
(b) likelihood that the harm that results from it will be great;
(c) inability to eliminate the risk by the exercise of reasonable care;
(d) extent to which the activity is not a matter of common usage;
(e) inappropriateness of the activity to the place where it is carried on; and
(f) extent to which its value to the community is outweighed by its dangerous attributes.

Those factors are to be viewed as a whole and the weight apportioned to each should be dependent upon the facts in each particular case. In this appeal, while we recognize that great harm might result from ingestion of asbestos fibers, the risk thereof resulting from Certified's limited activities, leaves that probability on the facts here, most improbable because its activities were in fact carried out safely and with the exercise of reasonable care. "An activity is not abnormally dangerous if the risks therefrom could be limited by the exercise of reasonable care." *G.J. Leasing Co.*, 854 F.Supp. at 568. "Clean up of PCB's from an industrial site is not an abnormally dangerous activity that warrants the application of strict liability." Certified's activities in this case were appropriate because in the demolition of buildings possibly containing asbestos it is necessary prior to demolition to inspect for asbestos in order to reduce potential health risks. Nothing required to be performed by Certified created or gave rise to the conditions complained of by the Splendorios. It was Bilray's unanticipated and unlawful actions that created the conditions complained of by them. Finally, and perhaps most importantly, the value to the community of Certified's activities far outweighed its dangerous attributes. "Cleanup operations serve the valuable and essential social function of reducing the danger" of potentially harmful substances such as asbestos. Therefore, public policy, as well as the other factors listed in Restatement (Second) Torts §520, support our conclusion that Certified could not on the facts present in this case be held strictly liable for its activities. Accordingly, Certified is not liable under the theory of strict liability to the Splendorios and the grant of Certified's motion for summary judgment was proper.

The Negligence Count

Before there could be any finding of negligence made against Certified, the Splendorios were first required to establish that (a) Certified owed them a legal duty to refrain from negligent activities; (b) that there was a breach of that duty; (c) that the breach proximately caused the Splendorios' injury; and (d) that there was actual loss or damage resulting. The linchpin in determining the existence of any duty owed to the Splendorios was the foreseeability of the risk of injury to them by Certified's actions. "The risk reasonably to be perceived defines the duty to be obeyed, and risk imports relation; it is risk to another or to others within the range of apprehension." *Builders Specialty Co. v. Goulet*, 639 A.2d 59, 60 (R.I.1994)(quoting *Palsgraf v. Long Island Railroad Co.*, 248 N.Y. 339, 344, 162 N.E. 99, 100 [1928]).

It is clear that Certified did not owe the Splendorios any duty. Its contractual obligation from which any duty emanated was to the PHA. Certified could not foresee any risk flowing to the Splendorios because it was not reasonably foreseeable that Bilray would transport any of the demolition debris to its wrecking yard in Johnston, contrary to the terms of its contract with PHA, and to the dictates of the law, and thereby create a risk to the Splendorios. Pursuant to §23–18.9–5, Bilray was required to deposit the demolition solid waste debris at a licensed solid waste facility. Bilray did not, however, obey that law. Certified cannot be held responsible for its not predicting and anticipating Bilray's breach of contract and illegal actions. Therefore, we are satisfied on the facts in this case that Certified did not owe any duty to the Splendorios, who were clearly outside the zone of any foreseeable danger created by Certified's activities under its contract with the PHA. In addition to the Splendorios' failure to establish any legal duty owed to them by Certified, the Splendorios have also failed to demonstrate any proximate cause between Certified's inspection actions and the Splendorios' alleged damages. Ordinarily the determination of proximate cause and, consequently, the existence of any superseding cause is a question of fact that should not be decided by summary judgment. However, one resisting summary judgment must assert "sufficient facts to satisfy the necessary elements of his or her negligence claim" and if a "plaintiff fails to present evidence identifying defendants' negligence as the proximate cause of his or her injury or from which a reasonable inference of proximate cause may be drawn," then summary judgment becomes proper. *Russian v. Life–Cap Tire Services, Inc.*, 608 A.2d 1145, 1147 (R.I.1992). On the record before us, there were insufficient facts alleged and presented to the trial justice to establish proximate cause between the inspection and certification activities of Certified and the alleged harm and damages to the Splendorios. The facts presented did not permit even an inference of proximate cause. The record demonstrates that it was Bilray's unforeseeable and illegal superseding act of depositing the demolition materials at its company wrecking yard that proximately caused the Splendorios' alleged harm and damages, thereby cutting off Certified's liability. Since Certified owed no legal duty to the Splendorios and because there was an insufficient showing of proximate cause between Certified's activities and the Splendorios' alleged harm and damages, summary judgment was properly granted in favor of Certified.

Accordingly, the summary judgment is affirmed, the Splendorios' appeal is denied and dismissed, and the papers of this case are remanded to the Superior Court.

SELWYN V. WARD
879 A.2D 882 (2005)

Opinion

PER CURIAM.

It's an all too familiar scenario — a group of high school students manage to procure some alcoholic beverages, act irresponsibly, and someone gets hurt. In this version, however, the injuries did not result from the consumption of illegally obtained alcohol but from a minor igniting it and causing an explosion. The plaintiff, Bridget Selwyn (Selwyn or plaintiff), is the victim in this tragedy, and she sought to recover for her injuries from several named defendants, including RC Liquors, Inc. (RC Liquors or defendant). It is from a grant of summary judgment in favor of that defendant that the plaintiff appeals.

This case came before the Supreme Court on May 12, 2005, pursuant to an order directing the parties to appear and show cause why the issues raised in this appeal should not summarily be decided. After hearing arguments of counsel and reviewing the memoranda submitted by the parties, we are satisfied that cause has not been shown. Accordingly, we shall decide the appeal at this time.

Facts and Travel

In the early morning of August 26, 2000, plaintiff and several others gathered at the home of Karen Ward (Ward), on Warwick Neck Avenue, in Warwick. The Ward property included an outbuilding, referred to as "the barn," in which Ward's son, Taylor, and his friends often socialized. On the night of the incident, the gathering at the barn consisted of: Bridget Selwyn, Taylor Ward, Michael A. Buonanno (Buonanno), John Cronin (Cronin), Eric Machala, Kathryn A. Marciano (Marciano), Peter Keene, Jason Petrarca, James Carvalho, and Richard Cole.

The accounts of the evening's events indicate that various people were smoking marijuana and/or ingesting ecstasy in the barn. There also was a partially consumed 1.75-liter bottle of 190-proof grain alcohol or "Everclear" in the barn. At about 4:30 A.M. on August 26, 2000, the bottle of Everclear became the catalyst for disaster when Buonanno poured some of the grain alcohol onto an open flame, causing an intense explosion that burned plaintiff, Marciano, and Cronin.

It was revealed during discovery that a bottle of Everclear had been purchased by another adolescent, Lauren Andrews (Andrews), for a gathering at the barn the previous month. Andrews said that she purchased the Everclear at RC Liquors and was not asked for proof of age. Earlier, at that gathering, Andrews mixed up a batch of "Jungle Juice" — a combination of "Kool-Aid, Everclear, and vodka" — and left the remaining grain alcohol in the barn.

The plaintiff amended her complaint to include RC Liquors as a party defendant. She alleged that defendant directly and proximately caused her injuries by providing Andrews with the grain alcohol when it "knew or should have known (1) that Andrews was underage to lawfully possess and/or consume alcoholic beverages; and (2) that it was unlawful and dangerous to others to provide grain alcohol to minors." RC Liquors moved for summary judgment.

In support of her opposition to defendant's motion, plaintiff submitted the affidavit of Thomas J. Paolino, Jr., M.D. (Dr. Paolino). Doctor Paolino is a physician and psychiatrist who devotes a substantial portion of his practice to treating substance abuse issues in adolescents and young adults. In the affidavit, he said that "the possession and use of grain alcohol by adolescents and young adults is extremely dangerous." He explained that consuming grain alcohol can lead to "rapid intoxication" and that "adolescents and young adults will typically engage in risky and dangerous behavior when severely impaired." He further averred that grain alcohol is extremely flammable and that "frequently adolescents and young adults who use grain alcohol light it on fire." Doctor Paolino expressed his opinion that: "It is very foreseeable that adolescents and young adults in the possession of grain alcohol will frequently light it on fire." The plaintiff also supplied a picture of the Everclear bottle, which includes a warning about the product's flammability.

The plaintiff argued that defendant breached its duty of care when it sold the grain alcohol to Andrews with actual or constructive knowledge of the "fire play" allegedly linked to Everclear. She conceded that there was "no allegation that this incident occurred due to the intoxication of a minor or that RC Liquors sold grain alcohol that occasioned, in whole or in part, the intoxication of a minor." She instead asserted that the cause of the incident was "horseplay." The plaintiff argued that "a number of drink recipes and web sites encourage this fire play" and that purveyors of grain alcohol should be aware that those drinks are lit on fire. The plaintiff also argued that defendant's violation of the state law prohibiting sales of liquor to minors was evidence of its negligence and that the statute is intended "to protect minors from injury by alcohol." Further, plaintiff asserts that the state Dram Shop Act "broadens liability."

The trial justice granted defendant's motion. After rejecting the testimony of Dr. Paolino on the ground that he was not qualified to give the proffered opinion, the trial justice ruled that plaintiff's claim failed on the element of foreseeability. The trial justice reasoned:

> There is no nexus, by statute or by common law, that would find that the conduct, if any, of the defendant in selling grain alcohol to the minor, who then allegedly gave it to her friend and went to Italy, would be liable under the circumstances of this case where there is no allegation that the injury occurred because any minor — or adult, for that matter — imbibing the alcohol, which caused, in whole or in part, that individual's intoxication. It would seem that there's no statutory authority for

> this cause of action and that the misconduct, if any, of the defendant was rendered remote by intervening independent acts of others.

Judgment entered pursuant to Rule 54(b) of the Superior Court Rules of Civil Procedure, and plaintiff filed a timely notice of appeal.

Issues on Appeal

The plaintiff argues that the trial justice erred by granting summary judgment in favor of RC Liquors because the documents produced illustrate that defendant negligently caused Selwyn's injuries by selling the Everclear to Andrews. In addition, plaintiff contends that defendant's alleged violation of state liquor laws establishes a cause of action in negligence against defendant under the Dram Shop Act. Lastly, plaintiff asserts that defendant can be held strictly liable because selling grain alcohol to a minor is an ultrahazardous activity.

Did Defendant Owe a Duty of Reasonable Care to Plaintiff?

To prevail on a claim of negligence, "a plaintiff must establish a legally cognizable duty owed by a defendant to a plaintiff, a breach of that duty, proximate causation between the conduct and the resulting injury, and the actual loss or damage." *Mills v. State Sales, Inc.*, 824 A.2d 461, 467-68 (R.I.2003). The crux of this appeal is whether defendant owed plaintiff a legal duty, which is a question of law. If no such duty exists, then plaintiff's claim must fail, as a matter of law. If the evidence establishes that a duty did run from defendant to plaintiff, then plaintiff is entitled to a determination of the remaining factual questions — did defendant breach the duty of care, and if so, was that breach the proximate cause of plaintiff's harm?

This Court determines whether a duty exists on a "case-by-case basis," considering "'all relevant factors, including the relationship between the parties, the scope and burden of the obligation to be imposed upon the defendant, public policy considerations,' and the 'foreseeability of harm to the plaintiff.'" The linchpin in the analysis of whether a duty flows from a defendant to a plaintiff is foreseeability. *Splendorio*, 682 A.2d at 466. As Justice Cardozo of the New York Court of Appeals said: "The risk reasonably to be perceived defines the duty to be obeyed, and risk imports relation; it is risk to another or to others within the range of apprehension." *Palsgraf v. Long Island Railroad Co.*, 248 N.Y. 339, 162 N.E. 99, 100 (1928). This Court has expressed this concept of limiting the scope of a defendant's duty according to risks he or she reasonably perceived, saying that a duty must be based on conduct "sufficiently likely to result in the kind of harm" suffered by the plaintiff, Volpe, 821 A.2d at 705, or that "in order to temper foreseeability an adequate nexus must exist between the foreseeability of plaintiff's harm and the actions of the defendant." *Marchetti v. Parsons*, 638 A.2d 1047, 1051 (R.I.1994).

The plaintiff argues that the risk of the type of harm she suffered was within defendant's range of apprehension because it knew or should have known that grain alcohol is commonly used by minors to engage in fire play. The only evidence plaintiff presented to support this contention was the opinion of Dr. Paolino. However, the trial justice rejected his opinion, saying: "He may well be qualified as an expert in psychiatry, in pharmacology, perhaps in treating those who suffer from substance abuse," but he is not qualified to give an opinion on whether it is foreseeable that adolescents would light grain alcohol on fire.

The admissibility of a proffered expert opinion is a matter left to the sound discretion of the trial justice; absent an abuse of that discretion, this Court will not disturb the trial justice's ruling. Having carefully reviewed the record, we are satisfied that the trial justice did not abuse her discretion by disregarding Dr. Paolino's opinion. From Dr. Paolino's education and experience, one could reasonably conclude that he was not qualified to give an opinion on a liquor store owner's actual or constructive knowledge about an adolescent's tendency to ignite grain alcohol for sport.

Further, we are not convinced that this type of harm is a foreseeable consequence of the sale of alcohol to minors. The plaintiff asserts that defendant owed her a duty arising out of G.L.1956 §3-8-5. She contends that her injuries were foreseeable by RC Liquors by virtue of the sheer quantity and volatile nature of the grain alcohol it allegedly sold to seventeen-year-old Andrews, in violation of §3-8-5. According to plaintiff, the size of the bottle of Everclear and the label warning of the product's flammability put defendant on notice that Andrews intended to share the grain alcohol with other minors and that one of those minors might get burned.

In *Martin*, 871 A.2d at 913, we held that a defendant-homeowner was not entitled to summary judgment in a suit to recover damages suffered by a minor who consumed alcohol on her property. The plaintiff was a guest at a party the defendant hosted for her daughter, with two kegs of beer and a port-a-john available; he admitted to drinking approximately six beers from the kegs. Id. at 914. There was an altercation, and the plaintiff was struck in the head by a baseball bat wielded by a third person, causing the injuries for which he sued the defendant and others. Id. The Superior Court granted the defendant's motion for summary judgment, finding that she had no duty to protect the plaintiff from the attack because it was unforeseeable. Id. This Court vacated the judgment, holding that a social host owes a special duty to his or her underage guests when he or she provides those guests with intoxicants. Id. at 915-16. We reasoned that holding social hosts to such a duty furthered the public policy reflected in our state laws banning underage drinking and prohibiting adults from supplying alcohol to minors. Id. at 916. Furthermore, we concluded that it was foreseeable that when upwards of fifty young people are at a party where alcohol is available, a violent altercation is foreseeable, because "the use of intoxicants frequently unduly excites the tempers, emotions and actions of those who indulge in them." Id. at 917.

The present case is distinguishable from Martin in two crucial ways. First, the minors in Martin were guests at the defendant's home and under her supervision while illegally consuming alcohol, whereas Buonanno, Selwyn, and the others gathered at the barn were neither on RC Liquors' property nor under its supervision when the fire injuring plaintiff occurred. Second, the evidence in Martin suggested that the defendant made alcohol available for consumption by the guests gathered at her house, giving rise to a special duty to protect those guests, but there has been no suggestion that RC Liquors sold grain alcohol to Andrews for the purpose of igniting it.

The public policy considerations that shaped the duty of care in Martin are not present in this case. At issue here is whether a purveyor of alcohol owes a duty to protect minors, to whom he or she allegedly supplied alcoholic beverages, from another person's deliberate act of pouring the alcohol over an open flame. The statutes regulating alcohol and minors reflect a public policy against underage drinking and not incendiary behavior. *Martin*, 871 A.2d at 916.

Moreover, as in *Martin*, 871 A.2d at 915, 917, public policy is not the sole factor; foreseeability limits the scope of duty. Even if we assume, as we are required to do for purposes of our review, that RC Liquors sold the grain alcohol to Andrews, a minor, we are satisfied that defendant could not reasonably perceive the risk that several weeks later, while the minor was out of the country, some other youth would pour the substance onto an open flame, causing flames to engulf Selwyn. Selwyn was not injured as a result of consumption of the grain alcohol nor was she vulnerable to a dangerous condition created by defendant. No special duty arises from RC Liquors' alleged illegal sale of the Everclear to protect those placed in harm's way by the deliberate ignition of the alcohol by a third person.

Does Plaintiff Have a Cause of Action Under a Strict Liability Theory?

The plaintiff asserts that selling grain alcohol to a minor is an ultrahazardous activity, warranting application of strict liability. Whether a defendant has engaged in an ultrahazardous or abnormally dangerous activity is a question of law. Strict liability attaches when a plaintiff's injuries are proximately caused by some ultrahazardous or abnormally dangerous activity of the defendant but not when they are caused by an ultrahazardous or abnormally dangerous material. Id. at 465-66. To determine whether an activity is ultrahazardous or abnormally dangerous, courts in this jurisdiction consider the following factors:

> (a) existence of high degree of risk of some harm to the person, land or chattels of others;
> (b) likelihood that the harm that results from it will be great;
> (c) inability to eliminate the risk by the exercise of reasonable care;
> (d) extent to which the activity is not a matter of common usage;
> (e) inappropriateness of the activity to the place where it is carried on; and
> (f) extent to which its value to the community is outweighed by its dangerous attributes. Id. at 466 (quoting 3 Restatement (Second) Torts §520 (1977)).

To give our analysis some perspective, the drafters explained that: "The harm threatened must be major in degree, and sufficiently serious in its possible consequences to justify holding the defendant strictly responsible for subjecting others to an unusual risk." 3 Restatement (Second) Torts §520, cmt. g at 38. They provided the following examples of the type of harm:

> Some activities, such as the use of atomic energy, necessarily and inevitably involve major risks of harm to others, no matter how or where they are carried on. Others, such as the storage of explosives, necessarily involve major risks unless they are conducted in a remote place or to a very limited extent. Still others, such as the operation of a ten-ton traction engine on the public highway, which

crushes conduits beneath it, involve such a risk only because of the place where they are carried on. Id.

With these benchmarks in mind, while we do not mean to trivialize the risks associated with providing minors with alcoholic beverages, flammable or otherwise, such activity does not rise to the level addressed by §520 of the restatement.

Conclusion

For the reasons set forth herein, the judgment is affirmed, and the papers in the case are remanded to the Superior Court.

Websites

▪ **Legal Information Institute**
www.law.cornell.edu/wex/products_liability

▪ **Overview of product liability**
www.law.cornell.edu/ (click "search sitewide" and enter "product liability" and/or "strict liability")

▪ **Consumer product warranties — Magnuson-Moss Act (U.S. Code)**
www4.law.cornell.edu/uscode/15/ch50.html

▪ **Model Punitive Damages Act — Products Liability Cases**
www.uniformlaws.org/ActSummary.aspx?title=Punitive%20Damages %20Act,%20Model

▪ **U.S. Consumer Product Safety Commission**
www.cpsc.gov

Forms and Court Documents

This is a complaint form, based on the factual scenario presented at the beginning of the chapter.

STATE OF PLACID   IN THE SUPERIOR COURT
COUNTY OF BARNES   FILE NUMBER: _____

Susan Wilson,   )   Complaint
Plaintiff   )
)
vs.   )
)

Haley Tire Company
Defendant

Product Liability Complaint

1.

Defendant Haley Tire Company (hereafter "Defendant") is a corporation organized under the laws of the State of Placid and is actively engaged in the manufacture and distribution of automobile tires commonly used on passenger automobiles.

2.

Defendant manufactured tires under the "Wild One," "One for the Road," and "Beast" brand names from 1999 through 2002 in the State of Placid.

3.

Defendant distributed the tires it manufactured through various wholesale and retail outlets, including Sam's Tahoe Dealership, located in Springfield, Placid.

4.

On May 15, 2000, the plaintiff purchased a 2001 model Orion Sports Utility Vehicle from Sam's Tahoe Dealership.

5.

This vehicle was equipped with "Beast" brand tires as standard equipment.

6.

On June 1, 2002, the plaintiff was operating her 2001 Orion Sports Utility Vehicle in a safe and reasonable manner, when the driver's side front tire suffered an explosive decompression, commonly called a "blowout."

7.

The tire blowout caused the plaintiff to lose control of her automobile and crash. She suffered extensive physical and emotional injuries.

8.

At the time of plaintiff's injuries, she was using the tires manufactured by the defendant in the manner and method anticipated by the defendant. Plaintiff was not aware of any defect in the tires, nor had the plaintiff been informed that the "Beast" brand tires on her automobile had been the subject of a nationwide recall commencing on May 28, 2002.

9.

When the plaintiff sustained her injuries more fully alleged below, the automobile tires were in a defective condition that caused them to be unreasonably dangerous to the plaintiff in that the tires had a pre-existing design defect that caused them to explosively decompress at high speeds.

10.

Plaintiff was not aware, and could not have become aware by reasonable inspection of said tires, that the tires were defective and dangerous.

11.

Defendants owed the plaintiff a duty to provide said automobile tires in a fit condition for use and free of defects. Defendant breached this duty to the plaintiff.

12.

The Defendant's breach was the sole and proximate cause of the plaintiff's injuries.

13.

As a result of the defendant's breach, plaintiff has sustained the following injuries, to wit . . .

WHEREFORE, the plaintiff prays that she have and recover of the defendant:
1. General compensatory damages in excess of $10,000.00.
2. Special damages in the amount of $305,712.00.
3. Such other relief as the court may deem just and equitable.

Respectfully submitted, this the _____ day of _____, 20_____.

_____

Clarence D. Arrow
Attorney for the Plaintiff

Key Terms

Privity   Ultra-hazardous
Products liability   Warranty
Strict liability

Review Questions

1 How is a strict liability action different from a negligence action?
2 Why does the law consider the defendant's care and correct procedures in a negligence case but ignore them in a strict liability lawsuit?
3 How is a strict liability lawsuit different from an intentional tort?
4 How would you define the term *abnormally dangerous activity*?
5 Explain the history of strict liability in the United States.
6 How have judicial rulings changed in strict liability cases from the mid-1800s through the 1900s?
7 What is the significance of the *Rylands* case?

8 Prior to the 1960s, if a person wished to sue a manufacturer of a defective or dangerous product, what series of recovery was available to him?

9 What is the significance of the *MacPherson* case?

10 What are the three theories of products liability lawsuits?

11 What are some of the alternative theories of recovery in products liability lawsuits?

12 How is the law of product liability applied to retailers?

13 What are examples of "inherently dangerous" objects?

14 Why is it important to preserve evidence?

15 What is the "chain of custody" for evidence?

Applying What You Have Learned

1 Ajax Company has come up with a new toy. This toy is a spaceship that when activated flies through the room in a great sweeping circle, spilling out candy. The spaceship is designed with sharp angles and points on the wings and nose. The first time it was used, the spaceship, while flying around the room, struck Toby in the face. He has been severely scarred. Does Toby have a products liability cause of action? If so, on what theories should he base his products liability lawsuit?

2 Does it matter in our products liability case against the tire manufacturer that Susan did not keep the tire? Would the tire be helpful in the lawsuit? If so, how?

3 ABC Computer Company has produced a new laptop computer that it says is "the most user-friendly computer in the world." Gene purchases the computer, and the first time he turns it on he receives a severe electric shock. Draft a products liability complaint on these facts using breach of warranty and strict liability theories.

Endnotes

[1] *Doundoulakis v. Hempstead,* 42 N.Y.2d 440, 398 N.Y.S.2d 401, 368 N.E.2d 24 (1977).

[2] *Hynes v. Energy West, Inc.,* 211 F.3d 1193 (Wyo. 2000).

[3] Lawrence Friedman, A History of American Law, Murray Printing Co., Forge Village, Mass., 1973, p. 425.

[4] *Ultramares Corp. v. Touche,* 255 N.Y. 170, 174 N.E. 441 (1931).

[5] Lawrence Friedman, *A History of American Law,* Murray Printing Co., Forge Village, Mass., 1973, p. 589.

[6] Miller & Lovell, Products Liability 7 (1977).

[7] *McCarty v. E. J. Korvette, Inc.,* 28 Md. App. 421, 347 A.2d 253, 264 (1975).

[8] Restatement (Second) of Torts §395, comment f.

[9] *Hoemke v. New York Blood Center,* 912 F.2d 550 (2d Cir. 1990).

[10] *Flagstar Enterprises, Inc. v. Davis,* 709 So. 2d 1132 (1997).

[11] *Zaccone v. American Red Cross,* 872 F. Supp. 457 (N.D. Ohio 1994).

[12] *Ruzzo v. LaRose Enterprises,* 748 A.2d 261 (2000).

[13] *Suter v. San Angelo Foundry & Mach. Co.,* 406 A.2d 140 (1979).

Crossword Puzzle

www.CrosswordWeaver.com

ACROSS

2 The liability assessed against a
manufacturer, seller, wholesaler, etc.,
for placing a dangerous or defective
product on the market that causes
injury or damage

4 The direct relationship between the
parties to a contract that arises from
their involvement in creating the
contract

5 A finding of liability regardless of fault

DOWN

1 A condition of special or unusual
dangerousness

3 A pledge, assurance, or guarantee
that a particular fact is true

Defamation

Chapter Objectives

- **Define defamation and apply it to factual situations**
- **Distinguish between libel and slander**
- **Explain slander per se**
- **Explain how damages are assessed in libel and slander cases**
- **Define the importance of "publication" in defamation cases**

I INTRODUCTION

Although we usually begin each chapter with a discussion of the Chumley case, this chapter, like the prior chapter, does not involve any of the legal issues raised in that case. Instead, we examine the facts of a different case here.

Susan is a college student and, like many students, she shops at stores close to the college campus. Susan writes checks to pay for her goods at these various stores, and she has always been scrupulous about keeping track of her money. One day, she walks into a local grocery store and sees a large sign by the main entrance. The sign reads: "These deadbeats have robbed us of money by passing bad checks at this establishment. If you see any of these people, tell them what you think about them — after all, because they violate the law, they raise your prices." Just below this statement, which is written in black, bold letters at least five inches tall, Susan sees her own name, among five others. She is immediately embarrassed and humiliated, all the more so because she knows that she has never written a bad check at this or any other store. She immediately approaches the store manager and tells him that there has been some error. The manager, in front of a large group of shoppers, says, "So, you're one of the deadbeats. Man, you people are all the same. Always making excuses. I should call the police on you right now. Get out of my store and don't come back until you pay off your bad checks!"

Susan has come to our firm for a consultation. She wants to know if she has a cause of action against the store for presenting false information about her to the public. We assess her case after addressing the topic of defamation.

DEFAMATION

Defamation is a rather strange tort. It is one of the few torts that provide a cause of action for injuring another person's reputation. Historically, defamation was one of a number of strict liability torts. Under the common law, for example, it was no defense to defamation that the statement was made innocently, that the plaintiff was a public figure, or that the statement was made on a matter of public concern by a media affiliate. The law of **defamation** has changed considerably in the past few decades.

Defamation
A false attack on the reputation or character of another.

A. WHAT IS DEFAMATION?

When a person falsely injures another person's reputation, or exposes that person to public humiliation or degradation, the person injured is permitted to bring suit against the other. A defamatory statement tends to harm the person's reputation in the community or cause others to stop associating with her.[1] Essentially, when a person is defamed, it injures her ability to deal with others in society.

The theory behind making defamatory statements actionable is that individuals should be free to enjoy their reputations and good names without the stigma of false statements. Allowing a plaintiff to bring suit for defamation is one way for an individual to protect her status in society.[2] Defamation is different from other torts in that the focus of the action is not the injury to the plaintiff's physical, financial, or emotional status, but the damage done to her reputation. See Figure 11-1 for the Restatement's position on defamation.

FIGURE 11-1

Restatement Position on Defamation

According to the Restatement of Torts, defamation consists of:

- A false and defamatory statement concerning the plaintiff;
- An unprivileged publication to a third party;
- Fault amounting to at least negligence on the part of the publisher; and
- Legal recognized cause of action for the statement or proof of special harm.*

*Restatement (Second) of Torts §558.

To defame someone is to make or write a statement that is false and that injures the plaintiff's character or reputation. Defamation requires that this statement be heard or seen by someone else.

TORT
BASICS
AT A
GLANCE

B. DEFAMATION COMES IN TWO FORMS

Defamation can occur in two ways. When a person makes a defamatory statement verbally, this is referred to as **slander.** When a person makes a defamatory statement in writing, this is referred to as **libel.**

Slander
Spoken defamation.

Libel
Written defamation.

Defamation comes in two forms: written and verbal. When someone defames another person in writing, that is libel. When someone defames another person verbally, that is slander.

TORT
BASICS
AT A
GLANCE

Because the elements for libel and slander are similar, we address the general elements of defamation and then discuss issues peculiar to each.

C. ELEMENTS OF DEFAMATION

In the following sections, we examine each of the elements of a defamation action (see Figure 11-2). In defamation cases, most jurisdictions follow the requirement that proof of the plaintiff's allegations must be **clear and convincing.** This is also the standard recommended by the Restatement of Torts.[3]

1. DEFAMATORY LANGUAGE

a. Definition

The first and most important element of any defamation action is that the words used actually defame the plaintiff. Defamatory language is any statement that subjects the plaintiff to public ridicule, hatred, or contempt. There are many types of vicious and unsavory statements that are not considered to be defamatory. Insults, for example, are generally not classified as defamation.

Sidebar

Libel and slander are generally considered to be different forms of defamation, with slightly different elements and different types of damages assessed. However, these differences are not as pronounced as other types of torts, such as the differences between the torts of assault and battery.

Clear and convincing
A measure of proof that is higher than preponderance of the evidence, but less than beyond a reasonable doubt; clear and convincing proof is evidence that is likely to be true under the facts.

FIGURE 11-2	In most jurisdictions, defamation consists of:
The Elements of Defamation	▪ Unprivileged ▪ Of false statements ▪ Publication ▪ That are the proximate cause of injury to another.*

*Barry College v. Hull, 353 So. 2d 575 (1977).

Statements that injure the plaintiff's feelings are also not defamatory. To be defamatory, the statement must injure the plaintiff's reputation or hold the plaintiff up to public ridicule, embarrassment, or humiliation. Insults do not meet this standard.

b. Opinions

Is an opinion defamation?

Example: John asks Ted what he thinks about Carl. John says, "I think he's dishonest." Is this a defamatory statement?

Answer: It depends. In most jurisdictions, a pure opinion is not actionable as defamation. However, this rule does have certain exceptions. For example, a statement that is otherwise an opinion may cross the line into defamation if we add some additional facts. For instance, suppose that John says, "I happen to know that Carl is dishonest." Although this statement sounds similar to the first, under defamation law, it is quite different. The second statement sounds as if it is based on some particular instance or on a fact that John has not yet stated. In such a situation, the closer the opinion comes to a factual statement, the more likely it is considered defamatory.

2. FALSE STATEMENTS

In addition to the language causing the plaintiff embarrassment or financial loss, the statement must also be false. One of the main defenses to a defamation action is that the statement is true. If the statement is true, it is not defamatory and therefore cannot form the basis of either a slander or libel action. We discuss this defense in greater detail later in this chapter.

3. THE STATEMENT REFERS TO THE PLAINTIFF

a. Burden of Proof

Although it sounds rather obvious, the plaintiff must prove that the defamatory statement was made about him. Sometimes this is difficult for the plaintiff to prove. Suppose that the defendant makes a statement such as, "He's a child molester." That statement certainly sounds as though it qualifies as defamation. However, before the jury could be allowed to reach that conclusion, the plaintiff would have to prove that the statement was made about him. If the defendant is pointing to a group of people that includes the plaintiff, how can anyone be sure that the defendant is referring to the plaintiff? These determinations depend on the unique facts of each case. If the defendant singles out the plaintiff in some way that it becomes clear to others that the defendant is talking about him, the plaintiff will probably prove his case. If not, then the plaintiff's case may fail. It is not a requirement that the defendant specifically name the plaintiff, as long as it is clear to others that the defendant is referring to the plaintiff.

A defamatory statement does not actually have to name the plaintiff. In most jurisdictions, if a statement can reasonably be interpreted as referring to the plaintiff, the courts will rule that the defendant has defamed the plaintiff even though the defendant never referred to the plaintiff by name.[4]

TORT
BASICS
AT A
GLANCE

What if the link to the plaintiff is tenuous? Is it enough that someone might have connected the plaintiff to the defamatory statement? Courts have consistently held that the statement must clearly refer to the plaintiff. A statement so vague that it may or may not have referred to the plaintiff is not actionable as defamation.[5]

b. Is It Possible to Defame a Group?

Suppose that Darrell Defendant makes the following statement: "It is well known that white males are incapable of telling the truth." John is a white male and doesn't like Darrell's statement. Can he bring a defamation action against Darrell?

Answer: No. To bring an action, John must prove that he, as an individual, was defamed. John has no cause of action simply because he belongs to a group that has been maligned.[6]

However, the rule changes when the group is small and readily identifiable. Suppose that Darrell's statement refers to a family. Darrell says, "That X family is full of liars and thieves." Can any member of that family bring suit against Darrell? In most jurisdictions, the answer is yes, because the statement was made about a clearly ascertainable plaintiff, that is, one of the members of that particular family.

4. PUBLICATION

In all jurisdictions, publication or communication of the defamatory statement is an essential requirement. Courts use the terms *publication* and *communication* interchangeably; we use the term *publication* for the remainder of the chapter. When a person publishes a defamatory statement, she communicates that statement to someone other than the plaintiff. When the defamation is slander, it must be heard and understood by someone other than the plaintiff. When the defamation is libel, or written, it must be read and understood by someone other than the plaintiff. If a writing is not intended to be published, and is accidentally read by a third person, most jurisdictions will hold that no publication occurred, and therefore there has been no defamation.

Example: Tina writes in her diary: "I know that Ted is a thief and a liar." Tina's mother, while cleaning her room, finds Tina's diary and reads this sentence. Ted files an action for libel. Can he prove publication?

Answer: No. Tina's diary was not intended for publication — in fact, one could argue that it was never intended to be read by anyone but Tina — so the accidental reading by Tina's mother will most likely not satisfy the publication requirement.

It is not enough that the plaintiff prove a mere possibility that someone might have heard or read the statement. The plaintiff must actually establish that the statement was communicated to someone other than herself.

In addition to the requirement that the statement be communicated to a third party, it is also essential that the third person realize the significance of the statement. Because of this requirement, a defamatory statement made in a language that no one but the defendant and the plaintiff can understand is not actionable.

TORT
BASICS
AT A
GLANCE

Publication refers to expressing a statement in writing or speaking it aloud.

---

5. INJURY TO THE PLAINTIFF'S REPUTATION

In addition to the other elements, the plaintiff must also prove that her reputation was damaged by the defendant's statement. As we see later, in libel and slander per se, damages are presumed. When the case involves "simple" slander or libel, the plaintiff must prove special damages. Damages and the methods used to assess them are discussed later in this chapter.

Are there plaintiffs who already have such bad reputations that they cannot be defamed? The answer seems to be yes. We'll use an extreme example here: Suppose that Adolf Hitler or Joseph Stalin were still alive. Is there anything that someone could say about them that would hurt their reputations?

On a more realistic level, suppose that John X is an admitted child molester. A local newspaper refers to him as an evil monster. Does John X have provable damages? In most cases, the answer would have to be no. Society clearly considers child molesters to be some of the lowest and most despicable criminals. Calling Mr. X a "monster" surely would not hold him up to any greater public humiliation than his self-confessed activities with children.[7]

D. SIMPLE LIBEL

The term *simple libel* is used in many jurisdictions to distinguish from other, and usually more complex, forms of libel, such as libel per quod and libel per se. When we speak of simple libel, we are referring to a defamatory writing. However, before we can examine the complexities of libel law, the issue we must address first is how the law defines *writing*. See Figure 11-3 for a list of the elements of libel.

Tech Topic
ONLINE DEFAMATION

Defamation has been around for eons, but the problem has taken on a new dimension as the Internet has become both a reporting and a social tool. The opportunities for online defamation are vast: videos, blogs, forums, and even social networking websites. Although many people believe that they can post whatever they want online without fear of repercussions, this simply is not the case. Defamation laws apply equally to online content.

Someone who has been defamed online has the same legal remedy that applies to other instances of defamation. The difficulty is in finding the person responsible. Under Section 230 of the 1996 Communications Decency Act, Internet service providers (ISPs) are immune from liability. They bear no responsibility for what users post. Nevertheless, someone who finds defamatory content can send a cease and desist letter to the ISP demanding that the comments be removed.

Furthermore, defamatory content is often posted anonymously. The libeled party can certainly request from the ISP the identity of the person responsible. However, if the defamatory content was posted from a public computer—say, in a library or a hotel—then it is almost impossible to find the culprit.

The best protection you can have against online defamation is to survey what is out there in cyberspace in your name. Google yourself, and if you find any negative results, you should at least be able to convince the ISP to remove the defamatory attack. At best, you can obtain a court order allowing you to subpoena the ISP to produce the identity of the poster. Armed with that identity, you can pursue a defamation lawsuit.

In most jurisdictions, libel consists of:		**FIGURE 11-3**
▪ Malicious ▪ Publication	▪ In print or in writing (including drawings)	Elements of Libel

*Ajouelo v. Auto-Soler Co., 61 Ga. App. 216, 6 S.E.2d 415 (1939).

Courts have ruled that any of the following can be considered libel:		**FIGURE 11-4**
▪ Cartoons* ▪ Movies**	▪ Signs ▪ Effigies	Types of Libel

*Russell v. McMillen, 685 P.2d 255 (1984).
**Brown v. Paramount Publix Corp., 270 N.Y.S. 544 (1934).

1. WHAT IS A WRITING?

In libel, the definition of a *writing* is often called into question. Courts have interpreted writing to include drawings, pictures, printed material, photographs, newspaper columns, books, and magazines, among others.[8] The significance of a writing is that it is usually considered to be a more permanent medium of expression than oral statements. A printed statement can reach many more people and for a longer period of time than a spoken statement. See Figure 11-4 for a list of the various items that constitute a writing.

2. LIBEL PER QUOD

When a statement must be interpreted before it is considered defamatory, many jurisdictions refer to it as *libel per quod.* Libel per quod is a statement that may appear innocuous standing by itself but becomes clearly defamatory when other facts are considered.

Example: A local newspaper prints the following announcement: "Mary Jones of 112 Elm Street announces the birth of a healthy, 7-pound baby boy on May 2."

Although this announcement does not appear to be defamatory, Mary Jones is a Catholic nun who has taken a vow of celibacy. This announcement, when understood in the context of other facts, creates a defamatory statement.

When libel per quod is alleged, the jury is called upon to evaluate the statement and determine if it was defamatory. The plaintiff must prove that the third party—in this case, the newspaper's readers—knew the extrinsic facts and could therefore connect the statement and the facts and create a defamatory conclusion.[9]

3. LIBEL PER SE

Libel per se is any writing (including a drawing) about a specific category of defamatory statements that is considered to be so serious that an injury to the plaintiff's reputation may be presumed. For example, when the defendant accuses the plaintiff of being a convicted felon or of having a sexually transmitted disease, these statements would be considered libel per se.

When the plaintiff presents proof of libel per se, she is entitled to a presumption that the defendant acted with malice and a presumption of recoverable damages that can be assessed by the jury. To satisfy the test of libel per se, the words used must be unambiguous and interpreted in a natural and reasonable way. See Figure 11-5 for examples of statements that are libel per se.

FIGURE 11-5	■ Accusations of a crime involving moral turpitude
Examples of Libel Per Se	■ Statements regarding the plaintiff's unfitness for his trade, business, or profession
	■ Statements that the plaintiff has a communicable, sexual disease

> "A libel per se is a malicious publication expressed in writing, printing, pictures, caricatures, signs, or other devices which upon its face and without aid of extrinsic proof is injurious and defamatory. . . . In its most general and comprehensive sense it may be said that any publication that is injurious to the reputation of another is a libel."[10]

TORT
BASICS
AT A
GLANCE

E. SLANDER

When a person is defamed verbally, this is slander. Generally, a slanderous statement must be stated loud enough for someone other than the plaintiff to hear it. The statement must be one that calls the plaintiff's character or reputation into question. Insults and cutting remarks are not slander. A slanderous statement must injure the plaintiff's reputation. Many courts hold slander to a higher burden of proof than libel. After all, a libelous statement can be produced on demand in a courtroom. The writing can be viewed by the jury and considered on its own merits. A verbal statement necessarily involves testimony from others about what they heard. The witnesses may remember the statement differently or differ about the context in which it was made. A libelous statement is permanent; a slanderous statement is, by its very nature, ephemeral. See Figure 11-6 for a list of the elements of slander.

1. DEFINING SLANDER

Slander refers to oral statements or, as some jurisdictions put it, a defamatory statement made in some way other than in writing. Slander includes not only statements but also gestures, sign language, or any other form of nonwritten communication.

2. SLANDER PER SE

Slander per se is similar to libel per se. When the defendant accuses the plaintiff of committing a crime involving theft or dishonesty, or of having a communicable sexual disease, slander per se is triggered and the plaintiff is entitled to special damages. Special damages are those damages that are beyond mere humiliation or embarrassment. When a statement is classified

---

In most jurisdictions, slander consists of the following:

- The speaking of
- Defamatory words

- That tends to expose the plaintiff to public contempt, hatred, or ridicule or interferes with the plaintiff's ability to earn a living in his business.*

FIGURE 11-6

The Elements of Slander

*Axelrod v. Califano, 357 So. 2d 1048 (1978).

as slander per se, malice and injury to reputation are presumed. See Figure 11-7 for the elements necessary to prove slander per se.

3. SPECIAL DAMAGES

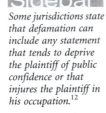

In slander, the plaintiff must show some form of special injury or that the statement falls into a category of legally recognized injurious statement before the plaintiff will be entitled to an award of damages.[11] For instance, the plaintiff would have to prove that her reputation was damaged or that her business suffered because of the slanderous statement. These damages must be tied to the defendant's slanderous statement.

4. IS LIBEL MORE SERIOUS THAN SLANDER?

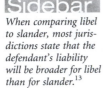

There is an interesting disparity between the application of written defamation and spoken defamation. Libel is considered to be more injurious to the plaintiff because the written word is more permanent. Writings can last for centuries and permanently ruin the plaintiff's reputation and good name in a way that slander is incapable of doing. Most jurisdictions consider libel to be more serious because writing is a process that takes time and thought. A person can blurt out something that she has not fully considered, but writing is a deliberate, drawn-out process that usually involves review by others and more than sufficient time for the author to modify a defamatory statement. When the author publishes a defamatory statement, it shows her clear intent to offer an injurious statement in a way that a slanderous statement usually cannot.

FIGURE 11-7 **Proving Slander Per Se**	In most jurisdictions, the elements necessary to prove slander per se include the following:
	▪ Defendant spoke defamatory words that tended to injure the plaintiff's reputation, trade, or livelihood. ▪ The statement was false. ▪ The statement was published or communicated to a third person.*

*Presnell v. Pell, 298 N.C. 715, 260 S.E.2d 611 (1979).

FIGURE 11-8 **Defenses Available in Defamation Actions**	▪ The statement is not defamatory. ▪ The person defamed is deceased. ▪ The defendant is protected by a privilege. ▪ The statement is the truth.

F. DEFENSES TO DEFAMATION

As we have seen in other chapters, some unique torts trigger unique defenses. Defamation is perhaps the best example of that axiom. There are defenses available in defamation actions that are rarely, if ever, seen in other causes of action. These defenses are summarized in Figure 11-8.

1. THE STATEMENT IS NOT DEFAMATORY

The most obvious defense to a suit for slander or libel is that the statement is not defamatory. As we have already seen, insulting, provocative, or annoying statements do not fall into the category of defamatory statements. If the defendant can establish that the statement does not qualify as defamatory, the court must dismiss the action.

2. THE DEFAMED PERSON IS DECEASED

In most situations, a person who has died cannot be defamed. Although this rule has certain specific exceptions, in general it means that the heirs and friends of a deceased individual do not have a cause of action for a defamatory statement made about the deceased. In a certain sense, deceased persons are fair game for nearly any statement.

3. PRIVILEGES

Certain individuals are protected under the law from defamation actions. The law recognizes that there are times when individuals should be allowed to speak freely, offer their opinions, and even make allegations without fear of being sued. When a person is protected from being sued, it is commonly called a privilege or immunity. This privilege can be raised as a defense and, if proved, will result in a dismissal of the action.

In most jurisdictions, the issue of privilege is an integral part of a defamation action. Whether a statement is privileged is contingent on several key features. First, the conditions under which the statement was made must be examined. If the defendant can show that the statement was made in a privileged circumstance — for example, a statement she made to her attorney or a member of the clergy — she has a defense to the defamatory statement. In such a situation, even though the defamatory statement was relayed to a third person, this person is bound by an oath of confidentiality. The law of privileges has a practical element here as well. If a plaintiff could allege slander by a statement that a person makes to her attorney, the entire conversation between the attorney and the defendant would be open to examination. This would have a chilling effect on the relationship and the free flow of information between attorneys and clients. The same rationale holds true for the other types of privileges recognized under defamation law.

FIGURE 11-9

Examples of
Absolute
Privileges

Statements made by:

- Judges in judicial proceedings
- Witnesses while testifying at trial
- Witnesses and experts in mental competency or commitment hearings

- Pleadings in civil cases
- Members of Congress while engaged in official duties

Members of Congress and state legislators are protected by a privilege against defamation for any comments that they make while the legislature is in session. This means that a senator can make a statement that would otherwise be deemed to be slander, but he cannot be sued for making that statement on the floor of the Senate. Politicians are not completely protected by this privilege. When Congress is not in session, or the politician is not meeting on government business, he or she has no greater protection than any other person.

a. Absolute Privileges

Some privileges are absolute, meaning that any defamatory statement made under specified circumstances can never be the basis of a defamation action. An example would be the private communication between a client and an attorney. See Figure 11-9 for examples of absolute privileges.

b. Qualified Privileges

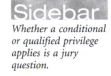

Whether a conditional or qualified privilege applies is a jury question.

Other privileges are considered to be qualified. A qualified privilege is one that protects the defendant from a defamation action as long as the defendant does not use the privilege as a ruse or abuse the privilege as a way of making defamatory statements without paying the consequences. In some jurisdictions, for instance, an attorney's closing argument in a trial enjoys a qualified privilege. An attorney's slanderous statement about a person may be protected, as long as it is made for purposes associated with the trial, not simply as a way for the attorney to slander an individual.

Qualified privileges come up in other contexts. Employers, for example, enjoy a qualified privilege for certain types of statements. For instance, if the employer is legally obligated to make a statement, such as in an accident report in which the employer states that the plaintiff was responsible for the accident, an action in defamation will not be permitted. Other situations that would trigger a qualified privilege are listed in Figure 11-10.

FIGURE 11-10

Qualified
Privileges

- Statements in which both parties have a business interest
- Statements criticizing employee work performance

- Statements regarding the factual reasons for an employee's dismissal
- Statements to law enforcement made on a good faith belief that a crime has been committed or is about to occur

4. THE STATEMENT IS TRUE

It is a classic defense in a defamation action that the defendant's statement was true. If the statement is true, the defendant has a complete defense, and the plaintiff's action should be dismissed.

Truth is a complete defense to a claim of defamation, even when the statement was made with malice.

TORT
BASICS
AT A
GLANCE

When truth is raised as a defense, it does not matter that the defendant acted with malice, ill will, or hatred in making the statement. Truth is an absolute bar to a defamation action. However, many jurisdictions provide that the statement must be true at the time that it is made, not one that becomes true later on.

Example: Paula Publisher accuses Ted of being a thief and an embezzler in an editorial she writes called "Local Scoundrels." Local grand jurors read the article and launch an investigation of Ted. Ted loses his job when his employer sees that he is being investigated. Ted then steals from his former employer because he can no longer pay his bills and is arrested on theft charges. Ted sues Paula for defamation. Paula counters that her statement was true. In support of her contention, she shows that Ted was arrested for theft. Ted shows that the statement was not true at the time that Paula made her statement, and therefore he is entitled to sue her for defamation. She files a motion for summary judgment. The court rules in Ted's favor. (Under this scenario, Ted's suit will not be dismissed, but his likelihood of being awarded a large amount of damages is low; after all, Ted actually is a thief.)

5. "GOOD FAITH" STATUTES

Some jurisdictions have so-called good faith statutes that have been specifically passed to insulate the press from defamation lawsuits for reporting on various issues of public concern. Under these statutes, if a reporter can show that she acted in good faith, a defamation action will not be permitted. In cases

---

■ The nature of the statement itself
■ The number of people to whom the statement was published
■ The effect of the statement on the plaintiff's reputation
■ The plaintiff's mental anguish, humiliation, and embarrassment

In cases where special damages must be proved:

■ The financial and property losses directly linked to the defendant's defamatory statement

FIGURE 11-11

Types of Evidence a Jury or Judge Can Consider in Awarding Damages in Defamation Cases.

where the press reports something incorrectly, some jurisdictions require that the press print a retraction before the good faith statute will protect the media from a defamation action.

G. DAMAGES IN DEFAMATION CASES

As we have already seen with libel per se and slander per se, harm may be presumed from certain types of defamatory statements. This harm may be limited to the damages for emotional distress, but the plaintiff is still permitted to recover.[14]

When the court awards damages to a plaintiff who has been libeled, the court takes into account the wider reach of a libelous statement compared to a slanderous statement. After all, a slanderous statement is often overheard by only a few people, while printed material can reach thousands. In the era of the Internet, libelous material could reach millions of people. Assessing damages for libel must take into account the fact that the defamatory statement will be read or seen by a much greater audience, with the result that the plaintiff will be injured far more severely than in most typical slander cases.

In making its decision about the amount of damages to award a plaintiff who has proved a defamation case, the jury is allowed to consider several different factors: the nature of the statement — that is, just how defamatory was the statement; how many people heard it or read it; what the plaintiff's character and reputation were before the incident and how they have been affected since; and to what extent the plaintiff suffered mental anguish, humiliation, or embarrassment because of the defamatory statement (see Figure 11-11).

When the statement is slander, the plaintiff must prove special damages. Special damages are the financial and other losses suffered by the plaintiff which are directly tied to the defendant's actions.

H. CONSTITUTIONAL LIMITS ON DEFAMATION ACTIONS

Defamation actions give plaintiffs the right to sue people who make statements about them. The First Amendment to the U.S. Constitution guarantees freedom of speech. Where is the dividing line between this right and the prohibition against defamatory statements? There is an immediate and obvious tension between defamation actions and the First Amendment. The right of freedom of speech was seen as vital by the framers of the Constitution; it was so important that it is embodied in the First Amendment, preceding even the right to jury trial and the presumption of innocence in criminal proceedings (Fifth Amendment). In evaluating any supposedly defamatory statement, the question often arises as to how the court balances the protections of the First Amendment against an individual's right to protect her reputation. See Figure 11-12 for some helpful questions in determining this balance.

Is the plaintiff:
    A public figure or a private figure?
Is the defendant:
    Media or non-media?
Is the statement:
    A matter of public or private concern?

Analyzing Constitutional Defenses to Defamation Actions

1. ANALYZING A DEFAMATION CASE FOR CONSTITUTIONAL IMPLICATIONS

The guarantees of the First Amendment are propounded in the U.S. Constitution, which is a federal document. Defamation actions are almost always brought in state courts, applying individual state laws. When a constitutional defense is raised, judges are faced with a multilayered analysis. They often follow this analysis:

1   Has the plaintiff proved defamation according to state law?
2   Is the plaintiff entitled to recover under state law?
3   If the answer to both questions 1 and 2 is yes, does the First Amendment protect the defendant's otherwise defamatory statement?

If the answer to question 3 is yes, the judge must dismiss the case against the defendant.

2. THE *NEW YORK TIMES* RULE

The Supreme Court was faced with the issue of balancing the constitutional guarantees against state-based defamation actions in *New York Times Co. v. Sullivan*.[16] The decision in that case brought about dramatic changes in how defamation actions are brought and also affected the standard of proof in such cases.

One of the biggest changes wrought by the *New York Times* case was that, to a certain extent, state law concerning defamation was "usurped" by a holding that essentially changed the rules. The U.S. Supreme Court held that when the plaintiff is a public person and the statement involves a matter of public concern, the standard of proof that the plaintiff must meet to prove a defamation case is much higher than when the case involves a private individual and a statement that does not involve a matter of public debate. In the first instance, public figures can "recover for injury to reputation only on clear and convincing proof that the defamatory falsehood was made with knowledge of its falsity or with reckless disregard for the truth."[17] In essence, the court ruled that a public figure could only recover when he could show that the statement was made with "actual malice." The court recognized that applying this high standard might mean that plaintiffs with legitimate concerns would be barred from bringing suits for defamation, but considered that

Sidebar

"Under the First Amendment, there is no such thing as a false idea. But there is no constitutional value in false statements of fact. . . . Our decisions recognize that a rule of strict liability that compels a publisher or broadcaster to guarantee the accuracy of his factual assertions may lead to intolerable self-censorship."[15]

public figures would have to pay the price to balance out the need for constitutional protections. However, the balance between individual concerns and constitutional protections shifts when the plaintiff is a private individual. Individual states are allowed to set their own standards for proof in such cases.

The actual malice test — sometimes called the *New York Times* Rule — held that when a public figure, such as a public official, raises a claim of defamation, she will not be entitled to damages unless she can present clear and convincing evidence that the statement was made with "actual malice."[18]

a. Malice

Malice
Reckless or false statements; legal malice is a court-created doctrine that supplies the element by assuming that certain phrases could only have been motivated by ill will. Examples would include falsely accusing someone of a crime or other despicable act.

In the context of defamation, **malice** refers to the defendant's hatred, ill will, or bad feelings toward the plaintiff. Malice has a fluid definition, however, depending on the nature of the communication. For a statement under the protection of the First Amendment, malice means the defendant's reckless or intentional statement of a false fact.

Although the plaintiff must normally prove malice, there are some statements that are considered under the law to be motivated by malice without the need of further proof. We have seen a similar approach adopted in libel per se and slander per se. Examples of these statements where malice would be inferred include the following:

- Implicating the defendant in a crime (in most jurisdictions there is no requirement that the crime be a felony)
- Making statements designed to show that the defendant is not legally entitled to practice her profession (e.g., that a lawyer has been disbarred or that a doctor has been stripped of her license to practice medicine, etc.)
- Accusing the plaintiff of having a communicable sexual disease (e.g., syphilis, AIDS, etc.)

When such statements are made, and they are false, the court will presume malice. In addition to presuming malice, courts will also presume some type of harm to the plaintiff. Under other situations, the plaintiff would have to show that the defamatory statement injured her reputation. However, when the

---

FIGURE 11-13

Examples of Actual Malice

Actual malice has been found in all of the following situations:

- A newspaper uses inflammatory headlines but then backtracks in the body of the article.
- A person accuses a public official of perjury when he knows the definition of perjury and also knows that the plaintiff did not commit that act.
- News media accuse the plaintiff of being the "prime suspect" in a heinous crime when they already have information that the police no longer classify the plaintiff as a suspect.

| ■ Private attorneys (not attorneys affiliated with city, county, or state government) | ■ Part-time deputies or "honorary" deputies
■ A person contesting a defamatory statement | **FIGURE 11-14**

Examples of People Who Have Been Ruled *Not* to Be Public Figures |

statement falls into one of the categories above, injury is presumed, and the plaintiff is entitled to some amount of damages to be determined by the jury.

If malice sounds like a slippery concept, no less a person than Justice Oliver Wendell Holmes would agree. In his famous book, *The Common Law,* Holmes addresses the issue of malice in slander cases:

> Malice must exist, but . . . it is presumed from the mere speaking of the words; that again you may rebut this presumption of malice by showing that the words were spoken under circumstances which made the communication privileged, — as for instance, by a lawyer in the necessary course of his argument — it is said that the plaintiff may meet this defence [sic] in some cases by showing that the words were spoken with actual malice.[19]

b. Malice and Negligent Investigation

There is no actual malice when the defendant did a poor job of investigating the claim against the plaintiff prior to publishing the statement. Malice requires some awareness that the statement is false or reckless disregard of the truth. See Figure 11-13 for examples of actual malice.

3. THE SHIFTING STANDARD DEPENDING ON THE PLAINTIFF'S NOTORIETY

When the plaintiff in a defamation case is a private individual, the plaintiff need only show simple fault or negligence on the part of the defendant. However, the rule changes when the plaintiff is famous (see Figure 11-14 and Figure 11-15). Celebrities, politicians, and other famous people have placed themselves in the public eye and enjoy less protection than private individuals. Public figures must show actual malice before they will be allowed to recover against the person making the defamatory statement.

Sidebar

Holmes was a law professor at Harvard Law School before serving on the Massachusetts Supreme Court. He was appointed to the U.S. Supreme Court by Theodore Roosevelt and served for 30 years.

Sidebar

Actual malice claims are usually based not on intentional actions, but on reckless disregard for the truth.[20]

| ■ Judges, including superior, state, district, probate judge, and so on[i]
■ Law enforcement officers (although some jurisdictions will consider this on a case-by-case basis)[ii]
■ Corrections officers[iii] | **FIGURE 11-15**

Examples of Individuals Who Have Been Held to Be Public Figures or Officials |

[i]*Times Pub. Co. v. Huffstetler,* 409 So. 2d 112 (1982).
[ii]*McCusker v. Valley News,* 121 N.H. 258, 428 A.2d 493 (1981).
[iii]*Sweeney v. Prisoners' Legal Servs.,* 146 App. Div. 2d 1, 538 N.Y.S.2d 370 (1989).

Example: Freddie Famous is a noted public figure. He is the governor of a large state. Reggie Reporter works for a national news agency. On the evening news, Reggie reports that Governor Famous has been squandering public funds on a secret love nest that he has built to share with one of his female staff workers, despite the fact that the governor has been married to Mrs. Famous for over 30 years. After Reggie files his report, the governor brings a defamation action against him. If the governor can show that Reggie was slipshod in his research and relied on untrustworthy sources for his information, will the governor win his defamation suit? In most cases, the answer is no. Simply showing that Reggie may have been negligent in his reporting may not be enough for the governor to recover against Reggie. The reason for this is that the facts of this case fall clearly into the arena of constitutional protections. First, the plaintiff is a public figure. Second, the defendant is a member of the media, and third, the report concerns a matter of public concern — improper use of government funds. Reggie will benefit from a finding that he had no actual malice in filing his report.[21]

Sidebar

When the question of the plaintiff's status as a public figure or public official surfaces in a defamation case, the judge must rule whether the plaintiff falls into that category.

The problem with the actual malice standard is that in everyday practice it often becomes confusing to apply. For instance, the Court in *New York Times v. Sullivan* did not provide any clear guidance about the basic ground rules for determining actual malice or even who should be considered a public figure or public official. Subsequent cases have sought to clear up these deficiencies, but this is an area of law that is bound to undergo more changes in the coming years.

I. DEFAMATION IN CYBERSPACE

The World Wide Web has created new and novel issues in defamation law. When a person is defamed on the Internet, what jurisdiction is empowered to hear the case? More specifically, where does the plaintiff file her suit? The Internet is truly a global phenomenon. A writer in Kiev can defame a person in New York City. Cyberspace raises a myriad of issues regarding jurisdiction and the lack of uniformity of laws among the states and throughout the international community.

Some states have taken the initiative in addressing these issues. Michigan and Alaska have expanded the definition of defamation and their criminal statutes on stalking to include harassment over the Internet. When a person uses the Internet to harass another, it is often referred to as *cyber-stalking*.

J. Invasion of Privacy

Closely related to the issue of defamation, especially in the age of the Internet and social media is the tort of invasion of privacy. Although not all states refer to this tort in the same way, the basics remain the same. It is an invasion of an individual's privacy to do any of the following:

- Intrude on a person's privacy
- Make public disclosure of private facts
- Use the person's name or likeness without permission

1. INTRUDE ON A PERSON'S PRIVACY

Although there are criminal statutes that criminalize behavior commonly referred to as "Peeping Tom," there are also states that allow individuals to bring a tort action for intrusion into privacy, whether as a type of nuisance action or as an outright invasion of personal privacy. Actions that would qualify as intrusion on a person's privacy would include intercepting and recording telephone calls, e-mail, or other communications (which is also a crime in most states). Intruding on someone's privacy would also include harassing phone calls. There is considerable overlap between this tort and criminal law, as harassing phone calls is also a crime in most states.

2. MAKE PUBLIC DISCLOSURE OF PRIVATE FACTS

Of all the invasion of privacy torts, this is the most problematic. Part of the problem stems from the protection of freedom of speech in the First Amendment. It is also the case that defamation exists as a cause of action to bring action against those making false statements. The release of accurate, but private, information may not be actionable in many states.

3. USE THE PERSON'S NAME OR LIKENESS WITHOUT PERMISSION

When someone uses your name or your likeness—such as a photograph—without your permission, that is also another form of invasion of privacy. The most common example is when a company uses a famous person's likeness without first obtaining permission, but it can also be brought by private individuals who have not given permission for their names or photographs to be used to promote a product.

Case Excerpt

LARUE V. BROWN
235 Ariz. 440, 333 P.3d 767 (2014)

Opinion

GOULD, Judge.

David and Sarah Brown ("Defendants") appeal from a judgment entered against them after a jury found them liable for defaming Mindi Larue and Jeremy Tucker ("Plaintiffs") on the Internet. Defendants argue Plaintiffs' defamation claim was barred by the statute of limitations because they filed it more than one year after the defamatory statements were published. We conclude, however, that Plaintiffs' defamation action was not time-barred because Defendants republished the statements less than one year before Plaintiffs filed their claim. We therefore affirm.

Facts and Procedural History

David Brown and Mindi Larue are former spouses who divorced in 2006. During the marriage, David and Mindi had two children. After the divorce, David married Sarah, and Mindi married Jeremy Tucker.

David and Mindi's divorce was very contentious, and resulted in a protracted custody battle over the children. In mid–2007 Defendants initiated a criminal investigation based on allegations Jeremy had abused one of the children. Defendants also filed an emergency petition to modify custody and parenting time in the family court. In March 2008, after a hearing on the petition to modify, the family court determined the allegations of abuse were not proven by a preponderance of the evidence.

On November 20 and 22, 2008, Sarah posted two articles on the website www.ripoffreport.com in which she accused Plaintiffs of sexual and criminal misconduct. Both articles revealed Plaintiffs' names, phone numbers, and address. The November 20 article is entitled, "Mindi Larue [f].n.a. Mindi Brown allowed physical abuse of daughter and protected boyfriend when daughter reported sexual abuse Phoenix Arizona." The article stated that "Mindi Larue is a despicable 'mother,'" and that "her live in boyfriend, Jeremy Tucker, molested and tortured her 4 year old daughter." The article notes that despite the child's statement to the police in Wisconsin about the abuse, no charges were filed, and as a result the child is "once again back in the home of the same man who tortured her" and sexually abused her. The article lists Jeremy Tucker's employer, and warns the reader that he "could be working at your business or company, or on nearby building projects. BEWARE."

The November 22 article is entitled, "Jeremy Tucker Child Molestor (sic), also tortures children with Tobasco sauce Phoenix Arizona." It alleged that "Jeremy Tucker is a sick sick pedophile who molested and tortured his girl friends (sic) 4 year old daughter," "touched her privates," and put "tobasco sauce in her panties." The article stated that charges were not filed and "this poor child is once again back in the home of the same man who tortured her with Tabasco sauce and touched her privates."

The website provided for interaction between readers and authors through a report and rebuttal forum which allowed interested readers to post questions and comments. On February 1, 2009, a reader posted a comment on the November 22 article entitled, "Where is the Little Girl's Biological Father? Where are her grandparents?" The reader then posed a series of questions, including, "Why hasn't the little girl said something to her father," and "Why hasn't someone called the child abuse hotline and reported this?"

On March 9, 2009, in response to the reader's comment, Sarah posted a statement on the November 20 article entitled "Answer to the WHY's." In this article, Sarah noted that the child did report the abuse to her biological father and the incident was reported to the police. Sarah then recited additional details of the child's interview with the police, and discussed the subsequent investigations conducted by CPS and the Arizona Ombudsman's Office. Sarah also stated that Jeremy Tucker "REFUSED (sic) to take a polygraph test on this matter." Sarah concluded that the case had been mishandled by CPS, "and as a result the child is now back in the home of the same man she was brave enough to speak against."

On June 1, 2009, a reader posted a comment on the November 22 article entitled, "What proof do you have?" In this comment, the reader stated "This is a 100% fake! I know this family very well and I also know the person who mailed this story to my whole neighborhood . . . He is just trying to get back at his ex-wife."

Later, on June 5, 2009, Defendants posted a response to a reader's comment and a "reply to everyone" on the November 22 article. In the response Defendants allege, "If you want proof of the fact that this man refused to take a polygraph test then look up PUBLIC records case [police report number]." Defendants then state "There is a substantial amount of proof," "do your research on child sexual abuse before you pipe off at the mouth while not having any evidence in front of you . . ." Then, on June 7, Defendants posted another comment on the November 22 article entitled, "reply to everyone." The reply stated, in part, "I am the biological father," and "I read the reply accusing me of seeking retribution. Who ever (sic) wrote that is a liar."

On December 23, 2009, Plaintiffs sued Defendants alleging the articles published by Defendants on the Internet were defamatory.

Defendants filed several motions to dismiss Plaintiffs' complaint on the grounds it was barred by the statute of limitations. The court denied all of Defendants' motions, and the case went to trial.

At the close of the evidence, Defendants asked the court to instruct the jury on their statute of limitations defense. Defendants sought language instructing the jury that it could not consider statements "made before December 23, 2008." The court did not include the requested language; instead, the court gave the following instruction:

> The statute of limitations for a defamation claim is one (1) year from the date the alleged defamatory statement was published to a third person. If a statement is re-published at a later date, the statute of limitations starts to run from the date of the republication. The lawsuit in this case was filed December 23, 2009. A statement is republished if it is published in a modified form.

The jury found Defendants liable for defamation. The jury awarded Plaintiffs $150,000.00 in compensatory damages against both Defendants and $50,000.00 in punitive damages against Sarah Brown.

Discussion

The only issue on appeal is whether the court erred in refusing to grant Defendants relief on their statute of limitations defense. Generally, Arizona provides that the statute of limitations for a defamation action begins to run upon publication of the defamatory statement. A plaintiff has one year after a defamation action accrues to commence and prosecute his claim. This appeal raises two issues of first impression in Arizona regarding the accrual date of a cause of action for defamation: (1) whether the single publication rule applies to defamatory statements published on the Internet, and (2) what constitutes a republication of a statement posted on the Internet.

I. Discovery Rule

Plaintiffs assert that the statute of limitations does not bar their defamation claim because they did not know who wrote the articles when they were posted in November 2008. Plaintiffs contend they did not learn that Defendants posted the articles until sometime later in 2009. Thus, based on the "discovery rule," Plaintiffs argue their cause of action did not accrue until they learned that Defendants authored the articles.

The discovery rule does not apply to this case. The record shows that Plaintiffs were aware of the articles, and were convinced Defendants had published them, as early as November 24, 2008. They cannot now assert the statements, or their author, were concealed from them.

II. The Single Publication Rule and Republication

Plaintiffs argue that Defendants' posts in March and June of 2009 were substantive modifications of the original articles posted in November 2008. As a result, Plaintiffs contend the later posts were republications that fell outside the single publication rule, thereby starting the accrual date for their defamation action anew.

A. Single Publication Rule

The single publication rule controls the point from which a defamation action accrues and when the statute of limitations begins to run. Under this rule, a cause of action for defamation arises at the time the statement is first published; later circulation of the original publication does not start the statute of limitations anew, nor does it give rise to a new cause of action.

Arizona has enacted the single publication rule by adopting the Uniform Single Publication Act, which provides:

> No person shall have more than one cause of action for damages for libel, slander, invasion of privacy or any other tort founded upon a single publication, exhibition or utterance, such as any one edition of a newspaper, book or magazine, any one presentation to an audience, any one broadcast over radio or television or any one exhibition of a motion picture. Recovery in any action shall include all damages for any such tort suffered by the plaintiff in all jurisdictions. A.R.S. §12–651(A).

The single publication rule protects defendants from being sued separately for each copy of a book or newspaper containing the allegedly defamatory statement. It also prevents the statute of limitations from being reset each time a copy of a publication is purchased or read.

The policy concerns behind the single publication rule apply with equal or more force to Internet publication. Given that "communications posted on Web sites may be viewed by thousands, if not millions, over an expansive geographic area for an indefinite period of time," allowing Internet publications to be subject to a multiple publication rule "would implicate an even greater potential for endless retriggering of the statute of limitations, multiplicity of suits and harassment of defendants. Inevitably, there would be a serious inhibitory effect on the open, pervasive dissemination of information and ideas over the Internet, which is, of course, its greatest beneficial promise." Oja, 440 F.3d at 1131-32. Recognizing these policy concerns, federal and state courts have uniformly applied the single publication rule to the Internet.

We agree with this reasoning from these other jurisdictions and conclude the single publication rule applies to Internet publications. Thus, in the case of Internet publications, the statute of limitations begins to run when the allegedly defamatory material is first made available to the public by posting it on a website.

In this case, Defendants published the defamatory statements on the website on November 20, 2008 and November 22, 2008, which is more than one year before Plaintiffs filed their complaint on December 23, 2009. As a result, unless Defendants republished the statements after December 23, 2008, Plaintiffs' claims are barred by the statute of limitations.

B. Republication

Generally, republishing material in a new edition, editing and republishing it, or placing it in a new form is a separate publication giving rise to a separate cause of action. Republication "occurs when a defamatory article is placed in a new form (paperback as opposed to hardcover) or edited in a new form." *Mitan v. Davis*, 243 F.Supp.2d 719, 722 (W.D.Ky.2003). A plaintiff has a new cause of action when "the defendant edits and retransmits the defamatory material, or distributes the defamatory material for a second time with the goal of reaching a new audience."

Because websites are subject to updates or modifications at any time that can be completely unrelated to their substantive content, the question of republication in the context of Internet publication focuses on whether the update or modification affects the substance of the allegedly defamatory material. "Mere modifications to the way information is accessed, as opposed to changes in the nature of the information itself, does not constitute republication."

Thus, republication does not occur every time a defendant adds to or revises the content of the website if the changes are unrelated to the alleged defamatory material. In *Churchill v. State*, 378 N.J.Super. 471, 876 A.2d 311 (App.Div.2005), the New Jersey appellate court concluded that changes to a website hosting a defamatory statement, such as moving and highlighting the website menu bar, did not constitute republications of the statement. Rather, the court concluded that the changes were technical, altering the means by which readers accessed the defamatory report, but not altering the substance or form of the report. Similarly, in *Atkinson*, the court concluded a website modification adding information unrelated to the defamatory statement was not a republication; the "modification did not change the content or substance of the website" and the update "did not reasonably result in communicating the alleged defamatory information to a new audience." And in *Firth*, the court recognized that although websites constantly change through the addition of new material, the changes are not republications unless they relate to and substantively modify the allegedly defamatory material. *Firth*, 98 N.Y.2d at 371-72, 747 N.Y.S.2d 69, 775 N.E.2d 463.

In contrast, the updates to the defamatory material in this case were not simply technical changes to the website or the addition of new, unrelated material. The facts before us more closely resemble those of Davis I. 334 B.R. at 884. In Davis I, the website was created by the defendants to document the purportedly criminal and unethical activities of the plaintiff. After the initial posting, the defendants made changes to the website by "adding 'Breaking News!' and 'Update!' sections and other sections containing additional substantive information and links to other websites containing substantive information." The court concluded that the changes to the website were republications because they "related to the original allegedly defamatory material" and they "altered both the substance and the form of the original material."

Here, in March and June 2009, Defendants replied to readers' comments made in response to their original defamatory articles. Defendants' "updates and rebuttals" were posted immediately below the text of the original articles, and the content of Defendants' replies referred to and re-alleged the substance of the original articles. Defendants' later comments also added to and altered the substance of the original material by providing additional information in response to a reader's questions, and re-urging the truth of the original articles in response to another reader's criticism. The Defendants' comments also altered the form of the original articles. The comments were displayed directly beneath the original articles, thereby implying they were supplements to the original articles. In addition, the submission dates of the new comments reflect the date the comments were added (March and June 2009), again implying they were updating the original articles.

Thus, Defendants republished the defamatory statements originally posted in November 2008 by replying to readers' comments in March and June of 2009. Accordingly, Plaintiffs' cause of action for defamation was not barred by the statute of limitations.

Conclusion

For the reasons discussed above, we affirm the judgment. Additionally, because Defendants have not prevailed in this appeal we decline Defendants' request that we asses fees against Plaintiffs pursuant to Arizona Rule of Civil Procedure 11 and A.R.S. §12-349.

Questions about the case:

1. What form did the defamation in this case take?
2. What award did the jury make?
3. Why was the statute of limitations an issue in this case?
4. How does "republication" affect the statute of limitations?

Now that we have reviewed the laws of defamation, let's return to the hypothetical case we addressed at the beginning of this chapter. To review the pertinent facts of Susan's case: First, her name has appeared on a sign in a store. The sign names her, among others, as a "deadbeat" and at the very least accuses her of committing a crime. Does she have a libel case against the store?

Taking the elements of defamation one by one, has the store manager published a defamatory statement? The sign can be, and certainly has been, read by other store customers. The statement is false, because Susan has never passed a bad check at the store. The statement is defamatory because it accuses her of a crime, and her reputation has been injured because this is a grocery store where she and many of her college friends routinely shop. The libel case seems fairly strong. Is there also a case for slander? Remember that when Susan approached the store manager, he accused her of being a deadbeat again, suggested that he would call the police to have her arrested, and banished her from the store while shouting that she had pending bad checks. This scenario would seem to qualify as a slander case. Susan has two potential claims against the store, one for libel and the other for slander. She will have to prove her damages to the jury, but the elements for both seem to be satisfied.

Chapter Summary

An action for defamation can be brought when a plaintiff believes that a statement has injured his reputation. Such an action is one of the few ways that a person can seek to protect his reputation from false allegations. To prove defamation, the plaintiff must show that a defamatory statement was made, that the statement was false, that it referred to the plaintiff, and that it injured the plaintiff's reputation. Defamation comes in two forms: libel and slander. Libel is written defamation, which can include books, cartoons, signs, and other objects. Slander is oral or spoken defamation and is usually limited to speech. The plaintiff's injury and awardable damages are presumed in specific situations, such as when the statement involves the false accusation of a crime, of an infectious disease, or of the legal inability to engage in the plaintiff's chosen trade. Traditional analysis of defamation actions changed significantly after the U.S. Supreme Court's decision in *New York Times v. Sullivan*. In that case, the Court ruled that the standard of proof in defamation actions depended on the classification of the plaintiff as a public or private figure. If classified as a public figure, the plaintiff could only recover if she could show actual malice on the defendant's part. If classified as a private individual, actual malice is not required. These rules reflect the fact that some individuals, such as celebrities, who deliberately seek fame and notoriety, must put up with more comments and discussions as compared to private individuals, who are entitled to greater protection.

 SKILLS YOU NEED IN THE REAL WORLD

Balancing School and Work

If you are like most paralegal students, you are trying to balance a job, a family, and a school career, all at the same time. When you walk such a tightrope, it is easy to fall off. One way to achieve balance is to do some studying during lunch or to work on class assignments after you are "off duty" at work.

Before you rush headlong into doing your studies and assignments at work, there are some important issues to consider. The most obvious is that you should not use the time your boss is paying you to work on your studies. You should remember that the firm is paying you for your efforts, so never, ever work on school assignments while you are being paid to work for the firm. In addition to that basic ground rule, there are some other important considerations for anyone trying to balance school and work.

Let's look at five simple rules that you should follow to achieve a greater balance between work and school and that will hopefully help you be better at both.

Rule 1. Get the Boss Involved

If you are going to do schoolwork at your job, get your boss involved. Explain to him or her that you will only be working on your schoolwork during your lunch break or after hours. You might be surprised how understanding most employers will be.

Emphasize that you will not work on schoolwork while you're being paid to work for the firm, but that during times when you are technically off the clock, you'd like to spend some time studying and working on school material.

Rule 2. Prioritize

Everyone has heard about prioritizing. Prioritizing is going through your in basket until everything is put in the out basket, right? Wrong. Prioritizing is putting first things first. Prioritizing takes discipline and time; that's why most people don't like to do it. Although there are as many rules for prioritizing as there are people, we'll focus on only one. We'll call this crisis prioritizing. Create a category labeled "top priority," or "absolute to do," or anything else you'd like to call it, and put only those tasks there that actually qualify. Look at it this way: Here is a list of items that you must take care of immediately or face real trouble. Only those items should be listed there. Force yourself to keep this particular category to a minimum.

Once you've established the crisis category, create a list of things that should be done soon. For a busy person, these are the only categories that you need. You could create a long-range to-do list, but chances are that you will never have time to look at it. For a busy student and full-time worker, you have two levels: crisis and soon-to-be crisis.

One secret of prioritizing is to schedule your work and studying around your own metabolism. If you are a morning person, do your studying before you go to work. If you are a night owl, schedule schoolwork then.

Rule 3. Delegate

If your response to delegation is, "Hey, I'm the low person on the totem pole; I don't have anyone to delegate to!" you may very well be wrong. You may not have anyone at work that you can delegate to, but you do have other people in your life. Get your kids involved in your studies. Have family members help you. Recruit friends, children, spouses, significant others, and anyone else you can find to help you.

Rule 4. It's Time to Get Organized

Organization actually takes time and effort, but it pays huge dividends. If your idea of organization is keeping a big stack of stuff on your living room table, you really aren't organized. Get some books on organization. Visit some of the websites mentioned at the end of this chapter. Get help and suggestions from others about how to get more organized — and how to stay that way.

One method used by many people to get organized is to create a master calendar. You could even go so far as to color-code various entries, but if that's a little over the top for you, a simple entry showing school assignments, test dates, and work assignments will be enough to give you an idea of what you're facing. The nice thing about writing this material down is that it lessens that two o'clock in the morning anxiety attack that all busy people have. You know the feeling: You suddenly bolt up in bed, convinced that you forgot to file an important pleading, or submit an important assignment, or any of the hundred other things that could have slipped by you. If you have a master calendar, you can climb out of bed and reassure yourself that the deadline isn't until next week, heave a sigh of relief, and go back to sleep.

Rule 5. Get Those Creative Juices Flowing

The real secret to getting a lot of things done isn't rigid schedules and unending work — it's getting creative. One paralegal has dictation software loaded on her laptop. On her 20-minute drive to work every morning, she dictates letters and other materials that she can print at work. Another paralegal carries a mini tape recorder with her wherever she goes. When she gets an idea, she dictates it to herself. Later, she plays the tape back and writes down any good ideas.

Many paralegals also get creative with their use of time. Pam Tallent studies whenever she has a chance. For instance, some paralegals study while they are waiting for the bus or when they are sitting in a doctor's waiting room.

If you follow these rules and use your own ingenuity, you'll find that it is easier to balance your school and work loads and free up some time to relax.

THE LIFE OF A PARALEGAL

The Life of a Brand-New Paralegal

When I showed up, no one even knew that I'd been hired. They were all surprised when they found out that I was there to replace a lady who'd put in her notice two days before. She trained me on her position, but I could tell that her heart really wasn't in it. I was on my own right from the start. I realized pretty quickly that if I were going to figure all of this stuff out, I'd have to get organized.

I took home copies of a lot of the basic forms that we used every day, and I made notes on them. I'd write on the margins what the different terms meant and why we would use this form in this particular case. Later, I started making up my own forms to help me keep track of things. The hardest part, at least at first, was learning the terminology. The legal terms were flying at me from day one, and I had to ask a lot of questions to get things clarified. I was doing all of this while having a lot of client contact. The phone rings all the time, and I'm talking to clients in between doing all of this other stuff. I am also a full-time student, so learning how to balance my time was crucial. I'm taking some classes during the day, one evening class, and an Internet class. While I'm learning my new job, I'm also trying to stay on top of my classes. It makes you a lot better at organization. I study for my classes on my lunch breaks and do a lot of schoolwork in the evenings.

I really enjoy the legal field. You are constantly getting new challenges and meeting people with new problems. It's a good feeling when you can help them out.

Christina Truitt, Paralegal

ETHICAL ISSUES FOR THE PARALEGAL: CONFLICTS OF INTEREST

One of the most important ethical issues for both attorneys and paralegals is avoiding a conflict of interest. At its simplest, a conflict of interest is any issue that arises between the client and the attorney in which the client's interest may be subordinated to some other concern. For instance, when an attorney represents both the plaintiff and the defendant in a lawsuit, there is a definite and obvious conflict of interest. After all, if the attorney represents both, whose interest is she safeguarding? Similar problems arise when an attorney is the business partner of the client. The lawyer's legal advice may be tainted by considerations of how the client's actions might affect their business relationship.

Ethical rules for both attorneys and paralegals emphasize avoiding even the appearance of a conflict of interest. Paralegals are often called upon to review the roster of clients to make sure that any newly acquired client does not have an interest that runs counter to that of a previous client. The prime example would be representing the husband in a divorce action and then the wife in a child custody dispute. Such representation would be considered a conflict of interest and would justify the firm refusing to represent the wife on the subsequent suit, especially because it was based in some part on the prior divorce action. Conflicts of interest can also come up in personal injury cases. If the potential plaintiff has met with the firm and discussed the possibility of representation in his personal injury suit against a particular defendant, the firm cannot then meet with the defendant, who is also seeking legal representation, even if the plaintiff did not actually hire the firm to represent him.

One method of avoiding potential conflicts of interest is by performing a "conflicts" check. Paralegals, attorneys, and secretaries routinely review new files to make sure that no potential conflicts are involved. There is even legal software available to help with this process.

Relevant Cases

PEROUTKA V. STRENG
116 MD.APP. 301, 695 A.2D 1287 (1997)

CATHELL, Judge.

Michael A. and Diane M. Peroutka appeal from the granting of a Motion of Summary Judgment in favor of Marsha Streng, appellee, by the Circuit Court for Baltimore County. This appeal involves an alleged defamatory statement made by appellee to appellant Diane M. Peroutka and her daughter. Appellants present one question on appeal: "Did the circuit court err when it granted appellee's Motion for Summary Judgment." We shall affirm.

The Facts

Prior to her marriage to Michael M. Peroutka, Diane M. Peroutka was married to Scott Hubbard, and two children resulted from Mrs. Peroutka's first marriage: Dawn M. Hubbard and Holly C. Hubbard. In roughly 1978, while the children were still very young, Mr. Hubbard died of leukemia. In August of 1985, Diane M. Peroutka and Michael A. Peroutka were married.

Sometime in 1989, when Dawn was approximately fourteen years old, she began believing that she had been sexually abused by Mr. Peroutka and that she had "repressed" all memory of those events. These memories were allegedly triggered by Dawn's discussions with her deceased father's sister, Marie Hubbard, and the book Courage to Heal. Dawn never discussed these allegations of sexual abuse with her family or anyone other than Marie Hubbard until 1992.

In the early part of 1992, Dawn discussed, with members of a youth group and a high school basketball coach, the alleged sexual abuse by Mr. Peroutka. At that time, Dawn was taken to the Child Advocacy Center and, ultimately, the Baltimore County Department of Social Services (BCDSS). The BCDSS conducted an investigation into the alleged abuse and found that Dawn's claims were unsubstantiated.

This, however, did not end Dawn's relations with the BCDSS. Due to these allegations of abuse, Mrs. Peroutka decided to waive her rights as a parent and have Dawn placed with the BCDSS. In May of 1992, Dawn was adjudicated a child in need of assistance and was placed in the custody of the State. At that time, appellee was Dawn's social worker. A few months later, Holly, Dawn's younger sister, was also placed with the BCDSS. Appellee was also Holly's social worker.

Sometime in March or April of 1993, Dawn began to realize that the allegations of sexual abuse were untrue. After working with Dr. McHugh, Dawn realized that she had never been abused by Mr. Peroutka. On 6 April 1994, the allegations of sexual abuse were "ruled out" by the BCDSS.

Despite the false allegations of child abuse, Dawn and appellee continued to communicate. In September of 1994, Dawn received a package from appellee that contained information regarding spousal abuse. At that time, Dawn was a psychology major in her sophomore year of college. A "cover letter" sent along with the materials stated: "I thought you might find some of this interesting—it also might be helpful in psychology class—

remember 'battering' doesn't have to be physical — emotional abuse can be just as devastating." It is important to note that apparently nowhere in this cover letter or the material was it asserted by appellee that appellant was "emotionally abused." It was, by the terms of the cover letter, forwarded for Dawn's interest.

Dawn showed the materials sent by appellee to Mrs. Peroutka on 12 January 1995. On that same day, Mrs. Peroutka confronted appellee regarding the materials. Appellee met with Mrs. Peroutka and Dawn in a BCDSS meeting room. At that meeting, Mrs. Peroutka repeatedly demanded to know whether appellee thought she was an emotionally abused spouse. Appellee eventually responded that she thought Mrs. Peroutka was an emotionally abused spouse. Appellee apparently based her opinion on Mrs. Peroutka's relationship with her daughters. Mrs. Peroutka told appellee that she was not emotionally abused. Appellee responded, "that's good" and left the room. On the following day, appellee called Dawn to apologize for leaving the room in an abrupt manner. During that conversation, appellee again expressed her opinion to Dawn that she thought Mrs. Peroutka was an emotionally abused spouse. Dawn subsequently republished appellee's statement to her sister Holly.

Appellants filed suit against appellee on 19 October 1995. The complaint alleged, in respect to Mr. Peroutka, that appellee's "defamation of him, consisted of her making, with malice, a false defamatory statement that he abused his spouse." Similarly, the complaint alleged, in respect to Mrs. Peroutka, that appellee's "defamation of her consisted of appellee making, with malice, a false defamatory statement that she was a battered spouse."

Appellee filed a Motion for Summary Judgment on 9 September 1996. A hearing on that motion was held on 16 October 1996. At that hearing, the trial court held:

The issue in this case is whether, and I would find as a matter of law, I have no difficulty in finding as a matter of law that this statement is not in the least bit defamatory to Mrs. Peroutka. The question is, is the statement defamatory to Mr. Peroutka? Could it be, is it in this case defamation?

The question is, is the statement made by Miss Streng at the specific request of Mrs. Peroutka made to Mrs. Peroutka and her daughter, who come to Mrs. Streng's office and who are inviting her to make, give her opinion, can that be construed as defamation to Mr. Peroutka?

In my view it is not defamatory. The statement is not defamation. It's an opinion. It's an opinion given at the specific request to give an opinion. That cannot constitute defamation. And it's clear from the authorities, Potomac Valve & Fitting Incorporated vs. Crawford Fitting Company, 829 F.2d 1280 (4 th Cir.1987), that an opinion cannot constitute actionable defamation. Adler vs. American Standard Corporation, 538 Fed. Supplement 572 (D.Md.1982), could also be stated as authority.

In my view the statement made by Miss Streng is an opinion. Even if the court were incorrect in stating that the statement was an opinion, the court would have little difficulty in establishing the statement, if it is not an opinion, if it is defamation, which I really don't think it is, if however it were defamation I would rule as a matter of law that the defamation is defamation per quod. . . .

Other facts are necessary to understand the statement as defamatory. Other facts are necessary to understand to even hold the statement to be defamatory. It is not on its face defamatory. And it would be defamation per quod if I thought it were defamatory.

In the case sub judice, there is no dispute as to the facts. In response to repeated questioning by Mrs. Peroutka, appellee, in the presence of Mrs. Peroutka and Dawn, responded that she thought Mrs. Peroutka was an emotionally abused spouse. This statement was subsequently republished by Dawn to her sister Holly. The only issue is whether the statement made by appellee was defamatory and, if so, whether the statement constituted defamation per quod or defamation per se.

Discussion

As this appeal concerns one person's right to freedom of speech and another's right to redress when his or her reputation is harmed by unprotected speech, the First Amendment of the United States Constitution, and Articles Forty and Nineteen of the Declaration of Rights of the Maryland Constitution, are implicated. In *Freedman v. State*, 233 Md. 498, 505, 197 A.2d 232 (1964), rev'd on other grounds, 380 U.S. 51, 85 S.Ct. 734, 13 L.Ed.2d 649 (1965), the Court of Appeals stated:

> The guaranty of freedom of speech and press ordained in Art. 40 would appear to be, in legal effect, substantially similar to that enunciated in the First Amendment, and it is significant that Art. 40 has been treated by this Court as in pari materia with the First Amendment.

In order to protect freedom of the press and freedom of speech, the Supreme Court, beginning with *New York Times Co. v. Sullivan*, 376 U.S. 254, 84 S.Ct. 710, 11 L.Ed.2d 686 (1964), made it more difficult for individuals to recover for defamation under state law. In *New York Times*, the Court held that for a public official to recover damages for defamation, he or she had to prove that the statement in regard to his or her official conduct was made with actual malice. This was defined by the *New York Times* Court as knowledge that the statement was false or reckless disregard for the statement's truth or falsity. The Court later held, in *Curtis Publishing Co. v. Butts*, 388 U.S. 130, 87 S.Ct. 1975, 18 L.Ed.2d 1094 (1967), that the requirement of actual malice also applied to "public figures" and that actual malice had to be proved by clear and convincing evidence in order for a "public official" or "public figure" to recover damages for defamation.

The Supreme Court also addressed the First Amendment's impact on state defamation law for individuals who were not public officials or public figures. In *Rosenbloom v. Metromedia, Inc.*, 403 U.S. 29, 31-32, 91 S.Ct. 1811, 1814, 29 L.Ed.2d 296 (1971), the Supreme Court examined "whether the *New York Times* knowing-or-reckless-falsity standard applies in a state civil libel action brought not by a 'public official' or a 'public figure' but by a private individual for a defamatory falsehood uttered in a news broadcast by a radio station about the individual's involvement in an event of public or general interest." In a plurality opinion, the Court indicated that when the matter was of public concern, the plaintiff, even if a private individual, had to show clear and convincing evidence of actual malice.

Three years later, the issue addressed in *Gertz v. Robert Welch*, Inc., 418 U.S. 323, 332, 94 S.Ct. 2997, 3003, 41 L.Ed.2d 789 (1974), was "whether a newspaper or broadcaster that publishes defamatory falsehoods about an individual who is neither a public official nor a public figure may claim a constitutional privilege against liability for the injury inflicted by those statements." The Court, in language that is particularly relevant to this case, stated:

> Under the First Amendment there is no such thing as a false idea. However pernicious an opinion may seem, we depend for its correction not on the conscience of judges and juries but on the competition of other ideas. But there is no constitutional value in false statements of fact.

When the speech is of public concern but the plaintiff is a private figure, as in Gertz, the Constitution still supplants the standards of the common law, but the constitutional requirements are, in at least some of their range, less forbidding than when the plaintiff is a public figure and the speech is of public concern. When the speech is of exclusively private concern and the plaintiff is a private figure, as in Dunn Dun & Bradstreet, the constitutional requirements do not necessarily force any change in at least some of the features of the common-law landscape.

In a case involving a plaintiff who is not a public figure, a prima facia case of defamation requires proof of the following elements:

> (1) that the defendant made a defamatory communication — i.e., that he communicated a statement

tending to expose the plaintiff to public scorn, hatred, contempt, or ridicule to a third person who reasonably recognized the statement as being defamatory; (2) that the statement was false; (3) that the defendant was at fault in communicating the statement; and (4) that the plaintiff suffered harm.

As to the first element, the determination of whether a statement "is reasonably capable of a defamatory interpretation is for the court upon reviewing the statement as a whole; words have different meanings depending on the context in which they are used and a meaning not warranted by the whole publication should not be imputed." *Batson v. Shiflett*, 325 Md. 684, 723, 602 A.2d 1191 (1992).

We agree with the trial court that the statement was not defamatory as to Mrs. Peroutka. Asserting that a person is emotionally abused is not the type of statement "which tends to expose a person to public scorn, hatred, contempt or ridicule, thereby discouraging others in the community from having a good opinion of, or from associating or dealing with, that person."

The more difficult question is whether the statement is defamatory as to Mr. Peroutka. Although it might be argued that the deceased first husband was the implied abusive spouse under the circumstances here present, the parties assumed that any implication as to the identity of the abuser would relate to Mr. Peroutka. The assertion that Mrs. Peroutka is an emotionally abused spouse, therefore, may imply that Mr. Peroutka is the abusing spouse. For purposes of this opinion, we shall assume, without deciding, that an assertion that a person emotionally abuses his or her spouse carries with it a defamatory meaning. The issue then becomes, whether, under the circumstances of this case, appellee's statement that she thought Mrs. Peroutka was an emotionally abused spouse was defamatory to Mr. Peroutka.

Emotional abuse is not a diagnosis — it is merely an opinion or an assessment. There is no listing for emotional abuse or excessive emotional coercion or pressure in the *Diagnos-*

tic and Statistical Manual of Mental Disorders-IV (*DSM-IV*). There are no defined set of clinically significant behavioral or psychological syndromes or patterns that occur in an individual that is associated with subjection to excessive emotional pressure, emotional coercion, or, as a lay-person might state, emotional abuse.

Maryland has consistently followed the majority rule — that defamatory misstatement of fact cannot be defended successfully as fair comment. The distinction between "fact" and "opinion," although theoretically and logically hard to draw, is usually reasonably determinable as a practical matter: Would an ordinary person, reading the matter complained of, be likely to understand it as an expression of the writer's opinion or as a declaration of an existing fact? An opinion may be so stated as to raise directly the inference of a factual basis, and the defense of fair comment usually has been held not to cover an opinion so stated.

We think that to sustain fair comment, facts which are set out in the publication must be truly stated (if they are unprivileged), and that such a fact which is not set out must both be true and be so referred to in the publication as to be either recognizable or be made identifiable and easily accessible.

Id. at 282, 176 A.2d 340. The Court ultimately held that the publisher did not set out the facts sufficiently in the editorial or reference them so as to inform a reader of the facts upon which the publisher based the opinion.

A review of the Maryland cases indicates that a statement, even if expressed in terms of an opinion, can be defamatory under certain circumstances regardless of whether the statement concerns a public figure or private person. When the underlying facts used to form the opinion are not given along with the defamatory statement, the statement itself may be treated as being factual and therefore potentially defamatory. If the facts from which an individual forms a conclusion are given but are false, the defendant is potentially subject to liability for defamatory speech based on the false statement of facts. If the facts from which a defendant forms his or her opinion are given or are readily available and those facts cannot be proved false, the defendant is not subject to liability for the opinion.

As we view the case sub judice, the ultimate issue revolves around the verifiability of the alleged defamatory statement. Section 566 of the Restatement (Second) of Torts, cited by the Court in Milkovich, provides:

> A defamatory communication may consist of a statement in the form of an opinion, but a statement of this nature is actionable only if it implied the allegation of undisclosed facts as the basis for the opinion.
>
> The Restatement distinguishes between "pure" opinion and "simple" opinion. A pure opinion is based on disclosed or known facts while a simple opinion is based on undisclosed facts. The Restatement divides the rule into four fact patterns:
>
> (1) If the defendant bases his expression of a derogatory opinion of the plaintiff on his own statement of false and defamatory facts, he is subject to liability for the factual statement but not for the expression of opinion.
>
> (2) If the defendant bases his expression of a derogatory opinion of the plaintiff on his own statement of facts that are not defamatory, he is not subject to liability for the factual statement — nor for the expression of opinion, so long as it does not reasonably indicate an assertion of the existence of other, defamatory, facts that would justify the forming of the opinion. The same result is reached if the statement of facts is defamatory but the facts are true . . . or if the defendant is not shown to be guilty of the requisite fault regarding the truth or defamatory character of the statement of facts. . . .
>
> (3) If the defendant bases his expression of a derogatory opinion on the existence of "facts" that he does not state but that are assumed to be true by both parties to the communication, and if the communication does not give rise to the reasonable inference that it is also based on other facts that are defamatory, he is not subject to liability, whether the assumed facts are defamatory or not.
>
> (4) If the defendant expresses a derogatory opinion without disclosing the facts on which it is based, he is subject to liability if the comment creates the reasonable inference that the opinion is justified by the existence of unexpressed defamatory facts. Restatement (Second) of Torts §566 cmt. c (1976).

Under the first fact pattern of the Restatement, liability is imposed on a defendant if he or she bases the opinion on his or her statement of false facts. The Maryland cases of *Hearst Corp. v. Hughes*, 297 Md. 112, 466 A.2d 486 (1983), *Berkey v. Delia*, 287 Md. 302, 413 A.2d 170 (1980), and *Hughley v. McDermott*, 72 Md.App. 391, 530 A.2d 13 (1987), are illustrative of the first fact pattern of the Restatement.

In the case sub judice, appellee did not base her opinion that Mrs. Peroutka was an emotionally abused spouse on facts disclosed in the opinion. Accordingly, this case is not similar to fact patterns number one or two of the Restatement. Although Maryland cases have addressed factual patterns similar to fact patterns 1, 2, and 4 of comment c to section 566 of the Restatement (Second) of Torts, we have not addressed whether a defendant should be held liable for an opinion that was based on facts known by the persons to whom the statement was published.

We shall hold, under the circumstances of this case, that appellee's statement was not defamatory. We explain.

The alleged defamatory statement was published to four persons: Mr. Peroutka, Mrs. Peroutka, Dawn, and Holly. All of these persons had firsthand knowledge of the facts that led appellee to form an opinion that Mrs. Peroutka was an emotionally abused spouse. In this context, it was evident that appellee was expressing an opinion. Comment b to section 566 of the Restatement provides:

> The pure type of expression of opinion may also occur when the maker of the comment does not himself express the alleged facts on which he bases the expression of opinion. This happens when both parties to the communication know the facts or assume their existence and the comment is clearly based on those assumed facts and does not imply the existence of other facts in order to justify the comment.

In the case sub judice, Mr. and Mrs. Peroutka, Dawn, Holly, and appellee knew that (1) Mrs. Peroutka had placed both Holly and Dawn in the custody of the BCDSS; (2) appellee was the foster care worker for both Dawn and Holly; (3) as Dawn's and Holly's social worker, appellee received information concerning their feelings and their family's interaction; (4) appellee had the opportunity to observe Mr. and Mrs. Peroutka's behavior in relation to Holly and Dawn; (5) when Dawn indicated that she thought she was sexually abused by Mr. Peroutka, Mrs. Peroutka wrote numerous letters to friends and acquaintances of the family that divulged personal and embarrassing information about Dawn; (6) Mr. and Mrs. Peroutka filed a Motion for a Restraining Order when Dawn went to visit her half-sibling shortly after she was placed in foster care; (7) neither Mr. Peroutka nor Mrs. Peroutka

visited Dawn while she was hospitalized for a severe eating disorder; and (8) when Dawn went to deliver a letter to Mr. and Mrs. Peroutka, in which she recanted her allegations of sexual abuse, a complaint for criminal trespass was filed against her. Because all the persons who received the alleged defamatory statement knew the underlying facts of the conflicts within this family unit giving rise to appellee's opinion, appellee is not subject to liability, although, as with any opinion, appellant is free to disagree.

We hold that the statement made by appellee was not defamatory as to either Mr. or Mrs. Peroutka. We, accordingly, affirm the grant of summary judgment by the trial court.

JUDGMENT AFFIRMED; COSTS TO BE PAID BY APPELLANTS.

PISCATELLI V. VAN SMITH
424 MD. 294, 35 A.3D 1140 (2012)

HARRELL, J.

American poet, author, and essayist William Carlos Williams wrote, "It is not what you say that matters but the manner in which you say it. There lies the secret of the ages." Selected Essays, preface at i (1954). Respondents in the present case, CEGW, Inc., owner of the Baltimore-based City Paper, and Van Smith (Smith), a reporter, published in 2006–07 two articles in the City Paper that reported on the 2003 double murder in Baltimore of Jason Convertino (Convertino) and Sean Wisniewski (Wisniewski). Petitioner, Nicholas A. Piscatelli (Piscatelli), who was mentioned unflatteringly in the articles, perceived that his reputation had been injured thereby and he had been portrayed in a false light. Piscatelli sued Respondents in the Circuit Court for Baltimore City for damages based on defamation and false light claims. The Circuit Court granted Respondents' motion for summary judgment, which judgment the Court of Special Appeals affirmed subsequently upon Piscatelli's appeal. Having granted Piscatelli's petition for writ of certiorari, we shall conclude

ultimately that the manner in which Respondent published those statements placed them within the protective embrace of the fair reporting and fair comment privileges, and consequently, Piscatelli's claims were not actionable. Therefore, we affirm as a matter of law.

I. Facts and Procedural History

In 2006 and 2007, Smith authored, and the City Paper published, two articles (one in each year) revisiting the 2003 murders of Convertino and Wisniewski and the trial of Anthony Jerome Miller (Miller) for those crimes. Respondents published the first article, entitled "Late Discovery," on 6 December 2006, and published the second, entitled "The Lonely Killer," on 20 June 2007. Both articles more than hinted that Piscatelli may have been involved in the murders, despite that he was not charged criminally in connection with the crimes.

Convertino and Wisniewski were murdered on or about 11 April 2003, in the Fells Point neighborhood of Baltimore. Prior to his death, Convertino worked for Redwood Trust, a Baltimore nightclub located in a former bank building (hence the name of the nightclub), managing and procuring music acts for the club. Wisniewski worked also for Redwood Trust, as well as for a nightlife promotions company that held events at Redwood Trust occasionally. Piscatelli owned Redwood Trust.

Two years after the murders, a police investigation concluded that Miller committed the crimes. The State charged him on 17 February 2006. Miller was tried and found guilty in the Circuit Court for Baltimore City of two counts of second degree murder and sentenced to two consecutive 30–year prison terms.

Insofar as Piscatelli was concerned, Respondents highlighted in their articles two particular aspects of the Miller trial. First, on or about 27 October 2006, the State's Attorney provided to Miller's defense counsel a memorandum containing supplemental discovery responses. The memorandum contained the following summary of a conversation Convertino's mother, Pam Morgan (Morgan), had with police detectives investigating the murders:

> Pam Morgan has stated that an unknown man approached her at a benefit in Binghamton, New York, held for her son's child shortly after his murder. The man advised her that Nick Piscatelli was behind her son's murder, he covered his tracks and hired someone to kill him.

This memorandum became part of the criminal case file and the public record, although it was not offered in evidence at Miller's trial.

The second feature of the newspaper reporting relevant to Piscatelli was that Miller's defense counsel and the prosecutor examined Piscatelli as a witness during Miller's trial. The prosecutor asked Piscatelli bluntly if he had anything to do with the murder of Convertino; Piscatelli responded that he did not. Piscatelli testified also that: Convertino had been planning to leave Redwood Trust for a similar position with a rival nightclub; Convertino planned to switch Sean "P. Diddy" Combs, a popular musician at that time, from performing at Redwood Trust to the rival nightclub; and, Piscatelli suspected Convertino of taking larger commissions than he was due during his employment at Redwood Trust.

Respondents reported the statement from the supplemental discovery memorandum in both articles and Piscatelli's Miller trial testimony in the 20 June 2007 article. Respondents included in the articles additional relevant comments that may be distilled into three themes: the double murder remains "mysterious," despite Miller's conviction; Piscatelli may have had a motive to kill Convertino; and, Morgan believed Piscatelli may be involved in her son's murder.

Based on these articles, Piscatelli filed a complaint in the Circuit Court on 5 December 2007, advancing counts of defamation and false light against Respondents, Smith and CEGW, Inc. Respondents retorted with a motion for summary judgment, arguing, as they do before us, that Piscatelli failed to establish that Respondents' statements were false and the fair reporting and fair comment privileges protected any allegedly defamatory material. Piscatelli, in his opposition to summary judgment in the trial court, contended that accusations of his involvement in the murders were false and Respondents abused their fair reporting and fair comment privileges. On 17 February 2009, the trial judge issued a written order stating, without further explication, that there was no dispute of material fact and Respondents were entitled to judgment as a matter of law.

Piscatelli filed timely an appeal to the Court of Special Appeals, maintaining that the Circuit Court granted improperly summary judgment because Respondents abused their fair reporting and fair comment privileges. The panel of the Court of Special Appeals concluded ultimately, in a reported opinion, that the trial judge granted properly summary judgment because Respondents' statements were privileged and not defamatory. *Piscatelli v. Smith*, 197 Md.App. 23, 41–42, 12 A.3d 164, 175 (2011).

Discussion

Piscatelli advanced two counts in his complaint: defamation and invasion of privacy (false light). We shall address in greatest detail Piscatelli's defamation claim, but need not address the false light claim separately. An allegation of false light must meet the same legal standards as an allegation of defamation.

In order to plead properly a defamation claim under Maryland law, a plaintiff must allege specific facts establishing four elements to the satisfaction of the fact-finder: "(1) that the defendant made a defamatory statement to a third person, (2) that the statement was false, (3) that the defendant was legally at fault in making the statement, and (4) that the plaintiff thereby suffered harm." *Indep. Newspapers, Inc. v. Brodie*, 407 Md. 415, 441, 966 A.2d 432, 448 (2009). For purposes of the first element, a "defamatory statement" is one that tends to expose a person to "public scorn, hatred, contempt, or ridicule," which, as a consequence, discourages "others in the community from having a good opinion of, or associating with, that person." Under the second element, a "false" statement is one "that is not substantially correct." The plaintiff carries the burden to prove falsity. Id. To determine whether a publication is defamatory, a question of law for the court, the publication must be read as a whole: "words have different meanings depending on the context in which they are used and a meaning not warranted by the whole publication should not be imputed."

Where a defendant asserts a privilege in a motion for summary judgment in a defamation action, we consider first whether the asserted privilege applies. Thus, we assume that the plaintiff's allegations of defamation are true for purposes of evaluating whether the privilege exists.

In some circumstances, an absolute or qualified privilege defeats a claim of defamation, if the defendant did not abuse that privilege. "An absolute privilege is distinguished from a qualified privilege in that the former provides immunity regardless of the purpose or motive of the defendant, or the reasonableness of his conduct, while the latter is conditioned upon the absence of malice and is forfeited if it is abused." *Smith v. Danielczyk*, 400 Md. 98, 117, 928 A.2d 795, 806 (2007).

Here, Respondents contended that two conditional privileges insulated their allegedly defamatory remarks: the fair reporting and fair comment privileges. Whether a conditional privilege exists is a question of law, and the defendant bears the burden of proof to establish the privilege. Once a prima facie case for a privilege is adduced, the plaintiff must produce facts, admissible in evidence, demonstrating the defendant abused the privilege, in order to generate a triable issue for the fact-finder. To demonstrate abuse of the privilege, the plaintiff must demonstrate that the defendant made his or her statements with malice, defined as "a person's actual knowledge that his or her statement is false, coupled with his or her intent to deceive another by means of that statement." All relevant circumstances are admissible when determining whether a defendant abused a common law defamation privilege, "including the defendant's reasonable belief in the truth of his statements, the excessive nature of the language used, whether the disclosures were unsolicited, and whether the communication was made in a proper manner and only to proper parties." While malice is usually a question for the fact-finder, it need not be submitted to the fact-finder when the plaintiff fails to allege or prove facts that would support a finding of malice.

A. The Fair Reporting Privilege

The fair reporting privilege is a qualified privilege to report legal and official proceedings that are, in and of themselves defamatory, so long as the account is "fair and substantially accurate." The privilege arises from the public's interest in having access to information about official proceedings and public meetings. A defendant abuses his or her fair reporting privilege, not upon a showing of actual malice (as with other common law conditional privileges), but when the defendant's account "fails the test of fairness and accuracy." Fairness and accuracy is satisfied when the reports are substantially correct, impartial, coherent, and bona fide.

2. The Fair Reporting Privilege Applies to Respondents' Reporting of the Supplemental Discovery Memorandum and Piscatelli's Trial Testimony

In the present case, the fair reporting privilege applies to Respondents' reporting of the excerpt from the supplemental discovery memorandum and the summary of Piscatelli's trial testimony. As to the supplemental discovery memorandum, Respondents wrote in the two articles:

> On Oct. 27, the prosecutor disclosed in a memorandum to the defense that "Pam Morgan Convertino's mother has stated that an unknown man approached her at a benefit in Binghamton, New York, held for her son's child shortly after his murder. The man advised her that Nick Piscatelli was behind her son's murder, he covered his tracks and hired someone to kill him." The memo does not indicate when Morgan shared this information with investigators, but she told City Paper during a Nov. 30 phone interview that the event was held in May 2003, just weeks after the murders.
>
> "At the benefit, this guy comes up to me and he says he knows who was behind my son's murder," Morgan recalls. "I didn't know Nick Piscatelli at that point." . . . "The unknown man came in, talked, and left," she continues. "I was like, 'Whoa!'" . . .
>
> One of the things she shared with the police had to do with Piscatelli. About a month after the killings, in May 2003, a benefit was held near Binghamton to raise money for Convertino's young daughter. About 500 people showed up, and while it was going on, Morgan says she was approached by a man she'd never seen before and hasn't seen since. "He said that Nick Piscatelli was behind my son's murder," Morgan recalls, "that Piscatelli had hired someone to do it, and that he'd covered his tracks."

These statements fall within the purview of the fair reporting privilege. In Chesapeake Publishing Corp., we concluded that information in a court case file is covered by the fair reporting privilege, if the reporter's account of that information is fair and substantially accurate. Here, the supplemental discovery memorandum was part of the Miller criminal case file and, despite not being offered in evidence at trial, was a public record that may be reported without liability for defamation, so long as the report is fair and accurate.

Respondents' summary of Piscatelli's testimony during Miller's trial was:

> Take, for instance, the motive that Convertino's boss may have had. Convertino was hired to manage Redwood Trust by Nicholas Piscatelli, a successful Baltimore real-estate developer. Piscatelli meticulously restored a historic downtown bank building that had survived the Great Baltimore Fire of 1904 to house his posh nightclub. Convertino, witnesses testified at Miller's trial, was planning to take his proven skills as a scene-maker to one of Redwood Trust's competitors, Bohager's Bar and Grill, when the murders happened. More specifically, Convertino was scheming to take a P. Diddy event that was scheduled to happen at Redwood Trust on April 13, 2003, to Bohager's instead; after the murders, on April 11, P. Diddy appeared at Redwood Trust, as originally planned. What's more, Piscatelli suspected Convertino of stealing not just shows, but money from Redwood Trust.

B. The Fair Comment Privilege

Piscatelli argues that the fair comment privilege is inapplicable because Respondents based their comments on purportedly defamatory, unprivileged facts. We disagree.

Maryland recognizes that, under the fair comment privilege, a newspaper like any member of the community may, without liability, honestly express a fair and reasonable opinion or comment on matters of legitimate public interest. The reason given is that such discussion is in the furtherance of an interest of social importance, and therefore it is held entitled to protection even at the expense of uncompensated harm to the plaintiff's reputation.

Thus, the fair comment privilege is available for opinions or comments regarding matters of legitimate public interest. In *Kirby*, we discussed the fair comment privilege regarding opinions expressed about a review hearing of a Baltimore police commissioner, inferring that it was a matter of legitimate public interest. 227 Md. at 282–83, 176 A.2d at 348–49. In *Kapiloff v. Dunn*, the Court of Special Appeals concluded that the performance ratings of high-school principals were also a matter of legitimate public interest. 27 Md.App. 514, 533–34, 343 A.2d 251, 264 (1975). Although Maryland case law has not addressed whether the occurrence or prosecution of crimes, and murder specifically, are matters of legitimate public interest, other courts have. This principle seems obvious. Therefore, the reporting about the murders and criminal trial of the presumed perpetrator at the bottom of this civil litigation are matters of legitimate public interest.

Whether a particular publication comes within the purview of this privilege "often turns on whether or not it contains misstatements of fact as distinguished from expression of opinion." The test for determining whether a published statement is a fact or opinion is, "Would an ordinary person, reading the matter complained of, be likely to understand it as an expression of the writer's opinion or as a declaration of an existing fact?" The fair comment privilege protects an opinion only where "the facts on which it is based are truly stated or privileged or otherwise known either because the facts are of common knowledge or because, though perhaps unknown to a particular recipient of the communication, they are readily accessible to him." Conversely, an opinion based on undisclosed facts, or that permits the inference of an undisclosed factual basis, is not privileged.

IV. Conclusion

Piscatelli failed to adduce facts that would be admissible in evidence to demonstrate that Respondents' reporting about Miller's trial was unfair and inaccurate, a burden he bore in order to present a triable issue for a jury as to whether Respondents abused the fair reporting privilege. Additionally, where Respondents expressed in the articles simple opinions based on disclosed, privileged statements, those opinions are themselves privileged as fair comment. For these reasons, the Circuit Court granted properly Respondents' motion for summary judgment.

JUDGMENT OF THE COURT OF SPECIAL APPEALS AFFIRMED; PETITIONER TO PAY COSTS IN THIS COURT AND THE COURT OF SPECIAL APPEALS.

Websites

◻ **Defining defamation**
http://dictionary.law.com/Default.aspx?selected=458

◻ **Find Law articles about defamation**
http://www.findlaw.com (click on "search findlaw" for defamation, slander, etcetera)

◻ **Legal search engines**
Using any search engine, type in "legal search engines," and then save the results for a search involving any of the issues raised in this chapter.

◻ **Timeslips (time and billing software for law offices)**
http://www.timeslips.com/

Forms and Court Documents

A complaint alleging libel.

STATE OF PLACID	IN THE SUPERIOR COURT
COUNTY OF BARNES	FILE NUMBER: _____

Lawrence Lookgood,	)	Complaint
Plaintiff	)	
	)	
vs.	)	
	)	
Placid News, Inc.,	)	
Defendant	)	

Complaint for Libel

COMES NOW the Plaintiff and complaining of the Defendant Placid News, Inc., alleges the following:

1.

Defendant Placid News, Inc. (hereinafter "Defendant") is a corporation incorporated under the laws of this State. Defendant's principal office is located at 1001 Burke Avenue, Barnes County, Pacific City, Placid.

2.

Defendant is the owner and principal publisher of the Placid News Herald. This is a newspaper, published daily and distributed statewide.

3.

On August 19, 2011, agents employed by the Defendant wrote an article about the Plaintiff. This article contained false and defamatory statements about the Plaintiff in that the article stated that the Plaintiff had fathered several children with his secretary, Lisa Doe. This statement was published in conjunction with another in which the Plaintiff was quoted as saying that he and his wife, Mrs. Julia Lookgood, had always enjoyed a happy and monogamous marriage. The clear implication of the article is that the Plaintiff engaged in an extramarital affair with his secretary and fathered children with her while he was married to Julia Lookgood.

4.

The defamatory article was distributed by the Defendant's agents to its distributors throughout the state. The defamatory article was read by thousands of individuals, including the Plaintiff's wife, children, and coworkers.

5.

The defamatory matter injured the Plaintiff's reputation, held him up to public ridicule and humiliation, and affected his ability to interact with his clients. The defamatory statement was intended to cause, and did cause, injury to the Plaintiff's reputation.

6.

Plaintiff is not a public figure and Defendant's agents knew that the statement was false, or acted with reckless disregard of the truth of the statement contained in said article.

WHEREFORE, Plaintiff prays that the Court award the following damages:

a. General damages in the amount of _____;
b. Special damages in the amount of _____; and
c. Punitive damages in an amount to be determined by the court.
d. Plaintiff also requests costs of suit; and
e. Such other and further relief as the court may deem just and proper.

Respectfully submitted, this the _____ day of _____, 20 ____.

_____

Clarence D. Arrow
Attorney for the Plaintiff

Key Terms

Clear and convincing proof	Libel
	Malice
Defamation	Slander

Review Questions

1   What is the difference between libel and slander?
2   How is libel per se different from slander per se?
3   Can a cartoon be considered defamatory? If so, what type of defamation is it?
4   How is the Restatement's definition of defamation (Figure 11-1) different from the general definition of defamation (Figure 11-2)?
5   Can a family be defamed? Why or why not?
6   Explain the term *publication*.
7   Why is it necessary that the plaintiff prove publication to be successful in her defamation action?
8   Mailing a letter to the plaintiff is usually not considered to be publication. Why?
9   How can the plaintiff prove that her reputation was damaged?
10   What is libel per quod?

11 In libel per se, malice is often presumed. Why?

12 Is libel potentially more damaging to the plaintiff than slander? If so, how?

13 It is often said that truth is an absolute defense to defamation. Explain.

14 Other than truth, what types of defense are available in a defamation action?

15 Explain the difference between an absolute privilege and a qualified privilege.

16 Why does a celebrity receive less protection under defamation law than a private person?

17 How do courts balance the First Amendment right of freedom of speech against a person's right to bring a defamation action?

18 What is the *New York Times* Rule?

19 What is actual malice?

Applying What You Have Learned

1 One evening, Ted, the news anchor on a local television show, reads the following from his prepared TV script: "In the news today, John Doe has been arrested and charged with child molestation." Ted pauses, and then, ad-libbing, says, "Man, that guy is always getting into trouble. Someone should teach that pedophile a lesson."

   In fact, John Doe has not been arrested or charged with any crime and has never been in trouble with the law before. Does John have a cause of action for defamation against Ted? If so, what type of action can he bring? Explain your answer.

2 Draft an answer to the complaint in the Forms and Court Documents section. What constitutional issues may also be involved in this case?

3 Draft a complaint based on the Case for Defamation. What are the possible defenses that a defendant might use in an answer?

4 Has your state expanded the definition of slander per se or libel per se? If so, what category of statements is covered?

5 What types of privileges and immunities are recognized in your state in regard to defamation actions? Are they more extensive than what the text suggests, or less so?

Endnotes

[1] *Swenson-Davis v. Martel*, 354 N.W.2d 288, 135 Mich. App. 632 (1984).

[2] *Berg v. Consolidated Freightways, Inc.*, 280 Pa. Super. 495, 421 A.2d 831 (1980).

[3] Restatement (Second) of Torts §580A, comment f.

[4] *Cosgrove Studio & Camera Shop, Inc. v. Pane*, 408 Pa. 314, 182 A.2d 751 (1962).

[5] *Weinstein v. Bullick*, 827 F. Supp. 1193 (E.D. Pa. 1993).

[6] *Cox Enters. v. Bakin*, 206 Ga. App. 813, 426 S.E.2d 651 (1992).

[7] *Wynberg v. National Enquirer, Inc.*, 564 F. Supp. 924 (D.C. Cal. 1982).

[8] *Ostrowe v. Lee,* 175 N.E. 505, 256 N.Y. 36 (1931).

[9] *Linebaugh v. Sheraton Mich. Corp.,* 198 Mich. App. 335, 497 N.W.2d 585 (1993).

[10] *Renwick v. News and Observer Pub. Co.,* 304 S.E.2d 593 (1983).

[11] *Reiman v. Pacific Development Soc.,* 284 P. 575, 132 Or. 82 (1930).

[12] *Miller v. Lear Siegler, Inc.,* 525 F. Supp. 46 (D.C. Kan. 1981).

[13] *Gonzalez v. Avon Products, Inc.,* 609 F. Supp. 1555 (D.C. Del. 1985).

[14] *Hearst Corp. v. Hughes,* 466 A.2d 486, 297 Md. 112 (1983).

[15] *Gertz v. Robert Welch, Inc.,* 418 U.S. 323 (1974).

[16] 376 U.S. 254, 11 L. Ed. 2d 686, 84 S. Ct. 710.

[17] *Gertz v. Robert Welch, Inc.,* 418 U.S. 323 (1974).

[18] *New York Times Co. v. Sullivan,* 376 U.S. 254, 11 L. Ed. 2d 686, 84 S. Ct. 710 (1964).

[19] Oliver Wendell Holmes, *The Common Law,* Little, Brown and Company, Boston (M. Howe ed., 1963).

[20] *Buendorf v. National Pub. Radio, Inc.,* 822 F. Supp. 6 (D.D.C. 1993).

[21] *Triangle Publications, Inc. v. Chumley,* 253 Ga. 179, 317 S.E.2d 534 (1984).

Crossword Puzzle

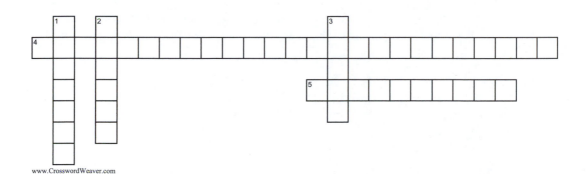

www.CrosswordWeaver.com

ACROSS

4 A measure of proof that is higher than preponderance of the evidence. Clear and convincing proof is evidence that is likely to be true under the facts. This standard of proof is less than beyond a reasonable doubt but higher than preponderance of the evidence.

5 An attack on the reputation or character of another

DOWN

1 Spoken defamation

2 Reckless or false statements; a court-created doctrine that supplies the element by assuming that certain phrases could only have been motivated by ill will. Examples would include falsely accusing someone of a crime or other despicable act.

3 Written defamation

Malpractice

- **Define medical malpractice**

- **Explain how a medical malpractice case can be based on different legal theories, such as contract or negligence**

- **Describe the standard of care for professionals**

- **Explain informed consent**

- **Describe how attorneys can avoid claims of legal malpractice**

CHUMLEY AND MALPRACTICE

When Mr. Chumley was airlifted from the crash scene to a local hospital, the attending physician failed to diagnose some of his internal injuries. Mr. Chumley suffered blunt trauma to his abdomen, but the physician failed to notice a potentially fatal spleen puncture. In fact, on the nurse's note that the firm has received through discovery, the message in Figure 12-1 appears.

The first hurdle is learning how to decipher this medical language. Unfortunately, that topic is too broad for a chapter that focuses on medical malpractice. The note actually says, "Patient complains of severe left-upper-quadrant pain upon palpation. Dr. Smith notified — DB."

FIGURE 12-1

Nurse's Note

Pt ℅ severe LLQ pain upon palpation. dr. Smith notified —db

Now that we know what the nurse's note says, do we have a case for medical malpractice against the attending physician? We answer that question over the course of this chapter.

II INTRODUCTION TO PROFESSIONAL MALPRACTICE

When professionals fail to live up to the standards of their profession, their clients may have a cause of action against them. In this chapter, we address the issue of malpractice cases. After defining what a malpractice case is, we then proceed to specific examples showing how such cases are proved. Although malpractice cases are brought against a wide variety of professions, the two most common are medical malpractice and legal malpractice.

III WHAT IS MEDICAL MALPRACTICE?

Malpractice
The failure of a professional to exercise an adequate degree of skill, expertise, and knowledge for the benefit of the client or patient; otherwise known as professional negligence.

In a suit for **malpractice,** the plaintiff is alleging that the defendant, who is a professional, injured the plaintiff while performing his profession. Although we proceed in the discussion as though malpractice is an entirely separate form of tort action, in fact it is not. Malpractice cases are usually based solidly in negligence theory, but because these cases raise so many unique issues, the topic of malpractice deserves a chapter to itself.

The basis of a malpractice action is that a person who claims to have special knowledge and skill causes personal injury or wrongful death to the plaintiff during the execution of that skill. The typical example of a malpractice action is when a doctor negligently injures his patient while treating him for some injury. The doctor's negligence in the treatment gives the plaintiff a cause of action against him.

Notice that malpractice actions are based on the negligent performance of the professional's duties. An essential part of any malpractice claim is that the injury occurred during, and as a direct result of, the professional's actions while performing his particular area of expertise. When the defendant is not acting in his professional capacity and causes injury, there is no cause of action for medical malpractice. Instead, that case would simply be treated as any other negligence action.

Example: Doctor Ted is driving home from work and fails to stop for a red light. He hits Frank's car. Frank brings a medical malpractice action against

Doctor Ted. Doctor Ted files a motion to dismiss for failure to state a valid cause of action. How does the judge rule?

Answer: The judge will dismiss the case. Doctor Ted was not acting in his professional capacity at the time of the accident, so a malpractice case is not authorized.

In malpractice cases, the defendant is held to a higher standard than what is seen in typical negligence cases. Recall that the standard of care in most negligence cases is the "reasonable person standard." Under that standard, the plaintiff must show that the defendant failed to act as a reasonable person would have done under similar circumstances and that this failure was a proximate cause of the plaintiff's injuries. This is not the standard used in malpractice cases. In malpractice cases, we use a variation of the reasonable person standard. Malpractice cases are also unique among negligence cases because the plaintiff must prove that there was a relationship between him and the professional. In fact, proof of a doctor-patient relationship is absolutely critical in proving medical malpractice. It is this relationship that gives rise to the special obligations that the defendant-doctor has toward the patient.

Medical malpractice cases have received a great deal of attention in the past couple of decades because of several large jury verdicts awarded to plaintiffs. Some of these awards have been enormous, stretching into hundreds of millions of dollars. As a result, the field has undergone dramatic changes. State legislatures have enacted new statutes to modify the statutes of limitation or to limit the size of verdicts that plaintiffs may receive in such cases. Many commentators have spoken of a "medical malpractice crisis" in which "runaway juries" constantly award huge verdicts to plaintiffs, which results in greater malpractice insurance premiums for doctors and may even drive some physicians out of the profession entirely. We address these issues as well, but first, we take a look at the history of medical malpractice actions.

If the plaintiff dies as a result of the malpractice — or dies while the case is pending — there are statutes that allow the case to continue. These "survival actions" allow heirs and family members of the deceased plaintiff to continue the suit in the name of the deceased plaintiff. Before these statutes were created, the general rule was that when a plaintiff died, his or her claim died, too.

A. A BRIEF HISTORY OF MEDICAL MALPRACTICE

Although medical malpractice cases seem like a relatively recent phenomenon, they have been around for hundreds of years. The first medical malpractice case in the United States was filed in 1794. However, these cases were few and far between. There has been a dramatic rise in these cases beginning after World War II, and they have been rising steadily ever since.

The medical profession has not always been held in high esteem. In the 1800s, physicians were often poorly trained and unlicensed.[2] Medical treatments were rudimentary and, by modern standards, lacking in proper hygiene and follow-up care. According to one commentator, "The notoriously low

From the first medical malpractice case in the United States: "Action of the case declaring that on the 10th of October 1791, the plaintiff's wife had a scrofulous tumor in one of her breasts, which required amputation; that the defendant, who then was, and for many years before had been a practicing physician, and professed to be well skilled in surgery, and in the amputation of limbs, applied to the plaintiff and affirmed to him that he had competent skill and knowledge to cut off his wife's breast, and to make a cure of it, and that he could and would for a reasonable reward, perform said operation, with skill and safety to his said wife; and the plaintiff relying upon the defendant's declarations aforesaid, consented to his performing said operation, and agreed to pay him therefor [sic] whatever should be a reasonable compensation; and the defendant in consideration thereof undertook and promised to perform said operation with skill and safety to the wife of the plaintiff; and that on the 10th of October aforesaid, the defendant did cut off the breast of his said wife, and performed said operation in the most unskillful, ignorant and cruel manner, contrary to all the well-known rules and principles of practice in such cases; and that after

(continued)

quality of medical training aggravated the profession's declining status."[3] There was a dramatic increase in medical malpractice cases in the 1840s and 1850s, and these cases brought about some important changes in the medical field, most notably licensing of physicians.

B. DEFINING MEDICAL MALPRACTICE

For our purposes, we use the following working definition of medical malpractice: when the physician's deviation from the accepted standard of care is a proximate cause of the patient's injury.

Malpractice cases can be based on any of several different theories. For instance, when a physician operates on the plaintiff without the plaintiff's consent, this is technically a battery. The doctor-patient relationship also has a contractual basis. One could argue that when the doctor violates the standard of care, she is essentially breaching a contractual term. However, the vast majority of malpractice cases are based on negligence theory and its concomitant requirement of proving duty to the plaintiff, breach of that duty, proximate causation, and resultant damages.

Medical malpractice cases are often brought not only against physicians, but also against nurses and other medical providers. For the sake of brevity, we simply refer to the "defendant-doctor" with the understanding that all of these medical providers may be named defendants in medical malpractice cases.

C. WHAT IS THE BASIS FOR A MEDICAL MALPRACTICE CASE?

As we noted above, a medical malpractice case can be based on any of several different theories. For instance, a medical malpractice case could be based in intentional tort theory.

1. BATTERY

When a patient alleges intentional contact of a harmful or offensive nature against a medical provider during the course of his treatment, the patient is essentially raising a battery claim. Almost all medical treatments involve some form of physical contact between the doctor and patient. If this is true, are all medical procedures batteries? If we analyze the elements of battery, we see that a medical procedure, such as invasive surgery, seems to satisfy all the elements of battery—except one. True, cutting open the plaintiff's body is a "harmful or offensive contact," but there is one important element missing. In most medical procedures, the doctor obtains consent from the patient before carrying out the procedure. In such a case, there is no battery, because the plaintiff has given the doctor permission to carry out the contact.

What happens in situations where the doctor does not obtain permission or when the doctor exceeds the scope of the permission?

Example: While Tom is waiting for the bus, he suddenly faints. Doctor Ted happens to be driving by, and when he sees Tom faint, he stops to lend a hand. Tom is obviously not in any immediate danger, so bystanders call for an ambulance. While they are waiting, Doctor Ted sees a cyst on Tom's hand and expertly cuts it off with a scalpel he happens to have with him. Has Doctor Ted battered Tom?

Answer: Yes. Tom did not give Doctor Ted consent to touch him or to operate on him.

An important caution about the hypothetical above: Had Tom's injury been life-threatening, the rules about consent would change. We explore this important exception surrounding medical emergencies later in this chapter.

When a battery does not occur within the scope of the physician's treatment, such as when a doctor happens to get involved in a fistfight with another man at a local grocery store, the other man cannot bring a malpractice action. Malpractice claims based on battery are limited to the arena of medical treatment.[4]

Similarly, when the doctor's contact with the patient exceeds the scope of the treatment, it may also provide the basis for a malpractice claim.

Example: While he is treating a young child, a doctor strikes the child in an effort to make her stop crying. Even when the doctor has a valid consent to perform the procedure, he does not have consent to strike the child.[5]

2. CONTRACT

Recovery in a medical malpractice case can also be premised on a contract theory. In most medical situations, a contract is either express or implied between the parties. The doctor provides professional medical services and skills in exchange for payment from the patient. Although some jurisdictions allow contractual relationship as one theory of recovery in medical malpractice cases, no jurisdiction limits such actions exclusively to this area of law. If a medical malpractice case were based solely on a contractual basis, this would dramatically limit the patient's ability to sue for negligent actions. It would also ignore some of the public considerations that are an important basis of medical practice.[6]

However, there is one element in a medical malpractice case that does resonate with contractual theory. As we see later in this chapter, the plaintiff must prove that there was a doctor-patient relationship between the two parties in the malpractice case.

3. NEGLIGENCE

The majority of medical malpractice cases are based on the theory of negligence. As such, these cases are based on a familiar formula:

1 Duty of the doctor to the plaintiff-patient
2 Breach of that duty
3 Proximate cause
4 Damages suffered by plaintiff

In a malpractice case, we could add one additional component to Element 1: proof of a doctor-patient relationship between the parties. We discuss each of these negligence elements in the next section.

IV. THE BASIC ELEMENTS OF A MEDICAL MALPRACTICE CLAIM

Although previous chapters have addressed the basic elements of any negligence claim, medical malpractice negligence cases involve special issues unique to these claims.

A. DUTY

Physician-patient relationship
The legally recognized relationship between a physician and patient in which the physician brings her skill to bear in the care and treatment of the patient; this relationship also triggers the evidentiary physician-patient privilege that protects the patient's communications with the physician from compulsory revelation.

When we discuss duty in the context of a medical malpractice case, we are talking about using a different standard to evaluate the defendant's actions. The duty imposed on a physician is to use reasonable skill, care, and expertise to ensure the safety and well-being of the patient.[7] This duty arises as a direct consequence of the **physician-patient relationship.** When a doctor takes on a patient, the doctor is required to use her skills in the best interests of the patient.

When does a physician's duty to a patient begin? Courts have been called upon to decide this issue many times and, over the decades, some basic factors have emerged to establish this relationship: the nature of the services that the physician will perform, the circumstances surrounding the plaintiff's request for medical assistance, and whether the physician takes a medical history from the patient.[8]

Among the duties that a physician owes a patient is the duty to diagnose the plaintiff's injury or sickness. Doctors must use reasonable skill and care in making this diagnosis, because it will determine the future course of the patient's treatment. A misdiagnosis could be as devastating to the patient as gross negligence in performing a procedure. See Figure 12-2 for a list of duties owed by doctors to their patients.

B. BREACH

The second element of a medical malpractice case is proof that the defendant-doctor breached the duty she owed to the patient. Unlike typical negligence

---

FIGURE 12-2

Other Duties That Doctors Owe Patients

- Duty to fully inform the patient about procedures, tests, and so on
- Duty to notify the patient about results of tests and procedures
- Duty to notify patient about the need for alternate treatment
- Duty to refer patient to another physician

cases that will often revolve around proof of causation or damages, medical malpractice cases often hinge on this single issue. In fact, our discussion of breach must encompass many different concepts and involve issues that are usually not seen in a typical negligence case.

When a plaintiff brings a medical malpractice case, the central issue frequently is whether the defendant-doctor breached her duty to the plaintiff. This proof of the breach of duty boils down to whether the defendant-doctor violated the standard of care. If she did, she has breached the duty; if she did not, then no breach occurred and she may be entitled to a verdict in her favor. Some commentators have said that the standard of care is the "threshold question" that must be determined in any malpractice case.[9]

1. DEFINING THE STANDARD OF CARE

The **standard of care** is an important issue in medical malpractice cases; here we define what this standard is and how it is applied. If the plaintiff can show that the defendant-doctor failed to exercise the same degree of skill, knowledge, and care as other doctors in the professional community, the plaintiff can establish that the doctor failed to use the appropriate standard of care in his case. However, medical treatment involves highly complex issues that the average person on a jury would find difficult, if not impossible, to understand. Diagnosis, treatment, and care of a patient, and the standard of care that prevails in the medical community at the time, are not matters of common knowledge. How then can a jury member decide if the defendant-doctor's behavior in a case violated the standard of care? The plaintiff must present expert testimony to explain the procedures, the course of treatment, the standard of care that should have been applied, and how the defendant-doctor's actions fell below that standard.[10]

Standard of care
The standard used by the law to determine negligence; the standard that dictates that the defendant must act in the same manner as a reasonable, prudent professional.

One of the essential elements of a claim for medical negligence is that the defendant breached the applicable standard of medical care owed to the plaintiff.[11]

TORT BASICS AT A GLANCE

---

2. MODERN APPROACHES TO STANDARD OF CARE

The standard of care applied in most jurisdictions relies heavily on testimony about particular procedures, the state of medical education and knowledge, and an examination of the techniques used by a physician to treat the plaintiff. In some jurisdictions, this standard of care is imposed by reference to the state of the medical field at the time of the treatment. We examine specific elements of this standard of care by reviewing the law applicable to the physician's experience level and the local and national standards, and by reference to statutory law.

a. Level of Experience

The applicable standard of care does not shift depending on the experience level of the practitioner. Newly licensed doctors do not enjoy a lower standard of care than seasoned veterans. All are held to the same standard.

b. National Versus Local Standards

Does the standard of care vary by location? For instance, is the standard of care for a rural doctor lower than the standard of care for an urban doctor? Historically, the answer was yes. Under the "locality rule," courts allowed a lower standard of care for rural doctors under the theory that they had less access to recent developments in medicine, had fewer opportunities for continuing medical education, and because communication to rural areas was difficult.

However, in recent years, this rule has come under increasing attack. Many have argued that although this rule might have had some relevance in the nineteenth and early twentieth centuries, in an age of telephones, the Internet, mandatory licensure, and required continuing education, such a rule makes little sense. In fact, many states that formerly followed the locality rule have begun to phase it out.

In the modern era, most jurisdictions follow the rule that requires a physician to treat the plaintiff with the same degree of reasonable, ordinary care and skill as any other physician in good standing in the same area of practice, whether that area encompasses rural or urban areas or both. There has been a gradual movement away from geographic limits on the standard of care in response to nationally standardized education at medical schools.

c. Establishing Standard of Care by Statute

Doctors are not held strictly liable for the outcomes of their treatments.

Although there has been a growing trend to "nationalize" the standard of care through case law decisions, there are states that have codified the standard of care. In these states, the standard of care is determined by statutes that not only establish the basic duty to the patient, but also enact other provisions that limit the application of the statute of limitations, provide greater procedural requirements, and limit the amount of damages that can be awarded in a particular case. A statute that codifies the standard of care is shown in Figure 12-3. We address some of the other legislative initiatives later in this chapter.

FIGURE 12-3

Standard of Care by Statute

In a malpractice action, the claimant shall have the burden of proving by evidence as provided by subsection (b):

    1 The recognized standard of acceptable professional practice in the profession and the specialty thereof, if any, that the defendant practices in the community in which the defendant practices or in a similar community at the time the alleged injury or wrongful action occurred;

    2 That the defendant acted with less than or failed to act with ordinary and reasonable care in accordance with such standard; and

    3 As a proximate result of the defendant's negligent act or omission, the plaintiff suffered injuries which would not otherwise have occurred.[*]

*Tenn. Code Ann. §§29-26-115 to -118 (2000).

d. Elements to Consider in Establishing the Standard of Care

In any medical malpractice case, the plaintiff's theory of negligence must eventually come down to proof. Specifically, how does the plaintiff prove that the physician violated the standard of care? One way is to present testimony from another expert witness, typically another physician, who will state that the defendant violated the standard of care. Some of the typical scenarios seen in medical malpractice cases are highlighted in Figure 12-4.

The standard of care is violated when the physician fails to:

■ recognize the extent of the plaintiff's injuries or his illness;
■ properly diagnose the plaintiff's illness; and/or
■ order additional diagnostic procedures that would have revealed the plaintiff's condition.

FIGURE 12-4

Violation of the Standard of Care

Tech Topic
MEDICAL TECHNOLOGY

Research scientists and physicians are constantly seeking new methods for treating diseases. Equally aggressive are their efforts to develop new diagnostic tools, and the results often seem as though they came straight from *Star Trek*.

One of the most well-known diagnostic tools is the endoscope, a small, flexible tube with a light and a camera on the end for looking into the esophagus, stomach, duodenum, or colon. Although endoscopes have been in use since the 1800s, they were of limited value until the late 1960s, when the imaging capability was perfected. Nowadays, colonoscopies and upper endoscopies are routine diagnostic procedures.

A more recent innovation is the "camera in a pill." The camera is about the size of a large vitamin pill and is easily swallowed with a glass of water. It is a noninvasive alternative to traditional endoscopy and is used to diagnose and evaluate diseases of the esophagus.

Another device is the remote heart-monitoring system. Devices worn by heart patients are able to wirelessly transmit data directly to the physician's computer for diagnosis or treatment. Even more impressive is the mobile application that allows doctors to get electrocardiograph data delivered to their iPads or iPhones so that they can remotely monitor patients' hearts.

While state-of-the-art diagnostic tools theoretically can help avoid malpractice lawsuits, an unexpected side effect has emerged. Patients have become more likely to ask for extreme diagnostic tests, even when they are not warranted. Fearful of malpractice, physicians tend to comply. The result is ever-increasing health care costs.

3. EXPERT TESTIMONY IN MEDICAL MALPRACTICE CASES

Before an expert is allowed to state his opinion to the jury, the attorney who called the expert to the stand must establish the expert's credentials. This is done by asking the expert about his education, credentials, membership in professional organizations, publications, and clinical experience. Once that information is brought out, the attorney is then allowed to submit the witness as an expert. This is called qualifying the witness. *If the judge accepts the witness as an expert, then, and only then, may the attorney ask about the specific medical issues involved in the plaintiff's case. A paralegal should learn the expert's credentials as early in the litigation process as possible to assist the attorney in qualifying the witness.*

Specialist
A person with expertise that exceeds that of a regular practitioner.

In many jurisdictions, it is not only a good idea to present expert testimony about the defendant's violation of the standard of care, it is actually a requirement. For instance, some states require that a medical malpractice complaint be accompanied by a sworn affidavit from an expert witness testifying to the defendant's negligence before the suit will be allowed to proceed. When an expert testifies at trial, the expert must present testimony showing what the standard of care was and how the defendant-doctor's treatment failed to live up to that standard, and establish a causal relationship between that failure and the injuries suffered by the plaintiff.[13] In many states, the rules of civil procedure require that the expert be actively involved in the practice of medicine.

There are specific limitations about what an expert can say. Because medical treatment is a highly specialized area, beyond the everyday experience of most jurors, the expert is allowed to testify about the treatment that the plaintiff should have received. The expert is also allowed to give an opinion that the defendant-doctor's treatment clearly violated that standard. However, an expert witness is not allowed to make any statements about who should prevail in the suit or to urge the jury to award specific types of damages. The expert's testimony is limited to the medical issues. The jury has the final say about the verdict and the award, if any.[14]

4. SPECIALISTS

When a medical malpractice case involves someone who is considered to be a **specialist** in a particular field, the standard of care the specialist must follow is higher than that of a general practitioner. Specialists are required to exercise the same degree of skill and care as other practicing specialists. Specialists are also required to know and apply the most recent advances in their specialties.[15] In many jurisdictions, the implicit geographical limitations on the standard of care for general practitioners are removed for specialists. A specialist must essentially meet the standard followed by similar specialists throughout the nation.[16] When a doctor is considered to be a specialist, she must not only exercise the same degree of skill and knowledge as a general practitioner, but also meet the standard for specialists in the same area.[17]

C. PROXIMATE CAUSE IN MEDICAL MALPRACTICE CASES

Just as we have seen with any other negligence case, a medical malpractice action must also establish a causal connection between the defendant-doctor's negligence and the resultant injuries to the plaintiff. Whether the plaintiff has actually presented sufficient proof on this point is an issue for the jury. In this context, proximate cause is defined in much the same way that it is in any negligence case. The plaintiff must show that the defendant is liable for the natural and probable consequences of his negligent act.

In a malpractice action, the plaintiff must prove that the defendant failed to follow the standard of care and that this failure was a proximate cause of his injuries.

D. DAMAGES

Just as we saw in negligence cases, the medical malpractice plaintiff must prove not only the first three elements of duty, breach of duty, and causation, but also that the defendant's actions resulted in legally recognizable damages. However, damages in medical malpractice cases often involve issues not seen in most other types of negligence cases. For one thing, the defendant is never liable for the plaintiff's original injury — that is, the injury that made the plaintiff seek medical treatment in the first place. In medical malpractice cases, the defendant is liable only for negligently treating the plaintiff. If the plaintiff suffers pain and discomfort during treatment that meets the standard of care, that pain and suffering are not recoverable. After all, the plaintiff would have suffered that pain anyway. The defendant-doctor is only liable for the pain and discomfort that flow directly from his negligence. As you can imagine, separating out the pain that the plaintiff would have suffered even under the best care from the additional pain that the plaintiff endured because of negligence is often a difficult task. To further complicate the issue of damages, the defendant-doctor is also not liable for a failed treatment, as long as this treatment was not below the applicable standard of care. Sometimes even the best medical care does not cure the patient. A doctor is not liable for failing to save the plaintiff; he is only liable for negligent care of the plaintiff.

In addition to these restrictions on damages, many states have enacted statutes that specifically insulate medical providers for good faith efforts or "honest mistakes."

Having specified what the plaintiff is not allowed to recover, we now address the issue of what types of damages the plaintiff *can* recover. As we have already stated, the plaintiff is allowed to recover for any pain and suffering directly attributable to the defendant's negligence. The plaintiff can also recover for any mental suffering tied to this same negligence.

If the plaintiff suffers any permanent injury, such as a scar or a loss of bodily function, he can recover for such losses. Suppose that the plaintiff can no longer carry on his previous employment. He would be permitted to sue for damages for the loss of his earning capacity. In addition to these damages, the jury is also allowed to consider the plaintiff's diminished life expectancy, increased chance of diseases or infections, and permanent disfigurement.

How does the jury put a monetary value on these types of damages? It is up to the plaintiff's attorney to present some yardstick for the jury to use in assessing damages. Obviously, the attorney will present testimony about the plaintiff's prior earning capacity or his favorite hobbies (which he can no longer enjoy). The attorney will often suggest a monetary amount for each of these items: pain and suffering, loss of earning capacity, and so on. (Loss of earning capacity will involve expert testimony.) The final amount, if any, the plaintiff will receive is up to the jury. Other factors to consider in assessing damages are found in Figure 12-5. See Figure 12-6 for limits to damages.

1. SPECIFIC TYPES OF INJURIES

In medical malpractice cases there are often injuries that are not seen in other types of negligence cases. Examples of these unique injuries are "wrongful birth" and "wrongful death" cases, among others.

a. Wrongful Birth

When a plaintiff brings a wrongful birth (sometimes called a "wrongful pregnancy" case), the plaintiff is alleging that a physician was negligent when he performed a sterilization procedure on the plaintiff. Often these cases are brought when patients seek to be sterilized because they have an increased chance of giving birth to a child with birth defects. They wish to avoid the pain of bringing a deformed child into existence by having themselves sterilized either through a tubal ligation (woman) or a vasectomy (man). In such a case, the parents may be entitled to general damages for the pregnancy, pain, and suffering for giving birth to a deformed child, and other out-of-pocket costs. However, many jurisdictions have been unwilling to assess the total cost of raising such a child against the doctor who performed the negligent sterilization procedure.

FIGURE 12-5

Assessing Damages

The jury can consider any or all of the following in assessing the plaintiff's damages:

- Permanency of injury
- Disfigurement
- Loss of earning capacity
- Shortened life expectancy
- Chances of further medical complications

- Loss of consortium (loss of companionship and services to a spouse)
- Estimate of costs of future medical care, in-home nursing, etc.

FIGURE 12-6

Statutory Limitations on Awards in Medical Malpractice Cases

States have followed different paths in their attempts to limit damage awards in medical malpractice cases. Their options include some or all of the following:

- Limiting the size of the total award for non-economic damages, such as pain and suffering
- Modifying or eliminating the concept of joint and several liability

- Limiting the amount of punitive damages
- Modifying how the jury is permitted to assess punitive damages

b. Wrongful Adoption

A wrongful adoption case is based on the premise that when an adoption agency conceals material facts about an adopted child's physical or mental condition, it is misrepresenting the facts to the adopting parents. This misrepresentation is especially important in the case of adopted children because the new parents have no way of knowing whether the child requires additional treatment that, if not given, could aggravate a pre-existing condition.

The elements of a wrongful adoption action include:

- false statements of material fact, such as the child's health history,
- made intentionally or with reckless disregard of the truth and
- provided to the adopting parents
- to induce them to adopt the child.
- Parents relied on this information.
- Parents adopted the child.

c. Wrongful Death

Wrongful death actions raise a whole host of legal issues and could easily justify an entire chapter by themselves. The basis of a wrongful death claim is that the defendant caused the death of another through his negligence. In a medical malpractice claim, this death is caused by the negligent treatment the deceased received. Usually, a cause of action in wrongful death is limited to those individuals who are the survivors of the deceased and dependent on him for support. When the decedent's survivors bring suit, they are allowed to sue for loss of companionship, mental pain and suffering, general compensatory damages for the loss of income that the deceased would have produced for the family, and medical and funeral expenses.

2. PUNITIVE DAMAGES

Punitive damages are allowed in medical malpractice cases. Usually, they are only awarded in cases in which the physician was grossly negligent or acted in bad faith. Some states limit the award of punitive damages to cases in which the jury finds "actual malice" on the part of the defendant-doctor[18] (Figure 12-7). Examples of actual malice include deliberately falsifying, destroying, or altering medical records or encouraging staff members to commit perjury.[19]

3. PUNITIVE DAMAGES AND TORT REFORM

The growing perception of runaway juries awarding millions of dollars to plaintiffs who have suffered relatively minor injuries has encouraged legislatures across the country to enact tort reform legislation. Almost every statute focuses on punitive damages awards in some capacity. Although the actual statistics might not support the perception of frivolous lawsuits and mega-verdicts, there is no question that affordable malpractice insurance for

FIGURE 12-7

Number of Plaintiffs Seeking Punitive Damages

Case type	Number of plaintiffs who sought punitive damages[a]	Punitive damages awarded[b]		Number of cases with punitive damages	
		Number	Median amount	Over $250,000	$1 million or more
All cases	1,823	700	$64,000	191	93
Tort cases[c]	822	254	$55,000	59	43
Medical malpractice	56	6	2,835,000	5	5
Intentional tort	141	126	81,000	13	4
Conversion	31	12	50,000	5	2
Slander/libel	38	24	13,000	9	6
Motor vehicle	417	67	7,500	9	8
Animal attack	23	0	/	/	/
Contract cases[c]	1,001	446	$69,000	132	50
Tortious interference	42	18	6,888,000	12	11
Employment discrimination	84	10	115,000	1	1
Fraud	259	151	100,000	67	7
Seller plaintiff	88	14	86,000	2	0
Buyer plaintiff	372	138	53,000	20	3
Other employment disputes	93	86	10,000	12	10

/No cases reported.
[a]Data on punitive damages sought are available for 99.9% of total trial cases with a plaintiff winner.
[b]Data on punitive damages awarded are available for 97.5% of total trial cases with a plaintiff winner. Median amounts are reported prior to adjustments, post-trial activity, or appeals and are rounded to the nearest thousand.
[c]Specific case types will not sum to tort and contract totals because not all case types are shown in the table.

Civil Bench and Jury Trials in State Courts, 2005, Bureau of Justice Statistics, U.S. Department of Justice.

physicians and other health care providers is becoming harder and harder to come by.

When physicians are sued for medical malpractice, and they have a malpractice insurance policy, the insurance company must provide legal counsel. Although the insurance company pays the attorney's fee, the attorney's responsibility is to protect the interests of the insured doctor. We discuss insurance issues in much greater depth in the next chapter; however, it is important to understand the role of malpractice insurance and the limitations placed on the medical profession because of it. If medical malpractice insurance premiums become too high, doctors are forced to choose between two unpleasant choices. On the one hand, they can simply leave the practice of medicine for some other profession in which insurance premiums are not so high, or they can pass the premium increases on to their patients in the form of higher fees for medical treatment. Doctors are often reluctant to do either but usually choose the latter.

In the 1980s, legislatures across the nation began enacting tort reform legislation as a way of limiting the number of malpractice cases and the amount of awards that insurance companies must pay, especially in the form of punitive damages. The most popular of these reforms is to limit the total amount of punitive damages that a jury can award. In many states, for example, plaintiffs are limited to specific amounts for punitive damages, no matter what the facts of a particular case may be. In other jurisdictions, punitive damages are capped as a multiple of the total compensatory damages. For instance, the State of Placid has a statute that limits punitive damages to three times the amount of compensatory damages. In this state, if John's damages are $10,000, but the doctor has acted in bad faith or with actual malice, the most that the jury could award John would be $30,000.[21] Whether these statutory limitations have actually cut down on the number of malpractice cases is a question open for debate.

INFORMED CONSENT

The general rule is that before a medical procedure can be performed, the doctor must obtain consent from the patient. This consent acts to insulate the doctor from any claim of battery, but it also serves another important function: It may prevent a medical malpractice claim. A patient is entitled to bring an action based on inadequate **informed consent.** The basis of this claim is that the patient was never made aware of the risks involved in the procedure or was never told about treatment alternatives so that she could make an informed decision about whether to risk the procedure in the first place. For a plaintiff to succeed on a claim of inadequate informed consent, she must prove the following:

Informed consent
An agreement by a person to allow some type of action after having been fully informed and after making a knowing and intelligent decision to allow the action.

1. The defendant-doctor failed to adequately describe the procedure to the patient, especially the treatment alternatives and the foreseeable risks involved.

2. A reasonable and prudent person would not have undergone the procedure if she had been adequately informed.

3. The lack of informed consent is a proximate cause of the plaintiff's injuries.[22]

Informed consent must be based on adequate information and the patient's understanding of what the procedure entails and what the risks of the procedure are. Whether informed consent was given in any particular case is a question for the jury. Part of what the jury will be called upon to evaluate is the manner of the interchange between the doctor and the patient, the patient's ability to ask questions, and the degree of explanation offered by the doctor. The jurors are often instructed that the test they should apply is what information a reasonable, prudent patient should have been given, not what the doctor, in his judgment, decided that the patient should know.

A. STATUTORY REQUIREMENTS IN INFORMED CONSENT

Many states have codified the informed consent requirement. See Figure 12-8 for Pennsylvania's informed consent statute.

FIGURE 12-8

Pennsylvania Statute on Informed Consent

Informed consent

    (a) Duty of physicians — Except in emergencies, a physician owes a duty to a patient to obtain the informed consent of the patient or the patient's authorized representative prior to conducting the following procedures:

    (1)   Performing surgery, including the related administration of anesthesia.

    (2)   Administering radiation or chemotherapy.

    (3)   Administering a blood transfusion.

    (4)   Inserting a surgical device or appliance.

    (5)   Administering an experimental medication, using an experimental device or using an approved medication or device in an experimental manner.

    (b)   Description of procedure — Consent is informed if the patient has been given a description of a procedure set forth in subsection (a) and the risks and alternatives that a reasonably prudent patient would require to make an informed decision as to that procedure. The physician shall be entitled to present evidence of the description of that procedure and those risks and alternatives that a physician acting in accordance with accepted medical standards of medical practice would provide.

    (c)   Expert testimony — Expert testimony is required to determine whether the procedure constituted the type of procedure set forth in subsection (a) and to identify the risks of that procedure, the alternatives to that procedure and the risks of these alternatives.

    (d)   Liability —

    (1)   A physician is liable for failure to obtain the informed consent only if the patient proves that receiving such information would have been a substantial factor in the patient's decision whether to undergo a procedure set forth in subsection (a).

    (2)   A physician may be held liable for failure to seek a patient's informed consent if the physician knowingly misrepresents to the patient his or her professional credentials, training or experience.[*]

[*]Pa. Stat. §1303.504

B. EMERGENCIES

One of the few exceptions to the requirement of informed consent is an emergency situation. When the patient is in a life-threatening situation, the physician is not required to seek informed consent from the patient or anyone else.[23] The reason for this rule is obvious. If a medical provider had to wait until she obtained valid consent from the patient, or a family member, the patient might well die.[24] In such cases, the court will imply consent to the treatment because most people would have consented to a life-saving procedure had they been able to.

When dealing with minors or others who are legally incapable of giving consent, the physician must obtain consent from a parent or guardian.

C. SCOPE OF INFORMED CONSENT

A validly obtained informed consent gives the physician permission to perform the procedure and essentially eliminates a medical malpractice claim on this ground. However, a question often arises in informed consent as to the scope of the consent. Just how far does this consent extend? For instance, can a physician claim that the patient consented to all types of actions, including negligent actions? Consider the following scenario:

Dr. X obtains a valid consent from Paula Patient to operate on her right kidney. However, he negligently operates on her left kidney. When Paula brings a medical malpractice claim, Dr. X claims that Paula consented to the procedure. How does the judge rule?

Answer: The judge will rule in Paula's favor. Paula's consent does not relieve the doctor of liability for his own negligence. On a practical level, nowhere in the informed consent did the doctor suggest that he would operate on the wrong kidney.

Would the answer to this question change if the surgeon exceeds the scope of the informed consent? Suppose that while the physician is operating on Paula, he discovers a lesion on her leg that he removes. The site of this surgery later becomes infected and causes Paula significant problems. Can she bring a medical malpractice action under this situation? Absolutely. Again, the physician did not mention anything about operating on Paula's leg in the context of a surgery on her kidney. Dr. X has exceeded the scope of the informed consent and he is liable to Paula for the resultant infection.[25]

Informed consent does not apply to negligent actions by the physician.

TORT
BASICS
AT A
GLANCE

PLEADINGS IN MEDICAL MALPRACTICE CASES

Pleadings in medical malpractice cases raise a host of issues not normally seen in other types of negligence actions. For one thing, many states require that a complaint be accompanied by a sworn affidavit from a medical expert detailing how the defendant violated the standard of care in the plaintiff's case. Another important point to consider is identifying the correct defendant. You should confirm that the right doctor is being sued. These days, many doctors can be involved in a patient's treatment. Identifying the actual negligent doctor may take a little extra time and digging, but will save time, effort, and an allegation of bad faith later on in the case.

Plaintiffs' attorneys often consider other elements of medical malpractice cases before deciding to accept them. These include the following:

- Is the case worth the time and effort it will take to complete it? Some commentators claim that a medical malpractice should be worth at least $30,000 before an attorney accepts it. After all, while the case is pending, the plaintiff's attorney must continue to pay his staff as well as rent and utilities.
- Does the attorney have enough time to devote to the case? The average medical malpractice case can take up to 100 hours of preparation. This time can increase dramatically if the attorney has never handled a medical malpractice case and must educate himself on the procedures.
- Is the plaintiff a sympathetic witness? If not, the jury may not like him and may be less inclined to award damages.
- How clear is the liability in the case? For instance, if the defendant-doctor is obviously at fault, that may be a factor weighing heavily toward accepting a case that would have been marginal for other reasons.
- How extensive are the damages? If the defendant-doctor was clearly negligent, but the plaintiff suffered few actual damages, it may not be worth the firm's time to accept the case.

See Figure 12-9 for guidance for drafting a medical malpractice complaint.

| **FIGURE 12-9**

Rules for Drafting a Medical Malpractice Complaint | **1** Check the applicable rules of civil procedure.
2 Has the correct defendant(s) been identified?
3 Notice pleading should raise all applicable issues and facts to back up the claims.
4 Has the investigative responsibility (Rule 11 under the Federal Rules of Civil Procedure) been satisfied? | **5** Is each paragraph worded clearly and concisely?
6 What is the jurisdiction and venue?
7 What is the prayer for relief?
8 Is it signed by plaintiff's attorney?
9 Are the proper attachments, including the expert's affidavit, included?
10 Is the certificate of service included? |

1. State in detail the medical history you obtained from the plaintiff on the first occasion that you met with plaintiff.
2. State in detail the plaintiff's medical history as it was relayed to you by plaintiff.
3. State in detail the symptoms that the plaintiff complained of.
4. Please state the following: the plaintiff's chief complaint, family history, personal history, and psychiatric history as you learned it from the plaintiff.

FIGURE 12-10

Sample Interrogatory Questions in Medical Malpractice Case

VII DISCOVERY ISSUES IN MEDICAL MALPRACTICE CASES

Once the pleadings have been filed and served on opposing sides, the discovery phase begins. In many ways, discovery in medical malpractice cases is very similar to other types of personal injury cases. Discovery takes place through oral depositions, requests for production of documents, and interrogatories (see Figure 12-10). However, medical malpractice cases also involve some unique discovery issues. For one thing, anyone reviewing the medical records must be proficient in the terminology and wording used in them to describe various symptoms and the procedures used to deal with them. For instance, can you decipher the nurse's note in Figure 12-11?

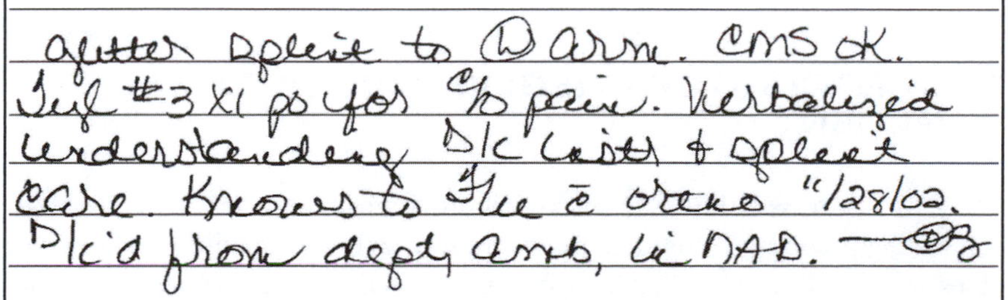
gutter splint to Ⓛ arm. CMS ok.
Tyl #3 x1 po for c/o pain. Verbalized
understanding D/C instr & splint
care. Knows to f/u c̄ ortho 11/28/02.
D/c'd from dept, amb, in NAD. —DB

Translation of the nurse's note:
Gutter splint to left arm. Circulation okay. Tylenol number 3 times 1 by mouth for complaint of pain. Verbalized understanding of discharge instructions and splint care. Knows to follow up with the orthopedic doctor November 28, 2002. Discharged from the department ambulatory in no acute distress. DB

FIGURE 12-11

Nurse's Note in Medical Record

VIII DEFENSES TO MEDICAL MALPRACTICE CLAIMS

Just as we have seen with the other elements of a medical malpractice claim, the defenses applicable to such a case often raise unique issues. A defense of statute of limitations is common enough in any negligence action, but when applied to a medical malpractice case a new issue arises: exactly *when* does negligence occur?

A. STATUTE OF LIMITATIONS

In many jurisdictions, the statute of limitations for a malpractice action is three to four years. But medical malpractice cases raise some interesting and unique issues when it comes to the cause of action. For instance, when does the cause of action begin? Does the plaintiff's cause of action, for calculating the statute of limitations, begin when the negligence occurs or when the patient discovers it? Unlike car wrecks, a patient may not know about a doctor's negligence for some time. For example, if a surgeon leaves a medical sponge inside the patient's body, the patient may not find out about it for weeks or even months. Does the statute begin running on the date of the surgery or when the patient discovers the negligence? Jurisdictions have been wrestling with this issue for years, and a general consensus has emerged. Many states follow the example set out in Figure 12-12. Under that construction, the statute of limitations begins running at the time of the negligent procedure and runs for three years, or it begins running when the patient discovers the negligent procedure and runs for one year after that point. The statute gives the patient the benefit of the doubt by explaining that the plaintiff's cause of action terminates on the expiration of whichever term is the longest.

B. CONTRIBUTORY NEGLIGENCE OF THE PATIENT

We have addressed the issue of contributory negligence in other contexts. Interestingly enough, this defense is often a factor in medical malpractice cases as well. Although called by different names in different states, the theory is simple enough. A defendant-doctor is permitted to raise a defense that the plaintiff's injuries were aggravated by the plaintiff's own failure to seek proper medical care or to follow medical procedures. Essentially, the defendant is stating that the plaintiff has caused his own aggravated symptoms and that the defendant should be relieved of liability because of it. See Figure 12-13 for jury instructions relating to contributory negligence.

(1) Except as provided by subs. (2) and (3), an action to recover damages for injury arising from any treatment or operation performed by, or from any omission by, a person who is a health care provider, regardless of the theory on which the action is based, shall be commenced within the later of:

    (a) Three years from the date of the injury, or

    (b) One year from the date the injury was discovered or, in the exercise of reasonable diligence should have been discovered, except that an action may not be commenced under this paragraph more than 5 years from the date of the act or omission.

(2) If a health care provider conceals from a patient a prior act or omission of the provider which has resulted in injury to the patient, an action shall be commenced within one year from the date the patient discovers the concealment or, in the exercise of reasonable diligence, should have discovered the concealment or within the time limitation provided by sub. (1), whichever is later.

(3) When a foreign object which has no therapeutic or diagnostic purpose or effect has been left in a patient's body, an action shall be commenced within one year after the patient is aware or, in the exercise of reasonable care, should have been aware of the presence of the object or within the time limitation provided by sub. (1), whichever is later.[*]

FIGURE 12-12

Wisconsin's Statute of Limitations for Medical Malpractice

[*] Wis. Stat. Ann. §893.55

"It is the duty of a patient to follow the reasonable instructions and submit to the reasonable treatment prescribed by his physician or surgeon."[*]

"If you decide that the defendant was negligent and that his negligence was a proximate cause of injury to the plaintiff, it is not a defense that something else may also have been a cause of the injury. However, if you decide that the sole proximate cause of injury to the plaintiff was something other than the conduct of the defendant, then your verdict should be for the defendant."[**]

FIGURE 12-13

Common Jury Instructions in Malpractice Cases

[*] *Merrill v. Odiorne,* 113 Me. 424, 94 A. 753 (1915)
[**] Illinois Pattern Jury Instruction, Civil, No. 12.05 (3d ed. 1995)

Case Excerpt

VERDON V. DUFFY
120 A.D.3d 1343, 993 N.Y.S.2d 96 (2014)

PETER B. SKELOS, J.P., THOMAS A. DICKERSON, LEONARD B. AUSTIN, and COLLEEN D. DUFFY, JJ.

In an action to recover damages for legal malpractice, the plaintiff appeals from an order of the Supreme Court, Westchester County (Tolbert, J.), entered July 3, 2012, which granted the defendants' motion for summary judgment dismissing the complaint.

ORDERED that the order is affirmed, with costs.

The plaintiff retained the defendants to commence an action to recover damages for, inter alia, personal injuries that she allegedly sustained in an automobile accident. The defendant in the underlying personal injury action moved for summary judgment dismissing the complaint, on the ground that the plaintiff did not suffer a serious injury within the meaning of Insurance Law §5102(d) as a result of the subject accident. While that motion was pending, the plaintiff accepted a certain sum of money to settle the action.

The plaintiff subsequently commenced this action against her attorneys to recover damages for legal malpractice. The plaintiff alleges that the defendants were negligent in their representation of her in the underlying personal injury action, in that they caused her to settle that action for far less than the fair value of her case. The defendants moved for summary judgment dismissing the complaint. The Supreme Court granted the motion.

To sustain a cause of action alleging legal malpractice, a plaintiff must establish that the attorney "failed to exercise the ordinary reasonable skill and knowledge commonly possessed by a member of the legal profession," and that the attorney's breach "proximately caused the plaintiff actual and ascertainable damages" (*Di Giacomo v. Langella*, 119 A.D.3d 636, 637, 990 N.Y.S.2d 221). "Even if a plaintiff establishes the first prong of a legal malpractice cause of action, the plaintiff must still demonstrate that he or she would have succeeded on the merits of the action but for the attorney's negligence" (*Di Giacomo v. Langella*, 119 A.D.3d at 638, 990 N.Y.S.2d 221). "'As to this second prong, the plaintiff must plead and prove actual, ascertainable damages as a result of the attorney's negligence.'"

"'To obtain summary judgment dismissing a complaint in an action to recover damages for legal malpractice, a defendant must demonstrate that the plaintiff is unable to prove at least one of the essential elements of [his or her] legal malpractice cause of action.'"

Here, in support of their motion for summary judgment dismissing the complaint, the defendants established, prima facie, that the plaintiff would not have succeeded on the merits of the underlying personal injury action, as there was insufficient evidence to establish that she sustained a serious injury within the meaning of Insurance Law §5102(d) as a result of the automobile accident. Consequently, the defendants also established that they did not "fail to exercise that degree of care, skill, and diligence commonly possessed by a member of the legal community" (*Porello v. Longworth*, 21 A.D.3d 541, 541, 799 N.Y.S.2d 918) when they advised her to accept a settlement offer in the sum that she ultimately accepted. In opposition, the plaintiff failed to raise a triable issue of fact.

Accordingly, the Supreme Court properly granted the defendants' motion for summary judgment dismissing the complaint.

Questions about the case:

1. What claim of legal malpractice does the plaintiff make in this case?
2. What standard is required to establish legal malpractice?
3. Did the plaintiff establish both elements of her legal malpractice claim?

 **THE CHUMLEY CASE: FOLLOW-UP ON MEDICAL MALPRACTICE ISSUE**

Now that we have examined the many issues involved in a medical malpractice case, we return to the question that began this chapter: Does Mr. Chumley, in addition to his other claims, also have a claim for medical malpractice against the attending physician? Yes, he does. The doctor's failure to examine and diagnose Mr. Chumley's spleen problem is clearly malpractice.

 LEGAL MALPRACTICE

In addition to medical malpractice claims, other professionals are increasingly becoming the targets of malpractice litigation. In the past decade, for instance, **legal malpractice** claims have risen dramatically. A legal malpractice claim is similar in some ways to a medical malpractice claim. When a plaintiff brings a legal malpractice claim, she is alleging that the attorney failed to perform his professional duties and that this failure resulted in an identifiable loss to the client. Legal malpractice, like medical malpractice, is a question of fact and must be determined by the jury (or judge, in a bench trial). See Figure 12-14 for a list of elements that must be included in proving legal malpractice and Figure 12-15 for examples of legal malpractice.

Legal malpractice
Professional negligence committed by an attorney during the course of his representation of a client.

A. THE ATTORNEY'S DUTY

A legal malpractice claim is not authorized when one person wishes to sue another person who happens to be an attorney. For instance, if an attorney and a non-attorney go into business together, the non-attorney is not allowed to bring a legal malpractice claim against the lawyer for some claim arising

---

When proving a legal malpractice case, the client must allege:

- The attorney owed a duty to the client.
- The attorney breached that duty, and the client would have been successful in the underlying legal action had it not been for the breach.
- The breach was the proximate cause of the client's loss.
- The client has provable damages for this breach.

FIGURE 12-14

Proving Legal Malpractice

- Abandonment of the case
- Inadequate preparation
- Inadequate representation
- Failure to keep client informed
- Failure to comply with court rules
- Absconding with funds
- Conflicts of interest

FIGURE 12-15

Examples of Legal Malpractice

from the business. A legal malpractice claim must be based on the attorney-client relationship. It is this relationship, like the doctor-patient relationship, that gives rise to the special duty owed by the attorney to the client, the breach of which gives the client a legal remedy.

B. BREACH OF DUTY

An attorney must exercise the same level of skill, legal knowledge, and ability for the client as is found in other members of the bar.[26] However, this standard does not require an attorney to live up to the same level of diligence and devotion seen by the most extraordinary attorneys in the area. Essentially, the law looks at an attorney's skill and knowledge and how it compares to an average cross section of the bar. If the attorney's actions fall below this general average, he can be said to have violated the standard of care. Generally, when an attorney acts with honesty and good faith, this will often negate many claims of legal malpractice.

1. ADDITIONAL PROOF OF BREACH REQUIRED

Legal malpractice actions are interesting in that many jurisdictions require that the plaintiff prove that, but for the attorney's negligence, she would have won the underlying suit or achieved a particular result. Often, the plaintiff has difficulty proving this element. Not all legal mistakes rise to the level of legal malpractice. How, for instance, would a client prove that but for the attorney's negligence, he would have won a jury trial? Absent obvious or gross negligence, an attorney could truthfully claim that no one ever knows for sure what a jury will do and the chances of the jury finding for the client were just as likely as the jury finding for the other party. However, not all legal malpractice cases involve jury trials. In a non-jury situation, the proof of negligence often becomes easier.

Is there a cause of action for negligence per se when an attorney violates an ethical rule? In most jurisdictions, the answer is no. Ethical rules are qualitatively different from the safety rules that form the basis for the traditional negligence per se claim.

2. EXPERT TESTIMONY

In some legal malpractice cases, the judge is called upon to determine the standard of care. After all, the judge is also an attorney.

Just as we saw in medical malpractice cases, expert testimony is also permissible, and sometimes mandatory, in establishing the standard of care that an attorney should have met in a particular case. For instance, some jurisdictions require expert testimony in malpractice cases in which the attorney is a certified specialist in a particular area of law.[27]

Example: Al Attorney has been retained to represent Sid. The case involves a simple and straightforward car crash. Sid, while stopped at a red light, was rear-ended by Terry. Sid retains Al to sue Terry for the damages to Sid's car and Sid's medical expenses. At the time that Al becomes Sid's attorney, there is over a year before the statute of limitations runs. Al fails to investigate the claim and waits too long to file Sid's complaint. The statute of limitations runs, and Sid's claim is barred. Sid brings a legal malpractice action against Al. Does he have a prima facie case against Al?

Answer: Absolutely. Sid can establish that there was an attorney-client relationship between himself and Al; he can also prove that Al failed to file a complaint prior to the expiration of the statute of limitations, despite the fact that Al had over a year to do so. Sid can prove the first two elements of his legal malpractice claim: Al's duty to him, and Al's breach of that duty. What about the third and fourth elements? Is there proximate cause between Al's breach and Sid's damages? Again the answer is yes. Sid would have been entitled to monetary damages if he had won his suit. Now he must pay those bills himself. His payments are directly caused by Al's breach of duty in failing to file a complaint.

C. PROVING DAMAGES

In legal malpractice, the client is permitted to recover for the loss of his claim, or, put another way, the amount of money he would have received if the attorney had not committed legal malpractice. What if the damages in the first case are not clearly established? In that case, the client must not only prove that the attorney's negligence cost him the damages he would have received in the underlying suit, but he must also prove what those damages would have been. The result is almost two trials in one: In the first, the client is proving the attorney's negligence; in the second, the client is proving the damages he would have received in the underlying case.

D. DEFENSES IN LEGAL MALPRACTICE CASES

Because legal malpractice resembles medical malpractice in so many ways, it should not be any surprise to learn that many of the same defenses are permissible in both types of cases. For instance, an attorney is permitted to raise the contributory negligence of the client as a defense to legal malpractice. How can a client be contributorily negligent? Suppose that the attorney asks the client to produce a specific document without which the attorney is unable to proceed, and the client never produces it. In such a case, the attorney's ineffectiveness was abetted by the client's refusal to cooperate. Other defenses available to the attorney include use of the attorney's best judgment. When a client hires an attorney, he is not hiring someone to simply speak for him; he is hiring a professional with a wealth of knowledge, experience, and skill. The client not only is relying on this skill, he also must understand that the attorney is prohibited from doing certain things because of it. What if the client wishes the attorney to fabricate court documents or suborn perjury and the attorney refuses to do so? Such a failure is not legal malpractice. See Figure 12-16 for a list of ways to avoid legal malpractice claims.

FIGURE 12-16 Ten Ways to Avoid Legal Malpractice Claims	**1** The firm should avoid marginal or questionable cases in the first place. **2** When turning down a case, explain to the person that the case is weak and why it is weak, and explain this in writing. **3** Always remind the person of the date the statute of limitations runs. **4** Keep track of all details by writing them down and putting them in the file. **5** Never promise the client that the case is a "winner," or that there is no doubt about the case. **6** Document everything, including contacts with the client. **7** Follow up with letters. **8** Keep track of client meetings, appointments, and so on (some malpractice insurers require a record system or time-management software). **9** Avoid "crisis management." **10** Anticipate problems and deal with them before they become crises.

XI   OTHER TYPES OF PROFESSIONAL MALPRACTICE

In recent years, other professionals have been targeted with malpractice claims. For instance, claims have been made against accountants for failing to properly document tax returns or account for funds. In some jurisdictions, counselors and even educators have been hit with malpractice claims. Whether malpractice claims will expand into other areas is a question that will be answered in the next few years.

Chapter Summary

Medical malpractice claims are a variation of a traditional negligence claim. In alleging malpractice, the plaintiff must prove that the defendant owed him a duty, that the physician violated that duty by failing to follow the established standard of care, and that this failure was a proximate cause of his injuries.

The physician's duty arises from the doctor-patient relationship. The physician must use the same level of skill, knowledge, and expertise as other physicians. Although medical malpractice claims appear to be a relatively recent phenomenon, actually they have been occurring for centuries. There has been an increase in medical malpractice claims in the last few decades, however. Whether this increase in claims has actually resulted in a dramatic increase in jury awards against doctors is a matter of some controversy. Medical malpractice cases almost always involve testimony by some expert, usually another physician, that establishes that the defendant's conduct in the case either was, or was not, in accord with the applicable standard of care. However, this testimony is not conclusive on the issue. It is up to the jury to decide if the defendant violated the standard of care. In recent years, legislatures across the country have enacted tort reform statutes that impose limits on a physician's liability or impose a cap on the amount of damages that a plaintiff can receive in a medical malpractice case.

Malpractice claims are not limited to medicine. Legal malpractice cases are becoming increasingly common as well. In a legal malpractice case, the plaintiff alleges that the attorney owed him a duty to act in conformity with the expertise, skill, and knowledge of other attorneys and breached this duty in a specific way. Usually, the plaintiff in a legal malpractice case must prove that absent the attorney's negligence, he would have succeeded in the underlying legal action that he claims the attorney mishandled.

SKILLS YOU NEED IN THE REAL WORLD

Reviewing and Summarizing Medical Records

When summarizing medical records, it is important to remember the purpose of the summary. Why summarize medical records at all? The first and most obvious answer is so that the attorney can have a handy reference. A reference should be short, concise, and helpful. It does not make any sense to prepare a medical records summary that is nearly as long and comprehensive as the records themselves. However, brevity is a skill and one not easily acquired. How do you know what to say—and what not to say?

Many paralegals, when faced with the prospect of summarizing a two-foot-high pile of medical documents, will take a deep breath and then begin to organize. One of the best organizational schemes, at least from a legal standpoint, is putting all medical records in chronological order. This makes them easier to understand and often will help with discovery questions dealing with the plaintiff's prior, unrelated medical claims and pre-existing injuries. At this point, the paralegal is not evaluating the actual treatment the plaintiff received. It is best not to attempt too many tasks at the same time. Getting the medical records in chronological order is sufficient at this stage.

Once the records are organized by date, what then? Now it is time to summarize. There are two generally accepted methods for summarizing medical records: narratives and page reference. The narrative summary consists of an overall description of the treatment that the plaintiff received, when he received it, and by whom. A page-reference summary provides page-by-page, and often line-by-line, summaries of what exactly happened in each record. Although these two approaches have different merits, many firms opt for a blended approach. They will prepare narrative summaries of the medical records overall, and then have the paralegal focus on particular entries to produce a page-by-page summary.

Here is an example of a narrative medical record summary in the Chumley case:

"The collision between Mr. Chumley's car and the locomotive occurred on August 23 of last year at 4:30 P.M. in the town of Cling, State of Placid.

"First responder was City of Cling EMT. They assisted firefighters in cutting Mr. Chumley out of the car. He was placed on a backboard and given the extensive nature of his injuries, Cling EMT called for Emergency Air Lift.

"EAL arrived at 4:49 P.M. and airlifted Mr. Chumley to Mission Hospital, which is three minutes away. In Mission Emergency Room, Mr. Chumley's medical condition was summarized as follows:

"Closed head injury; fractured left tibia; internal hemorrhaging; hemo-pneumothorax (air and blood in the pleural cavity); five broken ribs, all on his left side; left hip fracture and severe abdominal trauma. Mr. Chumley was unconscious at the time.

"On August 30, Mr. Chumley had a tracheotomy performed. Infection set in almost immediately. On August 31, attending physician Dr. Grubb, decided to . . ."

A page-by-page reference is provided in Appendices A–E, along with extensive information about the Chumley case.

THE LIFE OF A PARALEGAL

Screening and Evaluating Medical Malpractice Cases

Our firm handles strictly plaintiff work in medical malpractice cases. Normally, a potential client will call the office and I or one of the other legal assistants will take the call. There are a multitude of calls that are going to be received. Many of them complain about something that a doctor did or did not do. A large percentage of those complaints are things that are either not actionable as a medical malpractice claim or should be addressed by one of the many licensing boards, or at the least are questionable as to whether they are feasible to pursue, factoring in the potential expenses associated with bringing an action versus any potential recovery. Statistics in this state show that only a small percentage of the medical malpractice cases that are brought are successful.

When we are screening calls, especially ones with merit, we present them to one or all of the partners in the firm. Normally we will also have a weekly meeting where we go over all of the pending cases, their status, and any potential statute of limitations issues. We also have time to present cases that have been phone screened in order for the attorneys to decide as a firm whether they are matters regarding which they wish to meet with the potential clients and discuss in specific detail all aspects of the claims and investigate further. If it is a case, we make a follow-up call to the person and arrange a time to meet with one of the attorneys and a legal assistant to gather more information. During the interview with the client, we review all of the questionable medical treatment and subsequent treatment that they may have had. We also give an overview of what a medical malpractice action is, explain what is required of a plaintiff in order to substantiate or prove the case (burden of proof), the costs associated, the need for experts who are willing to offer opinions and potentially testify regarding the care provided by the potential defendant, and basically the pros and cons of a medical malpractice case. If the client understands all these issues and risks, have their questions addressed, and are willing to proceed, understanding the risks, we then proceed and have the person execute medical authorization release forms and some form of agreement with the firm, either to investigate the matter or a contract to represent.

Our investigation of the matter begins by obtaining a list of all physicians that the client has seen subsequent to the physician or care that is the reason that they have sought our firm out. Following that meeting, I or another legal assistant will proceed in obtaining copies of all medical records, including X-rays, pathology report, diagnostic reports, lab reports, MRIs, CT scans, and any other documents that will ultimately be needed to review the claim of malpractice by the attorneys and experts and organize them.

John Purvis, Legal Assistant

ETHICAL ISSUES FOR THE PARALEGAL: FEE SPLITTING OR SHARING

When dealing with malpractice cases, one particular area of ethical concern often surfaces. Suppose that the plaintiff's attorney has a standing agreement with a local physician or chiropractor that they will not only recommend the other's services to their clients, but they will also share the fees they receive on shared cases? Although it is not uncommon for attorneys to share fees with one another, such as when one attorney refers a client to another, sharing fees with non-lawyers is an area full of ethical minefields. For instance, when an attorney splits a fee with a physician, there is at least the appearance that an unethical relationship exists. Looking at the arrangement from the outside, it can appear that the physician is directing a patient to a particular lawyer simply to obtain the fee, and the lawyer could be directing the client to a particular doctor for the same reason. Although this might sound innocuous enough, just how far does this relationship go? For instance, does the physician have any say over which case the attorney accepts? Does the attorney have the right to influence the physician's diagnosis? As you can see, fee sharing with non-lawyers is fraught with difficulties. Non-lawyers also include legal assistants. Fee splitting between lawyers and legal assistants is considered to be unethical under the American Bar Association Ethics rules. Consider ABA Model Guideline 9: "A lawyer must not split legal fees with a legal assistant nor pay a legal assistant for the referral of legal business."[28]

Relevant Cases

DAVIS V. HOFFMAN
972 F. Supp. 308 (E.D. Pa., 1997)

Memorandum

GAWTHROP, District Judge.

This case involves the removal of the plaintiff's uterus, allegedly without her consent. Reading Hospital and Medical Center (the "Hospital") moves to dismiss or strike the plaintiff's claims for battery by lack of informed consent and for punitive damages. See Fed.R.Civ.P. 12(b)(6) and 12(f). Additionally, Nurse Susan B. Puchini moves to dismiss the Complaint against her for failure to state a claim. I shall grant the Hospital's Motion to Dismiss as to the battery claim, but deny it as to the punitive damages. I shall also deny its Motion to Strike.

Nurse Puchini's motion as to the plaintiff's claim of battery I shall grant, but shall deny it as to all other claims.

Background

According to the Complaint, the plaintiff, Roberta Davis, a resident of the State of New York, experienced pain in her lower abdomen and consulted Dr. David Hoffman. On August 1, 1994, he diagnosed her to be suffering from a fibroid uterus and prescribed a dilation-and-curettage procedure designed to remove the fibroids. The doctor further suggested a laparoscopy and hysteroscopy to search for cancer. The doctor's nurse, Susan Puchini, conducted a pre-surgical interview with the plaintiff in which she described a video hysteroscopy, a dilation-and-curettage procedure, a resectoscopic removal of submucous fibroids, a laparoscopy, and a laser myomectomy. The plaintiff avers that she specifically informed Dr. Hoffman and Nurse Puchini that she did not consent to a hysterectomy. They responded that they would awaken her during the operation to obtain her consent before proceeding to a hysterectomy. At no time did they inform the plaintiff that the doctor intended to perform a hysterectomy. On August 8, the plaintiff underwent a procedure that resulted in a hysterectomy, during which no one awakened her to discuss and explore possible alternatives, or if there was to be a hysterectomy, to first obtain her consent. Claiming that the hysterectomy caused her substantial injuries, she brings this diversity action against Dr. Hoffman, Nurse Puchini, and the Hospital.

I. The Reading Hospital's Motion to Dismiss Claim of Battery by Lack of Informed Consent
In response to the plaintiff's allegation that the Hospital committed battery by lack of informed consent to the hysterectomy, the Hospital asserts that Pennsylvania law places no duty on a hospital to obtain a patient's consent to an operation. It argues that Pennsylvania courts have applied the doctrine of informed consent only to physicians, not to hospitals.

The plaintiff responds that the Hospital gratuitously undertook to obtain her consent prior to the operation. Additionally, she contends that Pennsylvania law imposes on the Hospital respondeat superior liability for the torts of its agents, Dr. Hoffman and Nurse Puchini, under the doctrine of ostensible agency. Finally, she maintains that she has stated a cause of action against the Hospital sounding in negligence under corporate negligence theory. I examine below the three purported bases for the battery claim, but find all of them legally and factually insufficient.

Duty to Obtain Informed Consent

Pennsylvania law imposes on surgeons the duty to inform their patients of the material risks involved in operations, and to obtain their patients' consent to the operations before performing the surgery. Should a surgeon fail to obtain a patient's informed consent, a battery is committed when the scope of the operation exceeds the scope of the consent. This rule, however, applies only to the surgeon, and not to a hospital, which generally has no such duty, even if it is one of the hospital's surgeons who is operating in one of the hospital's operating rooms, working with the hospital's staff. There are, however, two exceptions to this rule. Both are inapposite.

In Friter, 414 Pa.Super. at 628–29, 607 A.2d at 1113–14 (1992), the court dealt with an unusual factual scenario. There, the hospital had contracted with the FDA to participate in a clinical study involving the implantation of experimental intra-ocular lenses. They were so experimental that they had not yet obtained FDA approval. Hence, the FDA promulgated regulations requiring the hospital to obtain informed consent, using a very detailed, five-page consent form, setting forth with particularity the possibility of the existence of unknown risks, since the lenses were still being tested. The court held that the failure to obtain informed consent, under those particular circumstances, was actionable. There is no such regulatory/experimental scenario here, and thus the exception does not apply.

In *Jones v. Philadelphia College of Osteopathic Medicine*, 813 F.Supp. 1125, 1131 (E.D.Pa.1993), the hospital itself, of its own volition, undertook to prepare a consent form, bearing the name and logo of the medical college and the hospital in question. The court concluded that although the hospital had no duty under Pennsylvania law to obtain informed consent, once it nevertheless voluntarily assumed that duty, it had better do it right. Otherwise, it would be held accountable in a court of law.

This is but an example, in the medical context, of general negligence law concerning duty. One has, for example, no duty to drive one's neighbor to the airport. But if one nevertheless volunteers to undertake that good-neighborly task, and then drives negligently, causing the neighbor to be injured en route, one is held legally accountable. It is no defense to the negligent driving that the good neighbor had no duty to take the neighbor to the airport in the first place. Here, as well, a consent form authored and printed by the Hospital was used. There is no suggestion, however, that the deficiency in consent was in any way causally inadequate in the form. Rather, any failure is attributed to the omissions in the way the form was filled in, or in the way the patient was not filled in as to what was to be the next phase of the operation. Thus the form was causally irrelevant and cannot be a basis for finding liability. Thus, neither discrete, narrow exception to the general rule that only surgeons have the duty to obtain informed consent applies here.

Corporate Negligence

Finally, the plaintiff seeks to recover under a theory of corporate negligence, whereby a hospital may be held liable for its own "failure to uphold the proper standard of care owed the patient." This theory of liability, however, is grounded upon mere negligence, as opposed to the requirement of intent, inherent in the intentional tort of failure to obtain informed consent. Under this doctrine, a hospital must: 1) "use reasonable care in the maintenance of safe and adequate facilities"; 2) "select and retain only competent physicians"; 3) "oversee all persons who practice medicine within its walls"; and 4) "formulate, adopt and enforce adequate rules and policies to ensure quality care." Id. Nonetheless, "a hospital cannot be sued for corporate negligence for failure to seek informed consent under the traditional battery theory." 158 F.R.D. at 73. Assuming arguendo that corporate negligence theory could include the duty to obtain informed consent, negligence could not satisfy the mental state requirement for battery. Therefore, the claim must fail.

Punitive Damages Claim

The Hospital contends that this court should dismiss the plaintiff's claim for punitive damages because she has not alleged that it engaged in conduct sufficiently egregious to support such an award. The plaintiff responds that the removal of her uterus without consent constitutes the reckless indifference or wanton misconduct necessary to support a claim for punitive damages. I agree it is patently egregious, amply sufficient to support an award of punitives. Therefore, I shall deny the Hospital's motion as to this claim.

II. Alternative Motion to Strike

The Hospital has moved in the alternative to strike the informed consent and punitive damages claims. I have just dismissed the informed consent claim, but the punitive damages claim I shall not strike. Federal Rule of Civil Procedure 12(f) permits a court to strike from any pleading any insufficient defense or any redundant, immaterial, impertinent, or scandalous matter, factors not present here. Thus, I shall deny the Motion to Strike.

III. Nurse Puchini's Motion

Negligence

Nurse Puchini argues that the plaintiff has failed to state a negligence claim against her for two reasons: (1) under Pennsylvania law, a nurse has no duty to obtain informed consent; and (2) Pennsylvania law does not permit a cause of action, grounded in negligence, to constitute battery; the act must be intentional. Plaintiff responds that Pennsylvania law imposes on nurses a duty of due care, distinct from any duty to obtain informed consent, and the facts of this case fall within the embrace of that general duty.

To the extent that the plaintiff could prove that Nurse Puchini's explanation of the operation fell short of the prudent nurse standard of care, she has stated a claim sounding in negligence. Pennsylvania law requires nurses to act in a reasonably prudent manner. The plaintiff alleges that Nurse Puchini did not advise her of any alternative testing, treatment, or procedures. She further alleges that the nurse failed to inform her properly of possible side effects and risks that could require a hysterectomy. Proof of these allegations could support a finding that Nurse Puchini acted negligently.

Negligent Infliction of Emotional Distress

As for Nurse Puchini's contention that the plaintiff has not stated a claim for the negligent infliction of emotional distress, I disagree. Pennsylvania law permits a plaintiff to recover for any mental suffering that results from physical injury, however slight, if the defendant's negligence caused the physical injury. The plaintiff alleges that, because of Nurse Puchini's negligence, she suffered physical injuries that have in turn resulted in emotional and psychological injuries. Proof of these allegations could support recovery.

Battery by Lack of Informed Consent

Nurse Puchini asserts that, as a physician's nurse, she had no duty to obtain the plaintiff's informed consent to surgery. She further

maintains that even if she did have such a duty, the allegations of her negligence do not support a claim for battery.

The plaintiff first responds that Nurse Puchini assumed the duty to obtain informed consent by giving her the Reading Hospital and Medical Center's informed consent form. In addition, she contends that Nurse Puchini incurred that duty through the doctrine of ostensible agency.

Duty to Obtain Informed Consent

Because nurses do not have a duty to obtain informed consent, the plaintiff has not stated a claim for battery by lack of informed consent against Nurse Puchini. Pennsylvania law generally imposes no duty on persons other than surgeons to obtain informed consent before performing surgery. Thus, courts have not imposed the duty on nurses. Persons who assist the "primary treating physician" have no duty to obtain the patient's informed consent. *Jones*, 813 F.Supp. at 1130.

Nor has the plaintiff stated a claim for battery by lack of informed consent, because there is no allegation that Nurse Puchini committed a battery. The tort of battery by lack of informed consent includes as one of its components "technical" battery, an intentional tort. *Shaw v. Kirschbaum*, 439 Pa.Super. 24, 34–35, 653 A.2d 12, 17 (1994). A plaintiff may not ground an informed consent claim on negligence. Instead, the defendant must actually intend contact with the plaintiff. Nothing in the Complaint supports the inference that Nurse Puchini intentionally touched the plaintiff.

Intentional Infliction of Emotional Distress

Nurse Puchini argues that the allegations of negligence are insufficient to satisfy the mental state requirement for the intentional infliction of emotional distress. I disagree. A jury could find that Nurse Puchini acted outrageously by not advising the plaintiff of the risks of the surgery. That would be enough to support recovery.

Punitive Damages

Nurse Puchini maintains that an award of punitive damages would not be justifiable. Noting that Pennsylvania law requires intentional, reckless, or malicious conduct to support a punitive damages claim, she asserts that the case involves only negligence. I disagree. The plaintiff responds that the unauthorized, intentional removal of her uterus could justify an award of punitive damages. I fully agree.

ORDER

AND NOW, this 7th day of July, 1997, for the reasons described in the accompanying memorandum:

1) Reading Hospital and Medical Center's Motion to Dismiss Counts VIII and X is GRANTED as to Count VIII but DENIED as to Count X, and Motion to Strike Counts VIII and X is DENIED; and

2) Susan Puchini's Motion to Dismiss the Complaint is GRANTED as to Count VII but DENIED as to all other Counts. Count VIII against the Reading Hospital and Count VII against Susan Puchini are DISMISSED with twenty days' leave to amend the Complaint.

HAWKINS V. ROSENBLOOM
17 S.W.3d 116 (1999)

Opinion

Guidugli, Judge.

This is an appeal by Robert A. Hawkins and Yvonne Hawkins (Hawkinses) from a judgment order, pursuant to a jury verdict of the Jefferson Circuit Court, which entered judgment for the appellee, Philip Rosenbloom, M.D. (Dr. Rosenbloom), and assessed all costs against the Hawkinses. We affirm in part, reverse in part, and remand.

On January 28, 1994, Dr. Rosenbloom performed elective gallbladder surgery on Mr. Hawkins at Baptist East Hospital in Louisville, Kentucky. On January 11, 1994, prior to undergoing gallbladder surgery, Mr. Hawkins met with Dr. Rosenbloom to discuss the general risks of surgery. As a result of this meeting, Dr. Rosenbloom caused to be prepared an office note stating that the general risks of surgery were discussed with Mr. Hawkins. Furthermore, Mr. Hawkins signed an informed consent form that stated his physician discussed with him the general risks of surgery. To remove Mr. Hawkins' gallbladder, Dr. Rosenbloom used a procedure called laparoscopic cholecystectomy, whereby several small incisions are made in the surgical area, a laparoscope is inserted into one and the gallbladder is removed through the others. Laparoscopic cholecystectomy is generally the preferred method of cholecystectomy (removal of gallbladder) as opposed to open cholecystectomy, whereby one's gallbladder is removed through a single standard incision.

Mr. Hawkins was scheduled for release from the hospital on January 30, 1994. However, Mrs. Hawkins discovered drainage around the laparoscopic incisions and the discharge was canceled. Thereafter, Dr. Rosenbloom performed exploratory surgery on Mr. Hawkins and discovered that a 1.5-cm perforation had been cut into Mr. Hawkins' bowel and that the bowel was leaking fecal material into Mr. Hawkins' abdomen. On February 4, 1994, Dr. Rosenbloom drained two abscesses due to infection caused by the leaking bowel. Mr. Hawkins remained in the hospital seventeen (17) days and thereafter was released with a full colostomy. On May 12, 1995, Mr. Hawkins underwent a fourth surgery to close the colostomy, which proved unsuccessful. However, the colostomy closed on its own several months later. In April of 1997, Mr. Hawkins underwent a fifth surgery for repair of a double hernia that was related directly to his January 30, 1994, colostomy.

The Hawkinses sued Dr. Rosenbloom for lack of informed consent and negligence among other things. The case went to trial and resulted in a jury verdict in favor of Dr. Rosenbloom. The Hawkinses raise three issues on appeal. First, before the trial of this matter, the trial court granted Dr. Rosenbloom's motion in limine excluding any evidence regarding informed consent at trial. The trial court granted said motion because the Hawkinses did not have an expert witness to testify with regard to the standard of care that an ordinary and careful physician would follow in obtaining informed consent. Furthermore, the trial court refused to instruct the jury on the law of informed consent. Second, the trial court refused to allow the Hawkinses' attorney to play video excerpts of testimony at trial during closing arguments. Third, during the trial of this matter, the trial court allowed Dr. Rosenbloom's attorney to cross-examine the Hawkinses' expert witness, Dr. Marco Bonta (Dr. Bonta), with a notarized letter from another physician.

With regard to their first argument, the Hawkinses maintain that no expert testimony was needed to establish the standard of care for informed consent. The law of informed consent, KRS 304.40–320, states as follows:

In any action brought for treating, examining, or operating on a claimant wherein the claimant's informed consent is an element, the claimant's informed consent shall be deemed to have been given where:

(1) The action of the health care provider in obtaining the consent of the patient or another person authorized to give consent for the patient was in accordance with the accepted standard of medical or dental practice among members of the profession with similar training and experience; and

(2) A reasonable individual, from the information provided by the health care provider under the circumstances, would have a general understanding of the procedure and medically or dentally acceptable alternative procedures or treatments and substantial risks and hazards inherent on the proposed treatment or procedures which are recognized among other health care providers who perform similar treatments or procedures;

(3) In an emergency situation where consent of the patient cannot reasonably be obtained before providing health care services, there is no requirement that a health care provider obtain a previous consent.

Part (2) deals specifically with what a reasonable person should be told before deemed to have been given informed consent. The Hawkinses' argument on this issue is two-fold. First, they argue that KRS 304.40–320 requires that a physician must meet the standard set out in both parts (1) and (2) of the statute for valid informed consent. Second, they argue that "the question of what a reasonable individual would understand does not require expert testimony." Therefore, they maintain, the trial court should have allowed them to present the issue of informed consent to the jury without expert testimony because Dr. Rosenbloom did not meet the standard set out under part (2) of the statute.

An action based on lack of informed consent "is in reality one for negligence in failing to conform to a proper professional standard. . . ." *Holton v. Pfingst*, Ky., 534 S.W.2d 786, 788 (1975). As in any medical malpractice case, the general rule is that expert testimony is required to negate informed consent. In Keel, the hospital administered a CT scan that involved injecting a contrast dye into the patient's system. The patient later developed thrombophlebitis at the site of the injection. The Supreme Court found that expert testimony was not required to establish informed consent in this case because the patient was given absolutely no information whatsoever regarding the risks and hazards of the procedure. In holding that expert testimony was not needed to establish informed consent in this case, the Court stated:

If we are to analogize consent actions to negligence actions, we must also acknowledge that a failure adequately to inform the patient need not be established by expert testimony where the failure is so apparent that layman may easily recognize it or infer it from evidence within the realm of common knowledge.

Thus, Keel is limited in its application to situations where no information is given to the patient regarding the risks and hazards of the procedure. However, in the case sub judice, we are not presented with the same or even similar circumstances as that in Keel. Mr. Hawkins met with Dr. Rosenbloom on January 11, 1994, to discuss the general risks of gallbladder surgery. During his deposition, Mr. Hawkins did not deny that Dr. Rosenbloom had discussed the general risks of gallbladder surgery with him but instead stated that "I don't remember that it happened." However, Mr. Hawkins signed an informed consent form that stated that his physician had discussed the general risks of gallbladder surgery with him. At trial, Mr. Hawkins testified that he signed the consent form but that he did not ask any questions or ask Dr. Rosenbloom to go over the form with him. Furthermore, as a result of the January 11, 1994, meeting, Dr. Rosenbloom caused to be prepared an office note stating that the general risks of surgery were discussed with Mr. Hawkins. Given these facts, we do not believe that any alleged failure on Dr. Rosenbloom's part was "so apparent that layman may easily recognize it or infer it from evidence within the realm of common knowledge." Thus, the trial court did not abuse its discretion by refusing to allow the Hawkinses to present evidence to the jury regarding lack of informed consent without expert testimony.

Finally, the Hawkinses argue that the trial court's decision to allow Dr. Rosenbloom's attorney to cross-examine their expert witness, Dr. Bonta, with a notarized letter from Dr. E. Christopher Ellison (Dr. Ellison) was an abuse of discretion and constituted prejudicial error. We must first decide whether the trial court

erred in allowing Dr. Rosenbloom's attorney to cross-examine Dr. Bonta with the letter. If the trial court did err, then we must decide whether such error was harmless or prejudicial to the Hawkinses' case.

Hearsay is defined as "a statement, other than one made by the declarant while testifying at the trial or hearing, offered in evidence to prove the truth of the matter asserted." Kentucky Rules of Evidence (KRE) 801(c). Hearsay is inadmissible during a trial except as provided by KRE or Supreme Court rules. KRE 802. Dr. Ellison's letter constituted hearsay. However, the trial court allowed Dr. Ellison's letter to be read into evidence under a hearsay exception, KRE 803, which states:

> The following are not excluded by the hearsay rules, even though the declarant is available as a witness:
>
> (18) Learned treatises. To the extent called to the attention of an expert witness upon cross-examination or relied upon by the expert witness in direct examination, statements contained in published treatises, periodicals, or pamphlets on a subject of history, medicine, or other science or art, established as a reliable authority by the testimony or admission of the witness or by judicial notice. If admitted, the statements may be read into evidence but may not be received as exhibits.

Dr. Ellison's notarized letter did not fall within one of the stated exceptions. It certainly did not constitute a published treatise, it did not appear in any journal, nor was it published as a pamphlet. Instead, the letter contained written responses to questions posed to Dr. Ellison by Dr. Rosenbloom's counsel or presumably from someone on his behalf. We do not know what material was provided to Dr. Ellison with regard to this case nor do we know exactly what questions were asked of him that caused the genesis of this letter. Further, we do not know the basis for his opinions. Dr. Rosenbloom had not listed him as a witness or, more specifically, an expert witness, and he had not been deposed for the case. He was not present at trial, did not testify, and the contents of the letter were never subject to cross-examination. In fact, Dr. Rosenbloom's counsel did not reveal the existence of this letter nor produce it to the Hawkinses' counsel until he sought the trial court's permission to use the letter to impeach Dr. Bonta at trial.

This letter does not qualify as a "learned treatise" and the trial court erred by allowing Dr. Rosenbloom's counsel to question Dr. Bonta concerning its contents. Dr. Rosenbloom argues that any error in the trial court's ruling regarding use of the letter was "harmless error and does not rise to the level of being reversible." We disagree. The Supreme Court, in *Crane v. Commonwealth*, Ky., 726 S.W.2d 302, 307 (1987), recently articulated the test for harmless error:2

> The test for harmless error is whether there is any reasonable possibility that absent error the verdict would have been different. . . . The question here is not whether the jury reached the right result regardless of the error, but whether there is a reasonable possibility that the error might have affected the jury's decision.

We believe it is reasonably possible that cross-examination of Dr. Bonta with the letter from Dr. Ellison affected the jury's decision. Essentially, Dr. Ellison was allowed to testify without Dr. Rosenbloom's counsel listing him as an expert witness or providing Civil Rule 26 disclosure. More important, however, is that the trial court allowed Dr. Ellison to testify in court without being subject to cross-examination by the Hawkinses' counsel. This allowed Dr. Rosenbloom to "pick and choose" amongst statements and opinions of Dr. Ellison knowing that Dr. Ellison would not be subjected to cross-examination with regard to those statements and opinions. In essence, the jury heard only one side of the story: the side most critical of the Hawkinses' case.

In fact, Dr. Ellison's "testimony" involved one of the central issues of the case: the standard of care employed by Dr. Rosenbloom in performing the surgery in question. Dr. Rosenbloom's counsel used Dr. Ellison's "testimony" to undermine and impeach the credibility of the Hawkinses' expert witness. Moreover, Dr. Rosenbloom's counsel emphasized the letter in closing arguments compounding the prejudicial effect of the hearsay testimony, all to the Hawkinses' detriment. We believe that use of the letter to cross-examine Dr. Bonta and in closing arguments constituted prejudicial error.

Accordingly, we affirm in part, reverse in part, and remand this case for proceedings consistent with this opinion.

ALL CONCUR.

Websites

■ *Washington Post* article: Medical Malpractice and the American Jury
http://www.washingtonpost.com/wp-srv/style/longterm/books/chap1/medical.htm

■ Consumer Action and Information Center of Hawaii
http://www.consumerlaw.com/medical.html

■ Insurance Information Institute
http://www.iii.org/

■ Defining Legal Malpractice
http://legal-dictionary.thefreedictionary.com/Legal+Malpractice

■ ABA Standing Committee on Legal Assistants
http://www.abanet.org/legalservices/paralegals/

Forms and Court Documents

Medical malpractice complaint.

STATE OF PLACID	IN THE SUPERIOR COURT
COUNTY OF BARNES	FILE NUMBER: _____

Charles Chumley,   )
Plaintiff   )
)
vs.   )
)
Joseph C. Doe, M.D.   )
Doe & Roe Medical Associates, P.A.,
Defendants

Complaint

COMES NOW, Charles Chumley, Plaintiff in the above-styled action and makes the following allegations:

1.

At all times pertinent to this action, Defendant Joseph C. Doe, M.D. (hereafter referred to as Defendant Doe) was a licensed medical doctor in the State of Placid.

2.

In Defendant Doe's capacity as a medical doctor, he was a managing partner in the firm of Doe & Roe Medical Associates, P.A. (hereafter referred to as Defendant Doe & Roe, P.A.), a registered Professional Association in the State of Placid.

3.

Both Dr. Doe and Doe & Roe, P.A. were engaged in the practice of medicine through their office located at 212 Alameda Canyon Road, City of Barnes, State of Placid.

4.

At all material and pertinent times to this complaint, Defendants Doe and Doe & Roe, P.A. had a physician-patient relationship with the plaintiff.

5.

On August 23, last year, the plaintiff was involved in an automobile-train collision that caused the plaintiff severe and life-threatening injuries.

6.

On August 23, last year, the plaintiff was transported to Mission Hospital and admitted into the Mission Emergency Room.

7.

Defendant Doe, in his capacity as Plaintiff's physician, visited him at the Mission-Barnes Emergency Room and examined the plaintiff.

8.

On August 23 and for all times afterward, Defendant Doe and Defendant Doe & Roe, owed a duty of reasonable care to plaintiff to use that knowledge, skill, and care that is generally used in similar cases and circumstances by physicians in communities having similar medical standards and available facilities, which duty these defendants breached by the following: Defendant Doe failed to diagnose plaintiff's severe abdominal injuries, including plaintiff's splenic injury.

9.

As a direct and proximate cause of Defendant Doe's failure to diagnose the plaintiff's medical injuries, he was not treated for his abdominal injuries for 28 hours following his admission to Mission-Barnes Hospital.

10.

As a direct and proximate cause of Defendant Doe's failure to diagnose and treat the plaintiff's injuries, plaintiff suffered from peritonitis. Plaintiff's spleen was removed on August 30, last year.

11.

As a direct and proximate cause of Defendant Doe's breach of the duty that he owed the plaintiff, Plaintiff incurred economic, physical, and mental damages in addition to and in aggravation of the injuries that he received as a result of the automobile-train collision that occurred on August 23, last year.

12.

As a direct and proximate result of Defendants' negligence, plaintiff suffered disability, disfigurement, mental anguish, loss of capacity for the enjoyment of life, expensive hospitalization, medical and nursing care and treatment, loss of earnings, loss of ability to earn money, and aggravation of a previously existing condition, to wit, his injuries from the automobile-train collision occurring on August 23, last year. These losses are permanent in nature. Plaintiff will suffer continued losses and impairments in the future.

WHEREFORE, the plaintiff requests judgment for damages against defendants, individually and jointly and severally, as follows:

Plaintiff prays that the Court award the following damages:

1. General damages in the amount of _____;
2. Special damages in the amount of _____; and

3. Punitive damages in an amount to be determined by the court;

4. Plaintiff also requests costs of suit; and

5. Such other and further relief as the court may deem just and proper;

6. Plaintiff also requests a trial by jury on the issues raised in this Complaint.

Respectfully submitted, this the _____ day of _____, 20 _____.

_____

Clarence D. Arrow
Attorney for the Plaintiff

Key Terms

Informed consent	Physician-patient	Standard of care
Legal malpractice	relationship	
Malpractice	Specialist	

Review Questions

1 If the first U.S. medical malpractice case was filed in 1794, why are medical malpractice cases considered to be such a pressing and immediate problem?

2 How has the medical profession's standard of care changed in the past two centuries? How has this standard of care and the treatment of patients affected the societal standing of physicians?

3 Medical malpractice cases can be based on one of at least three different theories. What are they?

4 Why are the courts reluctant to frame all medical malpractice cases in terms of contract theory? Is there some public consideration that puts the physician-patient relationship outside the framework of a simple contractual relationship?

5 What are the basic elements of a medical malpractice claim?

6 What are some examples of the ways in which a physician can breach her standard of care to the patient?

7 Why is expert testimony needed to prove the basic elements of the plaintiff's case?

8 Why would many states or jurisdictions require an expert's affidavit before the plaintiff's complaint can be filed? Is there some public policy behind this requirement?

9 Under the law of medical malpractice, a recent graduate of medical school and a seasoned physician are held to the same standard of care. Does this make sense? Why or why not?

10 Many jurisdictions have moved away from local definitions of the standard of care. Why?

11 A specialist is held to a different standard of care. What is that? Why should a specialist be held to a different standard of care than a general practitioner?

12   How have various tort reforms affected the way that a medical malpractice case is brought or how damages are assessed in such cases?

13   Why have many state legislatures enacted caps or limits on punitive damages awards?

14   Should punitive damages awards be limited in medical malpractice cases? Why or why not?

15   What is informed consent? What elements must be established to show that the plaintiff gave informed consent?

16   What is an exception to the requirement that informed consent must be obtained prior to carrying out any procedure?

17   Explain the scope of informed consent.

18   Some law firms employ legal nurse consultants or nurse paralegals to assist with medical malpractice cases. How could such individuals be helpful?

19   What are some of the defenses available in medical malpractice cases?

20   How is legal malpractice defined?

21   What is the attorney's duty to the client?

22   Is expert testimony ever used in legal malpractice cases? If so, how?

23   What are some ways that a paralegal can help a firm avoid a claim of legal malpractice?

24   Explain the difference between a narrative medical summary and a page-by-page medical summary.

Applying What You Have Learned

1   Nancy has decided to undergo a radical new therapy to cure her cancer. There is only one doctor in the country who practices this procedure. When Nancy meets with the physician, he takes great pains to point out to her what the risks of this procedure are. After listening to everything that the doctor has to say, Nancy decides to go ahead with the procedure. During the treatment, an unexpected complication develops. Nancy's doctor realizes that another procedure must be used. Should the doctor obtain a new informed consent from Nancy?

2   Drew, who suffers from obesity, decides that he wants to undergo an operation that will reduce the size of his stomach, commonly referred to as "stomach stapling." Drew will be physically unable to eat as much food as he was before the procedure and therefore should lose weight. When the doctor appears in Drew's hospital room to tell him all about the procedure and obtain Drew's informed consent, Drew says, "I don't want to know the details. It grosses me out. I'll get sick if you tell me anything. I trust you. Just do it." Is this a valid informed consent? Is there anything that the doctor can do to prevent, or at least minimize, any medical malpractice claim that Drew may have later because of lack of informed consent?

3   Draft a complaint based on the facts in the case excerpt. How would you allege a breach of the standard of care in that case?

4   Locate your state's statute of limitations on medical malpractice cases. What does it provide about a patient's cause of action

Endnotes

[1] *Cross v. Guthery,* 1 Am. Dec. 61 (1794).

[2] 69 Tenn. L. Rev. 385 (2002).

[3] 69 Tenn. L. Rev. 385 (2002).

[4] *Jure v. Raviotta,* 612 So. 2d 225, *cert. denied,* 614 So. 2d 1257 (1992).

[5] *Burton v. Leftwich,* 123 So. 2d 766 (1960).

[6] *Norton v. Hamilton,* 92 Ga. App. 727, 89 S.E.2d 809 (1955).

[7] *Hill v. Stewart,* 209 So. 2d 809 (1968).

[8] *Martinez v. Lewis,* 969 P.2d 213 (1998).

[9] 43 Baylor L. Rev. 1 Legal Malpractice in Texas, Beck (1991).

[10] *Jacoves v. United Merchandising Corp.,* 9 Cal. App. 4th 88, 11 Cal. Rptr. 2d 468 (1992).

[11] *Goins v. Puleo,* 350 N.C. 277, 512 S.E.2d 748 (1999).

[12] 43 Baylor L. Rev. 1 Legal Malpractice in Texas, Beck (1991).

[13] *Sayer v. Williams,* 962 P.2d 165 (1998).

[14] *Clark v. Sporre,* 777 N.E.2d 1166 (2002).

[15] *Heinrich v. Sweet,* 308 F.3d 48 (1st Cir. 2002).

[16] *Naccarato v. Grob,* 180 N.W.2d 788 (1970).

[17] *Vergara by Vergara v. Doan,* 593 N.E.2d 185 (1992).

[18] 43 Baylor L. Rev. 1 Legal Malpractice in Texas, Beck (1991). *Moskovitz v. Mt. Sinai Medical Ctr.,* 69 Ohio St. 3d 638, 635 N.E.2d 331 (1994), *cert. denied,* 130 L. Ed. 2d 602, 115 S. Ct. 668, _____ U.S. _____ (1994).

[19] Id.

[20] *Ditto v. McCurdy,* 86 Haw. 84, 947 P.2d 952 (1997).

[21] 13 Okla. City U. L. Rev. 135, Arancibia (1988).

[22] *Spano v. Bertocci,* 299 A.D.2d 335 (2002).

[23] *Hawkins v. Rosenbloom,* 17 S.W.3d 116 (1999).

[24] *Shine v. Vega,* 429 Mass. 456 (1999).

[25] *Davis v. Hoffman,* 972 F. Supp. 308 (E.D. Pa. 1997).

[26] *Babbitt v. Bumpus,* 73 Mich. 331 (1889).

[27] *Fidler v. Sullivan,* 93 App. Div. 2d 964, 463 N.Y.S.2d 279 (1983).

[28] ABA Model Guidelines for the Utilization of Legal Assistant Services, Guideline 9.

Crossword Puzzle

www.CrosswordWeaver.com

ACROSS

1 One who has become an expert in a particular field through education, training, or both
2 Professional negligence committed by an attorney during the course of her representation of a client
3 An agreement by a person to allow some type of action after having been fully informed and after making a knowing and intelligent decision to allow the action.
4 The failure of a professional to exercise an adequate degree of skill, expertise, and knowledge for an adequate benefit of the client/patient; otherwise known as professional negligence
5 The legally recognized relationship between a physician and patient in which the physician brings to bear her skill in the care and treatment of the patient; this relationship also triggers evidentiary privileges that protect the patient's communications with the physician from compulsory revelation

DOWN

1 The standard used to determine if a party has acted negligently in a particular case

Insurance

- Explain the role of insurance coverage in personal injury cases

- Describe how insurance policy limits affect settlement negotiations

- Define an insurance company's duty to defend its insured and when this obligation is triggered

- Explain "no-fault" insurance

- Describe and explain the basic components of an insurance policy

I   MR. CHUMLEY AND THE INSURANCE COMPANY

Mr. Chumley has a standard automobile insurance policy. This policy covers monetary losses from personal injuries, medical payments, and collision damage, among other things. As we have already seen, Mr. Chumley was severely injured in the collision with the train. He was rushed to the hospital shortly after the collision, where he began incurring huge medical bills. His car was also completely destroyed. His wife was killed, and there are funeral costs to pay. He cannot return to his job, so his income has been affected. Which of these losses is covered by his insurance? If the insurance company pays these claims, what effect does this have on his lawsuit against the railroad company? After all, if he is compensated for his medical bills, how can he sue the railroad company for recovery of bills that have already been paid? We examine all these issues in this chapter and provide a general framework for how law firms on both sides of a lawsuit deal with insurance companies. First, we discuss the general history and concepts of insurance.

II   INTRODUCTION

Although there are dozens of different forms of insurance, ranging from flood insurance to crop insurance, there are only a few types of insurance that figure prominently enough in tort law to justify a separate discussion. Broadly speaking, automobile insurance and homeowner's insurance are the two most important areas of insurance law, at least as they apply to personal injury cases and the other topics we cover in this chapter. An understanding of insurance law is crucial for anyone planning on entering the field of personal injury law. Even more important than understanding the underlying principles of the insurance industry is an understanding of how the individuals involved, from insurance agents to claims adjusters to insurance defense attorneys, function in the day-to-day world of slip-and-fall, car wreck, and personal injury lawsuits.

III   THE IMPACT OF INSURANCE ON CIVIL SUITS

Insurance coverage has an enormous impact on the course of a civil suit. When deciding whether to take a case, the plaintiff's attorney must consider the likelihood of recovering damages. If the defendant has no insurance and no assets, the potential recovery is almost nonexistent. In the pragmatic world of personal injury lawyers, no matter how good a case the plaintiff may have, if there is no possibility of recovery, the attorney will probably refuse to take the case. Plaintiffs' attorneys are almost always paid on a contingency fee, typically one-third of the total recovery. A case with clear defendant liability but no possibility of judgment means that the plaintiff's attorney has no financial incentive to take the case. Even if the attorney would like to take the case, just on "general principles," he has staff, rent, and other overhead costs to consider. When attorneys take on too many such cases, they lose money and jeopardize their ability to pay the costs of running a law office.

When the defendant has insurance coverage, the possibility of a recovery suddenly becomes greater. After all, the defendant's insurance coverage is specifically designed to pay out liability claims. A typical automobile insurance policy also provides an attorney to represent the defendant, under the "duty to defend" provision. This means that the plaintiff's attorney will be dealing with an attorney on the other side of the litigation, and that makes the entire process more predictable, although not necessarily any easier.

Determining whether the defendant has insurance coverage is usually simple. In most car collisions, the police have been called and an accident report has been filled out. Part of that report will include some basic information about the defendant's coverage. However, discovering how much coverage the defendant has (the policy limits) has traditionally been more difficult.

We explore a typical insurance policy in depth and focus on automobile insurance policies, but first we briefly address the development of insurance.

IV. HISTORY OF INSURANCE

The basic scheme behind insurance is deceptively simple: Individuals (policyholders) make payments (premiums) to the insurance company, which pools the money and uses this pool of money to pay out any claims made by a policyholder. This arrangement spreads the risk of loss over a wide group so that no one individual must bear the brunt of a large financial loss. Insurance companies are often seen as an important element of the economy because they guarantee that businesses and individuals will be able to recover from devastating losses, such as fires or automobile collisions. Without insurance, business owners would have no way of reestablishing themselves after a catastrophe. Given this crucial economic importance, and the fact that insurance companies have a great deal of leverage when dealing with the individual policyholder, all states have passed legislation restricting and regulating insurance companies.

Without insurance, there are only three possible methods to compensate an individual for a loss: (1) the individual bears the total burden, (2) the individual who caused the loss pays for it, or (3) a statute provides that some other agency, such as workers' compensation, pays the loss.

Insurance companies have existed for centuries. Lloyd's of London, the world's most famous insurance company, has existed since 1688. Lloyd's originally started out as a coffeehouse for merchant sailors and eventually branched out from coffee to insuring merchant fleets that undertook dangerous ocean voyages to secure spices, precious minerals, and, oddly enough, coffee.

Dislike or outright hatred of insurance companies is not a recent phenomenon. In many ways, this industry could qualify as the business most people love to hate. Statutes governing the insurance industry have existed since the 1800s, but the second half of the twentieth century saw the largest growth in insurance legislation. Much of the early insurance regulation was a direct response to outright corruption on the part of some insurance companies. For instance, a company might collect life insurance premium payments from an insured for years and then refuse to pay when she died, leaving her spouse and children in financial straits.[1] Part of this resentment of insurance companies was based on the perception that these large, faceless corporations cared more for profits than their responsibilities to their insured customers. One could argue that this sentiment is still prevalent.

Before 1944, the U.S. Supreme Court had consistently ruled that insurance was not *commerce* as that word is defined under the Commerce Clause of the U.S. Constitution. As such, Congress was prevented from enacting legislation to regulate the industry nationwide. However, after the decision in *United States v. South-Eastern Underwriters Association,* the Supreme Court's view changed.[2] Reversing its earlier position, the Court ruled that insurance was commerce and therefore could be regulated. Congress quickly took up the Supreme Court's suggestion by creating the first of many federal statutes regulating the insurance industry. The McCarran-Ferguson Act established that, in most questions regarding insurance law, state law would apply, except where insurance touched on national issues such as antitrust, federal taxation, and the jurisdiction of the Federal Trade Commission. In those situations, insurance companies come under the jurisdiction of federal statutes.

Sidebar

When researching insurance law, go to state law for insurance-related issues, such as policy provisions, exclusions, and duty to defend. Look to federal law when researching issues such as an insurance company's obligation to pay federal taxes, compliance with securities regulation, and labor issues.

V WHAT IS INSURANCE?

Premium
The insured's payment to the insurance company.

Indemnify
To compensate a person who has suffered a loss.

Insurance coverage is a type of contract between an individual (the insured) and an entity (the insurance company). The insured pays a **premium** (often a specific monthly amount) in exchange for the insurance company's promise to pay for (or **indemnify**) the insured's property loss, medical bills, funeral expenses, liability, and son on, up to a specified total amount.

Almost anything can be insured. Any potential loss is insurable, so long as it does not violate public policy or stem from the insured's intentional conduct or fraud. For example, some celebrities insure their faces against loss. If they are singers, they may insure their voices. A drug dealer, on the other hand, could not insure her consignment of cocaine, because such an insurance agreement would run counter to public policy (if not an actual criminal statute).

VI THE INSURANCE CONTRACT

Policy
A written insurance contract.

The insurance **policy** is actually a form of contract. As such, it has many of the same elements that are seen in any contract. However, unlike many other types of contracts, insurance policies are tightly regulated by state statutes. In fact, an insurance policy must conform to the applicable state statute, or it is void.

A. THE INSURANCE POLICY

If the insurance policy is a contract, what is the insured receiving in exchange for her premium payments? Actually, the insured receives three benefits:

1. The insurance company agrees to compensate the insured for specific losses covered by the policy.
2. The insurance company agrees to provide an attorney to the insured should the insured be sued for any actions covered by the policy.
3. The insurance company agrees to act as a **fiduciary** in handling the insured's policy matters (one bound by legal and ethical duties to act in the best interests of another).[3]

Fiduciary
A relationship in which one person, or entity, is obligated to act in a trustworthy relationship to the other; a fiduciary has the duty to act in the best interests of the other. A common example of a fiduciary relationship is the attorney-client relationship.

Should the insurance company breach any of these promises, it has violated the terms of a contract, and the insured is entitled to bring suit to enforce the contract provisions. The insurance contract is normally referred to as a policy, and we use that terminology for the rest of this chapter.

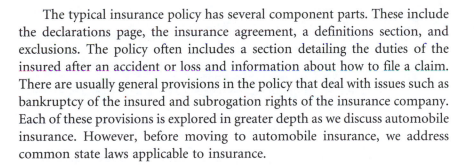

The terms *contract* and *policy* are used interchangeably by most legal authorities.

TORT BASICS AT A GLANCE

The typical insurance policy has several component parts. These include the declarations page, the insurance agreement, a definitions section, and exclusions. The policy often includes a section detailing the duties of the insured after an accident or loss and information about how to file a claim. There are usually general provisions in the policy that deal with issues such as bankruptcy of the insured and subrogation rights of the insurance company. Each of these provisions is explored in greater depth as we discuss automobile insurance. However, before moving to automobile insurance, we address common state laws applicable to insurance.

B. STATE LAWS REGARDING INSURANCE POLICIES

Insurance has been heavily regulated by the states for decades. These regulations affect everything from creating an office of state insurance commissioner (or similar title) to the size of the type font used in policies. In fact, many states have statutes that not only specify the size of the type used in the policy, but also require the use of boldface lettering for certain terms. These initiatives are all designed to make the policy easier to read and to avoid the old adage that "large print giveth and small print taketh away." In the past, small print,

States that have statutes setting out minimum print sizes and boldface requirements include California, Wisconsin, North Carolina, Idaho, Missouri, Louisiana, Oregon, Alabama, and New York, among many others.

buried in the policy, has been used to disguise policy limitations and other restrictions on the policyholder's rights.

In addition to requirements about what font size can be used in policies, some states go so far as to mandate the basic provisions of an insurance policy or to demand that an insurance policy's language be simplified so that policyholders can understand it. These "readable" insurance policies require that the language and terms used in the policy avoid legal and/or technical terms. See Figure 13-1 for an example of such a statute.

In addition to formatting requirements, there is one other important area of state law that factors prominently in civil suits: All states require that motorists possess minimum amounts of insurance coverage as a condition of receiving a valid driver's license from the state.

FIGURE 13-1

North Carolina "Readable Insurance Policy" Act

§58-38-20. Format requirements

(a) All insurance policies and contracts covered by G.S. 58-38-35 must be printed in a typeface at least as large as 10 point modern type, one point leaded, be written in a logical and clear order and form, and contain the following items:

    (1) On the cover, first, or insert page of the policy a statement that the policy is a legal contract between the policy owner and the insurer and the statement, printed in larger or other contrasting type or color, "Read your policy carefully";

    (2) An index of the major provisions of the policy, which may include the following items:
        a. The person or persons insured by the policy;
        b. The applicable events, occurrences, conditions, losses, or damages covered by the policy;
        c. The limitations or conditions on the coverage of the policy;
        d. Definitional sections of the policy;
        e. Provisions governing the procedure for filing a claim under the policy;
        f. Provisions governing cancellation, renewal, or amendment of the policy by either the insurer or the policyholder;
        g. Any options under the policy; and
        h. Provisions governing the insurer's duties and powers in the event that suit is filed against the insured.

(b) In determining whether or not a policy is written in a logical and clear order and form the Commissioner must consider the following factors:

    (1) The extent to which sections or provisions are set off and clearly identified by titles, headings, or margin notations;
    (2) The use of a more readable format, such as narrative or outline forms;
    (3) Margin size and the amount and use of space to separate sections of the policy; and
    (4) Contrast and legibility of the colors of the ink and paper and the use of contrasting titles or headings for sections.

VII   AUTOMOBILE INSURANCE

Lawsuits involving car crashes are the most common form of personal injury case. That fact alone would justify an extensive review of automobile insurance law. However, there is another element that makes a close study of automobile insurance law even more pertinent: Automobile insurance is required by law.

A. STATUTORY MINIMUM LIABILITY COVERAGE

All states have enacted statutes that dictate the minimum amount of insurance coverage that a car driver must have. Typically, the coverage falls into these categories:

- Liability coverage (including bodily injury)
- Property damage
- Medical payments
- Uninsured motorist/underinsured motorist

See Figure 13-2 for an example of mandatory minimum coverage.

B. LIABILITY COVERAGE

When the insured has liability coverage, it means that if he causes injuries to another person or damages property, the insurance company will compensate the injured party, up to the stated limit of the policy. Typically, this provision covers the injured person's medical and funeral expenses, lost wages, disability, pain and suffering, and legal fees, among others. Because this is a statutory requirement, liability coverage is usually broken down into two component parts: bodily injury and property damage.

FIGURE 13-2

California's Mandatory Minimum Automobile Insurance Coverage

§16451. Owner's policy
An owner's policy of motor vehicle liability insurance shall insure the named insured and any other person using any motor vehicle registered to the named insured with the express or implied permission of the named insured, against loss from the liability imposed by law for damages arising out of ownership, maintenance, or use of the motor vehicle within the continental limits of the United States to the extent and aggregate amount, exclusive of interest and costs, with respect to each motor vehicle, of fifteen thousand dollars ($15,000) for bodily injury to or death of each person as a result of any one accident and, subject to the limit as to one person, the amount of thirty thousand dollars ($30,000) for bodily injury to or death of all persons as a result of any one accident and the amount of five thousand dollars ($5,000) for damage to property of others as a result of any one accident.*

*Cal. Stat. §16451

C. BODILY INJURY

When an insurance policy insures against bodily injury, it usually refers to any injury, disease, wound, or sickness caused by the insured. This provision also covers the death of the injured party. The policy limits are usually stated as a total award per person injured or per accident. For instance, if a driver has policy limits of $300,000/$300,000, this means that the insured has a maximum policy limit of $300,000 for each person injured by her or $300,000 total payout for an accident, even if the actual proof of loss exceeds that amount. Most such policies contain language expressly limiting the extent of liability. For instance, the policy might contain a provision that reads:

> The limit of liability shown on the Declarations Pages for each person is the insurance company's maximum limit of liability for damages for bodily injury. These damages include damages for care of the injured person, loss of services or death that is the legal responsibility of the insured.

D. PROPERTY DAMAGE

When the insurance policy provides for property damage, this is usually construed to mean any type of property injury, loss, or destruction for which the insured is legally responsible. As we have seen in the previous example, policy limits of $300,000 means that the total payout for property damage is limited to that amount, even if the actual damages are higher.

E. MEDICAL PAYMENTS

The typical medical payments (MP) clause often states:

> The insurance company agrees to pay reasonable expenses incurred for necessary medical and funeral services because of bodily injury, as that term is defined in the Definitions section of this policy.[4]

This provision means that the insurance company will pay for medical (and often funeral) expenses incurred by the insured or anyone else covered by the policy. Most such policy provisions have specific limitations that do not apply medical payments to experimental procedures or treatments that are not commonly and customarily recognized throughout the medical profession. This exclusion often limits medical payments for **thermography,** acupuncture, or other nontraditional assessments and treatments.

Thermography
An assessment tool that can monitor temperature changes in the skin; often used by plaintiffs' attorneys as a way of showing that there is greater blood flow in an injured area, and is therefore a "picture of the pain."

F. UNINSURED MOTORIST COVERAGE

Uninsured motorist (UM) coverage was created as a way of protecting motorists from other drivers who do not have insurance. Although it is a legal requirement to have automobile insurance, that does not stop some drivers from operating cars without it. In situations in which these uninsured drivers cause accidents, the injured party would have no way to receive compensation. The injured party could attempt to sue the uninsured driver, but a person who cannot afford to pay her car insurance premiums usually has no other assets.

The standard uninsured motorist coverage clause usually provides the following:

> The insurance company agrees to pay compensatory damages which the insured is legally entitled to recover from the owner or operator of an uninsured motor vehicle when:
>
> - The insured incurs bodily injury caused by an accident and
> - Property damage is incurred due to an accident.
> - The owner/operator's liability for damages must arise out of the ownership, use, or maintenance of an uninsured motor vehicle.

Before a plaintiff can take advantage of the UM coverage provision in her policy, there are certain procedural steps that must be followed. In many states, for instance, the plaintiff/insured must give the insurance company 30 days' notice that she will request the full amount of the UM policy limits. Other common procedural steps include additional requirements if the potential claim is greater than the coverage. Before proceeding on a UM claim in any state, a paralegal should spend some time getting familiar with the procedural requirements.

G. UNDERINSURED MOTORIST COVERAGE

A standard underinsured motorist (UIM) coverage clause provides the following:

> The insurance company agrees to pay compensatory damages that the insured is legally entitled to recover from the owner or operator of an underinsured motor vehicle when:
>
> - The insured incurs bodily injury caused by an accident.
> - The owner/operator's liability for damages must arise out of the ownership, use, or maintenance of an underinsured motor vehicle. The insurance company will only pay such damages when the limits of liability under any applicable insurance policy have been exhausted.

Sidebar

Many states exclude punitive damages under UIM payments.

H. IMPORTANT PROVISIONS IN TYPICAL AUTOMOBILE POLICIES

Although an insurance policy can run to dozens of pages and contain language dealing with a wealth of issues (see Figure 13-3), for a paralegal working at either a plaintiffs' firm or a defense firm, there are only a handful of provisions that are critically important. Among these are the insurance company's duty to defend the insured, the insurance company's right of subrogation, and the topic of "stacking."

FIGURE 13-3	■ Declarations Page (lists the name of the insured, the automobiles covered, the policy limits, and any drivers who are covered by the policy) ■ Definitions ■ Coverage for Damage to Your Auto (Collision/Comprehensive Coverage)	■ Liability Coverage (Bodily Injury/ Property Damage) ■ Medical Payments ■ Uninsured Motorist Coverage ■ Underinsured Motorist Coverage ■ Insured's Duties After Accident ■ General Provisions
Parts of a Typical Automobile Insurance Policy		

1. DUTY TO DEFEND

One of the main duties that an insurance company has under its policy is to provide a legal defense for an insured when she is sued by someone and the suit is covered by the policy. In a typical example, the insured is involved in a car wreck and the other party sues her for negligence. Under this scenario, the insurance company has an obligation to provide a defense for the insured.

How does the insurance company meet this obligation? Usually, the insurance company hires an attorney to represent the insured in the lawsuit. This attorney represents the insured but is paid by the insurance company. The attorney who represents the insured owes her duty to the insured, even though the insurance company is paying for her services. This duty to defend has spawned a whole class of attorneys who specialize in insurance defense work. We discuss insurance defense firms (and plaintiffs' firms) later in this chapter.

Suppose, for example, that the insurance company wrongfully denies the insured paid legal counsel. What options does the insured have? The insured can bring suit against the insurance company seeking a court order declaring that the insurance company has a legal obligation to provide (and pay for) the insured's defense. This means that there would actually be two lawsuits pending: a negligence action, in which the insured is the defendant and the plaintiff is the person injured in the accident, and a second action based on breach of contract, in which the insured is the plaintiff and the insurance company is the defendant. This second action is usually in the form of an action for declaratory judgment. (An example of a declaratory judgment on this issue is provided at the end of this chapter, under Forms and Court Documents.)

2. SUBROGATION

Subrogation
In claiming a legal right or a debt, the substitution of one person for another.

The term **subrogation** refers to the insurance company's right to sue the tortfeasor in its own right to recover the money it has paid out to the insured. In essence, subrogation works this way: The insured files a claim for injuries caused by a negligent driver. The insurance company pays the claim, and the insured is satisfied. However, the insurance company is now out the money it has paid on the claim. If the insurance policy contains a subrogation claim, it permits the insurance company to file suit in its own right against the negligent driver to recover for the damages that she caused and that the insurance company subsequently paid out to its insured. Usually, this right to "stand in the shoes" of the insured is set out in the policy. Part of this right of subrogation may also include the insurance company's ability to call the insured to testify at trial. In fact, most insurance policies contain provisions in which the insured promises not to hinder the insurance company's subrogation action against another. See Figure 13-4 for an example of a subrogation clause.

One insurance company can file a subrogation claim against another insurance company. Suppose that Insurance Company A has paid more than its share of damages to an insured. It can seek reimbursement for the excess payment from Insurance Company B.

3. "STACKING" OF POLICIES

In situations in which the insured's policy limits are not enough to cover her medical payments, is there a way of increasing the available pool of funds? Is there a way, for instance, to add the policy limits of the insured's policy to that of another policy? The short answer is yes, with certain limitations. **Stacking** insurance policies means that two (or more) policies are combined, thus increasing the overall policy limits.

Example: Ted has been injured in a car accident. His policy limit for medical payments is $15,000. Ted's friend, John, was actually driving Ted's car at the time of the collision. John's medical payment policy limit is $50,000. Under certain circumstances, Ted can increase his overall policy limit to $65,000 by combining, or stacking, his insurance policy with John's policy.

a. Limit of Liability Provisions and Stacking

Insurance companies attempt to limit stacking by inserting language in the "limits of liability" clause of the policy that is usually some variation of the following:

> The insurance company's "limit of liability" shown on the Declarations Page of this policy is the maximum "limit of liability" for each person injured in any one accident, regardless of the number of:
>
> 1. claims made;
> 2. vehicles or premiums shown on the Declarations Page; or
> 3. vehicles involved in the accident.

Stacking
The policy limits of one policy are added to the policy limits of one or more other policies, increasing the available funds to the sum of all policies.

Stacking is commonly seen in cases involving underinsured motorist (UIM) and uninsured motorist (UM) cases.

This Company may require from the insured an assignment of all right of recovery against any party for loss to the extent that payment therefore is made by this Company.

FIGURE 13-4

Typical Subrogation Clause

When the policy does not specifically exclude stacking, policies can be combined in a variety of ways:

- For injury to the insured
- For injury to the insured's relative (while occupying a car covered by the policy)
- For an injury to the insured while occupying a car owned by the insured but not covered by the insured's policy
- For an injury to the insured while occupying another person's insured automobile
- For an injury to the insured when she was not occupying an automobile, but was injured by an insured driver in another vehicle

The rules regarding stacking vary considerably from state to state. When considering the applicability of stacking to the facts of a particular case, research stacking under your state's laws.

I. "NO-FAULT" INSURANCE

In the traditional approach to a personal injury case, the judge or jury ultimately determines who was at fault and then forces that person to pay the damages. There are at least two flaws in this system: It can take months, if not years, for a claim to be settled, and juries can sometimes be capricious in their awards. The concept of **no-fault insurance** was created to deal with both of these shortcomings.

Under a no-fault system, the insurance company pays for the insured's damages, whether the insured was at fault in the accident or not. Obviously, people who are insured under a no-fault system receive immediate compensation for damages, because there is no need for a trial to determine fault. But there is a quid pro quo. In a no-fault system, the insured is limited in the types of actions and damages she can receive from the other driver. For instance, in no-fault states, the injured party may not be entitled to pain and suffering

Sidebar

Among the states that have adopted no-fault insurance are Massachusetts, New Jersey, New York, Pennsylvania, Colorado, Florida, Hawaii, Kansas, Michigan, Minnesota, Utah, North Dakota, and Kentucky.

No-fault insurance
Insurance that requires an insurance company to pay for the insured's damages regardless of who was at fault in causing the damage.

Sidebar

In some states, no-fault coverage is referred to as "personal injury protection," or PIP.

FIGURE 13-5		
Advantages and Disadvantages of No-Fault Insurance	**Advantages:** ■ Faster payment of claims ■ Less litigation ■ Lower insurance rates (in theory) ■ Fewer large jury verdicts	**Disadvantages:** ■ Pain and suffering awards are not permitted ■ Negligent drivers are "protected" from their bad driving ■ Higher insurance rates (in practice) ■ Does not pay for property damage (usually covered by some other part of the policy)

awards. See Figure 13-5 for a comparison of the advantages and disadvantages of no-fault insurance.

If no-fault insurance sounds like a radical concept, it is interesting to note that all states have at least an element of no-fault in their automobile insurance policies. For instance, under most policies, medical payments and property damage are paid to the insured without regard to fault.

J. EXCLUSIONS

An insurance policy does not apply in all situations. For example, one evening, Ted has too much to drink at a local bar and decides to drive home. En route, he runs off the road and damages his car. He calls a tow truck, and while the tow-truck driver is pulling his car out of a ditch, a police officer drives up and begins questioning Ted. He smells alcohol on Ted's breath and eventually charges him with driving under the influence of alcohol. Later, when Ted files a claim for property damage to his car, the insurance company refuses to pay. The company cites its **exclusion** for damages caused by the insured while under the influence of alcohol. As proof that the exclusion applies, they point out that Ted was cited for DUI shortly after damaging his car.

Exclusion
The persons, types of losses, or damages not covered by an insurance policy.

1. INTENTIONAL INJURIES

Almost all insurance policies contain an exclusion for the intentional actions of the insured. A typical example would read:

> The insurance policy does not provide any coverage for an insured who intentionally causes bodily injury and/or property damage.

This provision prevents an insured from deliberately injuring another or damaging property and then being able to circumvent responsibility for her actions by requiring her insurance company to pay for her intentional violence.

"Vehicle" has been defined to include not only automobiles and motorcycles, but also other conveyances that would not, at first glance, appear to fall into the category, such as horse-drawn carts, rowboats, and speed-boats. Tractors and trailers, on the other hand, do not.[5]

Accident policies are often written with numerous exclusions that limit the insurance company's liability. When a specific incident falls within an exclusion, the insurance company will refuse to pay.

TORT BASICS AT A GLANCE

2. OTHER EXCLUSIONS

Among the other types of exclusions are provisions that limit payment to situations when the insured is in a vehicle. This often triggers some interesting litigation. For example, see Figure 13-6 for various tests to determine if a conveyance is a "vehicle" that is covered by the policy.

| **FIGURE 13-6**

Determining If an Object Is a "Vehicle" | When a question arises about whether a particular mode of transportation is covered by an insurance policy, the courts will look to:

■ how the vehicle was used;   ■ whether it was licensed by the
■ how it was constructed;   state; and
                                    ■ how risky it is to operate. |

VIII HOW INSURANCE COVERAGE AFFECTS SETTLEMENT

How is the word accident *defined? Is there a legal definition of this term that supplants the generally accepted definition? The answer is no.* Accident *and* accidental *have never been given an all-inclusive legal definition. Most jurisdictions simply require that this word, when found in an insurance policy, be construed in its common and ordinary way.*[6]

Because insurance is such an important issue in the lawsuit, the plaintiff's attorney wants to know, as early as possible, what amount of coverage the defendant has. If the defendant has only the minimum coverage required by law and the plaintiff's damages are extensive, this will affect how the attorney proceeds on the case or even her decision whether to accept the case.

A. DISCOVERY ISSUES WITH INSURANCE

For many years, the issue of revealing the defendant's policy limits was hotly contested. Defendants, and insurance companies, were usually reluctant to provide this information to the plaintiff, often in the belief that it would affect the way the suit was prosecuted. The issue was finally settled on the federal level by the passage of Rule 26 of the Federal Rules of Evidence. That rule is set out in Figure 13-7. Many states have followed the federal rule. With that change, learning the defendant's policy limits was made considerably easier.

Once the case is under way, the next consideration is settlement. Obviously, the plaintiff's attorney wishes to settle the case as early in the process as possible, while there may be several reasons why the defendant's attorney is in no particular hurry to settle. In situations in which the insurance company tenders the policy limits (i.e., they simply volunteer to pay the full amount of the insured's coverage), the pressure on the plaintiff to settle becomes intense. After all, the plaintiff will actually receive the policy limits, while she may not receive any additional money from the defendant individually, even if the jury awards her a large verdict.

| **FIGURE 13-7**

Rule 26, Federal Rules of Evidence. General Provisions Governing Discovery; Duty of Disclosure | (A) In General. Except as exempted by Rule 26(a)(1)(B) or as otherwise stipulated or ordered by the court, a party must, without awaiting a discovery request, provide to the other parties:

    (a)(1)(A)(iv) for inspection and copying as under Rule 34, any insurance agreement under which an insurance business may be liable to satisfy all or part of a possible judgment in the action or to indemnify or reimburse for payments made to satisfy the judgment. |

Settlement negotiations involve the plaintiff's attorney and the defendant's attorney. Before finishing our discussion of settlement, we take a slight side journey into the world of both of these legal teams so that we can understand the different types of pressures brought to bear on these attorneys and how they handle these pressures.

B. SPECIALIZATION AMONG PERSONAL INJURY ATTORNEYS

Attorneys who handle personal injury cases tend to specialize as either plaintiffs' attorneys or insurance defense attorneys. There are several reasons for this specialization. One reason is simple preference. Some attorneys enjoy representing plaintiffs and occasionally "taking on Goliath" to see if they can win. Other attorneys might find it more rewarding, both financially and emotionally, to represent defendants. Other reasons for this split are more practical. Once an attorney handles a number of plaintiffs' cases, he is better versed in that approach and might find changing sides a difficult adjustment. An insurance defense attorney, on the other hand, might find switching to the plaintiff's side not only impractical but also difficult because of conflict-of-interest claims. Consider an attorney who has worked with ABC Insurance Company for the past ten years, representing its policyholders in court, who then decides to take a plaintiff's case against the same company. This would raise a whole host of ethical problems. As a result, most attorneys spend their legal careers on one side or the other.

1. PLAINTIFFS' FIRMS

We discussed plaintiffs' firms in Chapter 4, but an additional word about them here is warranted. The attorney who represents the plaintiff in a personal injury case almost always does so under a contingency fee agreement. Under this agreement, the attorney is entitled to a percentage of the final award. The typical arrangement is for the attorney to receive 33 percent of the final recovery. If the jury awards a $3 million verdict, $1 million goes to the plaintiff's firm. However, if the plaintiff receives nothing at the end of the case, the attorney also receives nothing. This arrangement, although it induces an attorney to work hard to get the highest possible amount for the client, also puts a great deal of financial pressure on the plaintiff's attorney. Until the case is settled, there is essentially no money coming in. For a plaintiffs' attorney to remain in practice, he must have cases settling or reaching final verdict on a regular basis.

2. INSURANCE DEFENSE FIRMS

Attorneys and paralegals who work for insurance defense firms often have a standing agreement with one or more insurance companies that they will provide a legal defense to the insurance company's policyholders who are sued. Usually, insurance defense firms bill by the hour. It is virtually unheard of for an insurance defense attorney to work on a contingency basis for an insurance company. The insurance policy provides that the company will pay for the insured's legal defense. This means that the defendant's attorney represents the defendant but is actually paid by the insurance company. Any possible ethical complexities arising from this arrangement were settled decades ago by consistent court decisions that mandated that the defense attorney's responsibility is to the defendant, not the insurance company.

Insurance defense firms concentrate a great deal of energy on billing their clients. Usually, these firms bill insurance companies on a monthly basis. These bills are itemized so that the insurance companies can see exactly what the firm has done in the past four weeks. This system, although more financially stable than the plaintiffs' firm, brings its own pressures. For instance, some insurance defense firms have been known to overbill insurance companies or even charge for work that was not done. The financial temptation to bill for every possible legal activity sometimes becomes too great. Ethical insurance defense firms do not engage in such practices, but they often put great pressure on attorneys and paralegals to keep a strict accounting of the time they spend on individual cases to make sure that the firm is paid for the work that is actually done.

These are the two sides that are brought together in a personal injury suit. The plaintiff is represented by a capable attorney who will not earn her fee until the case ends successfully. The insurance defense attorney, on the other hand, makes the same amount of money per hour whether the case settles or not. Why then would the defendant's attorney ever seek to settle a case? Shouldn't all defense attorneys stand fast and never bargain in good faith? Certainly, the longer they work on the case, the more hours they can bill. But there are other considerations for insurance defense attorneys. For one thing, there are the ethical rules. If the defendant wishes to settle the case and reaching a settlement would be in the best interests of the client, the insurance company, and ultimately the overburdened court system, a lawyer will try to work out a settlement. There are other, more pragmatic concerns for the insurance defense attorney as well. If the attorney never seeks to settle cases and consistently loses cases at trial, the insurance company is likely to seek other counsel.

C. SETTLEMENT

When both sides to a suit seek to settle a case, they are actually engaging in a form of contract. One side promises to do something in exchange for a promise (or a payment) from the other side. We take an example from the Chumley case.

After extensively investigating the case, Mr. Chumley's attorney filed suit against the railroad company alleging negligence. Now, in an effort to bring the case to a conclusion, the plaintiff's attorney serves a settlement demand letter on the attorneys who represent the railroad company. The letter is set out in Figure 13-8.

For additional materials on the Chumley case, please see Appendices A–E.

D. RELEASES

Once a case is settled, the parties release one another from the claims in the lawsuit. A **release** is an official relinquishment of the plaintiff's claim against the defendant, in exchange for the money paid through the settlement. When a party signs a release, she is foregoing all possible actions she may have against the other. The end result of the settlement is a complete dismissal of the complaint, often in the form of a dismissal with prejudice (although it may be called by another name in some jurisdictions).

Release
To surrender or give up a legal right to sue another; the document or court filing in which this right is surrendered.

I. M. Lawyer, P.A.
444 Eaton Street
Beauty Spring, PL 28655
Phone: (828)439-4476
Fax: (828)439-4995 E-mail: lawyer@juno.com

April 24, 2003

Allnation Insurance Company
300 Dollar Street
Capitol City, PL 28888

Re: Claimant: Charles Chumley
    Insured: Charles Chumley
    Date of Loss: August 23, 2002
    Claim No.:   66563

Dear Sir or Madam:

I have been retained by Charles Chumley with respect to recovery of damages due to personal injuries suffered by Mr. Chumley in a train collision which occurred on August 23, 2002, and which involved your insured, National Railroad Company, Inc.

I have been directed to do everything that is necessary to present, settle, and collect this claim for damages.

I have evaluated this claim for settlement purposes. This letter and the enclosures are presented to you for the purpose of attempting to settle this claim.

I. Liability

National Railroad Company owns and maintains a section of railroad tracks passing through the Town of Cling, Placid, at an intersection with Morgan Street in that town (Railroad Crossing # 2156E). There are no railroad crossing arms or warning devices at that intersection. This intersection had vegetation and trees obstructing and/or severely restricting the view of Morgan Street. National Railroad Company failed to maintain the vegetation and trees growing at this intersection right-of-way. The railroad company owed a duty of care to reasonably and safely maintain the tracks and the right-of-way surrounding the tracks at this intersection.

FIGURE 13-8

Settlement
Letter in the
Chumley Case

FIGURE 13-8

(continued)

On August 23, 2002, at approximately 4:30 P.M., the Railroad's train struck Mr. Chumley's automobile as his automobile attempted to cross the tracks at Morgan Street. The train knocked Mr. Chumley's automobile off the road and pushed the car approximately 100 yards down the tracks from the point of impact. Mr. Chumley was severely injured, and his wife, Julia, was killed.

II. General Damages

As a result of the incident, Mr. Chumley has suffered a number of injuries, endured medical examinations, and suffered short-term and long-term health consequences. Injuries resulting from the collision include a closed-head injury, fractured left tibia, internal hemorrhaging, hemo-pneumothorax, and severe abdominal trauma. In addition, he had five broken ribs and a left hip fracture. Seven days after the collision, Mr. Chumley had a tracheostomy placed. Infection set in thereafter, causing acute and chronic bronchitis.

For several weeks after the collision, Mr. Chumley remained in a coma, with his breathing controlled by mechanical ventilation. It took several weeks after coming out of the coma for Mr. Chumley to reorient himself to his surroundings. Doctors noted that Mr. Chumley suffered from short-term memory loss.

In October 2002, Mr. Chumley was diagnosed with diabetes mellitus. He has no family history of this disease, but Mr. Chumley's doctors have determined that the severe trauma he received from the collision, to his head and abdomen, and the resulting injuries to both his brain and pancreas are the most likely cause of the diabetes mellitus.

III. Loss of Consortium

As a result of the collision, Mrs. Julia Chumley, Mr. Chumley's wife of many years, was killed. Because of her death, Mr. Chumley has lost his spousal relationship and her assistance in their family home. He and their children have lost her companionship and affection forever.

IV. Enclosures

Enclosed are the following records and reports for your review:

1. Emergency Room Record, Mission Hospital
2. Operative Report, Mission Hospital
3. Medical Report from Dr. Dexter Cleckner, M.D., Barnes County Hospital
4. Medical Report from Dr. Melissa Walker, M.D., Thorne Rehabilitative Hospital

V. Settlement

If this case can be resolved within 30 days and without the expense of litigation, I would recommend settlement in the amount of $3,000,000.00.

Very truly yours,

I. M. Lawyer
Placid State Bar # 006640

Tech Topic
INSURANCE AND TECHNOLOGY

Anyone who has applied for health insurance in recent years knows how scrupulous insurance companies are in gathering information about the applicant's medical history. Prior to the enactment of the new health care laws, pre-existing conditions were routinely used as the reason for denial of coverage. To maximize profits, insurance companies are beginning to use technologically savvy methods for amassing even more personal information about applicants to ferret out real or presumed preexisting conditions.

Consider Google. Google makes its money by collecting information about its users and selling it to advertisers — including insurance companies. If you use Gmail, Google has every e-mail you've ever sent or received. When you use Google to search the Web, it retains every search you've ever made. So if you e-mail your mother about how much weight you've gained or search online for information about diabetes, a subsequent application for health insurance might be denied because the insurance company has that information.

Likewise, Facebook has even more interesting information: your pictures, your comments, your likes, your friends, your activities. Again, all of this information is aggregated and sold to advertisers. Do you complain to your Facebook friends about your migraine headaches? Does a photo show you smoking a cigarette? An insurance company might see either of these as reasons to deny coverage.

Another potential tactic in the insurance game is genetic testing. If your DNA reveals a predisposition to a certain disease, insurance companies argue that they should have that information. Unfortunately, when one person carries a gene mutation, it is likely that other members of that person's family could as well. Thus, insurance companies could possibly deny coverage to the extended family.

So far, the U.S. legal system has not addressed these issues. But as technology continues to advance, maintaining privacy will become an even greater problem.

Case Excerpt

STATE FARM MUT. AUTO. INS. CO. v. SWARTZ
2006 WL 1118924 (Ohio App. 5 Dist. 2006)

EDWARDS, J.

Defendant-appellant Melvin R. Swartz appeals from the June 7, 2005, Judgment Entry of the Richland County Court of Common Pleas which entered judgment in favor of plaintiff-appellee State Farm Mutual Automobile Insurance Company against appellant in the amount of $30,000.00.

Statement of the Facts and Case

This case arises from a motor vehicle accident which occurred on March 25, 2002, in Mansfield, Ohio. The accident involved three motor vehicles. One of the vehicles was driven by Billy J. Stamper. Stamper had an automobile insurance policy with State Farm Mutual Automobile Insurance Company [hereinafter appellee]. Appellant was driving one of the other vehicles. Appellant failed to stop his vehicle at a stop sign at an intersection and attempted to make a right-hand turn onto another street. Appellant's vehicle was struck from behind by a southbound vehicle (the third vehicle involved) operated by Paul E. Temple, II, a non-party. After the impact, appellant's vehicle went left of center and struck, head on, the motor vehicle operated by Stamper. According to appellee and Stamper, Stamper incurred serious bodily injury as a direct and proximate result of the impact. Stamper submitted a claim to State Farm. State Farm paid $30,000.00 to/and on behalf of Mr. Stamper for personal injuries.

On May 24, 2004, appellee filed a complaint in the Richland County Court of Common Pleas. Appellee sought payment from appellant for the sum paid to Stamper claiming a right to subrogation. Subsequently, appellant filed a motion to dismiss alleging that appellee had failed to join an indispensable party, namely, Temple. The trial court overruled appellant's motion by a Judgment Entry filed June 2, 2004.

The case proceeded to trial on May 31, 2005. During the trial, appellant filed a motion for directed verdict. In that motion, appellant contended that appellee failed to prove it had a right to subrogation because it failed to present Stamper's insurance policy or otherwise prove a right to subrogation of Stamper's claim. The trial court granted the motion for directed verdict on the issues of statutory and contractual subrogation. However, the trial court overruled the motion for directed verdict on the issue of equitable subrogation. Ultimately, the jury returned a verdict in favor of appellee in the amount of $30,000.00. The Judgment Entry on Jury Verdict was filed on June 7, 2005.

It is from the June 7, 2005, Judgment Entry that appellant appeals, raising the following assignments of error:

> The Trial Court Erred in Not Directing the Verdict for the Defendant and Allowing This Case to Procedd [sic] to Jury Decision as the Plaintiff Produced No Evidence of a Contract or any Obligation on the Plaintiff's Part to Pay the Damages and Allowing Equitable Subrogation and the Plaintiff to Recover on That Inappropriate Claim.

In the third assignment of error, appellant argues that the trial court should have directed a verdict in favor of appellant because appellee failed to produce evidence of a contract or obligation on appellant's part to pay the damages suffered by Stamper and that appellee was not entitled to equitable subrogation. In other words, appellant contends that appellee failed to produce sufficient evidence to entitle appellee to a right of subrogation. We disagree.

As stated in assignment of error II, the standard of review for the grant or denial of a motion for directed verdict is as follows: whether there was probative evidence which, if believed, would permit reasonable minds to come to different conclusions as to the essential elements of the case, construing the evidence most strongly in favor of the non-movant. *Sanek v. Duracote Corp.* (1989), 43 Ohio St. 3d 169, 172, 539 N.E.2d 1114. This is a question of law, not one of fact. *Hargrove v. Tanner* (1990), 66 Ohio App. 3d 693, 695, 586 N.E.2d 141; *Vosgerichian v. Mancini Shah & Associates, et al.* (Feb. 29, 1996), Cuyahoga App. Nos. 68931 and 68943, 1996 WL 86684.

There are three distinct kinds of subrogation: legal (equitable), statutory and conventional (contractural). *Blue Cross & Blue Shield Mut. of Ohio v. Hrenko,* 72 Ohio St. 3d 120, 1995-Ohio-306, 647 N.E.2d 1358. The trial court sustained appellant's motion for directed verdict as to conventional (or contractual) subrogation and statutory subrogation. Specifically, the trial court found that appellee failed to provide proof that the contract of insurance between appellee and Stamper contained a subrogation clause and there was no applicable statutory right of subrogation. The trial court found that only an equitable (or legal) subrogation claim survived. Accordingly, the trial court's award of damages was premised upon an equitable subrogation claim.

Legal or equitable subrogation is a doctrine "under which, as a result of the payment of a debt by a person other than the principal debtor, there is a substitution of the former in the place of the creditor to whose rights he succeeds in relation to the obligation of the debtor, to the end that the burden of obligation be ultimately placed upon those to whom it primarily belongs, although in the recognition of the rights of others it may have been, for a time, borne by those who are only secondarily liable for the debt." *Maryland Cas. Co. v. Gough* (1946), 146 Ohio St. 305, 315, 65 N.E.2d 858. Equitable subrogation entitles an insurer to all the rights and remedies of the insured against a third party if: (1) the insurer indemnifies the insured for a loss occasioned by the third party; and (2) the loss is covered by the insurance policy.

Medical payment subrogation has been enforced under the doctrine of equitable subrogation. In *Allstate Ins. Co. v. LaCivita* (Aug. 9, 1996), Portage App. No. 94-P-0118, 1996 WL 494800, the court adopted the rationale that "the equitable right of subrogation is the legal effect of payment, and inures to the insurer without any formal assignment or any express stipulation to that effect in the policy." Id. at 6 (citing *State Farm Mut. Auto. Ins. Co. v. Scott* (Dec. 20, 1993), Clinton App. No. CA93-05-013); In accord, *Travelers Indemnity Co. v. Brooks* (1977), 60 Ohio App. 2d 37, 38-39, 395 N.E.2d 494. In *LaCivita,* the court held that because the insurer proved, through the testimony of the insured that it was her insurance company, that she made a claim for damages to the automobile, and that it paid the amount of damages to the vehicle, the doctrine of equitable subrogation was applicable.

We agree with the above cited decisions. Accordingly, we turn to the evidence to determine if appellee demonstrated an equitable claim. In this case, appellee presented testimony that Stamper had an automobile insurance policy from appellee, that Stamper made a claim for injuries sustained in the accident and that appellee paid for the damages arising from that injury. We find that appellee met its burden to prove an equitable subrogation claim.

For the foregoing reasons, appellant's third assignment of error is overruled.

The judgment of the Richland County Court of Appeals is affirmed.

GWIN, P.J. and FARMER, J. concur.

Judgment Entry

For the reasons stated in our accompanying Memorandum-Opinion on file, the judgment of the Richland County Court of Common Pleas is affirmed. Costs assessed to appellant.

Questions about the case:

1. What was the basis of the insurance company's action against Swartz?
2. What are the three distinct kinds of subrogation?
3. What is legal or equitable subrogation?
4. Where does the equitable right of subrogation come from?
5. Did the insurance company present enough evidence to justify receiving payment from Swartz for the medical payments it made on behalf of its insured? Explain.

Chapter Summary

Insurance is a complicated topic and involves many aspects of law. Insurance policies are actually contracts between the insurance company and the insured in which the insurance company promises to indemnify or reimburse the insured for losses covered by the policy in exchange for the insured's premium payments. Insurance coverage is a crucial issue in personal injury cases for several reasons. For one, the insurance policy's monetary limits often determine the size of the plaintiff's ultimate award in a case. For another, the insurance company has, among its other obligations, the duty to provide a legal defense to an insured who is being sued.

Interpreting how insurance law applies to a given factual situation is often difficult. For instance, in some cases, individual insurance policies can be combined, or "stacked," to provide additional coverage to a person who has suffered injury. In other situations, "no-fault" insurance may be state law. Under no-fault, the insurance company pays a claim without first determining who was the cause of the injury. Automobile insurance is further complicated by the fact that all states have statutes requiring that motorists possess at least a minimum amount of coverage before they are allowed to drive. These statutes not only regulate drivers; they also regulate insurance companies. The insurance industry is one of the most heavily regulated industries in the country, and this regulation applies not only to how individual policies are drafted, but also to the type of exclusions that an insurance company is allowed to make. An exclusion is a listed reason why the insurance company will not pay a claim. Typical exclusions include intentional destructive acts by the insured and alcohol or other drug use.

Finally, this chapter also explored the world of plaintiffs' and insurance defense law firms. These firms have very different approaches to cases that are not only the product of the different ways that they are compensated, but also stem from different demands placed on them by their clients. Insurance defense firms, for instance, are hired by insurance companies to defend policyholders who have been sued. They are, therefore, paid by the insurance company but owe their legal duty to the insured.

SKILLS YOU NEED IN THE REAL WORLD

Deciphering Insurance Policies

Many times during your legal career, you will find yourself reading insurance policies. Insurance policies are hard to read because they are lengthy documents filled with obscure terms and often include confusing subparts and references. When reviewing an insurance policy, here is a five-step process to help you master the details.

1. Start with the Declarations Page

The declarations page is a separate sheet that contains basic information about the policy. Some of the information that you will find on this page includes the following:

- The insurance policy number (critical for any correspondence with the insurance company)
- The date the policy became effective
- The named insured
- The vehicles covered

2. Review the Coverage

Once you have looked over and noted the basic identifying information, your next stop should be the information provided about coverage. A sample is provided in Figure 13-9.

3. Read through the Definitions

Most insurance policies contain a section entitled "definitions." This section specifically defines any important term used in the policy. If you wish to see how the insurance company defines "business purpose," you can find its definition here. Definitions can become crucial in any litigation with an insurance policy. Remember that most jurisdictions construe any ambiguities in the policy against the insurance company, so if there is a problem with a definition, better to know about it sooner rather than later.

FIGURE 13-9	Coverage	Limits
Coverage Provisions from a Sample Declarations Page	Liability Bodily Injury Each Person/Each Accident	$300,000/$300,000
	Property Damage Each Accident	$100,000
	Medical Payments Each Person	$1,000
	Combined UM/UIM Coverage Bodily Injury Liability Each Person/Each Accident	$300,000/$300,000
	Combined UM/UIM Coverage Property Damage	$100,000

4. Review the Limits of Liability

This important provision is where the insurance company spells out the conditions under which it will not be required to pay out damages. Review this section carefully to make sure that the accident or the people involved in your cases are not excluded under the terms of the policy. You should also confirm that there are no actions taken by the parties involved in the case that put them outside the insurance policy's coverage. A common example is the use of alcohol or drugs that caused the collision. Such behavior is frequently excluded from coverage in most insurance policies.

5. Confirm What Is Covered

Finally, go through the section marked "Insuring Agreement" or "Policy Agreement," and note exactly what the insurance policy does cover. For instance, under the Medical Payments Coverage section, does the company pay for acupuncture, chiropractic, or other categories of medical treatment? How does the insurance company limit or define medical fees? All of these points are critical in applying the insurance policy to the particular case.

 THE LIFE OF A PARALEGAL

Obtaining Records

I worked as a computer programs analyst for years before getting laid off and deciding to go back to school to become a paralegal. I went to work for a small firm almost as soon as I started my classes. I was surprised at how different a law office was from other types of offices. My biggest problem was that my "secretarial skills" — for want of a better term — weren't what they could have been. I had to learn some of the basics, like the right way to take a phone message. When I first started answering the phone, I'd just jot down the person's name and telephone number. When I handed it to the attorney, he'd say, "What's this about?" After that, I learned that you had to get more information. I had to learn how to type up letters and motions from a tape machine. The attorney I worked with just used a tape recorder. He'd dictate everything, and I'd have to type it up from the tapes.

The firm I work for handles just about everything, although we concentrate on personal injury cases. My particular specialty — learned through a lot of trial and error — is getting medical records. Contacts are everything when you're trying to get records. I think I was lucky when I first started doing it because I was honest with people. I'd call them up and say, "Hey, I don't know what I'm doing. I'm new, so forgive me if I mess up." Once I got a name, like someone at the hospital records department, whenever I called back, I'd always ask for that person. I still do that. If I'm not sure about exactly what I'm doing when I call someone up, I'll just tell them. Most people are really friendly to you. Once I get the records ordered, I keep track of them. I get them all organized and filed so that the attorney can go through them later and get what he needs out of them. I'll sift through them all and find out exactly what insurance paid and what the client paid. I'll summarize all of this information for ease of reference and make sure that the attorney sees it.

The way I see the role of the paralegal, I'm here to free up some of the attorney's time so that he can make more money. The more money he makes, the better it is for all of us. That's how I approach everything I do, from answering the phones to organizing medical records. What can I do that will make this easier on the attorney, and free him up to get some more clients so that he can keep paying me?

Leah Laidley, Paralegal

ETHICAL ISSUES FOR THE PARALEGAL: INSURANCE FRAUD

Studies have shown that one out of three automobile insurance claims involves some type of fraud. Fraudulent insurance claims account for 10 to 20 percent of the average premium. Insurance fraud arrests have also increased dramatically over the past three years and cost the economy over $80 billion a year. All of these factors point to a disturbing reality: If you work for a personal injury firm for any length of time, some of your clients will engage in insurance fraud.

Defrauding an insurance company appears to be one of the so-called victimless crimes. After all, who is going to feel sorry for a large corporation? Policyholders may sometimes feel that they are entitled to some return on the premiums they have been paying for years. Financial pressures may also figure prominently in the policyholder's decision to commit fraud. How can you, as a paralegal, avoid becoming involved in insurance fraud? Here are some telltale signs:

- The client continually inflates, exaggerates, or overstates her losses.
- The amount of loss seems to be out of line with the visual damages.
- The client has had numerous other claims with other insurance companies.

The good news for a paralegal is that the one thing you can do to avoid having the firm implicated in an insurance fraud case is the one thing you should be doing already: documenting the file. You should insist on proper documentation of every claim. No matter what loss the client claims he has suffered, you must have documentation of the extent of the loss and out-of-pocket expenses. You will need this information when you prepare for settlement anyway; getting it will also avoid any claim that you or your firm is involved in an insurance scam.

If you suspect that one of your clients is attempting to defraud the insurance company, report your suspicions to the attorney immediately. This may be a client that the firm would be better off not representing.

Relevant Cases

BIRTH CENTER V. ST. PAUL COMPANIES, INC.
567 Pa. 386, 787 A.2d 376 (2001)

Opinion
NEWMAN, Justice.

The St. Paul Companies, Inc. ("St. Paul") appeals from an Order of the Superior Court that reversed the Order of the Court of Common Pleas of Delaware County ("trial court"), which granted St. Paul's motion for judgment notwithstanding the verdict. The jury found, by clear and convincing evidence, that St. Paul acted in bad faith when it refused to settle a civil action against The Birth Center ("Birth Center"), and that St. Paul's bad faith conduct was a substantial factor in causing The Birth Center to incur compensatory damages in the amount of $700,000.00.

We affirm the decision of the Superior Court. Where an insurer refuses to settle a claim that could have been resolved within policy limits without "a bona fide belief . . . that it has a good possibility of winning," it breaches its contractual duty to act in good faith and its fiduciary duty to its insured. Therefore, the insurer is liable for the known and/or foreseeable compensatory damages of its insured that reasonably flow from the bad faith conduct of the insurer. The fact that the insurer's intransigent failure to engage in settlement negotiations forced it to pay damages far in excess of the policy limits

so as to avoid a punitive damages award, does not insulate the insurer from liability for its insured's compensatory damages where the insured can prove that the insurer's bad faith conduct caused the damages.

Factual and Procedural History

The Underlying Action—Norris v. The Birth Center

This claim arose out of St. Paul's bad faith refusal to engage in settlement negotiations in the underlying action, Norris. In that case, Gerald and Denise Norris ("Parents") filed suit on November 16, 1986 against Birth Center alleging that its negligence during the birth of their daughter Lindsey, caused her to suffer severe physical injury and permanent brain damage. After service of the complaint, The Birth Center turned to St. Paul, its professional liability insurance carrier, for its legal defense. St. Paul hired counsel to defend The Birth Center and undertook an investigation of the Parents' claim.

On August 2, 1991, the Parents proposed, on behalf of Lindsey, to settle the case within the limits of The Birth Center's professional liability insurance policy with St. Paul. The Birth Center notified St. Paul that it was making a firm demand to settle the case within its policy limits.

On August 7, 1991, St. Paul refused to settle or to even make an offer of settlement.

During the course of an August 8, 1991 pre-trial conference, the presiding judge recommended settlement of Norris within the limits of The Birth Center's insurance policy. Again, St. Paul refused. At a second pre-trial conference, a second judge assigned to the case also recommended settlement within Birth Center's policy limits. The Birth Center demanded settlement in accordance with the judge's recommendation; but St. Paul refused to negotiate or offer any money.

In January of 1992, St. Paul requested the defense attorneys for The Birth Center and one of the doctors involved in Lindsey's delivery to prepare pre-trial reports for St. Paul's consideration. In her report to St. Paul, defense counsel for The Birth Center stated that The Birth Center had, at best, a fifty-percent chance of successfully defending the lawsuit at trial. Furthermore, she advised that the jury verdict could range from $1,250,000.00 to $1,500,000.00. The doctor's defense counsel advised St. Paul that he believed that The Birth Center had a thirty-five percent chance of winning at trial and predicted a jury verdict of $5,000,000.00 to $6,000,000.00.

On January 27, 1992, the executive director of The Birth Center put St. Paul on written notice of the potential for compensatory damages and expressed her deep concerns regarding the possibility of a verdict in excess of Birth Center's policy limits. She explained that such a verdict would have devastating effects upon The Birth Center and could risk its continued existence. When expressing the same concerns to the St. Paul claims representative assigned to the case, the claims representative informed her that St. Paul tries "all of these bad baby cases, and we're going to trial."

Before the commencement of the Norris trial, a third judge, who ultimately presided over that trial, held another conference and recommended settlement within The Birth Center's policy limits. St. Paul refused to make any offer whatsoever. Then, on February

12, 1993, the Parents made a high/low offer of settlement, in which St. Paul would pay a non-refundable $300,000.00 amount regardless of the verdict. If, however, the jury returned a verdict in excess of Birth Center's policy limits, the Parents agreed to accept the policy limits as total satisfaction of the verdict. Finally, the settlement offer provided that if the jury returned a verdict lower than The Birth Center's maximum coverage, but higher than the low figure of $300,000.00, then the Parents would accept such verdict as full satisfaction of The Birth Center's liability. St. Paul refused this offer of settlement and made no counter-offer.

On February 16, 1993, the day of trial, a final pre-trial conference took place in the robing room of the trial judge. At this time, the Parents reasserted their high/low offer of settlement. The Birth Center expressed its desire that St. Paul agree to the Parents' proposal; but, a representative of St. Paul, present during the discussion in the robing room, rejected the high/low offer of settlement on the record. Following St. Paul's rejection, the judge stated that he believed that St. Paul's actions were in bad faith and that it was putting its interests ahead of those of its insured.

The Norris trial ensued. After the start of the trial, but before the jury returned a verdict, the trial judge instructed defense counsel for The Birth Center to contact St. Paul to see if it intended to make any offer of settlement. When counsel returned from her telephone conversation with St. Paul, she stated to those present in the robing room: "They must be crazy. They're not offering a dime. They won't give me authority to offer any money in this case, you know I can't believe it."

On March 4, 1993, the jury returned a verdict in favor of the Parents for $4,500,000.00, with The Birth Center liable for sixty percent of that amount. The final verdict was molded to include delay damages and interest and totaled $7,196,238. The Birth Center's ultimate liability amounted to $4,317,743.00. St. Paul agreed to indemnify The Birth Center for the entire verdict and the parties settled the case for $5,000,000. Before St. Paul paid the excess verdict, it requested that The Birth Center sign a release in exchange for the payment, but The Birth Center refused to sign the release. St. Paul paid on September 20, 1993.

The Birth Center v. St. Paul — The Bad Faith Action

On June 3, 1994, The Birth Center sued St. Paul, alleging that St. Paul breached its fiduciary duty to The Birth Center, its implied covenant of good faith, and its contract. The Birth Center also claimed that St. Paul's failure to settle Norris within its policy limits constituted negligence, reckless disregard for the rights of Birth Center, willful and wanton behavior and bad faith pursuant to the Bad Faith Statute, 42 Pa.C.S.A. §8371.

On May 3, 1996, the trial began. The Birth Center claimed that St. Paul's refusal to engage in reasonable settlement negotiations damaged "its business, reputation and credit." Appellee's Br. at 11. After the trial, the jury found, by clear and convincing evidence, that St. Paul acted in bad faith and that its actions were a substantial factor in bringing about harm to The Birth Center totaling, $700,000.00 in compensatory damages. The jury did not award punitive damages.

St. Paul moved for judgment notwithstanding the verdict. On February 7, 1997, the trial court granted St. Paul's motion. The trial court concluded that St. Paul's payment of the excess verdict nullified Birth Center's bad faith claim, that compensatory damages are not available pursuant to 42 Pa.C.S.A. §8371, and that, because it believed that it had not charged the jury on the breach of contract claim, that The Birth Center could not recover compensatory damages based on that theory. See *The Birth Center v. St. Paul Companies, Inc.*, No. 94-6492, slip op. at 9 (C.P. Delaware County Aug 11, 1997). The trial court denied The Birth Center's motion for reconsideration. On June 10, 1997, the trial court entered judgment in favor of St. Paul.

On appeal, the Superior Court determined that the payment of the excess verdict did not preclude the award of compensatory damages and that the trial court had charged the jury on breach of contract. Therefore, it reversed the decision of the trial court, reinstated the jury award, and remanded the case for a determination of The Birth Center's entitlement to interest, attorney's fees and costs pursuant to 42 Pa.C.S.A. §8371.

St. Paul appealed the Superior Court's decision to this Court.

Discussion

St. Paul's Arguments in Opposition to the Award of Compensatory Damages

St. Paul sets forth four reasons why it is not liable for Birth Center's compensatory damages. First, it asserts that its payment of the excess verdict barred Birth Center's bad faith claim. St. Paul argues that allowing bad faith claims despite an insurer's "voluntary" excess payment would discourage insurance companies from satisfying future excess verdicts. Second, St. Paul contends that *D'Ambrosio v. Pennsylvania National Mut. Ins.*, 494 Pa. 501, 431 A.2d 966 (1981) bars The Birth Center's claim. Third, St. Paul points to 42 Pa.C.S.A. §8371, which authorizes the award of punitive damages, attorneys' fees and costs when an insurer is found to have acted in bad faith, and asserts that because the statute does not mention compensatory damages, none are available. Fourth, St. Paul argues that the trial court did not charge the jury on The Birth Center's breach of contract claim and that, as a result, The Birth Center may not recover compensatory damages based on that claim. In turn, we address and reject St. Paul's arguments.

The Trial Court Charged the Jury on Breach of Contract

Although this is St. Paul's final argument, we address it first because if the trial court did not charge the jury on breach of contract, The Birth Center could only recover compensatory damages from St. Paul if some other theory provided a basis for recovery. As we discuss in this opinion, neither 42 Pa.C.S.A. §8371 nor any other relevant cause of action provide a basis for recovery. Thus, Birth Center's compensatory damage award depends on whether The Birth Center asserted a contract cause of action and whether the trial court charged the jury regarding that claim.

The Superior Court properly determined that The Birth Center asserted a breach of contract claim. Birth Center's Complaint requests compensatory damages based upon its insurance contract with St. Paul. Complaint ¶¶76-77. The Complaint provides:

> 76. By failing to settle the Norris claim within the limits of the insurance policy of The Birth Center, the Defendants herein breached their contractual obligations to The Birth Center under said policy of insurance, by failing to protect The Birth Center and their [sic] assets.
>
> 77. The Defendants herein, in the performance of the said contract, owed to The Birth Center, a fiduciary duty to act in good faith, and to use due care in representing The Birth Center's interests.
>
> WHEREFORE, Plaintiff The Birth Center demands judgment against Defendants in an amount in excess of . . . $50,000, plus additional compensatory and/or consequential damages allowed by law, together with interest thereon, Court costs, attorney's fees and such other relief as the Court deems just and proper.

Therefore, it is clear that The Birth Center alleged a claim sounding in contract.

Additionally, the trial court charged the jury with regard to The Birth Center's contract cause of action. The court charged the jurors, inter alia, that if they found that St. Paul breached its contract with The Birth Center, that they were to award compensatory damages if the breach caused the damages, and the damages were reasonably foreseeable at the time the parties entered into the contract

and at the time of the breach. Specifically, the trial judge charged, among other things, that:

> where one party to a contract breaches that contract, the other party may recover for those injuries which have been proved to you with reasonable certainty.
>
> If you find that defendant St. Paul breached its contract with the Birth Center, you must then decide based on all of the evidence presented what amount of money will compensate the Plaintiff for those injuries, which were a direct and foreseeable result of the breach by St. Paul which the parties could reasonably foresee at the time they made that contract and at the time of the Defendant's breach of the contract.

The jury returned a verdict finding that St. Paul acted in bad faith in its handling of the underlying Norris case, and that the bad faith conduct was a substantial factor in bringing about harm to The Birth Center in the amount of $700,000. The jury verdict sufficiently established that the jury considered the breach of contract claim. The jury found that St. Paul acted in bad faith; St. Paul had a contractual duty to act in good faith; therefore, St. Paul breached its contract.

In reviewing the propriety of an order granting or denying judgment notwithstanding the verdict, we must determine whether there was sufficient competent evidence to sustain the verdict. We view the evidence in the light most favorable to the verdict winner and give him or her the benefit of every reasonable inference arising there from while rejecting all unfavorable testimony and inferences.

A court may not vacate a jury's finding unless "the evidence was such that no two reasonable minds could disagree that the outcome should have been rendered in favor of the movant." While we respect Judge Koudelis' opinion that St. Paul's refusal to engage in settlement negotiations was not in bad faith, the jury was the finder of fact. It found that based upon all of the evidence that The Birth Center proved "by clear and convincing evidence that St. Paul acted in bad faith in handling the underlying case of *Norris v. The Birth Center*." We also note that Judge Clouse, who tried the underlying case, stated, the day of trial, that he believed that St. Paul's settlement posture was in bad faith and inconsistent with its fiduciary duty to the Birth Center. Specifically, Judge Clouse expressed his opinion that:

> There is a clear indication of bad faith here. I think the insurance company is not proceeding in a responsible manner and is not discharging its fiduciary obligation to its insureds in this case . . . I think this insurance company has operated in a highly irresponsible manner. I want it clear that they have turned this high/low offer of $300,000.00 down in which [sic] I think is a breach of their fiduciary responsibility to their insureds. And I want that clear on this record.

While Judge Clouse's opinion is arguably irrelevant to the jury's determination that St. Paul acted in bad faith, it is a compelling indication of how a reasonable jury could have come to a similar conclusion that St. Paul acted in bad faith.

42 Pa.C.S.A. §8371 Does Not Prohibit the Award of Compensatory Damages

In St. Paul's argument, it incorrectly asserts that compensatory damages may not be awarded when an insurer's bad faith conduct causes the insured to incur actual damages, because the damages are not mentioned in 42 Pa.C.S.A. §8371. While The Birth Center may not recover compensatory damages based on Section 8371, that Section does not alter The Birth Center's common law contract rights. We begin with the words of the statute. Section 8371 provides:

§8371. Actions on insurance policies

In an action arising under an insurance policy, if the court finds that the insurer has acted in bad faith toward the insured, the court may take all of the following actions:

(1) Award interest on the amount of the claim from the date the claim was made by the insured in an amount equal to the prime rate of interest plus 3%.

(2) Award punitive damages against the insurer.

(3) Assess court costs and attorney fees against the insurer. 42 Pa.C.S.A. §8371.

The statute does not prohibit the award of compensatory damages. It merely provides an additional remedy and authorizes the award of additional damages. Specifically, the statute authorizes courts, which find that an insurer has acted in bad faith toward its insured, to award punitive damages, attorneys' fees, interest and costs. Id. The statute does not reference the common law, does not explicitly reject it, and the application of the statute is not inconsistent with the common law. Consequently, the common law remedy survives. *Metropolitan Property and Liability Insurance Co. v. Insurance Commissioner of Pennsylvania*, 525 Pa. 306, 580 A.2d 300 (1990). In *Metropolitan Property*, we rejected an insured's argument that the Unfair Insurance Practices Act abrogated the insurer's contractual, common law right of rescission. Id. at 302-303. We explained that because the statute did not refer to the common law remedy of rescission and its concurrent application was not inconsistent with the statute that the legislature did not intend to preclude the remedy. Id.

Therefore, contrary to St. Paul's contention, Section 8371 does not prohibit courts from awarding compensatory damages that are otherwise available. In Section 8371, the legislature granted the court additional authority to award punitive damages, interest, costs and attorneys' fees. The fact that the statute authorized courts to award these damages does not prohibit them from granting other remedies that they theretofore had the power to award without the grant of additional authority.

Finally, St. Paul's argument that damages not mentioned by Section 8371 are not available is inconsistent with St. Paul's admission that other damages, not listed in Section 8371, remain viable. Appellant's Reply Br. at 3. Notwithstanding that Section 8371 does not provide that courts may require an insurer to pay an excess verdict when it refuses, in bad faith, to settle a case, St. Paul admits, as it must, that such an award is permissible. St. Paul states:

> It has long been held in this Common-wealth that when an insurance company fails to settle a third-party claim against its insured, the insurer can be liable for the full amount of any excess verdict, if the decision not to settle was made in bad faith. St. Paul also admits that this right has been held to be contractual in nature; it can be enforced by an action in assump-sit; and it is assignable to the injured third party.

St. Paul, thereby, concedes that an insurer who acts in bad faith may be subject to damages other than those set forth in Section 8371. Accordingly, just as courts may require an insurer to pay an excess verdict even though Section 8371 does not mention excess verdict liability, the absence of compensatory damages from Section 8371 does not alter the authority of courts to award compensatory damages.

Requiring insurers, who act in bad faith, to pay excess verdicts protects insured from liability that, absent the insurer's bad faith conduct, the insured would not have incurred. The insured's liability for an excess verdict is a type of compensatory damage for which this court has allowed recovery. Therefore, when an insurer breaches its insurance contract by a bad faith refusal to settle a case, it is appropriate to require it to pay other damages that it knew or should have known the insured would incur because of the bad faith conduct.

Because of the insurer's controlling role in the litigation, the insurer enters a fiduciary relationship with its insured and accepts the responsibility to protect the interests of its insured.

Notwithstanding the insurer's contractual duty to its insured, the interests of insurers and their insureds are not always consistent and are frequently in conflict with one another. Indeed, an insured's interests are particularly at risk when a plaintiff expresses a willingness to settle for the policy limits. When it becomes clear that an insurer could settle a third-party claim against its insured for the limits of the policy, and thereby release its insured from any worry about an excess verdict, the insurer must be vigilant to ensure that it has a reasonable basis to try the case and that it is not breaching its fiduciary duty to its insured, based upon a small chance of a defense verdict.

An insured's interests are particularly in jeopardy under the forgoing facts because whether the insurer settles for the policy limits or loses at trial, its risk is the same; in both instances, and absent bad faith, all it would have to pay would be the policy limits. Id. In such a situation, a faithless insurer would have nothing to lose by trying the case; it might as well take the risk and hope for a defense verdict. At the same time, the insured would have no reason to risk a trial.

The only applicable issue raised by the dissent is whether the Bad Faith Statute, 42 Pa.C.S.A. §8371, bars the recovery of compensatory damages. The provision does not prohibit the award of compensatory damages; it merely provides a basis to award additional damages. The statute does not reference the common law, does not explicitly reject it, and the application of the statute is not inconsistent with the common law. Accordingly, the remedy survives. We cannot countenance such a result because it directly conflicts with the one the legislature intended.

Conclusion

Today, we hold that where an insurer acts in bad faith, by unreasonably refusing to settle a claim, it breaches its contractual duty to act in good faith and its fiduciary duty to its insured.

Therefore, the insurer is liable for the known and/or foreseeable compensatory damages of its insured that reasonably flow from the insurer's bad faith conduct. Accordingly, we affirm the decision of the Superior Court,

reinstate the jury's verdict and remand this case to the trial court for a determination of The Birth Center's entitlement to interest, reasonable attorneys' fees and costs pursuant to 42 Pa.C.S.A. §8371.

FITZPATRICK V. STATE FARM INS. COMPANIES
NOT REPORTED IN F.SUPP.2D, 2010 WL 2103954, W.D.PA., 2010.

Memorandum Opinion
HAY, United States Chief Magistrate Judge.

Gregory L. Fitzpatrick ("Fitzpatrick" or "plaintiff") and Nancy L. Fitzpatrick, his wife, (collectively, "the Fitzpatricks" or "plaintiffs") bring this action against State Farm Insurance Companies and State Farm Mutual Automobile Insurance Company (collectively, "State Farm" or "defendants") seeking damages revolving around State Farm's conduct in settling the Fitzpatricks' claims for underinsured motorist benefits. In their Complaint, filed on October 19, 2009, in the Court of Common Pleas of Allegheny County, Pennsylvania, the Fitzpatricks assert four causes of action: bad faith in violation of 42 Pa.C.S.A. §8371 (Count I); breach of contract (Count II); breach of fiduciary duty (Count III); and a claim for violating the Unfair Trade Practice and Consumer Protection Law, 73 P.S. §201, et seq. ("UTPCPL") (Count IV). State Farm timely removed the case to this Court based on diversity and, on November 13, 2009, promptly filed a Motion to Dismiss asking that Counts II, III and IV be dismissed pursuant to Fed.R.Civ.P. 12(b)(6). Because the Fitzpatricks have failed to state claim with respect to Counts III and IV, the motion will be granted in part. Although their breach of contract claim brought at Count II survives, State Farm's motion is also granted to the extent that the Fitzpatricks seek attorney's fees in relation to the alleged breach.

Background

The Fitzpatricks maintained a motor vehicle insurance policy ("the Policy") with State

Farm that provided for medical benefits as well as underinsured motorist ("UIM") benefits of $1,000,000 per person, stacked, covering two vehicles. In March of 1997 and again in March of 1998, while the Policy was in effect, Fitzpatrick was involved in two separate automobile accidents in which he was seriously injured. Sometime thereafter State Farm was notified of Fitzpatrick's underlying liability claims and underinsurance claims on the Policy. Fitzpatrick settled all of the underlying liability claims between September of 2000 and February of 2001.

On October, 26, 2004, counsel for the Fitzpatricks notified State Farm's respective Claims Specialists of the Arbitrator he was naming in the underinsured motorist claims. Over the course of the next two years State Farm sought, and received, certain documentation and information on the claims including Fitzpatrick's medical records; discovery from the underlying liability cases; Fitzpatrick's school transcripts; plaintiffs' expert reports; Fitzpatrick's tax returns from 1993 through 1999 and from 2002 through 2004; and documentation of the salaries and bonuses of similarly situated attorneys at the law firm where Fitzpatrick had been employed. As well, State Farm took Fitzpatrick's Statement Under Oath, had him undergo a psychiatric evaluation and deposed a managing partner at Fitzpatrick's law firm.

On November 14, 2006, the Fitzpatricks made a demand of $1,750,000.00 to settle the claims. After several months of negotiations and counter-offers, the Fitzpatricks agreed to settle their claims for $915,000.00, which was paid by State Farm on May 25, 2007. Id. 50-57. The Fitzpatricks allege, however, that State Farm failed to fairly, objectively or diligently evaluate and settle their claims and by failing to act in good faith by, amongst other things, prolonging the process and making offers substantially less than the full value of their claims.

Discussion

A. Breach of Contract

State Farm first argues that the Fitzpatricks are unable to succeed on a claim for breach of contract because it has already tendered the proceeds of the Policy to them.

A plaintiff asserting a breach of contract claim under Pennsylvania law must establish three elements: (1) the existence of a contract; (2) a breach of a duty imposed by the contract; and (3) resultant damages. Generally, a breach of contract claim cannot be sustained where the proceeds of the policy have been paid since, if the plaintiff has received everything due under the policy, there are no damages.

The Restatement (Second) of Contracts §205, however, provides that "every contract imposes on each party a duty of good faith and fair dealing in its performance and its enforcement." Although the Pennsylvania Supreme Court has not formally adopted the Restatement in this regard, it has nevertheless suggested that parties to a contract have a duty to act in good faith and that their failure to do so constitutes a breach of contract.

Moreover, the Pennsylvania Supreme Court has found that even where payment has been made to an insured under an insurance policy, he or she may nevertheless have a cause of action for breach of contract against the insurer where he or she has suffered other damages because of the insurer's bad faith conduct in handling the claim. In *Birth Center v. St. Paul Companies, Inc.*, 567 Pa. 386, 787 A.2d 376, for instance, the insurance company refused to make a good faith effort to settle a case brought against its insured despite offers by the plaintiffs to settle the case within the policy limits. The case proceeded to trial resulting in a verdict against the insured in excess of those limits. Although the insurance company ultimately paid the excess verdict, the insured subsequently brought suit against the insurance company bringing claims for, inter alia, breaching its implied covenant of good faith as well as Pennsylvania's bad faith statute, 42 Pa.C.S.A. §8371. Id. The insurance company argued, much as State Farm has here, that its payment of the excess verdict precluded the plaintiff's bad faith claims. The Court, however, rejected that argument finding that "there is no reason to limit damages to the amount of the verdict where the insured can show that the insurer's bad faith conduct caused it additional damages." Id., 567 Pa. at 400, 787 A.2d at 385. The Court went on to explain that "where . . . the insured can prove that it sustained damages in excess of the verdict, the insurer's payment of the excess has little to do with the insured's damages. Accordingly, the insurer's payment of the excess should not free it from other known or foreseeable damages it has caused its insured to incur."

Here, like in *Birth Center*, the Fitzpatricks' breach of contract claim is not based on State Farm's failure to pay them the proceeds of the Policy nor do they seek the insurance proceeds. Rather, the Fitzpatricks' claim is premised on State Farm's contractual duty to act in good faith in handling their claim. They have alleged in the Complaint that State Farm breached that duty in a myriad of ways including unfairly evaluating their claims; being dilatory and failing to effectuate a prompt and equitable settlement of their claims; offering substantially less than the full value of their claims; and delaying payment of the claims. The Fitzpatricks seek interest on the claim or monies they allegedly would have had available to them if State Farm had complied with its duty to act in good faith and promptly settled the claim. Because the Fitzpatricks have alleged damages stemming from State Farm's performance of its duty under the Policy over and above payment of the proceeds, they have properly stated a claim for breach of contract.

State Farm also argues that even if the Fitzpatricks' breach of contract claim is not dismissed in its entirety, they are not entitled to attorney's fees for a breach of an insurance contract and that their request for attorney fees in Count II should therefore be dismissed. The Court agrees.

As pointed out by State Farm, attorney's fees are recoverable under Pennsylvania law only if there is statutory authority, a clear agreement between the parties that provides for such an award or some other established exception. Here, the Policy entered into between the parties does not provide for attorney's fees and there does not appear to be any statutory authority for the recovery of attorney's fees for breach of an insurance contract. Nor have the Fitzpatricks pointed to some other established exception which would entitled them to attorney's fees. Indeed, the Fitzpatricks have not addressed State Farm's argument in this regard at all and, thus, have seemingly conceded the issue. Accordingly, they are not entitled to recover such fees at Count II and that portion of their breach of contract claim is properly dismissed.

B. Breach of Fiduciary Duty

With respect to Count III, State Farm argues that the Fitzpatricks cannot assert a claim for breach of fiduciary duty under the facts alleged in the Complaint as a matter of law. Specifically, State Farm argues that, under Pennsylvania law, a life insurance company only has a fiduciary duty to an insured when a third party has asserted a claim against him or her.

Indeed, the Court of Appeals for the third Circuit has found that "under Pennsylvania law, a fiduciary duty higher than the duty of good faith and fair dealing does not arise out an insurance contract until an insurer asserts a stated right under the policy to handle all claims asserted against the insured." Thus, an insurer assumes a fiduciary duty toward an insured only when a third party has asserted a claim against the insured.

Because the instant case revolves around the Fitzpatricks' claims for UIM benefits under the Policy and does not involve claims by a third party, State Farm did not assume a fiduciary duty toward the Fitzpatricks. Since no duty was owed, it follows that State Farm could not have breached that duty and the Fitzpatricks' claim for breach of fiduciary duty must fail as a matter of law.

Conclusion

For the reasons set forth above, State Farm's Motion to Dismiss is GRANTED as to Counts III and IV, and to the extent the Fitzpatricks seek attorney's fees at Count II, and DENIED in all other respects.

Websites

■ **ABA Tort, Trial, and Insurance Practice Section**
http://www.abanet.org/tips/home.html

■ **New York State Department of Insurance**
http://www.ins.state.ny.us/puborder.htm

■ **Lloyd's of London**
http://www.lloyds.com

■ **Findlaw.com**
   http://www.findlaw.com (click on search box and enter "insurance," "declarations page," or "uninsured motorist coverage")

■ **Business Journal — World Insurance News**
   http://www.businessjournal.com/s/insurance/

Forms and Court Documents

Complaint form — insured sues insurance company for failure to defend under insurance policy.

In this pleading, Stanley Blue, the engineer of the train that struck Charles Chumley, is seeking a declaratory judgment from the court establishing that the insurance company is required, by the terms of the insurance, to provide a legal defense to him.

STATE OF PLACID	IN THE SUPERIOR COURT
COUNTY OF BARNES	FILE NUMBER: _____

Stanley Blue,	)
Petitioner	)
	)
vs.	)
	)
Bay Rock Insurance Company, Inc.,	)
Defendant	)

Petition for Declaratory Judgment

1.

At all times mentioned, Petitioner Stanley Blue (hereafter "Petitioner") was a resident of Barnes County, Placid, and an employee of Railroad Company.

2.

Defendant Bay Rock Insurance Company, Inc. (hereafter "Defendant") is and at all times mentioned was a corporation organized, existing, and doing business under and by virtue of the laws of this state.

3.

On May 5, last year, Defendant issued to Railroad Company an accident and liability policy (hereafter "the insurance policy") that insured the Railroad Company and "all of its employees" against liability or loss resulting from bodily injury or death caused by any person and resulting from the use of the Railroad's equipment.

4.

The accident and liability policy was issued and became effective on May 5, last year, and remained in effect until midnight, May 4, this year.

5.

The insurance policy, a copy of which is attached to this Complaint as Petitioner's Exhibit "A," provided that the Defendant would defend in the name and on behalf of Petitioner any suits which might at any time be brought against the company or its employees on account of personal injuries or death resulting from the operation or use of railroad equipment, including train locomotives such as the one Petitioner was operating. The policy states the Defendant's obligation to defend, at its own cost, all suits brought against the Railroad Company or its employees, on account of injuries or death resulting from the use of railroad equipment. The policy further provided that the Defendant had exclusive control of the defense of any suit brought against the Railroad Company or its employees for injuries specified in the policy.

6.

On August 23, last year, Petitioner was acting as engineer and operator of a locomotive engine and three cars (hereafter "the train"), two of which were carrying cargo, the remaining car being empty. As the train approached the intersection of the railroad track and Morgan Street, Town of Cling, State of Placid, Charles Chumley was driving his car south, towards the intersection of the railroad line with Morgan Street. As the train entered the intersection, it struck the car driven by Charles Chumley. As a result of the collision, Charles Chumley received severe personal injuries and the other occupant of the vehicle, Mrs. Julia Chumley, was killed.

7.

Charles Chumley eventually brought suit against the Railroad Company alleging negligence on the part of the Railroad Company in maintaining the intersection and in the operation of the train on the day of the incident. Petitioner Stanley Blue was named as a defendant in this action as well. A copy of *Chumley v. National Railroad Company, et al*, is provided as Petitioner's Exhibit "B" to this Complaint.

8.

Petitioner gave proper notice of the collision to his employer and proper notice to Defendant Insurance Company, as required under the terms of the insurance policy.

9.

On April 1 of this year, Defendant Insurance Company retained the services of Sterling and Silver, Attorneys at Law, to represent the Railroad Company in the action filed by Charles Chumley. However, Defendant Insurance did not provide legal counsel for Petitioner. In a letter dated April 4 of this year, Defendant Insurance Company notified Petitioner that it had no obligation to the Petitioner and would therefore provide no legal representation for the Petitioner in the action filed by Charles Chumley.

10.

Defendant's failure to provide legal counsel violated the insurance policy's duty to defend the Petitioner.

WHEREFORE, Petitioner respectfully requests that the court enter judgment declaring that:

1) The insurance policy issued to Railroad Company provides coverage for the Petitioner in this action; and

2) The Defendant, by the terms of said insurance policy, is obligated to provide a legal counsel and services per the insurance agreement, to represent the Petitioner in the underlying action, to wit: *Chumley v. National Railroad Company, Stanley Blue, and Town of Cling.*

Respectfully submitted,

This the _____ day of _____, 20_____

_____

Susan Vengeance
Attorney for Petitioner, Stanley Blue
State Bar No. 12345

Key Terms

Exclusion	Policy	Subrogation
Fiduciary	Premium	Thermography
Indemnify	Release	
No-fault insurance	Stacking	

Review Questions

1. How did the insurance industry develop over time? What impact does this history have on modern cases?

2. List and discuss the parties to an insurance policy. What responsibilities does each of these parties have?

3. How does insurance affect a civil suit?

4. What is an insurance premium?

5. How does an insurance company owe fiduciary duty to an insured?

6. How do states regulate the insurance industry?

7. Why do states require minimum automobile liability coverage for motorists?

8. Periodically, states enact new statutes requiring that insurance policies be readable or understandable. Why are such statutes necessary? Why don't insurance companies take the initiative and make their policies understandable without such statutes?

9   Explain the two components of liability coverage.

10 Explain the basic features of an automobile insurance policy.

11 What types of coverage are common in automobile insurance policies?

12 What is uninsured motorist coverage?

13 Compare and contrast uninsured motorist coverage with underinsured motorist coverage.

14 Explain the insurance company's "duty to defend."

15 List and explain the various parts of a typical insurance policy.

16 Explain subrogation.

17 Explain stacking insurance policies.

18 How does no-fault insurance differ from regular auto insurance?

19 What are the advantages of no-fault insurance?

20 What are some of the typical exclusions found in insurance policies?

21 Why are exclusions allowed in policies?

22 How does insurance coverage affect settlement?

23 When can a plaintiff use the discovery process to find out the limits of a defendant's policy?

24 How do plaintiffs' firms differ from insurance defense firms?

25 How are plaintiffs' firms and insurance defense firms compensated?

26 What is a settlement letter?

27 What is a release?

28 What steps should you follow when reviewing an insurance policy?

Applying What You Have Learned

1   According to one source, almost 15 percent of the average insured's premium is spent on bodily injury claims that are frivolous or fraudulent. Why is this so? Is there some way to correct the system to eliminate such claims?

2   Ted has been injured in an automobile collision. Another driver, Clark Collision, rear-ended Ted's car while Ted was stopped at a red light. The accident occurred on May 15 of this year. Ted's car was totaled. The car has a Blue Book value of $8,000. Ted's medical injuries were relatively minor: $3,000. He had arthroscopic surgery performed on his knee. Here is a summary of his medical bills:

Doctors' medical service	$1,500
Civil Rehabilitation Services	$1,500

3   Based on this information, prepare a settlement letter patterned on Figure 13-8, the Settlement Letter in the Chumley Case.

4   Does your state use the no-fault insurance system? What is the mandatory minimum coverage permissible in your state?

Endnotes

[1]Lawrence Friedman, *A History of American Law*, New York, Simon & Schuster, 1978, p. 476.

[2]322 U.S. 533 (1944).

[3]*Birth Center v. St. Paul Companies, Inc.*, 567 Pa. 386, 787 A.2d 376 (2001).

[4]Joint Economic Committee, Auto-Choice; Executive Summary (1998).

[5]Am. Jur. Insurance §633.

[6]Insurance §559, Am. Jur. 2d.

Crossword Puzzle

ACROSS

1 The policy limits of one policy are added to the policy limits of one or more other policies, increasing the available funds to the sum of all policies

7 Relationship in which one person, or entity, is obligated to act in a trustworthy relationship to the other. This person has the duty to act in the best interests of the other. A common example of such a relationship is the attorney-client relationship.

8 An assessment tool that can monitor temperature changes in the skin; often used by plaintiffs' attorneys as a way of showing that there is greater blood flow in an injured area and thereby providing a "picture of the pain."

9 A type of insurance that requires an insurance company to pay for the insured's damages regardless of who was at fault in causing the damage

DOWN

1 In claiming a legal right or a debt, the substitution of one person for another

2 The persons, types of losses, or damages not covered by an insurance policy

3 A written insurance contract

4 Surrender or give up a legal right to sue another; the document or court filing in which this right is surrendered

5 To compensate a person who has suffered a loss

6 The insured's payment to the insurance company

Fraud, Misrepresentation, and Business Torts

- ◼ **Explain how a civil action for fraud is brought**

- ◼ **Define negligent misrepresentation**

- ◼ **Detail the elements required to prove a negligent misrepresentation suit**

- ◼ **Explain the tort of interference with contract**

- ◼ **Define the concepts of dram shop liability and workers' compensation**

THE SHAREHOLDER'S SUIT

In the 1990s and early 2000s, the End-Run Corporation was a high flyer. Its stock price, which had remained around $20 per share in the 1980s, rose to over $100 per share in the last few years. End-Run posted huge profits and proclaimed a rosy future. End-Run executives received huge, and apparently well-earned, seven-figure salaries and a host of perquisites. Then a reporter for the local newspaper broke a story claiming that the "huge profits" of End-Run were actually part of a corporate scheme to fool stockholders and the public. In fact, End-Run was seriously in debt but had disguised the fact by clever (and illegal) accounting practices. Tom, who owns 1,000 End-Run shares, has just walked into our office. He wants to sue End-Run for what he says is outright fraud. Does he have a case? If so, what type of action can our firm file against

End-Run? Before we can analyze his case, we need a solid understanding of the law of fraud, deceit, and negligent misrepresentation.

INTRODUCTION

In this chapter we explore the various actions associated with fraud, deceit, and misrepresentation. We also examine the types of torts associated with business transactions, such as consumer actions and interference with contract rights.

Everyone knows that lying is something to be avoided. However, when does a lie, or a knowing misrepresentation, become actionable in tort law? Obviously not everyone who has told a lie has been sued. In fact, most lies are not actionable at all. However, under certain circumstances, a falsehood does give a person a cause of action against another person.

An outright lie can give rise to several possible actions. For instance, if the lie is in the context of a contractual agreement, this can provide the basis for a breach of contract suit. If the lie is unintentional, or made without concern for the actual truth, the plaintiff can sue for negligent misrepresentation. However, when and under what circumstances does a statement, or an action, become a misrepresentation? We begin with the simpler issue of fraud before moving into the more complex world of negligent misrepresentation.

FRAUD

The problem with words such as "fraud" and "deceit" is that they have been overused; their precise legal meanings have been diluted over time to the point that they are almost incapable of an exact definition.

Fraud is a word that lends itself to many possible definitions. People have been lying, cheating, and scamming each other forever. A basic definition of fraud could be a deceitful action against another to gain some form of advantage. Fraud includes outright lying, deceit, surprise, trickery, false claims, and the whole panoply of treachery practiced by human beings. While it may be difficult to define what fraud is, we can certainly say what fraud is not. Fraud is an intentional action. There is no negligent fraud. Fraud is an affirmative action and requires knowledge on the part of the person carrying it out that he is defrauding another. Later we discuss the tort of negligent misrepresentation, but for fraud, the plaintiff must show the defendant's intent. Fraud can occur when a person knowingly makes a false statement or when a person conceals or withholds a fact.

Example: One afternoon, Mary goes out shopping for antiques. She approaches John, who is standing beside a lovely nineteenth-century armoire with a "for sale" sign taped to it. Mary asks, "How much?" John responds, "How much are you offering?" She looks the armoire over again and offers $300. John says, "Okay." Mary has a friend help her load the armoire into her truck. Just as she is about to pull away, an irate man runs up to her and accuses her of theft. Mary explains that she bought the armoire from John, who has now disappeared. The irate man says that he is the rightful owner and that he did not intend to sell the armoire. Later, when Mary catches up with John and asks for her money back, John says, "I never told that you that I owned it." Can Mary sue John for fraud?

Answer: Yes. Although John did not make an actual statement claiming that he had the right to sell the armoire, he did withhold the fact that he did not have that right. Under these facts, withholding a fact is equivalent to making a false statement. Both are actionable.

Fraud involves any act (or omission) that conceals the breach of a legal duty or material fact. This act must cause injury to the plaintiff or give the defendant an unjustified or unconscionable advantage.

TORT
BASICS
AT A
GLANCE

A. PROVING FRAUD

To prove fraud, the plaintiff must show the following:

1. The defendant made a representation of a material fact or concealed a fact.
2. The representation was false.
3. The defendant knew the representation was false.
4. The defendant made the representation with the intent that the plaintiff would rely on it.
5. The plaintiff's reliance on the representation was reasonable under the circumstances.
6. The plaintiff suffered injury from his reliance on the representation.

One of the key elements involved in proof of fraud is that the representation involved a **material fact.** This is a fact that is crucial to the parties' understanding of the transaction or a key point of negotiation. In the example provided above, John's lack of ownership of the armoire was a material fact. It was a central point of the negotiations and an assumption that Mary made based on John's behavior. Many states have enacted statutes spelling out exactly what is a material fact. In fact, many refer to a misrepresentation of a "material past or present fact." A material past fact is simply a statement about a past fact, such as a statement detailing exactly where the armoire was manufactured and how it has been treated by previous owners. A material present fact refers to John's ownership of the armoire.

Material fact
A fact that is basic to a contract, one that the parties consider to be an essential ingredient of the negotiations.

FIGURE 14-1

Total Incoming
Cases Reported
by State
Trial Courts,
All States,
2003–2012

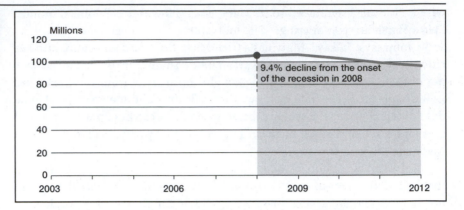

Source: Examining the Work of State Courts, An Overview of 2012 State Trial Court Caseloads, National Court Statistics Project, p. 3 (2014)

It is not fraud to make the types of statements we commonly associate with selling techniques. For instance, it is not a material misrepresentation to claim that a car is "the best car in the world." On the other hand, it is a material misrepresentation to claim that the car has never been in an accident when it actually has been. "Puffing" and other exaggerations are par for the course in a transaction, and most buyers do not take such claims seriously.

It is difficult to come up with a solid definition of a material fact that will work in all situations. Suffice to say that a material fact is one of those facts that would make or break the deal between the parties.

Example: John and Ted have decided to open a craft store together. They have extensively negotiated the partnership deal between them. The partnership takes effect on January 1 of next year, and each man will contribute $20,000 to the business. Both will work a minimum of 40 hours per week at the business. John prefers to work on Tuesdays and Thursday evenings, but he is flexible about other times. Ted is a morning person and plans on being at the store every morning at 8 A.M. Which of these facts is a material fact and which is not?

Answer: All of the contractual details concerning monetary contribution, the date that the partnership takes effect, and how many hours each man must work at the business are material facts. The nonmaterial facts include each man's stated preference about when he will actually work. Their preferences are not essential components to the contract and therefore are not material facts.

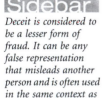

Deceit is considered to be a lesser form of fraud. It can be any false representation that misleads another person and is often used in the same context as fraud.

B. ALLEGING FRAUD IN THE COMPLAINT

When a complaint alleges fraud, the plaintiff must present enough detail in the complaint to show material facts, how these facts were untrue, and specific instances (times, places, and contents) of false representations.[2] Simply stating that the plaintiff was defrauded will not satisfy the requirements of notice pleading in most states.[3]

In most jurisdictions, fraud must be proven by **clear and convincing evidence.** This essentially means that someone alleging fraud has a higher standard to meet than allegations made in other types of civil cases (in which preponderance of the evidence is usually enough).

Clear and convincing evidence
A level of proof higher than mere preponderance of the evidence. In most civil trials, preponderance of the evidence is sufficient.

C. LIMITATIONS ON FRAUD ACTIONS

In some jurisdictions, omission of a material fact will not support a claim for fraud unless the defendant had a legal obligation to disclose it. Usually, the obligation to disclose a fact is limited to those with fiduciary responsibilities. As we have already seen, a fiduciary is a person or corporation that has a legal and ethical duty to act in the best interests of another. When a fiduciary fails to disclose a material fact, this failure can be the basis of a fraud claim. It can be the basis for other actions as well, including negligent misrepresentation.[4] See Figure 14-2 for a list of activities that are and are not considered fraud.

D. FRAUD AND CRIMINAL LAW

Civil actions for fraud are complicated by the fact that what makes a particular situation actionable under civil law also makes it punishable under criminal law. Fraud is a form of theft under criminal law. As a form of theft, fraud involves proof by the prosecution that the defendant used trickery, deceit, or deliberate falsehood to deprive the victim of his property. There is a reason that these elements sound similar to the elements of a civil action for fraud. The common law crime of fraud and the tort of fraud developed from the same legal source. In fact, several centuries ago, there was no clear distinction between civil and criminal actions. Fraud was fraud. Nowadays, that same confusion between civil and criminal actions still haunts any allegation of fraud. For instance, in the scenario we used to open the discussion of fraud—Mary's purchase of furniture she wrongfully believed was owned

---

Activities classified as fraud include the following:

▪ Any false statement that is reasonable and one upon which the plaintiff relies
▪ A willful, intentional misstatement that gives the defendant an unfair advantage over the plaintiff

Activities not classified as fraud include the following:

▪ Failing to fulfill a promise that was made in good faith
▪ Exaggerations or "puffing"
▪ Opinions (in most situations)

FIGURE 14-2

Activities That Are and Are Not Classified as Fraud

by John — are John's actions criminal or civil? Actually, they are both. Mary has a civil action against John for her monetary loss — the money she paid him believing that he was the owner — and the state also has an action against John for defrauding Mary of her property, namely, her money.

As we saw in Chapter 1, civil actions and criminal actions can be based on the same facts, but the litigation in each case proceeds independently of one another. The same witnesses may testify about the same events, but the end result of the two cases will be different. In the criminal case, John faces jail time and a fine. In the civil case, he faces a court order forcing him to repay Mary for her out-of-pocket expenses (and any other damages the court deems proper).

Although the topic of fraud has a great deal of potential for both civil and criminal actions, negligent misrepresentation does not. That action is usually a civil action only.

Tech Topic
INTERNET FRAUD

The number of ways to engage in fraudulent activity on the Internet is limited only by the perpetrator's imagination. Historically, auction fraud (from sites such as eBay) constituted the most frequent type of fraud. However, as the potential for fraudulent activity has diversified in recent years, incidences of auction fraud have dropped dramatically. Today, the most common types of Internet scams that might come your way are related to phishing, pharming, the "Nigerian letter," and the lottery.

In a phishing scam, you receive an e-mail from what appears to be your bank or another well-known company that asks you to click a link and visit its website to provide personal information. The website, however, is bogus, and its intent is to gather personal information such as account numbers. The ultimate goal is identity theft. A pharming attack is similar, but it instead redirects you to the bogus website even if you type the correct URL into your browser. Pharming scams are among the hardest types of Internet fraud to defend against.

The Nigerian letter scam involves an e-mail that asks for your help to access a large sum of money in a foreign bank account. The enticement is that you will get a percentage of the funds in exchange for your help. However, you will be required to provide an "advance fee" to help the deal go through. Once you do, the sender of the e-mail will disappear.

In a lottery scam, you receive an e-mail that claims you have won a great deal of money in an international lottery — even though you have never bought a ticket. Unfortunately, there is no lottery and no prize. If you were to reply to the message, you would be prompted to provide personal information or even to send money to cover expenses to deliver your so-called winnings.

Internet fraud is not likely to disappear, and it will continue to become more sophisticated and harder to detect.

IV NEGLIGENT MISREPRESENTATION

In many ways, negligent misrepresentation resembles an action for fraud, with one important difference: In fraud, the plaintiff must show that the defendant's false statement was made knowingly. In negligent misrepresentation, the plaintiff may simply show that the defendant was reckless or negligent in representing the truth to the plaintiff.[5] The important distinction between negligent misrepresentation and fraud is that a person may be liable for a statement made in good faith, but with careless disregard for its truth, under negligent misrepresentation, but will not be liable for the same statement under fraud. In many ways, this tort allows a cause of action for a simple misstatement. As such, most courts impose a higher standard of proof in such cases. This higher standard places more emphasis on the plaintiff's allegations.

Although most negligence cases do not require any relationship between the parties, negligent misrepresentation cases often do. After all, the plaintiff must prove that he relied on a statement by the defendant and that this reliance was reasonable under the circumstances. Often this proof of reasonable reliance springs from the fact that the plaintiff and defendant knew one another, that they did business together, or that there was some other relationship between them that made the plaintiff's actions understandable.

A. THE RESTATEMENT POSITION ON NEGLIGENT MISREPRESENTATION

The Restatement of Torts provides valuable guidance on the question of negligent misrepresentation. The Restatement position covers situations in which a person gives false information in the course of his business, profession, or employment (see Figure 14-3).

The Restatement makes it clear that when a person's only loss is monetary, the court should adopt a more "restricted rule of liability" than the standard used in fraud cases.[6] Many states have adopted the Restatement's position on negligent misrepresentation.

B. ELEMENTS OF NEGLIGENT MISREPRESENTATION

Negligent misrepresentation consists of the following elements:

1. The defendant, in the course of his business or profession, makes a false statement,
2. believing that the statement is true

FIGURE 14-3

Negligent Mis-
representation
Under the
Restatement
of Torts

(1) One who, in the course of his business, profession, or employment, or in any other transaction in which he has a pecuniary interest, supplies false information for the guidance of others in their business transactions, is subject to liability for pecuniary loss caused to them by their justifiable reliance upon the information, if he fails to exercise reasonable care or competence in obtaining or communicating the information.

(2) Except as stated in Subsection (3), the liability stated in Subsection (1) is limited to loss suffered

(a) by the person or one of a limited group of persons for whose benefit and guidance he intends to supply the information or knows that the recipient intends to supply it; and

(b) through reliance upon it in a transaction that he intends the information to influence or knows that the recipient so intends or in a substantially similar transaction.

(3) The liability of one who is under a public duty to give the information extends to loss suffered by any of the class of persons for whose benefit the duty is created, in any of the transactions in which it is intended to protect them.[*]

*Restatement (Second) of Torts §552

3. but without reasonable grounds for his belief or in reckless disregard of the truth.

4. The plaintiff suffers a financial loss because of his reasonable reliance on this false statement.

C. TRADITIONAL TORT ANALYSIS FOR NEGLIGENT MISREPRESENTATION

Negligent misrepresentation is a type of negligence, so the traditional tort analysis applies. In the next sections, we address the issues of the four-part test for negligence cases: duty, breach, causation, and damages.

1. DUTY AND BREACH OF DUTY

Duty in the context of negligent misrepresentation usually arises out of a relationship between the parties. Unlike other types of negligence, negligent misrepresentation resembles contractual actions more than personal injury cases. In contract cases, the right of the parties to sue one another is based on their contractual relationship. In order to sue, the parties must be in **privity** with one another. Because of this, actions for negligent misrepresentation are much closer to contract actions than they are to personal injury cases.

Privity
The direct relationship between the parties to a contract that arises from their involvement in creating the contract.

An exception to this general rule of privity between the parties is for businesses that supply information as their product. Businesses such as accounting or research firms owe a duty to exercise reasonable care and diligence in the way that they obtain their information and pass it along to others, even when those others are not in a direct, contractual relationship with them. As a corollary to this approach, however, most courts construe those who would reasonably rely on such a report as a small group — that is, the clients and those others who would foreseeably rely on the information provided.

The standard of care imposed on defendants in negligent misrepresentation cases is to use reasonable care in making statements. When a defendant has a business relationship with another person and supplies him with false information, either through incompetence or disregard of the truth, the defendant has violated his duty to the plaintiff. However, when the information is provided to another person with whom there is no business relationship, such as a favor to a friend, there is no duty to use reasonable care.

2. CAUSATION

The plaintiff's reliance on the information provided by the defendant must be reasonable for the element of causation to be satisfied. If the plaintiff's actions are unreasonable, the defendant can claim that the plaintiff contributed to his own damages. Contributory or comparative negligence is as much a defense to the tort of negligent misrepresentation as it is for other types of negligence.

However, as we have seen in other torts, the defendant takes the plaintiff as he finds him. Therefore, a plaintiff with slow mental abilities or one who is suffering from a particular handicap is held to the standard of a similarly situated plaintiff. This standard is imposed to protect the more vulnerable elements of society from others who would prey on their disabilities.[8]

3. DAMAGES

Payment of damages for negligent misrepresentation raises several interesting questions. For example, in our discussion of typical automobile negligence cases, the plaintiff was entitled to compensatory damages, such as pain and suffering, and special damages, such as medical bills. In those cases, the plaintiff was also entitled to punitive damages. In many ways, the damages available for negligent misrepresentation are more limited. According to the Restatement of Torts, the following types of damages are available in negligent misrepresentation cases:

Compensatory damages for monetary losses calculated as:
The difference between the purchase price of what the plaintiff received and the loss suffered from his reliance on the faulty information provided by the defendant.

In most jurisdictions, the plaintiff is entitled to any or all of the following types of damages:

- Fees associated with applications, licenses, permits, and so on
- Commission fees paid to real estate brokers, agents, or others who are paid on a commission basis
- Monetary difference between a loan that the plaintiff thought he was going to receive and the loan he finally received

■ Out-of-pocket expenses associated with finding, obtaining, and receiving a new service

■ In some cases, punitive damages, if the plaintiff can show malice on the part of the defendant

■ Attorney's fees for bringing an action against the defendant (when defendant acts with malice)

D. OPINIONS AND NEGLIGENT MISREPRESENTATION

Under negligent misrepresentation, an opinion may be grounds for a cause of action, but only when the opinion is presented as based on some fact. For instance, many jurisdictions apply the rule that a statement from a loan officer that the loan can be obtained is a mere opinion and does not provide a basis for a cause of action in negligent misrepresentation.

Example: Ted has applied for a loan at the local bank. Jack, the loan officer, looks over his paperwork and then tells Ted that the bank's underwriters must approve the loan. Ted asks, "How does it look?" Jack responds, "I think it looks pretty good."

Ted goes on a buying spree, believing that he will soon have the loan proceeds to pay for the items. Jack calls him later in the week with some bad news: "I'm afraid your loan application was turned down." Ted is furious and wants to sue the bank, and Jack, for negligent misrepresentation. Does he have a case?

Answer: No. Jack's statement to Ted was an opinion and was not apparently based on any fact. How could we change the scenario to give Ted a cause of action? Jack could make a statement such as, "I can tell you that they are going to approve this application. I've seen a dozen just like it this week, and every one of them was approved." When a statement is expressed as though it were a fact, the statement becomes actionable under negligent misrepresentation.[9] (For a similar situation, see the Case Excerpt.)

Negligent misrepresentation is also authorized in situations in which the speaker has special knowledge or expertise in a certain area, and the speaker makes a statement that a reasonable person would rely on.

Example: Arthur is a certified public accountant and has been asked to review the finances of XYZ Corporation. After several weeks, he issues a report stating that XYZ Corporation is in excellent financial health and poised for a major expansion. Myron, who is one of XYZ's employees and owns a few shares of the company's stock, decides to use his life savings to purchase 1,500 additional shares of XYZ stock as a way of beefing up his retirement holdings. Unfortunately, two days after Myron purchases the stock, the company announces that it is filing for bankruptcy. Arthur's report is filled with inaccuracies. Myron sues Arthur. Does he have a cause of action?

Answer: Yes. Many jurisdictions are now allowing a cause of action in such a case for anyone who could foreseeably rely on a CPA's report on the financial health of a company. Myron is an employee and a stockholder. He falls into that category.[10]

E. NEGLIGENT MISREPRESENTATION VERSUS MISTAKE

Where do we draw the line between a simple mistake and an action that can be characterized as negligent misrepresentation? In some ways, they are similar. After all, a party may be relieved of contractual obligations if he can show either negligent misrepresentation or mistake. However, the similarities end there. "Mistake" as a defense is available when both parties have made some error about the contract. When only one party makes a mistake about the contract, the contract continues to have legal effect.[11] Negligent misrepresentation, on the other hand, is made by only one party and, when proved, gives the other party the right to void the contract.

F. PLEADING NEGLIGENT MISREPRESENTATION

On a practical level, proving negligent misrepresentation is easier than proving fraud. Having said that, however, the plaintiff must still set out a clear case of negligence. Often that is quite difficult. The plaintiff must present evidence of the specific false statement or information provided by the defendant, how the plaintiff relied on this information, and that his reliance was reasonable. The plaintiff must also show proximate cause between that reliance and the monetary injury he suffered. Finally, the plaintiff must show a direct connection between a monetary loss and the defendant's actions. Unlike personal injury cases in which certain types of damages are obvious, the damages in negligent misrepresentation cases may be difficult to quantify. See Figure 14-4.

- Point to a specific conversation or communication in which false information was provided.
- Provide dates, times, and settings for this conversation or communication.
- Detail how the information was relayed and why, precisely, this information was false.
- Provide the background information (contract negotiation, buyer-seller transaction, etc.) if the information was provided in the context of a broader communication.
- Provide direct quotes (or close approximations) of exactly what the defendant stated.
- Explain the relationship between the plaintiff and defendant (fiduciary, partners, business associates, etc.).
- Detail how, precisely, the plaintiff relied on this information: Plaintiff purchased certain items because of the defendant's information; plaintiff undertook certain actions because of the defendant's information; plaintiff did/did not . . . .
- Show how the plaintiff's reliance on the false information was reasonable.
- Detail how the plaintiff's monetary losses were directly tied to the false information.
- Show how the plaintiff has suffered a financial loss by detailing exactly what extra money plaintiff has had to pay, or has lost, by his reliance on the defendant's statement.

FIGURE 14-4

Pleading Pointers in Negligent Misrepresentation Cases

G. DEFENSES TO NEGLIGENT MISREPRESENTATION

The defenses available in negligent misrepresentation cases are similar to the defenses available in most negligence cases. However, there are several other defenses that are more or less unique to this tort. They are as follows:

- Truth
- Opinion
- Statement that did not concern a material fact
- No detrimental reliance on the statement
- No damages
- Waiver

1. TRUTH

Perhaps the most obvious defense to negligent misrepresentation is that the statement was not false. After all, it is one of the essential elements of the claim that the plaintiff must prove that the statement was false or made in reckless disregard of the truth. If the statement is true, the plaintiff's case is essentially destroyed.

2. OPINION

In most situations, an opinion is not actionable. An opinion is simply the defendant's belief or "feeling" about a particular event and lacks a solid grounding in fact. The exception is when the opinion is offered as though it were a fact. Another exception concerns people who are in the business of giving opinions about specific issues. An attorney, for example, is often called upon to give an opinion about the law. The client is entitled to rely on that opinion.

3. STATEMENT THAT DID NOT CONCERN A MATERIAL FACT

The defendant can also raise the defense that her statement, even if false, was not about a material fact and, therefore, cannot be the basis of a negligent misrepresentation claim. Essentially, the defendant is claiming that her statement did not concern any fact that would cause another person to change his behavior or influence his conduct.

4. NO DETRIMENTAL RELIANCE ON THE STATEMENT

When the plaintiff hears a false statement but takes no action based on that false statement, he has not relied on it. It is not enough that the plaintiff prove that the defendant's statement was false; the plaintiff must also show that he relied on it in some way. If the plaintiff did not rely on the statement to his detriment, he has failed to prove an essential element of negligent misrepresentation.

5. NO DAMAGES

Similar to the last defense, a defendant is entitled to raise the defense that even if the statement was false and the plaintiff relied on it, the plaintiff suffered no damages because of it. Under the Restatement position, which has been adopted in one form or another by nearly all jurisdictions, pecuniary loss is an essential element of the claim. As far as this tort is concerned, mental pain and anguish are not damages. The plaintiff must show some form of monetary loss or he is not entitled to recover.

Sidebar

The plaintiff may be able to recover under some other tort for mental pain and anguish caused by the defendant's statement, such as infliction of emotional distress.

6. WAIVER

Finally, a defendant can claim that even if all of the elements are met, the plaintiff waived any right to pursue his action. A waiver occurs when the plaintiff signs a document officially relinquishing a legal right, or it can occur through conduct.

Example: During the course of Ted's business, Ted has made a statement that clearly constitutes a negligent misrepresentation. John, the person who received this false statement, acknowledges it and then continues to work with Ted anyway. Ted can now argue that because of John's **ratification,** he has waived any right to sue for the negligent misrepresentation.

Ratification
The process of confirming and accepting a previous action; a void contract can be ratified after the fact to make it legally enforceable.

H. DEFENSES THAT ARE UNAVAILABLE IN NEGLIGENT MISREPRESENTATION

It is not a defense to a claim of negligent misrepresentation that the defendant did not have a particular person in mind when he made his false statement. Anyone who could foreseeably have relied on her false statement has a potential claim against her. Other defenses that are not available to defendants in negligent misrepresentation cases are listed in Figure 14-5.

- That the defendant had no knowledge of the veracity of the statement
- That there was no privity of contract between the parties
- That the defendant acted in good faith

FIGURE 14-5

Defenses Not Available in Negligent Misrepresentation Cases

1. NO KNOWLEDGE

Defendants are not permitted to raise the defense that they had no knowledge of the accuracy of their statements at the time that they made them. A negligent misrepresentation case is based on the theory that the defendant failed to use reasonable care and competence in making her statement, so the fact that she failed to verify its accuracy actually helps the plaintiff prove one of his essential elements.[12] In fact, many jurisdictions allow a claim against the defendant precisely because he had no knowledge, at the time that he made the statement to the plaintiff, that it was true.[13]

2. LACK OF PRIVITY

Although we have said that privity of contract is often found in negligent misrepresentation cases, there is no requirement that it exist. Therefore, a defense of no privity of contract will not exempt the defendant from the consequences of her false statement. As long as the plaintiff can show that it was foreseeable that he would rely on the defendant's statements, and that his reliance was reasonable, the plaintiff has presented sufficient proof.[14]

3. GOOD FAITH

In many jurisdictions, the defendant's good faith in making the statement is also not a defense.[15] The true test is whether the defendant had reasonable grounds for believing that her statement was true. Without that reasonable belief, her good faith is immaterial.[16]

V | INTERFERENCE WITH CONTRACT

Sidebar

The scenario presented in this section is similar to the original English case that first brought the tort of interference with contract into prominence. In that case, a famous opera singer was lured away from performing at one opera house by the owner of another house. Lumley, the opera house owner who had a contract with the singer, sued Lye, who lured her away. He won his case and a place, or at least a footnote, in legal history.[17]

Suppose that the owner of a local stadium has entered into a contract with a famous rock band to perform six shows next month. The owner anticipates that the revenue from this show will be outstanding, and he has even installed extra seats, improved lighting, and hired additional security guards after signing the band to perform. Two weeks before the band is to perform, the stadium owner sees an article in the local paper advertising the band's performance but stating that the band will actually be performing at a local amphitheater, owned and operated by Al Amp. He calls the band's manager and learns that Al Amp contacted the band one day after the band signed with him and lured the band away by promising them more money and the chance to record a live album at the site. The stadium owner is furious and comes to our firm for advice. He knows that he can sue the band for breach of contract, but he wants to go after Al Amp. What kind of suit can he bring against him?

The tort of interference with contract, sometimes called interference with contractual relations, is a civil action that can be brought against a third party who interferes with the business relationship between two other parties. If the stadium owner can satisfy the elements of this tort, he may be able to win at trial.

A. ELEMENTS OF INTERFERENCE WITH CONTRACT

Interference with contract consists of the following elements:

1. There was a contract between the plaintiff and a third party.
2. The defendant knew that such a contract existed.
3. The defendant acted intentionally to induce the third party to breach the contract.
4. The defendant's actions were the proximate cause of the breach of contract.
5. The plaintiff suffered damages as a result of the breach of contract.[18]

While several of these elements are self-explanatory, the third element needs some additional clarification. What, for instance, is "intentional" conduct necessary to establish the third element of interference with contract? Is it enough that the defendant simply suggests to the third party that he walk away from a contract, or must the defendant do more before he will be liable? The answer, in most jurisdictions, is that the defendant must do more than simply suggest a contract breach.

Generally, the defendant must make a concerted effort to get the third party to breach his contract. The courts will examine not only what the defendant did, but also his motives for doing it. If the defendant induced the third party to breach the contract and then employed the third party for the same purpose, courts will consider that to be a major factor in determining the defendant's liability. However, the courts will also balance the actions of the defendant against the interests of society as a whole. Is there a good policy reason why the third party should be free to work with others? All of these factors make a determination of interference with contract difficult.[19]

Compare these two situations: XYZ Company is the largest employer in the area. Among its many interests is software design. The company insists that all employees, prior to hiring, sign a noncompete contract. This contract provides that if an employee leaves the company, for any reason, he or she cannot compete directly or indirectly with any of the company's interests for a period of five years within a 1,000-mile radius of the company's main headquarters. Steve is an XYZ employee who is approached by a landscape design company. They want to hire Steve to work for them to develop new landscape design software. Steve quits his job and goes to work for the company. XYZ sues the company on the theory of interference with contract because of the noncompete contract. As the basis of this contention, the company claims that it was considering creating landscape and home design software. How will the court rule on this suit?

Answer: In most jurisdictions, XYZ will lose. Although there is a noncompete contract and the landscape company did approach Steve and lure him away from his employment (essentially inducing Steve to breach his employment contract with XYZ), there is a larger, societal issue here. First, XYZ's noncompete contract is too broad. By insisting on a five-year, 1,000-mile radius of noncompetition, the company is stifling innovation and new businesses. Second, the courts are consistent in ruling that employees have the right to move on to new employment, and this right carries greater weight than a company's right to the employee's services.

Scenario 2: Sal works for Outdoor Advertising, Inc., a firm that markets and installs highway billboards. Sal believes that he can create a new company doing the same thing and make himself rich. When he leaves his old job, he takes the client list with him. He then begins contacting his old clients and asking them to switch to his new company. When several of the clients express concerns that they might have some legal liability for breach of contract, Steve assures them that he will help defray any legal costs if they should be sued. Outdoor Advertising learns what Steve is up to and brings an interference with contract suit against him. How will the court rule?

Answer: Steve is likely to lose. Although Steve has the right to leave the firm, and may even have the right to approach his old customers to see if they wish to change firms, he has certainly acted improperly by offering to pay their legal bills if they are sued. This undoubtedly induced many of Outdoor Advertising's customers to breach their contracts.[20]

In interference with contract, the defendant's actions do not have to be tortious. The tort does not spring from *how* the defendant interferes but simply the fact that he interfered. In such a case, the defendant does not have to engage in threats or battery or any other tortious activity. Simply luring the party away from the plaintiff is enough.[22]

Although we discuss interference with contract as a civil injury, it is important to point out that not all states categorize it this way. New York, for instance, classifies this as a cause of action based on breach of contract, not as a tort.[23]

Sidebar

The tort of interference with contract has a long history. Originally developed in ancient Rome, it was based on the theory that another person should not be allowed to interfere with someone's slave. Later, the concept was expanded to include employees and eventually parties to a contract.[21]

VI   DECEPTIVE TRADE PRACTICES

A. DECEPTIVE TRADE PRACTICES ACT

Sidebar

The Uniform Deceptive Trade Practices Act has been adopted, in whole or with modifications, in the following states: Colorado, Delaware, Georgia, Hawaii, Illinois, Maine, Minnesota, Nebraska, New Mexico, Ohio, Oklahoma, and Oregon.[24]

Most states have some type of statute that prohibits deceptive trade practices. The Uniform Deceptive Trade Practices Act, which has been adopted — although with substantial modifications — by a majority of states, provides that a person engages in deceptive trade practices when, during the course of his business, he:

1. passes off goods or services as his own when they are in fact someone else's;

2. sets out to confuse the origin, certification, or association of goods;
3. sets out to confuse the certification of the goods or their affiliation;
4. uses deceptive advertisements or statements to create the impression that the goods originated from one geographic area when they actually originated from another;
5. states that the goods have qualities that they in fact do not have; or
6. represents that the goods are new when in fact they are used.

The purpose of a deceptive trade practices act (DTPA) is to prevent merchants and others from tricking consumers into buying goods that they otherwise would not want. To bring an action under a state deceptive trade practices act, the plaintiff must show:

1. that the defendant took advantage of the plaintiff's lack of knowledge about an item
2. by engaging in one of the proscribed acts.[25]

B. PUBLIC AND PRIVATE ENFORCEMENT UNDER DTPA

The interesting thing about an action under the DPTA is that two actions are authorized. The Act permits private enforcement through a civil suit, but it also authorizes government actions. In many ways, a state DTPA resembles a criminal action. As we have seen in other contexts, a private action (battery, for example) can give rise to a civil cause of action and a criminal charge. Deceptive trade practices are similar in that the government and the individual can both bring actions. However, they are different in that the government action will not result in jail time. Instead, the defendant may be ordered to pay a civil judgment.

Sidebar

In states that authorize public and private enforcement of deceptive trade practices, the state attorney general is usually the person authorized to bring the public actions.

 **CONSUMER PROTECTION LAWS**

In addition to the other types of business torts we have discussed in this chapter, there are numerous "consumer protection" statutes that exist on the state and federal levels. Many of these statutes have tort-like features. These protections include the Federal Truth-in-Lending laws, the Uniform Commercial Code, and state limitations on debt collection practices. If a particular case involves a consumer-protection issue, both state and federal statutes should be reviewed to see if they apply.

VIII   SEXUAL HARASSMENT

In recent years, countless companies and several branches of the U.S. military have faced claims of sexual harassment. These claims are often expensive to resolve and, while pending, can have a debilitating effect on management and work relationships. When harassment occurs in the workplace, employee morale and productivity are often seriously affected. Even more important, the victim's sense of security is violated, and companies are often assessed with large verdicts for permitting such activity to occur.

A. SEXUAL HARASSMENT IN THE WORKPLACE

Everyone has the right to work in an environment free from sexual harassment and to be evaluated solely on work performance. Sexual harassment is defined in a variety of ways in different states. We address the basic issues found in such suits, but there is no substitute for reviewing state-specific law on this topic.

B. WHAT IS SEXUAL HARASSMENT?

Sexual harassment covers a wide range of behaviors, from obvious acts such as fondling someone's body to more subtle ones such as making suggestive comments. In general, sexual harassment is any unwelcome behavior in the workplace that

- relates to a person's gender or sexuality;
- is intentional and/or repeated;
- is unwanted and not returned; and
- interferes with a person's ability to do his or her job, or has an effect on working conditions.

There are two types of sexual harassment actions recognized in most jurisdictions: quid pro quo and hostile environment.

1. QUID PRO QUO SEXUAL HARASSMENT

In an action alleging quid pro quo sexual harassment, the plaintiff alleges that the defendant requested sexual acts as a basis for employment. Such cases are often seen in the context of a defendant offering the plaintiff favorable working conditions, promotions, or other incentives in exchange for sex.

2. HOSTILE ENVIRONMENT SEXUAL HARASSMENT

Hostile environment sexual harassment occurs when unwelcome sexual conduct interferes with an individual's job performance or creates a hostile, intimidating, or offensive work environment. Actions based on hostile environment can be brought even though the harassment did not result in tangible or economic job consequences. For example, plaintiffs do not have to allege that they were fired or passed over for a promotion when they refused to engage in sexual activity.

 ## DRAM SHOP LIABILITY

The vast majority of states have some form of dram shop liability. The basic premise behind dram shop liability is that a business (or, in some states, an individual) that furnishes alcohol to an obviously intoxicated person should bear part of the responsibility for the injuries this person later inflicts. Under the common law, there was no such cause of action against someone who furnished alcohol to another. Many states adopted dram shop liability by judicial interpretation of negligence law. Over the years, many state legislatures have codified dram shop liability. An example of a typical statute is found in Figure 14-6.

WORKERS' COMPENSATION

The topic of workers' compensation could easily fill an entire book. Although the basic idea behind workers' compensation statutes is deceptively simple, in practice it can often become quite complicated.

A. THE BASIC PREMISE OF WORKERS' COMPENSATION

Workers' compensation is based on the simple premise that workers who are injured on the job will receive a fixed, monetary award in return for giving up the right to sue their employer. The entire system is designed to short-circuit lengthy litigation by employees against employers for on-the-job injuries.

A person who sells or furnishes alcoholic beverages to a person of lawful drinking age shall not thereby become liable for injury or damage caused by or resulting from the intoxication of such person, except that a person who willfully and unlawfully sells or furnishes alcoholic beverages to a person who is not of lawful drinking age or who knowingly serves a person habitually addicted to the use of any or all alcoholic beverages may become liable for injury or damage caused by or resulting from the intoxication of such minor or person.	**FIGURE 14-6** Florida Statute §768.125. Liability for Injury or Damage Resulting from Intoxication

Workers' families are also entitled to an award in situations in which the worker is killed on the job. Employers pay into the system to compensate employees for their injuries. When an employee is injured on the job, he files a claim with the workers' compensation board, seeking reimbursement for medical payments and other financial losses. An employee covered by workers' compensation is prevented, in most cases, from bringing suit against the employer under traditional tort theory. The attraction of workers' compensation is that the employers receive some degree of assurance that they will not be sued by the employees, while the employees receive some amount of assurance that they will receive compensation for their claims without going through the burdensome process of filing a lawsuit.

B. BRINGING A CLAIM UNDER WORKERS' COMPENSATION

When an employee is injured on the job, he will file a claim under workers' compensation. If the injury is job related, the employee is entitled to payment for medical bills and associated costs. If the employee's injury is permanent in nature, the employee is entitled to a settlement that takes into account the degree of impairment and the effect of this impairment on future earnings. Instead of bringing a claim through the court system, an employee brings a claim through the state workers' compensation board. Although this board can be called many things in many states, the basic structure is the same. Claims are evaluated by administrative law judges, who are empowered to make decisions in such claims. Although they are not judges in the usual sense, they do have the power to render final decisions in claims.

C. THE ISSUES IN WORKERS' COMPENSATION

Although the premise of workers' compensation sounds simple, in practice it can often get bogged down in the details. For instance, suppose that Mary is injured on the job. She injures her right hand while loading some heavy boxes onto a shelf in the back storage room. The injury to her hand is severe. She has suffered some broken bones and what appears to be some permanent nerve damage. Mary is in constant pain. How does her claim proceed through workers' compensation?

When Mary is injured on the job, one of the first things that she is supposed to do is to report her injury to her employer. This report triggers several significant events. For one thing, it puts her employer on notice that she has been injured and that her injury should be cared for. If Mary fails to report her injury, her claim may be delayed or refused under workers' compensation. The reporting of the injury also gives the employer some relevant information upon which to begin an investigation.

D. ASSIGNING MONETARY VALUES TO INJURIES

One of the underlying theories of workers' compensation is that injuries to various parts of the employee's body have a set amount of recovery. This system of assigning monetary value to injuries is very much like the ancient system of tort law in which the loss of a hand justified more compensation for the victim than the loss of a toe. Under workers' compensation, the nature of the victim's injury, coupled with its permanence, will have a profound impact on the final monetary award. However, because the permanence of the worker's injury is often hotly debated, medical testimony is usually required to prove this point.

A physician may testify, usually through deposition, about the nature of the worker's injury. Returning to our example of Mary and her injured hand, suppose that a doctor determines that Mary has a permanent 50 percent loss of use of her right hand. In such a case, the workers' compensation administrative law judge will refer to a schedule to determine how much to award Mary for such a loss. This may sound simple and straightforward, but when it comes down to actual cases, the issues often become quite complicated. Suppose, for example, that Mary disputes the doctor's findings. Is she entitled to an independent doctor's opinion? The answer is usually yes. There are a host of other issues that could surface in a typical workers' compensation case, including an employer's contention that the employee's job duties did not include the activity in the course of which she was injured, the impact on her future employment, and the total amount of her award.

Attorneys and law firms that handle workers' compensation often develop a specialty in this area. Because of the complicated nature of cases, statutes, and rulings, most attorneys believe that they cannot do an adequate job in representing an injured worker or an employer unless they spend a great deal of time specializing in such cases. When a paralegal goes to work for a workers' compensation firm, the paralegal often finds that her duties involve workers' compensation cases exclusively.

Sidebar

In many ways, workers' compensation claims resemble abbreviated lawsuits. There is a claim raised by the employee; there is a response by the employer. Attorneys usually represent both sides. There is an administrative law judge whose responsibility involves ruling on the claim and deciding issues of law and fact. However, if you observed a workers' compensation hearing, the level of informality would probably surprise you. Workers' compensation hearings are frequently conducted in offices and conference rooms, not in courtrooms.

Case Excerpt

GUTIERREZ V. DEVINE
103 A.D.3d 1185, 958 N.Y.S.2d 566 (2013)

Memorandum

Plaintiff commenced this negligence and Dram Shop action seeking to recover damages for injuries she sustained when the vehicle in which she was a passenger struck a tree. The vehicle was operated by defendant Pierce A. Devine. Devine, a minor, tested positive for alcohol after the accident, and was charged with operating a motor vehicle while under the influence of alcohol (Vehicle and Traffic Law §1192[3]) and vehicular assault in the second degree (Penal

Law §120.03[1]). Before the accident, defendant Kyle Tatum, Tatum's girl-friend, and plaintiff drove to a gas station/convenience store owned and oper-ated by Lutz Brothers, Inc. (defendant), and Devine met them there. Tatum, who was 17 years old at the time, purchased beer from the store using false identification. The four minors then drove to a beach on Lake Erie, where they drank beer for approximately two hours. When it started to rain, they dropped Tatum's car off at Devine's house, and drove in Devine's car to the home of Tatum's girlfriend to pick up a movie. The accident occurred when the group was driving back to Devine's house. Plaintiff appeals from an order that, inter alia, granted defendant's motion for summary judgment dismissing the second amended complaint against it. We affirm.

We note at the outset that, although the second amended complaint asserts a violation of General Obligations Law §11–101, there is no claim or evidence that defendant sold alcohol to anyone who was visibly intoxicated at the time of the sale in violation of that statute. The analysis is therefore limited to whether plaintiff has a viable claim under General Obligations Law §11–100. That statute provides in relevant part that "any person who shall be injured in person . . . by reason of the intoxication or impairment of ability of any person under the age of 21 years . . . shall have a right of action to recover actual damages against any person who knowingly causes such intoxication or impairment of ability by unlawfully furnishing to or unlawfully assisting in procuring alcoholic beverages for such person with knowledge or reasonable cause to believe that such person was under the age of 21 years." Thus, the General Obligations Law "explicitly . . . limits liability for injuries caused by an intoxicated minor to the unlawful supply of alcoholic beverages to that person" (*Sherman v. Robinson*, 80 N.Y.2d 483, 487, 591 N.Y.S.2d 974, 606 N.E.2d 1365). "The plain language of the Dram Shop Act specifies that the individual who by reason of intoxication causes injury must be the very person to whom defendant furnished the alcoholic beverages, or for whom they were procured." Further, "liability under General Obligations Law §11–100 may be imposed only on a person who knowingly causes intoxication by furnishing alcohol to (or assisting in the procurement of alcohol for) persons known or reasonably believed to be underage" (*Sherman*, 80 N.Y.2d at 487–488, 591 N.Y.S.2d 974, 606 N.E.2d 1365).

Here, it is undisputed that defendant sold the alcohol at issue to Tatum and that Devine was the intoxicated person who caused plaintiff's injuries. There is no evidence that defendant knowingly sold or furnished alcoholic beverages to Devine, the underage tortfeasor, nor is there evidence that defendant assisted in procuring alcoholic beverages for Devine. Rather, the unlawful transaction was with Tatum.

Contrary to plaintiff's contention, "nothing in the General Obligations Law imposed upon defendant convenience store owner a duty . . . to inves-tigate possible ultimate consumers in the parking lot beyond its doors." Plain-tiff's reliance on our decision in *Krampen v. Foster*, 242 A.D.2d 913, 664 N.Y.S.2d 900 is misplaced. In *Krampen*, although the alcohol was not sold directly to the driver, the plaintiffs presented evidence that the store clerk knew both the purchaser and the driver (id. at 914, 664 N.Y.S.2d 900).

While the purchase took place, the store clerk looked out the window at the driver's car, which was parked directly in front of the store window, and the driver waved to the store clerk (id.). There is no such evidence in this case. Here, the record establishes that none of defendant's employees knew Tatum, Devine, or any of their companions, and the minors likewise did not know any of defendant's employees. Further, unlike in *Krampen*, plaintiff submitted no evidence that any of defendant's employees saw the people or activities in the parking lot. Thus, because plaintiff's injuries were not caused by the minor who purchased the alcohol, there can be no liability under the Dram Shop Act, and the court therefore properly granted that part of defendant's motion for summary judgment dismissing the Dram Shop cause of action against it.

Finally, it is well settled that there is no common-law cause of action for the negligent provision of alcohol and the court therefore also properly granted that part of defendant's motion for summary judgment dismissing the common-law negligence cause of action against defendant.

It is hereby ORDERED that the order so appealed from is unanimously affirmed without costs.

Questions about the case:

1. Which plaintiff was sold beer by the defendant?
2. Is there any allegation that the convenience store sold alcohol to someone who was obviously intoxicated?
3. How does the state Dram Shop Act factor into the facts of this case?

XI. FOLLOW-UP ON THE SHAREHOLDER'S SUIT

We began this chapter with a hypothetical situation involving the End-Run Corporation and a shareholder with 1,000 shares who wishes to sue the corporation for its false announcements and statements regarding the company's financial health. Now that we have reviewed the various types of business torts that could be brought in this situation, are any of them appropriate to this situation?

First, let's review the basic facts. Tom, who already owns 1,000 shares of End-Run stock, wants to sue the corporation for making false statements. Can he meet the essential elements of a fraud action? Remember that the elements for fraud consist of the following: (1) The defendant made a representation of a material fact or concealed a fact; (2) the representation was false; (3) the defendant knew the representation was false; (4) the defendant made the representation with the intent that the plaintiff would rely on it; (5) the plaintiff's reliance on the representation was reasonable under the circumstances; and (6) the plaintiff suffered injury from his reliance on the representation.

Assuming that Tom can present some proof to show that the company knew that it was making a false statement at the time it was made, the first three elements would seem fairly straightforward. What about the fourth element? There is no requirement that the plaintiff must show that the false statement was made with him in mind. If the plaintiff is in the group of people likely to be affected by the false statement, this element is met. Tom is a shareholder and falls into this category. We begin to run into problems, though, with the fifth element. Tom must show that his reliance on the representation was reasonable. This presupposes that Tom took some action with respect to the false information. We know that Tom already owns 1,000 shares. Unless we can show that Tom purchased more stock as a result, or took some other action, he cannot show any detrimental reliance on the information. We may also have some trouble with the last element. How does Tom show that he suffered economic injury? Surely the fact that he purchased the stock for a much higher price than it is worth now should be enough to prove damages, shouldn't it? In the pragmatic world of the courts, this may not be enough. The fact that Tom's stock was worth a lot more last year than it is worth this year may not be enough to prove an actual economic injury for Tom. There may be ways of dealing with this problem, but it is certainly an issue that the legal team must face.

Overall, Tom may not have a very strong case against End-Run, at least for fraudulent misrepresentation. His case for negligent misrepresentation also suffers from the same drawbacks.

Chapter Summary

In this chapter, we discussed torts that are normally associated with business dealings. When a plaintiff believes that he has been the victim of fraud, he can present a civil case in which he alleges that the defendant made a false statement to him, knowing that it was false, on which the plaintiff relied, and from which the plaintiff suffered some type of monetary damage. When the defendant makes a statement without knowing that it is true, or in reckless disregard of the truth, he can be sued for negligent misrepresentation. The essential elements of an action for negligent misrepresentation include a statement made by the defendant, in the course of the defendant's trade or occupation, upon which statement the plaintiff justifiably relied. Another essential element of a negligent misrepresentation action is that the plaintiff suffered some type of monetary loss as a result of the false statement.

There are several defenses available to a claim for negligent misrepresentation, including the truth of the statement made by the defendant, that the statement was an opinion, that the plaintiff did not actually rely on the statement to his detriment, or that the plaintiff suffered no monetary loss because of the false information.

In addition to actions for fraud and negligent misrepresentation, a plaintiff can bring other types of business torts, including interference with contract and deceptive trade practices. An action for deceptive trade practices can include not only a private action, but also a public action brought by the state attorney general.

SKILLS YOU NEED IN THE REAL WORLD

Helping to Try a Case

Up to now, we have discussed the preliminary work that goes into preparing for a civil trial. Now it is time to address actually trying a case. Although the paralegal will not be involved in questioning witnesses on the stand or making a closing argument to the jury, a paralegal can have an equally crucial role in the trial. As the paralegal, you will often be the one to act as the resource person: You will find crucial documents at critical times during the trial, you will coordinate witness appearances, you will help set up jury demonstrations, and you will research last-minute legal issues. As such, a good trial paralegal must be prepared to deal with a wide range of problems and be able to handle them efficiently.

We assume that settlement negotiations have broken down and the case is scheduled for trial. Barring any last-minute miracles, this case looks like it will actually go before a jury. The firm has gone into trial mode. The attorneys have locked themselves in their offices to review the file and to prepare. You must also get ready. Here are five things you should do before you begin any trial.

1. Get the Lay of the Land

When it seems likely that a particular case is actually going to go to trial, it's time for you to get into trial mode, too. If you think of a trial as a battle (and, in many ways, it is), you should do what military professionals do: reconnaissance work. Go to the courthouse and find out which courtroom is reserved for your case. If the courtroom is locked, ask courthouse personnel to open it for you. Explain to them that you are there getting ready for trial. Once you are inside, draw a basic diagram of the room. Locate the witness stand, judge's bench, and attorney tables. The plaintiff usually has the table closest to the jury box. Sit in the jury box and look at the room from their perspective. If you have a friend with you, have the friend talk in a normal tone of voice from the witness stand. Can you hear him? If not, is there a microphone? These are the things that you can tell witnesses later.

Next, locate electrical outlets. These days, attorneys and paralegals often bring laptop computers, overhead projectors, and even printers into the courtroom. Are there enough plugs to accommodate all of these devices? If not, will you need a power strip, extension cords, and so on? Will you need to tape the cords down so that people won't trip over them?

If the attorney wants to make notes during an opening or closing argument, is there a chalkboard, whiteboard, or easel? Make sure that you have backup supplies for whatever is available. Don't rely on the courthouse personnel to supply you with a dry-erase marker when the one in the courtroom goes dry just as the attorney is starting his closing argument.

2. Do a Trial Run with All Equipment

According to Murphy's Law, if it can go wrong, it will, and at the worst possible moment. Keep this in mind if your team is going to be using any equipment during the trial, such as an overhead projector. Do a trial run with the device shortly before the trial. If it is a digital projector, does it actually work with the attorney's laptop? Try it and see. Do you have backup lightbulbs and the right cable connectors? If possible, do a trial run with the equipment in the courtroom. In one case, an attorney had prepared a wonderful closing argument as a PowerPoint presentation. However, when it came time to present it to the jury, he suddenly realized that there was no place to project it. There was no screen and not even a blank wall in the courtroom. You can help avoid little disasters like this by doing a trial run with all equipment.

3. Check the Layout of the Courthouse

As part of your reconnaissance work at the courthouse, don't neglect the layout of the building outside the courtroom. If you are unfamiliar with the building, draw a map of the facility. You are going to have witnesses waiting around to testify. Where are they going to sit? What if they need to go to the bathroom or get a quick snack? If you know where these areas are, you can direct them — and also know where to look if they disappear. Take crucial witnesses to the courthouse and make sure that they know where to go. Take them right into the empty courtroom and show them where the witness stand is. Many witnesses are nervous about testifying, so this trip to the courtroom will give them a big boost of confidence just when they need it most.

4. Master the Trial Notebook or Case Files

By the time the case is actually about to go to trial, you should know the case file as well as the attorney, if not better. Test yourself: Can you find any particular document, transcript, motion, or pleading in less than ten seconds? If you can, you know the file; if you can't, you have more work to do. At some point during the trial, something unexpected will happen, and the attorney will need a document that you hadn't anticipated that you would need. Can you find it immediately? There is nothing more frustrating — and nerve-wracking — than floundering in the middle of a cross-examination because a particular document is lost.

5. Get Ready for Stress

If you are good at handling stress, you are in the right business. Unfortunately, most people aren't. Trials are stressful events. They will be stressful for you in ways that are different from the stress the attorneys will feel. You will find yourself constantly trying to anticipate where the case is going so that you can be ready with the right thing at the right time. There are ways that you can reduce stress, such as following the first four tips in this section, but there is no way to reduce all stress.

You know that both you and the attorney will be under a great deal of stress, so prepare ways to deal with it. If you like to exercise, don't neglect it during the trial. At least take a break at the end of the day to take a walk or do something else that you find enjoyable. Unfortunately, too many stressed-out people turn to alcohol or food or some other unhealthy diversion. Over time, these short-term responses will take their toll on you. The longer the trial, the more stress on everyone involved. You need to learn to deal with the stress or it will tear you apart—too often there is no middle ground.

THE LIFE OF A PARALEGAL

Going to Trial

When I start getting ready for trial, I first go through the discovery. I dig through it, pulling out pertinent documents that establish the crucial points in the case and show what the parties did. I put these all together and then make four copies of the whole package. One copy is for my attorney, one is for the judge, one is for the opposition, and one is for the witnesses. The reason that I make so many copies is that it helps speed things up and helps everyone stay focused. The judge and opposing attorney can follow along when my attorney is questioning a witness about a particular document. In some places, the court rules dictate that the opposing attorney gets a copy. But we do it even when the rules don't require it. We keep one copy of the package up at the witness box so that the attorney can direct the witness to a particular page. I separate out each exhibit, prepare a table of contents, and then put a tab on each specific document so that everyone can find it quickly. I number the documents sequentially, so that when the attorney asks the witness to turn to page 35, everyone else has the same page in front of them.

After I put the exhibits together, the next thing I focus on is the pleadings. I go through them thoroughly. I look for anything that either side has admitted, and I list it. Then I list the denials; that's what we will have to prove at trial. I've already gone through prior discovery responses and drafted follow-up questions. Now, I pull all of that information together.

These days, you get papered to death. You have to have a good handle on your file and be able to find your information quickly. That's not only true for trial preparation, but for settlement as well. A lot of times you might have an arbitration hearing, and you'll need to access this stuff quickly and efficiently. My rule is: you can't be too organized.

Jane Huffman, Paralegal

ETHICAL ISSUES FOR THE PARALEGAL: COACHING WITNESSES

When we discuss preparing for trial, there is one ethical issue that always rears its head: coaching witnesses. We have already seen that preparation for trial is critical, and that is no less true when talking about preparing witnesses to testify. However, when does preparation cross the line into coaching? First of all, what do we mean by "coaching" a witness? When a person coaches a witness, he is telling the witness what he should say when he is on the stand. That is clearly unethical and illegal. It is one thing to tell a witness what he should say; it is another to tell a witness what he is likely to hear. Although this sounds like splitting hairs, in the reality of a legal practice, this line is easy to maintain. You should never tell a witness how he or she should answer a specific question. You should never tell a witness to lie. Your advice to a witness should always be simple and direct. You should always tell the witness to tell the truth, even when the truth doesn't put the witness in a good light. Besides being unethical, a dishonest witness will almost always get caught. When a witness can be shown to be untruthful about one point in his testimony, the jury will probably discount all of his testimony.

When you assist in preparing a witness, it is common for you to tell the witness what he can expect during his time on the stand. You might tell him that he will be sworn and that he will be questioned about specific topics. You should tell a witness that he will be cross-examined and what the purpose of the cross-examination is. If there are unpleasant details in the testimony, you can advise the witness that he will, most likely, be asked about them. However, this preparation does not include rehearsing the witness in how he should answer particular questions. You should not "feed" the witness his lines. His testimony must be his own.

Relevant Cases

AMOURI V. SOUTHWEST TOYOTA, INC.
20 S.W.3d 165 (2000)

Opinion
Opinion by Chief Justice Cornelius.
Abdolhossein Amouri appeals from an adverse summary judgment rendered in his suit against Southwest Toyota, Inc. d/b/a Sterling McCall Toyota (Southwest). Amouri contends (1) the evidence raised a fact issue as to his claim that Southwest fraudulently induced him to sign a lease contract, and (2) the trial court improperly considered a defective transcript of Amouri's deposition in granting summary judgment. We reverse the judgment and remand the case for trial.

On September 4, 1997, Amouri visited Southwest, a Toyota dealership, intending to purchase a vehicle. A Southwest salesman, Apolo Lucci, assisted Amouri. Amouri selected a vehicle from the lot, test drove it, and decided he would buy it. Amouri contends that he and Lucci discussed only his purchasing the vehicle and the payment terms, and that they never discussed leasing the vehicle. To purchase the vehicle, Amouri proposed that he trade in his own car and make a substantial down payment and first installment payment. Nevertheless, after some discussion between Lucci and Southwest's managers, Lucci gave Amouri a document titled "Closed End Motor Vehicle Lease Agreement" and asked him to sign it. The document was in fact a lease agreement rather than a purchase agreement. Amouri signed the document believing he was purchasing the vehicle. Amouri traded in his car and made a substantial down payment and first installment payment, and then drove home in the vehicle he believed he had purchased.

Several days later, a friend of Amouri's, a former car salesman, inspected the paperwork Southwest had given Amouri and suggested that Amouri confirm that he had actually purchased the vehicle, rather than having leased it. Amouri telephoned Lucci, who reassured him that he had purchased the vehicle. The following day, Amouri returned to Southwest, where he met with several managers, each of whom told him that he had leased the vehicle. Amouri explained that if he were not purchasing the vehicle, he wanted the contract voided. He requested the return of his money and trade-in vehicle and offered to pay for his temporary use of the new vehicle. The managers refused his requests and stated there was nothing they could do. Amouri also requested a complete copy of the lease contract but was told that Southwest did not keep contracts and that he would receive a copy in two weeks. Within several days, Amouri returned the vehicle and keys to Southwest.

In October 1997, Amouri filed suit against Southwest for breach of contract, common law fraud, breach of the duty of good faith and fair dealing, and violations of the Deceptive Trade Practices Act-Consumer Protection Act, seeking the recovery of his initial down payment, installment payment, car rental expenses, and monetary damages for the damage done to his trade-in vehicle. In March 1999, Southwest filed a motion for summary judgment on the grounds that, as a matter of law, Amouri could not establish breach of contract or fraud. The trial court granted summary judgment, which Amouri now appeals only on the ground that summary judgment was improper because there is a genuine fact issue as to his claim that Southwest fraudulently induced him to sign the lease contract. In his first amended petition, Amouri alleged that Lucci and other Southwest employees induced him to sign the lease contract by fraudulently representing that they were assisting him in the purchase of the vehicle and by deliberately remaining silent when

they directed him to sign the lease contract. Pursuant to tex.R.App. P. 45, Southwest requests that this Court sanction Amouri for filing a frivolous appeal.

Fraudulent inducement is a type of fraud claim that shares the same elements as a simple fraud claim. Thus, to prove fraudulent inducement, Amouri had to show (1) that Southwest made a material misrepresentation that was false, (2) that it was either known to be false when made or was asserted without knowledge of its truth, and (3) that it was intended to be acted on, was relied on, and caused injury. In its motion, Southwest attacked the elements of misrepresentation and reliance. Citing two cases, *Brown v. Aztec Rig Equip., Inc.,* 921 S.W.2d 835 (1996), and *Plains Cotton Coop. Ass'n v. Wolf,* 553 S.W.2d 800 (1977), it contended that it was entitled to summary judgment as a matter of law because the law charges all competent persons with knowledge of the contents of the contracts they sign. According to Southwest, this rule necessarily forecloses any false representations contrary to the terms of the contract or any reliance thereon. It contends that the failure to read a contract constitutes negligence on the part of the signor, for which the signor is not excused, and that even illiteracy will not relieve a party of the consequences of his contract. At oral argument, counsel for Southwest cited Fisher Controls Int'l, Inc. v. Gibbons, 911 S.W.2d 135 (Tex.App.-Houston 1995, writ denied), as support for its contention that, because of this rule of law, fraudulent inducement cannot be established by misrepresentations that contradict the terms of a contract. Rather, it contends that fraudulent inducement is proven sometimes by evidence of a misrepresentation, but most often by evidence of a concealment of a material fact that is not thereafter contradicted by the written terms of a subsequent contract. In other words, Southwest argues that the concealment used to induce the agreement must involve something not provided for by the contract.

The general rule is that every person who has the capacity to enter into a contract is held to know what words were used in the contract, to know their meaning, and to understand their legal effect. The consequence of this rule is that a party to a contract may not successfully claim that he believed the provisions of the contract were different from those plainly set out in the agreement or that he did not understand the meaning of the language used. However, there is a long-established and well-known exception to the rule: Where the execution of a contract is procured by fraud, misrepresentation, or concealment, such that there is no real assent to the agreement, assent may be negated and the binding nature of the contract avoided.

Southwest's version of the general rule is incomplete. Even the failure to read a contract will be excused where the execution of the contract has been fraudulently induced. In *Plains Cotton Coop.*, the court stated:

> Where one party's false representations induce another party to contract, negligence of the second party cannot be raised to bar relief to him. . . . Thus, failure to read a contract before signing it, although it may constitute negligence, will not bar equitable relief to one who has executed a contract in reliance upon false representations made to him by the other contracting party. *Plains Cotton Coop. Ass'n v. Wolf*, 553 S.W.2d at 803.

In addition, illiteracy is irrelevant where the contract was procured through fraud. In Brown, while the court stated that "illiteracy will not relieve a party of the consequences of his contract," the court recognized that "every person having the capacity to enter into contracts, in the absence of fraud, misrepresentation or concealment, must be held to have known what words were used in the contract and to have known their meaning. . . ." *Brown v. Aztec Rig Equip., Inc.*, 921 S.W.2d at 846. Although the law charges parties with knowledge of the contents of the contracts they sign,

proof of fraudulent misrepresentations and reliance on such misrepresentations may permit parties to void their contracts.

Southwest contends that in order for Amouri to successfully assert a fraud claim, it either must have prevented Amouri from reading the lease or it must have physically forced him to sign it. It argues that Amouri denied in his deposition that either occurred. It is true that where a party resorts to trick or artifice in order to prevent another from reading the contract or having it read to him, the aggrieved party may void the contract. But this is not the only conduct that will give rise to a claim of fraudulent inducement. As we have noted, to prove fraudulent inducement, Amouri was required to show that Southwest made a material misrepresentation, which was false, and which was either known to be false when made or was asserted without knowledge of its truth, which was intended to be acted upon, which was relied upon, and which caused injury. Silence is equivalent to a false representation where circumstances impose a duty to speak and one deliberately remains silent. In short, to prove his fraud claim, Amouri was required to show that Southwest engaged in a misrepresentation or a concealment. Amouri was not required to show that Southwest prevented him from reading the contract or physically forced him to sign it.

At oral argument, Southwest's counsel suggested that fraudulent inducement is proven by evidence of a concealment of a material fact that is not thereafter contradicted by the terms of a written contract. He stated that *Fisher Controls Int'l, Inc. v. Gibbons* deals with a concealment. In *Fisher*, the court addressed whether the evidence was legally and factually sufficient to support a finding of fraud. *Fisher Controls Int'l, Inc. v. Gibbons*, 911 S.W.2d at 140–43. Actually, Gibbons brought suit for fraud based on alleged affirmative misrepresentations, as well as concealments. Id. at 140. Gibbons alleged in part that Fisher told him before he signed the contract, which provided that Gibbons would represent Fisher for a three-year term, that Fisher would later extend the term beyond three years. Id. The contract provided in part, "Nothing contained herein shall be deemed to create any express or implied obligation on either party to renew or extend this Agreement. . . ." Id. at 141. Therefore, Fisher's alleged statements contradicted the terms of the written contract. The court, finding no evidence of fraud, held that Gibbons could not recover for the statements. Id. However, the court based its finding of no fraud not on the ground that the statements contradicted the terms of the written contract, but on the ground that Gibbons knowingly agreed to the three-year term. In other words, he did not rely on any misrepresentations. The court noted:

> Gibbons testified that he had read and understood the renewal provisions in the contract; that he had tried but failed to get Fisher to agree to a five-year term; that his attorney had advised him a three-year term was less than he needed if he was signing a five-year note; and that contrary to the attorney's advice, he accepted a three-year term. Id.

As for the alleged fraudulent concealments, the Fisher court held that the plaintiff could not recover for them, not because they were contradicted by the express terms of the contract, but because the defendant had no duty to disclose the information. See id. at 143.

Southwest's contention that the law charges parties with knowledge of the contents of the contracts they sign is incomplete. That contention is true only absent fraud, misrepresentation, or concealment. Fraud through misrepresentation or concealment is what Amouri relies on to establish his cause of action. In its motion for summary judgment,

Southwest had the burden of proving that there was no genuine issue of material fact and that it was entitled to judgment as a matter of law. It did not succeed in disproving misrepresentation or reliance.

In its summary judgment motion, Southwest stated, "There is no evidence of a false representation or reliance in this case. This is one of the rare circumstances where nothing Plaintiff could say in an affidavit is sufficient to create a fact issue in this case." Southwest's real contention was that the law charges parties with knowledge of the contents of the contracts they sign, and thus there can be no evidence of misrepresentation or reliance. We have therefore construed the motion to be a traditional summary judgment motion. But, even if the language above placed the burden on Amouri to produce some evidence of misrepresentation and reliance, Southwest still would not be entitled to summary judgment. Amouri attached a controverting affidavit to his response to the motion for summary judgment, in which he alleged that Southwest discussed with him the form of payment he would use in purchasing the vehicle and at no time prior to signing the agreement did Southwest discuss his leasing the vehicle. He also alleged that he intended to purchase the vehicle and, based on what transpired at Southwest, believed he had done so. These allegations are sufficient to raise a fact issue regarding misrepresentation or concealment and reliance.

For the reasons stated, we hold that the trial court erred in granting summary judgment as to Amouri's causes of action based on fraudulent inducement only, and we deny Southwest's request for sanctions. We do not reach Amouri's second point. Accordingly, we reverse the summary judgment as to fraudulent inducement and remand the case to the trial court for trial of that issue.

MASOTTI V. BRISTOL SAV. BANK
43 Conn. Supp. 360, 653 A.2d 836 (1994)

BERGER, Judge.

The plaintiff in the present action alleges that on May 7, 1990, the defendant bank wrongfully withdrew $783,165.12 from her bank accounts. The defendant concedes that it withdrew this amount but maintains that the withdrawal was proper because the money was withdrawn from the joint accounts of the plaintiff and her husband, Vito Masotti, who was in default on an obligation in excess of the amount withdrawn. The plaintiff's complaint contains six counts: conversion, breach of contract, negligence, breach of duty of good faith and fair dealing, and, allegations of an unfair trade practice and a failure to disclose.

The defendant has filed the present motion for summary judgment maintaining that there is no genuine issue of material fact and that it is entitled to judgment as a matter of law.

In its motion, the defendant provides a lengthy history of the accounts owned by the plaintiff and her husband. On July 5, 1989, account no. 46510318 was opened as a joint savings account in the form of a certificate of deposit in the sum of $124,873. On May 7, 1990, the defendant withdrew $133,483.34.

On October 21, 1988, account no. 45000204 was opened as a joint savings account, also in the form of a certificate of deposit in the sum of $739,700.95. On April 28, 1989, Vito Masotti withdrew $181,922.58 and the balance was rolled into a new certificate. On May 7, 1990, the defendant withdrew the balance of $640,516.51.

The third account in contention, account no. 4133013, was also opened as a joint savings account on March 3, 1986. Over the next four years, Vito Masotti made several deposits and withdrawals to this account, including deposits of $115,000 and $50,000, and withdrawals of $112,019.21, $20,000, $10,000, and $24,000.

On May 7, 1990, the defendant withdrew $3,851.

According to the complaint, the plaintiff and the defendant entered into a deposit account contract when each account was opened. The contract indicates that either depositor could withdraw the funds and the defendant had a right of setoff. The plaintiff now argues that the contents of the contract were neither discussed nor did she sign such a contract although she did sign the signature card.

On December 20, 1988, the defendant loaned Vito Masotti's partnership, Village Gate Partnership, $15,000,000 for a project in Farmington. As a partner, Vito Massotti signed a guaranty that stated that the defendant had "a lien and right of set off for all the Borrower's Village Gate's Obligations upon and against the deposits, credits and property of each Guarantor now or hereafter in the Lender's possession or control or in transit to the Lender. The Lender may at any time apply the same or any part thereof to any of the Borrower's Obligations without notice and without first resorting to any other collateral."

By letter dated May 4, 1990, the defendant notified Vito Masotti, but not the plaintiff, that the $15,000,000 loan was in default and that there was a hold on his bank accounts. On May 7, 1990, the defendant notified both the plaintiff and her husband that the three aforementioned accounts were closed. While the notification was by certified mail, there is no proof of actual service to the plaintiff. On or about October 23, 1990, as part of a work out, the defendant reinstated the funds it withdrew as Vito Masotti pledged the money to secure new loans from the defendant. The plaintiff learned of the pledge on November 1, 1990, and while Vito Masotti released the defendant, the plaintiff did not.

The defendant argues that there are no genuine issues of material fact and as there is both a contractual and common law right of setoff, summary judgment must be granted. This court agrees. In her complaint, the plaintiff alleges that she entered into the contract and that §1.10 of the contract specifically authorizes the setoff. Section 1.10 states: "Unless this right is denied to us by law, we can take any funds in your account to pay any debt you owe us that is in default. This is called the right of set-off and applies to all funds of yours in our possession now or in the future. We can use this right of set-off without going through any legal process or court proceedings. If this is a joint account, this right of set-off applies to deposits of any of you to pay the debts owed to us by any or all of you."

The funds in the three accounts were the funds of both Vito Masotti and the plaintiff. In his guaranty agreement, Vito Masotti also agreed to such a setoff and as the Village Gate loan was in default, the defendant could set off those funds. The plaintiff now argues that she never signed or received a copy of the contract yet she pleaded the contract in her complaint. She also indicated, in response to discovery, that the contract was in the possession of the defendant. In her memorandum of law dated March 7, 1994, the plaintiff stated that "the contract is nothing more than a covenant . . . in which the defendant bank would hold the plaintiff's deposits and pay interest on these deposits until such time as they were withdrawn by the plaintiff." The plaintiff is attempting to assert her rights under the contract but is unwilling to acknowledge the rights of the defendant. She cannot have it both ways.

It should also be noted that under our common law, the defendant has a right of setoff. The coholders of a joint account are considered owners of the entire account and either may withdraw. As a result of Vito Masotti's guaranty and the default of Village Gate, the defendant had a right of setoff against the accounts. Under Connecticut law, "a creditor-bank has a right of set-off against funds in its possession belonging to a debtor-depositor."

The plaintiff has also argued in her memorandum of law in opposition to the defendant's motion (as opposed to her initial complaint or affidavit) that the funds were special purpose funds and thus unavailable for setoff under *Vic Gerard Golf Cars, Inc. v. Citizen's National Bank*, supra, 528 F.Supp. at 241. As noted by the Supreme Court in *Rosa v. Colonial Bank*, 207 Conn. 483, 494-95, 542 A.2d 1112 (1988): "A special purpose account however, is generally one over which the depositor has only limited dominion and control. The deposit is usually made with special restrictions or limitations agreed upon between the bank and depositor. . . . Common examples of special purpose accounts include payroll accounts in which the bank agrees to honor only certain checks payable to the depositor's employees . . . and trust or escrow accounts in which the bank has notice of third parties' interests in the account."

There are no facts in the present case to show that these accounts were special purpose funds. Accordingly, to the extent that the defendant had the right to set off the funds, and to the extent that there are no facts at issue, judgment enters as a matter of law, as to the first count, conversion, the second count, breach of the depositor's contract, the third count, negligence, the fourth count, alleged violation of good faith and fair dealing and the fifth count, the alleged unfair trade practice.

Count six alleges that the defendant and its officers acted deceitfully in failing "to communicate and negotiate with the plaintiff in a completely open, honest and fair fashion" and by failing "to make a full disclosure to the plaintiff of her rights or liability as a joint depositor." Thus, the plaintiff alleges that she was "deceptively induced into making the Depositor's contract. . . ." "The intentional withholding of information for the purpose of inducing action has been regarded, however, as equivalent to a fraudulent misrepresentation." *Pacelli Bros. Transportation, Inc. v. Pacelli*, 189 Conn. 401, 407, 456 A.2d 325 (1983). "To be actionable for fraud, the nondisclosure must be by a person intending or expecting thereby to cause a mistake by another to exist or to continue, in order to induce the latter to enter into or refrain from entering into a transaction." *Egan v. Hudson Nut Products, Inc.*, 142 Conn. 344, 347-48, 114 A.2d 213 (1955).

Notwithstanding the allegations of nondisclosure, the plaintiff has not submitted any proof that would indicate that a material fact exists. A material fact is one that will make a difference in the outcome of the case. She does not state any facts to support her conclusions other than that the agreement was not explained to her and that she did not sign it. This, however, is not enough to show fraud.

Fraud may not be presumed but must be strictly proven by "clear and satisfactory" evidence or "clear, precise and unequivocal evidence." *Kilduff v. Adams, Inc.*, 219 Conn. 314, 328, 593 A.2d 478 (1991). The plaintiff has not produced any facts on this issue. An honest mistake does not rise to the level of bad faith. *Wadia Enterprises, Inc. v. Hirschfeld*, 224 Conn. 240, 249, 618 A.2d 506 (1992).

Indeed, the plaintiff set forth no evidence that she ever deposited any money into these accounts.

In ruling on a motion for summary judgment, the test is whether a party would be entitled to a directed verdict on the same facts; and in the present case, without further evidence, the plaintiff cannot prevail. The motion for summary judgment as to the sixth count, therefore, is granted.

Websites

■ **Internet Fraud (FBI)**
http://www.fbi.gov (click on search box and enter "Internet fraud")

■ **Federal Trade Commission**
http://www.ftc.gov/

■ **U.S. Business Advisor**
http://www.business.gov/

Forms and Court Documents

A complaint alleging misrepresentation.

STATE OF PLACID   IN THE SUPERIOR COURT
COUNTY OF BARNES   FILE NUMBER: _____
Bart Bowler,
Plaintiff   )

)

)

vs.   )
)
Rockingham Finance, Inc. and   )
Mark Wolf,   )
Defendants

Complaint

COMES NOW, Bart Bowler, Plaintiff in the above-styled action and makes the following allegations:

1.

Plaintiff is and was at all times relevant to the allegations in this Complaint, a citizen of Barnes County, State of Placid.

2.

Defendant Rockingham Finance, Inc., (hereafter "Rockingham Finance") is a corporation organized under the laws of the state of Placid and maintains its headquarters in Barnes County.

3.

Defendant Mark Wolf is an employee of Rockingham Finance Corporation and was employed by Rockingham Finance as a loan officer at all times pertinent to the allegations in this Complaint.

4.

On September 6, 2011, Plaintiff entered into a sales contract with Able Properties to purchase the Fiesta Ball, a bowling alley, and the five acres of land surrounding it for $2 million. The agreement provided that the purchase was contingent upon Plaintiff's obtaining financing by October 10, 2002.

5.

Plaintiff tendered $10,000 earnest money to seller, and the same amount was due upon acceptance.

6.

Plaintiff contacted his banker, James Willoughby, at Placid State Bank to obtain financing. Placid State Bank was not interested in financing that large a loan, so Willoughby suggested Plaintiff contact Rockingham Finance.

7.

Willoughby and Plaintiff later met with Mark Wolf, a vice president of Rockingham Finance. The three discussed financing arrangements in general terms; Rockingham Finance was willing to lend 80 percent of the appraised value or the sale price, whichever was lower.

8.

The required appraisal, however, was not scheduled to be completed until after the financing contingency date set forth within Plaintiff's sales agreement.

9.

In early October, the appraiser verbally assured Plaintiff that the appraisal would be for at least $2 million. Plaintiff then called Wolf at Rockingham Finance, explained he was risking $20,000 earnest money, and requested assurance that Rockingham Finance would extend the loan. According to Plaintiff, Wolf responded affirmatively.

10.

On October 8, 2011, Plaintiff released the financing contingency in exchange for the seller's agreement to a 30-day extension of the November 1, 2011, closing date.

11.

Two days later, Plaintiff and Wolf discussed a repayment schedule and interest rates.

12.

In mid-November, the appraisal came in at $2.1 million. In late November, Wolf informed Plaintiff that Rockingham Finance National had rejected the loan.

13.

The Fiesta Ball was thereafter sold to another purchaser, and Plaintiff forfeited $5,000 earnest money.

14.

As a result of Defendant Wolf's false and misleading statement, Plaintiff incurred monetary losses.

15.

Defendant Wolf's statement concerning Rockingham Finance's approval of the Plaintiff's loan was made in reckless disregard of the truth.

16.

Defendant Wolf's statement was negligent misrepresentation of the actual facts involved in the loan approval process.

WHEREFORE, the plaintiff requests judgment for damages against defendants, individually and jointly and severally, as follows:
1. General damages in the amount of _____;
2. Special damages in the amount of _____; and
3. Punitive damages in an amount to be determined by the court;
4. Plaintiff also requests costs of suit; and
5. Such other and further relief as the court may deem just and proper;
6. Plaintiff also requests a trial by jury on the issues raised in this Complaint.

Respectfully submitted, this the _____ day of _____, 20 _____.

Clarence D. Arrow
Attorney for the Plaintiff

Key Terms

Clear and convincing   Material fact   Ratification
   evidence   Privity

Review Questions

1 Are there any factual changes that you could make to our Shareholder's Suit hypothetical that would give Tom a stronger case against End-Run?

2 What is fraud, and how does it differ from negligent misrepresentation?

3 What are the elements of fraud?

4 Some have said that fraud is not something that can be done unknowingly. Why?

5 Courts have consistently refused to limit the definition of what acts constitute fraud. Why have they been reluctant to do so?

6 What is a material fact?

7 How do normal salesmanship statements differ from fraud?

8 What is "clear and convincing" evidence, and how does this standard differ from "preponderance of the evidence"?

9 How does a fraud case change when the defendant is the plaintiff's fiduciary?

10 Actions that are classified as fraud can also be crimes. Explain the interplay between civil fraud and criminal fraud.

11 The Restatement of Torts limits actions for negligent misrepresentation to statements made by a defendant during the course of his business. Is this limitation too strict? Why would the drafters of the Restatement create this restriction?

12 What are the elements of negligent misrepresentation?

13 Why is there a requirement of the plaintiff's "reasonable reliance" on the defendant's statement in a negligent misrepresentation case?

14 Explain how the basic elements of a tort case (duty, breach, causation, and damages) are satisfied in a negligent misrepresentation case.

15 What is privity?

16 Opinions are usually not classified as negligent misrepresentations. Why? Are there situations in which an opinion can be actionable as a negligent misrepresentation? Explain.

17 What are some of the specifics that should be raised in a complaint alleging negligent misrepresentation?

18 Explain the defenses available in misrepresentation cases.

19 What is interference with contract? What are the elements of this tort?

20 Should interference with contract remain an actionable tort? Craft an argument against the continued existence of this tort.

21 Explain the public and private enforcement provisions of most states' deceptive trade practices acts.

Applying What You Have Learned

1 Should the contract between an attorney and her client receive the same level of protection as a typical business contract? Why or why not?

2 Draft an answer to the complaint presented in the "Forms and Court Documents" section of this chapter.

3 Draft a complaint for negligent misrepresentation using the facts presented in the beginning of this chapter in "Shareholder's Suit," with one important change: Instead of owning 1,000 shares of End-Run Corporation, Tom is now a major investor who has reviewed the bogus financial statements and has been induced by them to purchase a 51 percent share in the company. How do you address these issues in your complaint?

4 How does your state define *negligent misrepresentation*?

5 Does your state recognize the tort of interference with contract?

6 How does your state define *deceptive trade practices*?

Endnotes

[1] *Standard Oil Co. v. Hunt,* 121 S.E. 184 (1924).

[2] *Coley v. North Carolina National Bank,* 41 N.C. App. 121, 254 S.E.2d 217 (1979).

[3] *Patuxent Development Co. v. Bearden,* 227 N.C. 124, 128, 41 S.E.2d 85 (1947).

[4] *AMPAT/Midwest, Inc. v. Illinois Tool Works, Inc.,* 896 F.2d 1035, 1040 (7th Cir. 1990).

[5] *Board of Ed. v. A, C and S, Inc.,* 546 N.E.2d 580 (1989).

[6] Restatement (Second) of Torts §552, comment a.

[7] "Just in case you had any doubts — there is no tort of negligent misrepresentation in New York." Holahan 13 Pace L. Rev. 763 (1993).

[8] James & Gray, Misrepresentation, 37 M. L. Rev. 286 (1977).

[9] Am. Jur. 2d, Fraud and Deceit §143.

[10] *Bily v. Arthur Young & Co.,* 11 Cal. Rptr. 2d 51 (1992).

[11] *Baumann v. Florance,* 267 App. Div. 113, 114, 44 N.Y.S.2d 706, 707 (3d Dept. 1943).

[12] *Riley v. Bell,* 95 N.W. 170 (1903).

[13] *Wilson v. Murch,* 354 S.W.2d 332 (1962).

[14] *Hosford v. McKissack,* 589 So. 2d 108 (1991).

[15] *National Bank of Pawnee v. Hamilton,* 202 Ill. App. 516 (1916).

[16] *Vettleson v. Special School Dist. No. 1,* 361 N.W.2d 425 (1985).

[17] *Lumley v. Gye,* 2 El & Bl 216, 118 Eng. Rep. 749 (1853).

[18] *Petroleum Energy, Inc. v. Mid-America Petroleum, Inc.,* 775 F. Supp. 1420 (D. Kan. 1991).

[19] *Financial Marketing Services, Inc. v. Hawkeye Bank & Trust of Des Moines,* 588 N.W.2d 450 (1999).

[20] *Edward Vantine Studios, Inc. v. Fraternal Composite Service, Inc.,* 373 N.W.2d 512 (1985).

[21] Am. Jur. 2d Interference §37.

[22] *Diversey Corp. v. Chem-Source Corp.,* 965 P.2d 332 (1998).

[23] *IntelliSec v. Firecom, Inc.,* 2001 WL 218940 5 (E.D.N.Y. 2001).

[24] Am. Jur. 2d, Consumer §282.

[25] *Insurance Co. of North America v. Morris,* 981 S.W.2d 667 (1998).

Crossword Puzzle

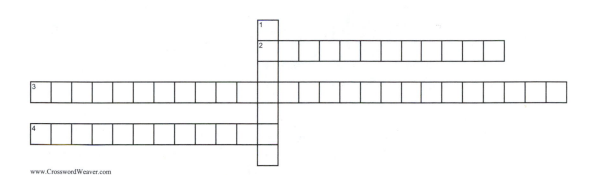

www.CrosswordWeaver.com

ACROSS

2 The process of confirming and accepting a previous action; a void contract can be ratified after the fact to make it legally enforceable

3 A level of proof higher than mere preponderance of the evidence. In most civil trials preponderance of the evidence is sufficient.

4 A fact that is basic to a contract, one that the parties consider to be an essential ingredient of the negotiations

DOWN

1 The direct relationship between the parties to a contract that arises from their involvement in creating the contract

Appendix A

CLIENT MATERIAL/DOCUMENTS

Clarence D. Arrow
Attorney at Law

CLIENT INTERVIEW — PERSONAL INJURY CASE

CLIENT'S NAME: Charles Allen Chumley
    ADDRESS: 17 Robin Hood Lane
    PHONE # WORK: *N/A, out of work since the accident*
    PHONE # HOME: 555-1212
HOW LONG AT PRESENT ADDRESS? *27 years*
WITH WHOM DOES CLIENT LIVE: *No one*
    SPOUSE: *Julia Lynn Chumley, killed in accident*
    CHILDREN: *Michael Allen Chumley* AGE: *26*
               John Page Chumley AGE: *24*

OTHER PRIOR RESIDENCES: *Lived in Akron, Ohio, until transferred here by Knight Manufacturing Co., 27 years ago*
PERSONS CLIENT SUPPORTS: *N/A, both children are grown and have moved out on their own*
CLIENT'S AGE: 57
CLIENT'S DATE OF BIRTH: May 5, 1946
CLIENT'S SOCIAL SECURITY NUMBER: 555-55-5555
CLIENT'S PLACE OF BIRTH: Akron, Ohio
CLIENT'S EDUCATIONAL BACKGROUND: *High school only*

CLIENT'S EMPLOYMENT HISTORY: *After leaving the military, he joined Knight Manufacturing Company as a "day press operator" and has slowly worked his way up to senior supervisor. Other than part-time jobs in high school, this is the only job he's ever had.*

CLIENT'S CURRENT EMPLOYMENT: Senior Supervisor Product Line
    EMPLOYER: Knight Manufacturing Company
    ADDRESS: 1001 Furniture Lane
    SUPERVISOR: Charles Dickens
    TYPE OF WORK: *Supervises extruded plastic pieces for formed furniture*
    LENGTH OF EMPLOYMENT: 27 years

PRESENT JOB STILL AVAILABLE? *Yes, employers have told him that he can return to work as soon as he is able.*
PAY: $32,000 per year

MILITARY HISTORY: *Served in Navy from 1964 to 1976. Left as a Chief Petty Officer.*

CLIENT EVER TREATED BY PSYCHIATRIST OR BEEN IN MENTAL INSTITUTION? *No*
PHYSICAL AILMENTS? *Suffers from severe pain, has difficulty walking, diabetes, memory loss, complications from several surgeries, some loss of brain function. (See medicals for additional details; client can't recall everything.)*
PHYSICAL AILMENTS OF FAMILY MEMBERS? *Family has always been in good health.* **No family history of diabetes.**
OTHER NAMES BY WHICH CLIENT HAS BEEN KNOWN? *"Chief," since his days in the military.*
BRIEF EXPLANATION OF WHAT HAPPENED: *Client says that he was crossing at a railroad/street intersection near his home and his car was hit (on driver's side) by train. Wife was killed. He was severely injured. No memory of actual accident. Memory loss of several weeks prior to accident. In coma following accident.*
DATE OF INCIDENT: **AUGUST 23, LAST YEAR.** *(Should be all right as far as Statute of Limitations goes.)*
PRIOR ACCIDENTS/LAWSUITS? *Client says never been in an accident, never been sued or brought suit before in his life.*

STATE OF PLACID

COUNTY OF BARNES

REPRESENTATION CONTRACT

THIS AGREEMENT, made and entered into this the 2nd day of February, 2003, between Charles Allen Chumley, hereinafter referred to as "Client"; and CLARENCE D. ARROW AND ASSOCIATES, P.A., hereinafter referred to as "Attorneys";

WITNESSETH:

WHEREAS, Client has a claim against National Railroad Company, Inc., and others, arising out of an accident that occurred on or about the 23rd day of August, last year, and desires to employ the Attorneys on a contingent fee basis;

NOW, THEREFORE, the Attorneys agree to represent, through trial court, as attorney for the Client and the Client agrees to pay the Attorneys

Thirty-Three and One-Third percent (33%) of the amount recovered or which may be recovered in this matter, whether by compromise or settlement at any time before suit is instituted or by compromise, settlement or judgment after suit is instituted, plus expenses incurred in the preparation of the case. Both parties agree that neither party will compromise or settle this action without consent of the other party.

This the 2nd day of February, 2003.

By: Clarence D. Arrow
Attorney at Law
Clarence D. Arrow and Associates, P.A.

To: Chumley File
        File Number 03-00045
From: C. Arrow
Re: Billing Info

Note that this is a standard contingency fee case. Client will have to pay court and other expenses. Please note this as a contingency fee in our billing software.

Client Expenses

Item	Amount	Paid
Copying client material at first meeting	22 pages	Not charged

STATE OF PLACID
BARNES COUNTY

AUTHORIZATION FOR RELEASE OF MEDICAL RECORDS

I, Charles Allen Chumley, hereby authorize all physicians, physician's assistants, hospital, and other medical and/or rescue squad and ambulance personnel having examined or treated me, and all other persons or companies possessing records or knowledge relating to such examination or treatment, to disclose or release the same upon request to any attorney or legal assistant of Clarence D. Arrow and Associates, P.A. (hereafter "the firm"), 1001 Burkemont Ave., Placid City, Placid 10000.

Information subject to this Release shall include that contained in all medical records including, but not limited to, rescue squad and ambulance records, emergency room reports, admission summaries, discharge summaries, doctors' orders, nurses' notes, temperature/pulse/respiration charts, anesthesia records, medication summaries, operative notes, consultation requests and reports, laboratory reports, radiology requests and reports, drug requests and reports, pharmaceutical records, and any and all other record of any kind whatsoever pertaining to me, including any and all x-rays, CAT scans, MRIs, and myelograms, and the reports from such tests: This request is made under further provisions of HIPAA. The undersigned expressly waives any privacy or confidentiality issues under HIPAA and further expressly consents under that Act to this release of Personal Health Information (PHI) to attorney.

I understand that the firm is not responsible for the costs of any copies or other expenses whatsoever for these matters. I understand and agree that I will arrange for payment for all copies or other expenses that may be incurred pursuant to P.C.A. §21-09-1245 or other.

A photocopy of the signed original of this Authorization for Release of Medical Records shall be sufficient and acceptable to all persons and entities from whom information or records are requested.

This the 2nd day of February, 2003.

Charles A. Chumley   **Charles Chumley**
Signature of Patient   Printed Full Name of Patient

555-55-5555   May 5, 1946
Social Security Number of Patient   Date of Birth of Patient

Appendix B

CORRESPONDENCE

Clarence D. Arrow & Associates, P.A.

Attorneys at Law

1001 Burkemont Ave.

Placid City, Placid 10000

Clarence D. Arrow, Esq.   TELEPHONE (555) 555-1212
                                                  Fax (555) 555-1213

Charles Chumley
17 Robin Hood Lane
Cling, PL 10001

RE: Contract of Representation and Follow-up Materials

Dear Mr. Chumley:

It was a pleasure to meet with you today. As we discussed during our meeting, there are some follow-up materials that we will need from you in order to continue our investigation of your claim against National Railroad Company, Inc., and others. Here is a list of the items that we need you to locate:

- Your income tax returns for the last three years
- Your personal calendar showing your appointments and movements up to the date of the accident
- Your job performance evaluations from Knight Manufacturing, Inc.
- The damage estimate for the damage to your auto

If you would like my paralegal, Paula, to come by your house and pick up these items, please feel free to give her a call at our main office number.

We look forward to serving you in this matter. If you have any questions about this case, you can reach Paula or me at the above telephone number.

Sincerely,

Clarence D. Arrow
Clarence D. Arrow & Associates, P.A.

CLARENCE D. ARROW & ASSOCIATES, P.A.
ATTORNEYS AT LAW
1001 BURKEMONT AVE.
PLACID CITY, PLACID 10000

CLARENCE D. ARROW, ESQ.   TELEPHONE (555) 555-1212
                                                        Fax (555) 555-1213

Matthew Mender, M.D.
Mender Clinic
17 Healing Lane
Placid City, PL 10000

RE: Patient — Charles A. Chumley
D/A: August 23rd, last year

Dear Dr. Mender:

We represent Mr. Charles Chumley in connection with personal injuries he sustained in an accident occurring on the above date. It is our understanding that you treated our client for these injuries. Please send us a narrative medical report describing those injuries, the treatment rendered by you, and the prognosis.

Also, please send us an itemized copy of your bill for such treatment.

A properly executed medical authorization is enclosed.

Thank you for your attention to this matter.

Sincerely,

Clarence D. Arrow
Clarence D. Arrow & Associates, P.A.

Appendix C

PLEADINGS

STATE OF PLACID
COUNTY OF BARNES

IN THE SUPERIOR COURT
FILE NUMBER: _____

Charles Chumley,)
Plaintiff)
)
) Complaint
vs.) Jury Trial Demanded
)
National Railroad Company, Inc.,)
Stanley W. Blue, and The Town)
of Cling, Defendants

Plaintiff, by and through his attorneys, complains of the defendant as follows:

1.

Plaintiff is, and all times hereafter was, a citizen and resident of the Town of CLING, County of BARNES, State of Placid.

2.

Plaintiff alleges upon information and belief that the defendant National Railroad Company (Railroad) is, and at all times hereafter was, a corporation organized and existing under the laws of the State of Placid, licensed to do business, and in fact doing business, in the State of Placid and having a registered agent for the service of process by the name of Richard Robin located at 230 N. Elm Street, Suite 2000, Greensboro, Placid, 27401.

3.

Plaintiff alleges upon information and belief that the defendant Town of CLING (Town) is a duly chartered municipality in the County of BARNES and the State of Placid.

4.

Plaintiff alleges upon information and belief that the defendant STANLEY W. BLUE is a citizen and resident of the County of Barnes, State of Placid.

5.

That at all times relevant to this Complaint the defendant STANLEY W. BLUE was an agent, servant, and employee of the defendant National Railroad Company (Railroad) and was acting within the course and scope of his employment with it.

6.

The plaintiff is informed and believes and therefore alleges that the Town has waived any sovereign immunity, which it otherwise might have through the purchase of liability insurance, thereby affording its residents and residents of other communities the right to sue for negligent acts, which it might commit.

7.

Railroad, at the time of the accident, owned, maintained, and used a set of railroad tracks laid in an east-west direction and passing through the Town.

8.

Morgan Street is a public street in the Town that runs in a north-south direction crossing the tracks.

9.

Plaintiff alleges, upon information and belief, that at the time of the accident, Railroad owned, maintained, and used the railroad tracks at railroad crossing number 728339E, which tracks cross and intersect with Morgan Street, in the Town of CLING, County of BARNES, Placid.

10.

On August 23, 2002, at approximately 4:30 P.M., plaintiff was driving his automobile south on Morgan Street approaching the railroad crossing. A train belonging to and being operated by Railroad, its agents, servants, and employees, was approaching the crossing from an easterly direction.

11.

At the crossing in question at the time of the accident, there were no mechanical devices to warn motorists of an approaching train; no blinking lights, automatic gates, bells or gongs, or stop bars were installed at the crossing.

12.

The northeast quadrant of the grade crossing, at the time of the accident, contained vegetation and trees in such a position that they obstructed and/ or severely restricted the view of the tracks or an approaching train by a motorist approaching the crossing. Upon information and belief, defendants, Railroad, Town, and STANLEY W. BLUE, were under a duty to maintain the area in question.

13.

That as the plaintiff approached the crossing, he stopped and looked both ways; however, he was unable to see the train approaching because of the vegetation and overgrowth which both the Town and the Railroad had negligently allowed to remain upon the right-of-way until such time as he was on the tracks and a collision was inevitable.

14.

Railroad's train struck plaintiff's automobile with great force as plaintiff attempted to cross the railroad track, knocked the car off the tracks in a southwesterly direction and dragged the car, which finally stopped approximately 100 yards from the point of impact.

15.

The Town and Railroad owed to the plaintiff a duty of due care to reasonably and safely maintain the tracks and the area surrounding such tracks, particularly at crossings, in order to provide adequate sight distance for motorists operating automobiles on streets that intersect such crossings.

16.

The Town breached this duty of due care by the following acts of negligence:

a. It failed to close the crossing pursuant to state law, when it knew, or in the exercise of due care should have known, that the crossing constituted an unreasonable hazard to vehicular or pedestrian traffic;

b. It failed to require the installation, construction, erection, or improvement, of warning signs, gates, lights, stop bars, or such other safety devices when it knew or should have known in the exercise of reasonable care that such devices were necessary;

c. It allowed the crossing to remain in use with absolutely no safety devices with total, wanton, and reckless disregard for the safety of vehicular and pedestrian traffic;

d. It allowed the vegetation and trees adjacent to the tracks to obstruct the view by motorists of the tracks and approaching trains when it knew, or in the exercise of due care should have known, that such vegetation and trees constituted an unreasonable hazard to vehicular and pedestrian traffic;

e. It failed to keep the public street free from unnecessary obstructions in violation of State law.

17.

Defendant STANLEY W. BLUE, while in the course and scope of his employment with defendant Railroad, was negligent, reckless, and careless in that he, among other things:

a. Permitted the crossing to remain in such a condition as to endanger the passage or transportation of persons or property across such crossing in violation of state law;

b. Failed to take such measures as to reasonably warn motorists of oncoming trains when it knew, or in the exercise of due care should have known, that the crossing was ultra-hazardous;

c. Failed to give the plaintiff a timely and reasonable warning of the approaching train;

d. Failed to keep a proper lookout for approaching motorists and to take action to avoid the collision between the plaintiff's automobile and the train;

e. Failed to require the installation, construction, erection, or improvement, of warning signs, gates, lights, stop bars, or such other safety devices when it knew or should have known in the exercise of reasonable care that such devices were necessary;

f. Allowed the crossing to remain in use with absolutely no safety devices with total, wanton, and reckless disregard for the safety of vehicular and pedestrian traffic;

g. Allowed the vegetation and trees adjacent to the tracks to obstruct the view by motorists of the tracks and approaching trains when it knew, or in the exercise of due care should have known, that such vegetation and trees constituted an unreasonable hazard to vehicular and pedestrian traffic;

h. Operated its train through a blind or obstructed crossing at an unreasonable rate of speed for the conditions;

i. Given the obstructed nature of the crossing, failed to give adequate warning of the approaching train;

j. Failed to maintain its tracks, crossings, and right-of-way in a condition that would allow for the necessary sight distance of approaching trains.

18.

Defendant Railroad was negligent, reckless, and careless in that it, among other things:

a. Permitted the crossing to remain in such condition as to endanger the passage or transportation of persons or property across such crossing in violation of state law;

b. Failed to take such measures as to reasonably warn motorists of oncoming trains when it knew, or in the exercise of due care should have known, that the crossing was ultra-hazardous;

c. Failed to give the plaintiff a timely and reasonable warning of the approaching train;

d. Failed to keep a proper lookout for approaching motorists and to take action to avoid the collision between the plaintiff's automobile and the train;

e. Failed to require the installation, construction, erection, or improvement, of warning signs, gates, lights, stop bars, or such other safety devices when it knew or should have known in the exercise of reasonable care that such devices were necessary;

f. Allowed the crossing to remain in use with absolutely no safety devices with total, wanton, and reckless disregard for the safety of vehicular and pedestrian traffic;

g. Allowed the vegetation and trees adjacent to the tracks to obstruct the view by motorists of the tracks and approaching trains when it knew, or in the exercise of due care should have known, that such vegetation and trees constituted an unreasonable hazard to vehicular and pedestrian traffic;

h. Operated its train through a blind or obstructed crossing at an unreasonable rate of speed for the conditions;

i. Given the obstructed nature of the crossing, failed to give adequate warning of the approaching train;

j. Failed to maintain its tracks, crossings, and right-of-way in a condition that would allow for the necessary sight distance of approaching trains.

19.

That the negligence of the defendants Town of CLING, National Railway, and STANLEY W. BLUE joined and concurred and combined in point of time and place proximately to cause the collision between plaintiff's vehicle and Railroad's train and plaintiff's resulting serious, painful, and permanent injuries and damages, all of which exceed the sum of Ten Thousand Dollars ($10,000.00), and which include, without limitation, the following:

(1) bodily injury and resulting pain and suffering;

(2) medical expenses, including the costs of therapy;

(3) loss of earnings and earning capacity;

(4) punitive damages as a result of the defendants' reckless and wanton conduct.

WHEREFORE, the plaintiff prays the Court as follows:

1. That the plaintiff have and recover from the defendants, jointly and severally, a sum in excess of Ten Thousand Dollars ($10,000.00) for compensatory and punitive damages as alleged above.

2. That the plaintiff have and recover the costs of this action.

3. For a trial by jury.

4. For such other and further relief as to the Court may seem just and proper.

This the _____ day of _____, 2015.

Clarence D. Arrow & Associates, P.A.

By: _____

Clarence D. Arrow, Esq.
State Bar No. 0000001
1001 Burkemont Ave.
Placid City, PL 10000
(555) 555-1212
Attorney for the Plaintiff

STATE OF PLACID

COUNTY OF BARNES

IN THE SUPERIOR COURT

FILE NUMBER: _____

Charles Chumley,   )

Plaintiff   )

)   Answer of National Railroad

vs.   )   Company, Inc. and Stanley W. Blue

)

National Railroad Company, Inc.,   )

Stanley W. Blue, and   )

The Town of Cling,

Defendants

COMES NOW the Defendants National Railroad Company, Inc. (hereafter "Defendant Railroad"), and Stanley W. Blue (hereafter "Defendant Blue") and, answering the Complaint herein, by alleging and saying as follows:

1. Upon information and belief, admitted.
2. Admitted.
3. Upon information and belief, admitted.
4. Admitted.
5. Admitted.
6. These Defendants are without sufficient information or knowledge to enable them to form a belief as to the veracity of the facts alleged in paragraph 6, and this paragraph is therefore denied.
7. Admitted.
8. Admitted.
9. Denied.
10. It is admitted that the Plaintiff was driving an automobile on August 23 of last year and that he was driving in a southerly direction on Morgan Street. It is also admitted that he approached an intersection with Morgan Street and a railroad that belonged to and was operated by Defendant Railroad and its employees. It is further admitted that a train, owned and operated by Defendant Railroad, was heading in a westerly direction toward this same intersection at the date and time alleged. Except as herein admitted, denied.
11. It is admitted that there were cross buck railroad signs positioned at the intersection. These signs were properly installed and clearly visible to motorists crossing the intersection from either the north or the south on Morgan Street. These cross buck signs were adequate warning for reasonable and prudent motorists. It is further admitted that there were no additional warning signs, mechanical gates, or flashing lights to warn motorists of the intersection of Morgan Street with the railroad. Except as herein admitted, denied.
12. Denied.
13. Denied.
14. It is admitted that there was a collision between the Plaintiff's automobile and the Railroad's train. It is further admitted that the Plaintiff's automobile traveled approximately 100 yards in a southwesterly direction immediately after the collision. Except as herein admitted, denied.

15. It is admitted that the Defendants Railroad and Town of Cling had a duty to maintain the railroad tracks and specific areas around the track in a reasonable and safe manner. Except as herein admitted, denied.

16. a. Denied.
    b. Denied.
    c. Denied.
    d. Denied.

17. a. Denied.
    b. Denied.
    c. Denied.
    d. Denied.
    e. Denied.
    f. Denied.
    g. Denied.
    h. Denied.
    i. Denied.
    j. Denied.

18. a. Denied.
    b. Denied.
    c. Denied.
    d. Denied.
    e. Denied.
    f. Denied.
    g. Denied.
    h. Denied.
    i. Denied.
    j. Denied.

19. Denied.

Defendant Railroad's and Defendant Blue's First Affirmative Defense

These Defendants show that the Plaintiff's own negligence was either a sole or contributing proximate cause of the collision that resulted in all of the injuries for which the Plaintiff now seeks recovery from these Defendants. Plaintiff's contributory/comparative negligence is hereby pled as a complete bar/partial bar to his recovery against these Defendants.

This the _____ day of _____, 2015.

_____
Perry E. Masson, Esq.
State Bar No. 11111111111
Hamilton Burger Lane
Placid City, PL 10000
(555) 333-1212
Attorney for the Defendants National Railway
Company, Inc. & Stanley W. Blue

STATE OF PLACID   IN THE SUPERIOR COURT
COUNTY OF BARNES   FILE NUMBER: _____

Charles Chumley,   )
Plaintiff   )
)   Answer of Town of Cling
vs.   )
)
National Railroad Company, Inc.,   )
Stanley W. Blue, and   )
The Town of Cling,
Defendants

Note: This Answer was substantially identical to National Railroad Company's Answer and will therefore be excluded from this section.

Appendix D

DISCOVERY

STATE OF PLACID   IN THE SUPERIOR
            COURT

COUNTY OF BARNES   FILE NUMBER: _____

Charles Chumley, Plaintiff	)	
	)	
	)	PLAINTIFF'S FIRST
vs.	)	INTERROGATORIES AND
	)	REQUEST FOR PRODUCT OF
National Railroad Company, Inc.,	)	DOCUMENTS
Stanley W. Blue, and	)	
The Town of Cling,		
Defendants		

Definitions

For the purpose of this set of Interrogatories, each undefined work shall have its usual and generally accepted meaning. Each defined word, and all variations thereof, shall have the meanings set forth below:

1. "Document"—any paper, file, tape, or similar material upon which verbal, graphic, or pictorial information or image is written, printed, typed, drawn, punched, produced, or reproduced in any fashion, including but not limited to all records, reports, correspondence, memoranda, notes, agreements, studies, minutes, photographs, drawings, sketches, maps, charts, brochures, photocopies, any computer cards, and tapes.
2. "He" and "his" refers to all genders.
3. "Identify" (or "state the identity of"):
   a. With respect to a document, means set forth the following information, if known:
      (i) a general description thereof (e.g., letter, memorandum, report, etc.);
      (ii) a brief summary of its contents;
      (iii) the name and address of the custodian of the original, or, if unavailable, of the custodian of a copy;
      (iv) the name and address of the person(s), if any, who drafted, prepared, compiled, or signed it;

(v)   any other descriptive information necessary in order to ade-
      quately describe it in a Subpoena Duces Tecum, or any motion
      or request for production thereof; and

(vi) a statement of whether or not the Plaintiff will voluntarily make
      it available to the Defendant for copying, and, if not, a state-
      ment of the specific reasons for not being willing or able to
      do so.

b.   With respect to any oral communication (including but not limited
     to conversations, discussions, or oral agreements), "identify" (or
     "state the identity of") means state the following current or last
     known information:

(i)   its type or nature (e.g., in person, by telephone, etc.);

(ii)   its date;

(iii) the identity of all present and/or participating; and

(iv)   a summary of what was said to whom and by whom.

c.   With respect to an individual, "identify" (or "state the identity of")
     means state the following current or last known information:

(i)   his name;

(ii)   his relationship to the Plaintiff at the time relative to the
       Interrogatory being answered;

(iii) his employer;

(iv)   his employment position;

(v)   his business address and telephone number; and

(vi)   his residence address.

d.   With respect to an association, partnership, or corporation, munic-
     ipality, State or Federal agency, "identify" (or "state the identity of")
     means state the following current or last known information:

(i)   its name;

(ii)   its type or nature (e.g., corporation, partnership, joint venture,
       etc.);

(iii) the nature of its business or primary activities;

(iv)   its address; and

(v)   its telephone number.

4. "Person" — any natural or artificial being including but not limited to
    any individual, corporation, partnership, voluntary association, munic-
    ipality, government, State or Federal agency.

5. "Occurrence" — the combined events and incidents that caused damage
    to the Plaintiff. The events leading up to and including the alleged mis-
    conduct of the Defendant.

Pursuant to Rule 33 of the State Rules of Civil Procedure, the following
questions must be answered fully and under oath, in the space following each
question (and on attached pages if the space provided is insufficient), and the
sworn answers served on the undersigned attorney within thirty (30) days of
service hereof.

These questions and the requests for production shall be continuing in nature so as to require supplemental answers as additional information becomes available as provided in the Rules of Civil Procedure.

1. Please describe in as much detail as possible the weather condition at the time and place of the alleged occurrence, including in your answer details of light, temperature, humidity, cloud cover, wind velocity, wind direction, and type of precipitation, if any.

2. Please describe as completely as you can the lighting conditions at the time and place of the alleged occurrence, including the amount of natural light and/or the amount of artificial lighting.

3. Please state what precautions, if any, were taken by you, or any agent or employee of the Defendant, prior to the Plaintiff's alleged occurrence, to prevent injuries to persons in the position of the Plaintiff.

4. Please describe all observations known by you to have been made of any hazard or danger that was involved in the alleged occurrence, including:
   a. the name and address of each person making each such observation;
   b. the date each such observation was made;
   c. the substance of each such observation.

5. Please describe all comments or complaints known by you to have been made regarding any hazard or danger that was involved in the alleged occurrence, including:

6. Please list all governmental standards and regulations governing conditions or activities involved in the alleged occurrence.

7. Please describe each standard and regulation listed in response to the preceding interrogatory, including:
   a. the government body responsible for each standard and regulation;
   b. the formal citation for each standard and regulation;
   c. the content of each such standard and regulation;
   d. the manner in which you became aware of each such standard and regulation;
   e. the date on which you became aware of each such standard and regulation.

8. Please describe each violation or noncompliance with a governmental standard or regulation governing conditions involved in the alleged occurrence, including:
   a. the formal citation for each such governmental standard or regulation that was violated or with which conditions did not comply;
   b. a description of the act or omission constituting each such violation or noncompliance;
   c. the date of each such act or omission.

9. Please list all industry, professional, and trade association standards and regulations governing conditions or activities involved in the alleged occurrence.

10. Please describe each standard and regulation listed in response to the preceding interrogatory, including:

a. the body responsible for each standard and regulation;

b. the formal citation of each standard and regulation;

c. the content of each such standard and regulation;

d. the manner in which you became aware of each such standard and regulation;

e. the date on which you became aware of each such standard and regulation.

11. Please describe each violation or noncompliance with an industry, professional, or trade association standard or regulation governing conditions involved in the occurrence, including:

a. the formal citation for each such standard or regulation that was violated or with which conditions did not comply;

b. a description of the act or omission constituting each such violation or noncompliance;

c. the date of each such act or omission.

12. Identify the operating rules, safety rules, and all other rules, bulletins, and writings of the Defendant that governed the conduct of the Defendant's employees at the time and place of the above-specified incident.

13. Identify the Telegraphic Accident Report prepared by the Defendant, its agents, servants, or employees in the ordinary course of Defendant's business and concerning the above-specified personal injury and/or accident.

14. Identify any (Repair) (Maintenance) (I.C.C. Inspection Reports) (Safety Appliance Reports) for a period of 12 months prior to the above-specified injury and/or accident to a period of 3 months subsequent to said injury or accident and specifically:

15. Identify any photographs taken prior to any changes in conditions that reflect the condition of same at the time of or immediately after the subject accident.

16. Identify the track survey kept in the ordinary course of the Defendant's business, reflecting the area of the subject accident. The request is for the last track survey prepared prior to the time of the subject accident and/or injury.

17. Identify the minutes and records of the meeting of the Defendant's safety committee and all "safety items" or similar reports kept or submitted in the ordinary course of the Defendant's business for three (3) years prior to the incident complained of.

18. Identify each member of the crew of Defendant's train involved in the subject accident and the respective crew titles of each.

19. Identify other persons aboard Defendant's train at the time of the subject accident who had any duties of any nature aboard said train, and state with respect to each, their job classification and the nature of their duties aboard said train.

20. Identify all other officers, agents, or employees of Defendant aboard Defendant's train at the time of the subject accident and the functions, if any, of each of such employees on said train.

21. State the location of each person listed in 18, 19, and 20 above at the time the subject accident occurred and the 60 seconds prior thereto.

22. State the name or designation, and location, of any brake control apparatus actually utilized to affect the movement of the train in question for 60 seconds before and 60 seconds after the time of the subject collision and the names of all persons who activated each such apparatus.

23. State the location (with reference to the roadway) of lead diesel unit, at the time the brakes on the train were first applied at or near the time of the collision; and
    a. Describe the type of brake application then made and the distance from the point of impact. (If subsequent brake application of a different type was made, state such location at the time and the type of application then made.)

24. State whether Defendant's railroad track was straight or curved within one mile of each side of the crossing where the subject accident occurred, and, if curved, state for what distance in each direction, and the direction of the curvature of the tracks.

25. State who owned and maintained the railroad track in question.

26. State whether you have in your possession photographs taken of and at the scene of the subject accident showing physical position or location of any warning signs, appliances, vehicles, or railroad equipment as same existed immediately after the happening of the accident and prior to any changes in their respective appearances, locations, or conditions.

27. State the exact width of the public roadway from edge to edge that the railroad tracks crossed upon or over at this crossing.

28. State the kind, type, and exact size and location of each and every fixed warning sign located at or in the vicinity of or approaches to the crossing at the time and place involved.

29. State the exact distance (or if not known, the approximate distance) traveled by the leading point of the Defendant's train from the following points until it came to a stop after the collision:
    a. From the first edge of the roadway passed by the lead unit or car;
    b. From the point of impact;
    c. From the last edge of the roadway passed by the lead unit or car;
    d. From the point where the last brake application prior to impact was made.

30. For the period of three months prior to the date of the subject accident, describe any inspections or repairs of any kind made to the brakes or brake system of any cars in Defendant's train, including each diesel unit, including:
    a. The date and kind of each such repair;
    b. The name and current address of each person making such repairs;
    c. The reason or reasons for each of such repairs.

31. State the exact time and date that an inspection was last made (prior to the occurrence of this accident) of the brake system or brakes on Defendant's train involved in the subject accident and the name and current address of each person who made such inspection.
    a. Give the same information for the first inspection after this accident.

32. State the speed of Defendant's train (if not known, give approximate speed) on the day of the subject accident at the following locations:
    a. One-half mile prior to the crossing;
    b. One thousand feet prior to the crossing;
    c. Five hundred feet prior to the crossing;
    d. Fifty feet prior to the crossing;
    e. At the initial edge of the crossing;
    f. At impact point.

33. State the distance required to stop a train of similar equipment and containing the same number of cars as the train involved in the subject accident, on similar track, with an emergency application of the brakes at the following speeds:
    a. 5 miles per hour;
    b. 10 miles per hour;
    c. 15 miles per hour;
    d. 20 miles per hour;
    e. At the speed that the train was going 50 feet from the subject crossing;
    f. At the speed that the train was going at the initial edge of the subject crossing.

34. State whether or not Defendant's train was moved at all after it first came to a stop following the impact of the subject accident and prior to full investigation by police and railroad crew; if so, state whether it was moved forward or backward, why it was moved forward or backward, and how far it was moved forward or backward.

35. State the name and current address of any Defendant's officers, agents, or employees who have actually inspected, or who have had the duty to inspect:
    a. Any signal devices at this crossing for the time one year prior to the subject accident to date;
    b. The physical condition of the crossing and its approaches or adjacent properties for the time one year prior to the subject accident to date.

36. State the names and last known addresses of each and every person known by you, your agents, servants, employees, or attorneys, to have been an eyewitness to the accident out of which this cause arose.

37. State the name and last known addresses of all persons known to you, your agents, servants, employees, or attorneys, who have any knowledge of the circumstances leading up to or surrounding the accident out of which the above cause arose, but are not eyewitnesses.

38. State the names and last known addresses of all persons from whom you, your agents, servants, employees, attorneys, or investigator have taken any written statements, or court reporters' statements in connection with any of the circumstances leading up to or surrounding the occurrence of the subject accident.

39. State whether or not at the time and on the day of the subject accident there were in effect any written side track agreements or other agreements (with respect to any side tracks located within one mile of the crossing where the accident occurred) between Defendant, or its predecessors, and

any person or persons, firm, corporation, partnership, or other business association, and, if so, state with respect thereto the following:

a. The date of each such agreement;

b. The names of the parties to each such agreement;

c. The names and addresses of the persons having custody or control of such agreements;

d. The exact location of any side track forming the subject matter of any such agreements.

40. State the date on which the last inspection (prior to the accident) was made by Defendant, through any of its officers, agents, or employees:

a. Of the crossing;

b. Of the warning devices thereat.

41. State the names and current residence addresses of every person who made or participated in the last inspection of the crossing or warning devices as specified in the answer above.

42. State the purpose and nature of the last inspection made of the crossing or warning devices as specified in the two answers above.

43. State the name and current address of any employees to whom you administered discipline of any description in connection with the subject accident or their actions relating thereto.

44. If you had received any communication whatsoever prior to this accident, from any person or entity whatsoever relating to the adequacy or performance of any signs or warning signals at this crossing, please state:

a. The name and current address of the sender;

b. The date received;

c. The form (written or verbal, etc.);

d. The name and address of Defendant's officer, agent, or employee who received it.

45. If you had received any communication whatsoever prior to this accident, from any person or entity whatsoever relating to the adequacy or performance of any signs or warning signals at this crossing, please state:

a. The name and current address of the sender;

b. The date received;

c. The form (written or verbal, etc.);

d. The name and address of defendant's officer, agent, or employee who received it.

46. State the cost or approximate cost of installing automatic crossing protection at the subject crossing at or about the time of the subject accident, and, specifically, the cost of:

a. Lights and bells (if not already installed);

b. Lights, gates, and bells (if not already installed).

47. Please state for a period of three (3) years prior to the subject accident the names and current addresses of all defendant's employees who made any report to defendant (including incident reports and safety items at safety meetings) of safety problems, incidents, or hazards at the subject crossing.

48. Give a complete description of the horn or whistle on defendant's loco-
    motives described above at the time of the subject accident, including but
    not limited to:
    a. The date of installation or approximate date thereof;
    b. The make and model number and the name of the manufacturer.
49. State which of the above-identified locomotives' horns were actually
    utilized by defendant for warning purposes at the time involved.
50. Was the defendant, at the time of the subject accident, a member of the
    American Association of Railroads (A.A.R.) and, if so, please:
    a. Describe and identify A.A.R. recommendations and/or standards as
        of the time of the subject accident pertaining to:
    b. Crossing protection for the type of crossing herein involved;
    c. Warning equipment on locomotives operating over crossings such as
        that located at the place of the subject accident herein.

This the _____ day of _____, 2015.
Clarence D. Arrow & Associates, P.A.

_____

Clarence D. Arrow, Esq.
State Bar No. 0000001
1001 Burkemont Ave.
Placid City, PL 10000
(555) 555-1212
Attorney for the Plaintiff

CERTIFICATE OF SERVICE

This is to certify that the undersigned has this date served the foregoing upon all other parties to this cause in the following manner:

- By delivering a copy thereof to the attorneys of record for said parties or to partners or employees at the office of such attorneys.
- By depositing a copy thereof in a postpaid wrapper in a post office or official depository under the exclusive care and custody of the United States Post Office Department properly addressed to the attorneys of record for said parties.

This the _____ day of _____, 2015.

Clarence D. Arrow & Associates, P.A.

_____

Clarence D. Arrow, Esq.
State Bar No. 0000001
1001 Burkemont Ave.
Placid City, PL 10000
(555) 555-1212
Attorney for the Plaintiff

_____

Exhibits provided in response to Interrogatories:

Police report
Photos
     Damage to plaintiff's car (2)
     RR crossing (8)

_____

Photos and Diagrams

This section contains photos of Mr. and Mrs. Chumley in happier times and a diagram of the accident scene.

Appendix E

MEDICAL

Medical Bill Totals for Charles Chumley

Mission Hospital	$219,380.01
Mission Clinic	$2,677.94
EMS	$65.50
Carter Surgical Associates	$12,935.00
Barnes Radiology	$4,561.00
Barnes Rehabilitation Hospital	$83,494.41
Barnes Bone and Joint Clinic	$6,151.20
Medical Internist's Association	$23,118.27
Doctor's Family Care	$760.00
Barnes Diabetes Medical Assoc.	$12,398.45
Joseph Frazier, M.D.	$5,692.02
Total	$371,233.80

BARNES REHABILITATION HOSPITAL
PLACID CITY, PL 10000

HISTORY AND EXAMINATION NOTES

PATIENT NAME: Chumley, Charles
ADMISSION DATE: 12-02-02
HOSPITAL NUMBER: 003-03-9087
HOSPITAL UNIT: HEAD TRAUMA

The medical records have been reviewed and the admitting Physician Assistant and Dr. Frazier have examined the patient.

Date of birth: 5-5-46

INFORMATION PROVIDED BY: Patient, patient's two sons, records from Mission Hospital.

PROFILE: This is the first admission to BRH of this 56-year-old, right-handed male, who previously lived with his wife, Julia, in Cling, Placid. Patient's wife was killed in the accident in which he received his injuries. The patient has a high school education. He worked at Knight Manufacturing Co. for 25+ years. His hobbies included playing golf and walking. He also enjoys watching professional football.

CHIEF COMPLAINT: "I was in an accident with a train and was in a coma for a couple of months."

HISTORY OF PRESENT ILLNESS: The patient was involved in an automobile-train accident in August of this year. The patient suffered multiple traumas. He was initially admitted to Cling Hospital immediately after the accident, but was then transferred to Mission Memorial. The patient's injuries included intraperitoneal hemorrhage, severely displaced left tibial plateau fracture, left hemo-pneumothorax, left elbow lacerations and a closed head injury. The patient underwent an ORIF for his left tibial plateau fracture as well as exploratory laparotomy with a splenectomy. The patient also had five broken ribs and a left hip fracture. The patient has a tracheostomy placed on August 30, 2002. The patient's hospital course was complicated by resistant organisms in the sputum causing acute and chronic bronchitis. The Infectious Disease Consultants for this followed him. The patient was also followed by Dr. Wellby for his pulmonary difficulties.

 The patient's hospital course was also complicated by the inability to pass a G-tube secondary to the patient's significant abdominal trauma. The patient has fistula development with infections of the fistula. The patient, therefore, required central hyper-alimentation. The patient has been receiving this via triple lumen catheter. Catheter was placed on October 14. The patient has tolerated this well and, in fact, has been able to eat some by mouth, having had a videofluoroscopy done on November 5.

PAST MEDICAL HISTORY: The patient has suffered the usual childhood diseases without sequelae.

Medically, the patient was diagnosed as having hypertension and was started on medication approximately one month prior to his injury. Trauma history — none, confirmed by both sons.

HABITS: Patient quit smoking about ten years ago. Previous to that, he smoked about 1 1/2 packs per day for 30+ years. The patient did not consume alcoholic beverages. He usually drinks sweet tea, diet soft drinks, and water.

ALLERGIES: NONE.

Glossary

Affirm   The appellate court agrees with the verdict, or some ruling, entered in the trial and votes to keep that decision in place.

Answer   The name of the document that the defendant serves on the plaintiff, outlining his defenses and any claims he may have against the plaintiff.

Assault   When the defendant causes the plaintiff to have fear or apprehension of a harmful or offensive contact.

Battery   When the defendant causes harmful or offensive contact to the plaintiff.

Breach   When the defendant fails to live up to a legal standard, or violates a duty.

Case law   The body of cases decided by judges who have interpreted statutes and prior cases.

Cause of action   A legal injury on which a lawsuit can be based.

Certiorari (cert.)   The power of a court to decide which cases it will hear and which it will not.

Chattel   Personal property, including animals.

Clear and convincing evidence   A level of proof higher than mere preponderance of the evidence. In most civil trials preponderance of the evidence is sufficient.

Clear and convincing proof   A measure of proof that is higher than preponderance of the evidence. Clear and convincing proof is evidence that is likely to be true under the facts. This standard of proof is less than beyond a reasonable doubt but higher than preponderance of the evidence.

Collateral source rule   An evidentiary rule that permits the jury to be told about the plaintiff's other sources of compensation, such as insurance, workers' compensation, and so on.

Comparative negligence   An approach to negligence cases that balances the negligence of the defendant against the negligence of the plaintiff and permits a reduced recovery for the plaintiff in proportion to the plaintiff's negligence.

Compensatory damages   An award by a judge or jury designed to compensate the plaintiff for his physical or financial losses.

Complaint   The first pleading in a suit, in which the plaintiff sets out his cause of action against the defendant and requests some form of remedy to be awarded by the court.

Compulsion   An overwhelming or irresistible impulse to perform some action.

Contributory negligence   A defense available in only a few jurisdictions that provides that a plaintiff who is even partially at fault is barred from any recovery.

Conversion   Exercising control over property and removing it from the possession of the rightful owner.

Custom   A practice that has acquired a legal status over time such that failing to follow the practice would result in liability.

Damages   Money that a court orders the losing side in a civil case to pay to the other side.

Declaratory judgment   A court order that specifies the duties and obligations of a party.

Defamation   An attack on the reputation or character of another.

Defendant   The legal title of the person who is served with the complaint.

Duress   When the defendant uses force, threat, or intimidation to overcome the plaintiff's will or to compel the plaintiff to perform (or not to perform) some action.

Duty   An obligation imposed by statute or common law.

Elements   The points raised by the plaintiff in his complaint that must also be proved at trial; failure to prove these points will often result in a dismissal of the plaintiff's case.

Equity The court's authority to order individuals and corporations to perform (or not to perform) certain activities because they are unjust.

Excessive force Force used in self-defense that is clearly disproportionate to the threat posed by another.

Exclusion The persons, types of losses, or damages not covered by an insurance policy.

Fair market value The amount that a willing buyer would pay for an item that a willing seller would be willing to accept.

Fiduciary A relationship in which one person, or entity, is obligated to act in a trustworthy relationship to the other. A fiduciary has the duty to act in the best interests of the other. A common example of a fiduciary relationship is the attorney-client relationship.

Foreseeability The legal requirement that the plaintiff be a person who would likely be injured by the defendant's conduct.

Foreseeable The outcome that a person should have known or been able to anticipate or predict based on certain facts.

General damages Those awards that are closely tied to the defendant's negligence.

Guilt The jury's determination that the defendant in a criminal case is responsible for committing a crime.

Immunity An exception or privilege granted by the law to an action that ordinarily would result in a cause of action.

Indemnify To compensate a person who has suffered a loss.

Indictment Official document issued by the grand jury, accusing the defendant of a criminal act.

Informed consent An agreement by a person to allow some type of action after having been fully informed and after making a knowing and intelligent decision to allow the action.

Injunction A court order that demands a certain action or that prohibits a certain action.

Intentional tort A civil action based on a defendant's purposeful, intentional act that causes harm, as opposed to a defendant who causes harm through negligence.

Intervening cause Any event that occurs after the initial plaintiff's injury that contributes to or aggravates those injuries.

Invitee A person who has a business purpose in coming onto the property.

Last clear chance A claim by a plaintiff in a contributory negligence allegation that the defendant was the person who had the last opportunity to avoid the event that caused the plaintiff's injuries and therefore the defendant should remain liable for the injuries, despite any negligence by the plaintiff.

Legal malpractice Professional negligence committed by an attorney during the course of her representation of a client.

Liable A finding that one of the parties in a civil case is obligated to pay damages to the other party.

Libel Written defamation.

Licensee Person who enters another person's premises for convenience, curiosity, or entertainment.

Loss of consortium A claim filed by the spouse of an injured party for the loss of companionship in the marriage caused by the injuries.

Malice Reckless or false statements. Legal malice is a court-created doctrine that supplies the element by assuming that certain phrases could only have been motivated by ill will. Examples would include falsely accusing someone of a crime or other despicable act.

Malpractice The failure of a professional to exercise an adequate degree of skill, expertise, and knowledge for an adequate benefit of the client/patient; otherwise known as professional negligence.

Material fact A fact that is basic to a contract, one that the parties consider to be an essential ingredient of the negotiations.

Mitigation of damages The responsibility of the plaintiff to lessen his potential injuries or losses by taking reasonable actions to seek medical treatment or take other precautions when a reasonable person in the same situation would have done so.

Motion for directed verdict A motion brought by the defense at the end of the plaintiff's case, asking that the case be dismissed because the plaintiff has failed to prove the claims raised in the complaint.

Mutual combat When the parties to a fight voluntarily engage in violence.

Negligence per se Negligence in and of itself; the principle that the violation of a safety statute establishes a presumption of breach of duty in a negligence action.

No-fault insurance A type of insurance that requires an insurance company to pay for the insured's damages regardless of who was at fault in causing the damage.

Nuisance A cause of action that is authorized when the defendant's behavior results in a loss of enjoyment or value in the plaintiff's property.

Per diem By the day or daily.

Physician-patient relationship The legally recognized relationship between a physician and patient in which the physician brings to bear her skill in the care and treatment of the patient; this relationship also triggers evidentiary privileges that protect the patient's communications with the physician from compulsory revelation.

Plaintiff The legal title of the person who brings a complaint.

Pleadings Documents that describe the legal injuries and counterclaims raised by the parties in a civil case.

Policy A written insurance contract.

Premium The insured's payment to the insurance company.

Prima facie (Latin) "At first sight;" the party has presented adequate evidence to prove a particular point.

Privilege A protection or advantage given to a class of persons for actions taken by them.

Privity The direct relationship between the parties to a contract that arises from their involvement in creating the contract.

Products liability Also known as "product liability," the liability assessed against a manufacturer, seller, wholesaler, and so on, for placing a dangerous or defective product on the market that causes injury or damage.

Professional Someone who either through education, training, or a combination of both, possesses skills that an average person does not.

Proximate causation The facts that show the defendant's legal responsibility for the injuries to the plaintiff, also known as legal cause.

Proximate cause Proof that the defendant's actions were the legal cause of the plaintiff's injuries (see Chapter 7).

Ratification The process of confirming and accepting a previous action; a void contract can be ratified after the fact to make it legally enforceable.

Reasonable person standard The standard used by the court to provide a yardstick by which it can evaluate the defendant's actions in a particular case.

Release Surrender or give up a legal right to sue another; the document or court filing in which this right is surrendered.

Remand The appellate court requires additional information or an evidentiary hearing; it cannot conduct such a hearing itself, so it sends the case back to the trial court for the hearing, and then considers the appeal based on that hearing.

Res ipsa loquitur (Latin) "the thing speaks for itself"; the principle that under certain circumstances, such as when the type of accident is one that would not ordinarily occur without some form of negligence, the defendant's negligence can be presumed.

Respondeat superior Liability imposed on an employer for the actions of the employee, when the employee is carrying out his duties for the employer.

Reverse To reverse a decision is to set it aside; an appellate court disagrees with the verdict, or some ruling, in the trial, and overturns that decision.

Self-defense When a person uses force (sometimes deadly force) to protect himself from an attack.

Slander Spoken defamation.

Special damages Those damages, such as medical bills, closely tied to the plaintiff's injuries and for which a specific amount can usually be calculated.

Specialist One who has become an expert in a particular field through education, training, or both.

Stacking The policy limits of one policy are added to the policy limits of one or more other policies, increasing the available funds to the sum of all policies.

Standard of care The standard used to determine if a party has acted negligently in a particular case.

Stare decisis The principle that courts will reach similar results as in prior cases involving similar facts and legal issues.

Strict liability A finding of liability regardless of fault.

Subrogation In claiming a legal right or a debt, the substitution of one person for another.

Sudden emergency A doctrine that relieves a person of the normal standard of care because of a swiftly developing and dangerous event.

Superseding cause An event that occurs after the initial plaintiff's injury which replaces one act of negligence with another.

Thermography An assessment tool that can monitor temperature changes in the skin; often used by plaintiffs' attorneys as a way of showing that there is greater blood flow in an injured area and thereby providing a "picture of the pain."

Trespasser A person who is on the property of another without permission.

Ultra-hazardous A condition of special or unusual dangerousness.

Verdict The jury's final decision in the case in which they decide questions of fact raised in the case.

Voir dire (French) "Look speak"; the process of questioning a juror to discover bias or prejudice or if she would make an acceptable juror to hear a case.

Warranty A pledge, assurance, or guarantee that a particular fact is true.

Index

A

Abnormally dangerous conditions, duty 159–160
Affirm 21
Age 80
Alienation of affections 52
Alternative dispute resolution 20
Answer 14
Appeals 21–24
Assault 40
Assault and battery 41–47
Asset searches 286
Attorneys, specialization 491–492
Attractive nuisance doctrine 157
Automobile insurance 483–488
    bodily injury 484
    duty to defend 486
    exclusions 489
    liability 483
    medical payments 484
    no-fault 488–489
    property damage 484
    stacking 487
    statutory limits 483
    subrogation 486–487
    underinsured motorist 485
    uninsured motorist 484–485

B

Bad-faith damages 278
Battery 40
    elements of 43–47
    harmful or offensive contact 46
    reasonable person standard 46–47
Breach, negligence 111
Breach of duty 183–188
    court doctrines 188–193
    custom or habit 187–188
    duty of jury 186
    emergencies 187
    expert evidence 199–200
    negligence per se 191–193
    objective standard 184–185
    physical characteristics 186–187
    professionals 188
    reasonable person standard 184
    res ipsa loquitur 189–191
    specialists 188

C

CAD, re-creating auto accidents 245
Case law, importance of 21–22
Causation, negligence 111
Cause of action 3
    rule 11 12
Certiorari 23
Chattels 60
    trespass to 60–61
Client
    authorizations from 123
    facts and photos 123–124
    obtain information from 123–126
Closing argument 19
Cloud computing 83
Coercion 78
Collateral source rule 275
Comparative negligence 316–322
    defenses 320
    defined 316
    history of 317
    mentally incompetent persons 320
    modified 318
    motion for directed verdict 321–322
    multiple defendants 321
    pleading 321
    proximate cause 319–320
    pure 318
    rescuer doctrine 320
    settlement issues 321
    slight-gross 318–319
    three models of 317–318
    Uniform Comparative Fault Act 317
Compensatory damages 269–271
Complaint 7
    filing 14
Compulsion 79
Consent 77
Consumer protection laws 533
Contract, interference with 530–532
Contributory negligence
    assumption of the risk 313–314
    "avoidable consequences" 309–310
    "contributory negligence per se" 310–311
    defined 304
    exceptions to 311–315
    history of 304–306
    introduction to 304–316

Contributory negligence (*continued*)
  jury question 315
  last clear chance 311–312
  plaintiff at fault 310
  rescuer doctrine 314–315
  sudden emergency 312–313
Conversion 61
Custom 147

D

Damages 8
  bad-faith 278
  collateral source rule 275
  compensatory 269–271
  emotional distress 276–277
  equitable remedies 284–285
  equity 284
  evaluating a case for 285–288
  future losses 273
  general 270
  loss of consortium 277
  lost wages 272
  medical bills 272–273
  mitigation 276
  negligence 112–113
  nominal 284
  pain and suffering 271
  per diem 271
  prior injuries 277
  proving property losses 274
  punitive 282–284
  special 272–276
  tobacco companies and the damages 282
  tort reform and punitive damages 282
Day in the life videos 274
Deceptive trade practices 532–533
Declaratory judgment 284
Defamation
  absolute privilege 402
  analyzing a case for 415
  burden of proof 394–395
  clear and convincing evidence 393
  constitutional limits 404–405
  cyberspace 408
  damages 404
  deceased persons 401
  defenses to 401–404
  defined 392
  elements of 393–400
  false statements 394
  "good faith" statutes 403–404
  libel 393
  libel per quod 398
  libel per se 398–399
  malice 406
  New York Times rule 405–406
  opinions 394
  privileges 401–402
  publication 395
  qualified privilege 402
  simple libel 396
  slander 393, 399–400
  slander per se 399–400
  writing 398
Defendant 10
Defense case 18
Defense firms 119
Defenses, false imprisonment 49
Depositions, discovery 15
Discovery
  depositions 15
  electronic 149
  in civil cases 14–15
  interrogatories 14
  request for physical and/or mental examination of
    party 15
  request for production of documents 15
  request to admit facts 15
Documenting intentional injuries 46
Documenting personal injury fraud 316
Dram shop liability 535
Duress 78
Duty
  abnormally dangerous conditions 159–160
  attractive nuisance doctrine 157
  defined 144
  "economic benefit test" 159
  guest statutes 160
  habit or custom 147–148
  how the courts determine 150–151
  invitee 158–159
  legal obligation 146–147
  licensee 158
  negligence 109
  professional status 148–149
  relationship 151
  rescue doctrine 158
  social relationship 152–154
  special relationships 151–152
  specialists 149
  third parties 161–162
  to defend, automobile insurance 486
  trespassers 156
  ultra-hazardous conditions 159–160
  using formulas 145–146
  victim's identity 146
  waiver 167
  when does it arise? 145

E

Economic benefit test, duty 159
Electronic data recorders 183
Electronic discovery 149
Elements 41

Elements of emotional distress 52
Elements of false imprisonment 47
Emotional distress
    damages 276–277
    elements of 52
    intentional infliction of 52–55
Equitable remedies 284–285
Equity 284
Evaluating a case for damages 285–288
Excessive force, self-defense 75
Exclusions, automobile insurance 489
Expert evidence, breach of duty
        199–200

F
Fair market value 274
False imprisonment 47–49
    defenses 49
    elements of 47
    unlawful restraint 48
Family Purpose Doctrine 92
Fear or apprehension, assault 42–43
Fiduciary, insurance 481
Foreseeability 44, 228
Fraud 518–522
    alleging in complaint 520–521
    criminal law 521–522
    Internet 522
    limitations on 521
    proving 519–520

G
Guest statutes, duty 160
Guilt 8

H
Harassment, sexual 534–535
Harmful or offensive contact
    assault 43
    battery 46

I
Immunity 82–83
    tort 56–57
Indemnify, insurance 480
Indictment 7
Informed consent
    defined 449
    emergencies 451
    malpractice 449–450
    scope 451
    statutory requirements 450
Injunction 284
Insanity 81–82
Insurance and technology 495
    automobile 483–488
    contract 480–481
    discovery issues 490–491

effect on settlement 490
fiduciary 481
history 479–480
impact on civil suits 478–479
indemnify 480
policy 480
premiums 480
releases 493
settlement 492–493
state laws 481–482
Intentional infliction of emotional distress 52–55
Intentional injuries, documenting 46
Intentional tort 39
Interference with contract 530–532
Internet fraud 522
Interrogatories, discovery 14
Intervening causes, proximate cause 247
Intoxication 79–80
    involuntary 79–80
    voluntary 79
Invitee, duty 158–159

J
Joint and several liability 88
Joint enterprise 92
Jury charge 19
Jury instructions 287–288
Jury selection 16

L
Law firm, contracting with 119
Law firms 117–119
Lawyer, becoming a 117
Legal malpractice 457–459
    defined 457
Liable 8
Libel 393
Licensee, duty 158
Litigation chart 12–13
Loss of consortium 277
Lost wages

M
MacPherson case, products liability 356
Malicious prosecution 55–56
Malpractice
    basic elements of 440–444
    basis for 438–440
    brief history of 437–438
    damages 445–449
    defenses 454–455
    defined 436
    discovery issues 453
    expert testimony 444
    informed consent 449–450
    legal 457–459
    physician-patient relationship 440
    pleadings 452–453

Malpractice (*continued*)
  proximate cause 444–445
  punitive damages 447
  specialists 444
  standard of care 441
  wrongful adoption 447
  wrongful birth 446
  wrongful death 447
Mediation 20
Medical bills 272–273
Medical technology 443
Mistake 80
Mitigation of damages 276
Model Uniform Products Liability Act 368
Motion for directed verdict 18

N

Necessity 78
Negligence
  breach 111
  causation 112
  damages 112–113
  duty 109
  four elements of 109–113
  history of 108
  per se 111, 191–193
  proximate causation 112
Negligent misrepresentation 523–530
  causation 525
  damages 525–526, 529
  defenses 528–529
  detrimental reliance 528–529
  duty 524–525
  elements 524–536
  good faith 530
  knowledge 530
  lack of privity 530
  mistake 527
  opinion 526, 528
  pleadings 527
  privity 524
  ratification 529
  restatement 524
  truth 528
  waiver 529
No-fault insurance, automobile insurance
      488–489
Nominal damages 284
Nuisance
  actions 59–60
  defined 59
  private 59
  public 59

O

Online defamation 397
Opening statement 17

P

Pain and suffering, damages 271
Palsgraf case 229–232
Per diem 271
Plaintiff 10
Plaintiff's firms 118
Plaintiff's case, trial 17–18
Pleadings 6–7
Policy, insurance 480
Premises liability 154–158
Premiums, insurance 480
Preponderance of the evidence 7–8
Prima facie 42
Private nuisance 59
Privilege 83–84
Privity, products liability 354
Products liability
  basic elements of 359
  consumer dissatisfaction 359–360
  defects in marketing 366
  defenses 375
  defined 354
  design defects 366
  discovery 368
  express warranties 362
  inherently dangerous objects 375
  manufacturer's duty 363–364
  manufacturing defects 366
  Model Uniform Products Liability Act 368
  pleading 366–367
  privity 354
  proving 365–367
  public policy arguments 365
  retailers and "mere conduits" 374–375
  standard of care 363–364
  the *MacPherson* case 356
  United States 354–356
  warranties 360–362
  warranty of fitness for purpose 360–361
  warranty of merchantability 360
Professionals
  breach of duty 188
  specialists 188
Property losses, damages 274
Proximate causation 44, 112, 220
Proximate cause
  acts of God 248–249
  "but for" 234
  court-created tests 233–234
  defendant's responsibility 227–228
  defense 243
  developing the concept 222
  evaluating a case for 226
  foreseeability 228
  historical development 222–223
  intervening causes 247
  jury question 243–244

law on 221
  malpractice 444–445
  multiple defendants 245–246
  "orbit of the risk" doctrine 232–233
  pleading 243–244
  problems defining 223
  proving 220
  remote causes 226
  Restatement position 224–225
  "substantial factor" test 234
  superseding causes 247–248
  working definition 223–224
Public nuisance 59
Punitive damages 282–284

R

Ratification 529
Reasonable person standard 184
  battery 46–47
Re-creating auto accidents with CAD 245
Relationship, duty 151
Releases, insurance 493
Remand 21
Request for physical and/or mental examination
  of a party 15
Request for production of documents 15
Request to admit facts 15
Res ispa loquitur, breach of duty 188–191
Rescue doctrine, duty 158
Respondeat superior 90
  limitations on 90–91
Reverse 21
Rule 11 11–12

S

Self-defense 74–77
  aggressor 75
  deadly force, property 76–77
  defending others 76
  excessive force 75
  limitations on 75–76
  martial artists 75
  mutual combat 77
Settlement, insurance 490
Sexual harassment 534–535
Slander 393, 399
  special damages 400
Social host liability 153
Social media 16
Social relationship, duty 152–154
Special relationships, duty 151–152
Specialists
  duty 149
  malpractice 444
Stacking, automobile insurance 487
Standard of care 144

Stare decisis 22
Statutes of limitation 87
Strict liability
  animals 353
  defined 350
  history of 351–353
  statute of limitations 353–354
  ultra-hazardous activity 350–351
Subrogation, automobile insurance 486–487
Superseding causes, proximate cause 247–248

T

Technology as the enemy 358
Third parties, duty 161–162
Tort, defined 2
Tort immunity 56–57
Tort law
  a short history of 9–11
  development of in the United States 10–11
Trespass 57–59
  to chattels 60–61
Trespassers 156
Trial
  closing argument 19
  defense case 18
  jury charge 19
  jury selection 16–17
  motion for directed verdict 18
  of a civil case 16–19
  opening statement 17
  plaintiff's case 17–18
  verdict 19

U

Ultra-hazardous activity 350–351
Ultra-hazardous conditions, duty 159–160
Underinsured motorist, automobile insurance 485
Unlawful restraint, false imprisonment 48

V

Verdict 19
Vicarious liability 89–92
Voir dire 17

W

Waiver, duty 167
Warranties 360–362
  defined 360–361
  express 362
  of fitness for purpose 360
  of merchantability 360
Witnesses, finding on the Internet 128
Workers' compensation 535–537
Wrongful adoption, malpractice 447
Wrongful birth, malpractice 446
Wrongful death, malpractice 447